# Modern Woodworking

## Tools, Materials, and Processes

by

**Willis H. Wagner**
Professor Emeritus, Industrial Technology
University of Northern Iowa, Cedar Falls

**Clois E. Kicklighter**
Dean, School of Technology
Professor, Construction Technology
Indiana State University, Terre Haute

**Publisher**
**THE GOODHEART-WILLCOX COMPANY, INC.**
**Tinley Park, Illinois**

## IMPORTANT SAFETY NOTICE

Work procedures and shop practices described in this book are effective methods of performing given operations. Use special tools and equipment as recommended. Carefully follow all safety warnings and cautions. Note that these warnings are not exhaustive. Proceed with care and under proper supervision to minimize the risk of personal injury or injury to others.

This book contains the most complete and accurate information that could be obtained from various authoritative sources at the time of publication. The Goodheart-Willcox Co., Inc. cannot assume responsibility for any changes, errors, or omissions.

**Library of Congress Cataloging-in-Publication Data**
Wagner, Willis H.
   Modern woodworking: tools, materials, and processes
/ Willis H. Wagner, Clois E. Kicklighter.
       p. cm.
   Includes index.
   ISBN 1-56637-618-1
   1. Woodwork (Manual training)  I. Kicklighter, Clois E.
II. Title.
TT185.W32 2000
684′ .08--dc21                                          99-10563
                                                        CIP

# Introduction

The 2000 edition of **Modern Woodworking** maintains its scope and depth, making it a state-of-the art text. The book includes updated information on the following topics:

- Adhesives
- Edgebanding
- Plate joinery
- Toggle clamps
- Solid surface materials
- 32mm construction
- New surface laminates
- CNC routers
- Detail and random orbit sanders
- Power compound miter saws
- Shop safety
- Wood finishing terms
- Water-based finishes
- Cordless drills
- Plunge routers
- Laser cutting tools
- Sliding tables
- Choosing the right solvent
- Pocket cutters
- New OSHA and EPA regulations

**Modern Woodworking** provides basic information about wood and wood products: selection, safe use, and care of hand and power tools; residential construction applications; and proper woodworking procedures. The text offers exploratory experiences designed to give the student insight into the major areas of woodworking and to serve as a reference for design and construction principles and methods. It is intended to help students develop competent technical skills for good performance in the broad areas of woodworking.

**Modern Woodworking** provides information and basic instruction in the areas of furniture and cabinetmaking, wood finishing, laminating and bending wood, plastic laminating, upholstery, and patternmaking. Also included is a chapter on special procedures in fine woodworking, to enable the advanced student to move on beyond standard woodworking techniques.

**Modern Woodworking** contains a chapter on mass production in the school shop. This unit provides sufficient instruction and examples to enable the instructor to develop a meaningful mass production product for any class. In addition, the technical aspects of wood structure, growth, and physical properties of wood are included to increase depth of understanding about wood.

**Modern Woodworking** describes and illustrates many industrial machines, methods, and processes. These examples are intended to broaden the scope of understanding for the typical woodworking student. The importance of safety is stressed throughout the text.

**Modern Woodworking** includes more than 1600 carefully selected illustrations which are coordinated with the text material. These illustrations help to communicate the important elements of the material presented. A special section showing 59 native and foreign species of wood is also included.

**Modern Woodworking** is intended for students in high schools, vocational/technical schools, colleges and universities, apprenticeship programs, and do-it-yourselfers. It can also serve as a valuable reference for students in architectural and interior design and construction.

Willis H. Wagner
Clois E. Kicklighter

# Contents

## Power Tools

## *Cabinetmaking and Furniture Making*

## Special Materials and Processes

## Construction

## Special Topics

# Acknowledgments

Examine the equipment, tools, and supplies you use in your woodworking activities. You will find a variety of manufacturer names affixed to these items. Likewise, you will find the names of a wide variety of outstanding manufacturers in this book. The Authors and Publisher wish to thank the following companies, individuals, and organizations for providing illustrations and technical information for this textbook.

3M Co.
Abitibi-Price Corp.
Adjustable Clamp Co.
AFM Corp.
Alcoa Building Products
Algoma Hardwoods, Inc.
American Institute of Timber Construction
American Plywood Association
Amerock Corp.
AMI, Ltd.
Anderson Corp.
Armstrong World Industries, Inc.
The ARO Corp.
Arvids Iriads
Ashdee Corp.
Bacon Veneer Co.
Baldwin Hardware Corp.
The Bartley Collection, Ltd.
Bertch Wood Specialities
Binks Mfg. Co.
Bird and Son, Inc.
Black & Decker
Black Brothers
Boise-Cascade Corp.
Bosch Power Tool Corp.
Bostitch
The Burke Co.
California Redwood Association
California Time/Westwood, Inc.
Campbellrhea Mfg., Inc.
Caradco Corp.
C.E. Morgan
Mark Clauss
CMT Tools
C.O. Porter Machinery Co.
Conwed Corp.
C.R. Onsrud, Inc.
Danley Machine Corp.
De-Sta-Co
Deft, Inc.
Delta International Machinery Corp.
DeVilbiss Co.
DeWalt
Dickinson Homes, Inc.
Digital Tool
Dremel
Drexel Heritage Furnishings, Inc.
Dry Clime Lamp Co.

Duo-Fast Corp.
E.I. DuPont DeNemours Co.
Ekstrom, Carlson and Co.
Enlon Import Corp.
Excalibur Machine and Tool Co.
Fastener Corp.
Fein Power Tools, Inc.
Fine Hardwoods Association
Fine Hardwoods—American Walnut Association
Fisher Controls
Flexsteel Industries, Inc.
Foley-Belsaw Co.
Wilson Forbes
Forest City Tool Co.
Forest Products Laboratory
Forestry Suppliers, Inc.
Formica Corp.
Frank Paxton Lumber Co.
Freeborn Tool Co., Inc.
Freud, USA
The Garlinghouse Company
Gasway Corp.
General Finishes
George Tanier Inc.
Georgia Pacific Corporation
The Gorilla Group
Gray and Rogers
Greenlee Bros. and Co.
Grizzly Imports, Inc.
Carl Grooms
Grosse Steel Co.
Haas Cabinet Co.
Handy Mfg. Co.
Mark Hazel
Herco, Inc.
Herman Miller Inc.
Hitachi Power Tools USA
Hyde Tools
Hydrocote Finishing Products
Independent Nail and Packing Co.
International Paper Co.
Ernie Ives
I-XL Furniture Co.
Jam Handy Organization
James L. Taylor Mfg. Co.
Jenkins, a division of Kohler General, Inc.
JET Equipment and Tools
J.M. Lancaster, Inc.

Jordan Millwork Co.
Julius Blum, Inc.
Kimball International
Knob Creek
Kohler General, Inc.
Koppers Co., Inc.
Kreg Tool Co.
Lamello AG
The Lane Company, Inc.
Leichtung, Inc.
Leigh Industries, Ltd.
Lodge and Shipley Co.
Lord and Burnham
Louisiana-Pacific Corp.
Lufkin Rule Co.
Makita Power Tools
Manville Building Materials Corp.
Dennis Marsh
Marvin Windows and Doors
Masonite Corp.
Noel Mast
Mattison Machine Works
Mead Publishing Paper Division
Memphis Hardwood Flooring Co.
Mepla, Inc.
Mereen-Johnson Machine Corp.
Merit Products, Inc.
Mersman Bros. Corp.
Michael Weing, Inc.
Millers Falls Co.
John Moeller
Nash–Bell–Challoner
National Building Code
National Forest Products Association
National Particle Board Association
National Plan Service, Inc.
National Rubber Bureau
Newman Machine Co.
Nicholson File Co.
NMC/Focal Point
North American Products Corp.
Northfield Foundry and Machine Co.
Northway Product Co.
Norton Co.
No-Sag Spring Div.
Oliver Machinery Co.
Osmose
Owens-Corning Fiberglas Corp.
Panel Clip Co.
Parker Mfg. Co.
Paslode Co., Div. of Signode
Paxton Lumber Co.
Period Furniture, Inc.
Porter Machinery Co.
Porter-Cable Corp.
Portland Cement Association
Potlach Corp.
Powermatic, Inc.
Pritam and Eames
Ransburg Electrostatic Equipment
Eldon Rebhorn

Red Cedar Shingle and Handsplit Shake Bureau
Redman Industries, Inc.
Rhode Island School of Design
Riveria Cabinets, Inc.
Rock Island Millwork
Rockwell International
Rogers Machinery Mfg. Co., Inc.
Rolscreen Co.
Ronthor Reiss Corp.
R.S. Brookman, Ltd.
Scholz Homes, Inc.
Selby Furniture Hardware
Senco Products, Inc.
Shaker Workshops
Shakertown Corp.
Sherwin-Williams Co.
Lear Siegler
Simonds Saw and Steel Co.
Skil Corp.
Sonoco Products Co.
Southern Forest Products Association
Speed Cut, Inc.
Spotnails, Inc.
Sprayon Products Inc.
Stanley Tools
Sunhill Machinery
Symons Corp.
Tarkett, Inc.
Te-Co
Therma-Tru, Div. of LST Corp.
Thomas Industries, Inc.
Thomasville Furniture Industries, Inc.
Tile Council of America
Timber Engineering Co.
Timesavers, Inc.
Triumph Twist Drill Co.
TrusWal Systems Corp.
Unit Structures, Inc.
United Brotherhood of Carpenters and Joiners of America
United Gilsonite Laboratories
United States Steel
Universal Clamp Corp.
Universal Form Clamp Co.
Upholsterers Supply Co.
USG Corp.
Veritas Tools, Inc.
Vermiculite Institute
Vocational Industrial Clubs of America (VICA)
Wadkin PLC
Bill Wagner
John Walker
David Welter
Western Wood Products Association
Weyerhauser Co.
Wilson Sporting Goods Co.
Wilsonart
Wisconsin Knife Works, Inc.
Woodcraft Supply Corporation
Woodland Pattern Co.
WorkRite Products Co.

Work quality and good design are evident in this English walnut, oak, and
Brazilian rosewood cabinet by James Krenov.
Dimensions: 23 1/2'' x 14'' x 57''.
(Pritam and Eames)

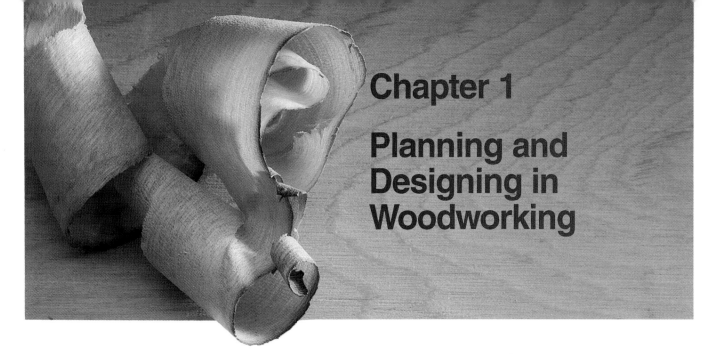

# Chapter 1

# Planning and Designing in Woodworking

Planning is a general term and may be as simple as determining activities for a day or as complicated as planning a house (Fig. 1-1), a school building, or even a space capsule. It means thinking through an activity before it is performed. In modern industry, planning is one of the chief functions of the engineering department. It includes such divisions as product selection and design, methods of fabrication, time schedules, plant layout, and equipment selection. Great emphasis is placed on this activity because careful planning can save time, materials, and energy. It also insures a good product and a profitable operation.

## PLANNING WOOD PRODUCTS

In the school shop, you will find that with careful planning you can avoid mistakes, get more work done, and do better work. A complete planning operation in woodworking will include the following activities: selecting the project, developing or refining the design, preparing presentation drawings and working drawings, developing procedures, listing materials, and estimating costs.

In order to do a good job of planning in woodworking, you must have some knowledge of tools, materials, and methods of construction. If you are in a beginning class your instructor will very likely provide specific directions and rather complete planning materials for your first construction activities. After you complete several projects and/or exercises, you will then be able to prepare some of your own plans and designs.

As you gain more "know-how" and experience in woodworking, you will be expected to build more difficult and complicated projects. These will intensify your interest and you will secure greater pleasure and satisfaction from the work. Pay careful attention to directions and demonstrations presented by your instructor. Study your textbook and

Fig. 1-1. Planning and design are an integral part of every sucessful project regardless of size.
(Marvin Windows and Doors)

other reference materials, and prepare and organize your planning materials so that you can make the best use of your class time.

## WOOD AS A CONSTRUCTION MATERIAL

Wood is one of our most popular and versatile raw materials. It can be easily formed, shaped, and smoothed, and offers a variety of tones, grain patterns, and surface textures. In products where the visual appearance is of major importance, the designer makes full use of these characteristics. Refer to Fig. 1-2.

The porosity or cellular structure of wood provides a material that is light in weight and relatively strong. It also makes possible the driving and fitting of nails, screws, and other metal fasteners. This porosity also accounts for its high insulating value (thermoresistivity) which makes wood seem warmer to the touch than a piece of metal. For example, touch a wooden bench top and then the metal jaw of a vise. Note that the metal seems cooler than the wood even though they are the same temperature. This is one of the reasons many people prefer furniture and cabinets made of wood to those made of metal or plastic.

### DESIGNING WOOD PRODUCTS

Designing is a complex activity that includes creating, inventing, searching, and developing. It is a selective process where ideas are studied, tried-out, analyzed, and finally either discarded or incorporated into the design. These ideas are recorded in words, drawings, or models.

At the outset, you should formulate a clear, concise statement of the problem, whether it be an original design or a modification and improvement of an existing design. This statement should include a description of the purpose and use of the product and any specific requirements concerning materials, size, and shape. Thorough study should then be given to the problem. Information is gathered and decisions are made concerning the kind of material and methods of fabrication. Other products of similar design are studied. As possible solutions are visualized, they should be recorded in sketch form. At times it may be helpful to experiment with a few pieces of the wood that has been selected. Test its workability and cut sample joints. A model or mock-up, built of a soft, inexpensive wood may provide a worthwhile check on certain designs. These activities will require considerable time but are fully justified when a major project is undertaken.

### DESIGN FACTORS

Fig. 1-3 shows the three chief considerations in design and how they relate. FUNCTIONAL requirements grow out of the use and purpose of the product. It must serve the purpose for which it is designed. A chair must provide comfortable support for the human anatomy. A chest should hold the articles for which it was designed. A tool holder must support tools securely, protect cutting edges, and permit easy removal. The function of a folding screen may be to separate space while the main purpose of a wood carving or wall plaque is simply to provide interest and beauty. When the function of a product has been clearly defined, certain guidelines will have been established concerning its form and other design requirements.

MATERIAL requirements are developed through a study of those materials that will be most suitable and appropriate. Consideration must be given to strength, beauty, durability, and economy. Softwoods may be perfectly satisfactory for one struc-

Fig. 1-2. This Queen Anne style highboy exhibits good proportions, sturdy construction, and functional design. (The Bartley Collection, Ltd.)

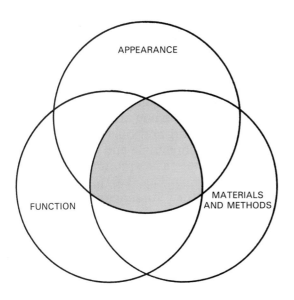

Fig. 1-3. Relationship of important design factors.

ture but unsatisfactory for another. For example: red cedar, which has many appropriate uses, has color, grain, and structural qualities that are unsatisfactory for furniture construction. Select a wood that has the qualities and characteristics required. If a dark tone is desired, it is best to use a dark wood. Staining one wood to imitate another tends to destroy the feeling of genuineness that is essential in good design.

Other materials can often be effectively combined with wood. Metal legs may provide the best solution in a table design. Be cautious of extreme contrasts. One material or kind of wood should dominate. Combinations of light and dark wood, sometimes used for turnings may detract from the basic form, resulting in a "flashy" or "gaudy" product that is soon discarded.

METHODS of construction must be given consideration as materials are selected. The size of structural parts and types of joints or fasteners used will not be the same for weak, soft-textured woods as for those that are strong and hard. Some experimentation with the material may result in improved joinery methods or a reduction in the size of parts. Make use of new glues and bonding methods, plywood and hardboard, laminated construction, special metal fasteners, and other new methods and products that extend the design potential of wood.

The APPEARANCE (visual aspect) of the design is the most difficult consideration to handle, especially for the beginner. In good design you must recognize such principles as proper balance, correct proportion, unity and harmony among the various elements, points of emphasis and interest, compatible colors, and interesting textures. There are no firmly established rules or standards that can be ap-

plied to appearance, and learning to recognize good design will take time and effort. Memorizing a list of principles will be of little value. Your ability in this area will grow through experience, practice, and reflection. Study articles that are well designed. Analyze them with respect to their function, materials used, construction features, and methods used to obtain an attractive and pleasing appearance.

Designers of wood products place great emphasis on function. They then build the design through the use of smooth, trim lines, simple shapes and forms, and interesting grain patterns, colors, and textures. They are cautious about using extra shapes, carvings, and inlays just to add to the appearance. Their purpose is to create pleasing visual aspects that seem to grow from and blend with the function, the materials, and practical construction techniques, as in Fig. 1-4.

Before preparing working drawings or starting the construction of a project, ask yourself some of these questions about your design. Will the article serve the function for which it was designed? Have the most appropriate kinds of wood and other materials been selected? Does the design make economical use of the material? Will construction methods be simple and practical to perform? Has proper attention been given to proportion and balance? Will the project be durable and easy to maintain? Is the

Fig. 1-4. The Shakers used folding screens in their hospitals to divide large spaces into smaller, more private ones. The frame is made of solid clear cherry, with inset cherry panels. The finish is oil. Dimensions of each panel: 16'' x 66 1/2''. (Shaker Workshops)

design free of superficial ornamentation? Will the product fit or blend into the surroundings in which it will be used?

## FURNITURE STYLES

Furniture styles have evolved through the years. Newer styles are often adaptations of those developed in an earlier period. Many of the period styles of furniture were developed in Europe during the eighteenth century. Kings and queens of the various countries employed skilled cabinetmakers who worked full time over a period of many years to produce elaborate, and often overdecorated, furniture to match their luxurious surroundings. Some of the designs produced were named for the ruler; some carried the name of the cabinetmaker.

Furniture styles are generally classified into three broad categories: TRADITIONAL (also known as PERIOD), EARLY 20th CENTURY INFLUENCES, and CONTEMPORARY. Each category contains several design or individual pieces which have become recognized by students of furniture as comprising a style. STYLE refers to a distinctive manner of designing which is typical of a specific person, place, time, or group.

Traditional furniture styles, Fig. 1-5, represent different periods of history in France, England, and the United States. Many European styles were inspired by rulers who commissioned for designs which they found appealing. For example, Napoleon inspired the French Empire Style. In other cases, styles were sometimes named after the currently reigning monarch, such as Louis XIII and Queen Anne. Some furniture styles were named after the gifted cabinetmaker who designed and built the furniture. Examples include Chippendale and Hepplewhite. Furniture of early America is a mixture of many styles from other countries, Fig. 1-6.

Early 20th century influences (modern) in furniture design was an effort to return to a more honest and simple design in reaction to the cluttered Victorian styles of the late 1800s. Examples of this influence on style include Art Nouveau furniture, the prairie homes of Frank Lloyd Wright, the Bauhaus school of design in Germany, and the International and Scandinavian Modern styles.

Natural, growing forms were chosen as the basis for Art Nouveau. In other words, furniture of this time was based on flowing, natural lines ending in a curve, similar to the bud of a plant. Frank Lloyd Wright's prairie homes were based on the idea that a structure, its surroundings, and its furnishings should be parts of the whole. His prairie furniture was composed of geometric shapes, slats, and flat surfaces which were usually natural and void of

Fig. 1-5.  Three traditional pieces from early America. Left. Architectural-style clock is walnut. (Mark Clauss) Center. Silver chest (circa 1850). Right. Desk on frame.   (The Bartley Collection, Ltd.)

Fig. 1-6. Queen Anne style chairs feature the cabriole leg. This design has remained popular through the years. (The Bartley Collection, Ltd.)

ornamentation. The Bauhaus style was one of simplicity. Mies Van der Rohe's Barcelona chair came to represent this style. After the Bauhaus school closed, Mies Van der Rohe and several others continued their design work. The result of this work was the International style. It is the outgrowth of the philosophy that "form follows function." This style is best characterized by abstract geometrical shapes and no decoration. Scandinavian Modern and Shaker furniture are sleek and clean-lined styles of furniture that are both functional and elegant, Fig. 1-7.

Contemporary furniture represents the very latest designs. It is composed of the new, the experimental, and the unclassified. Generally, contemporary furniture is thought of as representing developments since about 1950. It attempts to provide grace and charm through the use of interesting forms and shapes, constructed out of modern materials, and using the newest methods and procedures, Fig. 1-8. Beautiful grained hardwoods, especially walnut, are often used. Plastics and lighter weight metals are sometimes utilized.

A contemporary design must be carefully based on accepted principles. Lines and forms must be attractive and provide the utmost in function. Construction must be simple and light but still provide adequate strength. The development of the design

Fig. 1-7. The best known of all Shaker chairs is the so-called "slat back" or straight chair from the Canterbury, New Hampshire community. The tall back posts with their delicately rounded finials and the smooth curved slats give it a look of grace and beauty. The frame is rock maple. Dimensions: back 42'' high, seat 17'' high x 18 3/4'' wide x 14'' deep. (Shaker Workshops)

Fig. 1-8. Three examples of contemporary furniture. Top. Turtle table by Judy Kensley McKie made from walnut. Bottom. Chair and table by David Ebner.  (Pritam and Eames)

for a piece of contemporary furniture will generally require a great deal of thought, study, and experimentation to produce a lasting design.

## SKETCHING

The ability to develop your ideas through freehand sketches is desirable. The sketches can be made quickly, using a pencil and paper. They are a good way to record your ideas. Freehand sketches are also excellent for showing your instructor what you have in mind as you secure his or her approval and suggestions.

There are several methods of making a sketch. A beginner should use the procedure shown in Fig. 1-9. First, with the pencil held several inches from the point, make light block-in lines, Fig. 1-9A. Use sweeping strokes with the forearm pivoting at the elbow. It will be easiest to make a series of long dashes, aimed at a predetermined point. For vertical or diagonal lines that are long, revolve the paper and use the same stroking position. A finger movement can be used for short lines. The position, size, and overall proportion of your sketch will be determined by these block-in lines so try to apply good "eye" judgment to their spacing.

After major block-in lines are complete, darken the lines you want to show, Fig. 1-9B. Grip the pencil near the point and press down firmly. Follow along the block-in lines with a series of strokes formed by a wrist movement. Move your hand to a new position after several strokes are made. Vertical or diagonal lines may be made by shifting the paper or using a finger movement.

Details are sketched in about the same way, Fig. 1-9C. Sometimes it may be helpful to use a ruler to lay out a few sizes of a detail as shown. After the measurements are made, continue to draw the lines freehand. The keynote of the sketch is speed. If you take time to draw too many mechanical lines

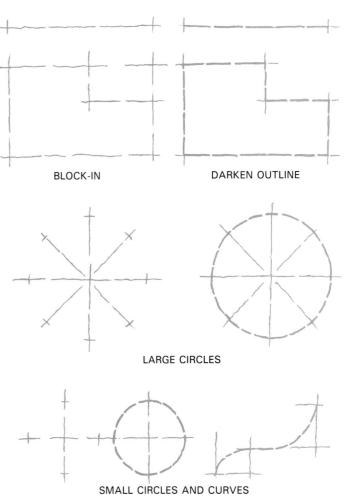

BLOCK-IN    DARKEN OUTLINE

LARGE CIRCLES

SMALL CIRCLES AND CURVES

Fig. 1-10. Sketching procedure.

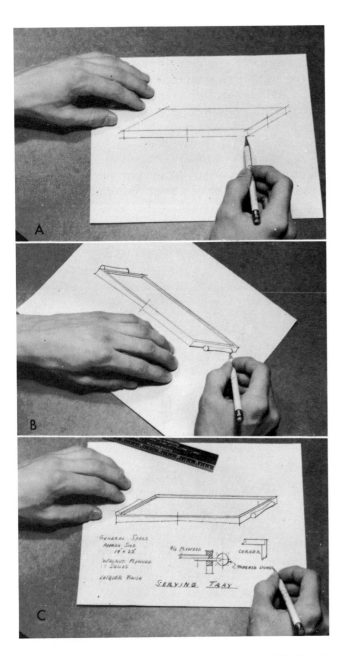

Fig. 1-9. Steps in making a freehand sketch. A—Blocking-in. B—Darkening outlines. C—Adding details.

you will defeat this purpose. Procedures for making circles and curves are shown in Fig. 1-10.

The degree of refinement in a sketch is determined by its use. Sketches, hurriedly made to supplement an oral description can be rough and incomplete. As you think through a problem, quick sketches will help you record your ideas so they will not be forgotten. Accurate and complete sketches can be made of final solutions.

The beginner may become discouraged with first attempts at sketching because he/she sets too high a standard in line quality. A great deal of practice is required before "snappy looking" drawings can be produced by this method. In freehand sketching, give most of your attention to approximate proportions and try to keep the lines running in about the correct direction. Do not attempt to produce perfectly straight and accurate lines. Drawings requiring this level of line quality should be made with instruments, Fig. 1-11.

Fig. 1-12 shows freehand sketching applied to the development of a design for a plant stand. The design problem included these specifications:

1. The stand must support two removable trays

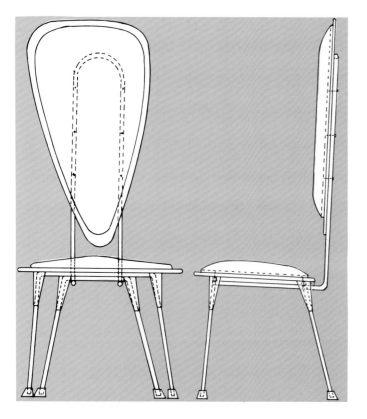

Fig. 1-11. Drawing is the language of design. The two views of this contemporary chair communicate essential information about the object to be constructed. (Mark Hazel)

at a height that is convenient for plant care and appropriate for viewing the plants.

2. The plant stand should provide space below the trays for additional plants which require less sun.
3. Construction should provide a strong, stable platform and add interest to the piece.
4. The plant stand should be made from a wood which will resist moisture and compliment the appearance of the plants.

As the basic design began to take shape, decorative joints were chosen to enhance the overall appearance as well as strengthen the construction. Function was always a major design consideration.

## PRESENTATION DRAWINGS

After your design is refined and fairly well developed, you should prepare a presentation drawing similar to the one shown in Fig. 1-13. It will serve to further organize your ideas and will provide a drawing that you can use to present your project proposal to your instructor. Presentation drawings will be especially helpful in the preparation of working drawings.

Presentation drawings are frequently freehand sketches, but may be drawn with instruments. Various types of pictorial drawing can be used.

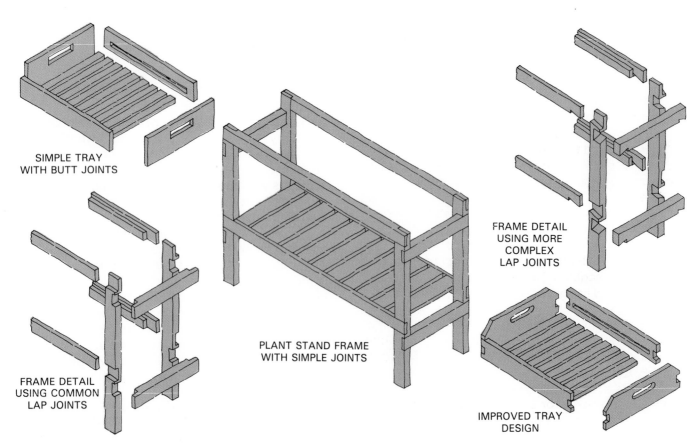

SIMPLE TRAY WITH BUTT JOINTS

FRAME DETAIL USING MORE COMPLEX LAP JOINTS

FRAME DETAIL USING COMMON LAP JOINTS

PLANT STAND FRAME WITH SIMPLE JOINTS

IMPROVED TRAY DESIGN

Fig. 1-12. Developing ideas for a plant stand with trays.

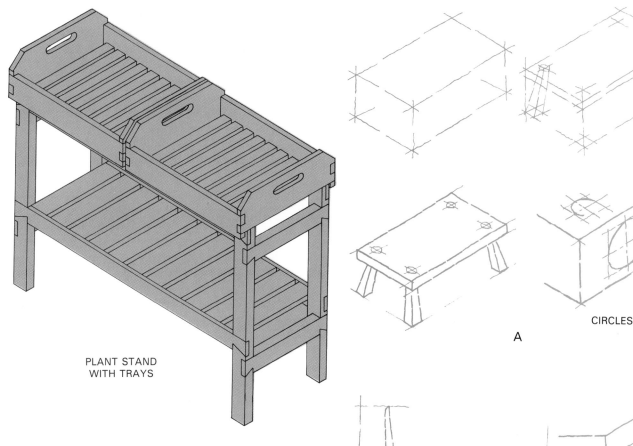

Fig. 1-13. Presentation drawing of plant stand.

PLANT STAND
WITH TRAYS

CIRCLES

A

REDUCE
ONE-HALF

CIRCLES

B

Fig. 1-14. Making pictorial sketches. A—Isometric. B—Oblique.

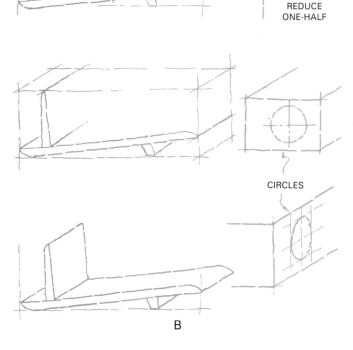

Isometric and oblique (note: ''cabinet'' is a type of oblique drawing), Fig. 1-14, are the easiest and most commonly used. In isometric drawings, first block in cubes and rectangles that hold the shapes and then locate finished outlines from the edges and surfaces of the block-in form.

For an oblique cabinet drawing make a profile or front view, and then secure the third dimension (picture effect) by drawing back at an angle. Make the lines drawn at an angle only about one-half their actual length to produce a more realistic appearance.

Show only visible outlines and keep the drawing as simple as possible. Dimensions should be kept to a minimum and in some instances may be given in note form. Include any key details that will be helpful in describing the methods and details of construction and list general specifications concerning materials and finish. Sometimes it may be desirable to add shading or color to the drawing to give a clearer picture of the finished product. Study a drafting textbook for suggestions and procedures in this technique.

MULTIVIEW PROJECTION (orthographic views) can also be used for presentation drawings, Fig. 1-15. When used for this purpose, only visible outlines are shown. Sometimes they are drawn to an accurate scale with mechanically made lines.

When made in this way they are especially valuable for checking the proportion, balance, and other visual aspects of the design. Multiview projections are often used when making working drawings.

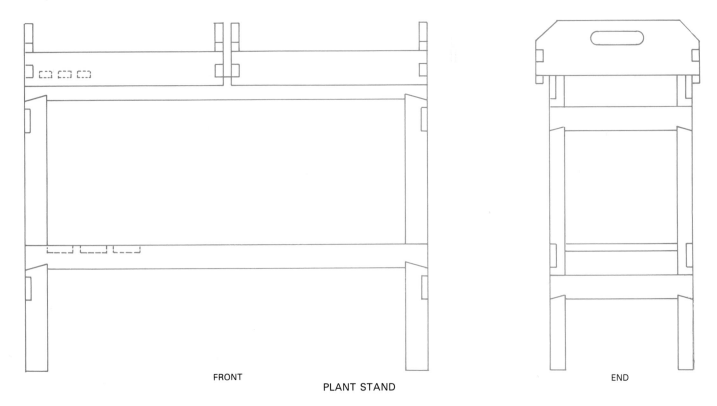

FRONT

PLANT STAND

END

Fig. 1-15. Multiview drawing showing front and end of plant stand.

## WORKING DRAWINGS

After you have secured approval of your project ideas through the use of presentation drawings, you are ready to prepare a WORKING DRAWING, Fig. 1-16. This drawing will provide complete shape and size description of the product and its various parts. The goal of the working drawing is to provide such a complete description that the product could be constructed by someone else without further explanations or information.

Working drawings must include assembled views of the product, complete with all size and location dimensions. Most wood construction will be of such a size that these views will need to be drawn to a smaller scale. Multiview projections are often used but various pictorial types of drawings may be satisfactory. In addition to assembled views, detailed views will be required to show the exact size and shape of parts, and the joints and fasteners used to assemble them. In woodworking drawings these details are often drawn full size and used as a pattern. Large pieces with an irregular contour are carefully drawn to scale and then a grid of squares is superimposed on the contour lines so that accurate patterns can be developed in the shop. In complicated assemblies, exploded pictorial drawings are often used to provide clear descriptions.

As you prepare a working drawing, decisions with respect to the methods and details of construction must be made. You must select the type and size of fasteners (nails and screws), proportion wood joints for the greatest strength, and determine the exact size of various parts. Study appropriate sections of this book and also reference books including a drafting textbook, for information and standards. A working drawing for a wooden product might also include a suggested design for a jig or fixture that could be used to insure accuracy in some important step of the fabrication processes.

## PLAN OF PROCEDURE

A plan of procedure is a carefully prepared list of the steps you propose to follow in the construction of your project. It requires a careful study of your drawings to recognize the various operations and work required. This is one of the very important parts of your project plans as it will help you organize your work and prevent mistakes.

Steps should be listed in outline form. The list should not be too brief; neither should it be too long and detailed. Usually listing the exact operations and defining the part involved will be sufficient. Some special or unusual process might be described in detail. It is not necessary to list the size of parts since the working drawing will supply this information. Listed below is a plan of procedure that could be used to construct the plant stand.

1.  From a study of the working drawings, prepare

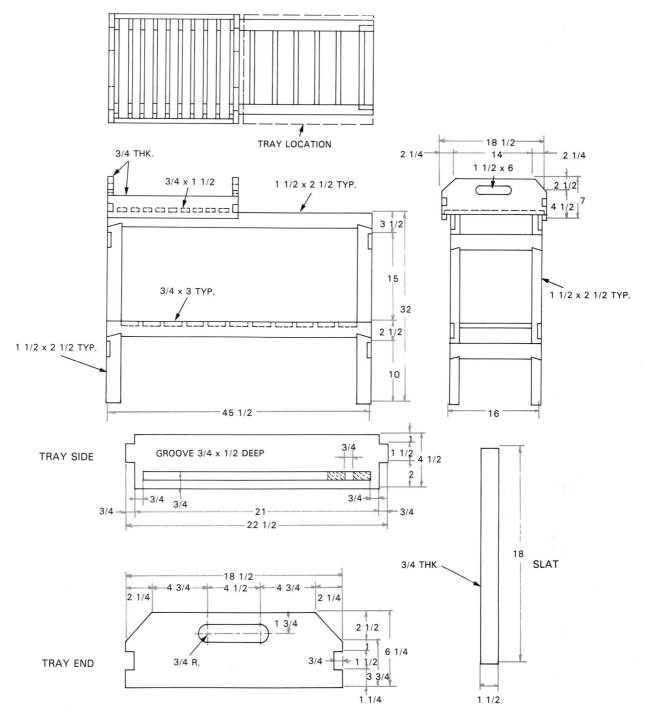

Fig. 1-16. Working drawings with dimensions in inches.

a bill of materials and a stock cutting list.
2. Select and cut out the stock.
3. Prepare the stock for the main structural members of the stand.
   a. Surface to finished thickness.
   b. Rip to width and cut to length.
   c. Lay out and cut joints on each piece.
4. Make a trial assembly of the main structural members to see that each piece fits properly.
5. Assemble the stand with water-resistant glue.

Use clamps to insure tight joints and proper adhesion. Check to see that the stand is plumb and square.

6. Disassemble and sand all surfaces.
7. Prepare the stock for the bottom shelf slats.
   a. Surface to finish thickness.
   b. Rip to width and cut to length.
8. Cut slats for bottom shelf to length and lay in place to check spacing. Mark the spacing or use a piece of scrap stock which is 3/4'' thick

to check spacing. Space between slats should be uniform.

9. Sand all surfaces of slats and attach to frame with small finishing nails. Glue may be used in addition to nails if desired.
10. Prepare the stock for the trays.
    a. Surface to finish thickness.
    b. Rip to width and cut to length.
11. Lay out curve, hand holes, and joints on tray ends. Cut ends to final shape.
12. Lay out tray sides and cut to final shape. Test for proper fit. Note: A plywood jig is desirable for accurate location of mortised holes. The bottom of slots should be in line with the bottom edge of tray ends.
13. Lay out and cut tray slats to proper length and width. Round the edge of slats with router or shaper before cutting each piece to length.
14. Make a trial assembly of each tray and check to see that it fits properly on the stand. Slats should be free to move slightly in the slots.
15. Disassemble and sand all sides.
16. Assemble trays with water-resistant glue. Use clamps and check to see that each assembly is square and plumb.
17. Finish sanding each assembly after proper gluing time.
18. No finish is recommended for this project because redwood will turn a uniform silver gray in time. In addition, chemicals in the finish may harm the plants. Fig. 1-17 shows a photograph of the completed plant stand.

## BILL OF MATERIAL

A bill of material is a detailed list of the items you need to build the project, Fig. 1-18. This includes: number of pieces, exact size (including allowance for joints), kind of wood, and name of the part. List

| No. | Size | Kind | Part |
|---|---|---|---|
| **(Stand)** | | | |
| 4 pcs. | 1 1/2 x 2 1/2 x 32 | Redwood | Legs |
| 4 pcs. | 1 1/2 x 2 1/2 x 45 1/2 | '' | Side rails |
| 4 pcs. | 1 1/2 x 2 x 16 | '' | End rails |
| 11 pcs. | 3/4 x 3 x 14 1/2 | '' | Slats |
| | | | |
| **(Trays)** | | | |
| 4 pcs. | 1 1/2 x 4 x 22 1/2 | Redwood | Sides |
| 4 pcs. | 3/4 x 6 x 18 | '' | Ends |
| 18 pcs. | 3/4 x 1 1/2 x 17 | '' | Slats |
| | | | |
| **(Fasteners)** | | | |
| 44 | 4d Finishing Nails (1 1/2'') | | |

Fig. 1-18. Bill of material for the plant stand.

the dimensions of your stock in this order: thickness x width x length. WIDTH is the dimension across the grain. LENGTH is the distance along the grain. A piece of stock could be wider than it is long. A complete bill of material includes hardware and finishing materials.

A stock cutting list can be developed from the bill of material. It is useful for estimating costs and checking out your lumber. Add about 1/16 in. to the thickness dimension if the stock must be planed. The width of each piece should be increased from 1/4 to 1/2 in. and the length about 1/2 to 1 in. A bill of material will list the actual size of finished pieces, while a stock cutting list should give the nominal (in name only) size of the lumber required. Try to group the parts as much as possible. Stock cutting lists may vary for a given bill of material depending on the sizes of lumber that are available. A stock cutting list for the plant stand is shown in Fig. 1-19. Study it carefully.

Fig. 1-17. Photograph of the completed plant stand.

| No. | Nominal Size | Kind | Parts |
|---|---|---|---|
| 1 pc. | 1 1/2 x 2 1/2 x 144 | Redwood | Stand legs |
| 2 pcs. | 1 1/2 x 2 x 144 | '' | Side & end rails |
| 1 pc. | 1 1/2 x 4 x 120 | '' | Tray sides |
| 1 pc. | 3/4 x 6 x 96 | '' | Tray ends |
| 2 pcs. | 3/4 x 1 1/2 x 120 | '' | Tray slats |
| 1 pc. | 3/4 x 1 1/2 x 72 | '' | Tray slats |
| 2 pcs. | 3/4 x 3 x 96 | '' | Stand slats |

Fig. 1-19. A stock cutting list for the plant stand.

Use good judgment in selecting stock. Allow for sufficient material for milling and trimming operations, but without incurring unnecessary waste. The sizes given in the stock cutting list can be used to estimate the cost of the wood. However, the actual cost may be somewhat more, depending on the sizes available in the stock room. For example, it may be necessary for you to purchase 1 in. (nominal size) stock for the items listed if no 3/4 in. is available. Softwood boards are generally available in multiples of 2 feet.

### TEST YOUR KNOWLEDGE, Chapter 1

Please do not write in the text. Place your answers on a separate sheet of paper.

1. When planning a woodworking project you must have some knowledge of tools, _____, and construction methods.
2. What is the first step in designing a wood product?
3. When designing a wood product you should give attention to its use and purpose, materials and methods, and _____.
4. The Queen Anne highboy is a familiar _____ furniture style.
5. The kind of wood most often used in contemporary furniture is _____.
6. Freehand _____ that are used to supplement an oral description may be rough and incomplete.
7. What should you draw first when making an oblique drawing?
8. _____ views are better than pictorial views for checking the proportion and balance of a design.
9. A typical item in a plan of procedure includes the name of the part and the _____ to be performed.
10. A bill of material should list the size, number of pieces, name of the part, and the _____.

### ACTIVITIES

1. Select a wood product you believe to be well designed. Prepare a written or an oral report analyzing its function, the materials and methods used in fabrication, and its appearance.
2. Prepare sketches and/or mechanical drawings that will describe some of the elements and principles of the visual aspects of design. Include line, shape, mass, formal and informal balance, proportion, harmony, repetition, gradation, texture, and color. Secure information from books and magazines.

This table was made in 1877 for use in the Brethren's shop at the Mt. Lebanon Shaker Village.
Dimensions: 42'' x 66'' x 29 1/2''.  (Shaker Workshops)

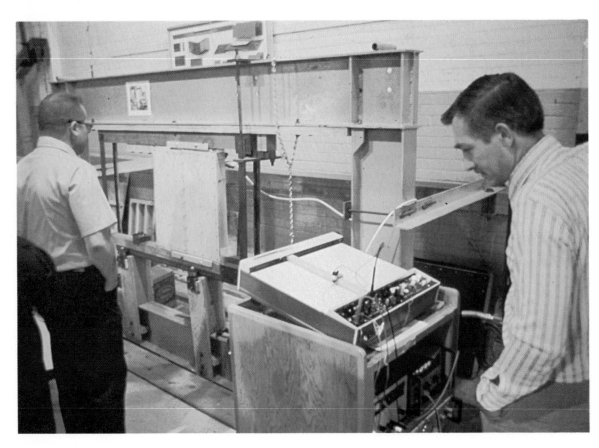

Top. Select hardwood logs ready for the mill. (Kimball International)    Bottom. The Forest Products Laboratory performs a variety of tests on wood and wood fabrications to determine properties. (Forest Products Laboratory)

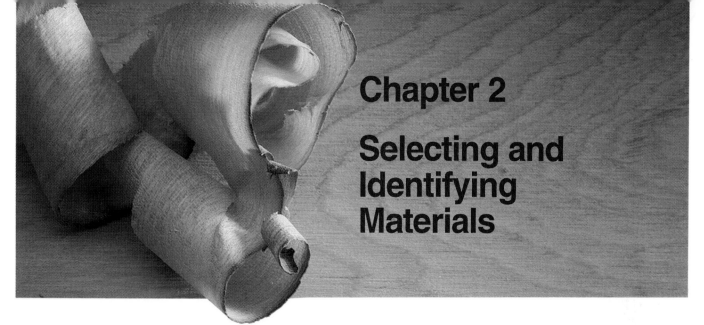

# Chapter 2

# Selecting and Identifying Materials

Lumber may be classified as either softwood or hardwood. SOFTWOOD comes from the evergreen or needle bearing trees. These are called CONIFERS because many of them bear cones. See Fig. 2-1. HARDWOOD comes from broadleafed (deciduous) trees that shed their leaves at the end of the growing season. This classification is somewhat confusing since many of the hardwood trees produce a softer wood than some softwood trees.

Some of the more common kinds of softwoods and hardwoods are listed in Fig. 2-2. THEY ARE GROUPED ACCORDING TO THE ACTUAL HARDNESS OF THE WOOD RATHER THAN THE CLASSIFICATION JUST DESCRIBED.

Some hardwoods have large pores in their cellular structure and are called OPEN GRAIN woods. They usually require special or additional operations in the finishing procedure.

In addition to hardness or softness, different kinds of wood will vary in weight, strength, color, texture, grain pattern, and odor. You should become familiar with these characteristics for the common

| SOFT | MED.-HARD | HARD |
|------|-----------|------|
| Balsa | CYPRESS | *Ash, White |
| Basswood | *Butternut | Beech |
| Cottonwood | DOUGLAS FIR | Birch |
| FIR, WHITE | Elm, American | Cherry, Black |
| PINE, PONDEROSA | HEMLOCK | *Hickory |
| PINE, WHITE- | *Limba (Korina) | Maple, Sugar |
| WESTERN | Magnolia | *Oak, Red |
| PINE, SUGAR | *Mahogany | *Oak, White |
| Poplar, Yellow | (Honduras) | *Walnut, Black |
| SPRUCE | *Mahogany | *Teak |
| REDWOOD | (Philippine) | |
| REDCEDAR, | *Prima Vera | |
| WESTERN | REDCEDAR, | |
| Willow, Black | EASTERN | |
| | Sweet Gum | |
| | Sycamore | |
| | Tupelo | |

*Open grained wood.
Note: Softwoods are set in caps. The others are classified as hardwoods.

Fig. 2-2. Common hardwoods and softwoods.

woods pictured in this section. To further develop your ability to identify various woods you will need to study actual specimens of the wood.

In wood identification it is often helpful to use a magnifying glass (about 10X) to study the cellular structure. For example, in order to distinguish White Oak from Red Oak, magnify the end grain and observe the tylosis (frothy growth) found in the cells of the White Oak.

Most of the samples shown in the color section, following page 27, were cut from plain-sawed or flat-grain boards. A view of the edge grain would look considerably different. The weight of the wood is given for one cubic foot, which would be equal to a board 1 in. thick, 12 in. wide, and 12 ft. long.

## SELECTING WOOD

As you become acquainted with the characteristics of various woods, you will also be able to

SOFTWOOD
(CONIFERS)

HARDWOOD
(BROAD-LEAVED)

Fig. 2-1. General classification of wood.
(Paxton Lumber Co.)

determine those that will be best suited for your work. For some of your first projects where you may be doing considerable work with hand tools, you will very likely want to select such woods as basswood, pine, poplar, or willow. These woods are easily worked and are fine for boxes, small cases, frames, toys, models, and similar items.

After you have gained some experience, you will probably want to select from the list of medium-hard woods that work well with both hand and power tools. They can be used in the construction of wall shelves, small radio cabinets, chests, lamps, trays, and many other household accessories.

When your project requires wide widths of stock you probably will want to consider using plywood. It takes time to glue up widths of solid stock. Plywood provides a saving in time and also greater dimensional stability and resistance to warpage. It is good practice to combine solid stock and plywood of the same species. Furniture manufacturers quite often do this and refer to the materials as SOLIDS AND VENEERS.

Advanced projects will usually be constructed with the aid of power machines. This will make it possible for you to use hardwoods. You should give careful attention to the selection of the kind of wood that will be appropriate for your design. Remember that the very best design, along with fine woodworking skills, cannot result in a satisfactory project if the kind and quality of the wood was not properly selected.

## GRADES OF LUMBER

The quality or grade of lumber depends on the size of the pieces and the amount of clear cuttings that they contain. Standards are established by associations of lumber producers and may vary somewhat, especially in the softwood classification.

### Softwood Grades

Softwood lumber grades are based on the American Softwood Lumber Standard PS 20-70 established by the United States Department of Commerce. Detailed rules are developed and applied by the various associations of lumber producers such as the Western Wood Products Association, Southern Forest Products Association, California Redwood Association, and similar groups. These agencies publish grading rules for the species of lumber in their regions. They also have qualified representatives at sawmills who supervise grading standards.

Softwood lumber is divided into three SIZE classifications: BOARDS, DIMENSION LUMBER, and TIMBERS. Each size classification has several grades within it. Fig. 2-3 shows the grades within each classification.

Another classification called FACTORY and SHOP LUMBER is graded primarily for remanufacturing purposes. It is used by millwork plants in the fabrication of doors, windows, moldings, and other trim items.

### Hardwood Grades

Grades for hardwood lumber are established by the National Hardwood Association. The best grade of hardwood lumber is FAS (firsts and seconds). This requires that pieces be not less than 6 in. wide by 8 ft. long and yield at least 83 1/3 percent clear cuttings. The next lower grade is SELECTS (sometimes called FAS 1 face) and permits pieces 4 in. wide by 6 ft. long with more defects on the second or back face (surface).

A still lower grade of hardwood is called No. 1 COMMON. It permits smaller pieces and yields 66 2/3 percent clear cuttings. No. 2 COMMON and No. 3 COMMON require 50 percent and 33 1/3 percent of clear cuttings but are not often listed in hardwood catalogues. Retailers usually cut out the defects in these grades and sell them as SHORTS (short lengths and narrow widths).

## LUMBER DEFECTS

A defect is an irregularity occurring in or on wood that reduces its strength, durability, or usefulness. It may or may not detract from appearance. For example, knots, commonly considered a defect, may add to the appearance of pine paneling. An imperfection that impairs only the appearance of wood is called a blemish. Some of the common defects include:

KNOTS: caused by an embedded limb or branch of the tree. It reduces the strength but in some cases may add to the appearance. See Fig. 2-4.

SPLITS and CHECKS: a separation of the wood along the grain and across the annual growth rings. See Fig. 2-5.

SHAKES: separations along the grain and between the annual growth rings. See Fig. 2-6.

PITCH POCKETS: internal cavities that contain, or have contained, pitch in solid or liquid form.

HONEYCOMBING: separation of the wood fibers in the interior of wood, usually along the wood rays. May not be visible at the surface.

WANE: the presence of bark or the absence of wood along the edge of a board. It forms a bevel and reduces the usable width.

BLUE STAIN: discoloration caused by a mold-like fungus. Though objectionable for appearance in some grades of lumber, it has little or no effect on strength.

DECAY: disintegration of wood fibers due to fungi. Early stages of decay may be difficult to recognize. In advanced stages wood is soft, spongy, and crumbles easily.

HOLES: caused by handling equipment or boring insects and worms. These will lower the lumber grade.

WARP: any variation from a true or plain surface, and may include any one or combination of the following: cup, bow, crook, and twist (also called wind). See Fig. 2-7.

## SEASONING LUMBER

The quality of lumber is also indicated by the method of drying. GREEN LUMBER from a freshly cut log will have an excessive amount of moisture (sap), most of which must be removed before it can be used. AIR DRIED (AD) lumber is simply exposed to the air over a period of time. By this method the

## boards

| APPEARANCE GRADES | SELECTS | B & BETTER (IWP—SUPREME)<br>C SELECT (IWP—CHOICE)<br>D SELECT (IWP—QUALITY) | | **SPECIFICATION CHECK LIST**<br>☐ Grades listed in order of quality.<br>☐ Include all species suited to project.<br>☐ For economy, specify lowest grade that will satisfy job requirement.<br>☐ Specify surface texture desired.<br>☐ Specify moisture content suited to project.<br>☐ Specify Ⓦ grade stamp. For finish and exposed pieces, specify stamp on back or ends. |
|---|---|---|---|---|
| | FINISH | SUPERIOR<br>PRIME<br>E | | |
| | PANELING | CLEAR (ANY SELECT OR FINISH GRADE)<br>NO. 2 COMMON SELECTED FOR KNOTTY PANELING<br>NO. 3 COMMON SELECTED FOR KNOTTY PANELING | | |
| | SIDING<br>(BEVEL,<br>BUNGALOW) | SUPERIOR<br>PRIME | | **WESTERN RED CEDAR** |
| | BOARDS<br>SHEATHING | NO. 1 COMMON (IWP—COLONIAL)<br>NO. 2 COMMON (IWP—STERLING)<br>NO. 3 COMMON (IWP—STANDARD)<br>NO. 4 COMMON (IWP—UTILITY) | ALTERNATE BOARD GRADES<br>SELECT MERCHANTABLE<br>CONSTRUCTION<br>STANDARD<br>UTILITY | FINISH PANELING AND CEILING — CLEAR HEART / A / B<br><br>BEVEL SIDING — CLEAR — V.G. HEART / A — BEVEL SIDING / B — BEVEL SIDING / C — BEVEL SIDING |

## dimension

| LIGHT FRAMING<br>2″ to 4″ Thick<br>2″ to 4″ Wide | CONSTRUCTION<br>STANDARD<br>UTILITY<br>ECONOMY | This category for use where high strength values are **NOT** required; such as studs, plates, sills, cripples, blocking, etc. |
|---|---|---|
| | STUD<br>ECONOMY STUD | An optional all-purpose grade limited to 10 feet and shorter. Characteristics affecting strength and stiffness values are limited so that the "Stud" grade is suitable for all stud uses, including load bearing walls. |
| STRUCTURAL LIGHT FRAMING<br>2″ to 4″ Thick<br>2″ to 4″ Wide | SELECT STRUCTURAL<br>NO. 1<br>NO. 2<br>NO. 3<br>ECONOMY | These grades are designed to fit those engineering applications where higher bending strength ratios are needed in light framing sizes. Typical uses would be for trusses, concrete pier wall forms, etc. |
| STRUCTURAL JOISTS & PLANKS<br>2″ to 4″ Thick<br>6″ and Wider | SELECT STRUCTURAL<br>NO. 1<br>NO. 2<br>NO. 3<br>ECONOMY | These grades are designed especially to fit in engineering applications for lumber six inches and wider, such as joists, rafters and general framing uses. |

## timbers

| BEAMS & STRINGERS | SELECT STRUCTURAL<br>NO. 1<br>NO. 2 (NO. 1 MINING)<br>NO. 3 (NO. 2 MINING) | POSTS & TIMBERS | SELECT STRUCTURAL<br>NO. 1<br>NO. 2 (NO. 1 MINING)<br>NO. 3 (NO. 2 MINING) |
|---|---|---|---|

Fig. 2-3. Softwood lumber classifications, grades, and standard lumber sizes. (Western Wood Products Association)

## BOARD MEASURE

The term "board measure" indicates that a board foot is the unit for measuring lumber. A board foot is one inch thick and 12 inches square.

The number of board feet in a piece is obtained by multiplying the nominal thickness in inches by the nominal width in inches by the length in feet and dividing by 12: $\frac{(T \times W \times L)}{12}$

Lumber less than one inch in thickness is figured as one-inch.

| | thickness in. | width in. | | thickness in. | width in. |
|---|---|---|---|---|---|
| board lumber | 1" | 2" or more | beams & stringers | 5" and thicker | more than 2" greater than thickness |
| light framing | 2" to 4" | 2" to 4" | posts & timbers | 5" x 5" and larger | not more than 2" greater than thickness |
| studs | 2" to 4" | 2" to 4" 10' and shorter | decking | 2" to 4" | 4" to 12" wide |
| structural light framing | 2" to 4" | 2" to 4" | siding | | thickness expressed by dimension of butt edge |
| joists & planks | 2" to 4" | 6" and wider | mouldings | | size at thickest and widest points |

Lengths of lumber generally are 6 feet and longer in multiples of 2'

## Standard Lumber Sizes / Nominal, Dressed, Based on WWPA Rules

| Product | Description | Nominal Size | | Dressed Dimensions | | |
|---|---|---|---|---|---|---|
| | | Thickness In. | Width In. | Thicknesses and Widths In. | | Lengths Ft. |
| | | | | Surfaced Dry | Surfaced Unseasoned | |
| **FRAMING** | S4S . . . . . . . . . . . . . . . . . . . . . | 2<br>3<br>4 | 2<br>3<br>4<br>6<br>8<br>10<br>12<br>Over 12 | 1-½<br>2-½<br>3-½<br>5-½<br>7-¼<br>9-¼<br>11-¼<br>Off ¾ | 1-⁹⁄₁₆<br>2-⁹⁄₁₆<br>3-⁹⁄₁₆<br>5-⅝<br>7-½<br>9-½<br>11-½<br>Off ½ | 6 ft. and longer in multiples of 1' |

| Product | Description | Nominal Size | Thickness In. | Width In. | Lengths Ft. |
|---|---|---|---|---|---|
| **TIMBERS** | Rough or S4S . . . . . . . . . . . . . . . . . . | 5 and Larger | ½ Off Nominal | | Same |

| Product | Description | Nominal Size | | Dressed Dimensions Surfaced Dry | | |
|---|---|---|---|---|---|---|
| | | Thickness In. | Width In. | Thickness In. | Width In. | Lengths Ft. |
| **DECKING** Decking is usually surfaced to single T&G in 2" thickness and double T&G in 3" and 4" thicknesses | 2" Single T&G . . . . . . . . . . . . . . . . | 2 | 6<br>8<br>10<br>12 | 1½ | 5<br>6¾<br>8¾<br>10¾ | 6 ft. and longer in multiples of 1' |
| | 3" and 4" Double T&G . . . . . . . . . . | 3<br>4 | 6 | 2½<br>3½ | 5¼ | |
| **FLOORING** | (D & M), (S2S & CM) . . . . . . . . . . | ⅜<br>½<br>⅝<br>1<br>1¼<br>1½ | 2<br>3<br>4<br>5<br>6 | ⁵⁄₁₆<br>⁷⁄₁₆<br>⁹⁄₁₆<br>¾<br>1<br>1¼ | 1⅛<br>2⅛<br>3⅛<br>4⅛<br>5⅛ | 4 ft. and longer in multiples of 1' |
| **CEILING AND PARTITION** | (S2S & CM) . . . . . . . . . . . . . . . . . . | ⅜<br>½<br>⅝<br>¾ | 3<br>4<br>5<br>6 | ⁵⁄₁₆<br>⁷⁄₁₆<br>⁹⁄₁₆<br>¹¹⁄₁₆ | 2⅛<br>3⅛<br>4⅛<br>5⅛ | 4 ft. and longer in multiples of 1' |
| **FACTORY AND SHOP LUMBER** | S2S . . . . . . . . . . . . . . . . . . . . . . . . | 1 (4/4)<br>1¼ (5/4)<br>1½ (6/4)<br>1¾ (7/4)<br>2 (8/4)<br>2½ (10/4)<br>3 (12/4)<br>4 (16/4) | 5 and wider (4" and wider in 4/4 No. 1 Shop and 4/4 No. 2 Shop) | ²⁵⁄₃₂ (4/4)<br>1⁵⁄₃₂ (5/4)<br>1¹³⁄₃₂ (6/4)<br>1¹⁹⁄₃₂ (7/4)<br>1¹³⁄₁₆ (8/4)<br>2⅜ (10/4)<br>2¾ (12/4)<br>3¾ (16/4) | Usually sold random width | 4 ft. and longer in multiples of 1' |

**ABBREVIATIONS**

Abbreviated descriptions appearing in the size table are explained below.

S1S — Surfaced one side.
S2S — Surfaced two sides.

S4S — Surfaced four sides.
S1S1E — Surfaced one side, one edge.
S1S2E — Surfaced one side, two edges
CM — Center matched.

D & M — Dressed and matched.
T & G — Tongue and grooved.
EV1S — Edge vee on one side.
S1E — Surfaced one edge.

Fig. 2-3 Continued.

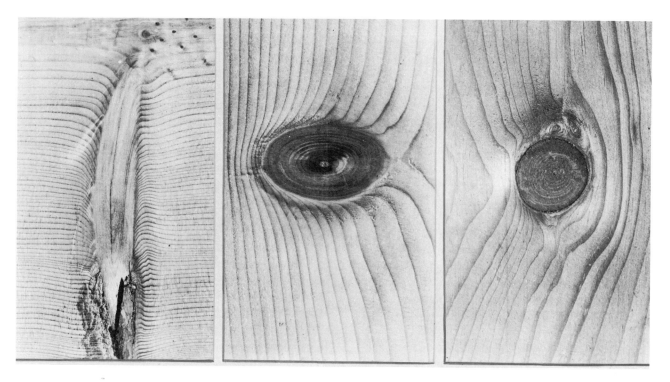

Fig. 2-4. Common kinds of knots. Left. Spike. Center. Intergrown. Right. Encased. The encased knot will probably loosen and fall out. (Forest Products Laboratory)

Fig. 2-5. Splits and checks.

Fig. 2-6. Shakes. (Forest Products Laboratory)

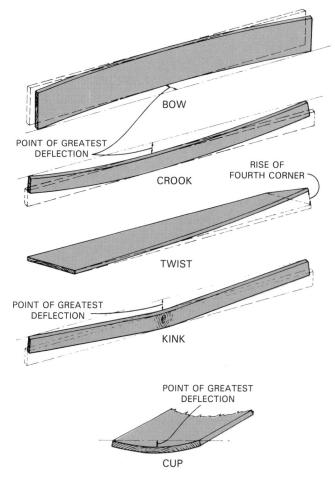

Fig. 2-7. Kinds of warp.

moisture content is reduced to 12 to 18 percent.

KILN DRIED (KD) lumber is dried in huge ovens where temperature and humidity are carefully controlled, Fig. 2-8. It will have a low moisture content (7 to 10 percent) and will be free of internal stresses that are often present in air dried lumber. Also, there usually will be fewer seasoning defects such as splits, checks, and warp. Lumber that is to be used for furniture, cabinetmaking, and other fine woodwork should be kiln dried.

### Moisture Meters

Two methods may be used to determine the moisture content of wood:
1. Oven drying a sample.
2. Using an electric moisture meter.

Although the oven drying method is the most accurate, meters are often used because readings can be secured rapidly and conveniently. The meters are usually calibrated to cover a range from 7 to 25 percent. Accuracy is plus or minus 1 percent of the moisture content.

There are two types of moisture meters. One determines the moisture content by measuring the electrical resistance between two pin-type electrodes that are driven into the wood. The other type measures the capacity of a condenser in a high-frequency circuit, where the wood serves as the dielectric (nonconducting) material of the condenser. See Fig. 2-9.

## CUTTING METHODS

Most lumber is cut in such a way that the annular rings form an angle less than 45 degrees with the surface of the board. This method produces lumber that is called FLAT-GRAINED (if it is softwood) or

Fig. 2-8. Kiln drying lumber in large quantities. (Forest Products Laboratory)

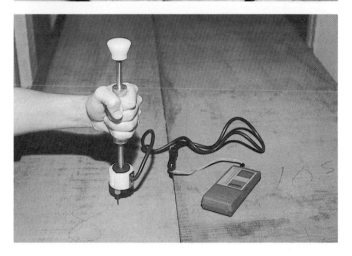

Fig. 2-9. Top. Modern digital moisture meter. LEDs indicate correct moisture percentage. Middle. Probes inserted into end cut. Bottom. Hammer probe provides readings up to 1 inch below surface. (Forestry Suppliers, Inc.)

PLAIN-SAWED (if it is hardwood).

Lumber can also be cut so that the annular rings form an angle of more than 45 degrees with the surface of the board. This method produces lumber that is called EDGE-GRAINED (if it is softwood) or QUARTER-SAWED (if it is hardwood). It is more difficult and expensive to use this method but it does result in lumber that is less likely to warp, and may

produce a more attractive grain pattern. The edge grain of some softwoods such as Douglas Fir, wears better than flat-grained surfaces.

## SURFACE AND SIZE

Softwoods are surfaced (planed) on all faces and edges (S4S). See Fig. 2-10. They are sold in specified widths from 2 in. to 12 in. in 2 in. intervals and in lengths of 8 to 20 ft. in 2 ft. intervals. Because the surfacing removes some of the wood, the thickness and width will actually measure less than the nominal size. Study the S4S sizes listed on this page.

Hardwoods can be purchased either rough (RGH) or surfaced on both sizes (S2S), Fig. 2-10. Surfaced thicknesses are somewhat different from those for softwoods, as shown in Fig. 2-11. Hardwoods are usually not cut to any standard width or length. They are cut and sold in RANDOM WIDTHS and LENGTHS (RW & L).

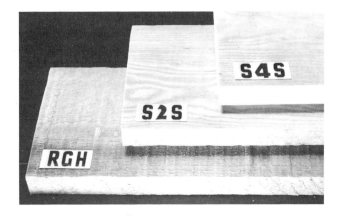

Fig. 2-10. Rough and surfaced lumber.

| SOFTWOODS | | HARDWOODS | |
|---|---|---|---|
| Rgh | S4S | Rgh | S2S |
| 1 x 2 | 3/4 x 1 1/2 | 3/8 | 3/16 |
| 1 x 4 | 3/4 x 3 1/2 | 1/2 | 5/16 |
| 1 x 6 | 3/4 x 3 1/2 | 5/8 | 7/16 |
| 1 x 8 | 3/4 x 7 1/4 | 3/4 | 9/16 |
| 1 x 10 | 3/4 x 9 1/4 | 1 (4/4) | 13/16 |
| 1 x 12 | 3/4 x 11 1/4 | 1 1/4 (5/4) | 1 1/16 |
| 2 x 2 | 1 1/2 x 1 1/2 | 1 1/2 (6/4) | 1 5/16 |
| 2 x 4 | 1 1/2 x 3 1/2 | 2 (8/4) | 1 3/4 |
| 2 x 6 | 1 1/2 x 5 1/2 | 2 1/2 | 2 1/4 |
| 2 x 8 | 1 1/2 x 7 1/4 | 3 | 2 3/4 |
| 2 x 10 | 1 1/2 x 9 1/4 | 3 1/2 | 3 1/4 |
| 4 x 4 | 3 1/2 x 3 1/2 | 4 | 3 3/4 |

Fig. 2-11. Rough and finished sizes.

## WOOD IDENTIFICATION

A key element in woodworking and in carpentry is the proper identification of the wood.

This insert, which is intended as a guide and an aid to the student in learning to identify various woods, shows typical color and grain characteristics of 59 different species.

**ASH, WHITE.** Strong, stiff, and fairly heavy (42 lbs. to cu. ft.). Works fairly well with hand tools but splits easily. Heartwood is a pale tan with a texture similar to Oak. Used for millwork, cabinets, furniture, upholstered frames, boxes and crates. Used extensively for baseball bats, tennis rackets, and other sporting equipment.

**ASPEN.** Soft, light, close-grained, and easy to work. White sapwood with light tan and brown streaked heartwood. Source: Europe, Western Asia and Middle Atlantic States. Used for furniture, and interior paneling.

**BALSA.** The lightest wood available (12 lbs. to cu. ft.). Very soft and easily cut with knives. Best known for its use in model aircraft construction. Also used for life rafts, duck decoys, hat blocks, and other lightweight items. Chief source is Ecuador.

**BASSWOOD.** The softest and lightest (26 lbs. to cu. ft.) hardwood in commercial use. Fine, even texture with straight grain. Especially easy to work with hand tools and highly resistant to warpage. Heartwood is a light yellowish-brown. Used for drawing boards, food containers, moldings, woodenware and core stock for plywood.

**BEECH.** Heavy, hard and strong. (44 lbs. to cu. ft.) A good substitute for Sugar Maple but somewhat darker in color, with a slightly coarser texture. Used for flooring, furniture, brush handles, food containers, and boxes and crates.

28

BELLA ROSA. Moderately hard, heavy and coarse textured. Striped and mottled grain patterns. Source: Philippine Islands. Available in veneer and lumber. Sample shows quartered veneer.

BIRCH. A hard, strong, wood (47 lbs. to cu. ft.). Works well with machines and has excellent finishing characteristics. Heartwood, reddish-brown with white sapwood. Fine grain and texture. Used extensively for quality furniture, cabinetwork, doors, interior trim, and plywood. Also used for dowels, spools, toothpicks, and clothespins.

BIRCH, WHITE. Selected sapwood rotary-cuttings of regular birch veneer. Same characteristics as birch except nearly white in color. Used to make plywood for installations requiring a very light, fine textured material.

BOXWOOD. Hard, close, and smooth grained. A very indistinct grain pattern with a light yellow color. Source: Europe, Asia, and West Indies. Used for inlays, marquetry, and instruments, especially fine rulers and scales.

BUCKEYE. A soft, close-grained wood that is not very strong. Nearly white in color, often blemished with dark stained lines. Source: Eastern United States. Rather scarce and usually available only in veneers.

BUTTERNUT. Fairly soft, weak, light in weight (27 lbs. to cu. ft.), with a coarse texture. Grain patterns resemble walnut. Large open pores require a paste filler. Works easily with hand or machine tools. Sometimes used for interior trim, cabinetwork, and wall paneling.

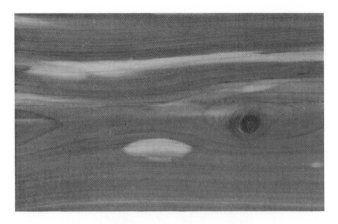

CEDAR, RED, EASTERN. Medium dense softwood, (34 lbs. to cu. ft.). Close grained and durable. Heartwood is red; sapwood is white. It has an aroma that inhibits the growth of moths. Knotty wood is available only in narrow widths. Used mostly for chests and novelty items.

CEDAR, RED, WESTERN. A soft wood, light in weight (23 lbs. per cu. ft.). Similar to redwood except for cedar-like odor. Pronounced transition from spring to summer growth (see edge-grain sample). Source: Western coast of North America, especially Washington. Used for shingles, siding, structural timbers and utility poles.

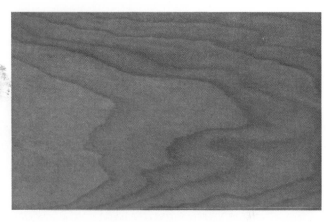

CHERRY, BLACK. Moderately hard, strong and heavy (36 lbs. to cu. ft.). A fine, close-grained wood that machines easily and can be sanded to a very smooth finish. Heartwood is a reddish-brown with beautiful grain patterns. One of the fine furniture woods, however, there is a scarcity of good grades of lumber.

CHESTNUT. Coarse textured, open grain, and very durable. Reddish brown heartwood. Easily worked with hand or machine tools. Source: Eastern United States. Available only in a wormy grade due to the "chestnut blight."

COCOBOLA. Dense, hard and oily. A difficult wood to work because of an interwoven grain. Bright red when freshly cut, but soon darkens. Source: Central America. Used for fancy cabinetwork and knife handles.

CYPRESS. Light in weight, soft and easily worked. Fairly coarse texture with annual growth rings clearly defined (sample shows edge grain). Source: Southeastern Coast of the United States. Noted for its durability against decay. Used for exterior construction and interior wall paneling.

EBONY. Extremely hard and so dense that it will not float in water. Difficult to work. Source: Ceylon, Africa and East Indies. The true black ebony comes from Ceylon and is expensive. Suitable for inlays, marquetry and small decorative articles.

ELM, AMERICAN. Strong and tough for its weight (36 lbs. to cu. ft.). Fairly coarse texture with open pores. Annular ring growth is clearly defined. Bends without breaking and machines well. Used for barrel staves, bent handles, baskets, and special types of furniture.

FIR, DOUGLAS. A strong, moderately heavy (34 lbs. to cu. ft.) softwood. Straight close grain with heavy contrast between spring and summer growth. Splinters easily. Used for wall and roof framing and other structural work. Vast amounts are used for plywood. Machines and sands poorly. Seldom used for finish.

GUM, SWEET. Also called Red Gum. Fairly hard and strong (36 lbs. to cu. ft.). A close grained wood that machines well but has a tendency to warp. Heartwood is reddish-brown and may be highly figured. Used extensively in furniture and cabinetmaking. Stains well, often used in combination with more expensive woods.

HAREWOOD. A close-grained wood nearly white in color. Grain pattern is often highly figured. Sometimes dyed to a gray color and called Silver Harewood. Source: England. Used for marquetry, inlay and paneling.

HEMLOCK. A softwood. Light in weight and moderately hard. Light reddish brown in color with a slight purplish cast. (Sample shows edge grain.) Source: Pacific Coast and Western States. Used for construction lumber and pulpwood; also for containers and plywood core stock.

IMBUYA.  Also called Brazilian Walnut. Moderately hard and heavy with an open-grain and fine texture. Source: Brazil. Used for high grade furniture, cabinetwork and paneling.

KOA.  Medium hard with a texture similar to walnut. Open-grained. Color is golden to dark brown, often with dark streaks. Polishes to a lustrous sheen. The best known hardwood of the Hawaiian Islands. Used for fine furniture, art objects, and musical instruments.

LACEWOOD.  Medium hard with flaky grain formed by wood rays. Usually quartered to produce small uniform flakes (as shown). Source: Australia. Occasionally used for decorative overlays on furniture and for wall paneling.

LIGNUM VITAE.  Very hard and heavy (specific gravity 1.20). Oily and mildly scented, with a fine interwoven grain texture that makes it hard to work. Source: Central America, West Indies, and Northern South America. Used for bearings, pulleys, brush backs, and similar items.

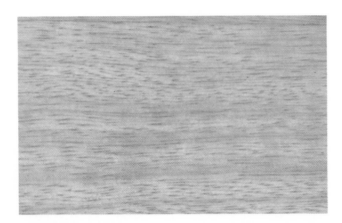

LIMBA.  A light blond wood from the Congo, often sold under the trade name Korina. It has an open grain with about the same texture and hardness of Mahogany. Works easily with either hand or machine tools. Used for furniture and fixtures, especially where light tones are required.

MAHOGANY, AFRICAN.  Characteristics are similar to American varieties. Slightly coarser texture and more pronounced grain patterns. Quarter sawing or slicing produces a ribbon grain effect (as shown). Source: Ivory Coast, Ghana and Nigeria. Used for fine furniture, interior finish, art objects and boats.

**MAHOGANY, HONDURAS.** Medium hard and dense (32 lbs. to cu. ft.). Excellent working and machining qualities. A very stable wood, with even texture, open pores, and beautiful grain patterns. Used for high grade foundry patterns and quality furniture. It turns and carves especially well.

**MAHOGANY, PHILIPPINE.** Medium density and hardness (37 lbs. to cu. ft.). Open grain and coarse texture. Works fairly well with hand or machine tools. Varies in color from dark red (Tanguile) to light tan (Lauan). Used for medium price furniture, fixtures, trim, wall paneling. Also, boat building and core stock in plywood.

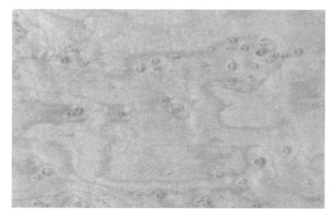

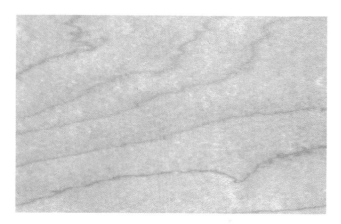

**MAPLE, BIRDSEYE.** Hard or Sugar Maple with tiny spots of curly grain that look like bird's eyes. The cause of this figure is not known. It may be distributed throughout the tree or located only in irregular stripes or patches. Used for highly decorative inlays and overlays.

**MAPLE, SUGAR.** Also called Hard Maple. It is hard, strong, and heavy (44 lbs. to cu. ft.). Fine texture and grain pattern. Light tan color, with occasional dark streaks. Hard to work with hand tools but machines easily. Is an excellent turning wood. Used for floors, bowling alleys, woodenware, handles, and quality furniture.

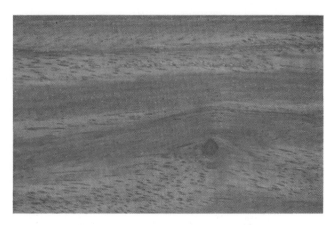

**MYRTLE.** Hard and strong with pore size and distribution about the same as walnut. Golden brown color with an olive green cast. Machines easily and can be polished to a high luster. Source: Southwestern Oregon. Used for decorative panels in furniture and architectural woodwork; also for art objects and novelties.

**NARRA.** Heavy, hard, and durable. Has a distinct grain pattern and open pores. Generally a golden yellow brown but may be found in a rose or deep red color. Source: Philippines and Malaysia. Used for high grade furniture and interior finish of ships.

33

OAK, ENGLISH. Open-grained with a texture similar to regular oak. Light tan to deep brown color with dark spots that create an unusual figure and grain character. Source: England. Used for fine furniture and special architectural woodwork.

OAK, QUARTERED. Sawing or slicing oak in a radial direction results in a striking pattern as shown. The "flakes" are formed by large wood rays that reflect light. Used where dramatic wood grain effects are desired.

OAK, RED. Heavy (45 lbs. to cu. ft.) and hard with the same general characteristics as White Oak. Heartwood is reddish-brown in color. No tyloses in wood pores. Used for flooring, millwork and inside trim. Difficult to work with hand tools.

OAK, WHITE. Heavy (47 lbs. to cu. ft.), very hard, durable, and strong. Works best with power tools. Heartwood is greyish-brown with open pores that are distinct and plugged with a hairlike growth called tyloses. Used for high quality millwork, interior finish, furniture, carvings, boat structures, barrels and kegs.

ORIENTALWOOD. Also called Australian Laurel. Medium weight with wood characteristics similar to walnut. Color is pinkish gray to brown with dark stripes as shown. Source: Australia. Used for highest quality furniture and cabinetwork.

PADOUK. Also called Vermillion. Hard firm texture with some interlocked grain that makes it difficult to work. Large open pores. Red color, may have streaks of yellow or brown. Source: Burma and West Africa. Used for art objects and novelties.

PALDAO. A fairly hard wood with large pores that are partially plugged. Grain patterns are striking and beautiful and provide an excellent example of an "exotic" wood. Source: Philippine Islands. Sometimes selected by architects for special fixtures or built-ins for public or institutional buildings.

PEARWOOD. A very fine textured, close-grained wood with pores that are indistinct. Subdued grain pattern, sometimes with mottled figure. Source: United States and Europe. Used for fine furniture, marquetry, saw handles and rulers.

PINE, PONDEROSA. Lightweight (28 lbs. to cu. ft.) and soft. Straight grained and uniform texture. Not a strong wood but works easily and has little tendency to warp. Heartwood is a light reddish-brown. Change from springwood to summerwood is abrupt. Used for window and door frames, moldings, and other millwork; toys, models.

PINE, SUGAR. Lightweight, (26 lbs. to cu. ft.) soft, and uniform texture. Heartwood, light brown with many tiny resin canals that appear as brown flecks. Straight grained and warp resistant. Cuts and works very easily with hand tools. Used for foundry patterns, sash and door construction, and quality millwork.

PINE, WHITE. Soft, light (28 lbs. to cu. ft.) and even texture. Cream colored with some resin canals but not as prevalent as in Sugar Pine. Used for interior and exterior trim and millwork items. Knotty grades often used for wall paneling. Works easily with hand or machine tools.

POPLAR, YELLOW. Moderately soft, light in weight (34 lbs. to cu. ft.), and even textured. Heartwood is a pale olive-brown and sapwood is greyish-white. Works well with hand or machine tools and resists warping. Used in a wide variety of products including inexpensive furniture, trunks, toys, and core stock for plywood.

**PRIMAVERA.** Sometimes called white or golden mahogany. Medium to coarse texture with straight and somewhat striped grain. Very similar to mahogany except for the color which is a light straw to golden yellow. Source: Southern Mexico, Guatemala, Honduras, and Salvador. One of the fine cabinet woods of the world.

**REDWOOD.** Soft and light in weight (28 lbs. to cu. ft.). Texture varies but is usually fine and even grained. Easy to work and durable. Heartwood is reddish-brown. Used for structures, outside finish and sometimes for interior paneling. Its durability makes it especially valuable for products exposed to water and moisture.

**ROSEWOOD, BRAZILIAN.** A very hard wood with large irregular pores. Various shades of dark brown with conspicuous black streaks. Rosewood with different colors and characteristics also comes from India, Ceylon, Madagascar and Central America. A beautiful wood used for art objects, levels, tool handles and musical instruments.

**SATINWOOD.** Fine grain texture, hard and heavy, with a slight oiliness. Golden yellow in color with beautiful wavy grain patterns that often give a mottled effect. Source: Puerto Rico. Honduras, Ceylon and East Indies. Used for inlays, marquetry, fine brush handles and similar items.

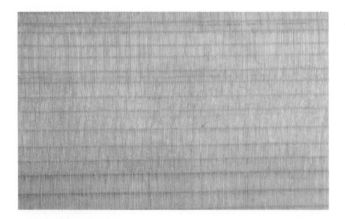

**SPRUCE.** A soft wood, light in weight (24 lbs. per cu. ft.). Transition from spring to summer growth is gradual (see edge grain sample). There are several species; Sitka, Englemen, and a general classification called Eastern. Source: various parts of the United States and Canada. Used for pulpwood, light construction and carpentry.

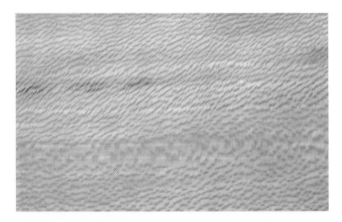

**SYCAMORE.** Medium density, hardness, and strength. A close-grained wood with a rather coarse texture. Easily identified by the flaky pattern of wood rays observed best in quartered stock. Source: Eastern half of United States. Used for drawer sides and lower priced furniture. Veneers are used for berry and fruit boxes.

**TAMO.** Also called Japanese Ash. The physical characteristics of the wood resembles American Ash. Grain patterns are extremely pronounced. Figures may consist of swirl, fiddleback or blister types. Source: Japan. Used for inlays and overlays where a highly decorative surface is required.

**TEAK.** Strong and quite hard. Resembles walnut except for a lighter tawny yellow color. Silicates and minerals in the wood give it an oily feel and dulls regular tools more quickly. Source: Burma, India, Thailand and Java. Used for fine furniture and paneling. Also used for ship building because of its great durability.

**TULIPWOOD.** Hard, medium textured, open-grained wood, with small pores that vary in size. Red and yellow color streaked with dark lines. Source: Northeastern Brazil. A highly decorative wood used for inlays, turnings, and novelties.

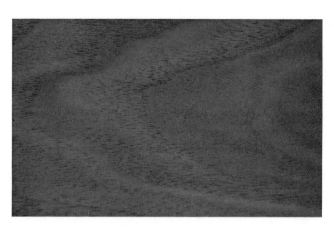

**WALNUT, BLACK.** Fairly dense and hard. Very strong in comparison to its weight (38 lbs. to cu. ft.). Excellent machining and finishing properties. A fine textured open grain wood with beautiful grain patterns. Heartwood is a chocolate brown with sapwood near white. Used on quality furniture, gun stocks, fine cabinetwork, etc.

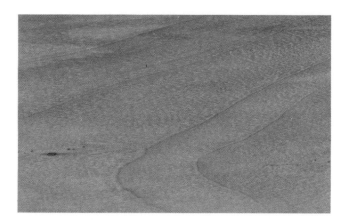

**WILLOW, BLACK.** Very soft and light in weight (27 lbs. to cu. ft.). Resembles basswood in workability, although there is some tendency for the machined surface to be fuzzy. Heartwood varies from light gray to dark brown. Used for some inexpensive furniture, core stock for plywood, wall paneling, toys, and novelty products.

**ZEBRAWOOD.** Also called Zebrano. Heavy, hard, open-grained wood with a medium texture. Light gold in color with narrow streaks of dark brown in quartered stock (see sample). A highly decorative wood from Central and West Africa. Made into quartered veneer and used where a spectacular effect is desired.

Standard thicknesses of hardwoods of one inch and over are sometimes designated in quarters of an inch and often referred to as four-quarter, five-quarter, etc. This also applies to White Pine and a few of the other softwoods.

### Metric Lumber Measure

Metric sized lumber gives thickness and width in millimeters (mm) and length in meters (m). There is little difference between metric and conventional dimensions for common sizes of lumber. For example, the common 1'' x 4'' board is 25 mm x 100 mm. Visually, they would appear to be about the same size. Metric lumber lengths start at 1.8 m (about 6 ft.) and increase in steps of 300 mm (about a foot) to 6.3 m. This is a little more than 20 ft. See Fig. 2-12 for a chart of standard sizes. Metric lumber is sold by the cubic meter (m³).

## PANEL MATERIALS

Wood panels are manufactured in several forms:
1. As plywood where thin plies are laminated to form various thicknesses.
2. As composite plywood where veneer faces are bonded to different kinds of wood cores.
3. As nonveneered panels including waferboard, particle board, and oriented strand board.

## PLYWOOD

Plywood is constructed by gluing together a number of layers (plies) of wood with the grain direction turned at right angles in each successive layer. An odd number (3, 5, 7, etc.) of plies are used so that they will be balanced on either side of a center core and so that the grain of the outside layers will run in the same direction. The outer plies

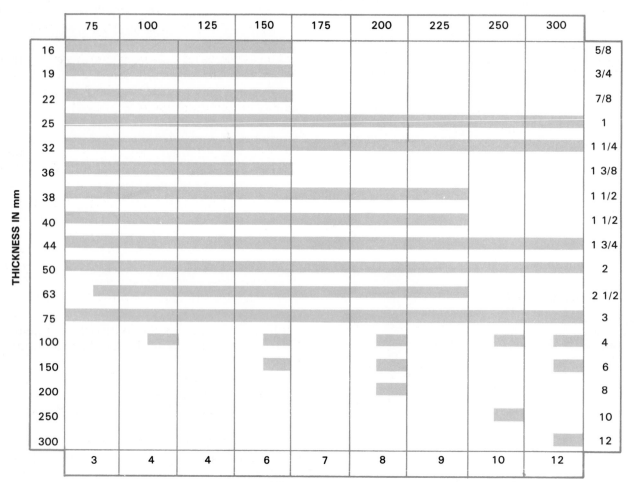

Fig. 2-12. Dimensions of metric lumber are given in millimeters. Lengths are always in meters and range from 1.8 m to 6.3 m in 0.3 m (about 1 ft.) increments.

are called FACES, or face and back. The next layers under these are called CROSSBANDS and the other inside layer or layers are called the CORE. See Fig. 2-13. A thin plywood panel made of three layers would consist of just faces and a core.

Plywood is classified as either hardwood or softwood depending upon the kind of wood used in the face veneers. It is available in nearly all of the fine hardwoods and many of the softwoods. The softwoods most generally available are Douglas Fir and Ponderosa Pine. More information concerning the manufacturing of plywood can be found in Unit 25.

There are two basic types of plywood; exterior and interior. EXTERIOR PLYWOOD is bonded with waterproof glues and can be used for boats, siding, concrete forms, and other construction that will be exposed to the weather or excessive moisture. INTERIOR PLYWOOD is bonded with glues that are not waterproof and is used for cabinets, furniture, and inside construction where the moisture content of the panels will not exceed 20 percent.

Plywood can be secured in thicknesses from 1/8 in. to more than 1 in., with the most common sizes being 1/4, 3/8, 1/2, 5/8, and 3/4 in. A standard panel size is 4 ft. wide by 8 ft. long. Smaller size panels are available in the hardwoods.

The grade of a plywood panel depends on the quality of the face and back veneers. In softwood, the highest grade is designated by the letter N and then ranges down through A, B, C, and D, Fig. 2-14. For example, a grade A-A panel would have a good grade of veneer on each side. An A-D grade, however, would specify a panel that was good on one side but had a back with knots, splits, etc.

## Softwood Plywood Grades

Softwood plywood is manufactured in accordance with U.S. Product Standard PS 1-74/ANSI

| VENEER GRADES | |
|---|---|
| N | Smooth surface "natural finish" veneer. Select, all heartwood or all sapwood. Free of open defects. Allows not more than 6 repairs, wood only, per 4 x 8 panel, made parallel to grain and well matched for grain and color. |
| A | Smooth, paintable. Not more than 18 neatly made repairs, boat, sled, or router type, and parallel to grain, permitted. May be used for natural finish in less demanding applications. |
| B | Solid surface. Shims, circular repair plugs, and tight knots to 1 inch across grain permitted. Some minor splits permitted. |
| C Plugged | Improved C veneer with splits limited to 1/8 inch width and knotholes and borer holes limited to 1/4 x 1/2 inch. Admits some broken grain. Synthetic repairs permitted. |
| C | Tight knots to 1 1/2 inch. Knotholes to 1 inch across grain and some to 1 1/2 inch if total width of knots and knotholes is within specified limits. Synthetic or wood repairs. Discoloration and sanding defects that do not impair strength permitted. Limited splits allowed. Stitching permitted. |
| D | Knots and knotholes to 2 1/2 inch width across grain and 1/2 inch larger within specified limits. Limited splits allowed. Stitching permitted. Limited to Interior, Exposure 1 and Exposure 2 panels. |

Fig. 2-14. Description of softwood plywood veneer grades. (American Plywood Association)

A199.1. This standard provides a system for designating the species, strengths, type of glue, and appearance.

Many species of softwood are used in making plywood. There are five separate plywood groups based on stiffness and strength. Group 1 includes the stiffest and strongest, Fig. 2-15.

## Hardwood Plywood Grades

The Hardwood Plywood Institute uses a number system (1, 2, 3, 4) for grading the faces and backs of a panel. A grading specification of 1-2 would require a good face with grain carefully matched, but a good back without careful grain matching. A number 3 back would permit noticeably more defects and patching, but would be generally sound. A special or PREMIUM grade of hardwood is known as "architectural" or "sequence-matched." This requires an order to a plywood mill for a series of matched plywood panels that result in a dramatic and beautiful effect when installed. It is quite expensive and usually limited to public or institutional buildings.

For either softwood or hardwood plywood it is common practice to designate in a general way the grade by G2S (good two sides) or G1S (good one side).

In addition to the various kinds, types, and grades, hardwood plywood is made with different core constructions. The two most common are the veneer core and the lumber core, as shown in Fig. 2-16. VENEER CORES are the least expensive, are stable and warp resistant. LUMBER CORES are easier to cut, have better edges for shaping and

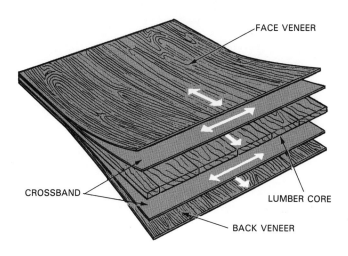

Fig. 2-13. Plywood construction. Top layer, face veneer; second, crossband; third, lumber core; fourth, crossband; bottom, back veneer. (Fine Hardwoods Association)

| GROUP 1 | GROUP 2 | GROUP 3 | GROUP 4 | GROUP 5 |
|---------|---------|---------|---------|---------|
| Apitong | Cedar, Port | Alder, Red | Aspen | Basswood |
| Beech, | Orford | Birch, Paper | Bigtooth | Fir, Balsam |
| American | Cypress | Cedar, Alaska | Quaking | Poplar, |
| Birch | Douglas | Fir, | Cativo | Balsam |
| Sweet | Fir 2 | Subalpine | Cedar | |
| Yellow | Fir | Hemlock, | Incense | |
| Douglas | California | Eastern | Western | |
| Fir 1[a] | Red | Maple, | Red | |
| Kapur | Grand | Bigleaf | Cottonwood | |
| Keruing | Noble | Pine | Eastern | |
| Larch, | Pacific | Jack | Black | |
| Western | Silver | Lodgepole | (Western | |
| Maple, Sugar | White | Ponderosa | Poplar) | |
| Pine | Hemlock, | Spruce | Pine | |
| Caribbean | Western | Redwood | Eastern | |
| Ocote | Lauan | Spruce | White | |
| Pine, South. | Almon | Black | Sugar | |
| Loblolly | Bagtikan | Engelmann | | |
| Longleaf | Mayapis | White | | |
| Shortleaf | Red Lauan | | | |
| Slash | Tangile | | | |
| Tanoak | White Lauan | | | |
| | Maple, Black | | | |
| | Mengkulang | | | |
| | Meranti, Red | | | |
| | Mersawa | | | |
| | Pine | | | |
| | Pond | | | |
| | Red | | | |
| | Virginia | | | |
| | Western | | | |
| | White | | | |
| | Spruce | | | |
| | Red | | | |
| | Sitka | | | |
| | Sweetgum | | | |
| | Tamarack | | | |
| | Yellow- | | | |
| | poplar | | | |

Fig. 2-15. Classification of softwood plywoods rates species for strength and stiffness. Group 1 represents strongest woods. (American Plywood Association)

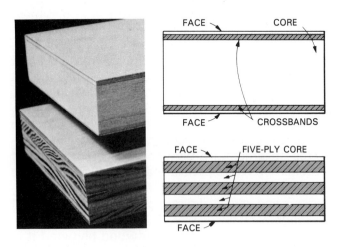

Fig. 2-16. Plywood. Above. Lumber core. Below. Veneer core.

finishing, and hold nails and screws better. Plywood is also manufactured with a particle board core. It is made by gluing 1/28 in. veneers directly to the particle board surface. The holding power of nails and screws is lessened with this type of plywood. However, it does provide a stable panel.

## COMPOSITE BOARD

Panels made up of a core of reconstituted wood with a thin veneer on either side are called composite board or composite panels. These materials are widely used in modern construction.

In cabinetwork, hardboard and particle board, Fig. 2-17, serve as appropriate materials for drawer bottoms and concealed panels in cases, cabinets, and chests. They are manufactured by many different companies and sold under various trade names.

### Hardboard

Hardboard is made of refined wood fibers, pressed together to form a hard, dense material (50-80 lbs. per cu. ft.). There are two types: STANDARD and TEMPERED. Tempered hardboard is impregnated with oils and resins that makes it harder, slightly heavier, more water resistant, and darker in appearance. Hardboard is manufactured with one side smooth (S1S) or both sides smooth

Fig. 2-17. Many structural wood panels are manufactured for construction uses. Products shown (top to bottom) include: waferboard, structural particle board, composite plywood, oriented strand board, and plywood. (Georgia Pacific Corporation)

(S2S). S1S has a reverse impression of a screen on the back side. Hardboard is available in thicknesses from 1/12 in. to 5/16 in., with the most common thickness being 1/8, 3/16, and 1/4 in. Panels are 4 ft. wide and come in standard lengths of 8, 10, 12, and 16 ft.

## Particle Board

Particle board is made of wood flakes, chips, and shavings bonded together with resins or adhesives. It is not as heavy as hardboard (about 40 lbs. per cu. ft.) and is available in thicker pieces. Particle board may be constructed of layers made of different size wood particles; large particles in the center to provide strength, and fine particles at the surface to provide smoothness.

Extensive use is made of particle board as a base or core for plastic laminates and veneers. It is an important material in the construction of counter tops, cabinets, drawers and shelving, many types of folding and sliding doors, room dividers, and a variety of built-ins.

It is popular because of its smooth, grain-free surface, and its stability. Its surface qualities make it a popular choice as a base for laminates. Doors made of it do not warp and require little adjustment following installation.

Particle board is available in thicknesses ranging from 1/4 in. to 1 7/8 in. The most common panel size is 4 x 8 ft.

## Waferboard

Waferboard, also called waferwood, is produced from high quality flakes of wood that are about 1 1/2 in. square. These flakes are bonded together under heat and pressure with phenolic resin, a waterproof adhesive. Both sides of waferboard have the same textured surface, Fig. 2-18. This surface has a natural slickness which can be minimized by special treatments. The density of waferboard is about 40 lbs. per square foot. Standard panel size is 4 x 8 ft. Thickness ranges from 1/4 in. to 3/4 in.

## Oriented Strand Board

Somewhat like waferboard in appearance, oriented strand board is also made up of wood fibers adhered to each other with suitable resins and glues, Fig. 2-19. The fibers are arranged in successive layers at right angles to one another. The panels can be used in applications similar to plywood and particle board.

Composite board products may be worked with regular woodworking machines and hand tools, using standard blades and knives. However, the resins in these products do wear cutting edges more rapidly than wood. Hard-tipped or carbide-tipped blades should be used if there is a large amount of cutting to be done.

Fig. 2-18. Waferboard consists of multilayers of wood wafers, bonded together under extreme heat and pressure with a waterproof phenolic resin. The result is a rigid, flat panel, dimensionally stable and equally strong in all directions. It may be used as an interior or exterior material. (Georgia Pacific Corporation)

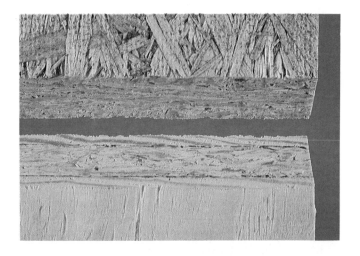

Fig. 2-19. Oriented strand board has layers of compressed strand-like particles arranged at right angles to each other. (Georgia Pacific Corporation)

## HANDLING AND STORING

Lumber that will be used for cabinetmaking and finished woodwork should be handled carefully, especially if it is surfaced. It should be protected from excessive moisture, dust and dirt, dents, and scars. Whether rough or surfaced it must be kept carefully stacked to minimize warpage.

A carefully laid stack of RW & L lumber is shown in Fig. 2-20. Long boards are placed in the bottom tiers (layers) and shorter ones on top, so that each board is completely supported. Wide and narrow

Fig. 2-20. A carefully built stack of RW & L lumber.

boards are laid so that "joints are broken" in each successive tier. One end of the stack is dressed (aligned) so that it will be easy to count the number of pieces and figure the footage. If the lumber is delivered with a considerably higher or lower moisture content than it will attain in the storage area, it should be open stacked with stickers (see Glossary) so that air can circulate freely around each piece.

Plywood, especially the fine hardwoods, must be handled with great care. The faces are sanded and they can easily become soiled and scarred. The best method of storing is to lay the panels flat. If they are stored in a vertical position, then pressure should be applied to the sides to keep them in a true plane.

### FIGURING BOARD FOOTAGE

The unit of measure for lumber is the board foot. This is a piece 1 in. thick and 12 in. square or its equivalent (144 cu. in.). You can figure the board feet in some pieces very easily. For example, a board 1 x 12 and 10 ft. long will contain 10 bd. ft. If it were only 6 in. wide it would be 5 bd. ft. If the original board had been 2 in. thick it would have contained 20 bd. ft. For most pieces of stock however, you will need to use the following formula (all of the sizes must be in inches):

$$\text{Bd. ft.} = \frac{\text{No. pcs. } \times T \times W \times L}{1 \times 12 \times 12}$$

For an example, find the number of board feet in 2 pieces of stock that are 1 x 9 x 36.

$$\text{Bd. ft.} = \frac{2 \times 1 \times \overset{3}{\cancel{9}} \times \overset{3}{\cancel{36}}}{1 \times \underset{4}{\cancel{12}} \times \underset{1}{\cancel{12}}} = \frac{18}{4} = 4\ 1/2$$

Stock that is less than 1 in. thick is figured as though it were 1 in. When the stock is thicker than 1 in. the nominal size is used. When this size contains a fraction such as 1 1/2, change it to an im-

proper fraction (3/2) and place the numerator above the formula line and the denominator below. For example, find the board footage in 3 pieces of stock 1 1/2 x 10 x 56.

$$\text{Bd. ft.} = \frac{\overset{3}{\cancel{3}}\text{ pcs. } \overset{1}{\cancel{3}} \times \overset{1}{\cancel{10}} \times \overset{\overset{7}{\cancel{14}}}{\cancel{56}}}{\underset{1}{\cancel{2}} \times \underset{\underset{1}{\cancel{3}}}{\cancel{12}} \times \underset{\underset{2}{\cancel{6}}}{\cancel{12}}} = \frac{35}{2} = 17\ 1/2$$

ALWAYS USE THE NOMINAL SIZE of lumber to figure the board footage. If the stock is long and the length is given in feet then one of the twelves (12s) can be dropped from the lower half of the formula. In random width lumber it is good practice to "round off" to the nearest inch. For example, if the board was anywhere between 7 1/2 to 8 1/2 in., figure it as 8 inches.

When working with large quantities of RW & L lumber, the use of the formula would be impractical. A BOARD RULE should then be used. See Fig. 2-21. On the metal head and also at the handle, are numbers for various lengths of boards. Running along the body from these numbers are tables that read in surface feet.

To use the board rule, first determine the length of the board and then place the rule across the surface with the head against one edge. Select the line that corresponds to the length and follow across to the other edge. Here you can read the board footage if the piece is 1 in. thick. If the nominal size of the board were 1 1/2 in., add 50 percent to the reading; for 2 in. stock double the reading.

Boards of the same length can be placed side by side and their total footage found in one reading. Board rules are available with various combinations of tables. A good one for hardwoods has five tables on each side, running in odd and even feet from 7 through 16.

The unit of measure for plywood, hardboard, and particle board is the SQUARE FOOT (sq. ft.). A standard 4 ft. x 8 ft. panel contains 32 sq. ft. Prices are quoted per square foot on the basis of full panel purchase, and vary widely depending on the kind, thickness, and grade of the wood.

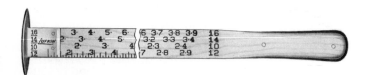

Fig. 2-21. Board rule. (Lufkin Rule Co.)

## TEST YOUR KNOWLEDGE, Chapter 2

Please do not write in the text. Place your answers on a separate sheet of paper.

1. Softwood comes from the evergreen or needle bearing trees that are called _____.
2. Which one of the following kinds of wood is classified as softwood: basswood, cottonwood, redwood, or willow?
3. Which one of the following kinds of wood is the heaviest: white ash, cherry, walnut, or white oak?
4. Softwood lumber is divided into three size classifications: _____, _____ lumber, and timber.
5. The highest appearance grade softwood boards are called _____.
6. The best grade of hardwood lumber that is generally available is _____.
7. One grade of hardwood lumber is called No. 1 common and contains _____ percent clear cuttings.
8. A defect caused by a separation between the annual growth rings is called a _____.
9. The warp in a board is more clearly defined by stating that it is cupped, bowed, _____, or twisted.
10. Quarter-sawed hardwood lumber is cut by the same method used to produce _____ softwood lumber.
11. One item on a hardwood purchase order reads: 200 bd. ft. — 4/4 walnut, FAS, KD, RW & L, Rgh. or S2S to 13/16. Define each of the abbreviations used.
12. A plywood panel that was listed as G2S would be _____ _____ _____.
13. Hardboard is _____ (lighter, heavier) than particle board.
14. Identify the two methods used to determine the moisture content of wood.
15. Name four types of composite board.
16. If 6/4 ponderosa pine is selling for 36 cents a board foot, a piece 10 in. by 24 in. would cost _____.

## ACTIVITIES

1. Plan and construct an electrically operated wood identification panel. It might operate in such a way that when the correct name is matched with the sample a light will glow or a buzzer will sound. You might build the parts in the shop and do the assembling and wiring at home. Wood sample kits can be secured from hardwood lumber dealers.
2. On a strip of heavy cardboard, develop the tables for a board rule that would measure stock 2, 3, 4, 5, and 6 ft. long. Try it out in the shop and check your readings with the board foot formula.
3. Prepare a sample board showing the various types of plywood and composite board.
4. Collect and mount samples of boards that illustrate the defects explained in this chapter.

These custom wooden gears were designed and fabricated for use in an authentic grist mill restoration project in Vigo County, Indiana. The gear bodies are white oak and the teeth are hard maple. (Mark Clauss)

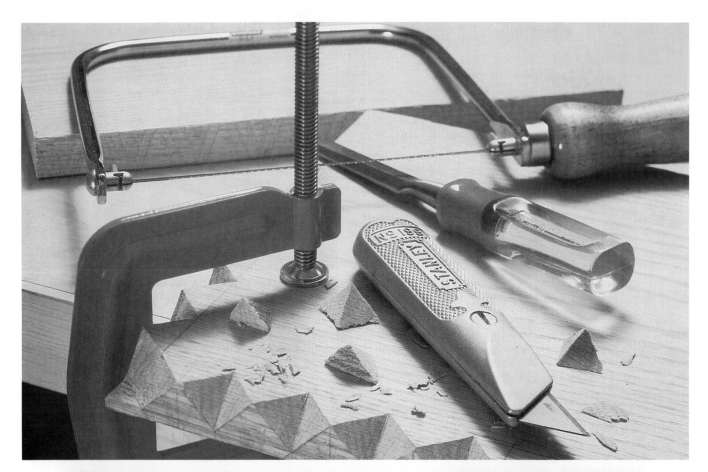

Top. Clamp your workpiece so that both hands may be used to guide sharp tools. (The Stanley Works).   Bottom. Wear eye protection whenever foreign material may be produced.   (Black & Decker)

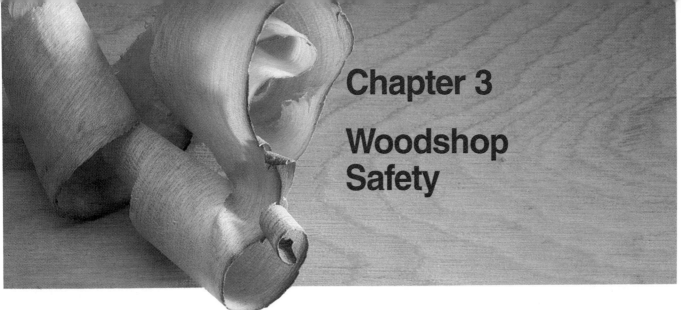

# Chapter 3

# Woodshop Safety

An important part of your experience in woodworking will be learning to follow practices and procedures that will prevent injuries to YOURSELF and OTHERS. Pay close attention to the instructions and demonstrations given by your instructor. Study the directions given in this book for using tools and machines. As you learn to use them the correct way, you also learn to use them the safe way.

Develop a good attitude toward safety. This means that you have a strong feeling toward the importance of safety and are willing to give time and attention to learning the safest way to perform your work. It means that you will be certain to work carefully and follow the rules—even when no one is watching you. A safe attitude will protect you and others, not only in the shop, but also in activities outside of school.

Carefully study the safety rules which follow. Your instructor may also recommend some additional rules. If you follow the rules and directions carefully, many of them will soon become safety habits that you will perform almost automatically.

## GENERAL SAFETY RULES

SECURE APPROVAL. Secure your instructor's approval for all work you plan to do in the shop. He or she is the one to decide if the work can and should be done, and will be able to suggest the best, easiest, and safest way to do it.

CLOTHING. Dress properly for your work. Remove coats and jackets, tuck in your tie, and roll up loose sleeves. It is advisable to wear a shop apron that is snugly tied.

EYE PROTECTION. Wear safety glasses or a face shield when doing any operation that may endanger your eyes. Be sure you have enough good light to see what you are doing without straining your eyes. Refer Fig. 3-1.

CLEAN HANDS. Keep your hands clean and free of oil or grease. You will do better and safer work, and the tools and your project will stay in good

Fig. 3-1. Always wear eye protection when performing any operation that may endanger your eyes. This hazardous job requires safety glasses. (Paslode Co., Div. of Signode)

condition.

CONSIDERATION OF OTHERS. Be thoughtful and helpful toward other students in the class. Be sure that the work you are doing does not endanger someone else. Caution other students if they are violating a safety rule.

TOOL SELECTION. Select the proper size and type of tool for your work. An expert never uses a tool unless it is sharp and in good condition, Fig. 3-2. Inform your instructor if tools are broken, have loose handles, or need adjustments.

Fig. 3-2. This sharp chisel is the proper tool for the installation of the lock set. It is very sharp, so use it with care. (The Stanley Works)

top of each other. Never allow edged or pointed tools to extend out over the edge of the bench. Close your vise when it is not in use and see that the handle is turned down. Keep drawers and cabinet doors closed.

FLOOR SAFETY. The floor should be clear of scrap blocks and excessive litter. Keep projects, sawhorses, and other equipment and materials you are using out of traffic lanes. Immediately wipe up any liquids spilled on the floor.

MATERIAL AND PROJECT STORAGE. Store and stack your project work carefully in assigned areas. If the storage is overhead, be sure the material will not fall off. Straighten the lumber rack when you remove a board. Do not leave narrow strips protruding from the end of the storage rack, especially at or near eye level.

LIFTING. Protect your back muscles when lifting heavy objects. Have someone help you. Lift with your arm and leg muscles. Secure help with long boards, even if they are not heavy.

FIRE PROTECTION. Many finishing materials, thinners, etc. are highly flammable. Others are toxic. Because of this, it is important that these materials be used only in approved areas. In addition, close cans of finishing materials and thinners immediately

CARRYING TOOLS. Keep sharp-edged and pointed tools turned down. Do not swing or raise your arms over your head while carrying tools. Carry only a few tools at one time, unless they are in a special holder. Do not carry sharp tools in the pocket of your clothes.

CLAMPING STOCK. Whenever possible, mount the work in a vise, clamp, or special holder, Fig. 3-3. This is especially important when using chisels, gouges, or portable electric tools.

USING TOOLS. Hold a tool in the correct position while using it. Most edged tools should be held in both hands with the cutting motion away from yourself and other students. Be careful when using your hand or fingers as a guide to start a cut. Test the sharpness of a tool with a strip of paper or a scrap or wood. DO NOT USE YOUR FINGERS.

WORKING SPEED. Do not "rush and tear" through your work. The good craftsworker knows that a steady, unhurried pace is safest and produces the best work.

BENCH ORGANIZATION. Keep your project materials carefully organized on your bench with tools located near the center. Do not pile tools on

Fig. 3-3. A bench vise is ideal for holding small pieces for an operation. (The Stanley Works)

after use. Use flammable liquids in very small quantities. Be sure the container is labeled. Dispose of oily rags and other combustible materials immediately, or store them in an approved container. Secure the instructor's approval before you bring any flammable liquids into the shop.

INJURIES. Report all injuries, even though slight, to your instructor.

## SHOP SAFETY

Woodworking is a very dangerous activity as many people know from firsthand experience. Shop safety is not just posting safety rules or talking about safe work practices. Shop safety should be a mental attitude that each of us develops and practices in our everyday work.

Naturally, you should do the typical things such as keeping the floor clean; picking up materials and tools before the work space becomes cluttered; and using safety devices such as safety glasses, ear protection, and machine guards. However, you should also select safer tools such as chip-limiting saw blades and cutters, Fig. 3-4. (Chip-limiting cutters help prevent overfeeding and are much safer than typical cutters.) You should read the owner's manuals frequently to refresh your memory on the safe procedures recommended for a particular piece of equipment. Pause to examine the total set-up before turning on a machine. All it takes is one small mistake to lose a finger or an eye. Be sure that safety guards are in place and used properly. More sensible and usable guards are being developed for most types of machines. Finally, know and respect your machines. They are designed to "cut" wood which is far tougher than your hand. Thinking safety pays dividends!

## POWER EQUIPMENT SAFETY RULES

Modern power woodworking machines can save large amounts of time. Learning how to use them safely will be an important part of your experience in the shop. Whether or not you are permitted to use power equipment will depend on your maturity and ability, along with policies established by your instructor.

Although beginning students will usually do most work with hand tools, there are certain basic machine operations that save time and may be appropriate if performed under close supervision.

Before operating any power tool or machine you must become thoroughly familiar with the way it works and the correct procedures to follow in its use. As you learn to use a machine the correct way, you will also be learning to use it the safe way.

Study the procedures outlined in the following chapters carefully. Pay close attention to the demonstrations and directions given by your instructor. Know and understand the following general safety rules that apply to power machine operation. You must also learn the specific safety rules that apply to each machine.

1. Always be sure you have the instructor's approval to operate a machine. Your instructor knows you and the machine, and can best decide whether you have "what it takes" to operate the machine safely.
2. Wear appropriate clothing. Remove coats or jackets, tuck in your tie, and roll up loose sleeves. Wear a shop apron and tie it snugly. See Fig. 3-5.

Fig. 3-4. Chip-limiting saw blades are much safer to use than blades that do not incorporate this feature. (Freud, Inc.)

Fig. 3-5. This student woodworker is wearing proper eye protection for the operation he is performing. (VICA)

3. You must be wide awake and alert. Never operate a machine when you are tired or ill.
4. Think through the operation before performing it. Know what you are going to do, and what the machine will do.
5. Make all the necessary adjustments before turning on the machine. Some adjustments on certain machines will require the instructor's approval, Fig. 3-6.
6. Never remove or adjust a safety guard without the instructor's permission.
7. Use approved push sticks, push blocks, feather boards, and other safety devices. Some operations may require the use of a special jig or fixture.
8. Keep the machine tables and working surfaces clear of tools, stock, and project materials. Also keep the floor free of scraps and excessive litter.
9. Allow the machine to reach its full operating speed before starting to feed the work.
10. Feed the work carefully and only as fast as the machine will easily cut.
11. Maintain the MARGIN OF SAFETY specified for the machine. This is the minimum distance your hands should ever come to the cutting tool while in operation.
12. If a machine is dull, out of adjustment, or not working properly, shut off the power immediately and inform the instructor.
13. When you are operating the machine, you are the only one to control it. Start and stop the machine yourself. If someone is helping you, be sure they understand that they are expected to know what to do and how to do it.
14. Do not allow your attention to be distracted while operating a machine. Also, be certain that you do not distract the attention of other machine operators.
15. Stay clear of machines being operated by other students. See that other students are "out of the way" when you are operating a machine.
16. When you have completed an operation on a machine, shut off the power. Wait until it stops before leaving the machine or setting up another cut. Never leave a machine running while unattended.
17. Machines should not be used for trivial operations, especially on small pieces of stock. Do not play with machines.
18. Do not "crowd around" or wait in line to use a machine. Ask the present operator to inform you at your work station when finished. Common standards of courtesy may slow you down, but they will make the shop a safer and more pleasant place to work.

## Safety Rules for Jointer

The jointer is one of the MOST DANGEROUS machines in the woodshop. Follow these safety rules carefully in addition to the general safety rules.
1. Be sure you have the instructor's approval to operate the machine.
2. Before turning on the machine, make adjustments for depth of cut and position of fence.
3. Do not adjust outfeed tables or remove guard without the instructor's approval, Fig. 3-7.
4. The maximum cut for jointing an edge is 1/8 in.; for a flat surface, 1/16 in.
5. Stock must be at least 12 in. long. Stock to be surfaced must be at least 3/8 in. thick, unless a special feather board is used.
6. Feed the work so the knives will cut "with the grain." Use only new stock that is free of knots, splits, and checks.
7. Keep your hands away from the cutterhead even though the guard is in position. Maintain at least a 4 in. margin of safety!
8. Use a push block when planing a flat surface, Fig. 3-8. Do not plane end grain unless the board is at least 12 in. wide.
9. The jointer knives must be sharp. Dull knives will vibrate the stock and may cause a kickback.

Fig. 3-6. Proper adjustment of a machine is important for safe operation. (Dremel)

Fig. 3-7. This jointer is fitted with a proper guard. Be sure that it works smoothly and it is in place for safe operation.

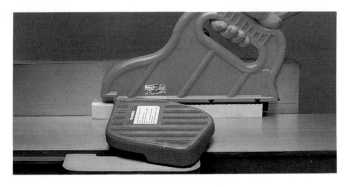

Fig. 3-8. This operator is using a pusher block to surface a short piece of stock. (CMT Tools)

Portable power tools, even though they are small, can be just as dangerous as stationary woodworking machines when not used properly. You should be certain that you know how to operate the equipment and then follow the safety rules.

### Safety Rules for Power Planes
1. Study the manufacturer's instructions for detailed information on adjustments and operation.
2. Be certain that the machine is properly grounded.
3. Hold the standard power plane in both hands before you pull the trigger switch. Continue to hold it in both hands until the motor stops after releasing the switch, Fig. 3-9.
4. Always be sure the work is securely clamped and held in the best position for performing the operation.
5. Do not attempt to operate with one hand a regular power plane designed for two hands.
6. Disconnect electrical cords before making adjustments or changing cutters.

### Safety Rules for Planers
1. Be sure you have the instructor's permission to operate the machine.

2. Adjust the machine to the correct thickness of cut before turning on the power.
3. Stock should be at least 12 in. long, or several inches longer than the distance between the centers of the feed rolls.
4. Surface only new lumber that is free of loose knots and serious defects.
5. Plane with the grain, or at a slight angle with the grain. Never attempt to plane cross grain.
6. Stand to one side of the work being fed through the machine, Fig. 3-10.
7. Do not look into the throat of the planer while it is running.
8. Do not feed stock of different thicknesses side by side through the machine, unless it is equipped with a sectional infeed roll.
9. Handle and hold the stock only in an area beyond the ends of the table.
10. If the machine is not working properly, shut off the power at once and inform the instructor.

### Safety Rules for Table Saws
1. Be certain the blade is sharp and the right one for your work.

Fig. 3-9. This operator is using the proper procedure to plane a surface with a portable electric plane. (Makita U.S.A., Inc.)

Fig. 3-10. Notice how this operator is standing to one side while operating this stationary planer. (Delta International Machinery Corp.)

2. The saw is equipped with a guard and a splitter. Be sure to use them, Fig. 3-11.
3. Set the blade so it extends about 1/4 in. above the stock to be cut.
4. Stand to one side of the operating blade and do not reach across it.
5. Maintain a 4 in. margin of safety. Fig. 3-12 shows one method to use for safely cutting a small piece of stock.
6. Stock should be surfaced, with at least one edge jointed before being cut on the saw.
7. The position of the stock must be controlled either by the fence or the miter gauge. NEVER CUT STOCK FREE HAND.
8. Use only new stock that is free of knots, splits, and warp.
9. Stop the saw before making adjustments to the fence or blade.
10. Do not let small scrap cuttings accumulate around the saw blade. Use a push stick to move them away.

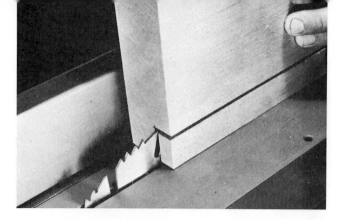

Fig. 3-13. The guard may not be used in this operation and, therefore, should be approved by the instructor.

11. Resawing and other special setups must be inspected by the instructor before power is turned on, Fig. 3-13.
12. The dado or any special blades should be removed from the saw after use.
13. Students helping to "tail-off" the saw should not push or pull on the stock but only support it. The operator must control the feed and direction of the cut.
14. As you complete your work, turn off the machine and remain until the blade has stopped. Clear the saw table and place waste cuttings in the scrap box.

**Safety Rules for Radial Arm Saws**
1. Stock must be held firmly on the table and against the fence for all crosscutting operations, Fig. 3-14. The ends of long boards must be supported level with the table.
2. Before turning on the motor be certain that all clamps and locking devices are tight and the depth of cut is correct.
3. Keep the guard and anti-kickback device in position. Do not remove them without your instructor's permission.
4. Always return the saw to the rear of the table after completing a crosscut or miter cut. Never remove stock from the table until the saw has been returned.
5. Maintain a 6 in. margin of safety.
6. Shut off the motor and wait for the blade to stop before making any adjustments.
7. Be sure the blade is stopped before you leave the machine.
8. Keep the table clean and free of wood scraps and excessive amounts of sawdust.
9. Secure approval from your instructor before making ripping cuts or other special setups. When ripping stock it must be flat and have one straight edge to move along the fence.
10. When ripping, always feed stock into the blade so that the bottom teeth are turning toward you. This will be the side opposite the anti-kickback fingers, Fig. 3-15.

Fig. 3-11. This student woodworker is using the guard and splitter in a safe manner. (Delta International Machinery Corp.)

Fig. 3-12. A small piece of stock may be cut safely on the table saw by clamping it securely to a larger piece.

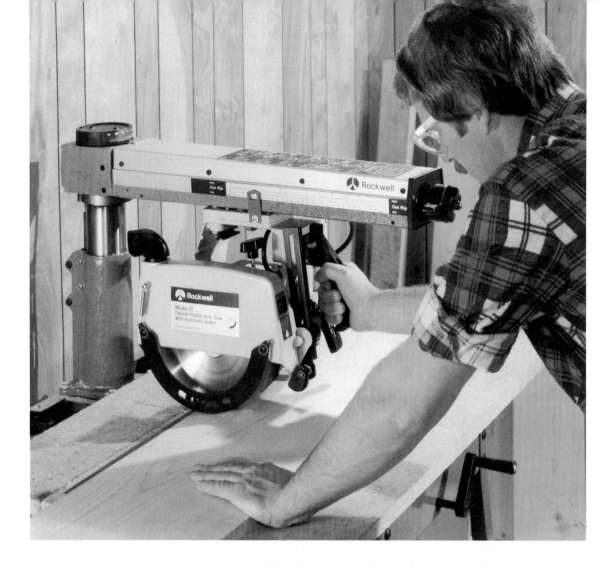

Fig. 3-14. This is the proper procedure for crosscutting stock on the radial arm saw.
(Delta International Machinery Corp.)

Fig. 3-15. The splitter and anti-kickback fingers should be properly adjusted when ripping on the radial arm saw.

## Safety Rules for Portable Circular Saws

1. Stock must be supported in such a way that the kerf will not close and bind the blade during the cut or at the end of the cut.
2. Thin materials should be supported on benches. Small pieces should be clamped in a vise or onto a bench top or sawhorse.
3. Be careful not to cut into the bench, sawhorse, or other supporting devices.
4. Adjust the depth of cut to the thickness of the stock, and add about 1/8 in.
5. Check the base and angle adjustment to be sure they are tight. Plug in the cord to a grounded outlet and be sure it will not become fouled in the work.
6. Always place the saw base on the stock, with the blade clear, before turning on the switch.
7. During the cut, stand to one side of the cutting line.
8. Large saws will have two handles. Keep both hands on them during the cutting operation. Small saws should also be guided with both hands when possible, Fig. 3-16.

Fig. 3-16. Notice that the base of the saw is resting on the stock as the blade is moved forward, the work is securely clamped, and the operator is using both hands to hold the saw. (Black & Decker)

9. Always unplug the machine to change blades or make major adjustments.
10. Always use a sharp blade with plenty of set.

### Safety Rules for Band Saws
1. Wheel guard doors must be closed, and the blade properly adjusted, before turning on the machine.
2. Adjust the upper guide assembly so it is 1/4 in. above the work, Fig. 3-17.
3. Allow the saw to reach full speed before feeding the work.
4. The stock must be held flat on the table.
5. Feed the saw only as fast as the teeth can easily remove the wood.
6. Maintain a 2 in. margin of safety!
7. Plan saw cuts to avoid backing out of curves whenever possible, Fig. 3-18.
8. Make turns carefully and do not cut radii so small that the blade is twisted.
9. Stop the machine before backing out of a long, curved cut.
10. Round stock should not be cut unless mounted securely in a jig or hand screw.
11. If you hear a clicking noise, turn off the machine at once. This indicates a crack in the blade. If the blade breaks, shut off the power and move away from the machine until both wheels stop.
12. Turn off the machine as soon as you have finished your work. If the machine has a brake, apply it smoothly. Do not leave the machine until it has stopped running.

### Safety Rules for Scroll Saws
1. Be certain the blade is properly installed. It

Fig. 3-17. The upper guide assembly of this band saw is properly adjusted for the thickness of stock being cut. (Black & Decker)

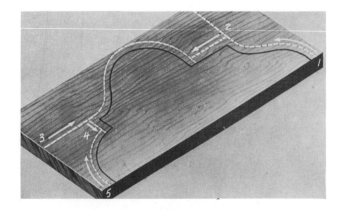

Fig. 3-18. The cutting sequence has been planned so that each operation will permit the next cut without backing out of a curve. (Jam Handy Organization)

should be in a vertical position with the teeth pointing down, Fig. 3-19.
2. Roll the machine over by hand to see if there is clearance for the blade, and if the tension sleeve has been properly set.
3. Check the belt guard to see that it is closed and tight.
4. Keep the hold-down adjusted so the work will not be raised off the table.

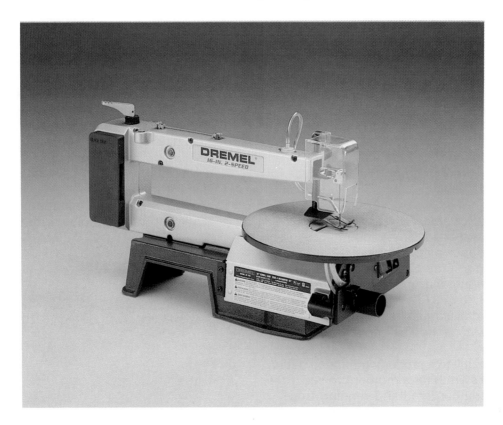

Fig. 3-19. This modern scroll saw is ready for work, with the blade installed properly (teeth pointing down) and held in place. (Dremel)

5. When the saw is running, do not permit your fingers to get directly in line with the blade. The work can usually be held on either side of the cutting line, as shown in Fig. 3-20.

## Safety Rules for Saber Saws
1. Make certain the saw is properly grounded through the electrical cord.
2. Select the correct blade for your work and be sure it is properly mounted.
3. Disconnect the saw to change blades or make adjustments.
4. Place the base of the saw firmly on the stock before starting the cut.
5. Turn on the motor before the blade contacts the work.
6. Do not attempt to cut curves so sharp that the blade will be twisted. Follow procedures described for band saw operation.
7. Make certain the work is well supported. Do not cut into sawhorses or other supports.

## Safety Rules for Drill Presses
1. Check the speed setting to see that it is correct for your work. Holes over 1/2 in. should be bored at the lowest speed.
2. Use only an approved type of bit. Bits with feed screws or those with excessive length should not be used.

3. Mount the bit securely to the full depth of the chuck and in the center. Remove the key immediately.
4. Position the table and adjust the feed stroke so there is no chance of the bit hitting the table.
5. The work should be placed on a wood pad when the holes are drilled all the way through.
6. Work that will be held by hand should be center punched.

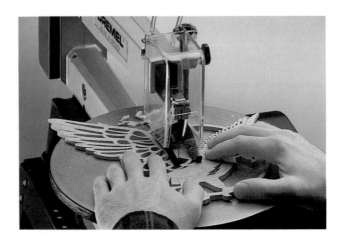

Fig. 3-20. Making a cut with fingers a safe distance from the blade. (Dremel)

7. Small or irregular shaped pieces must be clamped to the table or held in some special fixture, Fig. 3-21.
8. Feed the bit smoothly into the work. When the hole is deep, withdraw it frequently to clear the shavings and cool the bit.
9. When using special clamping setups, or a hole saw or fly cutter, have your instructor inspect it before turning it on. Fig. 3-22.
10. Always have your instructor check setups for routing and shaping.

**Safety Rules for Portable Electric Drills**
1. Select the correct drill or bit. Mount it securely to the full depth of the chuck.
2. Either clamp a scrap piece under work to prevent splintering the underside, or drill from both sides.
3. Stock to be drilled must be held in a stationary position so it cannot be moved during the operation.
4. Connect the drill to a properly grounded outlet.
5. Turn on the switch for a moment to see if the bit is properly centered and running true.
6. With the switch off, place the point of the bit

in the punched layout hole.
7. Hold the drill firmly in one or both hands and at the correct drilling angle, Fig. 3-23.
8. Turn on the switch and feed the drill into the work. The pressure required will vary with the size of the drill and the kind of wood.
9. During the operation, keep the drill aligned with the direction of the hole, Fig. 3-24.
10. When drilling deep holes, especially with a twist drill, withdraw the drill several times to clear the shavings.
11. Follow the same precautions and procedures as when drilling holes with the drill press.

Fig. 3-23. This drill is small enough to hold with one hand when drilling small holes. Two hands may be used, however, for added support. (Black & Decker)

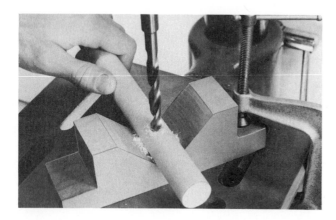

Fig. 3-21. Using a V-block to drill a hole in round stock is a safe practice.

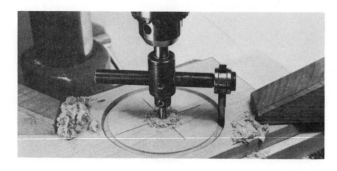

Fig. 3-22. The fly cutter is a dangerous tool. Be sure to clamp the work securely to the table when using this tool.

Fig. 3-24. A combination square may be used to keep the drill aligned with the direction of the hole while drilling. Lateral pressure may cause the drill to grab and twist out of your hand. (Black & Decker)

12. Always remove the bit from the chuck as soon as you have completed your work.

## Safety Rules for Lathes

1. Before starting the machine, be sure that spindle work has the cup center properly imbedded, tailstock and tool rest securely clamped, and proper clearance for the rotating stock.
2. Before starting the machine for faceplate work, check to see that the faceplate is tight against the spindle shoulder and the tool support has proper clearance.
3. Wear goggles or a face shield to protect your eyes, especially when roughing out work. The lathe should have a guard, Fig. 3-25.
4. Select turning speed carefully. Large diameters must be turned at the lowest speed. Always use the lowest speed to rough out work.
5. Wood with knots and splits should not be turned. Glued-up stock should cure the proper amount of time—at least 24 hours.
6. Keep the tool rest close to the work, Fig. 3-26.
7. Remove the tool rest for sanding and polishing operations.
8. Use a scraping cut for all faceplate work.
9. Remove both the spur and cup centers when they are not in use.
10. When you stop the lathe to check your work, also check and lubricate the cup center.
11. Keep the lathe tools sharp, hold them firmly and in the proper position.

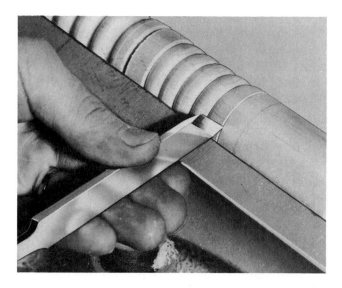

Fig. 3-26. The tool rest should be close to the work to prevent an accident.

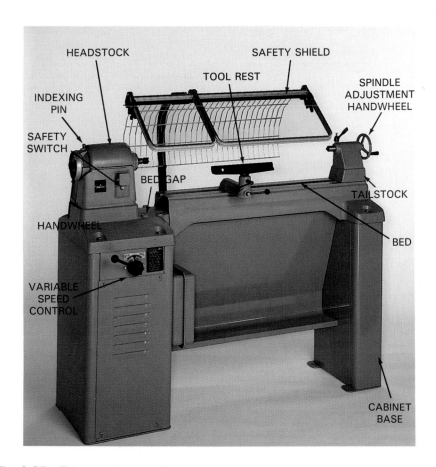

Fig. 3-25. This wood lathe is fitted with an approved safety shield. One section may be removed when doing faceplate turning. (Delta International Equipment Corp.)

12. Keep sleeves rolled up and loose clothing away from moving parts of the lathe and work.

## Safety Rules for Portable Routers

1. The bit must be securely mounted in the chuck to a depth of at least 1/2 in. The base must be tight.
2. As with all portable tools, be certain that the motor is properly grounded.
3. Wear eye protection when using the router.
4. Be certain the work is securely clamped and will remain stationary during the routing operation, Fig. 3-27.
5. Place the router base on the work or template, with the bit clear of the wood before turning on the power. Hold it firmly when turning on the motor to overcome starting torque.
6. Hold the router in both hands and feed it smoothly through the cut in the correct direction.
7. When the cut is complete, turn off the motor. Do not lift the machine from the work until the motor has stopped.
8. Always ask your instructor to check special setups before proceeding.
9. Always unplug the motor when mounting bits or making major adjustments.

## Safety Rules for Shapers

1. Be sure to get the instructor's permission before starting to set up and use the machine.
2. When possible, mount the cutter so that most of the cutting will be performed on the lower part of the edge. Any unused part of the cutter should be below the table, Fig. 3-28.
3. An approved lock washer must be located directly under the spindle nut. The nut must be set tight.
4. Use the fence for all straight line shaping cuts. Be certain it is properly adjusted and securely locked in place.
5. Use guards, feather-boards, and hold-down devices whenever possible, Fig. 3-29.
6. Maintain a 4 in. margin of safety when using the fence or miter gauge, and a 6 in. margin when using depth collars. If the part is too small to allow this margin, design and build a special holder or push board.
7. Cut only new stock that is straight, true, and free of splits, checks, and knots.
8. Roll the spindle over by hand to check clearance of complicated settings. Snap the

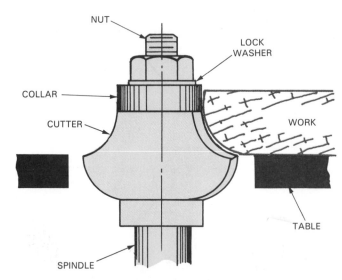

Fig. 3-28. The unused part of the cutter is positioned below the table for safety.

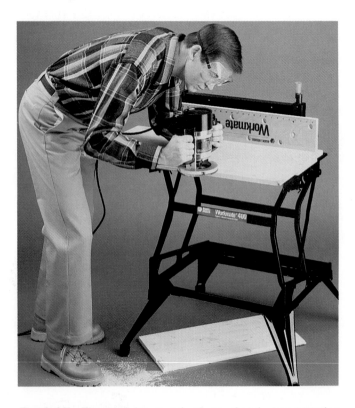

Fig. 3-27. The work is securely clamped and eye protection is being worn while operating the router. (Black & Decker)

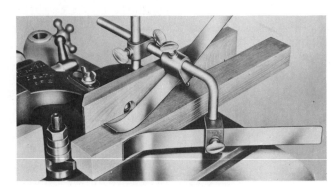

Fig. 3-29. Hold-downs help to make a smooth, safe cut on the shaper.

switch on and off quickly to check rotation of the cutter. Be certain the direction of feed is correct.

9. Have your instructor inspect the setup. Inform him or her of the direction and order of feed you plan to use.

10. Make a trial cut on an extra piece of stock that is the same thickness as your project work.

## Safety Rules for Sanding Machines

1. Be certain the belt or disc is correctly mounted. The belt must track in the center of the drums and platen. Do not operate the disc sander if the abrasive paper is loose.

2. Check the guards and table adjustments to see that they are in the correct position and locked securely in place.

3. Use the table, fence, and other guides to control the position of the work, whenever possible.

4. Small or irregular-shaped pieces should be held in a hand clamp, or a special jig or fixture.

5. When sanding the end grain of narrow pieces on the belt sander, always support the work against the table.

6. Sand only on the side of the disc sander that is moving toward the table. Move work along this surface so it will not burn, Fig. 3-30.

7. Always use a pad or push block when sanding thin pieces on the belt sander.

8. Do not use power sanders to form and shape parts when the operations could be better performed on other machines, Fig. 3-31.

Fig. 3-31. This small belt sander is being used to smooth the edge of an irregularly shaped piece. It is not being used to develop the basic shape. (Foley-Belsaw Co.)

9. Sand only clean new wood. Do not sand work that has excess glue or finish on the surface. These materials will load and foul the abrasive.

## Finishing Safety Rules

1. Wear safety glasses when applying finishing materials.

2. Wear rubber gloves, goggles, and rubber apron when applying bleaches and acids.

3. Thinners and reducers such as naphtha, benzene, lacquer thinner, and enamel reducer should be applied in a well-ventilated room. Fumes have a toxic effect.

4. Store all chemicals and soiled rags in proper, safe containers. Many chemicals and rags are highly flammable.

5. Wear an approved respirator for finishing operations that involve the use of toxic chemicals such as lacquer thinner and enamel reducer, Fig. 3-32.

6. Spraying should be performed in a well-ventilated booth to reduce toxic fumes.

7. Do not smoke while sanding or applying a finish. Not only does dust or vapor mixed with smoke create a hazard to your health, but it may start a fire.

8. Wash your hands well after applying a finish in order to remove any toxic materials that you

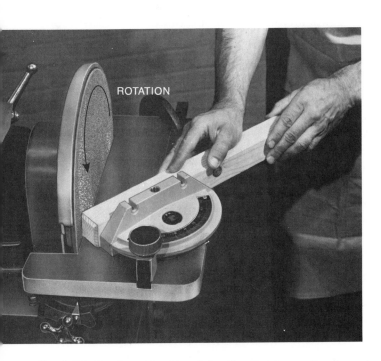

Fig. 3-30. Sand on the side of the disc that is moving down toward the table.

Fig. 3-32. An approved respirator is required when using toxic chemicals such as lacquer thinner and enamel reducer. (Campbellrhea Mfg., Inc.)

have handled.
9. Know where the sink, shower, or eye wash station is located in the event you are burned by a finishing material.
10. Provide an approved fire extinguisher in the finishing area.

## NEW OSHA RULES

### PERSONAL PROTECTIVE SAFETY EQUIPMENT

The Occupational Safety and Health Administration (OSHA) published a final rule on personal protective safety equipment in April 1994, which began in July 1994. States with their own health and safety plans were required to adopt similar standards by January 1995.

The rule affects woodworkers in the lumber, furniture, and wood products industries. Companies of all sizes must meet the requirements of the regulation. The regulation includes sections on guidance for the selection and use of personal protective safety equipment, performance requirements, employer hazard assessments, employee training in the use of personal protective safety equipment, and hand protection.

The hand protection section is the newest part of the regulation. Employers are mandated to require workers to wear personal protection safety equipment on their hands when skin absorption of harmful substances is possible. In addition, hand protection must be used where the threat of severe cuts, lacerations, abrasions, punctures, chemical burns, thermal burns, and harmful temperature exists. OSHA has identified gloves as the best available hand protection, but made employers responsible for identifying what kinds of gloves are best for their employees.

Wood industry-related jobs in the areas of chipping, grinding, machining, sawing, chiseling, and sanding require personal protection safety equipment. Face and eye protection for wood dust and chips includes goggles, masks, and respirators, Fig. 3-33.

## WOOD DUST EXPOSURE LIMITS

OSHA has established permissible exposure limits (PELs), effective June 1993, for several air contaminates in the workplace. Wood dust is among the list of air contaminates cited.

Wood dust is subject to total exposure limits of 15 milligrams per cubic meter of air and a limit of 5 for respirable dust. Both levels are measured over an eight-hour time-weighted average.

## EPA REGULATIONS FOR OZONE-DEPLETING CHEMICALS

Rules relating to ozone-depleting chemicals were adopted in 1993, and are being enforced by the Federal Environmental Protection Agency (EPA). These rules apply to companies of any size—one-person shop to large manufacturers. The regulations require labeling of all products that use ozone-

Fig. 3-33. This respirator could save your life or at least increase your comfort while working. (Grizzly Imports, Inc.)

depleting substances such as carbon tetrachloride, trichloroethane, and methyl chloroform. Methyl chloroform and trichloroethane are found in many solvents and adhesives used in the furniture industry. Further, chemical manufacturers must stop producing these ozone-depleting substances by January 1, 1996.

### TEST YOUR KNOWLEDGE, Chapter 3

Please do not write in the text. Place your answers on a separate piece of paper.

1. You should wear safety glasses in the shop:
   a. When working with sharp tools.
   b. When doing any work that may endanger your eyes.
   c. When you feel like wearing them.
   d. None of the above.
2. Why is it important to apply and handle finishing materials only in an approved area?
3. State 10 safety rules to follow when using power equipment.
4. The minimum distance your hands should ever come to a cutting tool while in operation is called the _____ ____ _____.
5. Portable power tools are much more dangerous than stationary woodworking machines. True or False?
6. The margin of safety for a jointer is:
   a. 8 inches.
   b. 1 inch.
   c. 4 inches.
   d. None of the above.
7. When feeding stock into a planer or table saw, stand (in front, to one side) of the work.
8. In general, the _____ should control the machine while in operation.
   a. Helper.
   b. Operator.
   c. Teacher.
   d. None of the above.
9. If possible, small saws should be guided with both hands. True or False?
10. When using a band saw, allow the saw to reach _____ speed before feeding the work.
11. A clicking noise on a band saw indicates a:
    a. Nothing of concern.
    b. A broken wheel guard.
    c. A crack in the blade.
    d. None of the above.
12. Power hand tools should be properly grounded through an _____ _____.
13. When working with both drill presses and electrical drills, any type of bit will do a good job. True or False?
14. What lathe speed should be used for turning large diameters and to rough out work?
15. Explain the proper way to hold a router for the best results.

### ACTIVITIES

1. Prepare a list of all the toxic chemicals used in your wood shop. Identify the appropriate safety precautions to be used with each chemical. Ask your instructor for Material Safety Data Sheets of each toxic chemical in the shop. Study each sheet and report the safety precautions for each chemical to the class. If they are not available, compile your own list of safety precautions and report them to the class.
2. Go to your school or local library and borrow a film about shop accidents. Arrange to show the film to your classmates.
3. Keep a log of unsafe work practices that you observe in your class for a period of two weeks. Report your observations to the class and emphasize the possible outcomes of each poor work practice.

The plate joiner is firmly held with both hands and safety glasses are worn to provide maximum safety. (DeWalt)

Left. Try Squares and "T" Bevels. (Stanley Tools). Right. Accurate measurement and careful work are necessary for the success of any woodworking project.   (The Stanley Works)

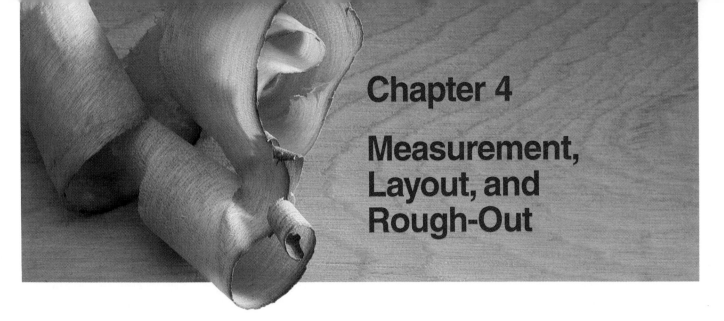

# Chapter 4

# Measurement, Layout, and Rough-Out

In Chapter 1 you have learned how to plan and design a woodworking project. The working drawings, plan of procedure, and bill of materials should be used to begin and complete the project. The basic procedures discussed in this unit are: measurement, selecting and laying out, cutting stock to rough length, ripping stock to rough width, laying out and cutting plywood, and sharpening a hand saw.

## MEASURING

Accurate measurement is necessary for the success of any woodworking project. Learning to measure accurately, therefore, is a necessity.

Most measuring performed in woodworking is straight line or LINEAR measurement. There are two kinds (systems) of linear measure in use today. They are CUSTOMARY and METRIC.

The INCH is the basic unit of measure in the customary system. Twelve inches equals one foot and 36 inches equals one yard. The yard is seldom used, but the foot is sometimes used on larger projects. The inch is divided into smaller units for finer measurement. Within the customary system, there are 2 methods for dividing the inch: COMMON FRACTIONS and DECIMAL FRACTIONS.

Common fractions divide the inch into 2, 4, 8, 16, 32, and 64 parts. The standard designation of each is 1/2, 1/4, 1/8, 1/16, 1/32, and 1/64 in. Only those fractions divisible by 2 are used. Fig. 4-1 shows an inch divided into common fractions.

Decimal fractions divide the inch into 10, 100, and 1000 parts. One tenth of an inch is designated as 0.10 in., one hundredth of an inch is designated as 0.01 in., and one thousandth of an inch is designated as 0.001 in. A special measuring device such as a micrometer or vernier caliper is required to measure in thousandths. That degree of accuracy is generally not required in woodworking projects. Tenths and hundreds are usually sufficient for woodworking. Fig. 4-2 shows an inch divided into decimal fractions.

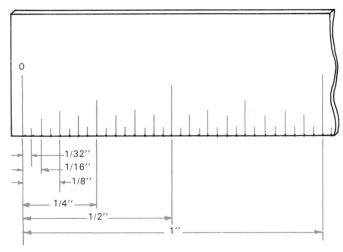

Fig. 4-1. An inch divided into common fractions.

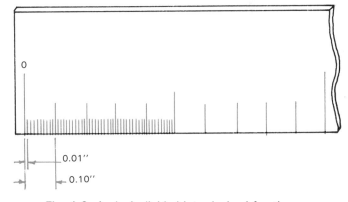

Fig. 4-2. An inch divided into decimal fractions.

## THE METRIC SYSTEM OF MEASURE

The METER is the basic unit of measure in the metric system. The meter is divided into finer parts for more precise measurement. The divisions are decimeters, centimeters, and millimeters. Each is based on the unit 10. For example, there are 10 decimeters in a meter, 10 centimeters in a decimeter, and 10 millimeters in a centimeter. Fig. 4-3 shows the metric units of linear measure that have application in typical woodworking projects.

The decimeter and meter are seldom used in woodworking. The centimeter is very useful for general size description while millimeters are needed for very precise measurements.

```
1 centimeter = 10 millimeters (mm)
1 decimeter  = 10 centimeters (cm)
1 meter      = 10 decimeters (dm)
1 meter      = 100 centimeters
1 meter      = 1000 millimeters
```

Fig. 4-3. Metric units of linear measure which are used in typical woodworking projects.

Metric symbols are used to identify each unit of measure. Each symbol is written in lower case letters as follows: millimeter (mm), centimeter (cm), decimeter (dm), and meter (m).

## CONVERSION FACTORS

The customary system is presently recognized in the United States as the primary system of linear measure. Movement is presently in the direction of adopting the metric system. While this process is underway, both systems will be used. Therefore, conversion tables are helpful when converting from one system to the other. Fig. 4-4 shows tables of inches to millimeters and millimeters to decimal inches. When tables are not available, inches can be converted to millimeters by multiplying by 25.4 (1 in. = 25.4 mm).

### FRACTIONAL INCHES TO MILLIMETERS

| In. | mm | In. | mm | In. | mm | In. | mm |
|---|---|---|---|---|---|---|---|
| 1/64 | 0.397 | 17/64 | 6.747 | 33/64 | 13.097 | 49/64 | 19.447 |
| 1/32 | 0.794 | 9/32 | 7.144 | 17/32 | 13.494 | 25/32 | 19.844 |
| 3/64 | 1.191 | 19/64 | 7.541 | 35/64 | 13.890 | 51/64 | 20.240 |
| 1/16 | 1.587 | 5/16 | 7.937 | 9/16 | 14.287 | 13/16 | 20.637 |
| 5/64 | 1.984 | 21/64 | 8.334 | 37/64 | 14.684 | 53/64 | 21.034 |
| 3/32 | 2.381 | 11/32 | 8.731 | 19/32 | 15.081 | 27/32 | 21.431 |
| 7/64 | 2.778 | 23/64 | 9.128 | 39/64 | 15.478 | 55/64 | 21.828 |
| 1/8 | 3.175 | 3/8 | 9.525 | 5/8 | 15.875 | 7/8 | 22.225 |
| 9/64 | 3.572 | 25/64 | 9.922 | 41/64 | 16.272 | 57/64 | 22.622 |
| 5/32 | 3.969 | 13/32 | 10.319 | 21/32 | 16.669 | 29/32 | 23.019 |
| 11/64 | 4.366 | 27/64 | 10.716 | 43/64 | 17.065 | 59/64 | 23.415 |
| 3/16 | 4.762 | 7/16 | 11.113 | 11/16 | 17.462 | 15/16 | 23.812 |
| 13/64 | 5.159 | 29/64 | 11.509 | 45/64 | 17.859 | 61/64 | 24.209 |
| 7/32 | 5.556 | 15/32 | 11.906 | 23/32 | 18.256 | 31/32 | 24.606 |
| 15/64 | 5.953 | 31/64 | 12.303 | 47/64 | 18.653 | 63/64 | 25.003 |
| 1/4 | 6.350 | 1/2 | 12.700 | 3/4 | 19.050 | 1 | 25.400 |

### MILLIMETERS TO DECIMAL INCHES

| mm | In. | mm | In. | mm | In. | mm | In. | mm | In. |
|---|---|---|---|---|---|---|---|---|---|
| 1 | 0.0394 | 21 | 0.8268 | 41 | 1.6142 | 61 | 2.4016 | 81 | 3.1890 |
| 2 | 0.0787 | 22 | 0.8662 | 42 | 1.6536 | 62 | 2.4410 | 82 | 3.2284 |
| 3 | 0.1181 | 23 | 0.9055 | 43 | 1.6929 | 63 | 2.4804 | 83 | 3.2678 |
| 4 | 0.1575 | 24 | 0.9449 | 44 | 1.7323 | 64 | 2.5197 | 84 | 3.3071 |
| 5 | 0.1969 | 25 | 0.9843 | 45 | 1.7717 | 65 | 2.5591 | 85 | 3.3465 |
| 6 | 0.2362 | 26 | 1.0236 | 46 | 1.8111 | 66 | 2.5985 | 86 | 3.3859 |
| 7 | 0.2756 | 27 | 1.0630 | 47 | 1.8504 | 67 | 2.6378 | 87 | 3.4253 |
| 8 | 0.3150 | 28 | 1.1024 | 48 | 1.8898 | 68 | 2.6772 | 88 | 3.4646 |
| 9 | 0.3543 | 29 | 1.1418 | 49 | 1.9292 | 69 | 2.7166 | 89 | 3.5040 |
| 10 | 0.3937 | 30 | 1.1811 | 50 | 1.9685 | 70 | 2.7560 | 90 | 3.5434 |
| 11 | 0.4331 | 31 | 1.2205 | 51 | 2.0079 | 71 | 2.7953 | 91 | 3.5827 |
| 12 | 0.4724 | 32 | 1.2599 | 52 | 2.0473 | 72 | 2.8247 | 92 | 3.6221 |
| 13 | 0.5118 | 33 | 1.2992 | 53 | 2.0867 | 73 | 2.8741 | 93 | 3.6615 |
| 14 | 0.5512 | 34 | 1.3386 | 54 | 2.1260 | 74 | 2.9134 | 94 | 3.7009 |
| 15 | 0.5906 | 35 | 1.3780 | 55 | 2.1654 | 75 | 2.9528 | 95 | 3.7402 |
| 16 | 0.6299 | 36 | 1.4173 | 56 | 2.2048 | 76 | 2.9922 | 96 | 3.7796 |
| 17 | 0.6693 | 37 | 1.4567 | 57 | 2.2441 | 77 | 3.0316 | 97 | 3.8190 |
| 18 | 0.7087 | 38 | 1.4961 | 58 | 2.2835 | 78 | 3.0709 | 98 | 3.8583 |
| 19 | 0.7480 | 39 | 1.5355 | 59 | 2.3229 | 79 | 3.1103 | 99 | 3.8977 |
| 20 | 0.7874 | 40 | 1.5748 | 60 | 2.3622 | 80 | 3.1497 | 100 | 3.9371 |

Fig. 4-4. Conversion tables for customary and metric measuring systems.

## SELECTING AND LAYING OUT

After you have made a stock cutting list you are ready to look over the lumber racks and select the items of stock best suited for your project. This requires a lot of good judgment. If you have not had much experience in woodworking, you should ask your instructor for help.

After you have selected a piece that appears to offer economical cuttings, look it over carefully on both sides for defects. Make a rough layout of the parts of the project using a bench ruler and/or a template. See Fig. 4-5. White chalk works fine for this since it can be easily wiped off if you want to try other arrangements. These lines will not be used for finished cutting but only to help you see how the piece will cut after it has been planed.

Be sure to look at the end of the stock. If it is rough, as it came from the sawmill, it will have small splits and checks that must be trimmed. You must allow for this in your rough layout. You will need to make your layout "around" other defects. However, some of them may be covered or placed on the back of your project. Very tight knots may even be desirable because of the interesting grain patterns around them.

In a rough layout, 1/16 in. extra thickness should be allowed for planing, about 1/4 in. for each width you will cut, and about 1/2 to 1 in. for each length. Check over your layout and be sure the grain is running in the right direction in each piece. Use the framing square to make a cutting line across the stock as shown in Fig. 4-6.

## CUTTING STOCK TO ROUGH LENGTH

Select a crosscut saw with 8 or 10 points to the inch. Fig. 4-7 shows the shape of crosscut teeth. They are beveled on each side to form a series of knife points that cut smoothly across the fibers of the wood. Note that the teeth are set (bent) out on alternate sides so that they will cut a kerf (groove)

Fig. 4-6. Marking a cutting line along the tongue of framing square. The blade is held against the edge of the stock.

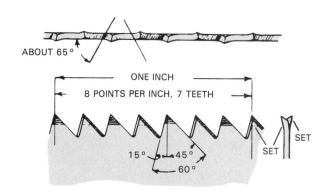

Fig. 4-7. Crosscut saw teeth. (The Stanley Works)

wider than the thickness of the blade. This permits it to move freely through the work, Fig. 4-8.

Place the board on sawhorses so that the position of the cut will be well supported. One knee can be placed on the board to hold it firmly. Hold the saw in your right hand (if you are right handed) and grasp the board in your left hand. Use your thumb as a guide, raising it well above the board so there is no danger of it being cut. Study Fig. 4-9. A block of wood, held in position at the cutting line could be used. Start the cut on the waste side of the line

Fig. 4-5. Using a template to determine size of rough cutting.

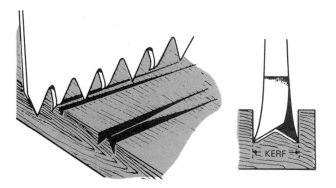

Fig. 4-8. How crosscut teeth cut.

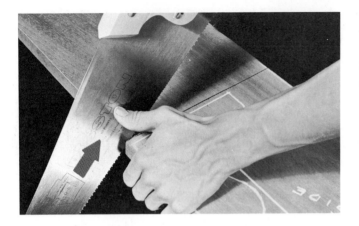

Fig. 4-9. Starting the cut.

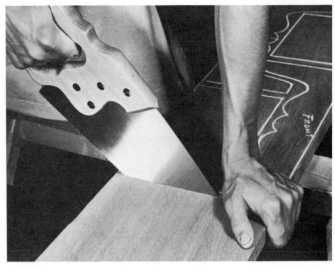

Fig. 4-11. Finishing the cut.

by pulling the saw toward you several times until you have cut a kerf 1/4 to 1/2 in. deep.

As soon as the saw is started, move your left hand away from the blade. With the saw held at about a 45 degree angle, take long, even strokes, using nearly the entire length of the saw. Apply just enough pressure so it cuts smoothly. See Fig. 4-10. If the saw starts to cut away from the line, you can bring it back by twisting it slightly.

Slow down as you near the end of the cut. Be sure both pieces are well supported. You may need to add another sawhorse or have someone assist you. If the board is wide you may be able to grasp both pieces as shown in Fig. 4-11.

Short pieces of stock are difficult to support and hold on sawhorses. It is better to clamp them in a vise as shown in Fig. 4-12.

## RIPPING STOCK TO ROUGH WIDTH

Select a rip saw with about 5 1/2 points to the inch. Fig. 4-13 shows the shape of rip teeth. They are filed approximately straight across and look like a series of narrow chisels. The cut left by rip saw

Fig. 4-12. Crosscutting with stock held in vise.

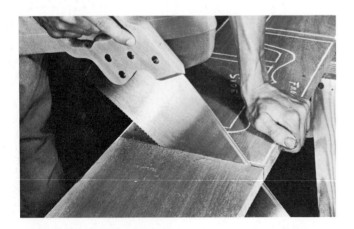

Fig. 4-10. Making the cut with full, smooth strokes.

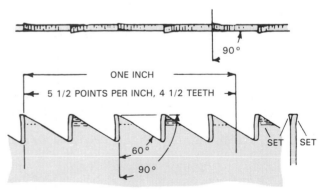

ONE INCH

5 1/2 POINTS PER INCH, 4 1/2 TEETH

90°

60°

90°

SET     SET

Fig. 4-13. Rip saw teeth. The 90 degree angle is often increased to give the tooth a negative rake. (The Stanley Works)

teeth is shown in Fig. 4-14.

Follow about the same procedure for ripping as crosscutting. The rip saw is held at about a 60 degree angle. Start the cut with the board extended out over the sawhorse and then move the sawhorse back as the cut is advanced. After cutting some distance, the sawhorse can be moved to a position in front of the saw as shown in Fig. 4-15. If the saw tends to bind in the kerf, a wedge can be inserted to hold it open.

The crosscut saw can be used for ripping but it will cut much slower. The rip saw, however, should not be used for crosscutting as it will not cut through cross grain fibers easily and will leave a very rough cut.

## LAYING OUT AND CUTTING PLYWOOD

Since plywood has a finished (sanded) surface and is expensive, especially in hardwood, it must be cut out carefully. If there are many pieces, or the parts are complicated, make a scaled drawing on paper before making the layout on the panel. This will insure the most economical layout and prevent errors such as cutting pieces with the grain running in the wrong direction.

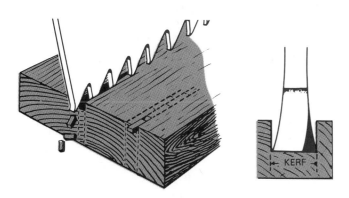

Fig. 4-14. How rip saw teeth cut.

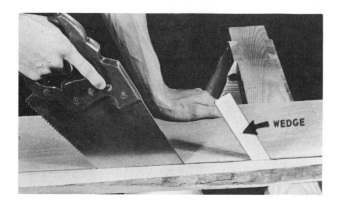

Fig. 4-15. Ripping stock to width. Note the defect called "wane" along the edge of the board.

Fig. 4-16. Laying out plywood cuttings using a double line.

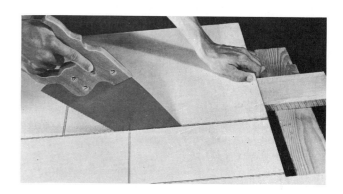

Fig. 4-17. Cutting plywood with a 10 point crosscut saw. Note the "stringers" placed on sawhorses to support the panel.

Since you will be cutting almost to finished size, it is good practice to use a DOUBLE LINE layout as shown in Fig. 4-16. The width of the cutting space will vary with the kind of plywood and type of saw used, in addition to the method used to smooth the edge. Use a 10 point (or finer) toothed CROSSCUT SAW for cutting plywood. See Fig. 4-17. Work carefully and try to avoid excessive splintering on the underside. Always be sure the panel is well supported and try to prevent any damage to the surface.

The portable saber saw is a good tool to use for cutting plywood, Fig. 4-18. It cuts on the upstroke, and this tends to splinter the top surface. Directions for using this tool are included in Chapter 13.

Use the same general procedures for cutting hardboard and particle board.

### SHARPENING A HAND SAW

Sharpening or refitting a hand saw is one of the more difficult processes in hand tool maintenance.

65

Fig. 4-18. Cutting plywood with a saber saw.    (DeWalt)

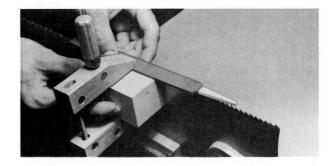

Fig. 4-19. Jointing a hand saw, using an 8 in. smooth mill file clamped to a square block of wood.

have a built-in file or abrasive stone, or hold a standard mill file.

## FILING

Filing a hand saw is done with a triangular saw file, like the one shown in Fig. 4-20. These saws are available in lengths from 4 to 8 in. Widths or cross sections are designated as regular taper, slim taper, extra slim taper, and double extra slim taper. For a 5 or 6 point rip saw, use a 7 in. slim taper. For a 10 point crosscut, a 5 in. extra slim taper is usually recommended. Be sure the file is equipped with a tight fitting handle.

Mount the saw in a regular saw-filing vise with the handle to your right. If one is not available, it can be mounted between two strips of wood in a regular woodworking vise. The teeth should project above the strips about 1/4 in. Start at the heel of the blade and work toward the toe. Place the file in the first gullet where it will contact the back of a tooth set away from you. Position the file to fit the bevel of the teeth so that you will file the front of a tooth and the back of an adjacent tooth in a single stroke.

Rip saw teeth are filed almost straight across with the handle end of the file just a few degrees below a horizontal line. See Fig. 4-21. Crosscut teeth are filed at an angle of about 65 degrees with the handle end of the file about 10 degrees below the horizontal, as shown in Fig. 4-22.

Use long, full strokes, with just enough pressure to make the file cut easily. Raise the file out of the gullet on the return stroke so that you can observe the work. Continue to file until you have removed about one-half of the "flat" of the teeth on each

However, as you gain skill and experience in woodworking you should not hesitate to undertake this task. Start with a saw that has become dull but still has well-shaped teeth. Sharpening a saw that is in poor condition with teeth out of shape is a challenge for even an experienced woodworker. Such saws should be sent to a local saw shop or to the factory where they can be machine filed or refitted by an expert.

The process of sharpening a saw includes three basic operations: JOINTING, SETTING, and FILING. While they are usually performed in this order, a heavy jointing operation will reduce the size of the teeth and they will need to be filed and reshaped before setting is possible. Since a saw can be lightly jointed and filed several times before additional set is required, these operations will be described first.

## JOINTING

Jointing is the operation of lightly filing off the points of the teeth so that they are all the same height. Clamp the saw in a vise and run a smooth mill file along the teeth. Clamping the file to a square block of wood, as shown in Fig. 4-19, will keep it in a horizontal position and guide it along the blade.

Move the file lightly over the teeth several times until tiny "flats" or "brights" are visible on the points of the teeth. The jointing process for the instructional pictures that follow was considerably overdone so that the flats could be easily seen. In actual practice, the jointing should be as light as possible and stopped just as soon as flats appear on nearly all of the teeth.

Patented saw jointing devices are available that

Fig. 4-20. Triangular taper saw file. (Nicholson File Co.)

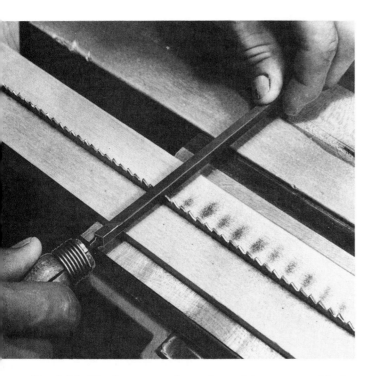

Fig. 4-21. File rip saw teeth nearly straight across, with the file handle down about 2 degrees.

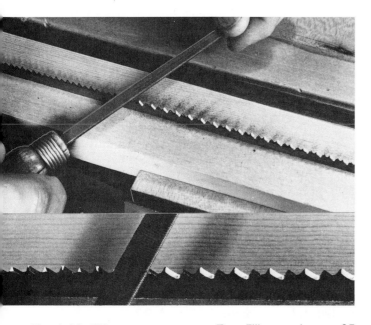

Fig. 4-22. Filing a crosscut saw. Top. Filing at about a 65 degree angle, with the handle down about 10 degrees. Bottom. Close-up view.

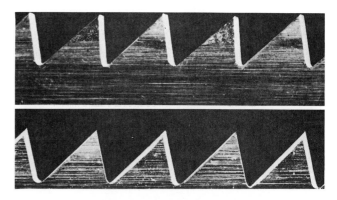

Fig. 4-23. Correctly filed saw teeth. Above. Rip teeth. Below. Crosscut teeth. (Nicholson File Co.)

Fig. 4-24. Setting the teeth. In this position the saw set will bend the teeth away from you.

## SETTING

Setting is the operation of bending the teeth slightly outward. The amount of set is determined by the points per inch. Most SAW SETS are calibrated on this basis. The proper amount of set should produce a saw kerf that is a little less than 1 1/2 times the thickness of the blade. This will require that each tooth be bent out slightly less than 1/4 of the blade thickness.

Study the manufacturer's directions and adjust the saw set. Clamp the saw in the vise and set the teeth bent away from you. See Fig. 4-24. Only about the upper half of the tooth should be set. Reverse the saw in the vise. Set the remaining teeth.

Automatic filing and setting machines are shown in Figs. 4-25 and Fig. 4-26. After these machines are set up and adjusted they can do a perfect job of filing and setting in minutes.

Take good care of your hand saws. Be sure the

side. File every other gullet until you reach the toe of the blade. Reverse the saw in the clamp and file the other gullets, stopping just as soon as the flats disappear. This is very important because when the flats are gone you will lose your reference point and may file some teeth shorter than others. Fig. 4-23 shows correctly filed crosscut and rip teeth.

Fig. 4-25. Automatic saw filer. After each file stroke, pawl engages teeth and moves blade into position for the next stroke. (Foley-Belsaw Co.)

Fig. 4-26. Automatic saw setting machine. After adjustments are made, it takes less than a minute to set a hand saw. The same machine can be used to set band saw blades. (Foley-Belsaw Co.)

lumber you cut with them is clean, dry, and free of nails. When not in use they should be kept in a tool rack or holder that will protect them from damage. Keep the screws tight in the handle. Wipe the blade frequently with a cloth lightly saturated with oil. Some woodworkers use a lemon oil furniture polish instead of machine oil. It has a slight cleaning action and leaves a light oily film that protects the metal surface from rust.

## TEST YOUR KNOWLEDGE, Chapter 4

Please do not write in the text. Place your answers on a separate sheet of paper.
1. The two systems of linear measure in use today are _____ and _____.
2. Make a _____ _____ _____ before selecting the stock best suited for your project.
3. How much extra stock is allowed in a rough layout for thickness?
   a. 1/2 in.
   b. 1/4 in.
   c. 1/16 in.
   d. None of the above.
4. How are crosscut saw teeth different from rip saw teeth?
5. Only half the entire length of the saw blade should be used when making a cut. True or False?
6. When cutting short pieces of wood, they should be held:
   a. By hand.
   b. In a vise.
   c. By another person.
   d. None of the above.
7. The _____ (rip saw, crosscut saw) can be used for both ripping and crosscutting.
8. The double line layout is used when laying out and cutting _____.
9. The three basic operations in the process of sharpening a saw are _____, _____, and _____.
10. Crosscut teeth are filed at an angle of about _____ degrees with the handle end of the file about _____ degrees below the horizontal.

## ACTIVITIES

1. Study the catalog of a supplier/manufacturer of hand tools. Develop a complete description

(kind, length, points per inch, etc.) for a number of hand saws. Include current retail prices for each. Note those that you would select for a home workshop.
2. From a study of reference materials, develop a list of saw file sizes to use when sharpening

saws ranging from 5 to 16 points per inch.
3. Prepare a wall chart which illustrates the various types of saws and explains the purpose of each.
4. Practice sharpening an old saw. Compare the cutting action before and after sharpening.

Grading southern yellow pine boards in a modern sawmill. (Southern Forest Products Association)

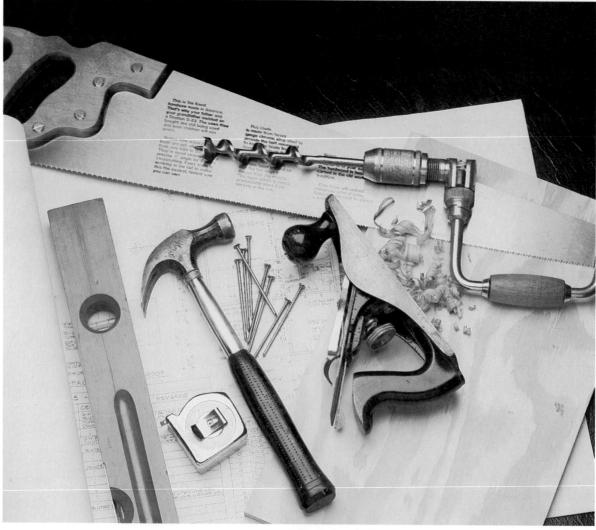

Hand tools, such as planes and saws, require skill and practice in order to produce parts to specified dimensions. (Top. The Stanley Works. Bottom. American Plywood Assoc.)

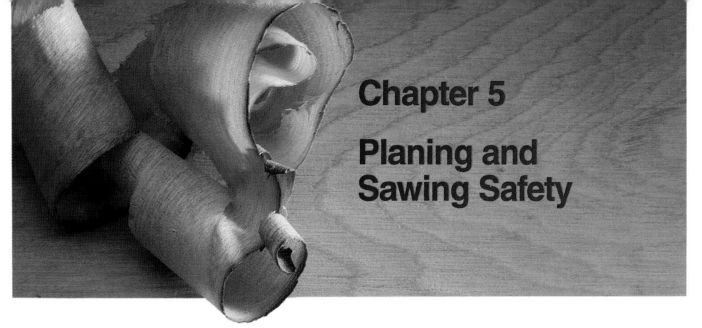

# Chapter 5

# Planing and Sawing Safety

This chapter and several that follow, deal with hand tool operations. They include basic skills that apply to a wide range of construction problems. As you gain experience in woodworking you will, of course, want to take advantage of the efficiency and time saving factors that power machines provide. If you have a good understanding of the correct procedures in using hand tools, you will develop skills in the use of the machines more rapidly.

As you undertake advanced projects involving the use of power machines, you will find that the need for hand tools continues to exist. The expert wood crafter knows how to use both hand tools and machine tools.

## KINDS AND SIZES OF PLANES

The standard hand plane is used to make a wood surface smooth and flat. Some of the common kinds of planes are shown in Fig. 5-1. Three of the planes are constructed in the same way and vary only in size. The SMOOTH PLANE is 9 in. long with a 2 in. cutter and is used on uneven surfaces and small pieces. The FORE PLANE is 18 in. long with a 2 3/8 in. cutter. It is used to plane large surfaces, especially the edges of long boards. The JACK PLANE is 14 in. long with a 2 in. cutter, and is a general purpose plane that can be used for many planing operations. While the sizes listed are the most common, other sizes are available. For example, the jack plane is available in lengths from 11 1/2 to 15 in., with a cutter width of 1 3/4 to 2 1/4 in.

You should become thoroughly acquainted with the standard plane, how it is assembled and adjusted. Study your plane. Refer to Fig. 5-2 to learn the name of the parts and how they fit together. To remove the plane iron (also called the cutter or blade) raise the lever on the lever cap and remove. The double plane iron (plane iron and plane iron cap) can now be lifted from the plane. To disassemble the double plane iron, loosen the cap screw, pull the cap iron back from the plane iron edge, turn it

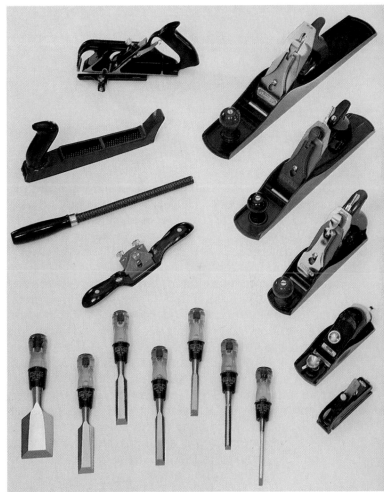

Fig. 5-1. Planes and chisels. (The Stanley Works)

sideways, and slide it toward the edge until the cap screw clears the hole in the plane iron.

## SHARPENING PLANE IRONS

Sharpening a plane iron includes the operations of honing (also called whetting) and grinding.

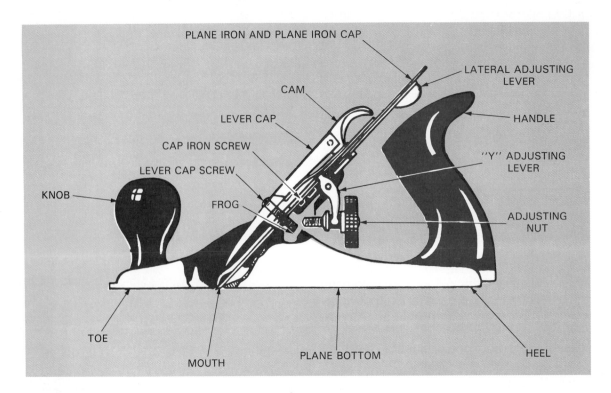

Fig. 5-2. Parts of a plane. (The Stanley Works)

GRINDING is the shaping and forming of the cutting edge and bevel. HONING involves working on the tip of the cutting edge to make it sharp. A plane iron that is in good condition can be honed a number of times before it will require grinding.

Oilstones used for honing are either natural or manufactured materials. One of the well-known NATURAL oilstones is the Arkansas, which is white to light gray in color and sometimes has darker streaks showing in the surface. It is made of natural novaculite stone, has a fine cutting surface and is used as the "final touch" for a razor-sharp edge. The ARTIFICIAL (manufactured) oilstones are made from aluminum-oxide (reddish-brown color) and silicon-carbide (dark gray colors). They are available in a large variety of shapes and sizes and are graded as coarse, medium, and fine. Aluminum-oxide stone is often referred to as an India oilstone. Silicon-carbide stones are sold under such trade names as Crestolon and Carborundum.

For HONING, apply a small amount of thin oil to the face of a medium grade oilstone and place the bevel of the plane iron flat on the surface. Now raise the other end a few degrees so that just the cutting edge rests on the stone. Maintain this angle and move the plane iron forward and backward over the entire surface as shown in Fig. 5-3A. Continue these strokes until you can feel a fine wire edge when you pull your finger out over the edge. This fine wire edge should exist all the way across the plane iron. Now turn the plane iron over, LAY IT

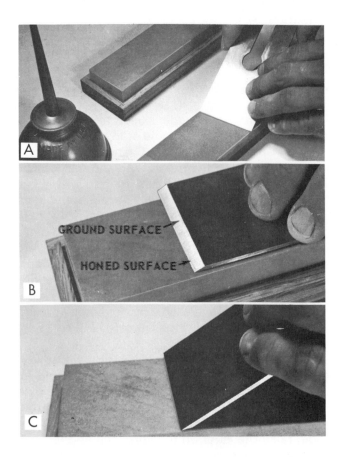

Fig. 5-3. Honing a plane iron. A—Honing beveled side until a slight wire edge is formed. B—Plane iron turned over and honed lightly while held flat on the stone. C—Final honing on a fine oilstone.

FLAT on a fine oilstone, and stroke it a few times as shown in Fig. 5-3B.

Turn the plane iron back to the bevel side on the fine stone for a few light strokes, then again stroke the top of the iron held flat on the oilstone, Fig. 5-3C. Repeat this procedure several times until the wire edge has disappeared. The edge should now be sharp, ''keen,'' and should cut a smooth, silky shaving when tested on a piece of wood. This is shown in Fig. 5-4.

Be sure to use sufficient oil on the surface of the oilstone. The oil will carry the fine steel cuttings away, preventing them from becoming embedded in the pores of the stone and glazing the surface. When you finish using the oilstone, wipe off the surface and replace the cover.

GRINDING requires forming an accurate bevel on a plane iron. The use of a guide or grinding attachment is necessary. Sometimes the cap iron can be turned crosswise and tightened to the plane iron so that it serves as a guide along the tool rest of the grinder, Fig. 5-5. Fig. 5-6 shows a plane iron clamped in a grinding attachment that makes it easy to form a bevel that is properly shaped.

When using a grinding attachment, first place the plane iron in the carrier with the bevel against the grinding wheel. Then adjust the angle of the attachment so that the surface of the bevel ground will be about two and one-third times the thickness of the plane iron, Fig. 5-7. Tighten the clamp that holds the plane iron and turn on the grinder. Take a light cut and check the grinding angle. If it is correct, grind the bevel by moving it back and forth across the wheel. Do not let the edge go beyond the center

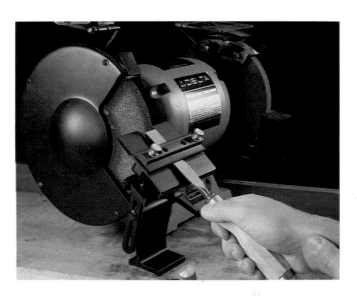

Fig. 5-6. Attachment for grinding plane irons, chisels, and other beveled edge woodworking tools. (Woodcraft Supply Corporation)

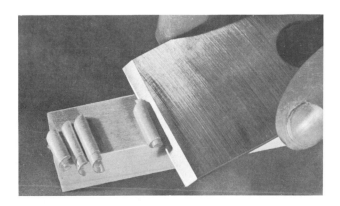

Fig. 5-4. Testing the sharpness of a plane iron. The iron should cut a fine, silky shaving when slight pressure is applied.

Fig. 5-5. A—Adjustable safety shield. B—3500 rpm motor. C—Wheel guard. D—Adjustable tool rest. E—Dust chute. F—6'' grinding wheel. G—Switch. (Delta International Machinery Corp.)

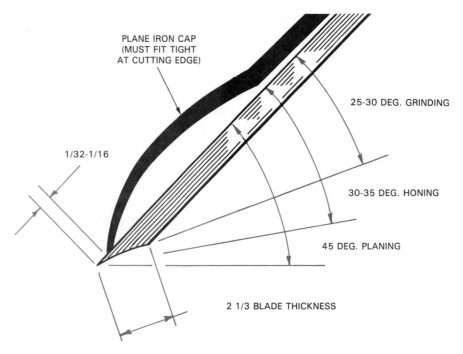

PLANE IRON CAP
(MUST FIT TIGHT
AT CUTTING EDGE)

25-30 DEG. GRINDING

1/32-1/16

30-35 DEG. HONING

45 DEG. PLANING

2 1/3 BLADE THICKNESS

Fig. 5-7. A double plane iron assembly showing the grinding and honing angles.

of the wheel face in either direction. Continue grinding until the edge is thin and a slight burr starts to form. Grind slightly more on the outside corners so they will be about 1/32 in. lower than the main part of the edge. Some woodworkers prefer to form this slight crown on the oilstone. Remove any burr that was formed in the grinding operation on a coarse or medium oilstone, then proceed to hone the plane iron as previously described.

*During the grinding operation, KEEP THE PLANE IRON COOL by dipping it in water. YOU MUST WEAR GOGGLES!*

## ADJUSTING PLANES

Position the plane iron cap on the plane iron as shown in Fig. 5-8, and tighten the cap iron screw. The edge of the plane iron cap must fit tight against the top of the plane iron. Otherwise, shavings will feed under it and prevent the plane from cutting properly. See Fig. 5-9.

Carefully place the double plane iron into the plane and secure its position with the lever cap. If necessary, adjust the setting of the lever cap screw so that the cam of the lever cap locks in place with smooth, firm pressure.

Turn the plane upside down and sight across the bottom. Look toward a window or other source of light. Turn the adjustment nut clockwise until the blade projects above the plane bottom about 1/16

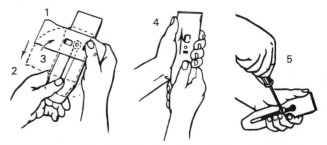

Fig. 5-8. Assembly of double plane iron. 1. Lay the plane iron cap on the plane iron with cap screw in slot. 2. Draw the cap back. 3. Turn it straight with the plane iron. 4. Advance the plane iron cap until it is within 1/16 to 1/32 in. of the cutting edge. 5. Tighten the cap screw.

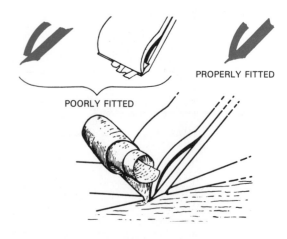

PROPERLY FITTED

POORLY FITTED

Fig. 5-9. The plane iron cap must fit tight to the plane iron. Its purpose is to break and curl the shavings, and prevent the wood from splitting ahead of the cutting edge. On crossgrained or curly-grained woods it should be close to the cutting edge. (The Stanley Works)

74

in. Now move the lateral adjustment lever from side to side until the cutting edge is parallel to the bottom of the plane. Turn the adjustment nut counterclockwise until the cutting edge is withdrawn below the surface of the plane bottom. Place the plane on the surface of the stock and turn the adjustment nut clockwise until the plane edge just begins to cut.

## PLANING A SURFACE

If you will look closely at lumber that has been surfaced you will find there are very small "waves" (called mill marks) which were formed by the rotating knives of a power planer. See Fig. 5-10. These should be removed with a hand plane. It takes a great amount of hand sanding to remove such marks, and since they are slightly compressed into the wood by the machine, there is a tendency for them to reappear when finish is applied. Hand planing may also be used to remove warp and other imperfections.

Plane the best face of the stock first. By examining the edge of the board try to determine the direction of the grain and clamp the stock in position so you will be planing WITH the grain. Most stock can be laid flat on a bench and clamped between a bench stop and vise dog as shown in Fig. 5-11.

Place the plane on the stock and move it over the surface, gradually turning the adjustment nut until a fine shaving is cut. You may find that the plane cuts in some spots and not in others. This indicates high places in the surface. Continue to plane these high spots until they disappear and the plane "takes" a shaving across the entire surface. Keep the plane set for a very fine cut. THE SHAVINGS SHOULD BE LIGHT AND FEATHERY. They should

seem to almost float when you drop a handful to the floor. Try to produce a smooth, true surface with as little planing as possible. Check the surface with a rule as shown in Fig. 5-12.

Generally, it is considered best to plane the surface of your stock while it is in one piece. If, however, there is much warpage present, it may be best to cut the stock into smaller pieces before

Fig. 5-11. Planing a surface.

Fig. 5-12. Checking the surface. The rule or straightedge must be placed diagonally across the stock to reveal twist (wind).

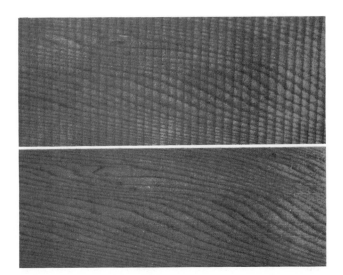

Fig. 5-10. Top. Millmarks on stock surfaced with a power planer. Bottom. The same surface after hand planing.

*Take good care of your plane. In addition to sharpening the plane iron, keep the knob, handle, and frog tightened. Keep the plane clean by wiping it with a slightly oiled cloth. You may apply a little paste wax to the bottom and sides to reduce friction and also to protect against rust.*

hand planing. Warped stock can be straightened by planing across the grain or diagonally with the grain.

Turn the stock end over end and plane the other side. Measure the stock at several points to determine finished thickness. A marking gauge can be used for this. Or you may wish to lay out a thickness measurement all the way around the edge as shown in Fig. 5-13.

On some work, the hand surfacing operation should be done later. If it is necessary to make edge joints to secure the required width of stock, then the hand surfacing operation should be left until after these joints have been made.

Small thin pieces are hard to clamp and hold while they are being planed. A board with a strip of hardboard glued to one end can be used, Fig. 5-14.

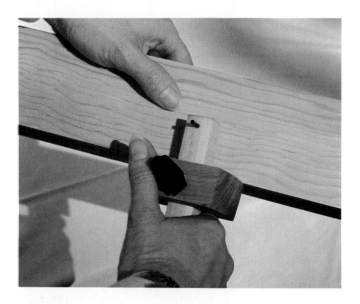

Fig. 5-13. Using a mortise gauge to lay out stock thickness.

## PLANING AN EDGE

After both surfaces have been planed, clamp the stock in the vise with the best edge up and the grain running in the right direction. The reason the best edge is planed first is that defects on the second edge will likely be removed when the stock is reduced to the required width.

Start the cut with most of the pressure on the plane knob and continue this pressure until the plane is well supported by the stock. Finish the cut with extra pressure on the plane handle. Fig. 5-15 shows a jack plane being used. A smooth plane will also work but may not produce as straight an edge.

In planing an edge, follow the same general procedure as in planing a surface, Fig. 5-16. Continue to plane until you can produce one continuous cut across the entire length of the board. Use the try square to check the edge for squareness with the face, Fig. 5-17.

From the finished edge, lay out the required width and draw a line down the length of the stock. Turning the stock end over end from the position used to plane the first edge should place the grain in the right direction. Some woodworkers prefer to square the ends to finished length before planing the second edge.

For very accurate planing it is sometimes helpful to hold the plane as shown in Fig. 5-18. The fingers under the plane serve as a guide to hold it in alignment throughout the cut. This will result in the shaving being cut by the same section of the plane iron.

Stock should always be held securely for planing operations. Fig. 5-19 shows some clamping setups. A long strip cannot be held in the vise because it will bend under the weight of the plane and prevent accurate work. In the same figure, note

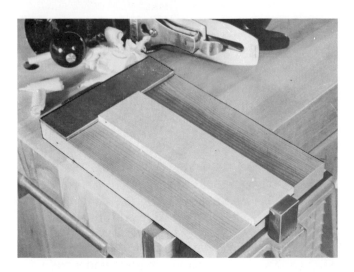

Fig. 5-14. Clamping thin pieces for planing. Keep the vise dog below the surface of the stock so it will not damage the plane.

Fig. 5-15. Planing an edge.

Fig. 5-16. Try to produce a smooth, true edge with as little planing as possible.
(The Stanley Works)

Fig. 5-17. Checking the edge to see that it is square with the face.

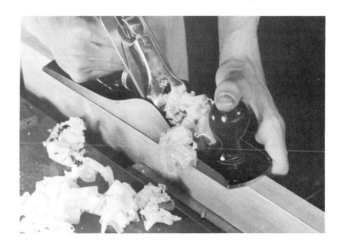

Fig. 5-18. Guiding the toe of the plane with fingers held on the plane bottom. Used for a fine and accurate cut.

that the good face of the plywood panel is being protected with a block of wood. Use care in handling stock that has been planed and smoothed so you will not need to remove nicks, dents, and soiled spots when you prepare your project for finish.

When the pieces of stock are very small it may be more practical to clamp or secure the tool and move the wood. A setup for planing the edge of small pieces of walnut is shown in Fig. 5-20. A carefully made straightedge is glued to a piece of flat stock. Then this unit and a jack plane are clamped in the vise.

## SQUARING STOCK TO LENGTH WITH BACKSAW

Lay out the position of the cut. Then mark a line across the surface using a try square and sharp pencil. Hold the handle of the try square against the edge of the stock and draw the line along the blade.

Fig. 5-19. Clamping methods. Left. A long strip needs the support of the bench top. Right. Large panel supported with the vise and a hand screw.

Fig. 5-20. Special setup for planing small pieces. The jack plane being used has a corrugated bottom, preferred by some workers because they feel it reduces friction.

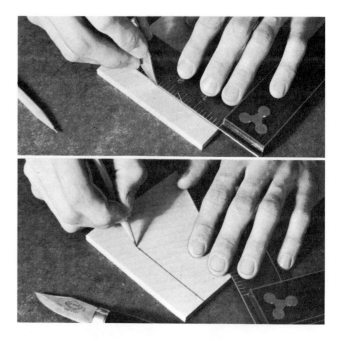

Fig. 5-21. Precision layout. Top. Knife drawn along the blade of a try square. Bottom. Sharp pencil drawn in the knife cut to make it easier to see.

For precision work use a knife or sharp pencil, as shown in Fig. 5-21.

The backsaw is used for making fine, accurate cuts. It has teeth similar to the crosscut saw but much finer (14 points). The blade is thin and reinforced with a heavy metal strip, Fig. 5-22.

When cutting with a backsaw, the stock is held in a horizontal position, in a vise, on a bench hook, or by other means. The saw cut is started in about the same manner as a regular handsaw but at a lower angle. After the cut is started, slowly lower the handle as you continue sawing and follow the cutting line across the surface of the stock. See Fig. 5-23. Use horizontal strokes to finish the cut.

For a precision cut with the backsaw, you may want to use the procedure shown in Fig. 5-24. It takes a little longer to set up, but since you are assured of a square cut that will require little or no planing, you may actually save time. An important part of this setup is an accurate "straightedge." This is a straight piece of stock with faces and edges perfectly square. Clamp the straightedge firmly along the cutting line. Tighten the outside spindle of the handscrew last since it provides the greatest amount of leverage.

Place the blade of the backsaw against the straightedge and start the cut. With the left hand, apply pressure to the side of the saw so the blade will be held snugly against the straightedge throughout the cut. A block of wood can be held against the blade as shown in Fig. 5-24A. The teeth of a

Fig. 5-22. These backsaws may be used to make fine, accurate cuts such as those required for joints. (Leichtung, Inc.)

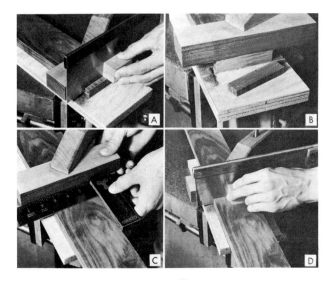

Fig. 5-24. Using a straightedge to guide backsaw. A—Holding saw against straightedge with block of wood. B—Completed cut. C—Setting straightedge for a second cut. D—Making second cut.

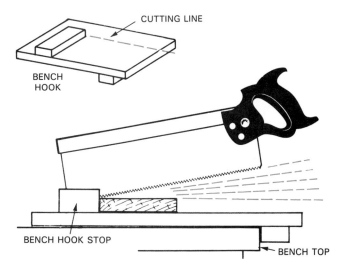

Fig. 5-23. A backsaw cut with the stock held on a bench hook. The bench hook stop serves as a guide for the saw when starting the cut.

backsaw are small and will not cut fast, so use long steady strokes. Sawdust cut near the center of the board must be moved to the edge of the stock, before it can be cleared from the saw kerf. Short strokes will not clear the sawdust. Instead it will work up along the sides of the saw and cause the blade to bind. Notice that the stock is clamped to a scrap piece that protects the saw from the vise and supports the wood fibers on the underside of the cut.

From the squared end lay out the finished length. Use the same procedure to cut off the second end. Whenever possible, clamp the straightedge on the stock so that the saw kerf will be on the ''waste''

side of the line. If you cannot do this, you will need to make an allowance for the width of the saw kerf.

## PLANING END GRAIN

End grain is hard to plane. Although a jack plane or smooth plane can be used, a BLOCK PLANE will do the best work. The blade of the block plane is positioned at a very low angle, with the BEVELED SIDE TURNED UP. It is designed to be held in one hand, leaving the other hand free to hold the work.

When planing end grain the cut should not continue over an edge or end unless the wood fibers are supported as shown in Fig. 5-25. When the

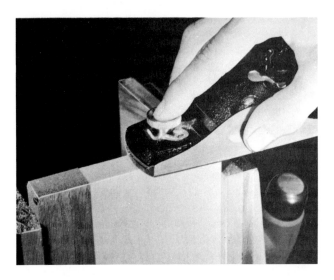

Fig. 5-25. Planing end grain. The edge is supported with scrap stock.

board is wide, plane in from each edge, toward the center. Always adjust the plane for a very light cut.

A good way to plane end grain is with a device called a "shooting-board" as shown in Fig. 5-26. It is constructed somewhat similar to a bench hook with the addition of a guide for the plane bottom. When using the shooting-board, the stock should be held firmly against the stop and fed into the cut after each stroke.

When planing the edge of plywood you will always be cutting some end grain. The block plane is a good tool to use for smoothing the edge of the plywood. Refer to Fig. 5-27.

## SQUARING SMALL PIECES OF STOCK

Small pieces and parts are difficult to plane and saw. They are hard to clamp and hold. Regular tools seem large and "clumsy." A sawing jig that works well is shown in Fig. 5-28. It clamps into the vise

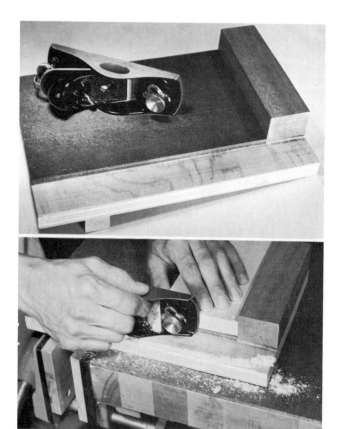

Fig. 5-26. Top. Block plane and shooting-board. Bottom. Planing end grain.

Fig. 5-27. Using block plane to smooth edge of plywood.

Fig. 5-28. A—Sawing jig for small parts. B—Cutting a small square block. C—Squaring-off piece of dowel. D—Cutting dowel at an angle.

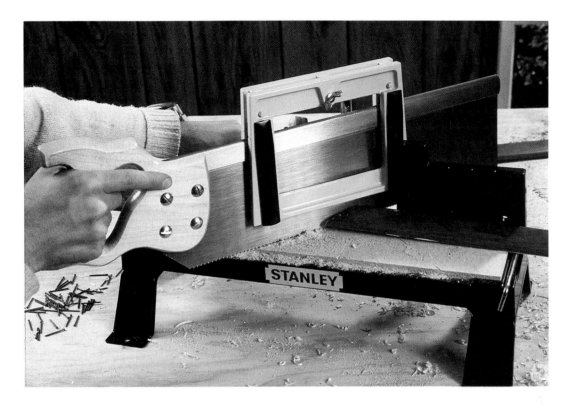

Fig. 5-29. The miter box will produce very accurate cuts at angles up to 45 degrees.
(The Stanley Works)

and operates similar to a miter box. The DOVETAIL SAW being used has fine teeth, a thin blade, and makes a smooth and accurate cut.

When constructing the jig, square the main center piece. Then cut it into parts with the miter box, Fig. 5-29. These pieces are carefully glued in place on the baseboard, using spacers equal to the saw blade thickness. Apply some paste wax to the slot to make the saw run smoothly.

Jigs like this are not hard to build and will help you do better work in less time. Some jigs may be specialized and designed to perform just one operation on a given part. They are used in mass production, where many identical parts are made.

Sanding should usually not be started until all edge tool operations are complete. Small parts, however, can be squared easily and quickly on a sanding board. They can be held perpendicular to the surface with a straightedge or a sliding carrier, Fig. 5-30. This carrier eliminates the tendency for the part to tip over as it is moved along the straightedge.

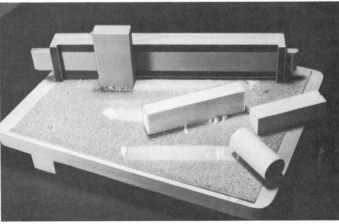

Fig. 5-30. Left. Squaring small parts on a sanding board using a sliding carrier. Right. View of the sliding carrier and finished pieces.

## TEST YOUR KNOWLEDGE, Chapter 5

Please do not write in the text. Place your answers on a separate sheet.

1. The smallest type of plane that uses a double plane iron assembly is called _____ plane.
2. The front end of the plane bottom is called the _____.
3. To remove the double plane iron from the jack plane you must first loosen and remove the _____.
4. An oilstone that is reddish-brown in color is made of a manufactured abrasive called _____.
5. Why is oil applied to the surface of the oilstone when honing an edge?
6. The bevel of a plane iron should be ground so that the included angle is from _____ to _____ degrees.
7. To increase the depth of cut of the jack plane the adjusting nut is turned _____ (clockwise, counterclockwise).
8. If the plane is not "taking" a shaving over the entire surface then the depth of cut should be increased. True or False?
9. To align the plane iron edge with the plane bottom the _____ adjustment lever is moved.
10. If the stock is to be edge-glued to form wider widths, then the surfacing operation is performed later. True or False?
11. The backsaw has "crosscut" shaped teeth that are small and number about _____ points per inch.
12. The blade of the block plane sets at a low angle with the beveled side turned _____.

## ACTIVITIES

1. Make a design sketch of a shooting-board that can be adjusted to plane the ends of pieces at 45, 60, and 90 degree angles.
2. Make a design sketch of a sawing jig that could be used to cut 100 pieces exactly 2 in. long, from strips of stock 3/4 in. square.
3. From the catalog of a supplier or manufacturer, develop a list of the various kinds of oilstones. Include a description of sizes, grades, materials, and current retail prices.
4. Visit a local hardware store and make a list of the types of hand planes on display. Include complete size description and current prices.

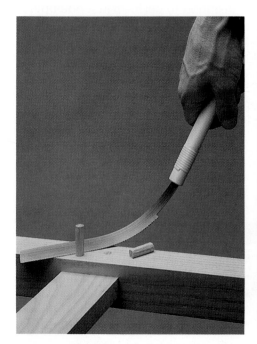 

Left. Japanese "Kugihiki" flush-cutting saw. Right. Lower right. Half-round spokeshave. Upper right. Radius spokeshave. (Woodcraft Supply Corporation)

Top left. Corrugated base plane, jointer plane, fore plane, jack plane, smoothing plane, and bench plane. Bottom left. Plough and combination planes. Right. Rabbet planes (bench, duplex, and side).    (Stanley Tools)

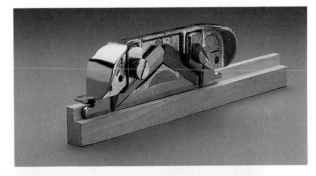

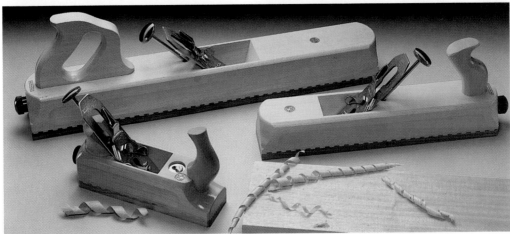

Top left. Router plane. Top right. Side rabbet plane. Bottom. Lower left. Deluxe primus smoothing plane. Upper left. Deluxe primus jointer plane. Middle right. Long pattern primus jack plane.    (Stanley Tools)

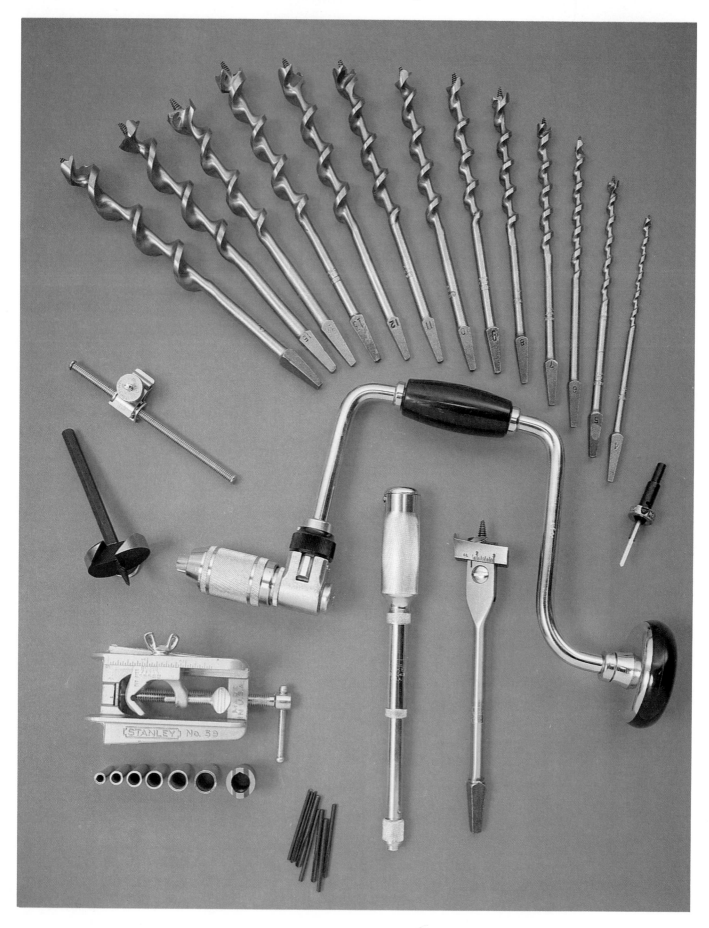

Tools for boring and drilling holes. (The Stanley Works)

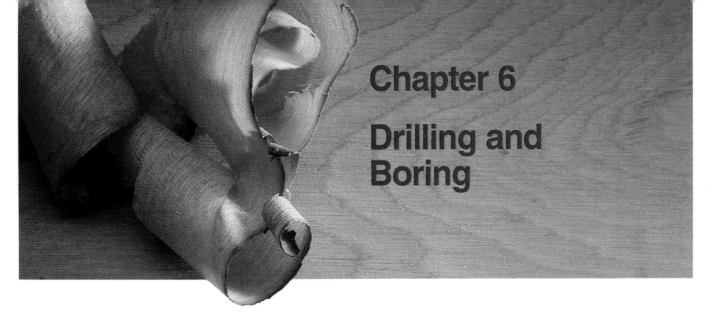

# Chapter 6

# Drilling and Boring

## BRACES AND AUGER BITS

In working with hand tools, holes larger than one quarter inch in diameter are bored with auger bits, Forstner bits, and expansion bits. These tools are mounted in a brace that holds them in position and provides the leverage to turn the bits into the wood. Holes 1/4 in. and smaller are usually drilled with a hand drill.

The parts of a standard ratchet brace are shown in Fig. 6-1. The shell and jaws form a chuck that is designed to hold the square shank of the various bits. The size of the brace is determined by its sweep. SWEEP is the diameter of the circle the handle forms as it is turned. Braces are available in sizes from 8 to 14 in. A good size for the school shop is 8 or 10 in. Most braces are equipped with a RATCHET. This permits boring in a corner even though a full revolution of the handle cannot be made. In heavy boring, the ratchet is helpful since the handle can be positioned for the greatest amount of leverage.

The brace requires little maintenance other than a few drops of fine oil on the threads of the chuck, and on the ratchet, handle, and head bearing from time to time.

Auger bits will vary in the shape and design of the twist, but all of them will have about the same parts as shown in Fig. 6-2. The FEED SCREW centers the bit and draws it into the wood. The pitch of the feed screw determines the rate of feed. Bits are available for fast, medium, and slow boring. The SPURS (also called nibs) score the perimeter of the hole as the LIPS (also called cutters) cut the shavings from the inside. After the shavings are cut, the TWIST moves them out of the hole.

The size (diameter) of standard bits range from 3/16 in. to as large as 2 in. The more common sizes are from 1/4 to 1 in. The size is stamped on the tang in sixteenths of an inch so that a 1/2 in. bit would carry a No. 8 (for 8/16 or 1/2 in.). For a 3/4 in. hole a No. 12 would be used. The length of auger bits range from 7 to 10 in., with the exception of dowel bits that are about 5 1/2 in.

## SHARPENING AN AUGER BIT

Sharpening an auger bit requires considerable skill and careful work. Check with your instructor before attempting this operation.

A special auger bit file is available for sharpening auger bits. However, other small, fine files can be used. Sharpen the lips or cutters first by stroking upward through the throat as shown in Fig. 6-3.

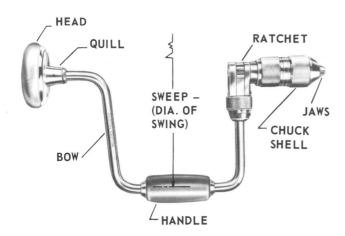

Fig. 6-1. Parts of a standard ratchet brace. (Millers Falls Co.)

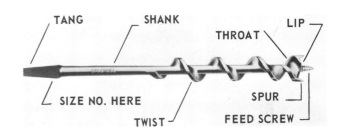

Fig. 6-2. Parts of a solid center type auger bit.

Fig. 6-3. Left. Filing the cutting lip. Right. Filing the spur. Try to maintain original bevel and do not file the outside.

Use medium pressure. Stop as soon as the cutters are sharp. Try to maintain the original bevel. Do not file the underside (side next to the screw). Turn the bit over, rest it on the edge of the bench and file the INSIDE OF THE SPURS. Try to keep the bit balanced by filing the same amount on each side.

## LAYOUT AND MARKING

Holes are usually bored and drilled after the stock has been surfaced and squared to finished size. Study your working drawings. Then with a rule, square, and sharp pencil, lay out the centerlines that will locate the exact position of the holes. See Fig. 6-4. Draw these lines lightly, so that those remaining after the holes are bored can be easily erased. Use a scratch awl to punch a hole where the centerlines intersect. This hole will make it easy to start the feed screw of the bit in the correct location.

## BORING $> = \frac{1}{4}''$

The stock should be securely held, either in the vise, or clamped to the bench. If the hole is to be bored all the way through, firmly clamp the stock to a piece of waste stock. This will support the wood around the edges of the hole when the bit cuts through the opposite side. The waste stock also provides material for the feed screw to enter and "pull" the bit through to complete the hole.

Select the correct size bit and insert it well into the chuck of the brace, with the corners of the tang held in the V of the jaws. Tighten the jaws on the bit by holding the chuck shell and turning the brace, as shown in Fig. 6-5.

Guide the bit with your left hand and set it into the hole marked with the awl. Turn the brace

*The edges of auger bits will stay sharp a long time if handled carefully. When not in use, keep them in special boxes or holders, or in fabric rolls. They will stay bright and shiny if you wipe them with a cloth lightly saturated with oil.*

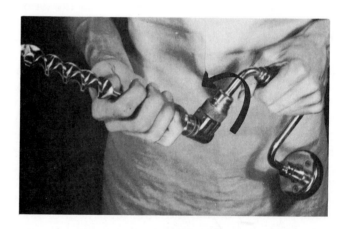

Fig. 6-5. Tightening the chuck of the brace by holding the shell and turning the handle.

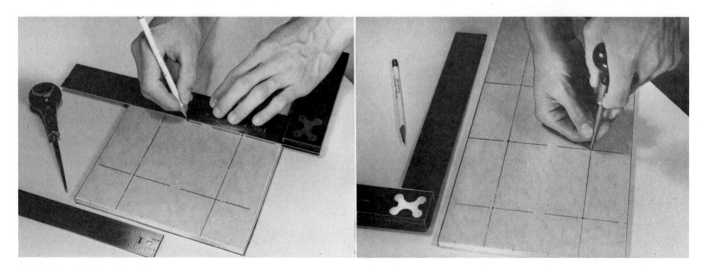

Fig. 6-4. Left. Laying out centerlines to locate the position of holes. Right. Making a hole for the feed screw of the bit.

clockwise and keep the bit perpendicular to the surface of the stock. Have another student help you "sight" this angle. Or you may keep the bit aligned with try squares as shown in Fig. 6-6.

It is usually easier to keep the bit perpendicular to the surface when boring in a vertical position, but on large holes you may not be able to exert enough pressure. This is especially true when boring holes into the end of stock because the feed screw will not "hold" in the end grain. You will need to apply extra pressure.

If it is not convenient to back up the work with waste stock the hole should be bored from both sides. Bore from one side until the feed screw just begins to come through, then reverse the stock and complete the hole as shown in Fig. 6-7. When boring a deep hole, withdraw the bit several times to cool it and clear the shavings. Lay out and bore the hole half way in from each end when boring lamp stems and similar pieces.

Use extra care when starting a hole in plywood or you may splinter the veneer around the edge of the hole. Start the feed screw and turn the bit until the spurs just begin to score the outside of the hole. Turn the bit about a half turn backward, and then forward, several times until the surface veneer is completely cut, before continuing to bore the hole. When boring a large hole in a small piece, especially near the end, you can help prevent splitting by applying pressure to the sides with a hand screw. Refer to Fig. 6-8.

Fig. 6-7. Top. Boring from the front side until the feed screw just starts to come through the back surface. Bottom. Stock is reversed and the holes finished from back surface. (A double twist type of bit is being used.)

Fig. 6-8. Clamping the sides of a narrow piece to help prevent splitting.

## BORING TO SPECIFIED DEPTH

There are several patented bit gauges available that will control the depth of the bored hole. They are usually clamped to the twist or shank of the bit and adjusted to provide the required depth. One type of gauge is shown in Fig. 6-9.

You can make a simple depth gauge by boring through a block of wood, cutting it to length and then slipping it over the bit so the bit extends an amount equal to the hole depth required.

If you have just a few holes to bore, you can wrap a small strip of masking tape around the twist at a position that will provide the required depth.

Fig. 6-6. Boring a hole in a vertical position using try squares to align the bit. Note the waste stock under the work. Be careful not to bore on through the waste stock and into the vise or bench.

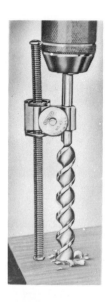

Fig. 6-9. A bit gauge is used to control the depth of the hole. This one is a spring type that will not mar the surface. (The Stanley Works)

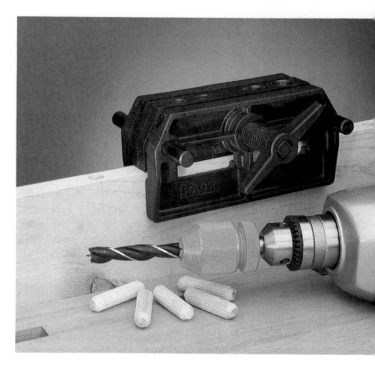

Fig. 6-11. Doweling jig with a self-centering guide block. (Leichtung, Inc.)

## DOWELING JIGS

Doweling jigs are specially designed for making dowel joints. However, they can also be used to insure straight holes in edges and ends of pieces.

Two types of jigs are shown in Figs. 6-10 and 6-11. The Universal doweling set (Fig. 6-10) is used to bore accurate dowel holes for edge-to-edge, T-butt, or corner joints without measuring. The self-aligning clamps accept stock 1/2" to 1" thick and drills of 1/4", 5/16", and 3/8". The other doweling jig (Fig. 6-11) has a center guide block that always remains centered between the two outside jaws. Holes 1/2 in. and under can be bored with this jig.

## COUNTERBORING

Sometimes it is necessary to have a hole of two different diameters. For example, you might want to place a screw or bolt head below the surface of the work. First bore the hole for the head to the required depth and then make the hole that will match the shank of the bolt or screw. See Fig. 6-12. It is important that you bore the holes in this order. If the small hore is bored first there will be no way to center the larger bit.

## BORING HOLES AT AN ANGLE

To bore a hole at an angle, set a T-bevel square at the required angle (use a protractor or the miter gauge of a table saw). Place it on the surface to be bored. Start the feed screw in the marked hole with the bit vertical, then tilt it to the required angle. Bring

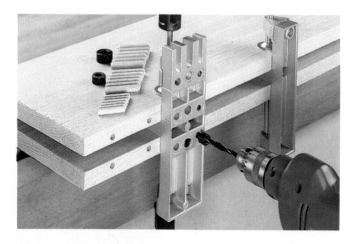

Fig. 6-10. The Universal doweling set may be used to bore accurate dowel holes for edge-to-edge, T-butt, or corner joints without measuring. The clamps are self-aligning. (Woodcraft Supply Corporation)

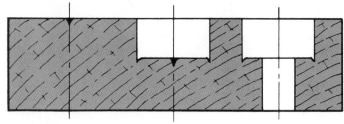

Fig. 6-12. Counterboring. Left. Position marked. Center. Large hole bored. Right. Smaller hole bored.

the blade of the T-bevel close to the bit and use it to align the hole as shown in Fig. 6-13.

When a number of holes must be bored at the same angle, you can do more accurate work by making a boring jig. There are many ways to make such a jig; the design and procedure will vary depending on the requirements of the work. Fig. 6-14 shows a jig that was designed to make a series of closely spaced holes on a wide board. Instead of boring the hole at an angle in the jig block, the hole was first bored square to the edge then the block was cut at the required angle.

## USING AN EXPANSIVE BIT

An expansive bit is used to bore holes from about 7/8 to 3 inches in diameter. It has adjustable cutters (usually two).

Adjust the cutter so the distance from the spur to the feed screw is equal to the radius of the hole. Some bits have a scale that will help you make this setting. After the setting is made lock the cutter securely. Start a test hole in a scrap block, checking the size before using it on your project.

In using an expansive bit to bore all the way through the stock, it is best to back up the work with a scrap piece as shown in Fig. 6-15. Large holes will require lots of "power," so it is advisable to use a large brace (10-12 in.) to give you the extra leverage that is needed.

## USING A FORSTNER BIT

A Forstner bit does not have a feed screw. It is used for boring holes that go only part way through

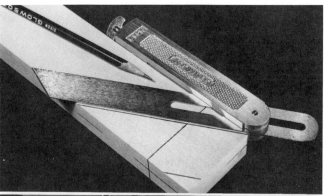
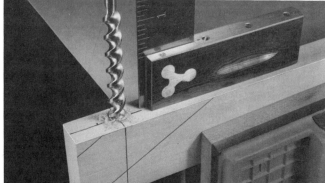

Fig. 6-14. Making and using a boring jig. Top. Laying out required angles. Center. Boring a perfectly straight hole. Bottom. Using the jig after it has been cut out. Note how it is aligned with the centerlines.

Fig. 6-13. Boring a hole at an angle.

Fig. 6-15. Boring a large hole with an expansive bit.

the stock and require a smooth flat bottom. It can be used to enlarge holes or bore holes in thin stock where the feed screw of a regular bit might cause the stock to split. A sharp Forstner bit works well for end grain boring. These bits are available in the same range of sizes as standard bits, Fig. 6-16.

Locate the position of holes to be bored with a Forstner bit by drawing a circle or square the size of the bit. Another method that works well is shown in Fig. 6-17. The hole is started with a standard bit and then completed with a Forstner bit.

### DRILLING HOLES $<=\frac{1}{4}''$

As mentioned before, holes 1/4 in. and smaller are usually drilled with a hand drill, using straight shank drills, Fig. 6-18. Study the parts of the standard model shown in Fig. 6-19. Apply a few drops of fine oil on the bearings of the gear and pinions when they need lubrication.

The size of a hand drill is determined by the capacity of its chuck. The most common size is 1/4 in.; a 3/8 in. size is also available. Twist drills are made in a wide range of sizes. A good set for use in the hand drill should range from 1/16 to 1/4 in. by thirty-seconds or sixty-fourths.

In drilling holes, use the same procedure as suggested for boring holes. It is important that the hole

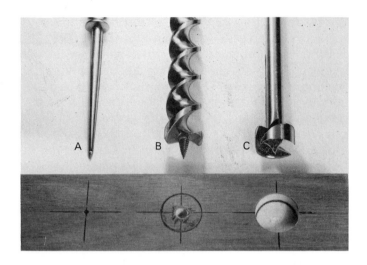

Fig. 6-17. Boring with a Forstner bit. Left. Standard layout procedure. Center. Score the hole with an auger bit. Right. Complete the hole with a Forstner bit.

be started with an awl since the twist drill has a blunt point. Place a twist drill all the way into the drill chuck and tighten the jaws. Open and close the jaws by holding the chuck and turning the crank.

Hold the handle in one hand and keep the drill perpendicular to the surface, while turning the crank with your other hand. Small drills will break if you

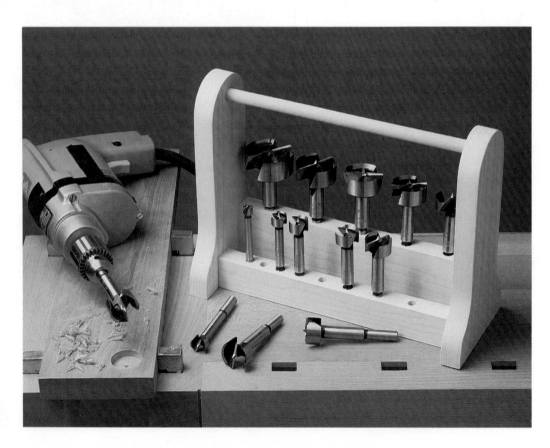

Fig. 6-16. Forstner bits produce a smooth, flat-bottomed hole. (Leichtung, Inc.)

do not work carefully.

Since there is no feed screw on a drill bit, you will control the feed by the pressure you apply. The amount of pressure to apply varies with the size of bit and the kind of wood. Drill to the required depth.

Continue to turn the drill while pulling it out of the hole. If the hole is deep, pull the drill out several times to clear the cuttings. Remove the drill from the chuck as soon as you have finished using it.

## AUTOMATIC DRILLS

Automatic drills (also called push drills) are designed to drill small holes rapidly. When the handle is pushed down the drill revolves. A spring inside the handle forces it back to its original position when pressure is released. Automatic drills use a fluted bit (drill point) that fits into a special chuck. Sizes range from 1/16 to about 3/16 in. Carpenters often use this type of drill to make holes for nails and screws. The main advantage of the automatic drill is that it can be operated with one hand as shown in Fig. 6-20.

Fig. 6-18. A hand drill is useful for drilling small holes. (The Stanley Works)

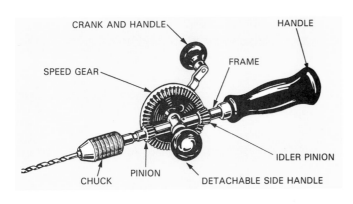

Fig. 6-19. Parts of a hand drill.

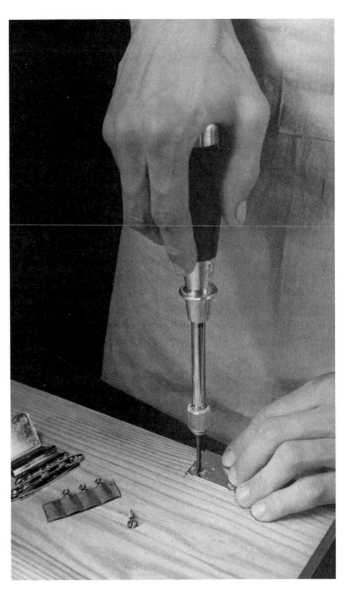

Fig. 6-20. Using an automatic drill to install a hinge.

## CORDLESS DRILLS

Cordless drills have become very popular because of their obvious advantages. New models have largely overcome the shortcomings of earlier designs—they were underpowered, the battery charge didn't last very long, and they took a long time to recharge. Over the years, the standard voltage increased from 7.2 volts to over 14 volts. At the same time, batteries improved and charging times decreased. These new tools, Fig. 6-21, can hold a charge for steady drilling for 30 minutes to almost an hour before recharging is required. Recharging takes from 10 minutes to 1 hour on most models. However, cordless drills are expensive when compared to a cord-type drill.

Fig. 6-21. New cordless drills have become very popular for anyone working with wood. Many styles are available. (Makita U.S.A., Inc. and Black & Decker)

### TEST YOUR KNOWLEDGE, Chapter 6

Please do not write in the text. Place your answers on a separate sheet of paper.

1. A brace that is equipped with a _____ can be used to bore holes even though a complete revolution of the handle cannot be made.
2. The _____ of the auger bit score the perimeter of the hole.
3. The number size of the auger bit is stamped on the _____.
4. What size hole will be bored by the following bits?
   a. No. 4.
   b. No. 7.
   c. No. 14.
5. The feed screw of the bit is easily started if a _____ _____ has been used to mark the center of the hole.
6. The threads in the chuck of the brace are _____ (right, left) handed.
7. End grain is usually easier to bore than side grain. True or False?
8. When making a counterbored hole the _____ (largest, smallest) hole is bored first.
9. A boring tool that can be adjusted to make various sized holes is called an _____ bit.
10. The size of a hand drill is determined by the size of its _____.
11. A _____ bit does not have a feed screw. It is used for boring holes that go only part way through the stock and require a smooth flat bottom.

### ACTIVITIES

1. Make a list of the boring and drilling hand tools useful in a home workshop. Include the size, description, and cost for each item. Refer to suppliers' and manufacturers' catalogs for information.
2. Develop both a presentation sketch and a working drawing of a tool holder for a complete set of standard auger bits. Design the holder so that it can be mounted on a vertical tool panel. A good tool holder will have many of the following features:
   a. Holds the tool securely.
   b. Holds the tool in correct position.
   c. Protects the tool from damage.
   d. Protects the worker from injury.
   e. Includes name and size.
   f. Is easily cleaned and maintained.
   g. Is attractive in appearance.

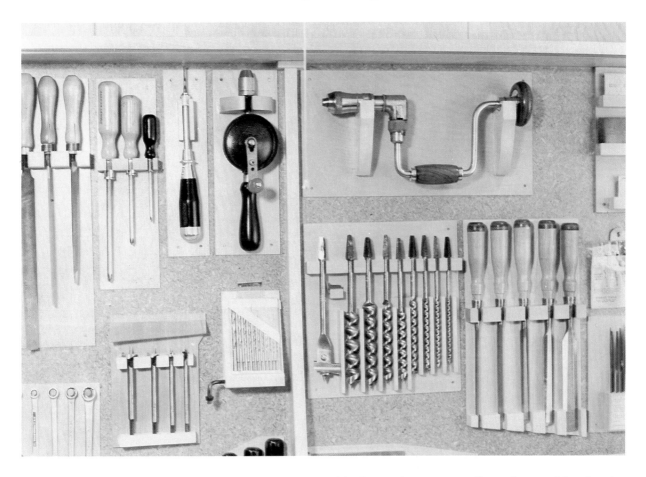

Custom-made tool holders can be used to store drilling and boring equipment, as well as other small hand tools.

Meetinghouse bench. This Shaker design was produced in Enfield, New Jersey around 1840 and is a refinement of the Windsor style. Dimensions: 31 1/2'' back height, 17'' seat height, 50'' width, and 18'' depth.
(Shaker Workshops)

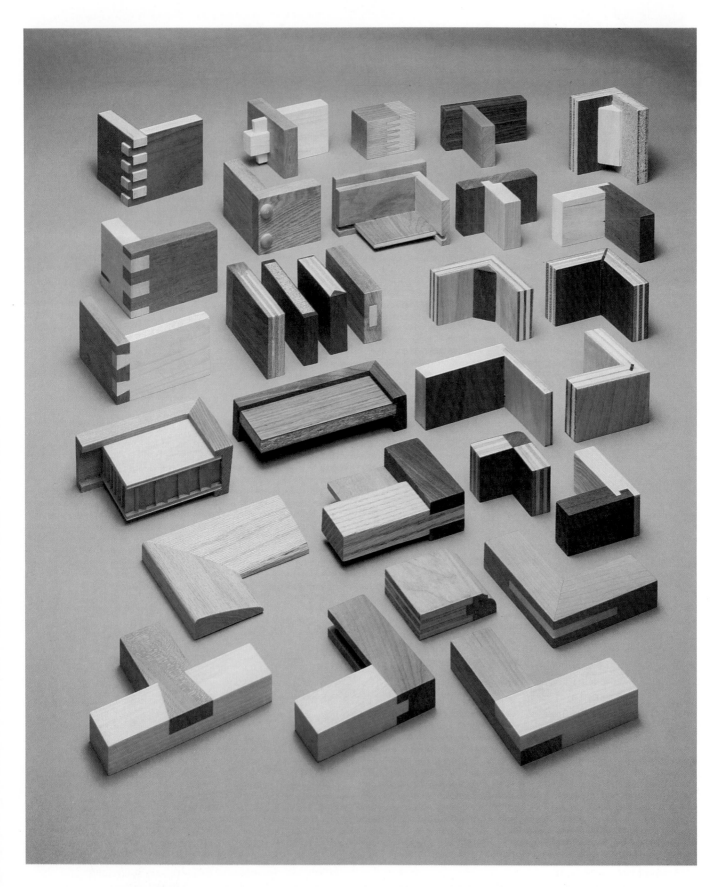

Wood joints that are visible on a workpiece must be strong and attractive. The beauty of any work would be enhanced by the wood joints shown here.

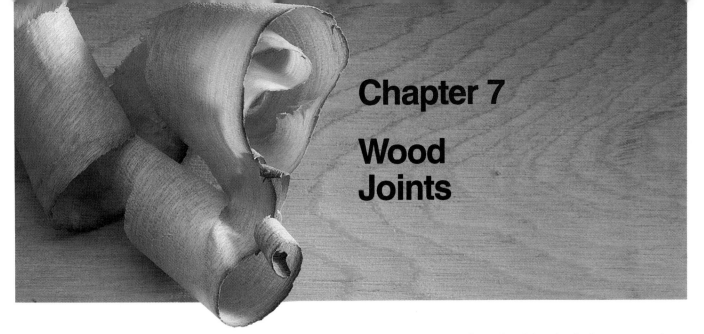

# Chapter 7

# Wood Joints

There are many kinds of wood joints used in building construction, cabinetmaking, and patternmaking. Some wood joints are simple and easily recognized; others are complicated, being a combination of several of the basic types.

Although many new and efficient metal fasteners have been designed, most fine furniture and cabinetwork is still assembled with glue. The strength of glued joints depends to a large extent on the contact area (the surface of one piece touching the other piece) and the quality of the fit. Some joints have interlocking features that may minimize the importance of the adhesive. Manufacturers of wood products often develop interlocking joints, held together with metal fasteners, that permit the article to be easily disassembled and reassembled. Such a feature helps to reduce storage space and simplify shipping problems.

When selecting wood joints for a project, give consideration to the strength, appearance, and difficulty of fabrication. This selection must also be based on the kind of wood you will use and the direction of the grain in the parts. In some projects, strength will be of primary importance. In others, appearance must be the major concern. For example, when building a tote tray for carpentry tools the strength of the corner joints is of primary importance. When building a silverware tray or chest, appearance is of greater importance. Desirable appearance does not necessarily mean the joint must be invisible. Carefully proportioned and fitted visible joints often add to the character and attractiveness of the design. A good rule to follow is to select the simplest joint that will satisfy the needs of the construction.

The pieces to be joined should first be cut and squared to size. For some joints you will need to allow extra stock to form the joint. Lay out the cuts carefully, using a sharp pencil or knife. When possible, it is good practice to mark one piece by holding the mating piece against it and in the correct position. Lay out all similar joints at one time. Usually this is done by clamping identical pieces together. Identify the members of each joint with a number or letter so that they can be easily matched during assembly.

In this chapter illustrations and instructions are given for making common joints with hand tools. See Fig. 7-1. Design, layout, and general procedures, however, will be about the same when using power equipment.

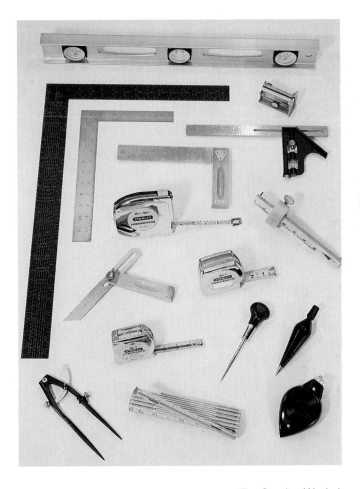

Fig. 7-1. Layout tools for woodworking. (The Stanley Works)

## BUTT AND EDGE JOINTS

A butt joint is easy to make but not as strong as many other joints. It is used extensively in house framing where overlays of additional material add to its strength. Simple boxes and frames are made with butt joints reinforced with nails, screws, and other metal fasteners. When the butt joint is reinforced with dowels, it is usually referred to as a dowel joint. Fig. 7-2 shows some typical butt joints. These are formed when the square end of one piece fits against the surface or edge of another piece.

The edge joint has many applications in building construction. In cabinetwork it is used to join narrow widths to form wider widths for table or desk tops, and other parts. There are many adaptations of the edge joint, Fig. 7-2.

Fig. 7-3. Making an edge joint. Left. Selecting the position of the stock and marking. Right. Planing the joint. Note how the toe of the plane is guided along the edge of stock.

The edge joint holds securely with glue and will be strong enough for most of your work if it is carefully made. A large piece, such as a table leaf, that will not be held by a frame or otherwise supported, should be reinforced with dowels or splines. Splines provide the greatest strength when they are cut with the grain across the joint. Dowels do not add a great amount of strength to the edge joint but help align the pieces when they are glued together.

To make a plain edge joint, position the pieces to be joined so the grain is matched and runs in the same direction. The annular rings should be reversed in every other piece as shown in Fig. 7-3. After the correct arrangement has been determined, make reference marks on the top surface at each joint.

Clamp two adjacent pieces together in the vise with the top surfaces turned to the outside, Fig. 7-4. Plane the edges until you are able to take a light, thin shaving along the entire length. Apply extra pressure to the toe of the plane at the beginning of the cut and extra pressure to the heel as the cut is finished. Remove the pieces from the vise and place them together to check the fit. Slight variations in the joint can now be corrected by planing each piece separately. Instructions for gluing edge joints are included in Chapter 17.

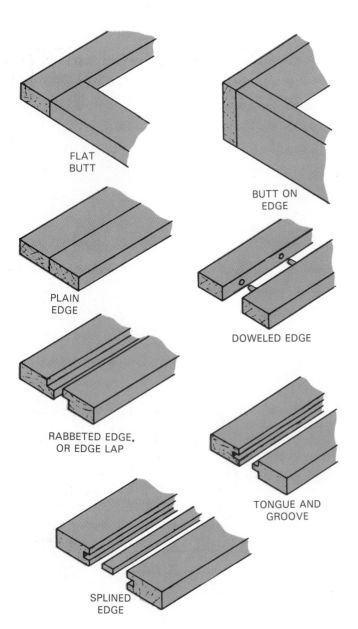

Fig. 7-2. Butt and edge joints.

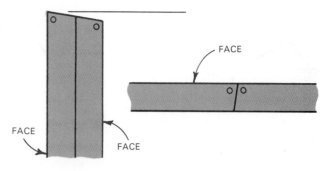

Fig. 7-4. How to clamp stock when planing an edge joint. This must be done carefully, since an error in the angle will result in a poor fit.

To install dowels in the edge joint, again clamp the pieces in the vise with the top surfaces outside, ends and edges even. Square lines across the edge where each dowel will be located, Fig. 7-5, top. Dowels should be spaced about 4 to 6 in. apart. A marking gauge is used to locate the center of each hole, from the top surface of each piece. If a doweling jig is used, this layout is not necessary.

Boring the holes with a doweling jig, in Fig. 7-5, bottom, saves time and insures accurate work. Mount a bit guide of the correct diameter in the jig. Position the carrier so the guide is located in the center of the stock. Place a depth gauge on the bit to provide a hole 1/16 in. deeper than half the dowel length. The dowels should enter each piece of wood a distance equal to about two and one-half times their diameter. The diameter of the dowels should be equal to one-half the thickness of the stock.

Line up the jig with the layout mark, clamp it securely, and bore the hole. Turn the jig around so the fence is on the other side, align it with the mark, and bore the matching hole. Follow the same procedure and bore all the other holes before removing the pieces from the vise. Make a trial assembly of the joint before gluing it together.

The edges of flooring and siding are joined with a tongue and groove or lap joint. In production woodwork, edges that will be glued together are often cut with a multiple tongue and groove.

## DADOS AND GROOVES

A dado joint is a rectangular recess, which is cut in the wood and runs across the wood grain. A groove is the same type of cut but runs along the grain. Both the dado and groove, Fig. 7-6, are usually cut to a depth equal to one-half the thickness of the stock. In some construction it should be less, especially when working with veneer core plywood or particle board.

The dado joint is used for such jobs as installing shelves, frames, and partitions in bookcases, chests, and cabinets. When carefully fitted and glued it makes a very strong joint. When dados are used to carry shelves or similar parts, the uprights should be clamped together and the position of the joints laid out along the edge, as shown in Fig. 7-7, top. Lines are then drawn across the surface, Fig. 7-7, bottom.

You can do a precision job of cutting a dado by following the procedure shown in Fig. 7-8. Clamp

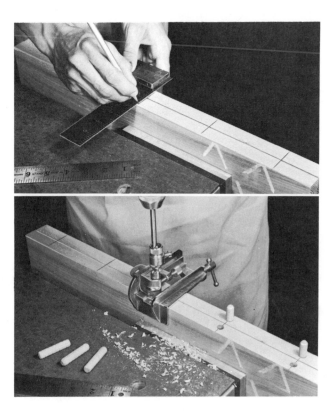

Fig. 7-5. Installing dowels in an edge joint. Top. Making the layout. Bottom. Boring the holes with a doweling jig.

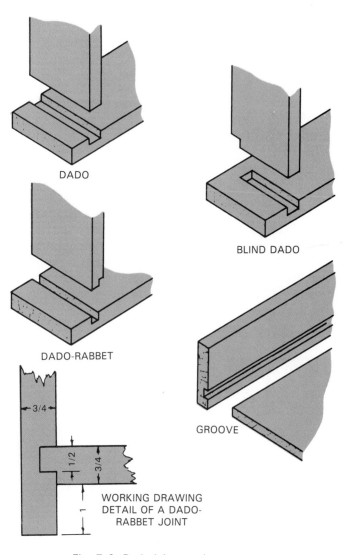

DADO

BLIND DADO

DADO-RABBET

GROOVE

3/4

1/2

3/4

WORKING DRAWING DETAIL OF A DADO-RABBET JOINT

Fig. 7-6. Dado joints and grooves.

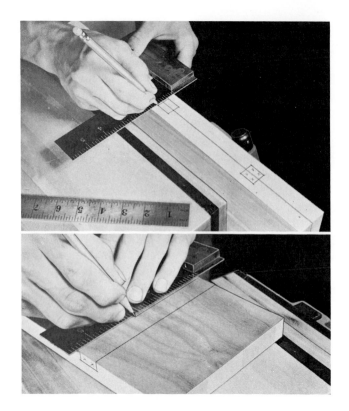

Fig. 7-9. Using a router plane to smooth the bottom of a dado joint.

Fig. 7-7. Laying out a dado joint. Top. On the edge. Bottom. Extending line across the face.

a straightedge along one of the lines so that the kerf will be on the waste side. Then make a cut to the proper depth with a backsaw. Move the straightedge to the other line and clamp it lightly. Place the part that will fit into the dado (mating part) against the straightedge and align its surface with the outside edge of the first saw cut. IF YOU MAKE THIS ADJUSTMENT CAREFULLY YOU WILL SECURE A PERFECT FIT. Clamp the straightedge securely, remove the mating part, and make the second cut. When sawing wide boards, use long strokes. This will insure that the sawdust that is cut in the center of the piece will be carried to the edge and removed from the saw kerf.

Use a chisel to remove the waste wood between the saw kerfs. The straightedge should be left in place, since it will serve as a guide for the chisel. Rough cuts should be made with the bevel of the chisel turned down or against the wood. For fine, finished cuts this position is reversed.

The dado can be finished with router plane as shown in Fig. 7-9. This will make the bottom of the dado level and true. Cut in from each side toward the center to prevent splitting the edges of the joint.

Grooves are used in drawer construction and panel work. They are usually cut on power machines but they can be cut by hand in about the same way as dados. The marking gauge can be used to lay out the groove and is especially helpful when working with long pieces. Use a straightedge to guide the saw when cutting the sides of the groove. The panel or mating part will help to position the straightedge for the second cut. Use a chisel to remove the wood from between the saw kerfs. A router plane can be used to finish the bottom of the groove.

The final trimming and fitting of grooves and dados can be done with a chisel. When making light paring cuts, lay the chisel flat on the work with the bevel turned out. If the joint is too tight, it is easier

Fig. 7-8. Cutting a dado joint. Left. Aligning the straightedge for the second cut. Center. Making the saw cut. Right. Removing waste stock with a wood chisel. Cut in from each side.

to plane off the thickness of the mating piece (not recommended for plywood), than to enlarge the width of the dado or groove.

## RABBET JOINTS

The rabbet joint is made by cutting a recess in one or both of the pieces to be joined, Fig. 7-10. The recess may be cut on the end or along the edge. Rabbet joints are easy to make and can be used for the corners of simple boxes, cases, and drawers. This joint is commonly used to install the back panel in a cabinet. If the joint will be assembled with glue, the depth of the shoulder cut should be equal to two-thirds of the thickness of the stock. However, when nails or screws are used, the depth is usually reduced to one-half. Fig. 7-11 shows the layout of a rabbet joint.

The end grain cut is difficult to make unless you use a simple jig like the one in Fig. 7-12. The jig is constructed by gluing a thin strip to a flat piece of stock. The thickness of the stripe is determined by the size of the joint.

Fig. 7-13 shows a rabbet joint being cut with the aid of the jig and a straightedge. After the setup is made, place the mating part in position to check the accuracy. Be sure the clamp is tight. The cross grain or shoulder cut is made by the same method used to square stock to length, except that the cut does not go all the way through. Hold the backsaw flat on the jig when making the end grain cut. Any irregularities in the saw cuts should be smoothed before removing the stock from the jig.

When cutting a rabbet along the edge of stock it is best to use the rabbet plane. This type plane, shown in Fig. 7-14, has an adjustable fence and

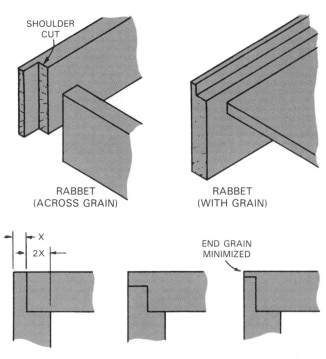

Fig. 7-10. Rabbet joints.

Fig. 7-12. A jig for making the end grain cut of a rabbet joint.

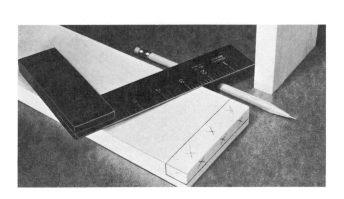

Fig. 7-11. Rabbet joint layout.

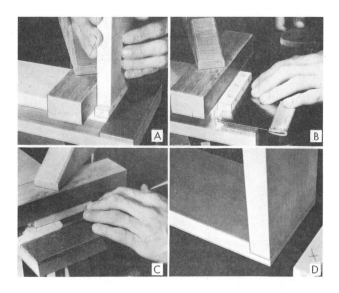

Fig. 7-13. Cutting a rabbet joint. A—Checking the straightedge setting. B—Making the end grain cut after completing the cross grain cut along the straightedge. C—Trimming the cut with a wood chisel. D—Completed joint.

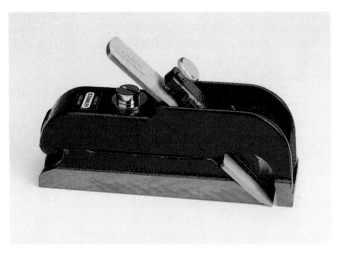

Fig. 7-14. Bullnose rabbet plane. (Stanley Tools)

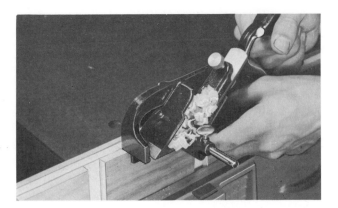

Fig. 7-16. Cutting a rabbet along the grain using a rabbet plane.

depth gauge. These control the width and depth of the cut. The plane blade is sharpened the same way as a regular plane iron.

After adjusting the fence and depth gauge, Fig. 7-15, set the blade for a fine cut. This is somewhat difficult to do because the plane has no adjustment screw or lateral adjustment lever. It is best to place the plane bottom on a flat surface, set the blade in position, and tighten the clamp.

Check the cut on a scrap piece of stock before working on your project. You may need to adjust the position of the blade several times before you secure a satisfactory cut. Fig. 7-16 shows the plane being used to cut a rabbet for a back panel. Fig. 7-17 shows an assembly made with both dado and rabbet joints.

## LAP JOINTS

In a lap joint an equal amount of wood is cut from each piece so that when the pieces are assembled

Fig. 7-17. An assembly made with dado and rabbet joints.

their surfaces are flush. There are several types of lap joints, Fig. 7-18. The HALF-LAP is used to splice two pieces of wood together, and the END-LAP is used as the corner joint for a simple frame. The CROSS-LAP is often used where the crossrails or braces of a table or bench join together. It is also used for grill work where parts running at different angles must form a flat plane. The MIDDLE-LAP provides a method of joining a brace to crossrails or midsections of a frame. The DOVETAIL LAP is made of a wedge-shaped mating part that fits into a matching kerf, Fig. 7-19.

Generally, the same procedure is used to lay out all of the lap joints. Fig. 7-20, left, shows both parts of a cross-lap placed side by side with their ends even while a centerline and cutting lines are laid out. The edges of each piece are laid out from the lines on the faces. A marking gauge (set at one-half the stock thickness) is used to mark the depth of the cut. For accurate work, the two pieces should be clamped together in the correct position and a knife used to mark the cutting line. See Fig. 7-20, right.

Use the same methods for sawing and removing waste stock as described for cutting rabbet and dado joints. If the stock is very wide, it may be

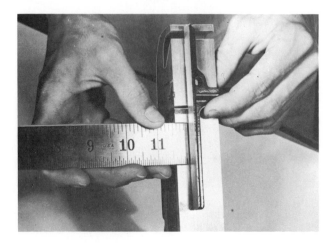

Fig. 7-15. Adjusting the fence of the rabbet plane.

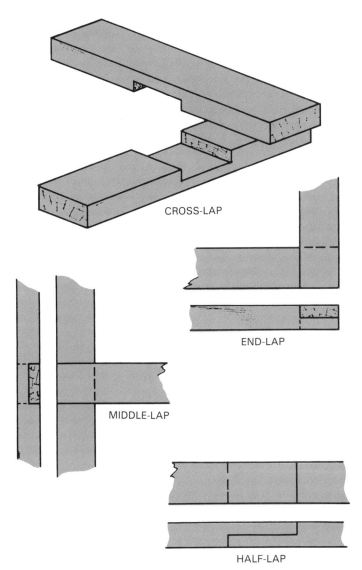

CROSS-LAP

END-LAP

MIDDLE-LAP

HALF-LAP

Fig. 7-18. Lap joints.

Fig. 7-20. Laying out a lap joint. Left. Marking the position on both parts. Right. Laying out the exact cutting line with a knife.

helpful to make several saw cuts in the waste stock before removing it with a chisel. If the joints fit too tightly, it is usually easier to reduce the width of the pieces than to trim the shoulder cuts.

## MORTISE-AND-TENON

A well-made mortise-and-tenon joint is one of the strongest wood joints. It is used to join legs and rails of tables, benches, and chairs. It is also used in quality frame and panel construction. The mortise-and-tenon comes in a variety of forms. The most common are shown in Fig. 7-21.

The BLIND mortise-and-tenon is a completely concealed joint. The thickness of the tenon should be not less than one-half the thickness of the stock. It usually has shoulder cuts on all sides so the mortise will be completely covered. The OPEN mortise-and-tenon (sometimes called a SLIP JOINT) makes a strong corner joint for a frame. It is somewhat easier to cut than the blind joint and is used extensively in cabinetwork. The HAUNCHED joint is used for the corners of a frame grooved to

Fig. 7-19. A dovetail lap joint provides exceptional strength against lateral stress.

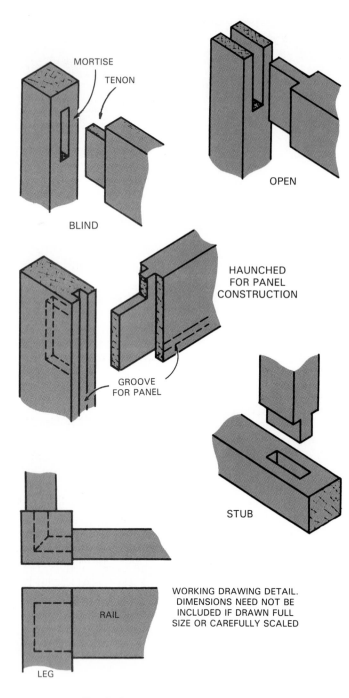

Fig. 7-21. Mortise-and-tenon joints.

1. Keep the cross section of the tenon large. It should be no less than one-half of the thickness of the stock.
2. The length of the tenon should be at least two and one-half times its thickness.
3. The position and size of the mortise should not reduce the strength of the part.
4. When the mortise is cut at the end of a member, it should not be closer than 1/2 in., or the end will break out.

When making a mortise-and-tenon joint, the mortise is done first since it is easier to adjust the size of the tenon than it is to change the mortise for a good fit. This joint is usually used in assemblies that require a number of joints of equal size, and therefore should be laid out at the same time. Fig. 7-22 shows the layout of a set of table legs. After the outside (best) sides have been selected, the legs are clamped together and lines squared across all of them at once. A marking gauge or mortise gauge can be used to lay out the sides.

The mortise can be made either by boring a series of adjoining holes and cleaning the opening with a chisel, or by cutting the entire opening with a chisel. Fig. 7-23 shows the first method. A doweling jig will insure an accurate boring job. However, if a centerline is laid out and the centers of the holes are carefully marked with the scratch awl, good results can be secured without the use of the jig.

Stock for the members (rails, stretchers) on which the tenons will be cut, must be squared to finished size with extra length allowed for the tenons. The tenons are carefully aligned and clamped together

carry a panel. The tenon is cut with a "haunch" or extension that fills the panel groove. When the design requires that the legs and rails be flush, the mortise for a regular tenon may be too close to the surface. For a joint of this kind, the tenon is cut with a shoulder only on the front side and referred to as a BAREFACED mortise-and-tenon.

To secure the full strength from a mortise-and-tenon joint, its parts must be carefully proportioned. This is especially true of the blind joint. You should keep the following in mind when designing and laying out such a joint:

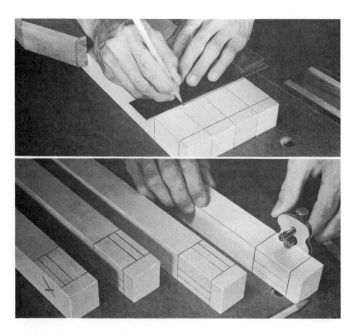

Fig. 7-22. Laying out mortises. Top. Length of mortise is marked on inside faces of legs. Bottom. A mortise gauge is used to lay out width.

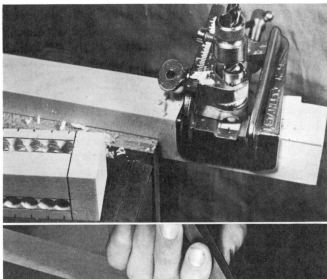

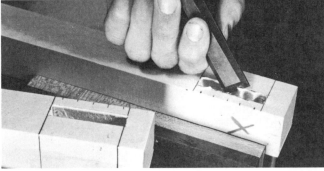

Fig. 7-23. Cutting the mortise. Top. Boring the mortise with the aid of a doweling jig. Bottom. Trimming with a chisel.

for the layout in about the same manner as the legs. See Fig. 7-24. Notice that a shoulder for the bottom edge is not included, since it would have reduced the width of the tenon too much to secure the required strength.

Fig. 7-24. Laying out tenons. Top. Shoulder cuts. Bottom. Using the mortise gauge to lay out cheek cuts.

Fig. 7-25. Cutting the tenon. A—Using a sawing jig to make the shoulder cut. B—Making the cheek cut. C—Trimming the cheek with a chisel. D—Completed joint.

Make the SHOULDER CUTS first. These cuts are made with the backsaw, using either a bench hook, straightedge, or a sawing jig as shown in Fig. 7-25A. Make these cuts carefully and to the exact depth required. If you cut too deep you will greatly reduce the strength of the tenon. Because the CHEEK CUTS are hard to make, you should use some kind of a sawing guide or jig. The one used in Fig. 7-25B is similar to the jig used for cutting rabbet joints.

After all the joints are cut they should be trimmed and fitted, Fig. 7-25C. This is usually done by working with each joint individually (selective fitting). Mark each member of the joint with a number or letter, so they can be easily and properly mated for final assembly, Fig. 7-25D.

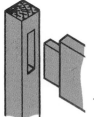

*Be especially careful when making the shoulder cuts on rabbets and tenons. If you cut below the required depth you will greatly reduce the strength of the joint.*

Mortises, especially those made by a machine, can be square, rectangular, or rectangular with rounded ends. A round mortise would simply be a hole. Tenons can be of the same shapes as mortises and also be round. The ROUND TENON is distinguished from the dowel by the fact that it is formed on the part and can therefore be much larger and stronger than an inserted dowel. The round tenon is used extensively in chair construction for joining turned legs to seats and joining rungs and legs. In industry, these round tenons are made on a CHUCKING MACHINE. It consists of a hollow cutter head, with knives on the inside surface that cut the shape quickly. Fig. 7-26 shows a procedure to follow in forming a round tenon by hand. Round tenons may also be made using a plug cutter. Refer to Fig. 7-27.

## DOWEL JOINTS

A carefully designed and fitted dowel joint is very strong. It is easier to make than the mortise-and-tenon. When carefully glued with one of the excellent adhesives now available, it can often be substituted for this joint.

Dowel joints are made in a wide variety of forms, Fig. 7-28. Some butt and edge joints are reinforced with dowels called DOWEL JOINTS. Dowels that are used for woodwork are round pieces of birch or maple, available either in the form of rods or pins. Dowel rods usually come in 3 ft. lengths in a diameter range of 1/8 in. to more than 1 in. Dowel pins are small pieces that are spiral grooved with rounded ends and ready to use. These are available in several sizes. The spiral groove permits air and excess glue to escape when the dowel pin is inserted into a hole during the gluing operation.

Use good judgment in spacing the dowels in a joint. Along an edge they may be 4 to 6 in. apart while in leg and rail assemblies, 3/8 in. dowels might be placed as close as 3/4 in. on center (OC). The diameter of the dowel should equal about one-half the thickness of the smallest member of the joint. The dowel should enter each piece of wood a distance equal to two and one-half times it diameter. The depth of the hole will need to provide from 1/16 to 1/8 in. clearance.

The layout of a dowel joint for leg and rail construction can be done in about the same manner as the mortises previously described. When possible, clamp the mating parts together so the centerlines for the holes can be laid out at one time. Dowel centers, as shown in Fig. 7-29, may be used to locate exact positions of the dowels in the mating parts. Instead of dowel centers you may use small brads. After making the layout on one part, drive small brads into the center points. Cut off the heads of the brads, align the pieces, and press them firmly together. This will mark the center points in the other piece.

Fig. 7-26. Top. Steps in making a round tenon. Bottom. Forming a round tenon with a wood file.

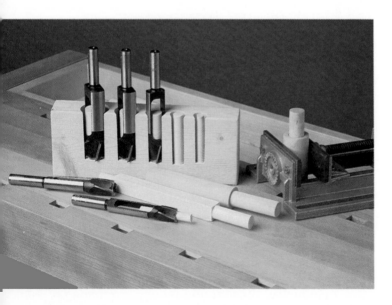

Fig. 7-27. A plug cutter may be used to make standard size plugs and round tenons. (Leichtung, Inc.)

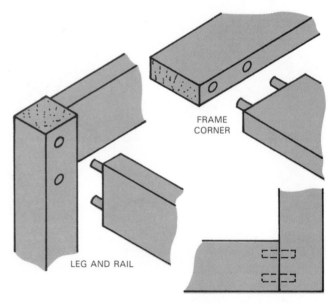

FRAME CORNER

LEG AND RAIL

Fig. 7-28. Dowel joints.

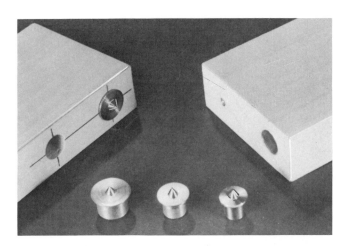

Fig. 7-29. Dowel centers.

Patented doweling jigs such as the one shown in Fig. 7-30 will save layout time and help you do accurate work. If you have a number of similar joints to make, you may want to make a jig somewhat like the one shown in Fig. 7-31. The parts do not need to be laid out. They are simply clamped in place and bored. A piece of hardboard is clamped under the rail to provide a 1/8 in. setback. The leg is clamped first on one side and then the other side. Fig. 7-32 shows a stool base assembled with dowels. Included in the view is the jig used to bore all the holes in the legs and rails.

## MITER JOINTS

The miter joint is formed by cutting an equal angle (usually 45 deg.) on each of the mating parts. In this type of joint there is no end grain visible. The plain miter joint does not have much strength and is often reinforced with wood splines, dowels, or metal fasteners.

The miter joint is used for picture frames and also for moldings on all kinds of furniture and cabinetwork. It is often selected for corner joints of boxes, cases, and cabinets. In house construction, it is used extensively for door and window casings and other interior and exterior trim members. Fig. 7-33 shows a plain miter joint and some of the ways it can be cut and reinforced to provide added strength. Fig. 7-34 shows two variations of feathered miter joints. Metal fasteners for miter joints are included in Chapter 8.

A plain miter joint can easily be cut with hand tools. The stock should be surfaced and planed to finished thickness and width. Lay out the length to the outside corner of the miter. When making a frame, always be sure to use the outside measurements. Use a combination square to lay out the 45 degree angle or, if the piece is wide or the angle is different, use a T-bevel square. Fig. 7-35 shows two methods of setting the T-bevel. Fig. 7-36 shows the T-bevel square being used to mark the angle.

Fig. 7-30. The edge-to-edge dowel jig enables up to four dowel holes to be drilled without moving the jig, achieving a high degree of accuracy. (Leichtung, Inc.)

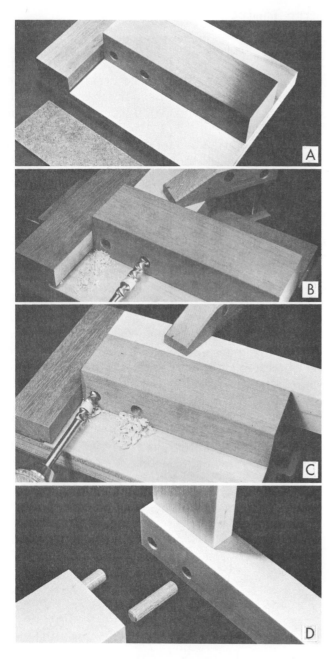

Fig. 7-31. Making a dowel joint with a jig. A—Doweling jig. B—Boring the rail. C—Boring the leg. D—Completed joint.

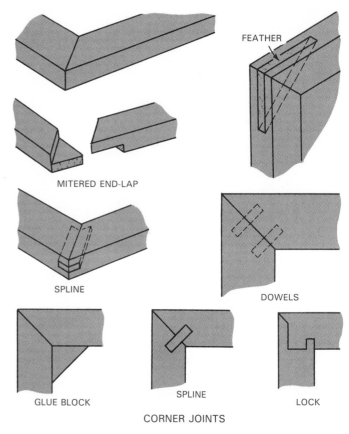

FEATHER

MITERED END-LAP

SPLINE

DOWELS

GLUE BLOCK

SPLINE

LOCK

CORNER JOINTS

Fig. 7-33. Miter joints.

Fig. 7-32. Stool base assembled with dowel joint. Note the boring jig.

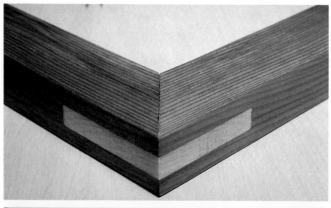

Fig. 7-34. Feather type miter joints.

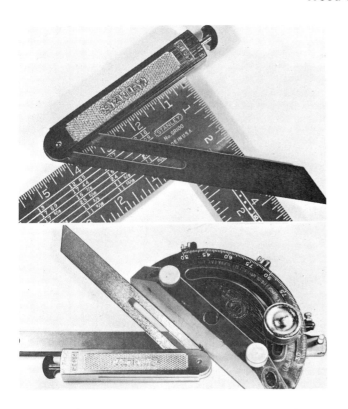

Fig. 7-35. Setting the T-bevel square. Top. With the framing square. Bottom. Using the miter gauge of a table saw.

The cut can be made with a backsaw and straightedge in about the same way as squaring stock to length. Fig. 7-37 shows the straightedge being accurately set. Wood is slightly more difficult to cut at an angle with the grain; give extra attention to keeping the saw blade firmly against the straightedge during the cut. Use long, full strokes and slowly feed the saw into the cut.

The miter box shown in Fig. 7-38 is designed especially for cutting angles. Swing the saw carrier to the required angle and hold the stock firmly on the bed and against the back. For accurate work, the stock should be clamped in position, either with a hand screw or special clamps provided on some miter boxes. Use long steady strokes while making the cut. The weight of the saw will be sufficient to feed it into the work. On small pieces it may be necessary to "hold up" on the saw so it will not cut too fast. To cut the miter on the other end of a piece that will be used in a frame, the carrier is moved to the opposite side.

After the miter joint is cut, hold the two pieces together against the inside or outside edge of a square to check the fit. If slight adjustments need to be made, this can be done by taking a few light cuts with the block plane.

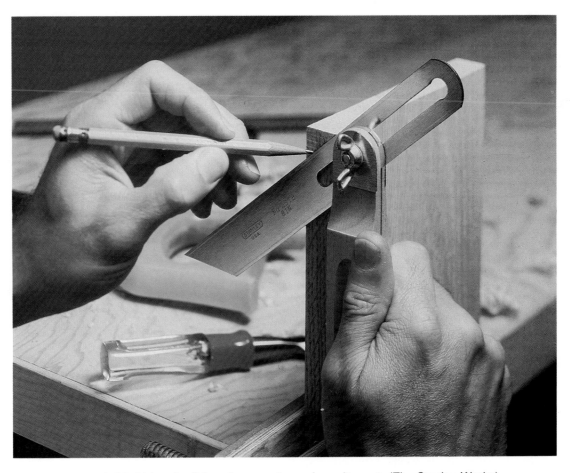

Fig. 7-36. Using the T-bevel square to mark a miter cut. (The Stanley Works)

Fig. 7-37. Setting a straightedge for a miter cut.

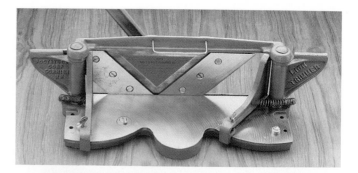

Fig. 7-39. Using a wood trimmer to finish a miter cut. Top. View showing table and guides. (Woodcraft Supply Corporation) Bottom. Shearing cut 1/16 in. thick.

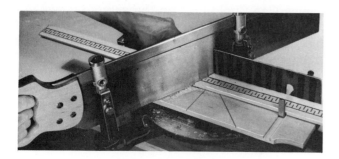

Fig. 7-38. Using the miter box to cut an angle.

Fig. 7-39 shows a WOOD TRIMMER being used to make a finished cut on a miter joint. This tool is often used by the carpenter for inside trim work. The patternmaker also uses it for fine, accurate cutting of end grain and various angle cuts. It consists of a table, guides, and a knife carriage, and is operated with a hand lever. The guides are adjustable so the stock can be securely held for the desired angle of cut. The wood trimmer is designed to make light shearing cuts so it is best to first rough out the angle with a saw. Generally, cuts of 1/16 to 1/8 in. can be easily made in softwood. Use finer cuts for hardwood. The knives are sharp and therefore should always be kept covered with a wooden guard block when not in use, to protect the edge and the worker.

The finished miter cut can also be modified using a disk sander with a miter gauge, Fig. 7-40.

## DOVETAIL AND BOX JOINTS

The dovetail joint is used in high quality furniture for drawer construction and other corner joints, Fig. 7-41. In furniture factories it is easily cut with specialized machines and can be rapidly assembled without the use of clamping devices. The multiple pin joint is difficult to cut with hand tools; in the

Fig. 7-40. The miter gauge may be used with a disk sander to modify or smooth a miter cut. (Foley-Belsaw Co.)

Fig. 7-41. Pins and tails of almost any thickness can be joined with the dovetail joint.    (Leigh Industries, Ltd.)

Fig. 7-42. Top. The guide finger spacing on this jig is infinitely variable. The tail boards are routed first. Bottom. The finger assembly may be rotated after routing the tail boards to the pin made to assure a perfect fit.    (Leigh Industries, Ltd.)

school shop it is usually made with a router and dovetailing fixture, Fig. 7-42.

Several other forms of a dovetail joint are shown in Fig. 7-43. Joints like the THROUGH DOVETAIL and the LAP DOVETAIL are excellent joints for some structures and can be made with hand tools. Their interlocking feature makes them strong and easy to assemble. They are an excellent solution for a rack or stand that could be easily assembled and held together with metal fasteners and then disassembled when not in use.

The box joint is strong and also easily assembled. It is often used in making high quality wooden shipping boxes. Like the multiple pin dovetail, it is hard to cut by hand. In Chapter 12 you will find an explanation of how it is cut on the table saw.

Fig. 7-44 shows a pair of sawing jigs used to cut a simple two-tail joint. The ''tail'' part is clamped in position and two cuts made. It is then reversed for the other pair of cuts. After the end grain cuts are made in each piece, waste stock is removed with a coping saw and chisel. The jigs must be laid out accurately. It will take time and careful work to produce the joints. This time and effort is justified if you are building a fancy jewelry chest of such woods as Teak, Rosewood, or Prima Vera.

## PLATE JOINERY

Plate joinery enables the woodworker to make fast, strong, and accurate joints. The joint is made with ''biscuits,'' ''wafers,'' or ''plates'' that are inserted into slots cut by a PLATE JOINING MACHINE, Fig. 7-45. The plate joining system can

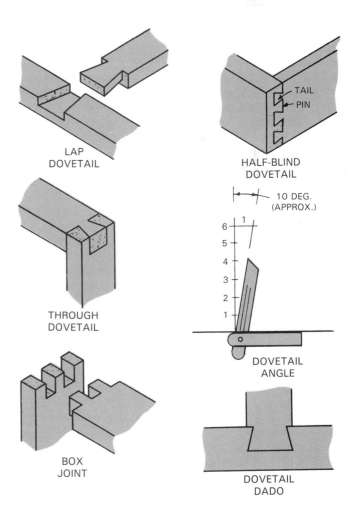

Fig. 7-43. Dovetail and box joints

Fig. 7-44. Top. Jigs for cutting dovetail joints. Bottom Completed joint.

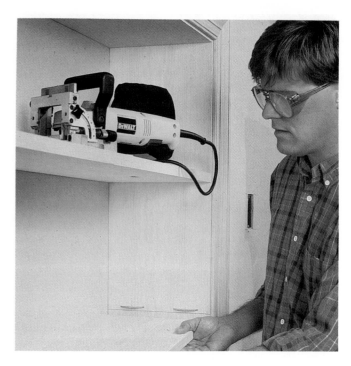

Fig. 7-46. Plate joinery may be used in the place of dowel or dado joints. (DeWalt)

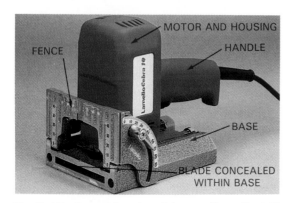

Fig. 7-45. Parts of a plate joiner. (Lamello AG)

be used for many applications, including, carcass shelves and divider frames (Fig. 7-46), and mitered frames. Plate joinery may be used in solid wood, plywood, and particle board.

A plate joint is similar to a splined joint. Special, compressed, die-cut football-shape wafers are inserted into 5/32 in. wide slots or kerfs cut into the pieces to be joined. The kerfs are cut with a plate joiner by plunging its carbide-tip saw blade into the workpiece.

## PLATE JOINERS

A PLATE JOINER is a portable power tool. Refer back to Fig. 7-45. It has a circular saw blade, motor and housing, base, fence, and handle. On most machines, the blade, arbor, and motor are mounted on a moving carriage that rides in the machine's baseplate. Pushing on the plate joiner's handle plunges the blade through the faceplate and into the workpiece. After a cut is made, a compressed spring causes the blade to retract behind the faceplate. While plate joiners are safe to operate, they are very loud and ear protection should be worn.

Workpieces should be securely clamped to prevent an accident that could result in an injury or ruined part or component. Goggles or a face mask should be worn during operation since dust and chips will be created. Keep your face away from the machine's dust chute.

Most plate joiners have adjustable (and removable) fences that are mounted on the machine's faceplate. The fence orientation and adjustment determines both the angle of the machine (cutter) and the placement of the slot on the edge of the stock. A track or guide keeps the fence parallel to the blade while the height is adjusted so the slots will be parallel. Most fences are reversible to cut slots on 45 degree edges.

## PLATES

The PLATES used in plate joinery, Fig. 7-47, are made of compressed beech or other materials and are available in three sizes:
1. #0   16 x 47mm
2. #10 20 x 52mm
3. #20 24 x 58mm

Fig. 7-47. Typical biscuits used in plate joinery. (Lamello AG)

Each size plate requires a slot with different depth and length. All require a slot that is 5/32 in. wide. Larger plates are used when they will provide the sole strength of the joint. However, the plate should not be placed too close to the face of the workpiece to avoid "puckering" the surface when the plate swells as it absorbs moisture from the glue.

## MAKING A PLATE JOINT

The following steps may be applied to make a typical edge-to-edge plate joint:
1. Align and butt together the edges of two boards to be joined. Mark across the boards where you want to place the plates. If they are being used mostly for alignment, they can be 11 or 12 inches apart. Place them closer together for more strength.
2. Adjust the cutter depth for the size of biscuit being used.
3. Adjust the machine fence to the proper depth and angle. The kerf should be in the middle of the panel edge.
4. Clamp the workpiece to the bench and line up the index mark on the fence with the layout line on the workpiece.
5. Turn on the machine and plunge the blade.
6. Release pressure and allow the cutter to return to its normal position behind the faceplate.
7. Move to the next location and cut the remaining slots using the same procedure.

## BUILDING JIGS

Building and working with jigs can provide interesting experiences. Their design and construction will test your creative and inventive ability and they should help you improve the quality of your project work. Quite often you may be able to save time by using a jig, especially when there are a number of similar parts to produce.

Jigs can be classified as specialized or general purpose. The boring jig for the stool is a good example of a specialized jig. Refer back to Fig. 7-32. It was designed to position and guide the bit at a specific place and angle. A general purpose jig and its operation are shown in Fig. 7-48. Such a jig will guide the saw for a precision job of squaring stock (3/8 in. and less in thickness) to length. It can be used to make both the shoulder cut and end grain cut of a rabbet joint in stock 5/16 in. thick. A miter joint can be cut in stock under 3/8 in.

You might want to construct a jig like this to use in your home workshop, because there will be times when you will need to cut small parts that would be dangerous to cut on a power saw.

When building a jig, maintain a high level of accuracy in its construction, otherwise it will not be of much value. Some jigs may be complicated and/or may employ a new idea. It will be necessary to build and rework them several times before a satisfactory model is completed.

## TEST YOUR KNOWLEDGE, Chapter 7

1. When selecting joints for your projects, you must consider the difficulty of fabrication, the strength, and the _____.
2. Joints should be laid out and cut before the pieces are squared and cut to size. True or False?
3. When reinforcing an edge joint, a _____ will provide greater strength than dowels.
4. In a dowel joint, the dowels should enter each member a distance equal to _____ times the diameter of the dowel.
5. A groove and _____ are the same kind of cut except that the groove is cut across the grain of the wood.
6. To install a back panel in a cabinet it is usually best to use a _____ joint.
7. When cutting a rabbet along the edge of stock, it is best to use the _____ plane.
8. The combination square can be used to lay out a 45 degree angle. True or False?
9. The lap joint that would be used for the corner of a frame is called a _____.
10. The open mortise-and-tenon is sometimes called a _____ joint.
11. When a shoulder is cut on only one side of a tenon the joint is called a _____ mortise-and-tenon.
12. When making a mortise-and-tenon joint, it is best to cut the _____ before cutting the _____.

Fig. 7-48. A—General purpose sawing jig. B—Squaring stock to length. C—Making the shoulder cut for a rabbet joint. D—Cutting a miter joint.

13. The cross section of a tenon can be rectangular, square, or round. True or False?
14. What devices may be used to reinforce miter joints?
15. The included angle of a tail of a dovetail joint is about _____ degrees.
16. A plate joint is similar to a _____ joint.
17. How many sizes of plates or "biscuits" are generally available for plate joinery?

## ACTIVITIES

1. Make a list of the common woodworking tools that are used for measuring and layout work. Include a brief description of each tool and how it is used.
2. Develop a table or chart that shows the measurement readings along the tongue and blade of a framing square, that can be used to set the T-bevel square at angles of 5, 10, 15, 22 1/2, 30, and 45 degrees.
3. Make a study of the various forms and adaptations of the mortise-and-tenon joint. Select a number of them you feel are practical, and prepare carefully proportioned detail drawings. If you do not draw them to scale, include dimensions.
4. Develop a working drawing sketch of a sawing jig to produce a MITERED HALF-LAP joint. Try to design a jig that will control the position and the depth of the cuts. Plan for it to be used to cut stock of a specific size. Write an explanation of how it works or include adequate notations on the drawings.

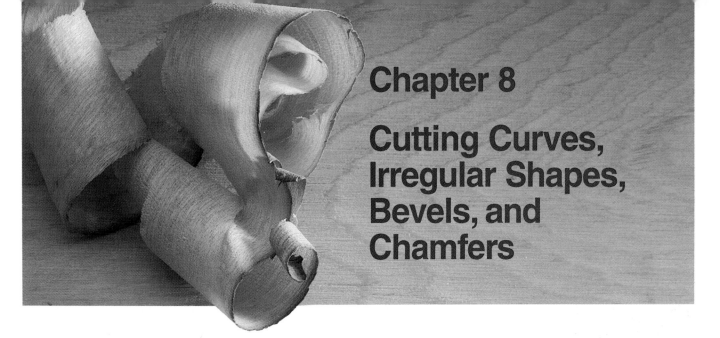

# Chapter 8

# Cutting Curves, Irregular Shapes, Bevels, and Chamfers

As you progress in woodworking, some of your projects will very likely contain curves and other irregular shapes. The cutting and forming operations for parts with irregular shapes are usually performed near the end of the fabrication sequence. Stock should be surfaced, squared to size, and the joints made and fitted before contours are cut and formed. There will be exceptions to this rule, however. For example, with some designs considerable stock can be saved by roughing out the shape in advance of squaring operations.

### LAYING OUT GEOMETRIC SHAPES

Circles and arcs can be laid out directly on the work, using dividers or a pencil compass, Fig. 8-1. Set the dividers at one-half the diameter (radius) of the required circle, and place one leg at the center point. Tilt the dividers slightly in the direction of movement as you draw the circle. When using the dividers, apply enough pressure to score a fine sharp line in the surface of the wood. For large circles you can use the trammel points or a piece of string. Fig. 8-2 shows how trammel points are used.

The dividers or compass can also be used to lay out triangles, hexagons, octagons, and other figures. See Fig. 8-3. A good drawing textbook will

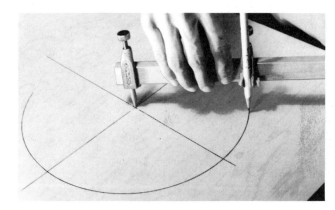

Fig. 8-2. Laying out a large circle with trammel points.

include many other geometric shapes, along with directions for constructing them.

Fig. 8-4 shows a practical way to lay out an ellipse and a spiral. You will need to experiment with the size of the string loop and the spacing of the nails to secure the desired shape and size of the ellipse. The spiral is formed as the string is unwrapped from a center post. The increase in the radius during a 360 deg. turn will be approximatley equal to the circumference of the center post ($2\pi R$).

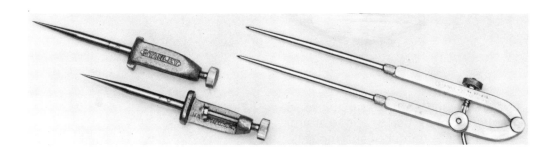

Fig. 8-1. Trammel points (left) and wing dividers (right) are two tools that can be used when laying out circles and arcs.

113

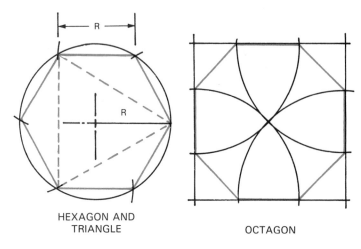

HEXAGON AND
TRIANGLE

OCTAGON

Fig. 8-3. Geometric constructions.

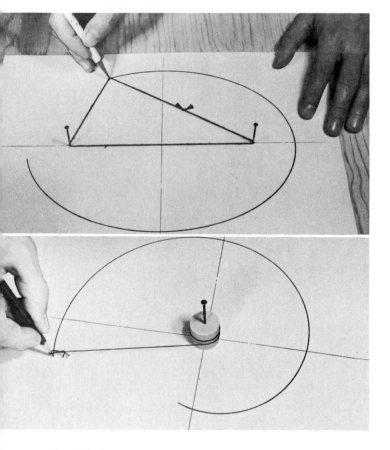

Fig. 8-4. Top. Using a string loop to draw an ellipse. Bottom.
Drawing a spiral.

## CURVES

In project design a smooth flowing curve is usually more interesting than a perfect circle or arc. You see these curves in the contour of automobiles, boats, and airplanes. They are applied to furniture designs with interesting and attractive results. The engineer or drafter calls them ''faired'' lines. They

are produced by drawing a smooth curve through a number of previously established points using a long plastic spline held in place with specially designed lead weights.

In the shop you can lay out a large smooth curve in about the same way the drafter uses a spline. For a single layout, bend a thin strip of wood into the curve you desire. Clamp or hold it in place and draw a line directly onto the wood. To develop a pattern, fasten a sheet of paper to a piece of cork board or soft wood, and set large pins or small nails at the points you want the curve to pass through. The wood strip is then ''threaded'' through these points and the line drawn as shown in Fig. 8-5. Small curves are laid out with an irregular curve. You probably have had experience with this operation in a drafting class.

## PATTERNS AND TEMPLATES

A pattern is a full-sized outline of an object drawn on paper. Some patterns can be developed from dimensions given on a drawing. Complicated curves and outlines are included in working drawings but are usually not full-size and need to be enlarged. This can be done easily by a method called ''enlarg-

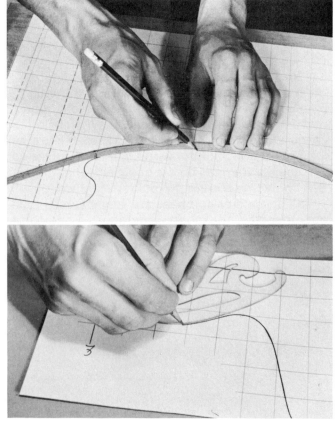

Fig. 8-5. Top. Laying out a smooth curve with a thin strip of wood. Bottom. Using an irregular curve.

ing with squares.'' It is accomplished by laying out small squares (if not included on the drawing) over the contour to be enlarged. On a sheet of paper lay out larger squares (size depends on the scale or ratio), and number them to correspond with the squares on the drawing. Work with one square at a time and draw a line through the large square in the same way it goes through the corresponding small square.

When a design is the same on both ends, you need only a half pattern. This is laid out on one side of a centerline, and then turned over and laid out on the other side as shown in Fig. 8-6. Some designs require only a quarter pattern.

You can transfer a pattern to wood by cutting it out and drawing around the edge, or by placing a piece of carbon paper between the pattern and the wood surface and tracing over the lines. Secure the pattern to the work with drafting tape or thumb tacks so it will not slip. When tracing a pattern onto the wood, use a straightedge and irregular curve to produce smooth lines on your work.

When you have a number of identical pieces to lay out, it is usually best to make a template. Glue your paper pattern (use rubber cement) onto a heavy piece of cardboard or a thin piece of plywood or hardboard. Cut out the contour carefully, and then smooth the edge with a fine file and sandpaper. See Fig. 8-7.

## CUTTING CURVES

The coping saw, compass saw, and keyhole saw are hand tools used to cut curves, Fig. 8-8.

### COPING SAW

The COPING SAW carries a blade that is easily replaced when it becomes dull or is broken. The blade has fine teeth, about 16 points per inch.

Coping saw work can be clamped in the vise, or supported on a sawing bracket as shown in Fig. 8-9. When the work is held in a vise, the blade should be mounted in the saw frame with the teeth pointing away from the handle. When using the sawing bracket the teeth should point downward or toward the handle.

Start the cut in the waste stock and then guide the saw to the edge of the cutting line. Use full, uniform strokes, keeping the blade perpendicular to the surface. Give the blade plenty of time to cut its way. Use extra strokes as you go around corners. Reposition the work as you progress, so the cutting will take place near the point of the V of the sawing bracket, or close to the jaws of the vise. Working slowly and carefully will actually save time because you will not need to do as much filing or sanding to finish the edges.

### COMPASS SAW

The blade of the COMPASS SAW runs to a point; it is 10 to 14 in. long and has about 8 points to the inch. It is used for cutting large curves and circles. The keyhole saw is similar except that it has a smaller blade and finer teeth. The pointed blade of these saws makes it possible to start the saw in a small hole and cut sharp curves.

Fig. 8-10 shows a compass saw being used to cut out a speaker opening in a panel for a stereo

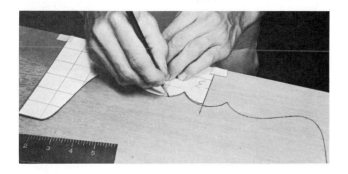

Fig. 8-6. Making a layout with a half pattern.

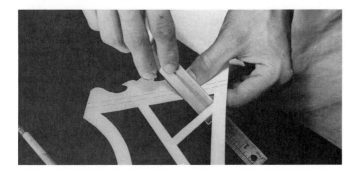

Fig. 8-7. Smoothing the edges of a template with sandpaper wrapped around a steel rule.

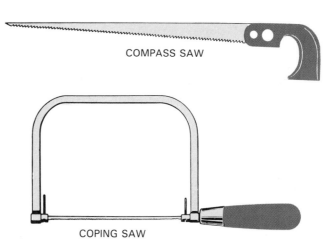

COMPASS SAW

COPING SAW

Fig. 8-8. Saws designed to cut curves.

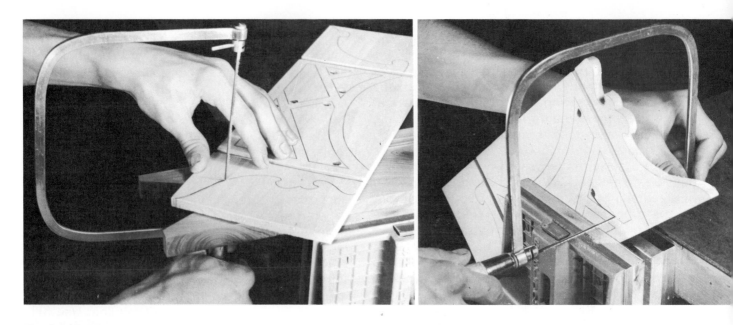

Fig. 8-9. Cutting with the coping saw. Left. Work held on a sawing bracket. Right. Work clamped in a vise. Note that the joints for the wall shelf have already been cut.

cabinet. A hole was bored in the waste stock to start the saw. When using this type saw the length of the stroke will vary with the sharpness of the curve. Sharp curves must be cut with the point of the blade while the entire blade can be used for curves with a large radius. The compass saw leaves a fairly rough edge, so keep the cut well into the waste stock to allow sufficient material for smoothing and finishing. The compass and keyhole saw can be sharpened by the same method used for regular hand saws.

## CHISELS

Curves that are formed by removing only a small amount of stock can be cut and smoothed with a chisel as shown in Fig. 8-11. CONCAVE (inside) curves are cut with the bevel held against the work.

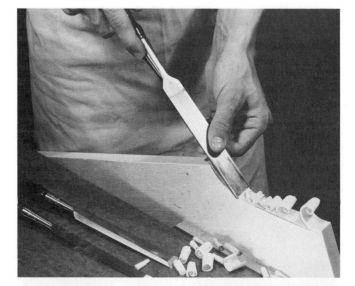

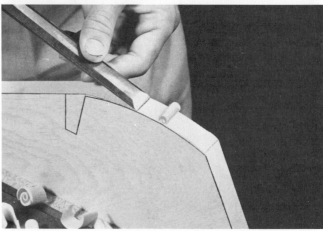

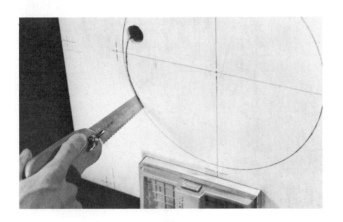

Fig. 8-10. Using compass saw to cut large, circular opening.

Fig. 8-11. Cutting curves with a chisel. Top. Concave or inside curves. Bottom. Convex or outside curves.

This way the depth of cut can be somewhat controlled by the angle of the chisel. The first heavy roughing cuts can be made by driving the chisel (use a socket type) with a mallet. Finished cuts should be made by hand, using very fine cuts as the layout line is reached. CONVEX (outside) curves are cut with the bevel turned up. Make a series of straight cuts tangent to the curve, then take a thin shaving along the layout line to finish the work. A shearing cut is usually made on end grain and hard woods.

The two general types of chisels are the SOCKET and the TANG. The handle of the socket chisel fits into a hollow cone. It should be used for heavy work, when the chisel is driven with a mallet, Fig. 8-12. The tang chisel has a lighter handle attachment, a thinner blade, and is used for light shaping and paring cuts. The size of a chisel is determined by the width of the blade. Chisels are sharpened (ground and honed) using the same method described for the plane blade. See Fig. 8-13.

### SMOOTHING CURVES AND EDGES

The SPOKESHAVE is a tool used for smoothing and shaping curved surfaces and edges. Fig. 8-14 shows a typical model with depth adjustment nuts and a blade that is 2 1/8 in. wide. The blade of the spokeshave is ground at the same angle and is honed in the same manner as a regular plane iron.

The spokeshave can be used for both concave and convex curves. It is usually held and used as shown in Fig. 8-15. However, it can be reversed

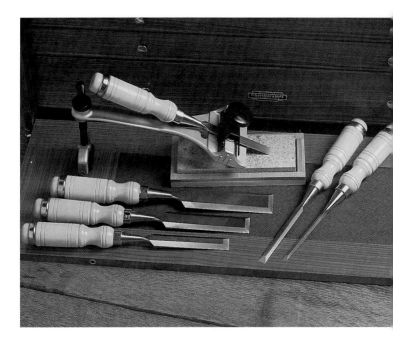

Fig. 8-13. Honing a chisel using a blade honing guide. (Leichtung, Inc.)

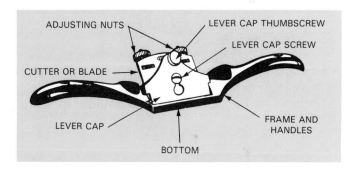

Fig. 8-14. Parts of the spokeshave. (The Stanley Works)

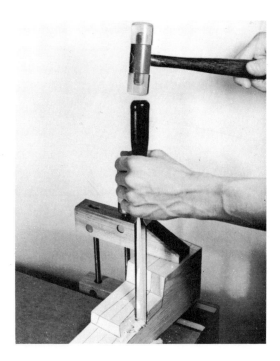

Fig. 8-12. Driving the chisel with a mallet. Always use a socket chisel for this operation.

Fig. 8-15. Using a spokeshave to shape and smooth a contour.

Fig. 8-16. Standard wood files. Top. Flat. Bottom. Half-round. (Nicholson File Co.)

and pushed instead of pulled. The setting for a fine shaving will vary with different shapes and sizes of curves. Hold the tool at an angle so it will make a shearing cut on end grain or hard wood.

A wood file is used for smoothing small pieces or pieces that have sharp curves. The most common files for woodworking are the round, half-round, and flat, Fig. 8-16. They are available in lengths of 8, 10, and 12 in. Small metal files are sometimes helpful in smoothing intricate work. The file should be fitted with a handle and held as shown in Fig. 8-17. When possible, use a stroking action rather than filing straight across an edge. Try to file in from each edge to prevent splitting the opposite side; this is especially important in working with plywood. Use a file card or file cleaner to keep the teeth clean, Fig. 8-18.

Two other shaping and rough smoothing tools are the tungsten carbide coated file, Fig. 8-19, and multiblade forming tool, Fig. 8-20. All of these tools cut rapidly and do a considerable amount of work

before they become dull. Fig. 8-21 shows the multiblade tool being used to finish a large, round hole. This tool is available in various sizes.

Sandpaper can be used for smoothing curves and rounding edges. It can be wrapped around various forms to fit the contour of the work. Coarse sandpaper will cut away the wood fibers rapidly when used across the grain. See Fig. 8-22.

Fig. 8-19. Tungsten carbide coated file. (Skil Corp.)

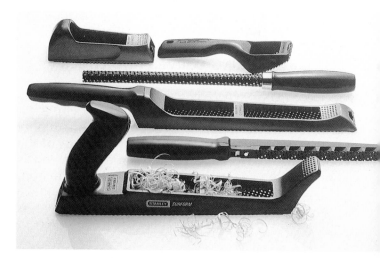

Fig. 8-20. Surform tools for shaping and rough smoothing. (The Stanley Works)

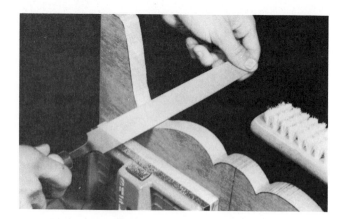

Fig. 8-17. Using the half-round wood file.

Fig. 8-18. File card and brush.

Fig. 8-21. Using a round, multiblade tool to smooth a hole. (The Stanley Works)

Fig. 8-22. Shaping and smoothing with coarse sandpaper.

## CARVING AND SHAPING

Gouges, chisels, knives, and scrapers of various shapes and sizes are used for carving wood, Fig. 8-23. Carving tools are usually sold in a set that consists of chisels, veiners, fluters, and gouges. They should be kept in a box or special holder. This will protect both the worker and the tools.

Fig. 8-23. Shavehook scrapers may be used to reach corners of flat and curved surfaces. (Leichtung, Inc.)

It takes a great deal of skill and patience to do fine wood carving. Always clamp the work securely, either in the vise or some special holder. Hold the tool in both hands and make the cuts by moving the cutting edge away from you. The angle of the tool edges will vary. However, most of them can be held at about a 30 deg. angle. Cut with the grain wherever possible.

An outside ground gouge, Fig. 8-24, is used to form the inside contour of trays and bowls. Start in the center and gradually enlarge the area. Cut long, thin shavings with the tool moving toward the center. Guide the blade with one hand and use the other hand to force it through the wood. Rolling the edge slightly back and forth will help it cut, especially on end grain. Fig. 8-25 shows a candy tray that required the use of a gouge on the inside contour.

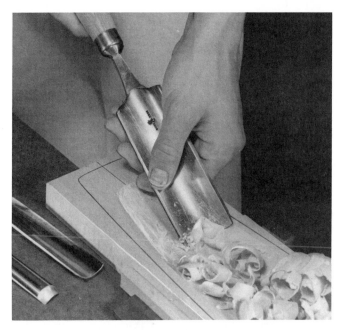

Fig. 8-24. Shaping an inside contour with an outside ground gouge.

*When using chisels and gouges always keep both hands behind the cutting edge, with the cutting motion away from you.*

Gouges and carving chisels require very sharp edges. They can be honed many times before grinding is required. When grinding, try to maintain the original shape of the tool. Fig. 8-26 shows an outside ground gouge being honed with a slip stone after the beveled side was honed on a regular oilstone.

Fig. 8-25. A finished tray that required the use of many forming and shaping tools.

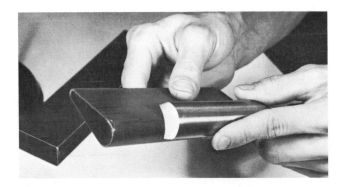

Fig. 8-26. Using a slip stone to hone a gouge.

## CHAMFERS, BEVELS, AND TAPERS

A CHAMFER removes the sharp corner from an edge and improves the appearance of some work. See Fig. 8-27. It is usually made at a 45 deg. angle with the surface or edge of the stock. Lay out a chamfer with a sharp pencil held so the fingers serve as a guide along the edge of the stock, as shown in Fig. 8-28. A marking gauge cannot be used since it will leave a groove.

Clamp the stock in a hand screw and clamp the hand screw in a vise, so the work will be held at an angle. Plane the edges first, and then the ends with the plane held at an angle to make a shearing cut. Use the block plane to chamfer small pieces.

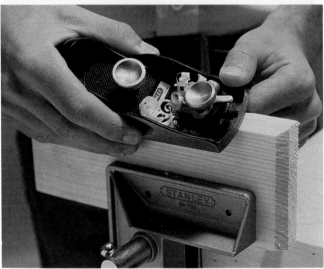

Fig. 8-28. Top. Laying out a chamfer. Bottom. Planing a chamfer. (The Stanley Works)

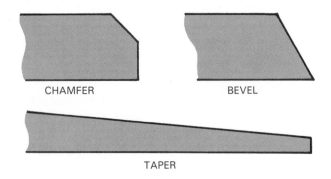

CHAMFER          BEVEL

TAPER

Fig. 8-27. Forms for wooden parts.

A BEVEL, Fig. 8-27, is a sloping edge that connects the two surfaces of the stock. It is planed in about the same manner as a chamfer. To lay out a bevel, the sliding T-bevel square is set at the required angle. It is then used to mark the angle on both ends of the stock. When possible, clamp the work so that the plane can be operated in a horizontal position. As the bevel nears completion, check it with the T-bevel square.

A TAPER, also shown in Fig. 8-27, runs along the length of the stock, making it smaller at one end. The legs of stools, chairs, and tables are often tapered to make them look lighter and more attractive. As in the forming of most irregular shapes, the tapering operation is performed after the work has been squared to size, the joints cut, and a trial assembly made.

Lay out the length of the section to be tapered. When there are a number of similar pieces, clamp them together to make this layout. Mark the size on the small end and then draw the line of the taper on each surface. See Fig. 8-29. Clamp the work securely and plane toward the smaller end. Start with the short strokes at the small end and gradually increase their length as you progress with the work, as described in Fig. 8-30. When tapering adjacent surfaces, you will remove the layout line on the surface being planed and it will need to be replaced. Note that the legs shown in the figures are tapered on only the inside surfaces. Tapers are sometimes hard to clamp in a vise. You may need to work out some special clamping arrangement.

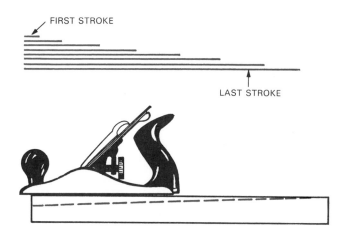

Fig. 8-30. Procedure for planing a taper.

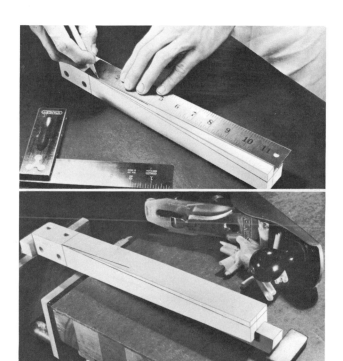

Fig. 8-29. Top. Laying out a taper. Bottom. Planing a taper.

## TEST YOUR KNOWLEDGE, Chapter 8

Please do not write in the text. Place your answers on a separate sheet of paper.

1. To lay out a large circle it is best to use a set of _____ _____.
2. What size of center post would you use to develop a spiral in which the radius increased approximately 1 1/2 in. in one revolution?
3. It is best to use a _____ to lay out many parts that have the same curved outline.
4. If a curved part is symmetrical, (the same on either side of a centerline) it will save time to develop and use a _____ pattern.
5. The teeth of a _____ saw blade may point toward or away from the handle depending whether the work is supported on a sawing bracket or held in a vise.
6. What hand tool would you use to cut a 12 in. hole in the center of a piece of plywood that is 2 ft. square?
7. When smoothing a convex curve with a chisel the bevel should be held against the work. True or False?
8. The most common shapes of woodworking files are round, flat, and _____.
9. When using gouges or chisels the work should be held in one hand and the tool in the other. True or False?
10. When planing a taper, the cut should usually be made toward the _____ (larger end, smaller end.)

## ACTIVITIES

1. Develop a selected list of hand forming tools (other than planes and chisels) that would be practical for use in a home workshop. Include a description of the shape and size of each item and its current price.
2. Select or design a small article such as an Early American wall shelf that includes some curved parts. Prepare a scaled working drawing. Then, use the enlarging with squares method, to make full-size patterns of the curved parts.

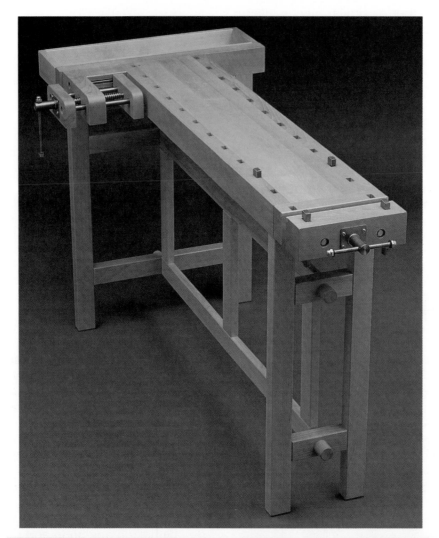

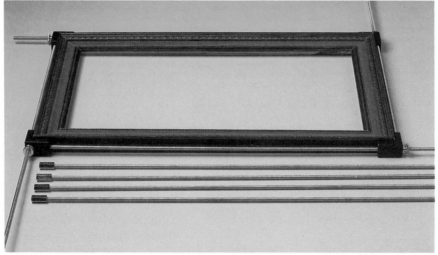

Top. Woodworking bench made from furniture quality Danish beech. Pieces were glued together and machined to close tolerances. Bottom. Adjustable size picture framing clamp. This clamp will hold any square or rectangular frame from 3 in. x 5 in. up to 4 ft. x 4 ft. (Leichtung, Inc.)

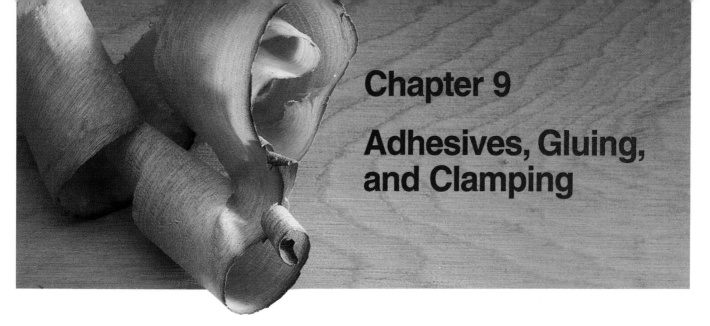

# Chapter 9

# Adhesives, Gluing, and Clamping

Gluing and clamping are important operations that are performed at various times during the total construction activity. At the outset, you may need to make edge or face joints to secure the wider widths or thicker pieces that your project requires. After parts are fabricated, there will be subassemblies and final assemblies to make. As the work nears completion, gluing operations may be included in the veneering of edges and the attachment of moldings and trim.

Gluing operations may involve the use of a number of different kinds of bonding materials. The term ADHESIVE is generally used to describe any substance or bonding material capable of holding objects together by surface attachment. However, adhesives, cements, and glues are somewhat different in composition.

The research laboratories of our chemical industries have developed many new and wonderful plastic materials from such raw materials as coal, air, water, petroleum, and natural gas. Among these have been a wide range of synthetic-resin adhesives that have revolutionized the methods and procedures in wood fabrication.

## ADHESIVES, CEMENTS, AND GLUES

Adhesives, cements, and glues are used to bond materials together. Adhesives are made from synthetic materials. Cements are generally rubber-based. Glues are made from natural materials. Since wood is a relatively weak material, most adhesives, cements, and glues produce bonds that are stronger than the material being bonded together. The most important characteristics are: setting rate, viscosity, water resistance, flexibility, color, sandability, and gap-filling properties.

## ADHESIVES

Adhesives are the most popular bonding agents in use today. There are two basic types of adhe-

sives: thermoplastics and thermosets. Each group has unique properties and applications.

### Thermoplastics

The most widely used adhesives in woodworking are thermoplastics. They are generally resistant to moisture, but are not waterproof. All thermoplastic adhesives soften with heat and therefore are not recommended for applications in high heat areas. There are six basic types of thermoplastic adhesives in common use: polyvinyl, acrylic resin, aliphatic thermoplastic resin, alpha cyanoacrylate, cross-linking PVA, and hot melts.

POLYVINYL ADHESIVES (PVA) are frequently called white glues, Fig. 9-1. They are very popular with both the do-it-yourselfer and industry. This adhesive is purchased ready-to-use. While it has a relatively short clamping time of 30 minutes, the piece should not be worked for 24 hours. The glue line is colorless and, therefore, will not detract from the finished appearance of the project. Since polyvinyl adhesives cure by the loss of moisture,

Fig. 9-1. Polyvinyl adhesive, commonly called white glue, is a thermoplastic adhesive.

it is necessary that the wood have a moisture content between 6 and 12 percent to develop a strong bond. A higher or lower moisture content will cause a weak joint. PVAs are nontoxic, have a rapid setting time, fair gap-filling qualities, are slightly flexible, and have a long shelf life. They are an excellent choice for general woodworking.

ACRYLIC RESIN adhesives are water-resistant and strong. They may be used to bond wood, metal, glass, and concrete. They are not recommended for plastics. Setting time is normally about 5 minutes with a recommended clamp time of 4 hours. Acetone is used to remove excess adhesive. Acrylic resin adhesives are used to bond edges of solid wood or composites to nonporous substrates like melamine or solid surface materials.

ALIPHATIC THERMOPLASTIC RESIN is also a form of polyvinyl resin, Fig. 9-2. It is yellow in color and somewhat stronger than other polyvinyl resins. Also it will not clog sandpaper, and is more resistant to lacquers and heat than polyvinyl adhesives. Because of its advantages, most woodworkers prefer aliphatic thermoplastic resin to polyvinyl. It does have a shorter shelf life than white glue.

CROSS-LINKING PVA adhesives represent the most advanced members of the PVA family. Chemical bonds formed within the adhesive as it dries improves the strength of the glue bond and increases its water resistance. It is similar to regular "yellow glue," but has a higher tack and a shorter drying time. Cleanup is done with water. This is the most widely used adhesive for radio frequency (RF) gluing. A popular name brand of this adhesive is Franklin's Titebond II, Fig. 9-3.

HOT MELTS are newcomers to the field of woodworking. They may be used to bond most any type

Fig. 9-3. Franklin's Titebond II (left) is a cross-linking PVA adhesive. It has high water resistance and good bond strength. (Woodcraft Supply Corporation)

of material and are sold in solid form. Hot melts are heated with a special applicator, Fig. 9-4. The adhesive is applied in molten form using an applicator. It is applied to only one surface and then brought together immediately with its matching surface. Bonding will occur in a short time, anywhere from a few seconds to three or four minutes. Short clamping time is an advantage of hot melts. Disadvantages include wide glue lines and low strength.

**Thermosets**

Thermosets are generally more costly than thermoplastics, but they are resistant to water and are not affected by heat. Curing is accomplished through a chemical reaction that begins when thermosets are mixed. There are six common types of thermosets: ureaformaldehyde, resorcinol-formaldehydes, phenol-and melamine-formaldehyde, epoxy polyurethanes, and reactive hot-melts.

ALPHA CYANOACRYLATE is frequently called "superglue." This adhesive, Fig. 9-5, works well with metals, glass, certain plastics, and other dense, nonporous materials. Outstanding characteristics include rapid drying time and extra strength. It

Fig. 9-2. Aliphatic thermoplastic resin glue is a form of polyvinyl resin glue. It is yellow in color and somewhat stronger than other polyvinyl resins.

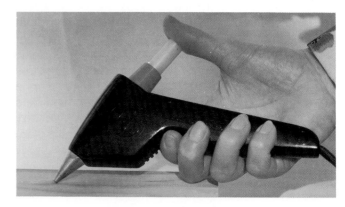
Fig. 9-4. Hot melt glues are applied using a special applicator, in this case, a glue gun.

Fig. 9-5. Alpha cyanoacrylate or "superglue" provides extra strength and rapid drying for dense, nonporous materials.

Fig. 9-6. Ureaformaldehyde resin glue. Top. Catalyst incorporated type mixed with water. Bottom. Liquid resin and powdered catalyst mixed for use.

reaches maximum strength in 24 hours and can be softened with acetone. It should not be allowed to touch the skin during application because it will bond the skin to anything it touches.

UREAFORMALDEHYDE is purchased in a powder form, Fig. 9-6. The addition of water starts a chemical reaction. Although not waterproof, urea-formaldehyde is more resistant to water than polyvinyl. This adhesive has poor gap-filling qualities and, therefore, requires close-fitting pieces. Clamping time is about 6 hours, but may be reduced with the application of heat or radio-frequency glue-drying equipment.

RESORCINOL-FORMALDEHYDE adhesives are expensive. They are very tough and are generally used where harsh conditions will be encountered, such as in boat use. They form a waterproof glue line, but stain wood a dark reddish-brown color. Resorcinols are packaged in two containers, Fig. 9-7. One contains a liquid resin and the other contains a catalyst. When they are mixed together, the reaction begins. The clamping time is long for resorcinols, which, in turn, can be a disadvantage with some assemblies.

PHENOL- and MELAMINE-FORMALDEHYDE adhesives are used for commercial applications. Exterior plywood uses phenol resin. Melamine frequently added to other adhesives to improve their adhesive properties. It is so expensive that it is seldom used alone.

EPOXY is not generally used as a wood adhesive. Epoxy also is packaged in two containers and must be mixed before using, Fig. 9-8. It produces one of the strongest glue joints, but is too expensive for large applications.

POLYURETHANE (ISOCYANATES) adhesives offer an option for exterior woodwork. They were developed as an alternative to epoxies and have been in use in Europe for several years, but are relatively new in the U.S. The key component in polyurethane adhesives is diphenylmethane diisocyanate (MDI). Isocyanates are highly reactive to moisture and develop a high-strength bond through molecular cross-linking. Wood with a moisture content of 8-20 percent is considered

Fig. 9-7. Resorcinol-formaldehyde resin glue.

Fig. 9-8. Epoxy resin glue.

optimum. Polyurethanes are available as two-part or one-part adhesives. Gorilla Glue™ is an example of this type of adhesive, Fig. 9-9.

REACTIVE HOT-MELT (POLYURETHANE) adhesives are solvent-free solids that are formed as pellets, sticks, granules, and liquid. They are then applied by melting in dispensing guns or other equipment. These glues have OPEN TIMES (the maximum amount of time between applying the adhesive and joining the substrates) from 30 seconds to 30 minutes, depending on the formula. Reactive hot-melts are waterproof, solvent-resistant, and will fill large gaps as they solidify. These adhesives can tolerate temperatures from -40 to 300 °F. Bond strength is significantly higher than standard hot-melt adhesives. Liquid reactive hot-melts are available in one- and two-part formulas. Reactive polyurethanes require specialized airtight application systems since they will begin curing when exposed to humidity.

Fig. 9-9. Gorilla Glue™ is a unique, environmentally friendly, one-part adhesive. It contains no solvents; therefore, it produces no harmful fumes as it cures. It is a waterproof general-purpose adhesive that will bond wood to wood, stone, cleaned brass, aluminum, iron, and plastic. (The Gorilla Group)

## CEMENTS

Cements are generally made from rubber suspended in a liquid. Some types of cements are flammable. The use of these requires special care and consideration. For this reason, they are not recommended for school use. Two types of cements that are generally recognized for school use are contact cement and mastic.

SOLVENT-BORNE CONTACT CEMENT is frequently used to bond veneer and plastic laminates to wood, Fig. 9-10. Solvent-borne cement emits large amounts of VOCs and the fumes pose a health risk. Some types are also highly flammable. The cement is applied to both surfaces to be bonded and allowed to dry before being brought together. Once the surfaces touch, bonding is immediate. Strength is very low when compared to other typical woodworking adhesives. High creep is another characteristic of contact cement. Safety is a consideration when using solvent-borne contact cement. Chlorinated-base cements are also available that are nonflammable. However, chlorine fumes can irritate the eyes.

WATERBORNE CONTACT CEMENT is nontoxic and nonflammable. It has similar strength and application characteristics to solvent-borne contact cement. However, from a safety point of view, waterborne contact cements are better to use than solvent-borne cements. Waterborne contact cements set up slower than solvent-borne cements, but "self drying" formulas are available to be used with spray equipment. Waterborne contact cement can be applied to foam plastics, and lacquered, painted, and varnished surfaces. Tools and spills can be cleaned with water while the cement is still wet. This cement should not be used with metal or wood veneer.

MASTIC is a thick contact cement which is generally used in the construction industry. It is frequently applied with a caulking gun to attach sheathing, dry wall, or subflooring, Fig. 9-11.

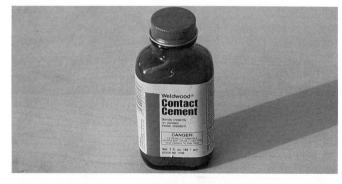

Fig. 9-10. Contact cement should be applied to both surfaces before bonding. Allow both surfaces to dry before bringing them together.

Fig. 9-11. Mastic adhesive has a thick consistency and is usually applied with a caulking gun.

## GLUES

Vegetable and animal products are used to make protein glues. Glues were once used extensively in woodworking, but today they have been largely replaced by adhesives and cements. The reason for this change is because adhesives and cements are generally believed to have superior qualities (strength, length of life, resistance to moisture, etc.) to glues. Also, traditional glues are not as readily available as modern adhesives.

Four basic types of glues are still available: hot animal glue; liquid hide glue; casein glue; and blood albumin, vegetable, and fish glues.

HOT ANIMAL GLUE may be purchased as dry powder or flakes, Fig. 9-12. It must be melted before use. As the liquid cools, it hardens and forms a bond. Speedy assembly is necessary when using hot animal glues to secure a good bond. This glue dries into a colorless, nontoxic, sandable glue line. Moist heat will soften the glue.

LIQUID HIDE GLUE is also a form of animal glue. It is available in a ready-to-use liquid. Refer back to Fig. 9-13. This glue is dark in color when curved and blends well with dark colored woods. It fills gaps well and develops moderate holding power. It, too, is sandable.

CASEIN GLUE is made from dried milk curds and is available as a powder, Fig. 9-14. It is mixed with water until it has the consistency of thick cream. The mixture is allowed to set about 15 minutes before being applied to the wood. Some types of casein glue will stain certain woods, but varieties are available which do not have this drawback. Casein glue is considered water-resistant, but will weaken if exposed to constant moisture. This glue can be applied as long as the temperature is above freezing, which is an advantage in construction. It cures by evaporation and chemical action. It may be used on woods containing up to 15 percent

Fig. 9-13. Hide glue has moderate holding power, is sandable, and blends well with dark colored woods. (Woodcraft Supply Corporation)

Fig. 9-14. Casein glue. Mix the powder with cold water.

moisture content and is particularly effective with oily woods such as teak, yew, and lemonwood.

BLOOD ALBUMIN, VEGETABLE, and FISH GLUES are used commercially. Blood albumin and vegetable glues are used to bond the veneers of interior plywood. Fish glues are used as the bonding agent on packaging tape and shipping boxes.

Fig. 9-15 is designed to be a useful reference when selecting a woodworking adhesive.

## PREPARING WOOD FOR GLUING

Wood pieces that are to be assembled with glue should all have the same moisture content. This will take place automatically if all pieces of the wood are stored in the same area for a period of time. The moisture content at the time of gluing should be equal to the moisture content the glued article will have when it is placed in service. The average moisture content for interior woodwork in the

Fig. 9-12. Animal glue. The flakes are prepared by soaking in water and then heating.

| WOODWORKING ADHESIVES | | | | |
|---|---|---|---|---|
| **THERMOPLASTICS** | | | | |
| Type | Common Form | Minimum Temp°F | Clamp Time | Characteristics/Use |
| Acrylic Resin | liquid | 50 | 4 hrs | Used to bond edges of solid wood or composites to nonporous substrates like melamine or solid surface materials |
| Aliphatic Resin (yellow glue) | liquid | 50 | 1 hr | Better water resistance, less creep, and faster tack than white PVA; nontoxic |
| Cross-linking PVA | liquid | 55 | 1 hr | Similar to yellow glue; high water resistance– appropriate for exterior use |
| Hot-melt (thermoplastic resin) | Granules, sticks, plugs | 350-400 | N/A | Used for fast tacking, or temporary assembly; bonds dissolve with heat; low bond strength |
| Polyvinyl Acetate (white glue) | liquid | 60 | 1 hr | High sheer strength and flexibility, rubbery glue line; no water resistance |
| **THERMOSETS** | | | | |
| Type | Common Form | Minimum Temp°F | Clamp Time | Characteristics/Use |
| Cyanoacrylate ("super glue") | liquid | 40 | N/A | Joints are strong and waterproof, low shock resistance; fast-setting; useful for small repairs in wood, plastic, or metals |
| Epoxy | Two-part heavy liquid | 32 | 1 hr | Must be mixed; useful for bonding difficult materials; waterproof; good gap-bridging strength; fumes pose health risk |
| Polyurethane (isocyanates) | liquid | 50 | 1-4 hrs | Moisture curing; very water resistant; may cause respiratory reaction; good for oily woods |
| Reactive Hot-melt (polyurethane) | Sealed cartridges or cans | 250 | N/A | Resists water and solvents; bond withstands heat; may cause respiratory reaction; special spray equipment needed |
| Resorcinol/phenol-resorcinol | two-part liquid | 70 | 4-10 hrs | Good water and solvent resistance; must be mixed; formaldehyde emissions are potential health hazzard |
| Urea Formaldehyde (plastic resin) | powder | 70 | 8-12 hrs | High strength; good moisture resistance; must be mixed; excellent for veneering; formaldehyde emissions are potential health hazzard |
| **CEMENTS** | | | | |
| Type | Common Form | Minimum Temp°F | Clamp Time | Characteristics/Use |
| Contact Cement (solvent-borne) | liquid | 40 | N/A | For bonding to wood composites; emits high VOC emissions, fumes pose health risk, some highly flammable |
| Contact Cement (waterborne) | liquid | 65 | N/A | Slow evaporation of water; catalyzed "self drying" formulas require special spray equipment |
| **GLUES** | | | | |
| Type | Common Form | Minimum Temp°F | Clamp Time | Characteristics/Use |
| Casein Glue | powder | 60 | 2-3 hrs | Moisture resistant but not waterproof; will bond species that feel oily such as teak; will stain dark or acid woods |
| Hide Glue | liquid and granules | 70 | 2-3 hrs | Bonds dissolve with moist heat; granules must be soaked in water and heated in a glue pot; repairs easily |
| Hot Animal Glue | powder or flakes | 145 | 2-3 hrs | Speedy assembly is necessary; dries into a colorless, nontoxic, sandable glue line; moisture will soften |
| Vegetable, Blood Albumin, and Fish Glue | powder or flakes | 70 to 230 | 2-3 hrs | Once used to bond interior plywood veneers, packing tapes and shipping boxes |

Fig. 9-15. This chart is intended as a general guide for woodworking adhesive characteristics. It contains four main categories: Thermoplastics, Thermosets, Cements, and Glues.

United States is about 8 percent but varies widely for different parts of the country. Exterior woodwork varies from 12 to 18 percent. High moisture contents (15 percent and above), will retard the curing time and may require the use of special glues.

The wood surfaces that will form the glue line should be dry, clean, smooth, and make good contact with each other, Fig. 9-16. This kind of surface is prepared with hand planes, chisels, and machines with sharp knives. Tests have proved that

Fig. 9-16. Parts ready for gluing. They are dry, clean, and fit together smoothly. Inside surfaces have been sanded.

Fig. 9-17. Checking trial assembly.

striating the surfaces with a sharp knife or scratch awl does not improve the strength of the joint. In fact, it may actually reduce the strength if loose wood fibers prevent the surfaces from making good contact.

For many years it was thought that glue held wood together through MECHANICAL ATTACHMENT. This concept proposed that the liquid glue flowed into the pores and cavities of the wood and then hardened to form an interlocking solid material. Today the more acceptable explanation is called SPECIFIC ADHESION. Briefly, this theory states that the molecular forces that cause certain molecules of different materials to be attracted to each other are the ones that operate in the gluing process. It is also believed that in some cases a kind of chemical reaction takes place that forms different molecules that add to these adhesive forces.

## TRIAL ASSEMBLIES

Before applying any kind of glue you should first place all of the parts together and check the fit. See Fig. 9-17. Check the squareness of individual parts and assembled parts. Check the clearance of interlocking joints so you can be sure they will slip together easily after the glue is applied. All joints and parts should fit together without excessive pressure from clamps. If you force an assembly together you will be gluing stresses into your project that may eventually cause the joints or structural members to fail.

When working with assemblies that are large and complicated, study and practice the sequence you will follow. If you are working with fast setting glue it is best to make several subassemblies rather than do all of the gluing at one time. Be certain that all parts are properly identified so you will not get them mixed or reversed during the gluing operation.

Adjust all the clamps and other gluing devices. Use small blocks of wood under the jaws of bar clamps to protect the smooth surfaces of final assemblies.

## PREPARING GLUE

Polyvinyl, liquid hide, and contact cement are ready to use when purchased, while many of the other glues will need to be mixed and prepared. When preparing powdered glues, mix just the amount you will need for each job. These glues have a working life (pot life) of only a few hours and then must be discarded. A paper cup makes a good small quantity mixing container.

Pour the dry powder into the cup and add a small amount of water. Stir with a stiff brush or stick until it forms a heavy ''gooey'' mass, then add a few drops of water at a time until you have reduced it to a smooth, creamy consistency. Manufacturers of urea resin glue usually recommend a proportion (by measure) of eight parts of powder to three parts of water. Casein glue is usually mixed in a proportion of one part of glue to two parts of water. If you use a brush to mix and apply the glue it can be cleaned with warm water and soap.

Study and follow the manufacturer's recommendation on the label of the container when working with glue, particularly resorcinol and epoxy glues. It is best to use sticks or a putty knife to mix and apply these glues, since they are difficult to remove from a brush.

## APPLYING GLUE

Applying the glue to the wood surface is called SPREADING. When the glue is applied to both wood surfaces to be joined it is called a DOUBLE SPREAD and when it is applied to only one surface it is called a SINGLE SPREAD. Glue can be spread with a stick, brush, knife, roller, or a mechanical spreader. On production work glue is sometimes applied with a spray gun. Woodworking industries often use a single spread since they have machinery that carefully controls the amount of glue applied. Fig. 9-18 shows a small single roll glue spreader and how it works.

For your work in the shop you should make a double spread. Use good judgment as to how much glue to apply. The surface should be thoroughly coated, yet not so heavy that you will have excessive "squeeze-out." This will make the work messy and will waste glue. Fig. 9-19 shows urea resin glue being spread on the faces of stock being used to form a larger blank. Note the approximately correct amount of squeeze-out on the assembled pieces. A good glue film is about .005 in. (5 mils) thick, however the thickness will vary with the material and kind of glue used.

The ASSEMBLY TIME refers to the total time between the spreading of the glue and the application of pressure. OPEN ASSEMBLY TIME is the period between glue spreading and the moment when the two surfaces are placed together. CLOSED ASSEMBLY TIME is the time the pieces remain in contact before pressure is applied. Open assembly time should usually be as short as possible. However, if the parts are immediately brought together and excessive pressure applied, too much glue may be squeezed out resulting in a "starved" joint. This is most likely to happen when gluing a hard, dense wood with urea resin.

You will need to know the assembly time of the glue you are using. For example, the blank of wood in Fig. 9-19 could not have been glued with polyvinyl by the method shown because the assembly time would have been too long. Polyvinyl glues have an assembly time of only about five minutes. The urea resin being used has an assembly time of 15 minutes at room temperature. To glue

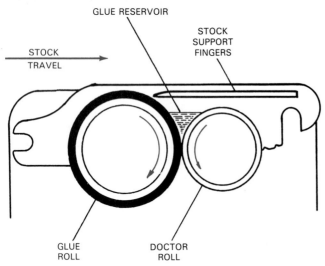

Fig. 9-18. A single roll glue spreader. Both rolls are powered. Adjustments between the glue roll and the doctor roll accurately controls the amount of glue spread. Coating speed is 100 lineal ft. per minute. Top. Spreader being used to coat a surface. Bottom. Section view showing roll arrangement.

Fig. 9-19. Top. Spreading urea resin glue with a brush. Bottom. Clamping the stock together. More pressure is applied by turning the assembly over and settting two more hand screws on the other side.

the blank successfully with polyvinyl, the pieces should be glued in pairs and then the two pairs glued together later. This would slow down the operation very little since polyvinyl work can be removed from the clamp in about 30 minutes.

Casein glue has an assembly time of about 20 minutes. Hide, resorcinol, and epoxy glues all have relatively long assembly times and seldom present any problem in this respect. Glues with long assembly times also require long clamping periods. For example, resorcinol glued joints should be kept clamped for about 10 hours.

## GLUING AN EDGE JOINT

Fig. 9-20 shows a suggested procedure for gluing an edge joint. The work is first assembled dry (without glue) and the clamps are adjusted. For joints of this kind the clamps are usually spaced about 12 to 16 in. apart. A rack or holder that will keep the bottom clamps on edge is helpful. Apply a bead of polyvinyl glue to one edge and then make the spread on both pieces by rubbing them together. Check the spread and apply additional glue to any areas that are not coated. After the spread is made on both joints, the pieces are carefully aligned and the clamps underneath are tightened. A third clamp is placed across the top surface and tightened. Note the paper towel laid between the clamp and the glue line so the corrosive action of the polyvinyl glue on the metal clamp will not stain the wood. This protection is not necessary if the clamps are removed within 1 hour.

Joints like this and others that are used to build up the required dimensions of the stock are usually not cleaned immediately. The squeeze-out line of glue is easily removed with a hand or cabinet scraper after the joint has set up.

Even though polyvinyl glue will set up so that most assemblies can be removed from the clamps in about 30 minutes, the joint will not gain its full strength for several hours. Edge joints for high quality work should have several days to cure so that the extra moisture at the glue line can dry out. If the joint is machined and planed too soon, extra wood (expanded by moisture) will be removed and this will form a depression after it dries. This is true of all glues that have a high moisture content.

The clamps used in Fig. 9-20 are called BAR CLAMPS. They are available in various lengths (maximum opening) from 2 to 8 ft. When tightened firmly with one hand they will exert about 600 lbs. of pressure. When tightened with both hands on the crank, you can apply pressure of well over 1200 lbs. Manufacturers of adhesives generally recommend 100 to 150 psi (pounds per square inch) for soft wood and 150 to 200 psi for hard wood. If one hand is used to tighten the clamps, Fig. 9-20C,

Fig. 9-20. Gluing and clamping edge joints. A—Applying a bead of glue on one edge. B—Rubbing the edges together to make a double spread. C—Tightening the bottom clamps. D—Applying a third clamp to the top surface.

then the three clamps will exert a total of about 1800 pounds of pressure. The stock is 3/4 in. thick and 24 in. long, making the area of the joint 18 sq. in. The pressure on the joint is therefore about 100 psi which is satisfactory for soft wood.

HAND SCREWS are ideal clamps for woodwork because the jaws are broad and distribute the pressure over a wide area. The greatest pressure can be attained by tightening the outside or "end" spindle as it provides greater leverage than the "middle" spindle. Hand screws are available in sizes (total length of jaws) from 4 to 24 in. Sizes most used in the school shop are 4, 6, 8, and 12 in.

C-CLAMPS provide a compact clamping device and are sometimes helpful in gluing operations. See Fig. 9-21. In woodworking they are often used to clamp parts to machines and make special setups. They are available in sizes (maximum opening) from 1 in. to 12 in., with smaller sizes of 2, 3, and 4 in. most often being used in woodworking.

Fig. 9-21. C-clamps in use. This type clamp is also called a carriage clamp.

## TOGGLE CLAMPS (QUICK CLAMPS)

Even though toggle clamps have been around for many years, they are just beginning to be used regularly by woodworkers. The advantages of toggle clamps make them well worth consideration. They have good holding power, positive locking action, and are fast and easy to use with one hand. In addition, they are reasonably priced.

Toggle clamps are ideal for clamping workpieces to shop tools, fixtures, and jigs. They operate through a combination of pivots and levers to apply force to the workpiece, Fig. 9-22. Toggle clamps are manufactured in many styles that include mechanical, pneumatic, and hydraulic variations— more varieties than any other type of clamp. Holding capacity of typical toggle clamps range from about 60 lbs. to 16,000 lbs.

## MECHANICAL TOGGLE CLAMPS

The basic mechanical toggle clamp is available in four different types: hold-down, straight-line, pull-action, and squeeze-action clamps. The two most popular types for woodworking are the straight line and hold-down types. Straight-line clamps provide a push or pull action. Pull-action clamps draw parts together while squeeze-action toggle clamps hold parts with a pinching action much like the action of a C-clamp.

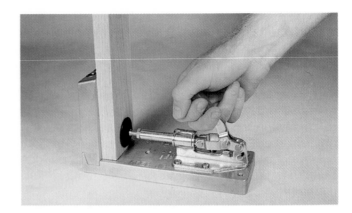

Fig. 9-22. Toggle clamps are now being widely used by woodworkers to hold workpieces in jigs and fixtures and for typical machining operations. (Kreg Tool Company)

### Hold-down Clamps

The most design variations of the toggle clamp are found with hold-down clamps, Fig. 9-23. Included in this group are T-handle or straight-handle clamps in a vertical or horizontal style; open or solid clamping arms with a high, low, or angled profile; and straight or flanged mounting bases. The greatest clamping flexibility is provided by the open-arm style. The threaded spindle can be adjusted to accommodate a variety of workpiece sizes.

The use of hold-down toggle clamps will increase safety and quality of work. They will eliminate stock creep when crosscutting miters, hold stock steady during routing, and eliminate spinning of stock during drilling operations. Safety is greatly increased by keeping fingers away from the cutters when template routing small pieces.

### Straight-line Clamps

Straight-line toggle clamps provide a pulling or pushing action, Fig. 9-24. Most will lock in the fully retracted or extended position. These clamps can be adjusted by moving the position of a hex nut. Straight-line toggle clamps have either a flange

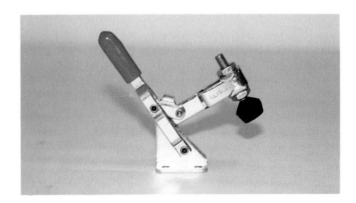

Fig. 9-23. Hold-down toggle clamps are available in several styles. (Te-Co)

Fig. 9-24. Straight-line toggle clamps provide a pulling or pushing action.    (Te-Co)

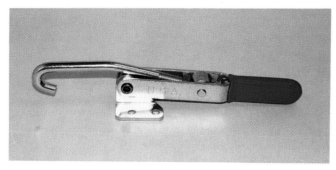

Fig. 9-25. Pull-action toggle clamps are also called latch clamps. They are used to pull two parts together.    (Te-Co)

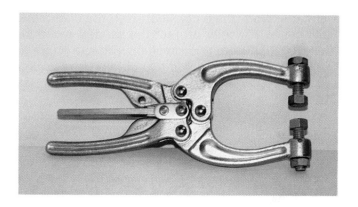

Fig. 9-26.  Squeeze-action toggle clamps are sometimes called toggle pliers. They are generally used where C-clamps might be used.    (Te-Co)

mount or threaded body for mounting the clamp directly through a panel, plate, or angle bracket.

Straight-line clamps are useful in gluing jigs where several items of the same size are to be assembled. They are also very useful for holding and positioning a piece for a machining operation.

### Pull-action Clamps

Pull-action clamps are also called LATCH CLAMPS, Fig. 9-25. They are designed to draw two parts together. The mechanism works by raising the handle to advance the clamping element, much like a toolbox latch. When the clamping element (hook or U-bolt) is engaged, the handle is moved to the horizontal position to pull the pieces together and lock the clamp.

### Squeeze-action Clamps

Squeeze-action toggle clamps combine the grip of a pair of pliers with toggle action, Fig. 9-26. In fact, the hand-held types are often called TOGGLE PLIERS. They are used where a C-clamp would generally be used. Squeeze-action clamps use either a threaded spindle with a fixed jaw or two threaded spindles to adjust the clamping thickness. Most clamps have a quick release handle for quick removal.

### Pneumatic Power Clamps

Pneumatic (or hydraulic) power clamps are used for repetitive production operations where set-up time is critical. A pneumatic or hydraulic cylinder provides the activating force. Some types of these clamps have a safety feature of being mechanically locked (when fully closed) so that even a loss of pressure will not cause them to cycle, Fig. 9-27. Pneumatic or hydraulic clamps are generally self-contained and simply need to be mounted and attached to air or hydraulic lines. The clamp shown in Fig. 9-27 provides 200 lbs. holding capacity in a package less than 7 in. long.

Fig. 9-27.  Self-contained pneumatic power clamps are ideal for repetitive production operations.    (De-Sta-Co)

## GLUING FRAMES AND FINISHED ASSEMBLIES

Before making the final glued assembly of paneled frames, legs and rails, and other structures, the parts should be sanded. This is especially important on inside surfaces. Always make a trial assembly, and determine the best and most efficient procedure to follow.

Fig. 9-28 shows the clamping of legs and rails. A subassembly of two legs and a rail are first made for each end of the table and then the final assembly

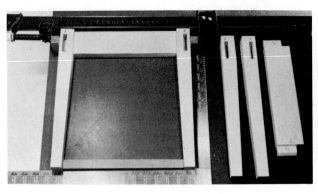

Fig. 9-28. Left. Subassembly. Note the spacer strip used to hold the bottom of the legs and correct distance apart. Right. Final assembly. Here a spacer strip is used to hold the frame square.

is made. Note the blocks between the clamp jaws and the work; they protect the sanded wood surfaces. By shifting their position you can apply the pressure at the right point to obtain correct alignment. Also note the "spacer" strips; one is used to hold the legs the correct distance apart in the subassembly and the other keeps the frame square in the final assembly.

It is important to work on a good, flat surface for assemblies like this because the parts of a structure must not only be square with each other but also lie in the correct plane. In frame assemblies the contact area of the joints is usually small so even a light pressure from the clamp will provide the required psi.

In Fig. 9-29 a large frame is being assembled. If the frame is not square you can shift one or two of the bar clamps to a slight angle with the work and use this diagonal force to pull it into the correct position. From a point level with the frame, sight across the horizontal plane that it forms to be sure it is not twisted.

After frame and panel or other assemblies are glued, it may be necessary to reinforce them with GLUE BLOCKS. A carefully squared piece of stock

is ripped across corners and then cut to 1 or 2 in. lengths. These blocks are coated with glue and set in position as shown in Fig. 9-30. Press firmly on the block and move it back and forth a few times to spread the glue and "set" it in place. It will stay in position and will not need to be clamped.

Fig. 9-31 shows a patented clamp that can be used for frames.

## CLEANING GLUED JOINTS

On final assemblies, where the wood surfaces have been sanded, extra precautions should be taken to keep them clean and free of glue. Even the slightest amount will seal the surface and cause a blemish in the finish. When the surface is bare of finish, glue "spots" may be hard to detect, but when finish is applied (especially stained work) they become noticeable.

Apply the glue carefully so there will be a minimum of squeeze-out. That which does appear

Fig. 9-29. Clamping arrangement for a large frame. (Adjustable Clamp Co.)

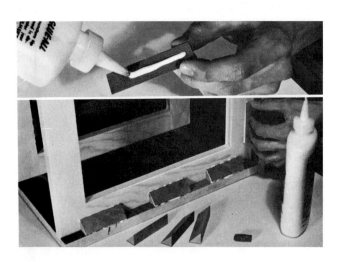

Fig. 9-30. Setting glue blocks. Top. Applying a bead of glue. Bottom. Setting the block with firm pressure and a slight back and forth movement.

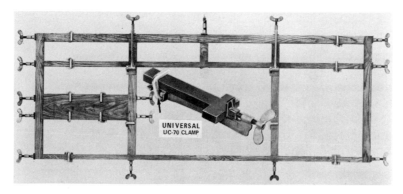

Fig. 9-31. Patented clamp replaces bar clamp in frame assemblies. U-device (arrow) grips rail firmly as screw is tightened. Can be equipped with antiscuff pad. (Universal Clamp Corp.)

around the joint (on front and top surfaces, and edges) should be removed. Use a sharp stick or wood chisel to remove as much as possible, then wipe the surface thoroughly with a sponge or cloth, moistened with hot water. See Fig. 9-32.

For extremely fine work, with joints that are hard to clean, apply masking tape around the edges of the joint to protect the surface from glue.

## GLUING MITER JOINTS

Miter joints are more difficult to clamp and glue. Fig. 9-33 shows some clamping devices that are designed for this purpose. The miter clamp, Fig. 9-33, left, is especially helpful for assembling picture frames. Glue can be applied to the joint and then it can be firmly held in the clamp for nailing. The miter clamps shown in Fig. 9-33 (right) fit into 5/8 in. blind holes bored in the back of the frame.

If no special miter clamps are available, assemble the miter joints as shown in Fig. 9-34. Small blocks of wood are temporarily glued to the sides of the frame, then split off after the glue has set.

Fig. 9-32. Cleaning a glue joint with a sponge moistened with hot water.

Fig. 9-34. Miter joints clamped by gluing small blocks on the frame.

Fig. 9-33. Left. Miter clamp especially designed for picture frames. Center. Frame clamp. Right. Miter clamps that require a hole on the backside of the frame.

Fig. 9-35 shows a band clamp being used to glue cube table together. It has many applications in gluing irregularly shaped objects. The canvas band is 2 in. wide and is available in several different lengths. A patented spring clamp, Fig. 9-36 (top), has pivoting jaws with serrated teeth along the edge. These teeth grip the surface of miter joints and other irregularly shaped parts. Another type of spring clamp is ideal for holding thin pieces together, Fig. 9-36 (bottom).

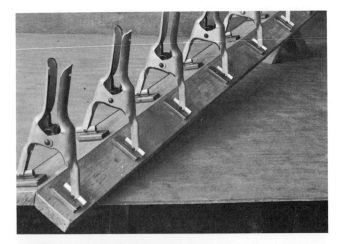

Fig. 9-35. Band clamp.

Fig. 9-36. Top. Patented spring clamps. (Arvids Iraids) Bottom. Another style of spring clamp.   (Grizzly Imports, Inc.)

## BUILDING CLAMPING DEVICES

You may wish to build a clamping device that you can use in the school shop or your home workshop. The press, Fig. 9-37, can be used to veneer panels, apply plastic laminates, clamp inlaid panels, and other similar operations. You will need to purchase four press screws which are available at hardware stores or industrial arts supply firms.

Figs. 9-38 and 9-39 show frame clamping jigs. One utilizes a standard hand screw to supply the pressure and can be adjusted to fit any size of frame. The other jig uses eccentrics to supply pressure and is adjustable for various sizes of small frames. Dovetail slots in the baseboard carry the eccentric units. Jigs may also be simple and designed for a single purpose.

## PRODUCTION METHODS AND EQUIPMENT

Clamping and gluing operations in industry are carefully planned and controlled. High efficiency is secured through the use of modern adhesives and the wide range of gluing equipment and machinery now available, Figs. 9-40 through 9-42.

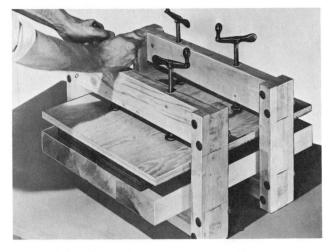

Fig. 9-37. Veneer press.   (Adjustable Clamp Co.)

Fig. 9-38. Adjustable frame clamp.

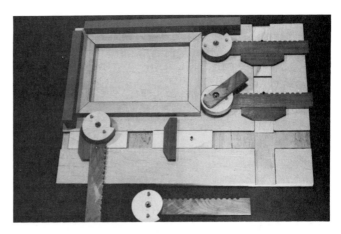

Fig. 9-39 Clamping jig for small frame. Pressure is supplied by eccentrics.

Fig. 9-40. This glue spreader applies adhesive to both the top and bottom surfaces of edge-glued lumber core stock. Eventually it will be bonded with veneer or high pressure decorative plastic laminate. (Black Brothers)

Fig. 9-41. A large air pod platen press. It is used to laminate flat stock such as plastic-faced panels, table tops, hollow-core flush doors, partitions, and countertops. (Black Brothers)

Fig. 9-42. Modern edge gluing machine for lumber 5/8 in. to 2 in. (16 mm to 51 mm) thick. Conveyor carries stock over glue applicator and stops when pieces contact the stop wand. Operator takes stock from top conveyor and lays up panels. When load is complete, it is moved into press by lower conveyor. Steam heated platens are pressed against the panel surfaces by air bags and edge pressure is supplied by air cylinders. Joints cure while operator lays up next load. (James L. Taylor Mfg. Co.)

Production spreaders can apply a precisely controlled film of glue to thousands of square feet of surface per hour. Pneumatic and hydraulic cylinders operate clamping devices and press platens smoothly and rapidly and provide the right amount of pressure.

Thermosetting resin glues used with steam, hot water, or electrically heated platens reduce the setting and curing time to just a few minutes. This feature, combined with automatic controls and equipment, permits one worker to glue edge joints in several thousand board feet of stock per day.

High frequency gluing has greatly reduced the setting and curing time for certain assemblies. In this type of gluing, high frequency (2 to 30 megacycles) radio waves are used to supply the heat. With heating methods commonly used (steam, hot water, and electricity) to apply the heat to the surface of the wood, some time is required for it to "soak in" to the glue line. With high frequency gluing the radio waves penetrate to the glue line immediately and the glue is set and cured in less than a minute even though the stock or lay-up is several inches thick. Fig. 9-43 shows a high frequency gluing operation.

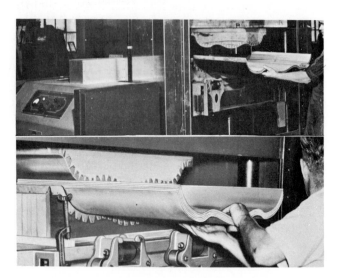

Fig. 9-43. Top. High frequency press with 30 kW generator. Dies are made of wood with a metal face that serves as the electrode. Press is closed and pressure applied by hydraulic power. Bottom. Removing finished panel, which will be used for serpentine drawer fronts. (Lodge and Shipley Co.)

### TEST YOUR KNOWLEDGE, Chapter 9

Please do not write in the text. Place your answers on a separate sheet of paper.
1. Adhesives are made from:
   a. Rubber-based materials.
   b. Natural materials.
   c. Synthetic materials.
   d. None of the above.
2. Glues are made from:
   a. Rubber-based materials.
   b. Natural materials.
   c. Synthetic materials.
   d. None of the above.
3. _____ and _____ are the two basic types of adhesives.
4. List the six types of thermoplastic adhesives.
5. _____ _____ is frequently called "super glue."
6. Which of the following is NOT a type of thermoset?
   a. Resorcinol-formaldehyde.
   b. Epoxy.
   c. Phenol- and melamine-formaldehyde.
   d. Mastic.
   e. All of the above.
7. _____ glue is a powdered glue that tends to stain certain woods.
8. When gluing a complicated structure, it is best to make several _____ rather than do all the gluing at one time.
9. What is spreading?
10. The greatest pressure can be applied by tightening the _____ (middle, end) spindle of the hand screw.
11. Excess glue or squeeze-out on edge joints should be removed after it has hardened by using a _____.
12. What are the two basic types of contact cement?
13. Name the four basic types of mechanical toggle clamps.

### ACTIVITIES

1. Prepare a chart that will provide information on adhesives commonly used in woodworking. List the kinds of glue along the left side of the chart and use such headings as preparation, assembly time, application instructions, and disadvantages across the top. Secure data from container labels, manufacturer's booklets, and reference books.
2. Conduct an experiment in curing thermosetting adhesives with heat. Use several kinds of joints and apply heat with such items as a discarded electric iron, heating pad, or infrared heat lamp. Prepare a written report of the results and include practical suggestions on how heat may be used to cure glue joints in the school shop.
3. Select or develop a working drawing for a small article, such as a book rack, wall shelf, box, toy, or model that includes some special gluing and assembly problem. Make design sketches of an assembly jig that would simplify and/or insure accurate construction. Include a written description of how it would be used.

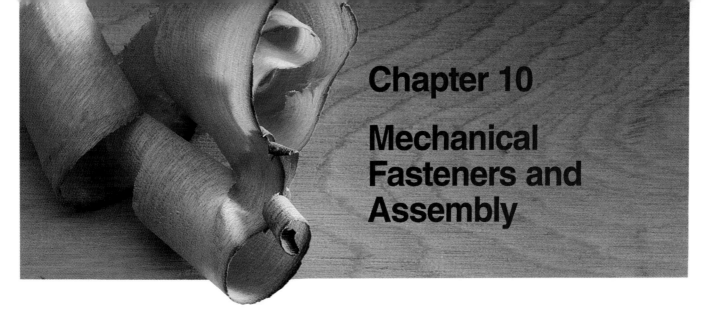

# Chapter 10

# Mechanical Fasteners and Assembly

Metal fasteners for woodworking include nails, screws, staples, bolts, splines, and many special items. Fasteners are used in nearly every type of construction. Nails and screws are still the most common. However, in industrial production where the work is done with power drivers, staples and patented fasteners are used extensively.

Fig. 10-1 includes a selection of hammers, screwdrivers, and other hand tools used to apply the more common wood fasteners.

## HAMMERS

Two shapes of nail hammer heads are in common use: the curved claw and the ripping (straight) claw. The curved claw is the most common and more suitable for pulling nails. The ripping claw can be driven between fastened pieces and works somewhat like a chisel in prying them apart.

The parts of a standard hammer are shown in Fig. 10-2. The face can either be flat or have a slightly rounded convex surface (called a BELL FACE). The bell face is used most often since it will drive nails flush with the surface without leaving hammer marks on the wood. The hammer head is forged of high quality steel and heat treated to give the poll and face extra hardness. The size of a claw hammer is determined by the weight of its head. It is available in a range of 7 oz. to 20 oz. The 10 oz. and 13 oz. are good sizes for work in the school shop. Carpenters usually select the 16 oz. or 20 oz. size for rough framing.

The hammer should receive good care. It is especially important to keep the handle tight and the face clean. If the handle becomes slightly loose

Fig. 10-1. Hand tools used to apply metal fasteners. (The Stanley Works)

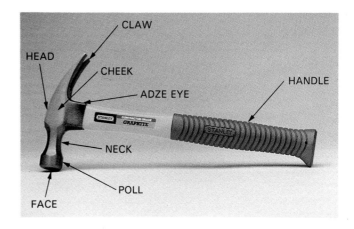

Fig. 10-2. Parts of a 16 oz. nail hammer with rip claw. (Stanley Tools)

bit can be tightened by immersing the head in linseed oil and leaving it for several days. It can also be tightened by driving the wedges deeper or installing new ones.

## NAILS

One of the easiest ways to fasten wood together is with nails. Nailed joints are not as attractive or strong as glued joints, but they are practical for packing boxes, crates, house frames, or for finish work where the nail heads can be covered.

There are many kinds and sizes of nails. Standard types that you should be able to identify are shown in Fig. 10-3.

Nails are usually made of mild steel. However, some are made of aluminum and others of mild steel with a galvanized coating for exterior work. The COMMON NAIL has a heavy cross section and is used for rough carpentry work. The lighter BOX NAIL is used for light construction, crates, and boxes. The CASING NAIL is the same weight as the box nail, but has a small conical head. It is used in finished carpentry work to attach door and window casings, and other interior trim. FINISH NAILS and BRADS are quite similar, and have the thinnest cross section and the smallest head. They are used for a great variety of small construction work.

The nail size unit is called a PENNY and is abbreviated with the lower case letter d. It indicates the length of the nail. A 2d (2 penny) nail is 1 in. long. A 6d (6 penny) nail is 2 in. long. See Fig. 10-4. This measurement applies to common, box, casing, and finish nails. Brads and very small box nails are specified by their actual length and gauge number. The gauge number varies from 12 to 20 with the highest number being the smallest diameter. Nails are priced and sold by the pound.

Fig. 10-5 shows a few of the many specialized nails available today. Each is designed for a special purpose with either annular or spiral threads for increased holding power. Some nails have special coatings of zinc, cement, or resin. Coating or threading a nail will increase its holding power to three or four times that of a smooth nail. These and various other forms of nails are made of such

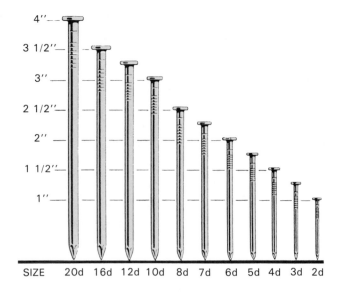

Fig. 10-4. Nail sizes. (United States Steel)

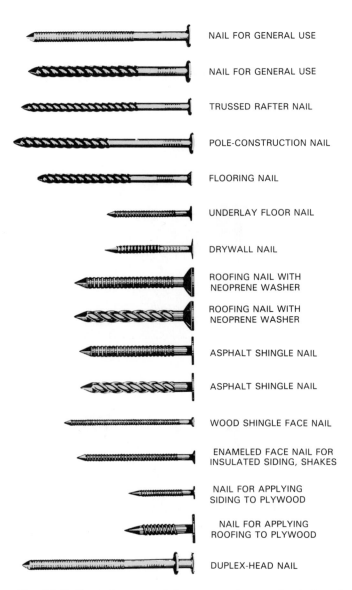

Fig. 10-5. Note the type of threads on these nails designed for special purposes. (Independent Nail and Packing Co.)

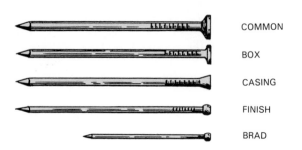

Fig. 10-3. Kinds of common nails.

material as iron, steel, copper, bronze, aluminum, and stainless steel. Nails for power nailers are available for most applications, Fig. 10-6.

## DRIVING NAILS

When driving nails, select an appropriate size hammer. Choose the nail with the smallest diameter, that will still provide the necessary holding power. On precise work you may need to lay out the nailing pattern or mark the position of the bottom member so that you can easily locate the proper position for each nail. Always nail through thin pieces into thicker pieces. When possible, drive the nails into cross grain rather than end grain so they will have maximum holding power.

Grip the hammer well back on the handle and use a wrist movement to start the nail as shown in Fig. 10-7. Once the nail is started, move the hand that held the nail out of the way. Use a full swing (arm and wrist) to get power in the stroke. Keep your eyes firmly fixed on the nail head. Ease up on the power of your strokes when the head gets close to the surface of the wood. Stop when the head is flush. Try to avoid denting the wood with marks from the hammer. If the nail begins to bend, remove it and start with a new one.

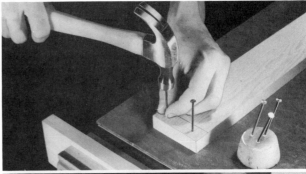
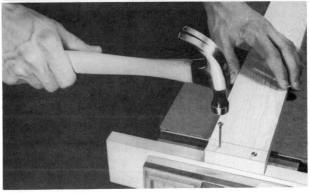

Fig. 10-7. Top. Start the nail with light strokes. Bottom. Drive the nail with wrist and arm movement.

*Use care when driving nails so that the hammer does not strike the surface of the wood. Hammer marks indicate work done by an amateur.*

Nails are easy to drive into soft wood but are difficult to drive into hard wood. When driving nails in hard wood, wax or soap placed on the point will help. Be sure to keep the face of the hammer clean. For wood that is very hard, it is best to drill a pilot hole for the nail. When nailing at the end of a board,

space the nail in from the end as far as possible while still retaining a good hold on the other member. Stagger the nailing pattern, Fig. 10-8, and avoid placing two nails close together along the same grain line. When there is danger of splitting the wood, blunt the sharp point of the nail with a hammer or cut it off with nippers. When the nail is slightly long for the work or you want to increase the holding power, drive it at an angle. In toenailing, Fig. 10-9, select the position and angle carefully, and stagger the nails so they will not intersect.

When driving casing nails or finish nails, leave the head slightly above the surface. Then use a nail set

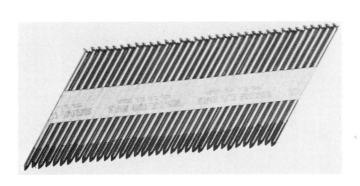

Fig. 10-6. This clip of nails is used with a power nailer. The ends are coated for easier driving and greater holding power. (Paslode Co., Div. of Signode)

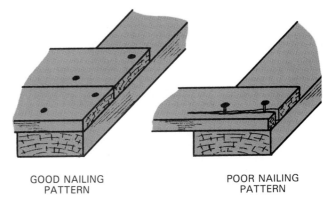

GOOD NAILING PATTERN          POOR NAILING PATTERN

Fig. 10-8. Always use a good nailing pattern. A poor pattern may cause the stock to split.

141

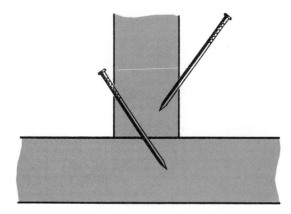

Fig. 10-9. Toenailing.

slightly smaller than the nail head to bring the head flush with the surface or about 1/16 in. below. See Fig. 10-10. The size of the nail set is determined by the size of its tip. Sizes range from 1/32 to 5/32 in. by thirty-seconds. The method for using a brad pusher or driver is shown in Fig. 10-11.

Fig. 10-12 shows the correct procedures for pulling a nail. Force the claw under the nail head and start the removal. On some work you should protect the surface with a putty knife (as shown) or scraper blade. After the nail is withdrawn part way, use a block of wood under the head to protect the surface of the work and increase leverage.

## WOOD SCREWS

Screws provide greater holding power than nails and offer the advantage of easy disassembly and reassembly of parts. Because they require more time to install, they are used mainly in high grade cabinetwork and furniture construction.

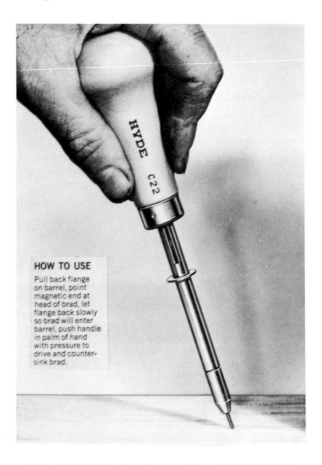

**HOW TO USE**
Pull back flange on barrel, point magnetic end at head of brad, let flange back slowly so brad will enter barrel, push handle in palm of hand with pressure to drive and countersink brad.

Fig. 10-11. Brad pusher or driver. (Hyde Tools)

Fig. 10-12. Pulling a nail. Top. Use a putty knife to protect the surface. Bottom. Use a block of wood to protect the surface and increase leverage.

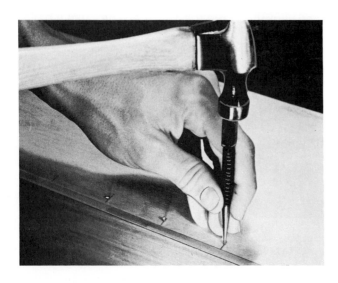

Fig. 10-10. Setting a nail.

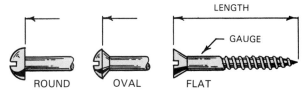

STANDARD SLOTTED SCREWS

SPECIAL DRIVER

PHILLIPS HEAD SCREW

Fig. 10-13. Kinds of wood screws.

Wood screw size is determined by the length and diameter (gauge number). Screws are classified according to the shape of head, surface finish, and the material from which they are made. See Figs. 10-13 and 10-14. Wood screws are available in lengths from 1/4 to 6 in. and in gauge numbers from 0 to 24. The gauge number can vary for a given length of screw. For example, a 3/4 in. screw is available in gauge numbers of 4 through 12. The No. 4 would be a thin screw while the No. 12 would be a thick screw. From one gauge number to the next, the size of the wood screw changes by 13 thousandths (.013) of an inch.

Most wood screws are made of mild steel with no special surface finish. They are usually concealed in the cabinet or furniture structure. Such screws are labeled as F.H.B., which stands for FLAT HEAD BRIGHT. When screws will be visible in high quali-ty work, they should be nickel or chromium plated or made of brass. The heads should be round or oval. Wood screws are priced and sold by the box which contains one hundred (100). To completely specify wood screws they should be listed like this:

10 — 1 1/2 x No. 10 — Oval Head — Nickel.

Give careful consideration to the selection of the kind and size of screw that will be best suited for your work. To secure the maximum holding power the screw should enter the base piece of wood the entire length of the threads. This is about two-thirds of its length. This may not be possible in thin stock. Where the screw will be anchored in end grain you will need to use extra length since end grain does not hold screws well. It is good practice to use the smallest screw diameter that will provide the required holding power.

## DRILLING HOLES FOR WOOD SCREWS

When fastening wood with screws, two different size holes should be drilled. One should be the size of the screw shank. The other should be a little smaller than the root diameter of the screw thread, see Fig. 10-15.

Use good judgment in selecting the size of the drill bits. The size of the shank hole should be just large enough that the screw can be pushed in with the fingers. The size of the pilot hole (also called an anchor hole) for a given screw will vary depending on the hardness of the wood. For soft wood use a hole that is about equal to 70 percent of the root diameter; and for hard wood about 90 percent. When working with hard wood, the pilot hole should be drilled almost as deep as the screw will go. For

|  | 0 | 1 | 2 | 3 | 4 | 5 | 6 | 7 | 8 | 9 | 10 | 11 | 12 | 14 | 16 | 18 | 20 |
|---|---|---|---|---|---|---|---|---|---|---|---|---|---|---|---|---|---|
| Diameter Dimensions In Inches At Body | .060 | .073 | .086 | .099 | .112 | .125 | .138 | .151 | .164 | .177 | .190 | .203 | .216 | .242 | .268 | .294 | .320 |
| **TWIST BIT SIZES For Round, Flat and Oval Head Screws in Drilling Shank and Pilot Holes.** | | | | | | | | | | | | | | | | | |
| Shank Hole Hard & Soft Wood | 1/16 | 5/64 | 3/32 | 7/64 | 7/64 | 1/8 | 9/64 | 5/32 | 11/64 | 3/16 | 3/16 | 13/64 | 7/32 | 1/4 | 17/64 | 19/64 | 21/64 |
| Pilot Hole Soft Wood | 1/64 | 1/32 | 1/32 | 3/64 | 3/64 | 1/16 | 1/16 | 1/16 | 5/64 | 5/64 | 3/32 | 3/32 | 7/64 | 7/64 | 9/64 | 9/64 | 11/64 |
| Pilot Hole Hard Wood | 1/32 | 1/32 | 3/64 | 1/16 | 1/16 | 5/64 | 5/64 | 3/32 | 3/32 | 7/64 | 7/64 | 1/8 | 1/8 | 9/64 | 5/32 | 3/16 | 13/64 |
| Auger Bit Sizes For Countersunk Heads | | | 3 | 4 | 4 | 4 | 5 | 5 | 6 | 6 | 6 | 7 | 7 | 8 | 9 | 10 | 11 |

Fig. 10-14. Wood screw sizes.

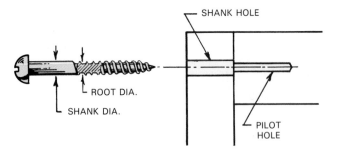

Fig. 10-15. Holes for wood screws.

Fig. 10-16. Drilling holes for screws. Top. Shank hole. Center. Countersinking. Bottom. Pilot hole. Note masking tape wrapped around drill to mark hole depth.

soft wood the pilot hole is drilled to about one-half of this depth. If you are using a large number of screws of equal size in an assembly, you may want to experiment with scrap wood to determine just the right pilot hole for the size of screw and kind of wood you are using.

Use centerlines to mark the position of the screws. Make this layout carefully so the screws will be properly spaced, especially if the screw heads will be visible. Fig. 10-16 shows a sequence of operations for drilling the holes. After the center of the screw hole is marked with a scratch awl, the shank hole is drilled. A countersink bit mounted in the brace is then used to countersink the hole to a size that will exactly match the screw head. The second piece of stock is then clamped in position and the pilot holes are drilled.

Both flat and oval head screws need to be countersunk. Use care in doing the countersinking so the head will fit correctly, Fig. 10-17. Flat headed screws look especially bad if not perfectly aligned with the surface. Your work may require that the screw head be recessed and the hole plugged. For this the shank hole will need to be counterbored. Remember to bore the large hole (size of the screw head) first and then drill the shank hole.

## SETTING SCREWS

The parts of a standard screwdriver are shown in Fig. 10-18. A number of sizes and styles are available. The size is specified by giving the length of the blade, measuring from the ferrule to the tip. The most common sizes for woodworking range from 1 1/2 to 6 in.

The size of a Phillips screwdriver is given in a point size that ranges from a No. 0, the smallest, to a No. 4. Size numbers 1, 2, and 3 will fit most of the screws used in the school shop.

Tips of screwdrivers must be carefully shaped, and should look somewhat like those shown in Fig. 10-19. For a slotted screw they must be square, the correct width, and fit snugly into the screw. The width of the tip should be equal to the length of the bottom of the screw slot. The sides of the screw-

Fig. 10-17. Drilling and countersinking for a flat head screw.

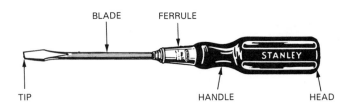

Fig. 10-18. Parts of a standard screwdriver.

144

Fig. 10-19. Screwdriver tips. Left. Phillips. Center. Standard. Right. Cabinet.

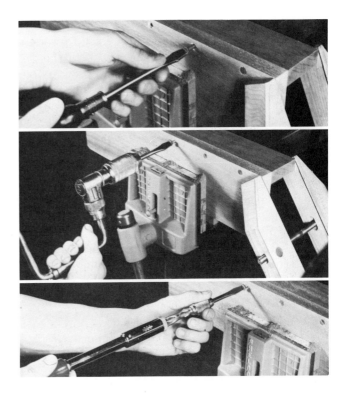

Fig. 10-21. Setting wood screws. Top. Screwdriver. Center. Screwdriver bit mounted in brace. Bottom. Spiral ratchet screwdriver.

driver tip should be carefully ground to an included angle of not more than 8 deg. and to a thickness that will fit the screw slot. Use the side of the grinding wheel to form a flat surface. If the grinding is done across the sides, the tip will hold in the screw slot better. See Fig. 10-20.

If you have properly drilled holes for the screw, it is an easy matter to insert the screw in the shank hole and drive it "home" with the screwdriver, Fig. 10-21. Use care that the screwdriver does not slip out of the slot and dent the surface of your work. Using Phillips type screws helps eliminate this problem because the tip cannot easily slip out of the screw slot. A screwdriver bit mounted in a brace is a good way to set large screws. The brace provides a great deal of leverage. Be careful that you do not twist off the screw or damage the head. A spiral ratchet (automatic) screwdriver, will save time when you have a large number of screws to set.

A little wax or soap on the threads will make it easier to drive screws into hard wood. Do not apply too much force or the screw will twist off in the wood. Screws usually break just where the threads start, and the part embedded in the wood is very difficult to remove. If the screw turns too hard, it indicates that the holes were not properly drilled. Remove the screw and make the holes larger.

Brass screws are much softer than steel screws and are easily twisted off or otherwise damaged. On very fine work it is often worthwhile to first drive a steel screw of the same size (this will cut the threads in the pilot hole), then remove it and set the brass screw.

When drilling holes for a large number of screws a great amount of time can be saved by using a special multioperational bit like the one shown in Fig. 10-22. In a single stroke it will drill the pilot

*When setting screws, if you use too much force or a poorly shaped screwdriver tip, you will damage the slot in the screw heads and your work will appear shoddy.*

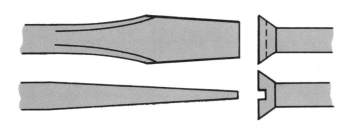

Fig. 10-20. The screwdriver must fit the screw.

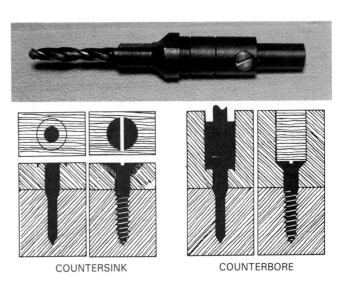

COUNTERSINK          COUNTERBORE

Fig. 10-22. Special bit for screw holes. (The Stanley Works)

hole, shank hole, and either score the surface for countersinking or counterbore the work for recessing the screw head. Fig. 10-23 shows a similar type of bit designed for drilling and countersinking being used in an electric drill. Drill bits of this kind are designed to match standard screw sizes. Bits are available for the commonly used screw sizes.

## SPECIAL FASTENERS

Fig. 10-24 shows a number of metal fasteners especially designed for woodworking. The HANGER BOLT has wood screw threads on one end and machine threads on the other. LAG SCREWS and CARRIAGE BOLTS are often used for rough construction or for concealed work in cabinetmaking.

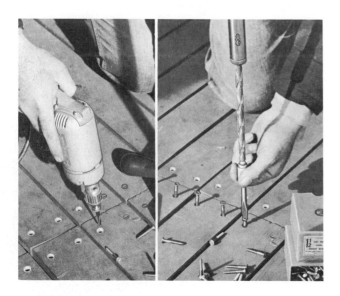

Fig. 10-23. Left. Drilling countersunk holes with special bit. Right. Setting screws with a spiral ratchet screwdriver.

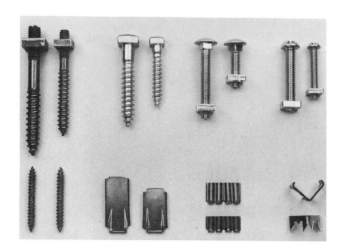

Fig. 10-24. Special fasteners. Top row. Hanger bolts, lag screws, carriage bolts, stove bolts. Bottom row. Dowel screws, splines, corrugated fasteners, chevrons.

STOVE BOLTS are used frequently in metalworking and are sometimes useful in joining certain parts of woodwork.

Corrugated fasteners are used for rough work and can be applied quickly. They drive and hold best when set at an angle with the wood grain. For an installation like the one in Fig. 10-25, they should penetrate the wood about one-half of its thickness. Hold or clamp the parts in position. Drive the fastener into one side and then the other. The fasteners set in the opposite side should be staggered so they are not aligned with the ones on the face side. Corrugated fasteners are available in sizes of 1/4 to 3/4 in. They are packed in units of 100.

Steel splines can be driven into soft wood along the grain but it is better to cut a saw kerf first. Clamp the stock together so you can cut into the edges or ends of both pieces at the same time. Use a backsaw or dovetail saw and cut to a depth equal to one-half of the spline width. Clamp or hold the pieces together and drive in the spline as shown in Fig. 10-26. The spline length should be about equal

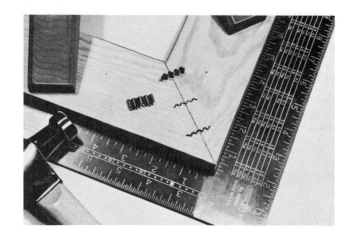

Fig. 10-25. Using corrugated fasteners to hold miter joint.

Fig. 10-26. Fastening a butt joint with steel splines.

Fig. 10-27. Left. Flat corner plate. Center. Bent corner iron. Right. T-plate.

to the thickness of the stock. Splines are available in several sizes and are sold in lots of 100. Chevrons work in about the same way as splines but are designed especially for miter joints.

Dowel screws have wood screw threads on each end. When set in two pieces of the same kind of wood, they will penetrate each piece an equal distance—if the holes are drilled exactly the same. To set only one end, clamp the other end between two hard wood blocks. Do not use pliers or you will damage the threads.

Metal plates and angles, Fig. 10-27, can be used in many ways to assemble parts and reinforce wood joints. They are attached with screws. Since they are unattractive they should be used only where they can be concealed.

## PRODUCTION EQUIPMENT

Today the building trades and industrial plants use automatic fastening equipment and machines. They save a tremendous amount of hand labor. This results in better quality control of their products. A wide variety of equipment is available, from hand operated staplers to large multiunit power drivers, Fig. 10-28.

This equipment is used extensively in cabinet

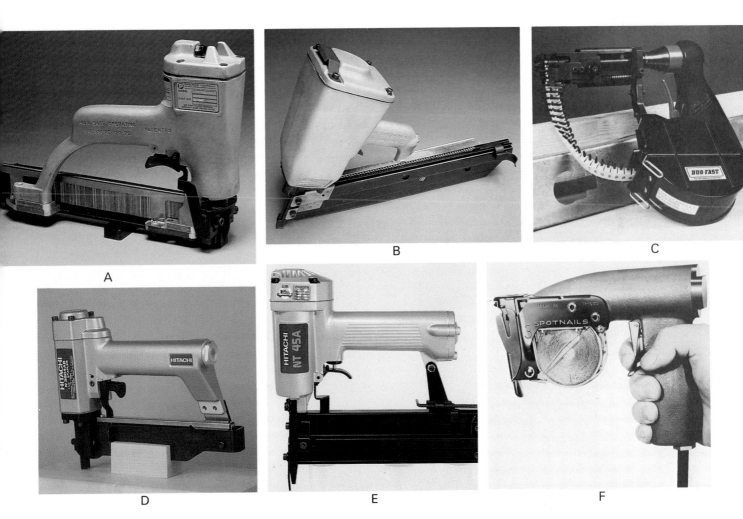

Fig. 10-28. Tackers, staplers, and nailers. A—Medium duty air-powered staple gun. B—Heavy duty air-powered power nailer. (Paslode Co., Div., of Signode) C—Self-feeding screw system. D—Narrow crown finish stapler. (Hitachi Power Tools) E—Finish nailer that uses 18 gauge brads. (Hitachi Power Tools) F—Air tacker. Holds up to 5,000 staples in one cartridge. (Spotnails, Inc.)

shops, furniture factories, sash and millwork plants, toy factories, and many other industries that work with wood and wood products. Pneumatic (air) powered tackers and nailers are popular because the power mechanism can be built of lightweight materials, making a unit that is easily handled. Nearly all the portable tools can be operated with one hand which frees the other hand to hold and position the material. See Figs. 10-29 to 10-35.

Automatic nailing machines are adaptable to light or heavy work. They press the wood members

Fig. 10-31. Attaching trim to chair frame with headless pin tacker. Tacker is air powered and drives 18 gauge pins in three lengths. (Senco Products, Inc.)

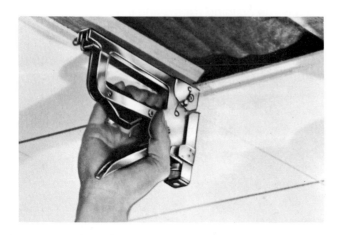

Fig. 10-29. Hand powered gun tacker being used to staple ceiling tile to wood furring strips.

Fig. 10-30. Attaching a panel using a light duty air-powered brad nailer. (Paslode Co., Div. of Signode)

Fig. 10-32. General purpose nailers such as this one can speed construction and improve quality. (Paslode Co., Div. of Signode)

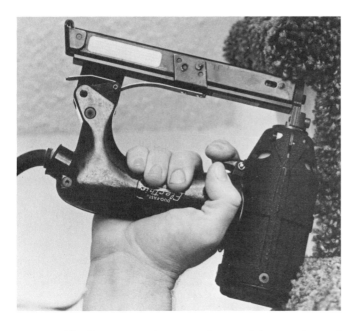

Fig. 10-33. Electric staplers may be used in a variety of fastening jobs. (Duo-Fast Corp.)

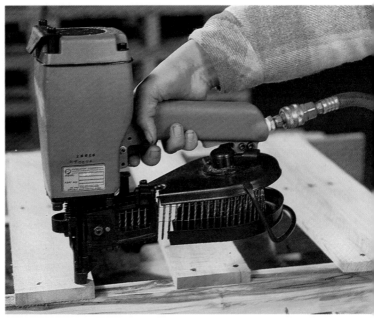

Fig. 10-35. This portable pneumatic nailer drives round headed nails, 6d through 9d. It is 4 to 5 times faster than driving the same nails by hand. (Paslode Co., Div. of Signode)

together and hold them while the nails are driven. Many of the newer machines make their own nails from coils of special threaded wire. The threads run in a spiral around the wire to provide greater holding power (much like the threaded nails shown previously in this unit). At a touch of the foot control, wire is fed into the machine, a nail is made and driven instantly. Adjustments can be made for different nail lengths, and to provide for setting and clinching. Figs. 10-36 to 10-39 show several models and sizes of nailing machines in operation.

Fig. 10-36. Multihead nailing machine equipped with five units. Nail pattern selector can be programmed to automatically drive nails in specified locations at a rate of 145 per minute. (Bostitch)

Fig. 10-34. Nailing drawer slides in place with a long nose staple nailer. It is air operated. (Fastener Corp.)

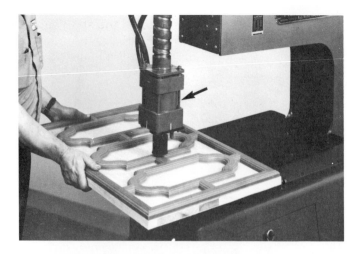

Fig. 10-37. Nailing machine blind nails overlay to furniture panel. Air cylinder (arrow) presses parts together tightly as screw nail is driven from below. Air pressure requirements are 60 to 100 psi or 414 to 690 kPa. (Bostitch)

Fig. 10-38. Using a heavy-duty portable nailer for in-plant assembly of exterior wall frame. Nailer drives smooth shank nails up to 3 1/2 in. (89 mm) long. Operating air pressure 100 psi (690 kPa). (Senco Products Inc.)

Fig. 10-39. Gang of air driven nailers being used to attach 1/2 in. (12.7 mm) plywood sheathing to house wall section. Each unit is equipped with remote firing mechanism connected to operator's console.

### TEST YOUR KNOWLEDGE, Chapter 10

Please do not write in the text. Place your answers on a separate sheet of paper.

1. Name the two types of nail hammers commonly used.
2. How is the size of a claw hammer determined?
3. The only difference between the box nail and the casing nail is the shape of the _____.
4. The difference in length between a 6d nail and an 8d nail is:
   a. 1 inch.
   b. 3 inches.
   c. 1/2 inch.
   d. 1/4 inch.
5. Threaded or _____ nails will have three or four times the holding power of a smooth nail.
6. The sizes of nail sets vary by sixty-fourths, with the largest size being about _____ in.
7. What is F.H.B. an abbreviation for?
8. From one gauge number to the next, the size of a wood screw changes by:
   a. 1/13 inch.
   b. 13 thousandths of an inch.
   c. 13 one hundredths of an inch.
   d. 1 inch.
9. When drilling holes for screws the shank hole must be made larger than the _____ hole.
10. The _____ screw should be countersunk so that the head is flush with the surface of the wood.
11. Large screws can be set with a screwdriver bit mounted in a _____.
12. A bolt with wood screw threads on one end and machine screw threads on the other is called a _____ (carriage, hanger) bolt.
13. Corrugated _____ will drive into end grain easier than into side grain.

### ACTIVITIES

1. Make a visual aid by mounting nails, screws, and other metal fasteners on a framed panel. Include some threaded or coated nails. You might want to use epoxy glue for mounting these metal parts. Include a carefully lettered or typewritten label with each item.
2. Design one or several practical joints that are held together with a hanger bolt. Keep the metal fastener concealed as well as possible. Rapid assembly and disassembly could be a feature of the joint. Carefully prepare orthographic or pictorial drawings of your design.

The craftsmanship found in these pieces is an accomplishment for any woodworker. Left. Roll top desk. This oak roll top desk is an appropriate project for an advanced woodworker. (Mark Clauss). Right. Three-drawer file cabinet. The frame and panel construction of this piece is strong and attractive. (Mark Clauss)

These beautiful furniture pieces required a great deal of sanding and preparation for the final finish. Top. Corner cabinet of curly maple, satinwood, and ebony by George Gordon. Bottom. Writing table of kingwood, Honduras rosewood, and ebony inlay by Craig Marks. (Pritam and Eames)

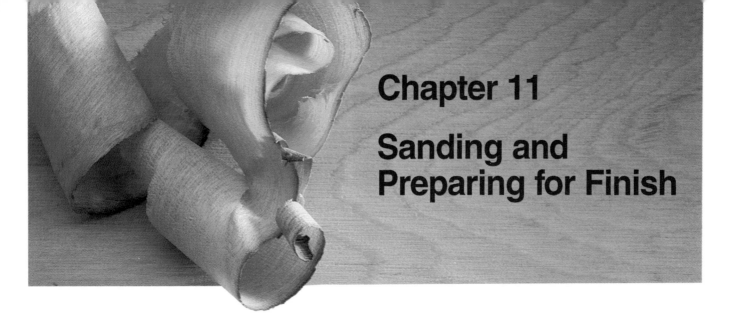

# Chapter 11

# Sanding and Preparing for Finish

SANDING is the process where wood fibers are cut with an abrasive (a hard material that cuts and wears away a softer material). This smooths the wood surface and prepares it for finishing coats.

Sanding operations are usually not performed until all edge tool work has been completed. However, there are exceptions. For example, when cutting out small intricate parts it may be better to sand the surface of the blank first. There will be times when a coarse sanding operation can be used to shape and form parts. Such operations are usually performed with power sanders. You should not, however, try to substitute a sanding operation for those that can best be performed with planes, chisels, and other tools. Individual parts, especially their inside surfaces, are always sanded before the final assembly. A final touchup sanding is then given to all exposed surfaces just before the finish is applied.

## COATED ABRASIVES

Since sandpaper is not made of sand, industry has adopted and uses the term COATED ABRASIVE. This is a more descriptive term for abrasive materials that are applied to paper or cloth, made into sheets, discs, drums, belts, and other forms. There are four kinds of abrasive material used for woodworking: FLINT and GARNET which are natural (mined or quarried) materials; and ALUMINUM OXIDE and SILICON CARBIDE which are artificial (manufactured) materials. See Fig. 11-1.

FLINT is actually quartz (silicon dioxide) which is found in natural deposits and is one of the oldest abrasives used for woodworking. It has been largely replaced by newer and better materials. It is, still used, however, for maintenance work and operations such as removing paint and varnish. GARNET is reddish brown in color and is the same natural mineral as the semiprecious jewel. It is the most widely used natural abrasive material. It is an excellent abrasive, especially for hand sanding.

ALUMINUM OXIDE, made of bauxite, coke, and

Fig. 11-1. Types of abrasive paper (from left to right): silicon carbide (blue black), aluminum oxide (tan), flint paper (colorless), and garnet paper (reddish brown).

iron fillings, is a brown material that appears more tan in color in the finer grades. It is hard and tough, and although it is more expensive than natural abrasives, it will cut faster and wear longer. SILICON CARBIDE, made of silica (sand) and coke, is blue-black in color and the sharpest and hardest of the four abrasives. Silicon carbide is used extensively in production work. In the school shop it is the abrasive usually found on wet-or-dry papers that are designed for sanding finishes.

### MAKING ABRASIVES

Abrasive materials are crushed and then sifted through accurately woven silk screens as shown in Fig. 11-2. The mesh of the screens are numbered according to the openings per linear inch. This number is used to designate the grit size or grade of the abrasive. For example, a medium grade of

Fig. 11-2. Batteries of vibrating silk cloth screen sift and separate abrasive grains into various sizes.

abrasive is No. 80 and is sifted through a screen that has 80 openings per inch along one side. The screen actually has a total of 6400 openings per square inch. Screens are used to sift grades from 12 to 220. Finer grades (240—600) are sifted by special processes called HYDRAULIC SEDIMENTA-TION and AIR FLOTATION.

## Backing Materials

The abrasive grains are glued to backing materials such as paper, cloth, paper/cloth combinations, and fiber. Paper weights are designated by the letters A, C, D, and E. The lightest weight is A and is used for the finer grades of finishing papers. E is the heaviest and is used for belts, discs, and drums on sanding machines. Cloth weights include J, or Jeans cloth and X, or Drills cloth. Jeans cloth is light and flexible, and used to make belts for such operations as sanding molding. X weight is used for flat sanding belts on large production machines.

## Coating Processes

A "making machine," Fig. 11-3, is used to glue the abrasives to the backing. This will take backing material up to 50 in. wide and has a production capacity of 30,000 yards per day. The backing material is first printed with the trademark, grade size, paper weight, and other markings. An accurate coating of glue is then applied with rollers and the backing moves into chambers where the abrasive is deposited, either by gravity or an electrostatic process. The coated abrasive is then allowed to predry as it travels in long festoons. It is then given a

Fig. 11-3. Front end of a machine that makes coated abrasives. It consists of in-feed roll rack, rotary two-color printer, adhesive roll coater, abrasive grain dispenser, sizing machine or sizer, drying chambers, and traveling racks.

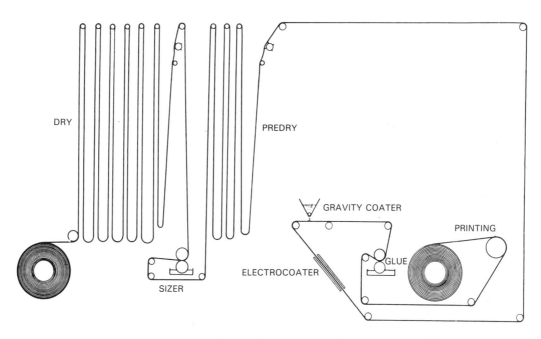

Fig. 11-4. This diagram shows the operation of a "making" machine.

second, or SIZING COAT, of glue and the final drying takes place. Study the drawing, Fig. 11-4.

The electrostatic coating process (also known as electrocoating) is shown in Fig. 11-5. The abrasive grains are carried between two electrodes which create an electrical field of 50,000 volts. The electrical charge drives the grains upward into the glue where they are embedded vertically to form the abrasive surface.

Abrasives are applied to the backing to form either a closed coat or an open coat. In CLOSED COATING the grains are packed closely together and cover the surface completely. Closed coat abrasives are used for heavy sanding operations, especially on power machines. OPEN COATING leaves spaces between the grains so that only about 70 percent of the surface is covered. This helps keep the abrasive

from "loading-up," especially on soft materials. The spaces let most of the cuttings drop free from the backing. See Fig. 11-6.

After the coated abrasives have cured they are FLEXED. In this process a tightly drawn sheet of the material is passed over a metal edge to break the stiffness of the glue bond and make it more flexible. Large sheets are then cut into standard forms. These forms include sheets, rolls, belts, discs, and specialties. They have a wide variety of uses. See Fig. 11-7.

Fig. 11-5. Diagram of electrostatic coating process. Abrasive grains are imbedded vertically in glued backing.

Fig. 11-6. Typical abrasive paper markings. Light toned sheets are open coated; dark sheets are closed coated.

Fig. 11-7. Forms of coated abrasives used for woodwork include cones, sleeves, strips, slotted discs, cartridge rolls, and bands. Some forms are shown here. (Norton Co.)

## ABRASIVE GRADES AND SELECTION

The grade of an abrasive depends on the size of the abrasive grains or particles. The older method of grading refers to an aught number or symbol. The newer system, already mentioned, indicates the number of openings in each inch of the silk mesh through which the abrasive grains are screened. Current listings of abrasive paper grades may include both the aught symbol and the mesh number. A wide range of abrasive grades are available as shown in the table in Fig. 11-8. The coarse, very coarse, and extra coarse grades are seldom used in the school shop. They are used in heavy sanding operations on industrial machines. Notice that flint paper does not carry a grade number but is listed under five descriptive grade titles.

Abrasive papers are packaged in lots of 25, 50, and 100 sheets. The lots are called SLEEVES. Ten sleeves are called a UNIT. The standard sheet size is 9 in. by 11 in. Flint paper is sold in 9 in. by 10 in. sheets.

The grade of abrasive paper you select will make considerable difference in the speed and quality of your work. A carefully planed surface can be sanded with a No. 150 paper and be nearly ready for finish. If light tool marks show on the surface it would be best to start with a 100 and finish with a 150. The exact grade of paper that you will need depends on the kind of wood, the surface condition, and the type or quality of work you are doing. When changing from a coarse grade to a finer grade, do not move more than two grade numbers. It would take

| GRAIN TYPES | SILICON CARBIDE | | | ALUMINUM OXIDE | | | GARNET | | | FLINT |
|---|---|---|---|---|---|---|---|---|---|---|
| Extra Coarse | 12 | 16 | 20 | 16<br>4 | 20<br>3½ | | 16<br>4 | 20<br>3½ | | |
| Very Coarse | 24 | 30 | 36 | 24<br>3 | 30<br>2½ | 36<br>2 | 24<br>3 | 30<br>2½ | 36<br>2 | Extra Coarse |
| Coarse | 40 | 50 | | 40<br>1½ | 50<br>1 | | 40<br>1½ | 50<br>1 | | Coarse |
| Medium | 60 | 80 | 100 | 60<br>1/2 | 80<br>0 | 100<br>2/0 | 60<br>1/2 | 80<br>0 | 100<br>2/0 | Medium |
| Fine | 120 | 150 | 180 | 120<br>3/0 | 150<br>4/0 | 180<br>5/0 | 120<br>3/0 | 150<br>4/0 | 180<br>5/0 | Fine |
| Very Fine | 220 | 240 | 280 | 220<br>6/0 | 240<br>7/0 | 280<br>8/0 | 220<br>6/0 | 240<br>7/0 | 280<br>8/0 | Extra Fine |
| Extra Fine | 320 360 400<br>500 600 | | | 320<br>9/0 | 400<br>10/0 | | 320<br>9/0 | 400<br>10/0 | | |

Fig. 11-8. Grade sizes for those coated abrasives used in woodworking. The aught symbol is listed directly below the mesh number of the kinds and grades where it is still used.

a great deal of sanding with a No. 180 paper to remove the heavy scratches left by a No. 80 paper. Coarse grades of paper are used for shaping edges or removing gouge marks.

## SANDING

A full sheet of abrasive paper will usually be too large for your work. You will need to divide it into several smaller pieces. Lay the sheet grain side down on a flat surface and tear it along a steel bench rule, as shown in Fig. 11-9. When working with coarse grades or using a wooden straightedge it is best to scribe a line in the paper with a sharp scratch awl. Paper can also be folded and firmly creased, then torn along the fold line.

## SANDING FLAT SURFACES

When sanding flat surfaces, the paper should be mounted or held on a sanding block. The paper will last longer, resist loading, and do better work if the block has a rubber or felt cushion. The rubber sanding block shown in Fig. 11-10 holds one-fourth of a standard sheet.

Before sanding a surface, remove pencil marks with a rubber eraser or a scraper. Keep your hands clean during sanding operations and during the time you handle the work after sanding. While abrasive paper will cut faster across the grain, SANDING SHOULD BE DONE IN THE DIRECTION OF THE WOOD GRAIN. If you have a heavy defect to remove, you may want to cut across the grain. But remember, you will need to do a great amount of sanding WITH the grain to remove the "cross grain" scratches.

Both pressure and motion are necessary to make abrasive paper cut. You can apply these best when the wood is held in a vise or clamped to a bench top. See Fig. 11-11. Protect sanded surfaces and edges with smooth blocks of scrap wood. Use full strokes and move uniformly over the whole surface. Sand just enough to produce a smooth surface. Ex-

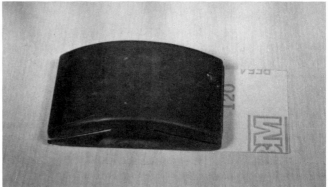

Fig. 11-10. Attaching abrasive paper to rubber sanding block. Top. Place one edge of paper in jaw, abrasive side up. Center. Stretch across bottom of block. Bottom. Place other end in jaw. Be sure paper is properly aligned before closing jaws.

cessive sanding on some woods will undercut the soft grain between annular rings and produce a wavy surface. Thin veneers of hardwood plywood must be sanded lightly and carefully.

## SANDING EDGES, CHAMFERS, AND BEVELS

A sanding block should be used when sanding edges, chamfers, and bevels. Try to keep the block

Fig. 11-9. Tearing a sheet of abrasive paper into smaller pieces.

157

Fig. 11-11. Sanding a surface.

Fig. 11-13. Cleaning sanded work with vacuum cleaner.

from rocking so these surfaces will stay flat and not become rounded. End grain is hard to sand. It is usually best to sand it in only one direction, lifting the block on the return stroke. Fig. 11-12 shows a setup that prevents the end of a board from becoming rounded during a sanding operation. Cut out special blocks to fit concave curves and irregular shapes. Some shapes can be sanded with the paper wrapped around a dowel rod or a wood file. For small intricate parts, tear the paper into narrow strips and use it in this form or glue it (use rubber cement) to thin narrow strips of wood.

## CLEANING SANDED WORK

Complete the sanding operation by brushing off the sand dust and cleaning your workbench. Brush away the dust carefully so you do not fan it into the air and cause it to spread throughout the shop. A vacuum cleaner, Fig. 11-13, will be helpful in this cleanup. It also is very effective in removing dust from the surface, wood pores, and joints of your work. Because sanding creates a large amount of

fine dust, it is advisable to wear a dust mask or respirator while hand sanding.

*Sanding is an important woodworking operation. Select the proper grade of abrasive paper for your work and sand just enough to smooth the surface. Excessive sanding may undercut soft spots in the wood grain and corners and edges may become rounded and uneven.*

Sanding leaves tiny wood fibers only partially cut from the wood surface. A light application of moisture from a damp sponge will cause these fibers to swell and raise above the surface. After they dry they will feel like whiskers and can be removed with a few light strokes of fine paper. This operation is called RAISING THE GRAIN and is an important operation in high quality work. In Fig. 11-14 the

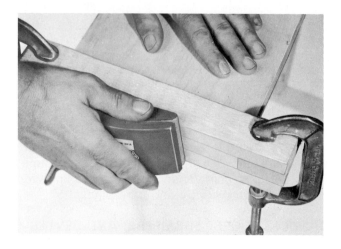

Fig. 11-12. A setup for sanding end of board when it must be kept straight and true.

Fig. 11-14. Using moisture to raise the wood grain.

grain is being raised only on the inside surfaces of a project. After assembly and final touch-up sanding, the other surfaces will receive the same treatment, Fig. 11-15.

## SANDING SMALL PIECES

When wood parts are small it is often easier to clamp or hold the abrasive paper against a flat surface and move the wood over it. Fig. 11-16 shows such a procedure using a SANDING BOARD. The board holds a full sheet of paper that is attached with masking tape. A cleat along the underside of the board is clamped in the vise to hold the board in position.

## USING A WOOD SCRAPER

Cross-grained, curly, or wavy-grained wood is very difficult to plane and should be smoothed with

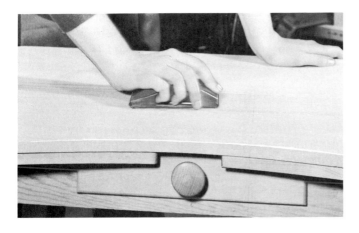

Fig. 11-15. Some surfaces can be sanded best after the article is assembled.

Fig. 11-16. Using sanding board to sand small pieces.

Fig. 11-17. Using hand scraper.

a wood scraper. A scraper will not insure a perfectly flat surface, so a plane should be used first. Take very light cuts and plane across the grain if necessary. The scraper can then be used to smooth the surface before the sanding operation.

## HAND SCRAPER

The hand scraper, Fig. 11-17, can be either pulled or pushed. It is held at an angle of about 75 deg. The angle will vary depending on the way the scraper was sharpened. Heavier cuts can be made when the scraper is pushed. Grip the scraper between the thumb and fingers on each end. Then move the thumbs nearer the center and use them to apply the force.

To sharpen a scraper, first lay the scraper flat on the bench, then draw the burnisher (hardened steel rod) over each side. Place it in the vise and draw file the edge square with the sides as shown in Fig. 11-18. The corners become very sharp and are somewhat dangerous, so it is good practice to round

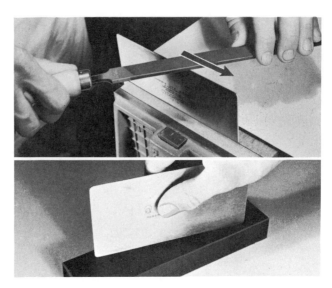

Fig. 11-18. Sharpening a hand scraper. Top. Filing the edge. Bottom. Honing the edge.

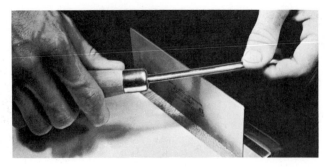

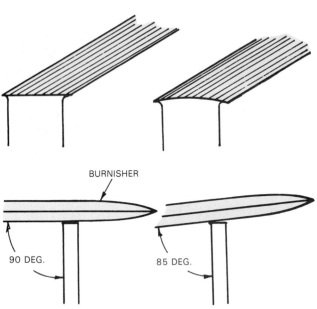

BURNISHER

90 DEG.

85 DEG.

Fig. 11-19. Top. Using a burnisher to form cutting edges. Bottom. Drawings of edges and angles.

them slightly. Hone the edge on an oilstone until it is smooth and sharp on each side. It can be laid flat on the stone for a few strokes to remove any wire edge that may have formed. With the scraper again held in a vise, run a burnisher along the edge. Hold the burnisher at an angle of 90 deg. with the sides for the first stroke. Then gradualy tilt it for the next three or four strokes until it reaches an angle of about 85 deg. Repeat this operation with the burnisher tilted toward the opposite side, Fig. 11-19. Use a drop of oil on the burnisher and press it down firmly. This will form a slight hook on each corner of the edge that will cut a fine silky shaving. A scraper can be sharpened several times with the burnisher before it will need to be filed and honed.

## CABINET SCRAPER

The cabinet scraper, Fig. 11-20, works like the hand scraper. It is easier to hold and better to use if you have a large amount of heavy scraping to do. To adjust the cut, first turn the adjusting thumbscrew out and clear of contact with the blade. Set the scraper on a flat surface and place the blade in

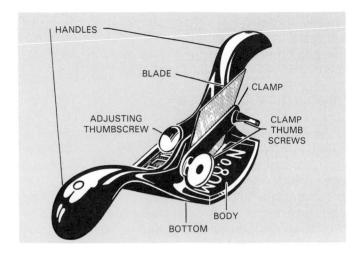

HANDLES

BLADE

CLAMP

ADJUSTING THUMBSCREW

CLAMP THUMB SCREWS

No 80 M

BODY

BOTTOM

Fig. 11-20. Parts of a cabinet scraper. (The Stanley Works)

position with it resting on the surface. Then tighten the clamp thumbscrews. By turning the adjusting thumbscrew you bend the blade slightly, causing it to cut into the surface of the work, Fig. 11-21.

The blade of the cabinet scraper is sharpened by the same method as the hand scraper with the exception that the edge is usually filed to form a 45 deg. bevel.

## REPAIRING DEFECTS

Large defects in wood can be repaired by cutting out the area with a chisel, then carefully fitting in a piece of wood of similar grain and color. This repair takes considerable time, but will hardly be noticed if done skillfully.

To repair a small dent in wood, place a drop of water in the depression. The water will soak into the wood fibers and swell them back to near their original position. When the dent is large, use a hot soldering iron and damp cloth, Fig. 11-22. Too much steaming or wetting is undesirable, especially when working with interior plywood. Allow the sur-

Fig. 11-21. Using the cabinet scraper.

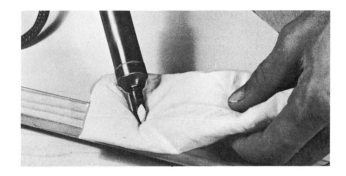

Fig. 11-22. Using a hot soldering iron and a damp cloth to swell a large dent.

face to dry thoroughly before sanding.

Checks, cracks, and holes can be filled with stick shellac, wood putty, or plastic wood. Because these materials will not take stain properly, select a color that will match the final finish. Stick shellac comes in various colors and can be melted and applied with an electrically heated knife. Colors can be mixed to secure the proper shade. See Fig. 11-23. Wood putty is mixed with water for use. It will take stain fairly well. However, it is usually better to color it with dry powders if the required shade is considerably different. On work that will be finished with paint or enamel, the color of the patch need not be considered. Plastic wood is available in several colors. A natural shade can be tinted with colors-in-oil. Place a bit of the color on a paper towel, then mix it with a small portion of plastic wood using a putty knife. Keep the can covered except when removing material. If the plastic wood becomes too hard, it can be softened with lacquer thinner.

Plastic wood shrinks when it dries, so large patches should be filled above the level of the wood. Sand the patches smooth with the surface of the wood after they have hardened.

## THE FINAL TOUCH

After your project is assembled and all defects have been repaired, give it a final light sanding with 150 to 220 paper, Fig. 11-24. Use a block on large surfaces. Use a small pad on edges, ends, and other areas, Fig. 11-25. Use the pad to soften all corners and arrises. With these very slightly round corners there will be less danger of cutting through when rubbing down a coat of finish. Softened corners feel much better to the touch and they also wear better.

Fig. 11-23. Repairing a wood surface. Top. Melting stick shellac into the defect with a burn-in knife. Center. Wood putty is easy to mix and use. Bottom. Adding color to natural shade of plastic wood.

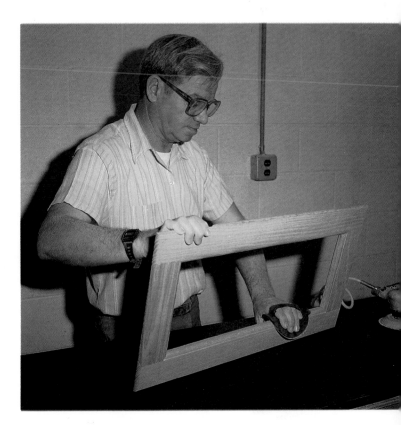

Fig. 11-24. Final sanding before finish is applied. (Campbellrhea Mfg., Inc.)

161

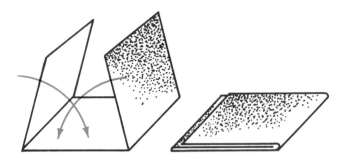

Fig. 11-25. A finger tip and pad for final touch-up sanding. Fold as shown. Use both sides and then interchange the flaps.

Be careful that the abrasive paper does not pick up wood splinters along a sharp edge of the work, especially when sanding the edge of plywood.

Inspect the wood surfaces carefully. You can do this with a close visual inspection and also by feeling them with your hand. Your fingertips are sensitive and can detect variations as fine as a few thousandths of an inch.

Finally, give the project a grain raising operation if necessary and then dust it carefully. Use a brush or a vacuum cleaner to remove all dust and lint. It is now ready for the first coat of finish.

### TEST YOUR KNOWLEDGE, Chapter 11

Please do not write in this text. Place your answers on a separate sheet of paper.

1. This abrasive material has been used through the years for sanding wood and is made from quartz.
   a. Garnet.
   b. Aluminum oxide.
   c. Flint.
   d. None of the above.
2. Which one of the following abrasive materials is not used for wood sanding?
   a. Garnet.
   b. Aluminum oxide.
   c. Emery.
   d. Silicon carbide.
3. The mesh of the screens used to sift abrasive grains are listed by the number of openings _____ _____ _____.
4. The weights of paper used for coated abrasive backings are designated by the letters A, C, D, and _____.
5. Name the two methods for depositing abrasives to backing.
6. Explain the difference between open coated paper and closed coated paper.
7. Standard lots of abrasive paper sheets are called _____.
8. The hand scraper should be used when their is a large amount of heavy scraping to do. True or False?

### ACTIVITIES

1. Prepare a visual aid showing the various kinds and grades of abrasive paper and/or cloth. Attach small swatches of the material to a panel and label them carefully.
2. Develop several sample pieces of wood showing the results of improper sanding. Include a piece of fir that has been oversanded, and a piece with cross-grain scratches, rounded edges or corners. Include others that you feel are important.

The natural beauty of wood adds interest and function to these objects.    (Mark Clauss)

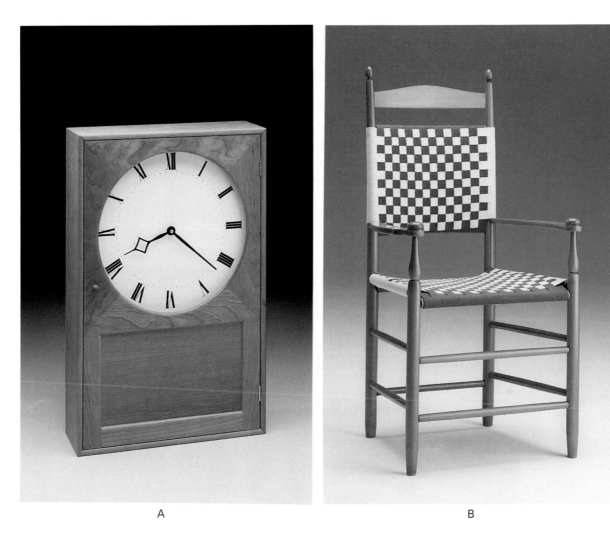

A                                    B

A—Wall clock. This clock is the work of Issac N. Youngs of New Lebanon, New York. The case is cherry with a pine back and the finish is oil. Dimensions: 20 1/2'' x 13 1/2'' x 4''. (Shaker Workshops)   B—Tape back dining armchair. This comfortable chair is simple, functional, and well-constructed. The backposts are bent to the rear and the back rails are curved. Dimensions: 40 3/4'' back height, 25 1/8'' height of arms, 17 1/2'' seat height, 20 3/4'' seat width, and 17 1/8'' depth of seat.   (Shaker Workshops)

Top—Exotic hardwood bowls. The pinstripe bowl is made from Bloodwood, Zircote, and selected veneers. The anasazi bowl is made from Purpleheart, Holly, tropical Walnut, Pau Cetim, and selected veneers. Dimensions: about 4'' x 4''. (Woodcraft Supply Corporation)    Bottom—Burl Bowls. These bowls were made from Big Leaf Maple burls. Burl is a natural growth in trees that produces remarkable and unique distortion in the grain and colors within the wood.
(Woodcraft Supply Corporation)

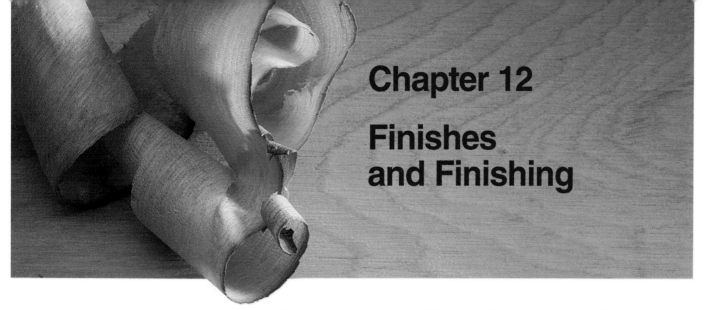

# Chapter 12

# Finishes and Finishing

Wood is a porous, and therefore, absorbent material. If left unfinished, it will absorb moisture, oils, and dirt. As a result of general use, unfinished wood discolors, shrinks, swells, checks, or warps. Finishes can help protect the wood against these conditions and enhance the beauty as well. Finishes, therefore, are important to the appearance and usefulness of the final product, Fig. 12-1.

To do a good job of wood finishing, you must know the properties of the wood, the characteristics of the finish, and the correct and safe methods of application.

## FINISHING SAFETY RULES

1. Wear safety glasses when applying finishing materials.
2. Wear rubber gloves, goggles, and a rubber apron when applying bleaches and acids. These are dangerous materials.
3. Thinners and reducers such as naphtha, benzene, lacquer thinner, and enamel reducer should be applied in a well-ventilated room. Their fumes are toxic.
4. Store all chemicals and soiled rags in proper, safe containers. Many chemicals and the rags used with them are flammable, Fig. 12-2.
5. Wear an approved respirator for finishing operations that involve the use of toxic chemicals such as lacquer thinner and enamel reducers.
6. Spraying should be performed in a well-ventilated booth to reduce toxic fumes.
7. Do not smoke while sanding or applying a finish. Not only will the dust or vapor mix with the smoke creating a hazard to your health, but it may well start a fire.
8. After applying a finish, wash your hands well to remove any toxic materials that you may have handled.
9. Know where the sink, shower, or eye wash station is located in the event you are burned by a finishing material.
10. Provide an approved fire extinguisher(s) in the finishing area.

## WOOD FINISHING TERMS

Knowing the proper term is important when discussing wood finishing materials, procedures,

Fig. 12-1. The beauty of natural wood in this modern kitchen is emphasized and protected by a clear finish. (Haas Cabinet Co.)

Fig. 12-2. Safety containers for volatile thinners. Springs keep spouts closed when not in use.

and conditions. The following terms are commonly used:

ANTIQUING is a process which ages the piece.

BLEACHING removes unwanted natural coloring from wood.

BUILT-UP FINISH does not penetrate the wood, but forms a film on the surface.

DISTRESSING a surface involves intentionally marring a wood surface to create the effect of longtime use and wear. Chains or hammers are commonly used to ''distress'' surfaces.

DRYING TIME consists of two stages: setting and curing. When setting, the volatile liquid evaporates from the finish material. Further drying occurs during curing when a chemical change occurs and the oils and resins harden.

FILLER is a liquid or paste material that contains finely powdered silica and a resin.

FILM FINISH is any finish that can be built by repeated applications to a hard, thick layer on wood.

FISHEYES are small crater-like marks in a finish.

GILDING is the addition of gold accents, especially on edges.

GLOSS TOPCOATING is shiny, smooth, and nearly transparent if it is a clear coating.

GRAINING produces an opaque surface that resembles wood grain.

MARBLIZING gives wood the appearance of marble.

MOTTLING produces the visual effect of texturing even though the surface is smooth.

PATINA is primarily the mellowing and color changes that occur in wood over time.

PENETRATING FINISH is typically a natural oil finish such as linseed oil, tung oil, and wax. Synthetic materials include alkyd and phenotic resin-oil coatings.

PENETRATING STAIN contains dyes and resins that are almost totally absorbed into the wood.

PIGMENT is finely ground powders that are insoluble and provide color and body to a finishing material.

PIGMENT STAIN contains insoluble powdered colors which bond to the wood surface with resins.

POLISHING involves buffing the surface with wax.

PRIMER prepares surfaces for opaque coatings.

SATIN TOPCOATING has a distinct amount of surface texture which diffuses light reflection.

SEALER is a thin clear coat that fills wood pores and serves as a barrier coating.

SEMIGLOSS TOPCOATING is not as shiny or as clear as a clear gloss topcoating.

SHEEN is the degree of gloss in a cured finish.

SOLVENT is any evaporating liquid that will dissolve a cured finish, stain, glaze, or paste-wood filler.

STAIN changes the color, tone, and/or shade of wood.

THINNER is any evaporating liquid—water, mineral spirits, naphtha, lacquer thinner, alcohol—that can be used to thin a finish, stain, glaze, etc., so it can be applied with a brush, cloth, or spray gun.

TOPCOATING is the final protective film that resists moisture, dirt, chemicals, or other harmful substances.

WASHCOAT is a thinned coat of sealer that is often applied before stain.

## BRUSHES

Perhaps the most important tool used during finishing processes is the brush. The skilled woodworker takes pride in having quality tools for the forming and shaping of wood; he or she also gives careful attention to the selection of quality brushes for finishing operations. There are many grades, kinds, and sizes of brushes. Several of the most common brushes are shown in Fig. 12-3.

Fig. 12-4 shows the parts of a brush. The bristle used in brushes is obtained from animals (particularly Chinese hogs which grow long hair), and from manufactured synthetic bristle. Hog bristles are oval in cross section, and have naturally tapered and flagged (split) ends. These flagged ends provide paint holding ability through capillary action. Nylon and polyester (manufactured materials) are also used extensively for brushes. The material is made into filaments that are soft, fine, tapered, and flagged on the end like hog bristles. Nylon or polyester stock will wear longer than natural bristles, and are well suited for water base finishes. Other materials used for brushes include: horse, ox, and fitch hair, and tampico (cactus) fibers.

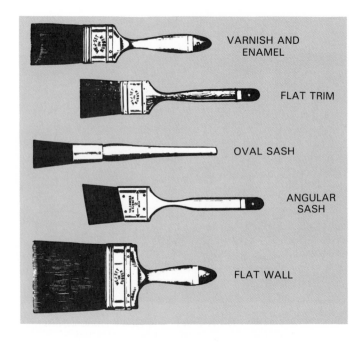

VARNISH AND ENAMEL

FLAT TRIM

OVAL SASH

ANGULAR SASH

FLAT WALL

Fig. 12-3. Five kinds of brushes.

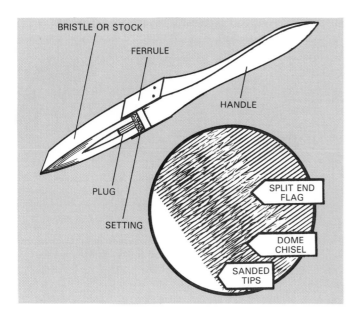

Fig. 12-4. Parts of a brush. Inset shows the tip of a quality brush.

Fig. 12-5. Dip a brush into finishing material one-third to one-half of its bristle length.

A quality brush will have a smooth taper from the ferrule to the tip, formed by varying lengths of bristle. Inside the brush is a PLUG made of wood, metal, fiber, or plastic that forms a reservoir to hold the paint. It must be properly proportioned. Low-quality brushes are often made with an oversize plug to make the brush appear thicker. The SETTING holds the bristle or stock together in the ferrule. Rubber settings have been used extensively. Today, however, they are rapidly being replaced with epoxy resin settings that are tough, durable, and resistant to solvents and thinners.

The sizes of brushes are determined by their width, thickness, and length of the exposed bristle. The thickness is sometimes specified as single (X), double (XX), or triple (XXX).

## USING AND CLEANING BRUSHES

Before using brush, remove any loose bristles and soak the brush in linseed oil for a short time. Soaking is not required for nylon brushes.

When using a brush, dip it into the paint or material only about one-third to one-half of the bristle length. Then pull it lightly over the edge of the container or a large strike wire to remove excess material on the outside, Fig. 12-5.

Select the correct size and kind of brush for the work. Usually it is best to use the smallest size that will still do the work satisfactorily. Avoid using the brush edgewise or jabbing it into corners, cracks, or holes. Do not allow the brush to stand on its bristles either in the finishing material or in a thinner.

Brushes that are used from day to day may be kept suspended in a thinner (never water) or in some cases the finish being used. Rubber brush holders,

like that shown in Fig. 12-13, work well when using shellac, lacquer, and certain synthetic finishes. They are not satisfactory when using finishes with an oil base. In all cases, it is best to thoroughly clean a brush after it has been used. See Fig. 12-6.

To clean a brush, first remove as much of the material as possible by pulling it over the edge of the container and wiping it with a rag or paper towel. Wash the brush thoroughly in the correct thinner and again, wipe it off as much as possible. Do not clean a nylon or polyester brush in paint and varnish remover, or materials containing acetone or lacquer thinner. Now wash the brush in a commercial brush cleaner or a detergent and rinse well in clear water. Carefully strip out the excess water, straighten the bristles or stock and wrap in a paper towel. After it is dry, the brush can be left in this wrapping or replaced in its original jacket.

## PREPARING SURFACES FOR FINISHING

Before an exposed surface can be finished, all surface dents must be removed or repaired. Minor

Fig. 12-6. Materials for cleaning a brush.

defects like machine marks, small scratches, and excess glue can be removed with light sanding. More serious defects such as dents and holes will require repair work.

## REPAIRING DENTS

Dents caused by machining operations, clamping, etc. frequently appear during the construction of a project. Small dents can generally be removed by applying a drop of warm water to the spot. If the dent is too deep to be removed with water alone, it can be removed with an iron (clothes or soldering) and a damp cloth. To use this method, first form a thin pad from several layers of clean cloth. Wet it thoroughly and then wring it out. Place the damp pad over the dent and apply heat with the iron, Fig. 12-7. Move the iron back and forth to prevent the wood from burning. When the surface is dry, it may be sanded smooth.

## FILLING HOLES

Several types of holes or open defects are common in woodworking. Included are open joints, cracks, splits, and gouges. Some type of filler is required for their repair. The basic types of fillers include plugs, plastic wood, wood putty, stick shellac, and wax sticks, Fig. 12-8.

PLUGS are made from an actual piece of wood that is forced into the hole or crack. The advantage of plugs is they have characteristics similar to the surrounding area. The disadvantage is the time required for making, placing, and trimming the plug.

PLASTIC WOOD is a combination of wood powder and plastic hardener. It is available in many colors and can be mixed to match most any wood. Plastic wood applies and dries quickly. Disadvantages of plastic wood include shrinkage, lack of grain pattern, and resistance to stain.

Fig. 12-8. Materials for filling holes and open defects in wood: wood plug, plastic wood, wood putty, stick shellac, and wax sticks.

WOOD PUTTY is a mixture of wood and adhesive in powder form. It is mixed with water to a dough-like consistency. Wood putty is easy to apply, inexpensive, and quick to dry. However, wood putty does not have a grain pattern and shrinks when dry. Water stain can be mixed with it, but it will not take oil stain.

STICK SHELLAC is colored shellac. It is applied with a heated knife. The shellac must match the finished color of the wood since it will not receive stain. It is a hard, durable filler which requires no drying time. Like plastic wood and wood putty, stick shellac has no grain pattern.

WAX STICKS are colored wax that resemble crayons. They are applied by forcing them into the defect and wiping with a cloth. Wax sticks are easy to apply and require no drying time. On the other hand, wax sticks do not take stain, will melt when heated, do not have a grain pattern, and may be dissolved by some finishing solvents.

The best method for repairing a major defect will depend on its size, location, and severity. After gaining experience using these methods, the proper selection will be easier.

## CLEANING AND DISASSEMBLY

Exposed surfaces to be finished must be smooth and free of dust, dirt, glue, and grease. Bottoms, backs, and inside surfaces are usually given at least a sealer coat and should not show unnecessary pencil marks, dirt, or serious blemishes.

Usually it is best to disassemble large pieces as much as possible. For example, removing the back panel of a bookcase will make it easier to brush or spray the shelves as well as the panel. Hardware that has been prefitted should be removed, Fig. 12-9. For some objects, a special hanger or pallet will support the work during the application and/or drying of the finishing coats.

Fig. 12-7. Small dents may be steamed out using a damp pad and heat from an iron.

Fig. 12-9. Prefitted hardware being removed before finish is applied. (The Stanley Works)

## BLEACHING

Wood bleaching is the process of removing some of the natural color from the wood. If a light tone is required it is usually best to select a light colored wood. However, there may be some situations where it is necessary to lighten a dark wood or change the stained color of an article being refinished.

Bleaches commonly used by students are commercially prepared and consist of two solutions. The solutions are mixed together in a glass or porcelain container and the mixture is applied to the bare wood with a rubber sponge or cotton rag. Since woods will vary in the way they respond to bleaching, it is essential that test strips be made on inconspicuous places or on sample stock. WEAR RUBBER GLOVES AND A FACE SHIELD throughout the operation, Fig. 12-10. Most wood bleaches are highly caustic and, therefore, dangerous. Use special care when handling these materials.

When the bleach has surface-dried, sponge lightly with clear water to remove any residue. Allow the surface to dry for at least 12 hours. Sand lightly and proceed with the finishing schedule.

## WOOD FILLERS

The traditional wood filler used by most serious woodworkers is paste wood filler. However, latex fillers and liquid fillers provide additional choices.

### Paste Filler

Walnut, oak, ash, mahogany, and butternut are some of the common hardwoods that have large open pores. They are referred to as OPEN-GRAIN WOODS. See Fig. 12-11. For a smooth surface finish these pores need to be filled with a paste filler.

Paste filler contains silex (powdered quartz), linseed oil, turpentine, and driers. It can be purchased in a natural shade (light buff) and in several colors. Natural paste filler can be colored by adding colors ground in oil. See Fig. 12-12. For a walnut shade use Vandyke brown and burnt umber. For mahogany use Vandyke brown and Venetian red. Filler can also be colored with oil stains. Stir the material thoroughly, then thin with mineral spirits or naphtha to a creamy consistency. Use a thin mix for woods with small pores and a heavier mix for woods with large pores.

Prepare wood for filler by applying a wash coat of shellac or lacquer, Fig. 12-13. A wash coat can be prepared by reducing one part sanding sealer with five parts lacquer thinner, or by reducing one part shellac with seven parts alcohol. After the wash coat is dry, sand it with a 220 paper. Work with the grain. This thin coating will also seal a previously applied stain coat. It makes the surface smooth and somewhat harder so that it will take the filler better. Excess filler will also be easier to remove. This wash coat also prevents staining action by the filler.

Apply the filler with a stiff brush. Thoroughly coat the surface by first brushing with the grain, Fig.

Fig. 12-10. Mixing a commercial wood bleach. Note that the worker is wearing rubber gloves. (Sherwin-Williams Co.)

Fig. 12-11. This photo shows the surface of mahogany. It generally has large pores that require filler to obtain a smooth surface.

Fig. 12-12. Colors in oil on the left can be used to color paste filler on the right.

Fig. 12-13. Applying wash coat of shellac.

Fig. 12-14. Top. Applying paste filler. Center. Wiping off. Bottom. Close-up view.

12-14, and then across the grain. On a small surface, simply pour out a small amount of filler and spread it with your finger tips or the palm of your hand. In a short time (10—20 minutes) the filler will lose its wet or shiny appearance. The excess should be wiped off at this time. Use a coarse rag or piece of burlap and WIPE ACROSS THE GRAIN. Use the palm of your hand to smooth the surface and pack the paste into the wood pores. The filler should be in the pores of the wood and not on the surface. Finish by wiping with the grain, using very light pressure. Use a rag wrapped around a small stick to remove excess filler from corners and small openings.

Once the filler has hardened it is difficult to remove. Therefore apply filler only to sections or areas that can be wiped before it becomes too hard. A cloth lightly saturated with mineral spirits may be used to remove filler that has partially hardened.

Inspect the surface carefully, Fig. 12-15. If the pores are not properly filled repeat the operation after one hour. After the filled surface has dried overnight it can be sanded lightly with fine paper.

### Latex Fillers

Latex fillers are emulsion compounds, similar to latex primers and primer-sealers. They do not raise the wood fibers as do solvent-thinned fillers. Latex fillers also dry quickly and wash off equipment quickly and easily. Follow the manufacturer's instructions for application.

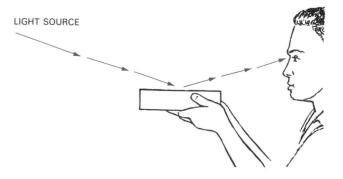

Fig. 12-15. How to inspect a finish. Light rays reflected from the surface will amplify imperfections.

### Clear Fillers

Whenever a paste or latex filler is not desirable, a clear liquid filler may be used to fill the pores of an open-grained wood. Several coats of varnish or lacquer will do the job. They both produce a bright and deep appearance, but considerable time and effort are necessary for their application. If the final coat of the piece will be lacquer, it may be easier to fill the pores with several coats of sanding sealer. It is easy to sand and is less expensive than lacquer. Each coat should be sanded, but not through the finish.

Clear fillers produce a deeper finish than paste or latex fillers, but require more time and work. Clear fillers may be applied with brushes or spraying equipment.

## FINISHING OPERATIONS

Once all defects are repaired, all pores filled, and all final sanding and disassembly completed, the finishing schedule can continue.

## CHOOSING THE RIGHT SOLVENT

Even though water-based finishes and adhesives are becoming more widespread, solvents other than water will be useful from time to time.

Solvents are one of two types—INERT SOLVENTS and REACTIVE SOLVENTS. Substances like mineral spirits and lacquer thinner are inert solvents. They reduce the viscosity of finishes and allow deeper penetration, faster drying, and more uniform application. These solvents don't alter the composition of the oils or resins used in the finish. Inert solvents make good thinners, degreasers, and cleaners because they can mix freely with a substance without disturbing its molecular structure.

Reactive solvents can dissolve stains or adhesives and strip finishes because they break apart the molecular bonds. Reactive solvents change substances permanently. Therefore, they cannot be used to thin paint. Strange as it may seem, water is a reactive solvent when it is used with soap. It alters the structure of grease and dirt molecules, making them water soluble.

You should always use less-dangerous chemicals instead of highly toxic solvents whenever possible. For example, use lacquer thinner for thinning lacquer not cleaning brushes. Use ethanol (denatured, ethyl, or grain alcohol) to dilute shellac instead of the more toxic wood or methyl alcohol. Never use carbon tetrachloride as a degreaser because a single exposure to its strong vapors could be fatal. Instead, use mineral spirits or naphtha to remove oil or wax residue. Methylene chloride is a major ingredient in most paint removers and non-flammable types of contact cement. The vapors of this chemical have a strong effect and may disrupt your heartbeat. Methylene chloride is also one of two solvents that pass freely through the filter cartridges of organic-vapor respirators. (The other is methyl alcohol.) Use goggles because a small droplet can cause serious eye damage. The chart in Fig. 12-16 lists common solvents and their uses.

Use brushes and rollers whenever possible to reduce toxic vapors because the dilutents used in both compressor-powered sprayers and spray can finishes are also highly toxic. Most of these solvents (dilutents) are some type of petroleum distillates and can cause eye and throat irritation, nerve damage, liver and kidney injury, and blood diseases.

The least-hazardous choice for brush-on varnish and paint thinner is mineral spirits. Turpentine also has low toxicity, but it is more likely to cause an

| COMMON SHOP SOLVENTS | | | |
|---|---|---|---|
| Solvent | Uses/Applications | Chemical Type | Usual Route of Absorption |
| Acetone | Cleaner, thinner for epoxy and plastic cement, degrease base metal | Reactive | Lungs |
| Ethanol (denatured or ethyl alcohol) | Shellac, spirit stain thinner | Reactive | Lungs |
| Ethyl acetate | Aerosols, plastic cement | Reactive | Lungs and skin |
| Halogenated solvents | Paint and varnish remover, refinishers, contact cements, aerosols adhesives, some paints, degreasers | Inert | Lungs and skin |
| Hexane | Rubber and contact cements | Inert | Lungs and skin |
| Isopropanol (isopropyl or rubbing alcohol) | Surface cleaner | Reactive | Lungs and skin |
| Lacquer thinner | Quick-dry thinner, thinner for two-part epoxies, degrease base metal | Inert | Lungs and skin |
| Methanol (methyl alcohol) | Shellac, spirit stain thinner, finish stripper, blush | Reactive | Lungs and skin |
| Methyl ethyl ketone | Aerosols, plastic cement | Reactive | Lungs |
| Methyl isobutyl ketone | Aerosols, plastic cement | Reactive | Lungs |
| Mineral spirits | General-purpose thinner, degreaser, brush cleaner, wood filler | Inert | Lungs and skin |
| Turpentine | General-purpose thinner, degreaser, brush cleaner, wood filler | Inert | Lungs and skin |
| VM&P naphtha (Benzine) | Quickdry thinner, degreaser cleaner | Inert | Lungs and skin |

Fig. 12-16. Be sure you have the right solvent for your application.

allergic skin reaction. Repeated skin exposure to most solvents except water can cause skin irritation.

The most flammable shop solvent is acetone. It, as well as quick-dry solvents, poses a serious fire hazard. Proper storage and disposal of these dangerous chemicals is very important. Flammable chemicals should be stored in approved, sealed containers in a steel cabinet that is vented to the outside. A metal bucket with a lid will provide safe storage for solvent-laden rags until they can be disposed of.

The following suggestions may be helpful in disposing of solvents in a responsible manner.
1. Never pour flammable solvents or hazardous waste compounds down the drain.
2. Never pour hazardous liquids in surface water or ditches as they may enter the groundwater.
3. Mix hazardous liquids with non-reactive absorbents (like cat litter) and dry the material or seal it in a container. Do not use sawdust because that could lead to spontaneous combustion.
4. Air-dry brushes, rags, and the hazardous liquids remaining in containers outside or in a well-ventilated area before disposal.
5. Recycle waste finishes and solvents by brushing them on an old board or take advantage of community recycling efforts or exchange programs for paints and varnishes.
6. Rethink your finishing processes to reduce or eliminate hazardous materials.

## PROPER VENTILATION AND FIRE SAFETY

Adequate ventilation requires a steady flow of fresh air across a work area in a direction that carries fumes away from the worker. This means CROSS VENTILATION. If you smell a strong odor or become dizzy, you should leave the room immediately. However, some solvents are dangerous long before you can smell them. For example, a safe level of methyl alcohol is 200 ppm (parts per million), but most people can't smell it until the vapor level reaches 2000 to 6000 ppm. Remember that most solvent vapors are two to four times heavier than air and will accumulate near the floor. This is especially important in basement shops and storage areas. An air-to-air exchanger and a spark-free fan are ideal for basements.

Records compiled by the National Fire Protection Association show that spontaneous combustion is a leading cause of woodshop fires. Turpentine and oil finishes are especially hazardous because they tend to oxidize in air. A pile of oil- or turpentine-soaked rags can reach ignition temperature in a few hours. Dispose of waste each day to reduce the hazard.

## STAINING

Staining will emphasize or de-emphasize the grain and will add color to the wood surface. Most stains used on exterior woodwork have a preservative feature. Staining is not essential in obtaining a finished surface. Many woods have the most beauty when finished using clear finish.

Stains are generally classified in three groups. They are water, oil, and spirit (alcohol or acetone base). SPIRIT STAINS dry and set up rapidly. Their use is generally limited to spray application. Industry uses a stain similar to spirit stain called non-grain-raising (NGR). It is fast drying like spirit stain but has better clarity and fade resistance.

There are two general types of OIL STAIN: penetrating and pigmented. See Fig. 12-17. PENETRATING STAINS are brushed on and the excess is wiped off. A cloth pad can be used for the application. The stain should dry 24 hours. Then it should be sealed with a thin coat of shellac or other sealer. The sealer is especially important on dark stains such as mahogany or walnut to prevent the stain color from "bleeding" into the finished coats. Lighter tones can be produced by thinning or by wiping dark stain immediatley after application. Soft porous woods are usually given a wash coat of shellac (seven parts alcohol, one part shellac) before applying a penetrating stain. End grain may be coated with mineral spirits or thinned linseed oil before applying an oil type stain. This prevents excessive penetration. Fig. 12-18 shows the application of an oil stain.

PIGMENTED STAINS are applied in about the same manner as penetrating stains. For heavy "toning" effects, allow these stains to dry without wiping. They dry in about 12 hours, and usually do not require a shellac sealer. Carefully study the

Fig. 12-17. This oil base stain cleans up with soap and water. A clear coat over the stained surface is required to seal in the stain. (Deft, Inc.)

Fig. 12-18. Applying an oil base stain with a cloth. Do not allow the stain to dry before it is wiped. Wipe with the grain to remove the excess. (Deft, Inc.)

manufacturer's directions. Try the stain on a scrap of wood before applying it to your project. You can see the final appearance better if you coat the sample with sealer. Once the stain is applied, it is difficult to change the effect obtained. Therefore, it is important that it be done right the first time. Use turpentine or a turpentine substitute (mineral spirits) for a thinner.

WATER STAINS are made by mixing dry powders and water. They come in a variety of colors and shades. The grain of the wood should always be raised before using this type of stain. Water stains penetrate deeply and have little tendency to fade. Additional coats can be applied to darken the wood. If the wood is too dark, it can be lightened, using a sponge and hot water. Fig. 12-19 shows water stain being used to color a sap streak. After it dries, the entire surface should be given a light coat of stain. Reduce the strength of the stain on end grain or apply a wash coat of shellac to prevent excessive penetration. Allow water stain to dry at least 12 hours before completing the finishing schedule.

Ready-made water base stains are also available. These are applied with a brush, roller, or cloth pad. They are then wiped in about the same way as

Fig. 12-19. Using water stain to darken sap streak in walnut. To make stain, mix a small amount of dry powder in warm water.

described for pigmented oil stains. They dry rapidly, so on large projects individual sections should be completed before proceeding to others. Ready-made water base stains do not raise the grain as much as regular water stain and do not penetrate very deep. They should not be sanded until after a sealer coat has been applied. They work best on wood that does not require a paste filler.

## SEALERS

A sealer coat "ties down" the stain and filler already applied and prevents absorption of the finish coat into the wood. When working with a closed-grain wood that is not stained, the sealer will be the first coat of finishing material applied. It will seal the porous wood and act as a foundation for surface coats. Its purpose is to seal out moisture and dirt. Therefore, a sealer coat should be applied to all surfaces of your project, whether they are beneath the surface, otherwise hidden, or surfaces that may not receive any additional finish. For example, always seal the bottom side of a chair seat or tabletop. Moisture may cause dimensional change and/or warpage.

Shellac is used extensively as a sealer. It dries dust free in about 15 minutes and can be rubbed or recoated in about two hours. Only fresh shellac should be used. Mixtures over six months old tend to deteriorate and do not dry properly. When using shellac for a sealer coat, a 4 lb. cut should be reduced with an equal amount of alcohol. Coats of shellac are usually smoothed with steel wool because they will load dry papers.

Lacquer base sealer (called sanding sealer) is designed for spray application but can be brushed on smaller projects. It will dry in about 10 minutes, and can be sanded with a 6/0 dry paper in about 30 minutes. It cuts off as a powder, does not load the paper, and provides a smooth surface on which to apply finish coats.

Shellac is not waterproof and will water spot. Sanding sealer is soft and does not resist wear, for which reason it is not well suited for use as finish coat. Additional coats of shellac or sanding sealer may be used for final coats for small projects where a tough finish is not required.

In addition to shellac and lacquer, there are many oil-base and latex sealers available that can be applied by brushing or spraying. These provide an excellent sealer for wood and have good sanding qualities. They usually require overnight drying.

## SHADING AND GLAZING

With the surface filled, sealed, and ready for final coats, shading or glazing may be undertaken. The shading operation is usually performed by spraying a dye tinted lacquer (shading lacquer) over the surface. This adds a light tone or shade of color, making it more uniform. It also can be used for special effects or variations. Similar results can be secured by adding the required color tint to a commercial glazing liquid, brushing it on, then wiping it off with a rag or clean brush. Most glazes have an oil base and require several hours to dry.

Special effects can be secured by applying tinted or shaded glaze to carvings or moldings, wiping the glaze from the high spots, and leaving it in the recesses. The procedure is sometimes used when restoring and refinishing furniture. This gives it an "antique" effect, Fig. 12-20.

## CLEAR FINISHES

Clear finishes may be categorized as PENETRATING FINISHES and SURFACE FINISHES. Each group has special attributes which makes it useful for certain applications.

PENETRATING FINISHES. There are penetrating finishes available referred to as "rub-on" or "close-to-the-wood" finishes. These finishes penetrate into the wood surface and bring out the beauty of the grain, Fig. 12-21. Some penetrating finishes never dry completely, while others harden in the wood. Penetrating oil finishes cannot be applied over woods that have been sealed. They should be used on raw wood or over penetrating oil.

DRYING OILS, such as linseed oil, are available raw or boiled. Raw linseed oil should be avoided because it never hardens. Boiled linseed oil is a true drying oil and produces a solid film. The film, however, will remain comparatively soft even after an extended period. Boiled linseed oil is usually applied in a number of thin coats and rubbed in by hand. This finish should never be overcoated with shellac or lacquer because the penetrated linseed

Fig. 12-21. These penetrating finishes are used together to seal and coat. (General Finishes)

oil will remain semisoft. This will cause poor surface adhesion. Linseed oil was used extensively in the past because it was readily available and easy to apply. However, it was also found to have poor resistance to wear, poor resistance to moisture, and a need for frequent reapplication.

A modern alternative to boiled linseed oil is a product that uses linseed oil in a resin form. It is commonly known as Danish oil finish. It penetrates into the cell cavities and solidifies. It is very easy to apply—brush the finish material on raw wood until it cannot absorb any more. Then wipe the surface dry with a cloth. Repeat the procedure the next day until the surface attains the desired degree of luster. Danish oil finish discolors wood slightly and darkens with age, but is a very popular finishing material.

Tung oil (China wood oil) can also be used in place of boiled linseed oil. It dries to a harder film than linseed oil and is more resistant to moisture. This oil dries to a dull, nonglossy finish even when applied in several thin coats. Heavy coats tend to wrinkle.

As an alternative to tung oil, there are several products that contain very effective dryers. These products produce hard, dry finishes. The finish is applied by wiping it on the surface where it acts as a penetrating sealer. Additional coats will produce a more lustrous finish.

RUBBING OILS are available in several formulas. Most are just a diluted varnish combined with a large amount of oil. These products usually penetrate well, dry hard, and produce an attractive finish. Rubbing oils cause very little surface buildup. Application procedures vary somewhat. Follow the manufacturer's directions.

It is important to keep all penetrating oil finishes sealed tightly when they are not in use. Oxygen in the air will mix with the oil in the finish and dry to form a hard skin on the surface. This layer must be removed before use again as it will not dissolve.

Fig. 12-20. Skilled workers wipe glaze-coated surfaces to produce highlights and special effects. (Thomasville Furniture Industries, Inc.)

Penetrating finishes may be maintained by applying a wax or furniture polish, or mineral oil. Add a small amount of vinegar and turpentine to mineral oil for an effective cleaner for penetrating finishes.

SURFACE FINISHES. Clear surface finishes that are popular for wood include shellac, varnish, lacquer, and acrylic finishes.

SHELLAC is used as a surface finish on wood, but is more frequently used as a surface sealer. This finish dries (dust free in 30 minutes) by evaporation of a solvent—called denatured alcohol.

The shellac resin is a product of the lac bug and may be purchased in ready-to-use alcoholic solution as either orange or white shellac, Fig. 12-22. Orange shellac will give some color to the wood, but white shellac will not. Orange shellac is more moisture resistant than white shellac, but neither are suitable for exterior finish. Water turns shellac white and alcohol dissolves a shellac finish. Shellac has a shelf life of about six months.

Shellac is thinned with denatured alcohol to the desired cut. CUT means the number of pounds of shellac dissolved in a U.S. gallon of alcohol or 4/5 of an imperial gallon. A two- or three-pound cut is recommended for most furniture work.

A shellac finish may be applied with a brush or spray gun. Use thin coats and work quickly. Avoid repeating brush strokes to eliminate brush marks due to rapid drying. The surface should be lightly sanded between coats with 220 to 230 grit silicon carbide abrasive. Apply at least three coats to obtain a suitable finish. After the final coat, the finish may be rubbed out with pumice and rottenstone, steel wool, or commercial rubbing compound, Fig. 12-23. Brushes or spraying equipment may be cleaned with denatured alcohol.

FRENCH POLISH is a mixture of two parts shellac (three- or four-pound cut), two parts denatured

Fig. 12-23. Commercial rubbing compound is used to provide a smooth finished coat.

alcohol, and one part boiled linseed oil. The linseed oil acts as a lubricant for the shellac. The mixture is rubbed onto the wood surface using a special cloth pad of tightly woven cotton or linen. The pad being rubbed against the surface of the wood creates heat and speeds the drying. As the polish builds on the wood surface, a deep gloss will begin to appear, Fig. 12-24. Any swirl marks left by the pad may be wiped out using a cloth dampened in denatured alcohol.

French polish is available commercially. Specific instructions for the application of the products are given on the container.

VARNISH is a mixture of oil, resin, solvent, and drier. There are four types of varnish: oil varnish, polyurethane varnish, acrylic varnish, and spirit varnish.

Fig. 12-22. White shellac is an excellent surface sealer, but may also be used as a surface finish.

Fig. 12-24. Applying French polish with a cloth. French polish is a mixture of shellac, alcohol, and boiled linseed oil.

OIL VARNISHES are made from fossil gums or resins in oil, turpentine or mineral spirits, and driers. The amount of oil in the mixture greatly affects the resistance to water and alcohol, elasticity of the film, and brittleness. Spar varnish has a high percentage of oil and is classified as a long-oil varnish. This means it is highly resistant to water and alcohol. Short-oil varnish has a small amount of oil. It rubs well, but is brittle. Medium-oil varnish is an all-purpose varnish which is reasonably tough and elastic, Fig. 12-25.

POLYURETHANE VARNISH is a synthetic varnish, made from resins and polymers, thinned with mineral spirits. This type of varnish has no oil and dries by moisture-curing. Polyurethane varnish has improved weather resistance and better drying properties, is very tough and flexible, and has superior resistance to chipping and abrasion. It dries to the touch in 20 minutes and is hard in four to five hours, Fig. 12-26.

ACRYLIC VARNISH is non-yellowing and colorless. It is composed of acrylic-resin glycols, mineral spirits, and water. This finish is hard, tough, and comparatively brittle. It dries in 2 hours and has little odor. The surface has good abrasion resistance. Recoating requires sanding down to bare wood and starting over. Acrylic varnish can be thinned by adding water. It can be colored with universal tinting colors. Clean tools with warm, soapy water.

SPIRIT VARNISH is made from resins or gums and a solvent such as alcohol or turpentine. (Shellac is a spirit varnish.) This finish material dries quickly through evaporation of the solvent and provides a finish that is less durable than other varnishes.

WATER-BASED VARNISH has been developed because of pressure from OSHA and EPA. Both OSHA and EPA seek finishes that do not rely so much on VOLATILE ORGANIC COMPOUNDS (VOCs). Water-Reducible Conversion Varnish is a new product that meets VOC regulations.

Fig. 12-26. Polyurethane varnish contains no oil. It is weather resistant and is very tough and flexible. (United Gilsonite Laboratories)

Water-based varnish has an appearance like traditional solvent-based varnishes and does not produce the hazy appearance of some water-based finishes. The finish is designed for use on furniture, cabinets, and other interior wood products. One such product, Sher-Wood Kemvar "W" Water Reducible Conversion Varnish, is compatible with Sher-Wood solvent stains and waterborne wiping stains. This finishing system meets the test requirements of the Kitchen Cabinet Manufacturers Association.

Water-based finishes do, however, tend to raise the grain of wood more than solvent-based finishes. Therefore, more sanding is required, but that isn't a bad tradeoff for a safer product.

The Water-Reducible Varnish is catalyzed. It consists of two components—a base and a catalyzer—which must be mixed by the user. Water-based varnish can be applied with most commercial spraying equipment and dries in 20 to 30 minutes.

LACQUER generally has the following ingredients: nitrocellulose, a solvent (such as acetone), varnish resins, a diluting agent (such as benzene or toluene), and plasticizers or softeners (to produce a more elastic finish). Many kinds of lacquer products are available to the woodworker.

Lacquer produces a clear, hard finish that dries very quickly. Spraying and brushing lacquers are essentially the same except that the solvent/thinner evaporates more slowly in brushing lacquer. This allows brush marks to level out before the surface hardens. Brushing lacquer is very seldom ever thinned, but spraying lacquer is always thinned. Spraying is the preferred method of application. Use a pure bristle brush for brushing lacquer.

Fig. 12-25. These two surfaces were finished with medium-oil varnish over 25 years ago. They are still beautiful, with no cracks or chips.

A lacquer finish may be rubbed or polished to almost any degree of gloss, Fig. 12-27. However, many coats are required to develop the same thickness produced in one application of varnish. Thinners made by one company are not recommended for use with lacquer products from another company because of the wide variety of formulas used.

Lacquer fumes are toxic and application should be performed in a well-ventilated room or spray booth. Lacquer is also flammable and should be kept away from open flames. Wear an approved respirator when spraying lacquer, Fig. 12-28.

ACRYLIC finishes are similar in quality to lacquer finishes, but have none of the fire hazard characteristics. These finishes use water as a solvent and will cause exposed bare metal fasteners to rust if not covered with wood filler. Acrylic finishes may be sprayed or brushed. Always wear a respirator when spraying acrylic finishes. A nylon bristle brush should be used for brushing acrylic materials.

Acrylic finishes have a milky appearance when they are applied, but this will disappear as the finish dries, Fig. 12-29. Acrylic can be applied over most any other finish. Each coat should be sanded with 320 grit silicon carbide abrasive to improve bond between coats. Acrylic finish material can be cleaned by using soap and warm water.

## PAINT AND ENAMEL

If you build your project of a softwood or of a wood that does not have an attractive grain pattern, you may want to finish it with paint or enamel.

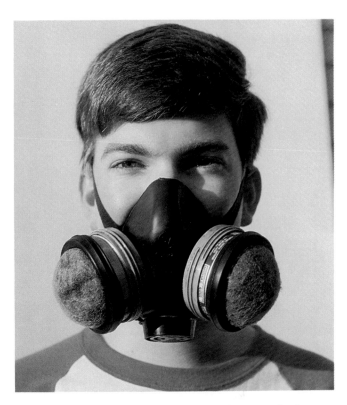

Fig. 12-28. This respirator can be used when spraying lacquer.

Fig. 12-29. Even after a coat of clear acrylic was applied to these brass parts, they still showed tarnish that resulted from exposure to air. (Amerock Corp.)

PAINT is a general term used to identify opaque finishes. Paint is a mixture of oils, emulsions, driers, and pigments. ENAMELS consist of natural or synthetic varnishes with pigments added.

Surfaces need not be as carefully prepared for opaque finishes as for clear finishes; they should be smooth and clean. Small checks, cracks, and nail holes can be filled with water putty, preferably after the undercoater or primer has been applied. Knits or sap streaks (often present in wood such as pine) should be sealed with a coat of shellac before painting.

Enamel finishing materials are shown in Fig. 12-30. Brush on a coat of undercoater or primer.

Fig. 12-27. The finish on this wood car body was produced with several coats of lacquer. Each coat was rubbed before the next one was applied.

Fig. 12-30. Materials for an enamel finish: enamel, reducer, and primer.

The undercoater will seal the wood pores and form a foundation for the finish coats. After it is dry, sand lightly, wipe off the surface carefully, and apply a coat of enamel. If a second coat of enamel is necessary, the first coat should be cut lightly with a fine abrasive paper. The final coat should not be rubbed. If a soft sheen is desired, a semigloss enamel or paint should be selected.

Oil base paints are prepared and applied in about the same way as enamel. Use turpentine or mineral spirits for thinning these materials and also for cleaning brushes. Always mix paint and enamels thoroughly before using.

## Color Selection

Color selection is an important consideration when working with paints and enamels. Study

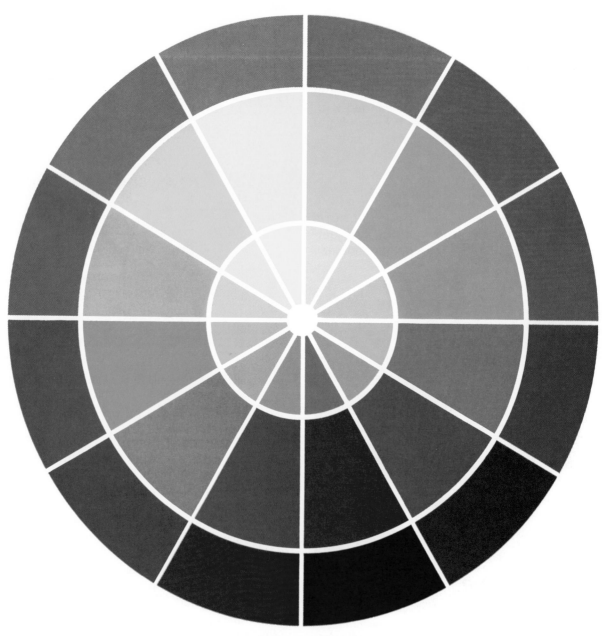
Fig. 12-31. Color wheel.

178

reference materials to learn more about the principles that apply. Here are a few of the basic terms and definitions with which you should be familiar:

HUE: A particular name of a color, like red or orange.

PRIMARY COLORS: Red, blue, yellow.

SECONDARY COLORS: Violet, green, orange.

INTERMEDIARY COLORS: Red-violet, blue-violet, blue-green, yellow-orange, red-orange.

RELATED COLORS: Hues side by side on the color wheel. See Fig. 12-31.

COMPLEMENTARY COLORS: Hues opposite each other on the color wheel.

VALUE: The lightness or darkness of a color.

TINT: Color nearer white in value. Pure color with white added.

SHADE: Color nearer black in value. Pure color with black added.

## Painting

When working with several colors or intricate patterns and designs, masking tape will often help secure a professional job. Masking takes a little more time at the start but usually results in overall time savings. Apply the tape carefully and avoid stretching as much as possible. Remove it as soon as the finish has set by pulling it from the work at about a 90 deg. angle. Masking (pressure-sensitive) tape is perishable and should not be stored for long.

Latex emulsion paints are a satisfactory finish for wall shelves, picture frames, and other projects that are not subjected to hard use. These paints apply easily, dry quickly, require no primer, and use water as a thinner. They are available in a wide range of colors and can be applied with a spray gun, brush, or roller. See Fig. 12-32.

When painting large surfaces a roller can often be used to good advantage. See Fig. 12-33. A brush with nylon bristles is recommended for water base finishes. Brushes with regular bristles will absorb moisture and will become "soggy" and lose

Fig. 12-33. Using roller to apply latex wall paint. (Sherwin-Williams Co.)

their rigidity and snap. Brushes and rollers should be cleaned in soap and water immediately after use. Brushes or equipment used in the application of some exterior latex paints must be cleaned in a commercial brush cleaner. Spatters and drops of latex emulsion paint are easily wiped up with a damp rag immediately after they are spilled. However, they are difficult to remove after they have set for 15 minutes or more. Application of latex exterior paint is shown in Fig. 12-34.

## EPOXY AND POLYESTER RESIN

Epoxy resin finish can be applied to wood, metal, fiberglass, and nearly any other type of surface. It too has high resistance to moisture, acid, abrasion, and weathering. Industry uses epoxy resin coatings on foundry patterns, printed electrical circuits, bows and arrows, fiberglass products, and many other products that require an unusually tough finish.

Fig. 12-32. Latex emulsion paint. Polyester brushes are also recommended.

Fig. 12-34. Exterior latex (water-base) paint being applied to exterior surface. This paint has high resistance to blistering and peeling. (Sherwin-Williams Co.)

Epoxy resin is a two-part product. The two containers are sometimes fastened together as in Fig. 12-35. Shake the containers and then pour equal amounts into a mixing pot. Stir for several minutes, then let the mixture set for 30 minutes before applying. The first coat on new wood should be reduced with a special thinner that is also used for cleaning brushes and equipment. It will be dry to the touch in about one hour, and can be recoated in about four hours. Pot life (length of time mixed portion in pot should be used) is 24 hours, but it can be kept longer if refrigerated. Manufacturers provide specific instruction for their product. Follow these closely.

Polyester resin films are clear and hard and form a surface that is quite comparable to that of a plastic laminate material. The liquid resin must be mixed with a catalyst (substance which by its presence produces reaction between other substances). It is then applied in a heavy coat to form a film (4 to 10 mils). The strength and hardness of a polyester finish is not secured in films as thin as conventional finishes. Since work with this resin must be carefully controlled, its application is largely limited to industrial production, where it is used extensively for the finish on desk and table tops.

## WATER-BASED FINISHES

Many water-based wood-finishing products have become available in recent years. Each promises to be environmentally safe and easy to clean up. These products are generally safer to use, but they have properties that are very different from their traditional, solvent-based equivalents. Mixing and thinning them is different. Applying them is also different. They even appear different straight from the can. (Learning to use them to achieve a high-quality finish will take some time even for the experienced finisher.)

The reason for the development of new water-based wood finishes is largely in response to recent governmental regulations restricting the amount of solvent or volatile organic compounds (VOCs) in finishing materials, such as clear finishes, sealers, fillers, stains, and paints. As a result of this regulation, fewer solvent-based products will be available in the future.

Most oil finishes such as 100 percent tung oil and boiled or raw linseed oil, will not be affected. Oil-varnish mixtures, like Watco Danish Oil, may be changed slightly to reduce VOCs and commercially prepared shellac will be available in not less than a 3-lb. cut. High solids varnish (not water-based) are already in compliance with reduced VOCs.

Most finishes used in a typical woodworking shop have been solvent-based which includes traditional

Fig. 12-35. Mixing epoxy resin. The two cans are permanently attached.

lacquers, varnishes, polyurethanes, and shellac. Water-based finishes use the same general resin types as solvent-based finishes—polyurethane and acrylic—but formulations are much more complicated. Water-based finishes, Fig. 12-36, also generally contain surfactants, defoamers, thickeners, flow-out additives, mar reducers, and other additives necessary to make the resin compatible with water. However, they are non-flammable, easy to clean up, mostly non-toxic, and low in odor. These characteristics can result in lower insurance rates and no need for an explosion-proof spray booth.

Water-based finishes do have some problems, though. They sometimes develop poor film properties when dried in a humid environment. Storage areas must always stay above freezing. Many water-based finishes are not easy to apply. They also typically raise the grain more than solvent-based finishes. Some of them may not be compatible with traditional oil-based stains, sealers, and fillers. Finally, some water-based finishes won't tolerate thinning. Only distilled water should be used as a thinner since water containing minerals can cause sand-like specks in the finish.

Fig. 12-36. This clear satin lacquer is non-toxic, non-flammable, and environmentally safe.
(Hydrocote Finishing Products)

## FINISHING ROOM

Most school shops have a separate enclosed area for the application of finishes. This area should be well lighted and properly heated. In addition, special attention should be given to ventilation and cleanliness. The air should be free of dust and have a humidity range of 25 to 40 percent. The room temperature should be 70 degrees or above.

Materials and supplies, Fig. 12-37, should be carefully organized. There should be space for bulk storage and easily accessible space for small working quantities. Arrange containers in an orderly manner and in such a way that the labels can be read without turning them around. All containers should have neat and accurate labels.

Working surfaces (tables or bench tops) should be of metal or composition material that will not be harmed by the finishes. Walls, ceilings, and floors should be of materials that can be easily cleaned.

Wood finishing requires extra attention to maintenance and housekeeping responsibilities. You might leave lumber racks and tools in disorder and be able to correct them the next day but in the finishing room, paint filled brushes, open containers, and spilled materials must be cared for at once or loss and damage will result. Below is a list of directions to follow as you perform your finishing operations.

1. Clean up your materials and return them to their proper place as soon as you have finished your work.
2. Close containers by first wiping out the lip and then sealing the lid tightly. Wipe off the outside. See Fig. 12-38. Open containers by prying carefully all the way around the lid.
3. Keep storage shelves in order with materials in their proper places and labels turned to the front.
4. Clean brushes carefully and return them to their place of storage.
5. Clean any working surfaces that you have used.
6. Rags that contain finishing materials should be discarded by taking them directly to the school incinerator or storing them in a metal container.
7. Store your project in an approved location.
8. Use care while working around other students' projects.
9. Do not use the finishing area for sanding, rubbing, or polishing a finish.
10. The finishing room is designed for the mixing, application, and drying of finishes. Its use should be restricted to these activities.

## APPLYING TOPCOATS

After the wood has been stained, filled, and sealed, you are ready to apply the final surface finishes.

When applying lacquer and synthetic varnish, as in applying all finishes, the SURFACES OF YOUR PROJECT MUST BE CLEAN. Brush carefully and then wipe with a tack cloth (cloth treated so it will pick up lint and dust). Commercially prepared tack cloths are available at reasonable cost, Fig. 12-39.

Thin the finish if necessary, so it will flow easily. Dip the brush in the material about one-third of the bristle length and then rub the brush against the inside edge of the container to remove the excess material. When applying finishing material to your

Fig. 12-37. Finishing materials in working quantities.

Fig. 12-38. Be sure to wipe out lip before closing container.

Fig. 12-39. Wiping surface lightly with a tack cloth before applying final coat.

Fig. 12-41. Good lighting is important. Keep the work between you and a major source of light.

project, move the brush over the surface with just enough pressure to cause the bristles to bend a little, Fig. 12-40. Use fairly long strokes, working in the direction of the grain of the wood. Work rather quickly, completing one section at a time. On some slower drying finishes you can brush first across the grain and then finish with the grain. When using fast drying finishes, move the loaded brush from the dry surface into the wet surface. Do not go back over the work after it has been coated. Keep the surface being coated between you and a major light source so you will have a good view of the work and will not miss any spots, Fig. 12-41.

Usually it is best to coat "hard-to-reach" surfaces first. Brush edges and ends before the faces; bottoms before the tops. On some jobs you may find it best to coat the bottom surfaces, allow them to dry, then turn the project over and do the sides and top. See Fig. 12-42. You can make a tripod on which to rest the work by driving nails all the way through a thin piece of wood. Fig. 12-43 shows a project with small nails driven into the underside to support it during the application and drying of finishing coats. Some pieces may be coated all over, then hung by a string or wire to dry.

Most projects require at least two coats of varnish or lacquer. The first coat should be cut down

Fig. 12-42. Coating bottom surfaces first.

Fig. 12-43. Work supported on small nails driven into underside.

dry with 3/0 steel wool or 6/0 finishing paper. Clean the surface carefully. Apply a second coat.

Rubber brush holders and mason jars save a lot of brush cleaning when these finishes are used a great deal. They are not "foolproof," however, and will require complete cleaning from time to time. Each time you finish using the material, wipe off the jar and bring the level of the finish to a midpoint on the bristles of the brush.

Fig. 12-40. Brushing finish coat. (Deft, Inc.)

Fig. 12-44. Top. Materials for cutting down a finish. Bottom. Cutting a finished surface with wet-or-dry paper held on a felt pad. Oil is being used as a lubricant.

Fig. 12-45. Top. Materials for polishing a finish. Bottom. Rubbing a final coat with rottenstone and oil. Felt pads that have been used for a coarse abrasive should not be used for a fine abrasive.

## SANDING AND RUBBING

Cutting down finished surfaces with abrasive paper, steel wool, or a powdered abrasive is an important part of producing a good finish. If brush marks, dust specks, and other imperfections are not removed, they will form a part of the finish and become even more noticeable as the next coat is applied. Always be sure the finish is dry and hard. Overnight curing at room temperature with normal humidity is usually sufficient for most synthetics.

First coats should be rubbed with dry finishing paper (6/0—8/0) or fine steel wool. At this stage the finish is quite thin and water or other lubricants could easily get under the surface. Use a small piece of abrasive paper and fold it twice into equal sections. This makes a good pad with the grain side of one flap interlocking with the paper side of the other flap. Attach the paper to a sanding block when working with large flat surfaces. Always clean the surface carefully after rubbing, especially when steel wool is used.

When cutting the second coat, or any additional coats, use a wet-or-dry silicon carbide paper with water or rubbing oil. The paper will cut rapidly with water, and will cut a little slower and finer with oil, Fig. 12-44. Work carefully so you smooth the surface but do not cut through. A 400 or 500 grade paper will remove imperfections and leave a dull sheen to the surface. A brighter sheen can be obtained by rubbing with pumice stone and oil, or rottenstone and oil, as shown in Fig. 12-45. A commercially prepared rubbing compound is recommended for polishing the final coat of hard lacquer and synthetic finishes, Fig. 12-46. FINISHES SHOULD ALWAYS BE RUBBED IN THE DIRECTION OF THE WOOD GRAIN.

Finishes are available that dry to a soft, rubbed-effect luster without final rubbing or polishing. These however, do not usually have the fine appearance of a carefully hand rubbed finish.

### FINISHING SCHEDULES

It is good practice to develop a finishing schedule for major projects and include it in your plan of pro-

Fig. 12-46. Commercial rubbing compound.

cedure. This will make it easy for your instructor to check your ideas and make suggestions. It will also help you plan your work. You may want to experiment with several of the operations in the schedule in order to check the materials or improve the procedures. Considerable experimentation is usually done by furniture manufacturers to get the best tone, shade, or finish, before starting full production. Following are several schedules to guide you as you prepare a schedule of your own.

## SCHEDULE FOR NATURAL FINISH ON WALNUT (VARNISH)

1. Apply water stain. Allow to dry for 12 hours.
2. Shellac wash coat (7-1). Dry 30 minutes and sand with 5/0 dry paper. Clean surface.
3. Fill with walnut paste filler. Dry 24 hours. Sand lightly.
4. Apply sanding sealer. Dry one hour and sand with 5/0 dry paper. Clean surface.
5. Apply synthetic varnish. Dry overnight and sand with 6/0 dry paper.
6. Apply second coat of synthetic varnish. Dry overnight. Sand with No. 400 wet-or-dry paper and water.
7. Rub to satin finish with pumice stone and oil.

## SCHEDULE FOR LIGHT, CLOSE GRAINED WOOD (LACQUER)

1. Apply a brown pigmented oil stain. Allow to set for 10 minutes and wipe lightly. Dry 12 hours.
2. Spray sanding sealer. Dry 30 minutes and sand with 5/0 dry paper. Clean surface.
3. Spray clear gloss lacquer. Dry two hours. Sand lightly with 5/0 dry paper to remove any imperfections. Clean surface.
4. Spray semi-gloss coat of clear lacquer.

## SCHEDULE FOR NATURAL FINISH ON ANY WOOD (DANISH OIL FINISH)

1. Completely dry wood. Clean wood of all wax, dirt, and old surface finishes.
2. Sand wood smooth with very fine sandpaper. Remove all dust with vacuum or brush.
3. In a well-ventilated area, apply a liberal amount of finish. Spread it on as thick as possible with a brush, cloth, roller, or very fine (#0000) steel wool. Pour it on flat wood surfaces. Spray it on large or detailed areas.
4. Keep the surface wet with the finish material for 30 minutes. Apply more oil to any dry or dull spots that may develop. Rub the wet surface with very fine (#600) sandpaper or very fine (#0000) steel wool to achieve extra smoothness. Wipe off all surplus oil.

5. After 60 minutes, reapply a liberal amount of finish. Keep the surface wet with the oil for 30 minutes. Wipe off all surplus oil. Wipe dry with clean cloths. Do not allow any excess oil to dry on the surface. Allow it to cure overnight before using. Waxing is not necessary.

## SPRAYING, COATING, AND DRYING

### SPRAY EQUIPMENT

Modern woodworking plants employ a wide range of spray equipment in their finishing departments. Many of the new fast-drying finishes are designed especially for spray applications. See Fig. 12-47.

Conventional spraying equipment consists of a compressor, transformer, hose, hand guns, and an approved spray booth. It is usually included in the school shop layout. If the shop equipment at your school includes spray equipment, you will want to become experienced in its use.

COMPRESSORS are either piston or diaphragm type. The piston type requires a reserve pressure tank. Portable compressors are usually the diaphragm type. These deliver a relatively large volume of air at a lower pressure. Fig. 12-48 shows a small 1/2 hp oil-less piston air compressor that will provide sufficient volume of air and pressure for small spray painting jobs. Many different types are available.

An AIR TRANSFORMER is shown in Fig. 12-49. It is a device that filters out oil, dust, and moisture, and regulates the air pressure.

Fig. 12-47. A glaze coating is applied in an industry spray booth. An advanced air washer design helps trap the glaze overspray before it reaches the outside atmosphere.
(DeVilbiss Co.)

The AIR HOSE carries the compressed air from the transformer to the gun. Refer back to Fig. 12-48. It is reinforced with fabric embedded in the rubber or on the outside surface. The minimum size of hose needed to operate a single gun is 1/4 in. ID. Too long a length of small hose will result in excessive pressure drop.

Fig. 12-48. A small piston air compressor, hose, and spray gun. (Thomas Industries, Inc.)

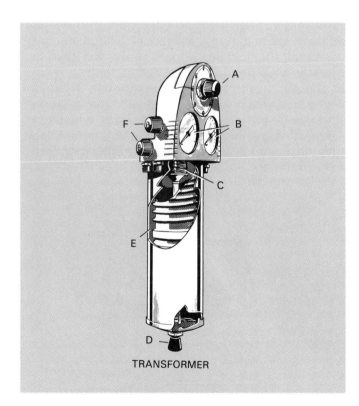

Fig. 12-49. Compressed air equipment. The transformer consists of: A—Air regulator. B—Pressure gauges. C—Filter. D—Drain. E—Condenser. F—Outlet valves.

SPRAY BOOTHS are compartments or enclosures designed to confine and exhaust or filter overspray and fumes created by the spraying operation. They are essential for the safe indoor operation of spray equipment. The type is determined by the method used to trap or dissipate the overspray. Fig. 12-50 shows some standard types. The dry baffle type, in which the exhaust air goes directly to the outside, is most commonly used in school shops.

The SPRAY GUN, Fig. 12-51, uses compressed air to atomize the material and spread it on the surface of the work in a controlled pattern. Spray guns may have either an attached container, Fig. 12-51, or a separate container. They also may be classified as a BLEEDER type or NONBLEEDER type. In the nonbleeder gun the trigger controls both air and material flow. In the bleeder gun, air continuously

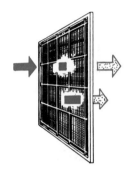

**WATER WASH BOOTH.** Literally washes paint pigments out of the exhaust air. Most efficient for removal of paint pigments from exhaust air regardless of paint viscosity or drying speed. Most acceptable to all fire, health, and building codes. Use where production is continuous.

**FILTER BOOTH.** Traps overspray particles in filter elements. Suitable for production work with slow drying or light viscosity materials, and intermittent or light production with all types of materials. Regularly scheduled filter replacement keeps booth at top efficiency.

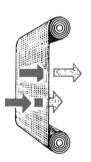

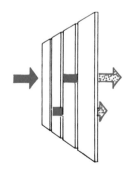

**DISPO BOOTH.** Similar to the filter booth. Filter element is a cloth curtain placed on rollers. As the cloth becomes saturated with pigments, new cloth is gradually rolled into place, either manually or automatically. Cloth rolls easily replaced.

**BAFFLE BOOTH.** Use where exhaust air to the outside does not have to be free of paint particles. Suitable for intermittent production with quick drying materials. Baffles assure an even air flow distribution through the spray booth work area.

Fig. 12-50. Four types of spray booths. (Binks Mfg. Co.)

passes through the gun and prevents pressure build-up in the lines. It is the type that is used with small diaphragm compressors that do not have a pressure tank.

Spray guns may have either an internal mix or external mix spraying head, Fig. 12-52. The external mix gun is used to apply fast drying materials and is easier to clean. It also provides greater control of the spray pattern. The internal mix gun is

used for slow drying materials and is the best type to use when air pressures are limited.

Guns may vary in the way the material is fed. In the SUCTION FEED GUN, the stream of compressed air passing over the fluid tip creates a vacuum allowing atmospheric pressure to force the material from the cup. In the PRESSURE FEED GUN, air pressure enters the cup and the material is forced to the fluid tip. This is the type of gun used in production work where the material is brought to the gun through a hose connected to a pressurized supply tank. Fig. 12-53 shows a cross section of a nonbleeder, external mix, suction feed type spray gun.

**Adjusting the Gun**

Most finishing materials will need to be reduced for spraying. Standard lacquers are reduced about 25 percent. The material should be thoroughly mixed and strained into the cup. Attach the cup to the gun and adjust the air pressure to about 25 lbs.

Open the fluid adjustment screw and check the pattern by triggering the gun while it is held stationary and aimed at a test surface. The shape of the spray pattern can be changed by turning the spreader adjustment valve. With the adjustment closed you will secure a perfectly round shape and then as it is opened, air flows through the wings of the air cap and forms an elliptical pattern. See Fig. 12-54. Spray patterns for internal mix gun heads are varied by using different shaped nozzles.

After you have selected a desirable pattern for your work, you will need to adjust the material or fluid flow. Large patterns will require a large amount of material; the fluid adjustment screw will need to be nearly wide open. You may also need to readjust the air pressure at the transformer. Always select a size of spray pattern that will fit your work. Using a large pattern on a small surface will result in excessive overspray and loss of material. Too much air pressure will cause overatomization and waste material.

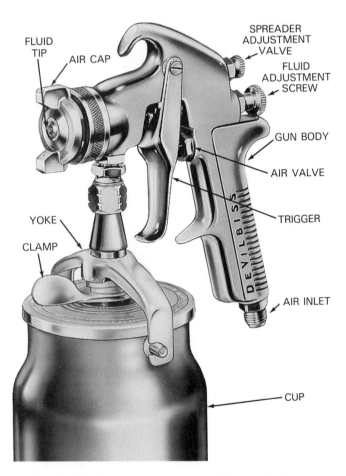

Fig. 12-51. Parts of a spray gun with attached cup.

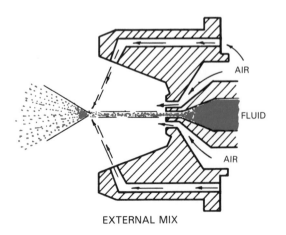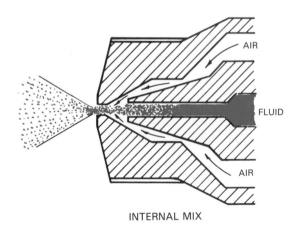

Fig. 12-52. Types of spray heads. The spray head, or nozzle, consists of an air cap and a fluid tip.

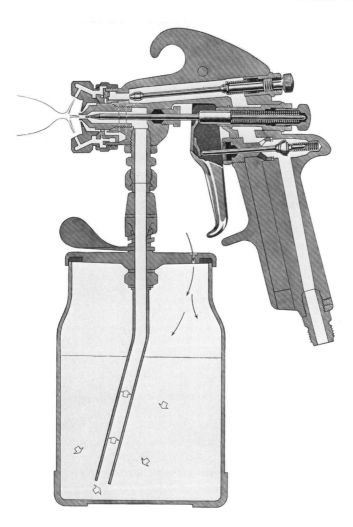

Fig. 12-53. A section view of a nonbleeder, external mix, suction feed type spray gun. (DeVilbiss Co.)

*To reduce overspray and obtain maximum efficiency always spray with the lowest possible air pressure.*

## Using the Gun

Practice using the spray gun by coating a test panel. The gun should be held perpendicular to the surface and moved in even strokes parallel to it as shown in Figs. 12-55 and 12-56. The stroke should be started before the trigger is pulled and released before the stroke is finished.

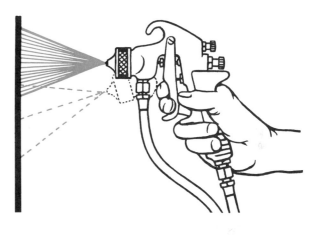

Fig. 12-55. Hold the gun perpendicular to the surface. Tilting (dotted lines) will result in an uneven pattern.

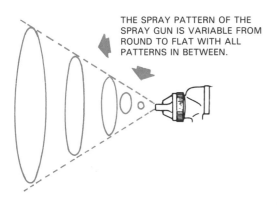

THE SPRAY PATTERN OF THE SPRAY GUN IS VARIABLE FROM ROUND TO FLAT WITH ALL PATTERNS IN BETWEEN.

IN NORMAL OPERATION, THE WINGS ON THE NOZZLE ARE HORIZONTAL AS ILLUSTRATED HERE. THIS PROVIDES A VERTICAL FAN SHAPED PATTERN WHICH GIVES MAXIMUM COVERAGE AS THE GUN IS MOVED BACK AND FORTH PARALLEL TO THE SURFACE BEING FINISHED.

Fig. 12-54. Spray patterns of the external mix gun.

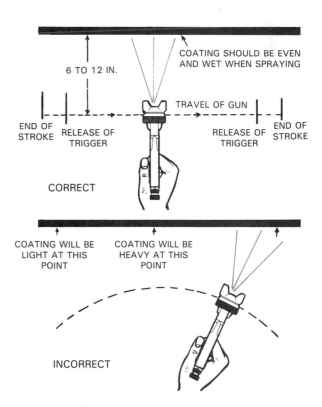

COATING SHOULD BE EVEN AND WET WHEN SPRAYING

6 TO 12 IN.

TRAVEL OF GUN

END OF STROKE    RELEASE OF TRIGGER    RELEASE OF TRIGGER    END OF STROKE

CORRECT

COATING WILL BE LIGHT AT THIS POINT    COATING WILL BE HEAVY AT THIS POINT

INCORRECT

Fig. 12-56. Stroking procedure.

The weight of the coat will vary with the speed of the stroke and the distance between the gun and the surface. Try to lay down an even, wet coat. If the gun is held too far from the surface, the coat will be light. If the gun is held too closely and moved too slowly, you will build too heavy a coat and it will sag. LAP EACH STROKE HALF WAY over the preceding stroke for a uniform finish, Fig. 12-57.

To set up your project work for spraying, disassemble it and handle it in about the same way as for a finish with a brush. If possible, the project should be supported on a turntable as shown in Fig. 12-58. This will make it easier to move the work as you proceed from one surface to the next. Keep the surface being coated between you and a major light source for the best view of the coat being applied. It is easier to spray a horizontal surface than a vertical one, so try and arrange your work so that most of it can be coated in the horizontal position.

Spray hard-to-reach surfaces and edges first, Fig. 12-59. The face of the panel is then filled in. When spraying a level surface, always work from the closest side to the farthest side. The movement of the air toward the booth will pull the overspray away from the wet surface. To minimize overspray, edges should be sprayed with the gun set at a small pattern. A fuller pattern can be used, if the gun is held closely and stroked rapidly.

You will need to study your work and determine the best procedure to follow. Fig. 12-60 shows a suggested sequence of strokes for use with rectangular pieces.

Fig. 12-58. Work set on a turntable in the spray booth. The wings of the air cap are in a vertical position to form a horizontal pattern as the gun is stroked up and down with the grain.

Fig. 12-59. Spray edges first, then top surface.

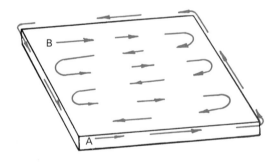

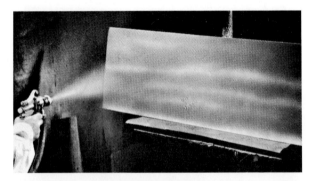

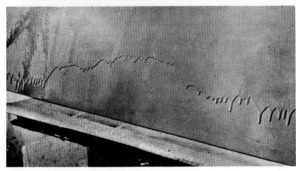

Fig. 12-57. Top. Gun held too far away. Bottom. Gun held too closely and stroked too slowly. (E.I. DuPont DeNemours Co.)

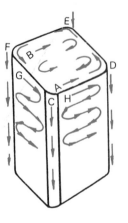

Fig. 12-60. Spraying sequence for rectangular pieces.

## Faulty Operation

Unsatisfactory work may be caused by defective equipment or poor operational technique. Study the manufacturer's manual for directions concerning the style or type of gun you are using. In general, problems which may be encountered include:

FAULTY PATTERNS. Usually caused by dirty or clogged air caps or fluid tips. Remove and clean them in correct thinner. Too much pressure used with a thin material can cause trouble.

RUNS AND SAGS. Can be caused by excessive material in patterns, material that is too thin, a gun held too closely to surface, and/or motion that is too slow.

ORANGE PEEL. Caused by material that does not flow together smoothly because it is too heavy and dry when it reaches the surface. Hold the gun closer and thin material properly.

BLUSHING. A cloudy appearance in the film due to moisture. Caused by high humidity and thinners that evaporate too rapidly.

SPITTING GUN. Caused by air entering the material line through the packing around the needle valve (oil and tighten). Check for a loose connection between the siphon cup and gun. Vent hole in the cup may be plugged.

## Gun Cleaning and Care

A spray gun is easy to maintain and clean, if you have extra cups for materials as shown in Fig. 12-61. When you have finished with the gun, release it from the cup and loosen the air cap. Hold a cloth over the cap, pull the trigger and force material back into the cup, Fig. 12-62. Attach a cup that is about half filled with thinner; shake and trigger the gun several times while it is held in the spray booth. Wipe off the outside of the gun and disconnect the air hose. The air cap should be removed and placed in thinner, especially if it is an internal mix type, and the fluid tip should be wiped clean. Guns that will be stored for a period of time

Fig. 12-62. Forcing material from the gun back into the cup. (DeVilbiss Co.)

should be disassembled and completely cleaned and dried. Do not soak the entire gun in thinner as it will dissolve the lubricant in the valve packings.

Proper lubrication is important. The fluid needle packing gland should be oiled often. Also place a drop of oil on the air valve stem and the trigger bearing screw, Fig. 12-63. When cleaning clogged holes in the cap or fluid tip always use a wooden match stick or toothpick. Do not use wire, nails, or metal tools, Fig. 12-64.

Fig. 12-61. Spray gun with extra cups for different material.

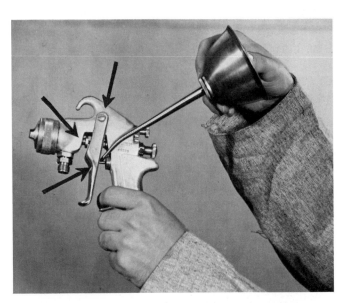

Fig. 12-63. When oiling the spray gun the fluid needle packing gland, the air valve, and the trigger bearing screw should all be oiled as shown by the arrows.

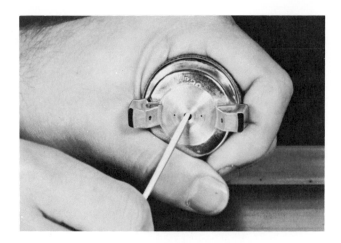

Fig. 12-64. Cleaning the air cap.

Fig. 12-66. A small, self-powered spray unit can be loaded with spray materials used by a regular gun.

## SELF-SPRAYING CANS

Many finishing materials are available in self-spraying cans. These are handy for small jobs.

The pressurized gas that atomizes the material and carries it to the surface being finished is propane isobutane. This gas, in liquid form, is loaded in the spray can along with the material. It creates pressure of about 40 psi (280 kPa) at 70°F (21°C). When the valve of the can is pushed, the mixture is released and forms a spray as it is emitted from a tiny opening.

Mix the material by shaking the can, then swirling the metal ball (located in the container) around the bottom. Hold the valve 10 to 12 in. from the surface, Fig. 12-65. After use, wipe the valve, invert the can and release the valve to allow a small amount of clear gas to clean the opening.

Cans of gas propellant are available for use with a small spray gun, Fig. 12-66. This self-powered unit can be loaded with materials used by a regular gun. The materials should be thinned and the spray unit handled in the same way as a regular spray gun. A unit of this type will work satisfactory on many small articles, Fig. 12-67.

*Self-spraying cans should not be exposed to temperatures above 120°F. Do not place them where they will be exposed to sunlight shining through glass. Never puncture or incinerate the can even though it appears empty.*

Fig. 12-65. Using a spray can for touch-up work. (Sprayon Products Inc.)

Fig. 12-67. These small articles can be finished quickly and easily with the spray unit shown in Fig. 12-66. (Eldon Rebhorn)

## INDUSTRIAL SPRAYING

Special considerations must be given to industrial spray equipment. Due to the many pieces that must be sprayed, the equipment must work quickly and efficiently.

Guns with cups are seldom used in production work. Rather, pressure fed guns are used. Material is supplied through hose lines and pipes that are connected to pressurized tanks or special pumps, Fig. 12-68. The spray operator can work continuously without interruption.

Production setups often employ automatic gun heads that are pneumatically or electrically operated. These guns are mounted on carriers that move back and forth or up and down as the work moves along a conveyor line or around a revolving table. Fig. 12-69 shows an electrostatic painting machine.

A spindle spraying setup is shown in Fig. 12-70. The work is placed on conveyorized spindles, sometimes called a chain-on-edge machine. As the spindles pass in front of the spray guns, they are automatically rotated, and the guns are triggered to provide a uniform coat on all sides of the work.

In AIRLESS SPRAYING the material is atomized by high (hydraulic) pressure rather than compressed air. Fig. 12-71 compares the equipment arrangement of airless spraying with that of conventional spraying. In the airless spraying method, a special pump delivers paint to the spray gun under fluid pressures as high as 3000 psi. Atomization occurs as the material is forced through the small gun nozzle opening. The valve seat, needle, and tip are

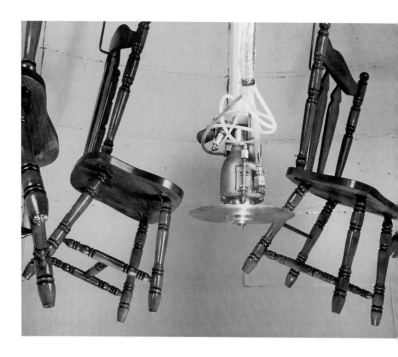

Fig. 12-69. Industrial electrostatic painting equipment applying the final coat to these chairs. A conveyor carries the work past the painting unit. (Ransburg Electrostatic Equipment)

Fig. 12-70. Top. Automatic spraying of turned legs, stain coat. Legs move into an infrared drying oven. Bottom. Close-up showing a spraying station equipped with three automatic guns. Only two are being used for the legs in process. Legs rotate as they pass by the guns.

Fig. 12-68. On this production line, the final coat of lacquer is supplied through a hose. (Ransburg Electrostatic Equipment)

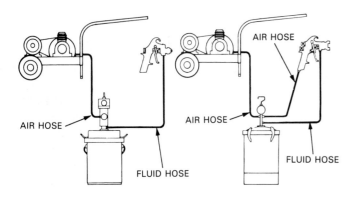

Fig. 12-71. Left. Airless spraying. Right. Conventional spraying.

made of tungsten carbide to resist the excessive wear caused by the material passing through the nozzle at such high pressure, Fig. 12-72. Heavy coats can be applied without fogging or overspray.

The HOT-SPRAYING of materials, either by conventional or airless methods is often employed in production work. By heating the material, the viscosity of a high solids product can be reduced without the addition of extra solvent. This results in a reduction of the number of coats, the finish has less tendency to sag, and such problems as blushing (finish taking on grayish cast while drying) are eliminated. In this process the material is heated to a temperature of 160 to 200°F. Gun cups are available that have thermostatically controlled heating units.

ELECTROSTATIC SPRAYING is used extensively in the metalworking industry. It cannot be used successfully in wood finishing without first applying a conductive material to the wood surface. In the electrostatic process the material receives a negative charge from a special spray gun, or a revolving disc that throws the material into the air by centrifugal force. The negatively charged particles of material are attracted to the product which has received a positive charge. Even coats can be applied and there is little overspray or loss of material, Fig. 12-73.

## ROLLER COATING

In roller coating the work is passed between synthetic rubber rollers that carry a film of the finishing material. The rollers revolve in a reservoir of the material, then against a chromium plated doctor roll that controls the film thickness. Roller coaters can be used to apply nearly any type of finishing material to plywood, hardboard, particle board, metal sheets, and other flat work, Fig. 12-74.

An important roller coating process utilizes the reverse roll filling machine. After the filler is applied with a regular roller, a wiping roller (turning in the opposite direction) packs the material into pores of the substrate and wipes off the excess, Fig. 12-75.

Fig. 12-76 shows a modern finishing system that consists mainly of roller coating equipment. It is designed to apply a woodgrain finish to particle board or hardboard panels. After precision sanding, the panels move through a reverse roll filling machine that applies a coat of polyester filler. The filler is cured almost instantly as the panels pass through an ultraviolet processor where ultraviolet light waves (not heat) cause polymerization. This process is commonly referred to as UV curing. A single-head sander smooths the filler coat and precision roller coaters apply a basecoat. After the panels pass through a drying oven and grain printer, a polyester topcoat is applied and cured. Fig. 12-77 shows key views of the system.

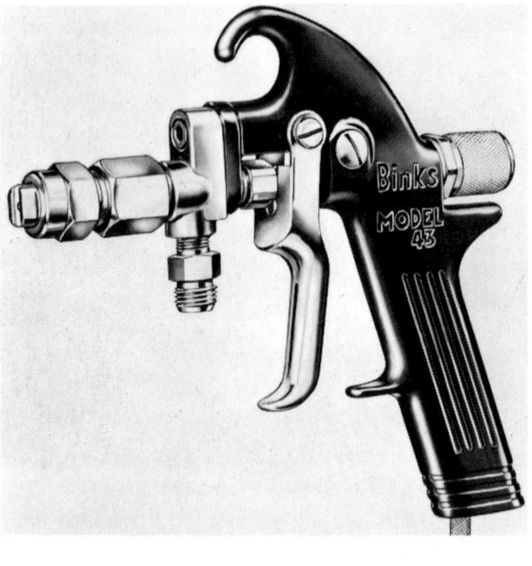

Fig. 12-72. Airless spray gun. Spray tip is made of tungsten carbide.

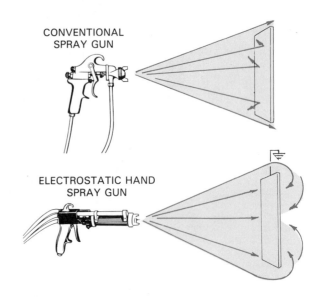

Fig. 12-73. Electrostatic spraying. (Ashdee Corp.)

ROLL ARRANGEMENTS

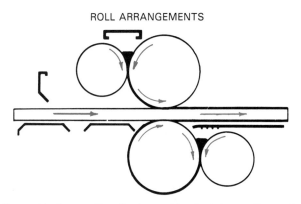

1. Top and bottom coating. Can be used for single top coating or single bottom coating, if desired.

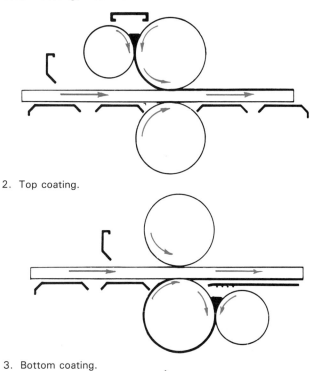

2. Top coating.

3. Bottom coating.

A

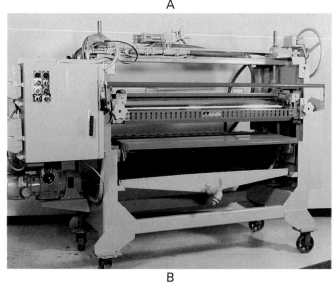

B

Fig. 12-74. A—Typical roll arrangements in regular roller coating machine. B—Top and bottom coating machine. (Black Brothers)

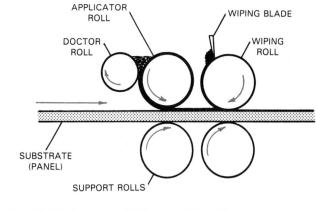

Fig. 12-75. Reverse roll filling machine. Wiping blade removes and recycles excess filler. Wiping roller is chrome coated and polished.

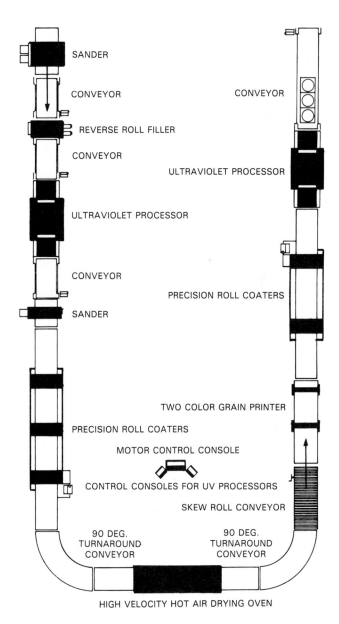

Fig. 12-76. Diagram shows modern finishing system for flat panels. Line operates at 60 to 75 fpm (18.3 to 22.9 mpm). (Black Brothers)

193

Fig. 12-77. Top. Infeed side of reverse roll filling machine. Just beyond is UV processor and precision sander. Center. Panels, filled and base coated, move into two-color grain printer. Bottom. Two precision roller coaters in tandem lay on topcoat. This double-coating operation is called "wet on wet." The panels then move into second UV processor. (Black Bros.)

## CURTAIN COATING

Curtain coating is a high speed production process where the work is passed through a falling,

continuous stream (curtain) of finishing material. The curtain is formed by flowing the finishing material over a weir or dam. It then drops from the skirt of the weir by gravity, either onto the work or into a gutter which returns the material to a reservoir to be recirculated. The thickness of the film varies with the rate of flow and the speed at which the work moves. Accurate films of from 1 to 25 mils can be applied with a machine like the one shown in Fig. 12-78.

Fig. 12-79 shows a diagram of a pressure curtain coater. The three main components are the curtain forming head, the conveyor belt, and the material circulating and filtering system. The opening for the head is composed of a stationary knife and a movable knife that can be accurately adjusted to provide the required curtain thickness. Application speeds may run as high as 800 fpm. At this rate of application, it is often necessary to heat the surface of the wood to reduce the dry time. Intense electric radiant heat can raise the surface temperature of a wood panel to 200°F in as little as 10 seconds. The panel is then passed through the curtain coater and the finish dries in two or three minutes.

## FLOW COATING AND DIPPING

In the flow coating method, the work is carried by an overhead conveyor, or placed in a chamber where a bank of low pressure nozzles eject streams of the finishing material. The excess drains off into catch basins and is recirculated through the system. In dipping, the product is completely immersed into a tank. The viscosity of the finishing material must be carefully controlled to prevent lower surfaces and edges from holding an excessive film. The position of the parts, and dripping and drying procedures must be correct in order to prevent tears, curtains, and sags.

## TUMBLING

This method is often used to finish knobs, buttons, golf tees, beads, and other small wooden objects. Parts are placed in a drum or barrel with a small amount of lacquer, enamel, or wax. The barrel revolves at about 25 rpm causing the parts to tumble over each other. Additional finishing material is placed in the barrel as required. As they dry, the parts polish each other to a smooth, satiny finish.

## FORCE DRYING

Finishing materials dry, harden, and cure by evaporation, oxidation, and polymerization (mixing of compounds causes them to have different properties). All of these actions take place more rapidly

Fig. 12-78. Modern curtain coating machine. Conveyor belt speeds are adjustable from 100 to 450 fpm (30.5 to 137 mpm). (Gasway Corp.)

at elevated temperatures.

In high volume production it is important to dry the finish as rapidly as possible. Wet parts or assemblies are placed on conveyors that carry them through heated ovens. Radiant heat (produced by infrared bulbs or special ceramic generators) is often used because it penetrates the finish coating, thus reducing the curing time, Fig. 12-80.

UV radiation is commonly used to cure flat work coated with specially formulated finishes (usually polyester resin or acrylics). The finishing coat is not cured by heat, but by light rays. The fluid coating is converted to a tough, solid film in a few seconds, through chemical reaction (polymerization) triggered by exposure to ultraviolet radiation.

Some wet surfaces cannot be exposed to high temperatures immediately or they will bubble and blister. They are usually given a "flash-off" period to allow excess thinners and solvents to evaporate. This may be done at room temperature or in an enclosure where warm air is circulated and exhausted.

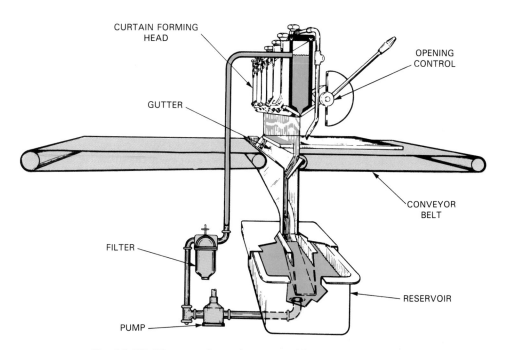

Fig. 12-79. Diagram of curtain coater with pressure type head.

Fig. 12-80. Large pieces of furniture moving into a radiant heated oven on a floor-based conveyor. (Dry Clime Lamp Corp.)

Fig. 12-81. Hand rubbing kitchen cabinet doors that are carried on free-turning rollers. (International Paper Co.)

## CONVEYOR LINES

Production finishing systems require some type of conveyor line to move the product from one station or stage of the process to the next. They may consist of an overhead monorail or floor-based equipment. Usually they are powered. Sometimes the product is pushed along by hand over free moving balls or rollers. Powered floor-based equipment consists of a slowly moving chain that carries pallets (bases for the product) along two parallel rails on which skate wheels are mounted. See Figs. 12-81 and 12-82. The pallets can be spread wide apart for application or rubbing operations, and brought together (close-packed) for a drying stage.

In small plants a closed loop system, Fig. 12-83, may be used where the product is moved around the same conveyor line several times before the finish is complete. Large plants employ a complete single conveyor line where the product is completely finished when it reaches the end. Fig. 12-84 shows a layout of such a system in a large factory where 480 TV and stereo cabinets are finished in an eight hour period (one per minute).

Fig. 12-82. Tables rest on pallets which are moved along conveyor by a chain located in center channel (arrow). (Binks Mfg. Co.)

## TEST YOUR KNOWLEDGE, Chapter 12

Please do not write in the text. Place your answers on a separate sheet of paper.
1. List five safety precautions to follow when working with finishes.
2. The size of a brush is determined by the _____, _____, and _____ of the exposed bristles.

Fig. 12-83. Closed loop conveyor line. Only the section through the drying oven is powered. Cabinets make two complete circuits in the finishing process. (Northway Products Co.)

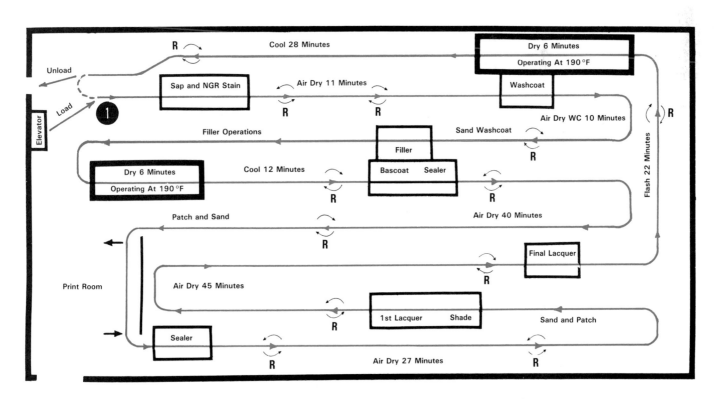

Fig. 12-84. Layout of a finishing system in a large furniture plant. Cabinets are loaded on conveyor line from elevator in upper left corner. Points marked R indicate rotation of cabinets from width to breadth or vice versa to take up less space on line. Conveyor moves at 6.11 fpm (1.86 mpm).

3. Which of the following is NOT used to fill holes in wood?
   a. Stick shellac.
   b. Plugs.
   c. Penetrating stain.
   d. Plastic wood.
4. _____ will emphasize or de-emphasize the grain and will add color to the wood surface.
5. Name the three general classifications of wood stains.
6. The purpose of sealer is to:
   a. Tie down stain and filler already applied.
   b. Prevent absorption of the finish coat.
   c. Seal out moisture and dirt.
   d. None of the above.
   e. All of the above.
7. Varnish is a mixture of oil, resin, solvent, and drier. True or False?
8. _____ consists of oils, emulsions, driers, and pigments. _____ consists of natural or synthetic varnishes with pigments added.
9. Explain the difference between ''tint'' and ''shade.''
10. List five guidelines to follow when working in the finishing room.
11. The first topcoat of finish should be rubbed with _____ finishing paper.
12. Name the five components of conventional spraying equipment.
13. When spraying a surface, the spray gun is held perpendicular to the surface and moved in semicircular strokes. True or False?
14. When material is atomized by hydraulic pressure rather than compressed air, this is known as:
    a. Conventional spraying.
    b. Air spraying.
    c. Airless spraying.
    d. None of the above.
15. Small crater-like marks in a finish are called _____.
16. What are the two types of solvents?
17. What are VOCs?

## ACTIVITIES

1. Prepare a sample finishing board using stain and paste filler. As you apply each coat, mask out a part of the previously applied finish so that when it is completed you can see each stage of the schedule. Label each part.
2. Write manufacturers of paint and other wood finishing products for their latest literature.
3. Prepare a chart listing basic kinds of finishing material. Along the sides and across the top include such headings as purpose and use, drying time, thinners, how applied, and special directions.
4. Prepare sample panels finished with shellac, lacquer, varnish, penetrating finishes, etc. Conduct controlled tests of these surfaces by submitting them to abrasions, scratches, dents, heat, and common household materials like detergents, fruit acids, cooking oil, and grease. Prepare a paper describing the tests and listing results and conclusions.

This detail sander can reach into spaces not previously accessible by power sanders.
(Fein Power Tools Inc.)

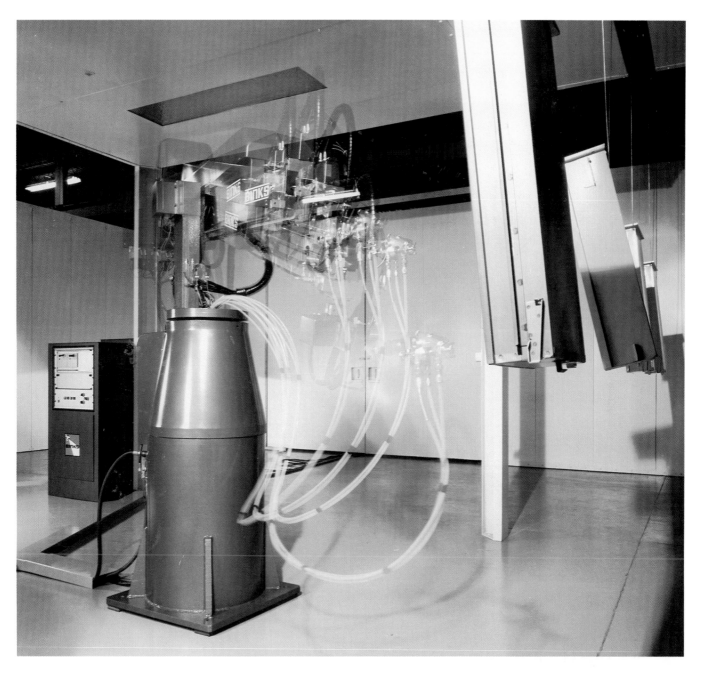

Multi-exposure photo shows operation of robot spraying machine. To program machine, skilled operator guides spray gun through best sequence for product. Movement through six axes of motion are recorded on cassette tape. When tape is played back, machine automatically duplicates recorded motions. Arm movements are powered by hydraulic cylinders and wrist movements by electric motors. (Binks Mfg. Co.)

Planing stock to desired thickness is required for most woodworking projects. This serving tray and stand have several thicknesses of material which were produced by planing equipment. (The Bartley Collection, Ltd.)

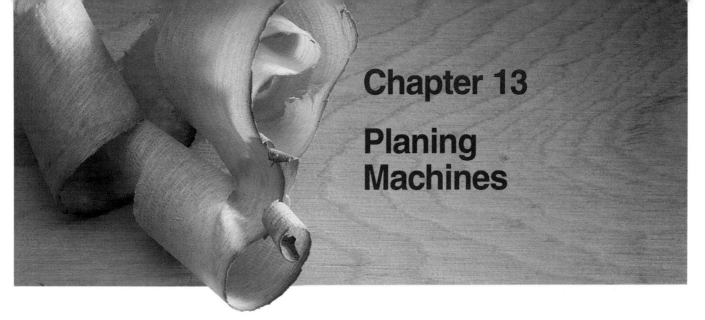

# Chapter 13

# Planing Machines

The jointer and planer (also called a surfacer) are power planing machines that smooth the surfaces of lumber, and form faces and edges that are straight and true. The JOINTER is the most versatile of the two machines and is a direct counterpart of the hand plane. It will plane surfaces, edges, bevels, chamfers, and tapers. The PLANER is a single purpose machine that planes the stock to a uniform thickness. See Fig. 13-1.

## POWER EQUIPMENT SAFETY

As with all machinery, the jointer and planer must be used carefully and cautiously. Before continuing with this unit, review the power equipment safety rules which follow.

1. Always be sure you have the instructor's approval to operate a machine. Your instructor knows you and the machine, and can best decide whether you have "what it takes" to operate the machine safely.
2. Wear appropriate clothing. Remove coats or jackets, tuck in ties, and roll up loose sleeves. Wear a shop apron and tie it snugly.
3. You must be wide awake and alert. Never operate a machine when you are tired or ill.
4. Think through the operation before performing it. Know what you are going to do, in addition to what the machine will do.
5. Make all the necessary adjustments before turning on the machine. Adjustments on certain machines will require the instructor's approval.
6. Never remove or adjust a safety guard without the instructor's permission.
7. Use approved push sticks, push block, feather boards, and safety devices. Some operations require the use of a special jig or fixture.
8. Keep the machine tables and working surfaces clear of tools, stock, and project materials. Also keep the floor free of scraps and excessive litter.
9. Allow the machine to reach its full operating speed before feeding the work.
10. Feed the work carefully and only as fast as the machine will easily cut.
11. Maintain the MARGIN OF SAFETY specified for the machine. This is the minimum distance your hands should ever come to the cutting tool while in operation.
12. If a machine is dull, out of adjustment, or not working properly, shut off the power immediately and inform the instructor.
13. When you are operating the machine, you are the only one to control it. Start and stop the machine yourself. If someone is helping you, be sure they understand that they are expected to know what to do and how to do it.
14. Do not allow your attention to be distracted while operating a machine. Also, be certain that you do not distract the attention of other machine operators.
15. Stay clear of machines being operated by other students. See that other students are out of the way when you are operating a machine.
16. When you have completed an operation on a machine, shut off the power. Wait until it stops before leaving the machine or setting up another cut. Never leave a machine running while unattended.
17. Machines should not be used for trivial operations, especially on small pieces of stock. Do not play with machines.
18. Do not "crowd around" or wait in line to use a machine. Ask the present operator to inform you at your work station when finished. Common standards of courtesy may slow you down, but they will make the shop a safer and more pleasant place to work.

## PLANING SEQUENCE

The sequence of operations for planing and squaring stock on power machines is about the same as

Fig. 13-1. Planing machines. A—20 inch single surface planer. (Grizzly Imports, Inc.)   B—Planer-molder. (Foley-Belsaw Co.)
C—18 inch planer is popular for school and industrial use. (Powermatic)   D—13 inch planer on stand with extension tables.
(Delta International Machinery Corp.)   E—20 inch planer with table extensions. (Enlon Import Corp.)   F—12 inch planer.
(Makita U.S.A., Inc.)

for hand tools. First, select the best face and plane it on the jointer. The jointer table works like the hand plane bed or bottom: it guides the cutting edge, planing off the high places until a flat, true surface is formed. The planer, on the other hand, will only partially straighten a surface. Its bed is relatively small and if the stock has cup or bow, the pressure of the rollers tend to flatten it during the planing operation and the stock then springs back into a warped form as it leaves the machine. The planer will remove a small amount of warp after a number of passes through the machine. This, however, may result in the stock becoming too thin.

Next, select and plane the best edge with the planed surface held against the fence of the jointer. If the grain is running in the wrong direction, this operation can be delayed until the second face has been planed.

Now move to the planer and plane the second face parallel to the first face and bring the stock to the required thickness. If a planer is not available this operation can be performed on the jointer. However, the thickness cannot be as accurately controlled. With the stock straight and true on two faces and one edge, you are ready to rip it to the required width on the table saw, Fig. 13-2.

When the stock is straight and there are no serious defects, the procedure is simple. If the stock is warped, it will be necessary to rough cut large pieces into smaller ones before planing and surfacing to finished size, if full thickness is required, Fig. 13-3. Rough cuts to length can be made with a handsaw, radial arm saw, or band saw. Ripping cuts in rough stock can be made with the handsaw or band saw. Do not use the table saw for ripping or crosscutting until at least one surface and one edge are straight and true.

Give careful attention to rough cutting of your stock. Cut it into smaller pieces only to the extent necessary to maintain the required thickness. Many small pieces will require extra handling and may be under the required size for safe machine operation.

Boards that are too wide for the jointer can be rough ripped into narrower widths. They may be rough planed with a hand plane to secure one flat face and then both surfaces can be finished on the planer. Be certain to turn the flat face down as the stock is fed into the machine for the first cut.

## JOINTER

### PARTS AND ADJUSTMENTS

Principal parts of a jointer are shown in Fig. 13-4. The cutterhead (not shown in the photo) holds three knives and revolves at a speed of about 4500 rpm. The size of the jointer is determined by the length of these knives. This also determines the maximum width of stock the jointer will handle.

The three main parts that can be adjusted are the infeed table, the outfeed table, and the fence. The outfeed table must be level with the knife edges at their highest point of rotation. This is a critical adjustment. If the table is too high the stock will be gradually raised out of the cut and a slight taper will be formed. If it is too low the tail end of the stock

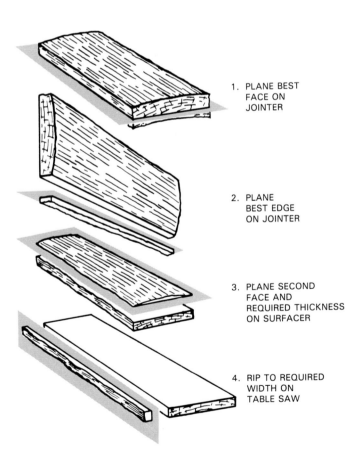

1. PLANE BEST FACE ON JOINTER

2. PLANE BEST EDGE ON JOINTER

3. PLANE SECOND FACE AND REQUIRED THICKNESS ON SURFACER

4. RIP TO REQUIRED WIDTH ON TABLE SAW

Fig. 13-2. Sequence for planing stock on power machines. An excessive amount of stock is being removed to make the drawings clear. In actual practice a much smaller amount is used.

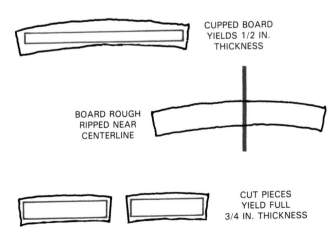

CUPPED BOARD YIELDS 1/2 IN. THICKNESS

BOARD ROUGH RIPPED NEAR CENTERLINE

CUT PIECES YIELD FULL 3/4 IN. THICKNESS

Fig. 13-3. Rough cut cupped lumber to maintain thickness. This also applies to lumber that is bowed.

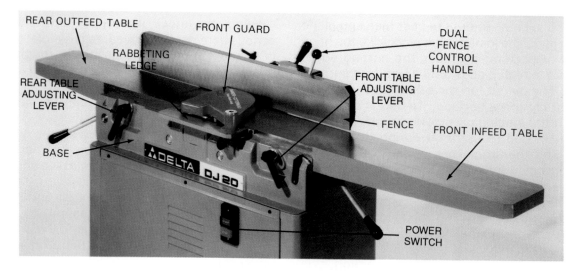

REAR OUTFEED TABLE

FRONT GUARD

DUAL FENCE CONTROL HANDLE

RABBETING LEDGE

REAR TABLE ADJUSTING LEVER

FRONT TABLE ADJUSTING LEVER

FENCE

FRONT INFEED TABLE

BASE

POWER SWITCH

Fig. 13-4. Parts of a jointer. (Delta International Machinery Corp.)

will drop as it leaves the infeed table and cause a "bite" in the surface or edge. Check with your instructor before making any changes in the setting of the outfeed table.

The fence guides the stock over the table and knives. When jointing an edge or squaring stock, it should be perpendicular to the table surface. The fence can be tilted to other angles when cutting chamfers or bevels.

To make a cut on the jointer, the infeed table is set below the level of both the knives and outfeed table as shown in Fig. 13-5. Most jointers have a scale that indicates this distance, which is referred to as the "depth of cut."

## JOINTER SAFETY

1. Be sure you have the instructor's approval to operate the machine.
2. Before turning on the machine, make adjustments for depth of cut and position of fence.
3. Do not adjust the outfeed tables or remove guard without the instructor's approval.

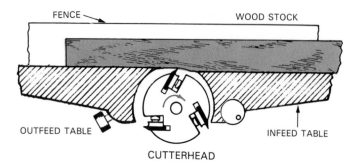

FENCE

WOOD STOCK

OUTFEED TABLE

INFEED TABLE

CUTTERHEAD

Fig. 13-5. How the jointer works. Note the direction of the wood grain.

4. The maximum cut for jointing an edge is 1/8 in.; for a flat surface, 1/16 in.
5. Stock must be at least 12 in. long. Stock to be surfaced must be at least 3/8 in. thick, unless a special feather board is used.
6. Feed the work so the knives will cut "with the grain." Use only new stock that is free of knots, splits, and checks.
7. Keep your hands away from the cutterhead even though the guard is in position. Maintain at least a 4 in. margin of safety.
8. Use a push block when planing a flat surface. Do not plane end grain unless the board is at least 12 in. wide.
9. The jointer knives must be sharp. Dull knives will vibrate the stock and may cause a kickback.

*The jointer is one of the most dangerous machines in the woodshop. Review the following jointer safety rules, in addition to the general safety rules outlined in the beginning of the unit.*

## PLANING AN EDGE

This operation is also called jointing an edge. Examine your stock and determine the direction of the grain. Turn it so it will feed properly. Be certain that the fence is square and tight, and that the guard is in position and properly adjusted. Set the infeed table for the correct depth of cut and turn on the machine.

Place the stock on the infeed table and press it lightly against the fence. Stand close to the machine so you can work in a natural position without bending over or reaching out too far. Move the stock into and through the cut, Fig. 13-6. Step your hands alternately to new positions on the stock, feeding with first one hand, then the other so the cut will be continuous and smooth. The rate of feed will vary with the kind and size of wood and the depth of cut. It should seldom be slower than 10 fpm.

When planing narrow stock, follow the procedure shown in Fig. 13-7. Start the cut, keeping your left hand well back of the cutterhead. When a foot or more of the stock has passed over the knives, step the left hand across the knives and press the stock against the fence and outfeed table as you continue to move it forward. Feed the stock as previously described with the left hand over the outfeed table and the right hand over the infeed table. Neither

hand should pass over the knives and violate the 4 IN. MARGIN OF SAFETY. Finish the cut with the left hand, or step the right hand over the knives and finish the cut with both hands.

Narrow pieces of stock that are close to the 12 in. minimum length should be handled with a push stick as shown in Fig. 13-8.

## PLANING A SURFACE

Turn your stock so you will be feeding the grain of the wood in the right direction. If there is some warp in the board, turn the concave (dished in) surface down so the stock will not rock on the table. Set the depth of cut at about 1/16 in., check the fence and guard, and turn on the machine.

Place the stock on the infeed table and move it into the knives. The left hand should be kept well back of the knives and then stepped over them to hold the stock down on the outfeed table. Finish the cut by placing a pusher block on the end of the board as shown in Fig. 13-9. Boards with twist or "wind" create an extra problem. Apply pressure on the low points. Try to keep the board from rocking during the cut.

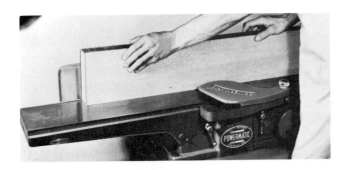

Fig. 13-6. Planing the edge of a large piece of stock.

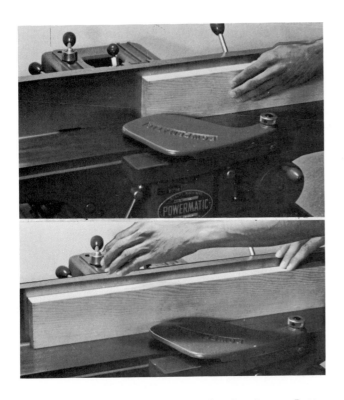

Fig. 13-7. Planing narrow stock. Top. Starting the cut. Bottom. Stepping the left hand across the knives.

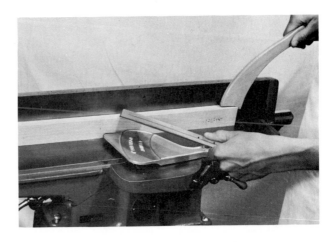

Fig. 13-8. Using push stick on a small piece of stock.

Fig. 13-9. Using a pusher block for a surface cut.

Thin, narrow strips can be surfaced safely by using the setup shown in Fig. 13-10. Here a feather board is clamped to the fence so that it applies firm pressure to the stock as it passes over the knives. Feed the stock in about half way, then move around to the outfeed table and pull it through. The stock should be at least 2 ft. long.

## PLANING END GRAIN

End grain or plywood can be planed without splitting off the edge by following the procedure shown in Fig. 13-11. First make a cut about one inch in from the edge. Then reverse the piece and finish the cut. The board should be at least 12 in. wide. The cut should be light and the feed slow. A feed that is too slow, however, will dull the knives excessively and may burn the wood.

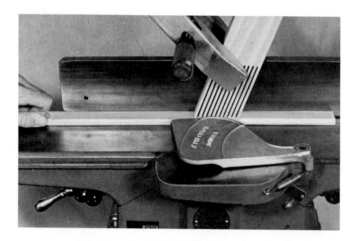

Fig. 13-10. Thin strips can be surfaced safely with the use of a feather board.

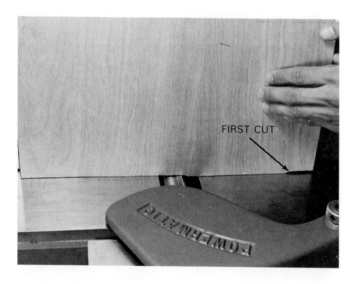

Fig. 13-11. Planing end grain. The guard has been pulled away to show the cut.

## BEVELS AND CHAMFERS

To cut bevels and chamfers the fence is set at an angle with the table. Machines will vary in the way this adjustment is made. The fence can be set either away from the table or toward the table, Fig. 13-12. When possible the fence should be tilted toward the table as it is usually easier to hold the stock in position. A series of cuts will be required to complete the work.

## PLANING A TAPER

Lay out the taper on the work and mark a line at the point where it starts. Then place the part on the infeed table with the mark about 1/2 in. beyond the high point of the knives. Clamp a stop block onto the table so it just touches the end to be tapered. Lower the infeed table an amount equal to the taper or some even proportion of it.

Start the machine, set the end of the piece against the stop, pull the guard open, and carefully lower the piece onto the outfeed table and knives as shown in Fig. 13-13. Using a pusher block or push stick, move the part forward, keeping the tapered end firmly on the infeed table as shown. In the example, the depth of cut was set at one-half the total taper required and the part was passed over the jointer twice. Duplicate parts do not need to be laid out when cut with the same setting.

The cutterhead will dig in a little at the start of the taper. This is the reason for setting up the cut to start slightly back of the exact point. After the taper is cut, this can be smoothed with one light pass over the jointer set for a standard cut, or by using a hand plane. If the piece to be tapered is longer than the infeed table, mark the midpoint and plane the tapered end (as previously described) to one-half the amount required. With the part resting on this surface, take regular jointer cuts until the total taper is formed.

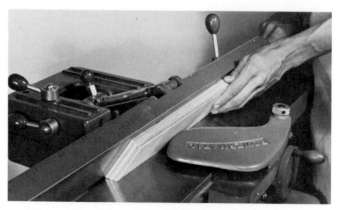

Fig. 13-12. Planing a bevel. Final cut is being made.

Fig. 13-13. Planing a taper. Top. Lowering work onto knives. Bottom. First cut half finished. Note: the guard has been held open to show the cut.

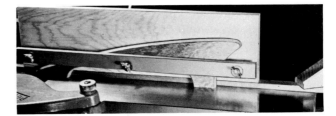

Fig. 13-15. This special carrier is used for cutting odd-shaped parts.

## PLANING A RABBET

To plane a rabbet, first set the fence to provide the correct width. This is done by measuring the exact distance from the end of the knives to the fence. Lower the infeed table to provide the required depth, then feed the stock as shown in Fig. 13-14. When cutting a large rabbet in hard wood it is usually best to set the infeed table to only part of the required depth and form the rabbet in several passes over the machine. You will need to lower the table after each pass until the required depth is attained.

## SPECIAL SETUPS

Various fixtures can be designed and built to do specialized operations on the jointer. Fig. 13-15 shows a carrier being used to machine a small surface on a tripod lamp leg. The same carrier can be used to hold other small parts. Usually such setups are used only when pieces are being mass produced. Always have your instructor check any special setup before you operate it.

For regular project work, where only a few pieces will be planed, making special setups to handle small parts will usually not justify the time required. The work should be done by hand. If you plan your work carefully you will be able to machine most of your stock while it is in large pieces.

## SHARPENING JOINTER KNIVES

Jointer knives must be kept keen and sharp in order to do good work. Dull knives will vibrate the stock, cause "kickbacks," and increase the hazards of operation.

### Honing

If there are no serious nicks in the edges, the knives can be honed a number of times before grinding is required. To hone the knives use the following procedure:
1. Disconnect the electrical power by pulling the plug or turning off the main switch and locking the panel.
2. Remove the fence, lower the infeed table, and clean the cutterhead.
3. Lower the outfeed table until a straightedge resting on it aligns with the knife bevel with about 5 deg. of clearance, Fig. 13-16.

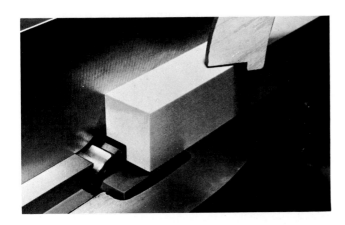

Fig. 13-14. Cutting a rabbet. Work carefully since the guard cannot be used.

Fig. 13-16. Setting cutterhead to hone knives. Outfeed table is lowered slightly.

4. A gauge block can be made so that the infeed table can be adjusted to this setting. The other knives are then easily set in the same position.

5. Drive a wooden wedge between the cutterhead and frame to lock it in position.

6. Wrap a piece of paper around one end of a silicon carbide oilstone, saturate it with oil, and hone the knife edge, Fig. 13-17. Stop as soon as a slight wire edge starts to form.

7. Repeat the operation on the other two knives. Try to hone each knife the same amount.

8. Use a fine slip stone and lightly stroke the front of the knife to remove the wire edge. Keep the stone aligned with the surface of the knife.

9. Clean the machine and readjust the table, fence, and guard. Inspect all settings carefully, connect the power, and make several trial cuts.

The knives may be jointed lightly before the honing operation, by holding an oilstone on the table and just touching the high point of the rotating edge. The cutterhead should be turned by hand unless the machine is equipped with a special jointing attachment.

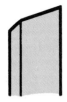
*Be careful when honing jointer knives; they become razor sharp! You can receive a serious cut if your fingers should slide along one of them.*

Fig. 13-17. Top. Honing knives with a fine oilstone. Bottom. Close-up view.

## Grinding

After the knives have been honed a number of times they will require grinding. This is a tricky job, unless you have specialized grinders that will insure an accurate bevel (30-35 deg. included angle) with the edge straight. The knives must also be balanced. Usually it is best to remove the knives from the machine and send them to a saw shop where they can be ground by an expert. On some machines it is easy to remove the entire cutterhead for grinding and adjustment.

There are a number of procedures that can be followed when setting jointer knives. A typical procedure that will work for most machines includes the following steps:

1. Disconnect electrical power, remove fence, and lower infeed table. Clean all parts and apply a light film of oil.

2. Place a knife and gib in position. Tighten gib screws just enough to hold them in place.

3. Adjust the position of the knife so that the heel extends above the cutterhead about 1/16 in. Shift the horizontal position of the knife so that the end extends about 1/32 in. beyond the edge of the outfeed table.

4. Adjust the outfeed table to align with the high point of the knife.

5. Place a bar magnet on the outfeed table and over the knife. Loosen the knife and allow the magnet to hold it in position. Roll the cutterhead so the edge of the knife is above the centerline (high point of the knife rotation). Tighten the gib screws. Perform this operation on each end of the knife.

6. Repeat these operations for the other two knives.

7. Check the height of each knife with a straightedge as shown in Fig. 13-18. Lower the outfeed table slightly and with the straightedge in position, roll the cutterhead so the knives will move the straightedge about 1/8 in. Make a mark at the edge of the table for each knife movement. The distance be-

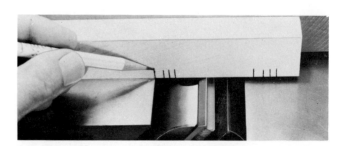
Fig. 13-18. Checking the height of the knives with a wooden straightedge. The cutterhead is turned by hand and each knife should move the straightedge an equal amount. Note that the No. 3 knife is too high.

tween these marks should be equal. Readjust any knife that is high or low.

8. Check the height at both ends of each knife.
9. Tighten each gib screw securely, going over the entire cutterhead several times.
10. Adjust the outfeed table and replace the fence and guard. Turn on the machine and make several trial cuts.

Jointer designs will vary with different makes and models. Study the manufacturer's instruction manual for details concerning a given machine. Some cutter heads are equipped with screw lifters that simplify knife setting, Fig. 13-19. Manufacturers provide various devices for checking and adjusting the jointer knives such as the gauge, Fig. 13-20.

Some jointers, especially larger machines, can be equipped with a knife grinding attachment, Fig. 13-21. Here the knives are precision ground without removing them from the cutterhead.

## LUBRICATION

Modern machines are often equipped with sealed bearings that seldom need attention. Check and follow the manufacturer's recommendation for lubrication schedules. All machines will require a

Fig. 13-21. Motor driven knife grinding and jointing attachment. (Oliver Machinery Co.)

few drops of oil on controls and adjustments at regular intervals. Clean and polish working surfaces with 600 wet-or-dry paper and oil when required. These surfaces can be kept smooth and clean by wiping them often with a light oil or furniture polish. Some crafters apply a coat of paste wax to protect the surface and reduce friction.

## PORTABLE PLANES

When the work to be planed is large and heavy, it is easier to move the tool than the work. The portable electric plane is powered equipment that can be used for jobs such as planing doors, beams, and assembled work. It will perform heavy planing jobs with speed and accuracy.

Fig. 13-22 shows the parts of a typical electric plane. The motor operates at a speed of 15,000 rpm and provides for a 3 1/4 in. planing width and a rabbeting depth of 13/16 in. The cutters are often carbide-tipped. The adjustments of the plane work like a jointer turned upside down. The depth of cut is controlled by either raising or lowering the front shoe which corresponds to the infeed table of the jointer. The rear shoe, like the outfeed table,

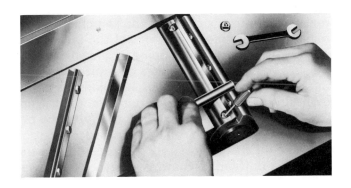

Fig. 13-19. Setting jointer knives. The height of the knife is being adjusted by turning a screw lifter.

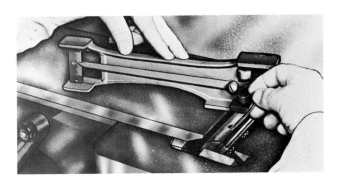

Fig. 13-20. Checking the height of the knife with a special gauge. (Powermatic, Inc.)

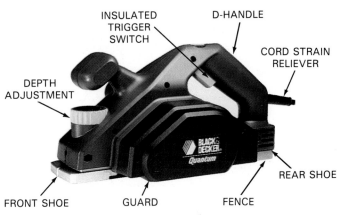

Fig. 13-22. Parts of an electric plane. (Black & Decker)

209

cutter. The fence of the plane is adjustable for planing bevels or can be removed for a surfacing operation as shown in Fig. 13-23.

Hold and operate the power plane in about the same manner as a hand plane. The work should be securely held in such a position that the operation can be easily performed. Start the cut with the front shoe resting firmly on the work and the cutterhead slightly behind the surface. Be sure the electrical cord is clear and will not become fouled. With your hands gripping the toe or knob, and the handle, start the motor and move the plane forward with smooth even pressure on the work. When finishing the cut, apply extra pressure on the rear shoe, Fig. 13-24.

### POWER PLANE SAFETY

1. Study the manufacturer's instructions for detailed information on adjustments and operation.
2. Be certain that the machine is properly grounded.
3. Hold the standard power plane in both hands before you pull the trigger switch. Continue to hold it in both hands until the motor stops after releasing the switch.

4. Always be sure the work is securely clamped and held in the best position for performing the operation.
5. Do not attempt to operate with one hand a regular power plane designed for two hands.
6. Disconnect electrical cords before making adjustments or changing cutters.

The power block plane, Fig. 13-25, is a small, light machine that can be used on small surfaces and edges. It has about the same features and adjustments as the regular power plane, but is designed to operate with one hand. When using this tool, work should be securely held or clamped in place. Control surfaces are small and kickbacks can occur. Be sure your free hand is kept out of the way. The power block plane is a convenient tool for many cabinet making operations, but its use should be limited to the experienced woodcrafter.

## PLANER

### PARTS AND ADJUSTMENTS

The planer is also known as a thickness planer or a SURFACER. Planer size is determined by the widest stock it will plane, Fig. 13-26.

The surfacer or planer is a self-feeding machine. As the stock enters the machine the top surface is gripped by a corrugated feed roll that moves the stock forward. The stock next moves under the chip breaker and into the cutterhead. The chip breaker presses down on stock in front of the cutterhead and prevents excessive chipping by the knives. The pressure bar is located behind the cutterhead and rides on the planed surface. It holds the stock down firmly on the bed and prevents it from vibrating and chattering. Behind the pressure bar is the powered outfeed roll which moves the stock out of the machine, Fig. 13-27. Directly under the infeed and outfeed rolls are two rolls that are set slightly above the surface of the table and help carry the stock. They are usually free-turning on small machines, while on larger machines they are

Fig. 13-23. Using a portable electric plane to surface a large beam. (Skil Corp.)

Fig. 13-24. Using a portable electric plane to trim the edge of a piece of stock. (Makita U.S.A., Inc.)

Fig. 13-25. Planing a chamfer with a power block plane. The gauge sets the chamfer angle.

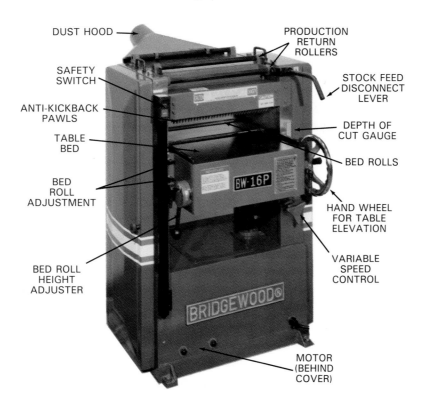

DUST HOOD

PRODUCTION RETURN ROLLERS

SAFETY SWITCH

STOCK FEED DISCONNECT LEVER

ANTI-KICKBACK PAWLS

DEPTH OF CUT GAUGE

TABLE BED

BED ROLLS

BED ROLL ADJUSTMENT

BW-16P

HAND WHEEL FOR TABLE ELEVATION

BRIDGEWOOD®

BED ROLL HEIGHT ADJUSTER

VARIABLE SPEED CONTROL

MOTOR (BEHIND COVER)

Fig. 13-26. Parts of a standard 16 in. (406 mm) planer.

powered. The table and lower roll assembly is adjustable for various thicknesses of stock.

The speed of the cutterhead usually ranges from 3000 to 3600 rpm. It may be directly driven or belt driven. The feeding mechanism may be powered by the cutterhead motor or by a separate motor, and can be adjusted to provide speeds of 10 to 50 fpm.

Planers produce a large amount of fine shavings and wood dust. They should not be operated without an adequate dust collection arrangement. Dust collectors are of two general types: a CENTRAL SYSTEM where ducts from a number of machines are connected to a single blower and filter, or UNIT COLLECTORS that are attached directly to one machine and contain the blower and filtering unit in a single cabinet.

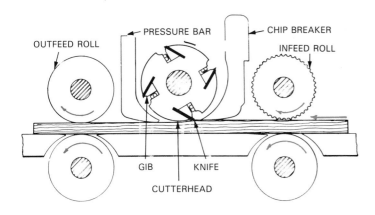

Fig. 13-27. Planer operation. (Forest Products Laboratory)

OUTFEED ROLL

PRESSURE BAR

CHIP BREAKER

INFEED ROLL

GIB

KNIFE

CUTTERHEAD

## PLANER SAFETY

1. Be sure you have the instructor's permission to operate the machine.
2. Adjust the machine to the correct thickness of cut before turning on the power.
3. Stock should be at least 12 in. long, or several inches longer than the distance between the centers of the feed rolls.
4. Surface only new lumber that is free of loose knots and serious defects.
5. Plane with the grain, or at a slight angle with the grain. Never attempt to plane cross grain.
6. Stand to one side of the work being fed through the machine.
7. Do not look into the throat of the planer while it is running.
8. Do not feed stock of different thicknesses side by side through the machine, unless it is equipped with a sectional infeed roll.
9. Handle and hold the stock only in an area beyond the ends of the table.
10. If the machine is not working properly, shut off the power at once and inform your instructor.

## OPERATING THE PLANER

Adjust the height of the bed so that the thickness gauge reads about 1/16 in. less than the thickness of the stock. Examine the stock and determine the

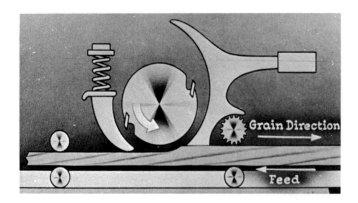

Fig. 13-28. Planer feed and grain direction.
(Jam Handy Organization)

direction of the grain. Be sure the bottom surface of the board is flat. See Fig. 13-28.

Turn the machine on, lay the end of the stock on the table, and feed it into the machine as shown in Fig. 13-29. Raise up on the other end until the stock has progressed beyond the pressure bar. Move to the rear of the machine and support long boards as they come from the machine. If these boards are not supported, they will tend to force

up the pressure bar and a nick will be made in the end of the board, Fig. 13-30.

Return the stock to the front of the machine without turning it over or changing its position. Check the thickness. If a second cut is necessary, set the machine. See if the second cut should be made on the opposite side of the stock. If so, turn it END OVER END so the grain will be feeding in the correct direction.

When surfacing a number of pieces to a given thickness, run the thickest pieces first. As they are reduced to the thickness of the other pieces, run all of them through the machine at the same setting. The thickness of the cut will be determined by width of the stock, hardness of the wood and finish desired. An average cut is about 1/16 in.

When surfacing several pieces of short stock, they should be fed as shown in Fig. 13-31. By butting the ends together the pieces will push each other out of the machine and they will be less likely to stick under the pressure bar.

Thin stock (under 3/8 in.) should be surfaced by placing it on top of a carrier board. This board must be straight and true and somewhat longer and wider than the stock. A strip of thin wood glued to the end of the carrier will help keep the stock in posi-

Fig. 13-29. Stand to the side when feeding stock into the planer.
(Delta International Machinery Corp.)

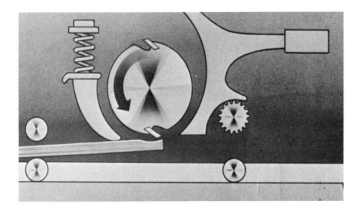

Fig. 13-30. To prevent nicking, support long boards as they enter and leave the planer.

tion during the planing operation.

Square parts, such as legs, can be planed to finished size by first squaring two adjacent faces on the jointer and then planing the two opposite faces at the same thickness setting.

## ADJUSTING AND SHARPENING THE PLANER

Requirements and recommendations for planer maintenance will vary with different makes and models. Study the manufacturer's maintenance manual for detailed instructions.

The bed of the planer must be parallel with the cutterhead and must move smoothly up and down. Adjustments involve the jack screws and gibs. The maintenance manual should be checked before any of these adjustments are made. The lower rolls carry the stock slightly above the surface of the bed. The height will vary with the kind and condition of the stock. Rough stock will require a high setting (0.25 in.) while hard, smooth lumber can be planed at a low setting (.005 in.). For general purpose work a setting of .010 to .015 in. is usually satisfactory. When rolls are set too high, a snipe or bite will appear on the ends. If set too low, the stock will not feed through the machine easily.

Fig. 13-31. Butt the ends of short pieces together. They also can be turned at a slight angle to provide a smoother feed.

The pressure bar is spring mounted and adjustable. The setting should provide enough pressure on the stock to prevent vibration. It should not be so great however, that it restricts the movement of the stock through the machine. This is one of the most important adjustments on the planer. Check the maintenance manual for directions.

Planer knives can be honed in somewhat the same manner as jointer knives. Some machines may have a frame that will support one end of the oilstone or a metal clip that can be attached so that it will ride on the cutterhead as shown in Fig. 13-32. Some machines are equipped with a jointing attachment that can be used lightly before the honing operation.

Knives can be ground by removing them from the machine and resetting them with a special gauge or dial indicator. Many modern machines are equipped with a knife grinding attachment as shown in Figs. 13-33 and 13-34. The device consists of a motor driven grinding unit that slides back and forth along a bar mounted on the machine. Since

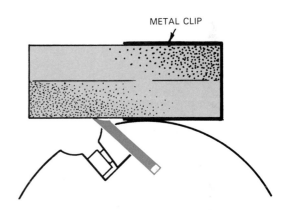

Fig. 13-32. Honing planer knives with an oilstone.

Fig. 13-33. Knife grinding attachment mounted on an 18 in. planer.

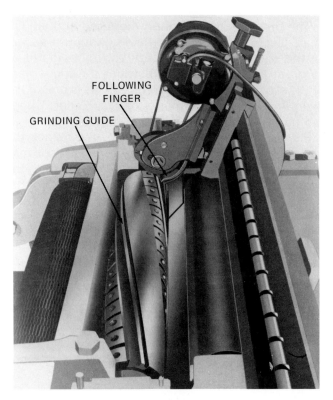

FOLLOWING FINGER

GRINDING GUIDE

Fig. 13-34. Grinding spiral cutterhead knives. Following finger slides along the grinding guide and rotates the cutterhead into the correct position as the grinding wheel is fed along the knife. Spiral knives produce less noise than straight knives. (Wisconsin Knife Works, Inc.)

it is so important that all knives be exactly the same height, the attachment usually includes a jointing device. This abrasive stone is held in a carrier against the knives while the machine is running. After jointing, the knives are ground, Fig. 13-35.

The rolls, cutterhead, and bed must be kept clean and free of gum and pitch. Gum on the rolls tends to hold wood chips. These chips indent the surface of the stock as it passes through. Use a cloth saturated with kerosene or mineral spirits to clean the machine parts. Heavy coatings of pitch or gum may require the use of a fine grade of steel wool.

Lubrication schedules will vary depending on the make or model. Check the manufacturer's recommendations and follow them carefully.

## INDUSTRIAL PLANING MACHINES

To plane a flat surface on warped lumber, industry employs a machine called a facer, Fig. 13-36. The machine resembles the regular jointer with the addition of a special feeding mechanism. This mechanism consists of a belt or chain studded with spring loaded shoes or rubber toes. They feed and hold the lumber firmly but do not flatten it, as it moves over the cutterhead in about the same manner as you feed stock on a regular jointer. The feeding mechanism can be raised or lowered for various stock thicknesses. Machine widths vary from 24 to 36 in. with feeding rates of 40 to 100 fpm.

Industrial surfacers and planing machines are manufactured in a wide range of sizes. Fig. 13-37 shows a heavy-duty machine that is available in a width of 60 in. Production machines are usually equipped with knives that are jointed and ground in the machine with diamond grinding wheels. They are manufactured with such precision that accuracies of .001 in. can be maintained in surfacing operations. In addition to wood they are used to plane rubber or vinyl tile, hardboard, fiberboard, composition siding, and plastic laminated sheets. Double surface planers, with a cutter head above and below the bed or table are available and are often used in production work.

Facers and planers are usually combined in a production planing operation, Fig. 13-38. Power operated cut-off saws are used to cut the rough

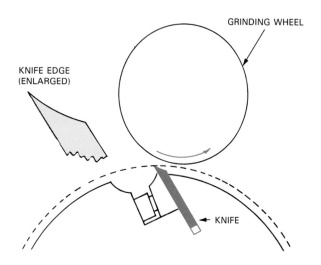

GRINDING WHEEL

KNIFE EDGE (ENLARGED)

← KNIFE

Fig. 13-35. Grinding planer knives.

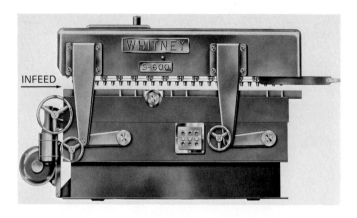

INFEED

Fig. 13-36. 36 in. facer. The cutterhead has a diameter of 5 1/2 in. and is driven by a 15 hp motor at a speed of 4200 rpm. The overhead feed belt is driven by a 1 1/2 hp motor. (Newman Machine Co.)

Fig. 13-37. Machine operator feeds lumber into double-surface planer. Machine's rate of feed is adjustable from 20 to 120 fpm (6.1 to 36.6 mpm). (Jordan Millwork Co.)

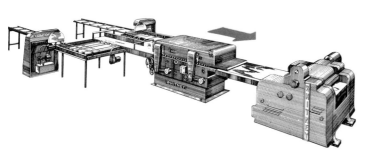

Fig. 13-38. Facer and single surfacer connected with conveyors to make a continuous planing operation.

Fig. 13-39. A combination jointing and surfacing machine. Cutterheads are 6 in. in diameter and directly driven by 15 hp motors. A 3 hp motor is used for the variable feed mechanism.

lumber to length and remove serious defects. A transverse conveyor carries it to the infeed conveyor of the facer where the bottom surface is planed flat and true. From the facer the stock moves into the planer and the top surface is planed to provide the required thickness.

The operations of the facer and single surfacer or planer are combined in a production machine called a "straitoplane," Fig. 13-39. Lumber is carried over a table and cutterhead in the same manner as the facer and then goes through a single surfacer located on the outfeed table.

Fig. 13-40 shows an abrasive planer in operation. This machine will produce a smooth surface on stock up to 64 in. wide.

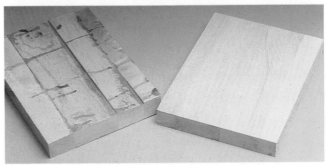

Fig. 13-40. Top. Modern abrasive planer. Capacity of the machine is 64 inches in width. (Timesavers, Inc.) Bottom. Results of a single pass through the abrasive planer.

## TEST YOUR KNOWLEDGE, Chapter 13

Please do not write in the text. Place your answers on a separate sheet of paper.

1. The _____ is the most versatile of the two power planing machines. The _____ is a single purpose machine.
2. List the four steps in the sequence for planing stock.
3. The size of a jointer is determined by the length of the:
   a. Fence.
   b. Infeed table.
   c. Knives.
   d. Outfeed table.
   e. None of the above.
4. Why must the outfeed table be level with the knife edges at the highest point of rotation?
5. Narrow pieces of stock can be planed using a _____ _____.
6. Knives must be ground every time they are honed. True or False?
7. The _____ _____ on a portable plane corresponds with the infeed table on the jointer.
   a. Rear shoe.
   b. Chip deflector.
   c. Depth adjustment.
   d. Front shoe.
   e. None of the above.
8. Name the two types of dust collector systems used with planers.

## ACTIVITIES

1. Select a small jointer that would be satisfactory for a home workshop. Prepare complete specifications including size, length of bed, speed, adjustment features, motor size, and other items. Include a cost estimate.
2. Prepare complete specifications for a planer that would be appropriate for a school shop. Include size, cutterhead speed and diameter, cutterhead motor size, rates of feed, motor size for feed mechanism, floor space, net weight, and other items. Secure information from supplier's and manufacturer's catalogs.
3. Prepare and present to the class a report on dust collection systems. Include both central systems and unit collectors. Use blackboard drawings to describe how cyclones work. Suggest ways to control dust in the home workshop either with homemade or purchased equipment. Write to manufacturers for descriptive literature. You can secure addresses from your local lumber dealer or from woodworking magazines.

 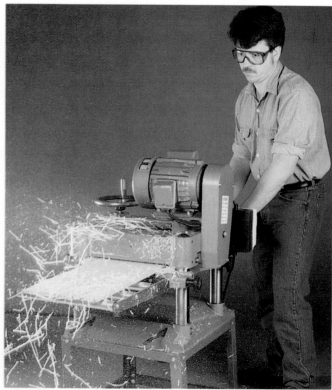

These planers can handle big jobs. (Left. Delta International Machinery Corp. Right. Grizzly Imports, Inc.)

On this abrasive planing machine a wide sanding belt, traveling at high speed, removes stock quickly and quietly. Modern woodworking plants often use this method to surface glued-up solid stock and panels of particle board. Contact roll is 10 in. in diameter. Feed rates vary from 30 to 75 fpm (9 to 23 mpm). (Timesavers, Inc.)

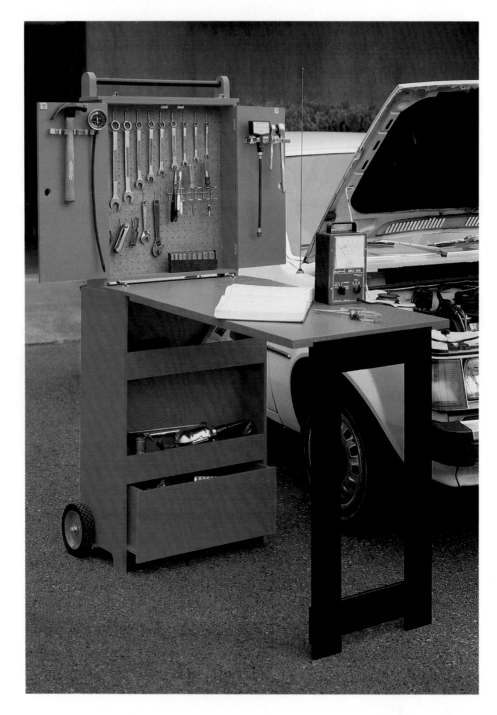

Most of the cutting required for this plywood project was performed on the table saw.
(American Plywood Association)

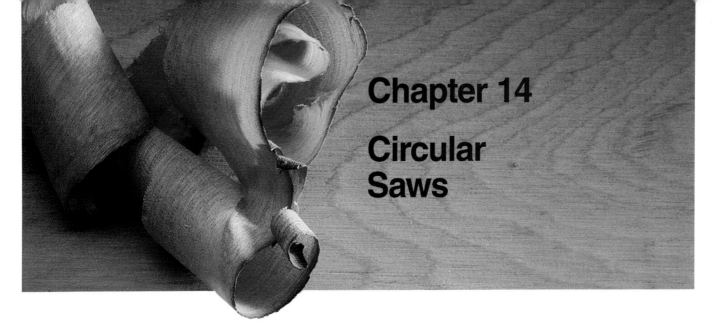

# Chapter 14

# Circular Saws

There are many kinds and sizes of saws that use a circular blade. In the school shop you will learn to use a table saw. In addition, you may have experience with a radial arm saw and a portable electric saw. Industry uses circular saw blades on a wide range of specialized production machines, some of which are described later in this unit.

## TABLE SAW

The table saw is also called a CIRCULAR SAW or BENCH SAW. Sometimes it is referred to as a variety saw, because of the many sawing operations it will perform. Fig. 14-1 shows a standard tilting arbor table saw. The arbor is the shaft on which the blade is mounted. It can be set to cut angles with the table remaining horizontal. Some smaller table saws have a fixed arbor and the table is tilted to make angular cuts. The tilting arbor saw is generally considered to be more accurate and easier to operate than the tilting table saw.

On some saws the section of table to the left of the blade is mounted on bearings and can be moved forward and backward, Fig. 14-2. This permits

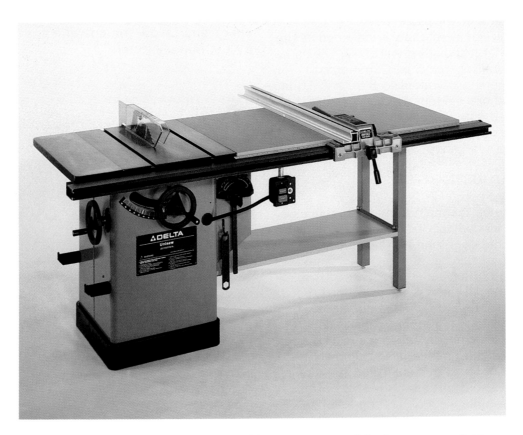

Fig. 14-1. The Delta Unisaw is considered by many as one of the best saws available. (Delta International Machinery Corp.)

Fig. 14-2. This table saw has a tilting arbor and movable table. (Delta International Machinery Corp.)

Fig. 14-3. This planer-molder saw planes, rips, and shapes in one pass. (Foley-Belsaw Co.)

accuracy and easy stock handling when crosscutting wide boards. The table can be locked into position for ripping cuts. Still another type of saw is called a UNIVERSAL SAW. It has two saw arbors mounted on a large trunnion. By placing a crosscut blade on one and a rip blade on the other, a shift from ripping to crosscutting is easily made by turning a handwheel. This brings the correct blade above the surface of the table.

The general size of a table saw is indicated by the diameter of the largest blade it will carry. The usual size range is from 8 in. to 16 in. Common sizes for home use are generally limited to 8 in. and 10 in. saws. School shops seldom use saws larger than 12 in. Fig. 14-3 shows a versatile planer-molder saw; it is an excellent multipurpose machine for home or school workshop.

## PARTS AND ADJUSTMENTS

Fig. 14-4 shows the main parts of a table saw. There are two handwheels located under the table: one for tilting the arbor, one for raising and lowering the blade. The table has a throat insert plate that can be removed when mounting blades. It is replaced with a special insert when the dado is used. The fence is adjustable to various positions along the table, and guides the stock when making ripping cuts. On some models the fence can be tilted at an angle. The miter gauge, also called a cut-off gauge, slides in grooves that are milled in the table, and is used for crosscutting.

An under-the-table view of a tilting arbor saw is shown in Fig. 14-5. The arbor carries the saw blade which is mounted between a flange and a collar. The collar is held in place with a nut which may have

left-handed threads. Procedures for aligning the table and blade, as well as other adjustments, will vary with different makes and models. Always check and follow the operator's manual provided by the manufacturer.

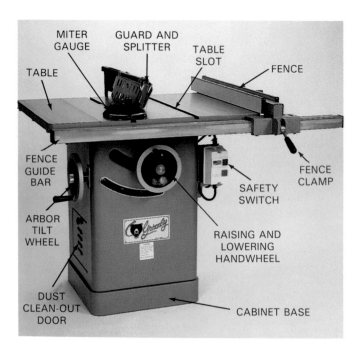

Fig. 14-4. Parts of a tilting arbor table saw. (Grizzly Imports, Inc.)

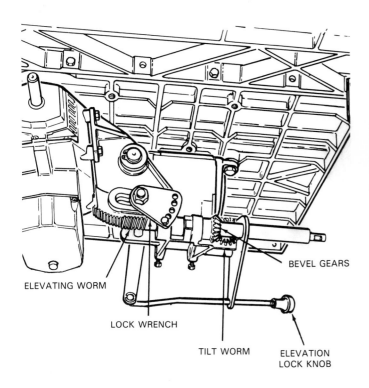

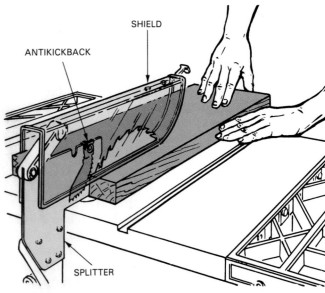

Fig. 14-6. Note the location of the splitter and the antikickback devices on this table saw.

Fig. 14-5. Tilting and elevating mechanism for a tilting arbor table saw. (Sears, Roebuck and Co.)

## GUARDS

Saw guards are not foolproof and their use will not completely eliminate the hazards of table saw operation. They should however, be standard equipment on all machines and used for all operations.

A good guard covers the blade but does not completely hide it from view. It should include a splitter that prevents the saw kerf from closing behind the blade and also prevents stock from feeding back over the top of the blade. The guard should be equipped with an antikickback device to prevent the blade from throwing the work back toward the operator. A good guard should be easy to use and adjust. Fig. 14-6 shows a guard that has plastic shields, a splitter, and antikickback feature.

## SAW BLADES

To specify a circular saw blade, list the kind, diameter, gauge, number of teeth, and arbor hole size. The common kinds of blades are the RIP, CROSSCUT, ROUGH CUT (RC) COMBINATION, STANDARD or FLAT GROUND COMBINATION, and HOLLOW GROUND COMBINATION. There are other kinds designed for special work. Examples of these include the trimmer, edger, groover, inserted tooth groover, and concave groover.

The GAUGE (thickness) of a blade varies with its diameter. A large blade will require a greater thickness to support the rim and prevent it from

vibrating. Heavy cuts in hard wood will require extra blade thickness. The gauge of the blade however, must be kept to a minimum; a thick blade will cut a wide kerf, waste stock, and require more power. Saw manufacturers use the Birmingham and Stubbs gauge for indicating blade thickness.

The NUMBER OF TEETH will indicate blade size and coarseness of the cut. It will also determine the rate of feed. Fine tooth saws must be fed slowly because the gullets are too small to handle sawdust from heavy cuts. Large teeth can be fed rapidly but make a rough cut. The following table lists some gauges and numbers of teeth appropriate for average work in the school shop.

| SIZE | 8 in. | 10 in. | 12 in. | 14 in. |
|---|---|---|---|---|
| GAUGE | 18 | 16 | 14 | 13-12 |
| DECIMAL EQUIVALENT | .049 | .065 | .083 | .095-.109 |
| NO. TEETH RIP | 36-40 | 30-36 | 24-36 | 24-36 |
| NO. TEETH CROSSCUT | 100-120 | 72-100 | 72-100 | 60-100 |
| NO. TEETH R.C. COMB. | 30-44 | 36-44 | 40-44 | 44 |
| NO. SECTIONS STAN. COMB. | 12-14 | 14-16 | 16-18 | 18-20 |

ARBOR HOLES for 8 and 10 in. blades are usually 5/8 in. in diameter. Blades 12 in. and 14 in. in diameter usually have a 3/4 or 1 in. arbor hole.

Rip and crosscut blades, Fig. 14-7, are for a single purpose. The rip blade teeth are filed straight across to form chisel shapes that do a fast and efficient job of cutting along the grain. The hook angle is at least 30 deg. Crosscut blades have teeth that are filed to a point. These teeth cut through the wood fibers easily when fed across the grain. The rip blade leaves a rough cut when used for cutoff work. The crosscut saw should be used only for cutoff or miter work. If it is used for ripping it will rapidly heat and dull. This is especially true when it is used to cut end grain, such as cheek cuts of tenons.

Fig. 14-8 shows two types of combination blades. They cut well both with the grain and across the grain. Combination blades do not work as efficiently or stay sharp as long as the rip or crosscut blades when applied to the latter's specific operation, so are seldom used in production work. For example, in a production ripping operation the best blade to use would be a rip blade. Combination blades, however, are suitable for use on a single arbor saw for general purpose work. In addition, they save a great deal of blade changing time.

The rough cut combination has teeth that look like rip teeth but with a smaller hook angle. The teeth are filed at an angle across the top to form a modified chisel shape. The standard combination has some crosscut teeth and some rip teeth. The rip teeth, called RAKERS, are filed straight across and are not set.

Fig. 14-7. Left. Rip saw blade. Right. Crosscut blade.

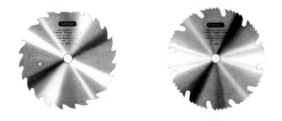

Fig. 14-8. Combination blades are useful for general purpose work. Left. Rough cut combination. Right. Standard combination or miter.

Fig. 14-9. Hollow ground combination.

A hollow ground combination blade is shown in Fig. 14-9. The shape of the teeth is similar to that of the standard combination, but is not set. The clearance for the blade is secured by grinding a gradual taper from the rim to the hub or collar area. The thickness is usually reduced about three gauges. For example, one manufacturer's 10 in. hollow ground blade has a rim gauge of 14 and tapers to a gauge of 17 at the edge of the saw collar. This kind of blade is often called a planer blade since the sides of the teeth actually plane the wood, resulting in a very smooth surface. Use should be limited to high quality finish work on stock that is straight and true. Since the clearance is so slight, it will burn easily if there is binding of the kerf caused by warped or casehardened stock.

A variety of saw blades are available, in addition to those just discussed. Fig. 14-10, left, shows a blade designed especially for making fine cuts in hardwood plywood. Fig. 14-10, right, shows a carbide tipped blade. This type of blade is used extensively in production work because it will stay sharp at least 10 times longer than a standard blade. The teeth are not dulled by hardboard, plastic laminates, or other materials that have an abrasive effect on regular blades. Wear a faceshield when using a carbide tipped blade, because the teeth do occasionally break loose from the blade.

Fig. 14-11 shows a carbide tipped blade being sharpened with a special saw tooth grinder. Note the teeth have been brazed to the blade. In addition to the face, each tooth must be individually ground to shape on the side and top, Fig. 14-12.

There is also a special hardened steel tooth blade available that stays sharp longer than a conventional blade. It cannot be filed and is sharpened by grinding. Fig. 14-13 shows a typical sharpening operation for a specially hardened steel blade.

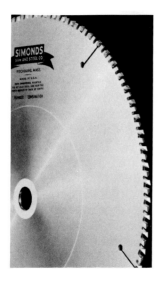

Fig. 14-10. Left. Plywood blade. Right. Carbide tipped blade designed for either crosscutting or ripping.

Fig. 14-11. Grinding the teeth to proper shape is one of the important steps in the manufacture of high quality saw blades. (Foley-Belsaw Co.)

## SAFETY RULES FOR THE TABLE SAW

The following safety rules should be observed when working with the table saw. In addition, review the power equipment safety rules given in Chapter 3.

1. Be certain the blade is sharp and the right one for your work.
2. The saw is equipped with a guard and a splitter. Be sure to use them.
3. Set the blade so it extends about 1/4 in. above the stock to be cut.
4. Stand to one side of the operating blade and do not reach across it.
5. MAINTAIN A 4 IN. MARGIN OF SAFETY. (Do not let your hands come closer than 4 in. to the operating blade even though the guard is in position.)
6. Stock should be surfaced and at least one edge jointed before being cut on the saw.
7. The position of the stock must be controlled either by the fence or the miter gauge. NEVER CUT STOCK FREE HAND.
8. Use only new stock that is free of knots, splits, and warp.
9. Stop the saw before making adjustments to the fence or blade.
10. Do not let small scrap cuttings accumulate around the saw blade. Use a push stick to move them away.
11. Resawing and other special setups must be inspected by the instructor before power is turned on.
12. The dado or any special blades should be removed from the saw after use.
13. Students helping to ''tail-off'' the saw should not push or pull on the stock but only support

Fig. 14-12. Each tooth is individually ground to shape on a carbide blade. Top. Grinding the side. Bottom. Grinding the top. (Foley-Belsaw Co.)

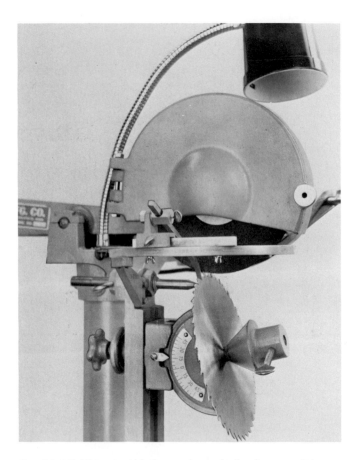

Fig. 14-13. This steel blade requires grinding because it is too hard to file. (Foley-Belsaw Co.)

it. The operator must control the feed and direction of the cut.

14. Wear a faceshield when using a carbide tipped blade. This will provide extra protection in the event a tooth should come loose from the blade.

15. As you complete your work, turn off the machine and remain until the blade has stopped. Clear the saw table and place waste cuttings in the scrap box.

## CHANGING SAW BLADES

Remove the TABLE INSERT PLATE (also called a throat plate) and raise the arbor to its highest point. On universal saws the work can be done under the table, with the blade at its lowest point. Place a wrench on the arbor nut and turn it in the same direction that the saw turns when in operation. This will be counterclockwise on most machines. Hold the blade stationary with a piece of wood wedged between the teeth and the table or frame. Remove the nut, collar, and blade. Do not lay the blade on the table or a metal surface.

Before mounting another blade, check the arbor, flange, collar, and nut. They must be clean and free

of pitch, gum, and rust. Use a cloth lightly saturated with kerosene or mineral spirits to clean the saw parts. Rust should be removed with a piece of 600 wet-or-dry abrasive paper.

The arbor flange should have a small notch or punched hole on the outside edge that is turned up when the blade is mounted. Place the saw on the arbor with the teeth pointing in the correct direction and the trademark turned up. Replace the collar with the recessed side against the blade. Hold the blade with a piece of wood and tighten the nut by turning it in the opposite direction of blade rotation, Fig. 14-14. Replace the table insert.

By always mounting the blade with the arbor in the same position and with the trademark up, the perimeter of the blade should run true. The clearance of the arbor hole will always be located in the same position and correction will be made if the arbor is slightly off center.

## RIPPING TO WIDTH

Stock to be ripped must have at least one flat face to rest on the table and one straight edge to run along the rip fence.

Raise the blade until it projects above the table a distance equal to the thickness of the stock, PLUS 1/4 in. Unlock the fence and move it along the guide bar to the required width. For an accurate setting check the measurement between the fence and a point of a tooth on the blade that is set toward the fence, Fig. 14-15. Lock the fence in position, place the guard over the blade, and start the machine.

Place the stock flat on the table with the straight edge against the fence and move the stock into the blade. Be sure the guard with splitter is properly positioned for the operation. Continue a steady feed

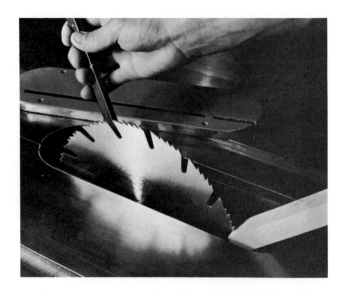

Fig. 14-14. Tightening saw arbor nut.

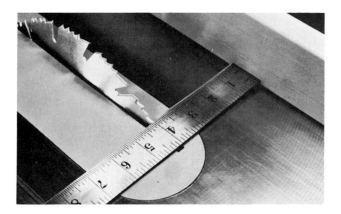

Fig. 14-15. Setting the fence.

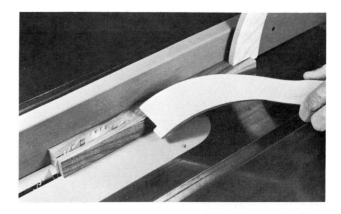

Fig. 14-17. Ripping small pieces. Be careful! Guard cannot be used.

through the entire cut. Keep your hands at least 4 in. away from the blade even though it is covered by a guard, Fig. 14-16. When the saw is operating, stand slightly to one side of the cutting line. When cutting long boards have someone support the stock as it leaves the table. Avoid reaching over the saw to ''catch'' short pieces. Have a helper take them, or let them fall into a stock cart or to the floor.

### Ripping Small Pieces and Strips

Narrow strips and short pieces can be ripped as shown in Fig. 14-17. Use a push stick in each hand. For this job THE GUARD CANNOT BE USED, so

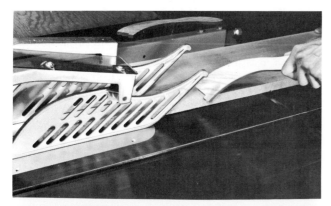

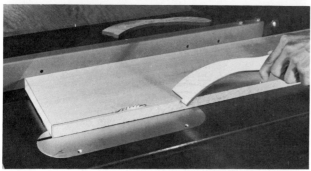

Fig. 14-16. Ripping stock to width. Top. Guard in position. Bottom. Guard and splitter removed to show operation.

special care must be taken when performing this operation.

Standard practice places the stock between the fence and the blade with the waste to the outside. Very thin strips however, will be fouled between the fence and blade so they are usually cut as shown in Fig. 14-18, top. The edges of the stock must be parallel and the rip fence reset after each cut. Sometimes the edge is jointed and sanded before it is ripped, thus providing a finished strip for veneering or inlay. By another method, the thin strips are first formed by cuts made in the edge of the piece and then all of them are ripped off at once, Fig. 14-18, bottom.

When cutting thin strips and veneers, the slit in the table insert may be too wide or the veneer may slip under the fence. An auxiliary table surface should be used. It can be made by setting the fence, lowering the blade below the table and then clamping a piece of 1/8 in. hardboard to the table. Turn on the saw and then elevate the blade so it cuts through the hardboard and to the height required.

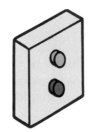

*Always think through the operation before turning on the machine. Know what you are going to do and what the machine will do. If you have the slightest doubt about how it will work, check with your instructor first.*

### RESAWING

Resawing is a ripping operation in which the stock is cut on edge into two thinner pieces. If the width of the stock does not exceed the maximum height that the blade can be raised, the operation can be completed in one cut. For wider boards set the saw to cut a little above the centerline and make two

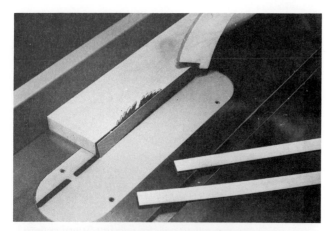

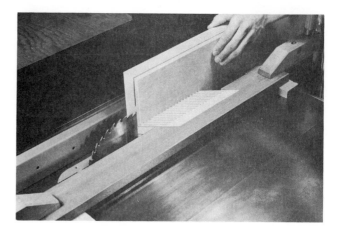

Fig. 14-19. Making the second cut of a resawing operation.

Fig. 14-18. Top. Ripping a single strip. Below. Ripping off thin strips after they were formed by edge cuts. Note that push sticks being used and the guard has been removed to show the operation.

## CROSSCUTTING TO A LINE

When you have only a few cuts to make, it is easiest to square lines across the surface of the stock and follow them in the crosscutting operation. Make a check mark on the side of the line where the saw kerf will be located. The guard tends to obscure the blade and it is often helpful when aligning the cut to use a line scribed in the table surface. Since most of your work will be located to the left, it should extend back from the left side of the blade as shown in Fig. 14-20. When using this line, allowances will need to be made for blades of different gauges or settings.

Set the height of the blade 1/4 in. above the work. Move the fence to one side and well out of the way. Place the miter gauge in the table slot and set it for a right angle (90 deg. mark on the protractor scale). Check the guard to see that it is in position and properly aligned.

Hold the stock against the miter gauge with your left hand. Align the cutting mark with the saw blade, or the scribed line, so that the saw kerf will be on the waste side of the line. Turn on the motor, grasp

cuts. Keep the same face of the stock against the fence for both cuts. Using a feather board increases the accuracy and safety of the resawing operation. Wide boards can first be cut on the table saw. After that operation, the center section can be cut apart on the band saw.

A feather board may be made by ripping a series of saw kerfs about 1/8 in. apart in the end of a board that has been cut off at an angle of approximately 30 deg. The strips that are formed are similar to a series of "springs" that apply a smooth, even pressure. For ripping operations the feather board should be set in a position so it will hold the stock against the fence, but will not close the saw kerf and pinch the saw.

Beginning students should perform their first resawing operations by setting the saw slightly below the center of the work, leaving about 1/4 in. to hold the two pieces together after the second cut, Fig. 14-19. The pieces can then be cut apart with a handsaw.

Since resawing operations require heavy ripping cuts, always use a sharp rip blade.

Fig. 14-20. Aligning stock with line scribed in saw table.

the knob of the gauge in your right hand, and move the stock through the cut, Fig. 14-21.

Use a push stick to move waste cuttings away from the blade and make additional cuttings as required. When you complete your work, turn off the motor and wait for the blade to stop before leaving the machine. Clear the table, and pick up waste cuttings and place them in the scrap box.

Maintain the same margin of safety (4 in.) as for ripping. If you have small pieces to cut, you should do the work by hand or clamp the stock to another piece, Fig. 14-22. The guard cannot be used for the setup shown so you should be especially careful.

## CUTTING DUPLICATE PARTS TO LENGTH

When you have a number of pieces to cut that are 6 in. or longer in length, you can use a stop rod mounted in the miter gauge as shown in Fig. 14-23. The work is fed in from the right side to the stop and then moved through the saw. The guard will not interfere with this operation and should be used. Be certain the metal stop rod is not in the cutting path of the blade.

Pieces can be cut to the same length by attaching

Fig. 14-22. Cutting small piece by clamping it to a larger one.

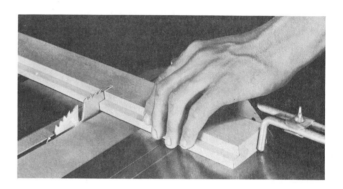

Fig. 14-23. Cutting duplicate lengths using stop rod. Guard can be used for this, but has been removed to show this operation.

Fig. 14-21. Top. Squaring stock to a marked line. Bottom. Guard removed to show operation.

a clearance block to the fence, Fig. 14-24. The block must be thick enough so the distance between the fence and the blade will be greater than the diagonal measurement of the pieces being cut. This will prevent the pieces from flying off the table if they cock while going through the cutting path. Square the end of the stock, and then move it from the left along the miter gauge until it is against the clearance block. Hold the stock firmly to the miter gauge and make the cut. Repeat the operation for additional pieces. The clearance block should be located back of the saw blade a distance equal to the width of the stock.

Duplicate parts may be cut to length between the fence and blade if HELD FIRMLY AGAINST THE MITER GAUGE THROUGHOUT THE OPERATION. As the stock is cut off, you must continue to hold it against the miter gauge as you move it clear of the saw, either out to the rear of the table or back to the starting position. If the cut piece is left unsupported between the blade and fence it may

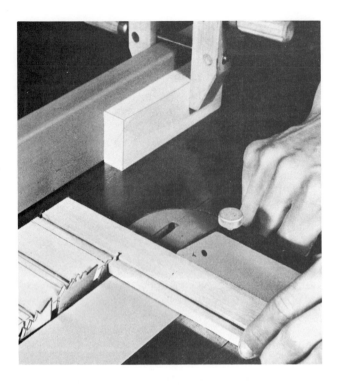

Fig. 14-24. Using clearance block to cut duplicate parts.

turn in a diagonal position and be thrown back violently by the blade.

## CUTTING PLYWOOD

Special attention must be given to crosscutting plywood because the pieces are usually wider and there is a tendency for fine hardwood veneers to splinter along the surface. Ripping does not usually create any extra problems. Lines should be squared across the pieces and followed while making the cut, Fig. 14-25. Sometimes it is better on wide pieces to reverse the position of the miter gauge and hold it against the front edge of the work. For a fine finish use a special plywood or hollow ground

blade. The combination blade may work better if it is raised higher than 1/4 in. above the surface of the stock, but always check with your instructor before doing this. Very large pieces of plywood are difficult to handle on the table saw. For these cuts use a handsaw, portable circular saw, or sabre saw.

## CUTTING ANGLES, BEVELS, AND TAPERS

Angles are cut across the face of the stock by holding the stock against the miter gauge which is set at the required angle. There is a tendency for the stock to "creep" along the face of the gauge so it must be held firmly. This movement can also be prevented by gluing (use rubber cement) a piece of abrasive paper to the face of the gauge. Some miter gauges can be equipped with a clamping attachment, Fig. 14-26. Compound angles are formed by tilting the blade and setting the gauge at an angle.

Bevels and chamfers may be cut by tilting the blade and using the miter gauge to guide flat, rectangular stock. On some pieces, especially long strips, it will be best to rip the bevel as shown in Fig. 14-27. The fence must be moved to the left of the saw blade, otherwise the stock may wedge between it and the blade and be kicked back. When you are performing any of these opertions for the first time, always have your instructor check your setup before turning on the machine.

Cutting a taper on the table saw using a special fixture is shown in Fig. 14-28. The stock is held at an angle while it is fed through the cut. The notches in the tail of the fixture can be cut on the band saw to provide the required taper. After the notched block is cut away by many different setups, a new one can be glued on. When cutting a taper on two opposite edges, as shown, you will need to make two notches: one for the first cut and one

Fig. 14-25. Cutting plywood with a special blade. Guard should be used. It has been removed here to show the operation.

Fig. 14-26. Cutting a compound angle using a miter gauge clamp.

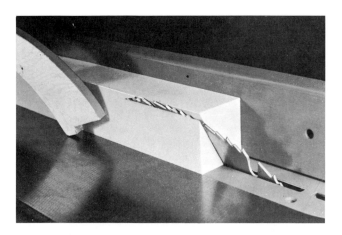

Fig. 14-27. Ripping a bevel. Fence is positioned on the left side of the blade.

Fig. 14-28. Cutting a taper with a special fixture. Splitter guard should be used.

for the second. Use a push stick to hold the stock in the fixture. A splitter guard will also help hold the work. It is usually best to move the work through the cut and have a helper remove it after it has cleared the back of the blade.

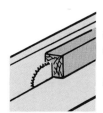 *Have your instructor check all special setups before performing the operation. You will then know if the cut can be made safely.*

## CUTTING RABBETS, DADOS, AND GROOVES

These joints can be cut rapidly and accurately with a dado head. When only a few joints need to

be cut however, the time required to mount the dado head may not be justified. In this instance, it is best to use a single blade.

To cut a rabbet, first lay out the width and depth on the front end of the piece. Raise the blade to the correct height to cut the depth and set the fence to the width. Measure from the outside of the blade to the fence. Make the first cut with the stock held flat on the table and against the fence. Next, raise the blade to equal the width and adjust the fence so this cut will meet the one made for depth. Fig. 14-29 shows this cut being made. Making the cuts in this sequence will prevent the waste strip from being trapped between the fence, blade, and work.

Use the same procedure to form a rabbet on the end of wide stock. For stock that is narrow, use both the fence and miter gauge. Set the fence to provide the correct width and raise the blade to cut the depth. Hold the stock against the miter gauge and fence, then make the first cut. Remove the waste with a series of cuts, moving the stock a little further away from the fence on each stroke, while holding it securely against the miter gauge.

Fig. 14-30 shows a dado being cut with a single blade. Set the blade to the correct height and then make a series of cuts inside the layout lines. All of the waste can be removed with the blade or a chisel. If you are cutting several duplicate pieces, use the fence to make the outside cuts.

A groove can be formed by making a series of cuts with a single blade, Fig. 14-31. The outside cut is made first, as shown. Move the fence toward the blade a distance equal to the kerf width for each cut until the other side of the groove is reached. When cutting duplicate parts, run each piece over the machine before changing the fence setting.

Fig. 14-29. Making the second cut on a rabbet. This procedure prevents the waste from being trapped.

Fig. 14-30. Cutting a dado with a series of cuts. Guard can be used.

Fig. 14-32. Parts of a dado head.

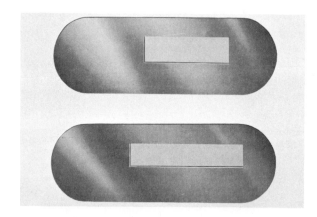

Fig. 14-33. Table inserts for dado heads.

Fig. 14-31. Cutting a groove with a single blade.

## MOUNTING A DADO HEAD

The dado head, Fig. 14-32, consists of two blades and a number of chippers. By assembling various combinations, widths of 1/4 in. to 13/16 in. (in increments of sixteenths) can be made. A single blade will cut a width of 1/8 in. Diameters of 6, 8, and 10 in. are the most common blade sizes, but larger sizes are available. A special table insert must be used, Fig. 14-33. You can make a wooden insert by shaping a piece the same size as the metal part. The dado can be mounted, lowered below the table and the insert set in place. With the dado running, raise it through the insert to cut the slot. Be sure the insert is held firmly in place while making the cut.

The dado head is mounted on the arbor with the blades on the outside. The arrangement of the chip-

pers is not critical except that the ones next to the blades must be set so their wide, swaged edges are located in the gullets as shown in Fig. 14-34. The cutting edges of the chippers overlap so it is possible to use paper washers between them to secure a slightly wider make-up.

## USING A DADO HEAD

The dado head can be used to cut dados, grooves, lap joints, rabbets, and interlocking joints. The stock can be held and controlled with the fence or miter gauge, used separately or in combination.

To cut a groove, raise the dado head to the correct height and adjust the fence. Feed the stock

Fig. 14-34. Mounting a dado head. Note position of swaged chipper (arrow).

through the machine as shown in Fig. 14-35. Since a large amount of waste is being removed, feed the work slower than when using a regular saw blade. If the groove does not continue all the way along the piece, a stop can be preset on the fence.

When cutting dados, the stock is held against the miter gauge. On some work both the miter gauge and fence can be used, Fig. 14-36. Extra care must be given to dado work to prevent splintering, especially when cutting plywood made of fine hardwood veneers. Always try a scrap piece first to check the work and to see if the width and depth are correct. If there is a tendency for the wood to splinter, lower the dado head and take a first cut that just scores the surface (about 1/16 in. deep). Then set to the required depth and take the final cut.

Rabbets can be quickly and accurately cut using the dado head as shown in Fig. 14-37. A wood pad is clamped or screwed to the fence and then set in the required position with the dado below the table. With the dado head running, raise it and allow it to cut into the wood pad to the required height. When doing this, always be certain that the dado will not strike the metal fence.

*Remove the dado head, or any other special setup you have made, as soon as you have finished your work. Clear the saw table and place waste cuttings in the scrap box.*

## SPECIAL FIXTURES AND SETUPS

Many special setups and fixtures can be used on the table saw to insure accuracy and safety in its use. Shop-built fixtures should be carefully made and finished. A coat of paste wax on sliding surfaces will usually make them easier to operate.

Fig. 14-38 shows a special setup for cutting a

Fig. 14-35. Cutting a groove with the dado head. Guard has been removed to show operation.

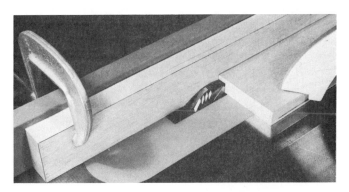
Fig. 14-37. Cutting a rabbet with the dado head.

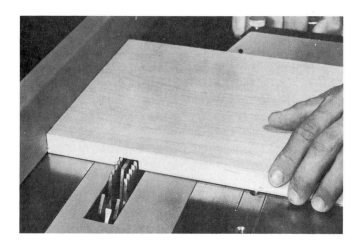
Fig. 14-36. Cutting a dado using both the fence and miter gauge. Guard has been removed to show operation.

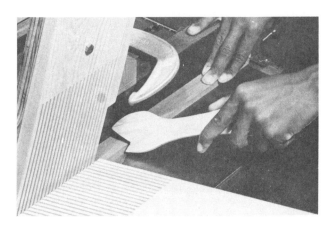
Fig. 14-38. Cutting a groove in a thin, narrow strip.

231

groove. Light pressure is applied to the workpiece by feather boards clamped to the table and fence. A shop-built fixture is shown in Fig. 14-39. It rides on the table and is guided by the fence. The top view shows the fixture being used for end grain cuts which are hazardous to make without some special support. The other side of the fixture is used to cut slots for feathers in miter joints. The frames were glued together and then the feather reinforcement was added.

Flat miter joints are easily and safely cut with the fixture shown in Fig. 14-40. The auxiliary table rides on the saw table and is guided by the splines in the table slots. To assemble the fixture accurately, the splines were placed in the slots, a bead of glue applied, and then the auxiliary table was clamped in place.

Miter joints on the edge of stock, especially plywood, are difficult to form. Fig. 14-41 shows a setup that insures accurate work and prevents

Fig. 14-40. Cutting miter joints with a special fixture. Guard can be used.

Fig. 14-41. Setup for cutting edge miters.

Fig. 14-39. Top. Making cheek cuts on a tenon with a shop-built fixture. Bottom. Opposite side being used to cut slots for a feather in a miter joint.

splintered edges. A wood pad is attached to the fence and then positioned so that the distance from the outside of the blade to the pad equals the thickness of the stock. The blade is lowered below the table and tilted to a 45 deg. angle. With the blade running, it is raised through the table and allowed to cut into the pad to about the depth shown. DO NOT RUN IT INTO THE METAL FENCE! If the setup is correct, the blade will cut from the exact corner of the surface. The waste strip is trapped between the blade and fence and must be removed with care.

In Fig. 14-42 a box joint is being cut with the dado head and a fixture attached to the miter gauge. A square pin the exact size of the slot in the joint is used to position the cuts. After each slot is cut, it is slipped on the pin and the next one is cut. When making the setup, first mount the pin on the backboard and then attach the backboard to the miter gauge so the cut will be exactly in the correct position. A side and end of the box are usually clamped together and cut at the same time. They must be offset an amount equal to the slot or pin width.

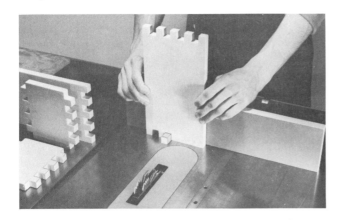

Fig. 14-42. Cutting box joints.

LOCK MITER JOINT

FOLLOW THESE STEPS TO MAKE PART A

WOOD PAD

SAW FENCE

SAW BLADE

STEP 1

MAKE THREE CUTS IN ORDER SHOWN

MULTICUT OR DADO    3-2-1

STEP 2

STEP 3

FOLLOW THESE STEPS TO MAKE PART B

STEP 1

STEP 2

STEP 3

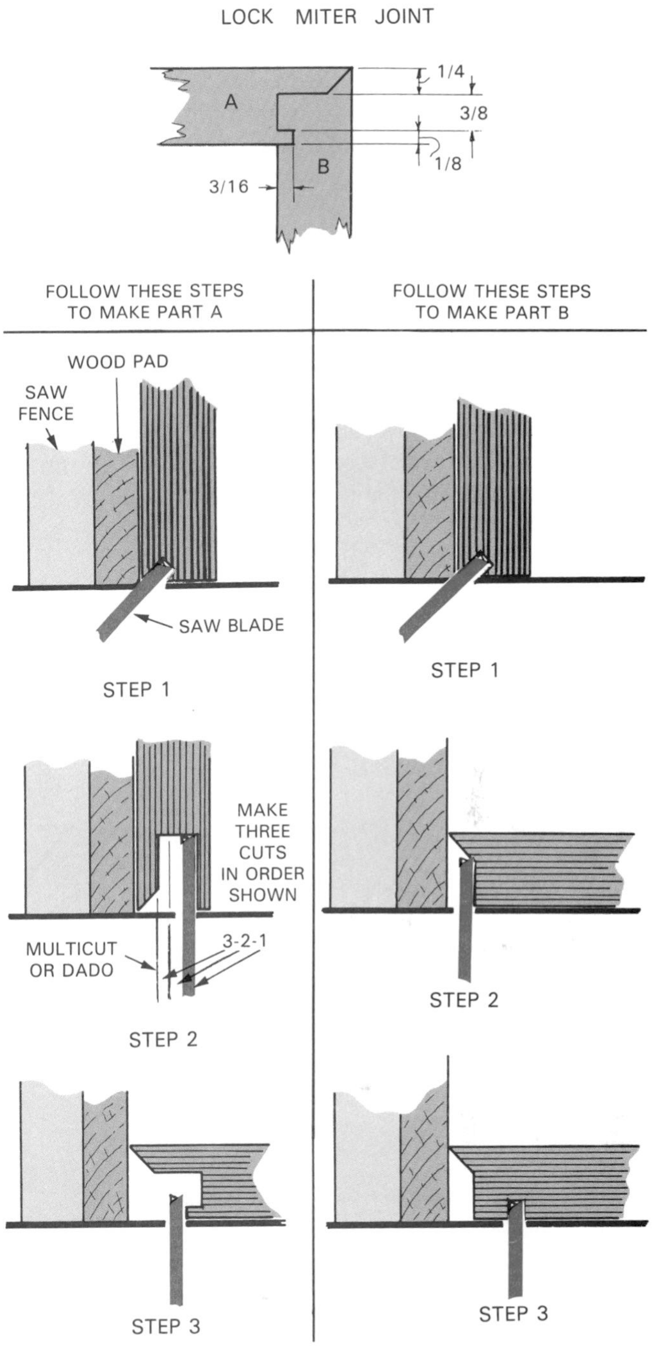

Fig. 14-44. Cutting sequence for a lock miter joint. These joints should be made before any other cuts.

## SLIDING TABLES

Sliding or rolling tables have long been available on industrial saws. In recent years, sliding tables have become common on standard table saws used by typical woodworkers. They are useful any time a woodworker needs to cut a large piece of stock. Sliding tables also "improve" accuracy.

Most models extend the work surface from 2 to 5 feet to the left of the saw blade. The fence can be positioned either at the front or back of the table depending on the stock size. The sliding table can also be used for mitering. See Fig. 14-43.

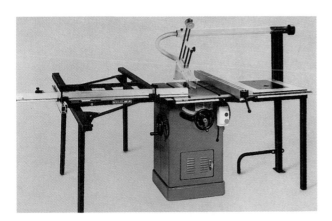

Fig. 14-43. This typical tilting arbor table saw is equipped with a sliding table (left), T-slot saw fence (right center), and overarm bladecover. (Excalibur Machine and Tool Company)

## CUTTING SEQUENCE

Complicated joints and work on the table saw may require a series of cuts. The cuts must be carefully planned. Some cuts that can easily be made at first may be difficult or impossible to make at the end of the sequence. For example, the miter cut of the joint shown in Fig. 14-44 would be difficult to make after all the other cuts were complete.

## SHARPENING CIRCULAR SAW BLADES

Sharp saw blades are a pleasure to use. They produce fine, accurate work quickly and safely. Dull blades are dangerous to use because they resist the stock being fed into them and are more likely to cause kickbacks. Also, they tend to heat, causing pitch and gum to build on the blade. This adds more friction and creates more heat, possibly causing the edge of the blade to snake (warp).

Blades should be kept bright and clean. Small amounts of pitch or rosin can be removed by wiping the blade with a cloth saturated with a special pitch and gum remover, kerosene, or mineral spirits. The teeth, Fig. 14-45, should also be wiped clean. A good way to remove a heavy coating of pitch is to soak the blade in warm water. Wipe dry and oil lightly. Do not scrape the surface of the blade with a metal tool or coarse abrasive. Rust spots should be polished off with 600 wet-or-dry paper and oil. Always clean the saw blade before sharpening it.

Considerable skill and certain equipment are needed to completely refit (sharpen) circular saw blades. However, they can be filed a number of times before a complete sharpening job is required. Many woodworkers file their saws three or four

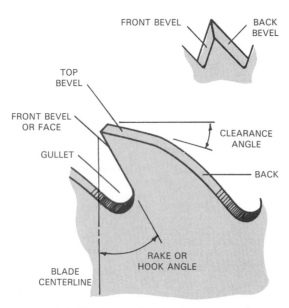

Fig. 14-45. Parts of a circular saw tooth.

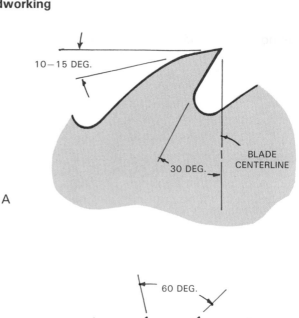

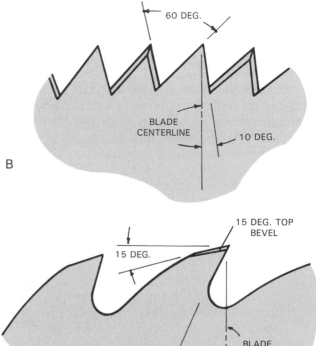

times, then send them to a saw shop for a complete machine sharpening operation. This will be described later in the unit.

Basic kinds of saw blades were described in the section on the table saw. Each of these blades is available in a wide variety of tooth sizes and shapes. When sharpening, the original shape of the teeth should be maintained. Sometimes it is helpful to trace around a section of the teeth of a new blade and refer to this pattern during sharpening operations. Fig. 14-46 shows a profile of saw teeth, with suggested filing angles.

## JOINTING BLADES

Jointing is the operation of "rounding" the blade so that all the teeth will be exactly the same height.

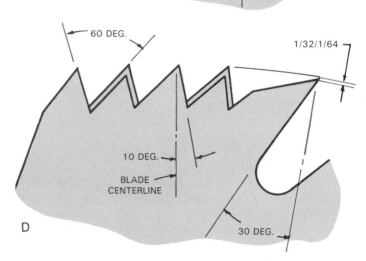

Fig. 14-46. Suggested filing angles for four common saw teeth. A—Rip. B—Crosscut. C—R.C. combination. D—Combination.

It does not need to be performed each time before the saw is filed, but the tiny flats formed on the points of the teeth by jointing are a helpful guide to the inexperienced worker.

Be certain the blade is in the correct position by loosening the arbor nut and retightening with the flange mark and trademark up. Clamp an abrasive stone to the miter gauge and raise the blade until it just touches the stone. Turn on the machine and move the stone over the blade, Fig. 14-47. Stop the saw and examine the blade. Tiny "flats" or "brights" should be visible on the points of the teeth. Rejoint if necessary. If the saw is in poor shape it may be impractical to strike the very short teeth. Instead, it may be better to allow these to remain short until the next time the saw is filed or completely reconditioned. The jointing should always be done as lightly as possible, so that during the filing operation just a few strokes of the file will form a new point or edge.

## FILING SAW TEETH

Mount the saw in a filing clamp. Commercial clamps are available that will hold different blade sizes and adjust to various filing angles. A shop-built clamp, Fig. 14-48, may also be used.

Fig. 14-48. Shop-built saw clamp. A strip of leather is glued along the top edge of the jaws which are hinged at the bottom.

For rip and rough cut combination blades, select an 8 in. smooth or dead smooth mill file. Set the blade so the teeth are supported close to the saw clamp and file the top bevel of teeth that are set away from you. File rip teeth straight across. For combination teeth drop the file handle about 15 deg. Use light full strokes, forming a bevel with the required clearance. The file will cut smoother and easier if you use a diagonal stroke, Fig. 14-49. Watch jointed flat and stop just as soon as it disappears. Filing beyond this point will lower the tooth,

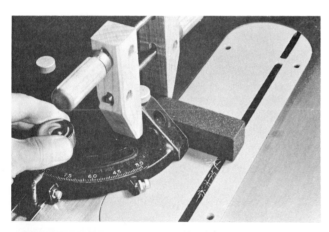

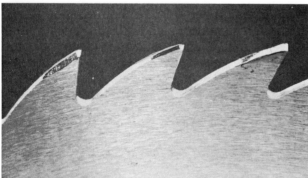

Fig. 14-47. Top. Jointing a blade. Wear goggles for this operation. Bottom. Jointed blade. Note flats. Jointing has been heavier than normal so it would show in photograph.

Fig. 14-49. Arrows point out two teeth of the combination blade that have been filed.

then it will not do its share of cutting. After you have filed all the teeth set away from you, reverse the blade in the clamp and file the remaining teeth. The teeth of some combination blades have a front bevel that may be filed very lightly.

Crosscut teeth on small blades are usually shaped so they can be filed with a taper file, Fig. 14-50. Position the file so it will cut the back bevel of one tooth and the front bevel of an adjacent tooth. The file will usually cut smoother if the handle is dropped slightly. Since most of the filing is done on the back bevel, file this bevel first on all teeth set away from you. Stop filing as soon as about one-half of the jointed flat has been removed. Reverse the blade in the clamp to file the remaining bevels and remove the balance of the flats. Large blades may have a rounded gullet (area between the teeth); use a special crosscut saw file with a rounded edge. BE SURE TO MAINTAIN THE ORIGINAL TOOTH SHAPE WHILE FILING EACH BEVEL SEPARATELY.

The crosscut teeth of regular combination blades are filed in the same way as just described. The raker tooth is filed straight across and about 1/64 in. lower than the points of the crosscut teeth.

## SETTING TEETH

After a number of sharpenings, the teeth will require additional set. The amount of this set will vary with the type of work. Generally blades used on table saws are given two gauges of set on each side. Blades for portable saws are set 2 1/2 gauges on each side. Too much set is undesirable because it produces a rough cut, creates extra strain on the blade, and requires extra power. A blade with four gauges of set (two on each side) will make a kerf that is about 1 1/2 times the thickness of the blade. Refer to Fig. 14-51.

Saws of 14 gauge and lighter can be set with a hand set, Fig. 14-52. Follow the manufacturer's directions in adjusting the set. Only the top 1/8 to 5/32 in. of the tooth should be set. Observe the direction of the previous setting and follow the same

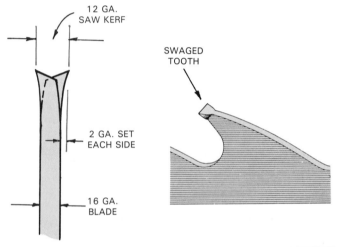

| BLADE THICKNESS | SAW KERF (2 GAUGES OF SET ON EACH SIDE) | INCREASE |
|---|---|---|
| 18 ga. (0.49) | 14 ga. (.083) | .034 |
| 16 ga. (0.65) | 12 ga. (.109) | .044 |
| 14 ga. (.083) | 10 ga. (.134) | .051 |
| 12 ga. (.109) | 8 ga. (.165) | .056 |

Fig. 14-51. Gauges of set and saw kerf width.

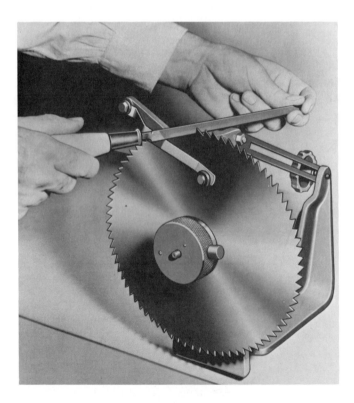

Fig. 14-50. Crosscut blade being filed. Notice that the file position reaches both the back bevel of one tooth and the front bevel of the adjacent tooth. (Foley-Belsaw Co.)

Fig. 14-52. Setting circular saw teeth with a hand set.

236

pattern. You can check your work by sighting across the flat surface of the blade, toward a major light source. Never set the raker teeth of combination blades, or any of the teeth of hollow ground blades. Large, heavy gauge saws will require special setting equipment.

Some saws have swaged teeth instead of set to provide clearance. In this process the ends of the teeth are made wider by upsetting or flattening them with a special tool.

## GUMMING

Gumming is the process of grinding and shaping the saw gullets. The edge of a thin abrasive wheel is shaped to the required contour and the saw is held in a special fixture, Fig. 14-53. With this fixture, the depth of the cut can be accurately controlled. When gumming a blade without special equipment, a reference circle should be made on the blade, Fig. 14-54. Lines should be laid out from the front bevel

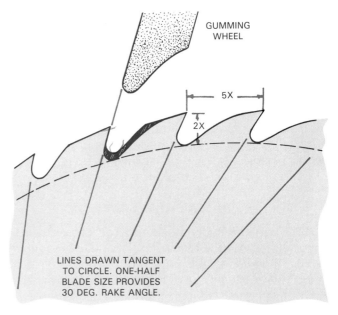

Fig. 14-55. Gumming layout for rip teeth.

or face of each tooth to serve as a guide during the grinding operation. The depth of the gullet should equal about two-fifths of the distance between the points of the teeth, Fig. 14-55. The face of the tooth is ground only just enough to clean the surface so that correct spacing can be easily maintained. Heavy grinding will produce too much heat and burn the teeth. It is best to grind lightly, skip every other gullet, and go around the blade several times until the required depth is attained.

## DADO HEADS

To sharpen a dado head, the entire assembly should be mounted on the arbor and jointed. The blades are then filed in about the same way as a combination saw blade, Fig. 14-56. A special file

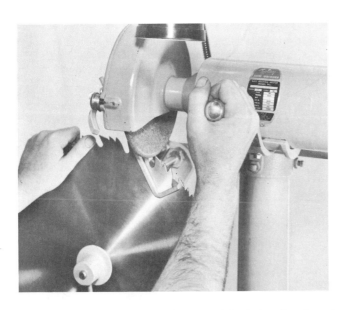

Fig. 14-53. Gumming a saw with a special grinder. Depth and shape can be accurately controlled. (Foley-Belsaw Co.)

Fig. 14-54. Marking a reference circle for a gumming operation.

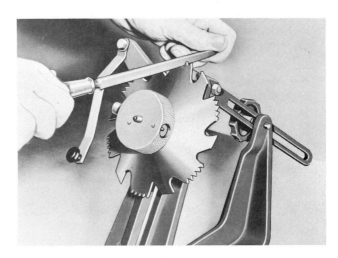

Fig. 14-56. Filing a dado blade held in a commercial saw clamp.

may be required. On some blades a smooth, square file will fit the teeth best. Chippers are filed straight across with a clearance angle of about 15 deg.

When the teeth of circular saw blades and dado heads become badly misshapen, they should be sent to a saw shop or factory where they can be completely refitted by experts, Fig. 14-57. Here precision machines and equipment will be used to grind, file, set, and tension the blade so that it will be like new. Fig. 14-58 shows a special filing machine being used to sharpen a circular saw.

## RADIAL ARM SAW

Although originally designed for crosscutting, improvements in the radial arm saw have broadened its use. It is especially suited for cutting boards to length. One advantage of the radial arm saw is that the board is held against the fence while the saw moves across the board. This prevents kickbacks and reduces the chance of stock slipping to one side as the cut is made. The main disadvantage is the length of cut which can be made when crosscutting.

## PARTS AND DESCRIPTION

In this machine the motor and blade are carried

Fig. 14-58. Saw filing machine set up to sharpen flat ground combination blade. (Foley-Belsaw Co.)

Fig. 14-57. Left. Using a diamond wheel to face grind carbide-tipped teeth. Right. Using a straight edge to check the blade body for "bumps" or other misalignments. (North American Products Corp.)

by an overhead arm while the stock is held stationary on a table. The arm is attached to a vertical column at the back of the table and can be set at various angles. The depth of cut is controlled by raising or lowering the overhead arm. Fig. 14-59 shows the parts of a typical model.

The motor is mounted in a yoke so that it can be tilted for angle cuts. The yoke is suspended from the arm on a pivot which permits the motor to be rotated in a horizontal plane. Various adjustments make it possible to perform many sawing operations. The radial arm saw is used in woodworking shops and is valuable to the building trades (where large pieces are cut). It is easy to hold the work stationary and move the saw blade.

When crosscutting, mitering, beveling, and dadoing, the work is held firmly on the table and the saw is pulled through the cut. For ripping and grooving, the blade is turned parallel with the table and locked into position. Stock is then fed into the blade in somewhat the same manner as a table saw.

The radial arm saw uses the same kind of blades as a table saw. Size is determined by the diameter of the largest blade it will carry. Blades are mounted by the same method as used for the table saw.

## RADIAL ARM SAW SAFETY

Follow these safety procedures when operating a radial arm saw, in addition to the power equipment safety procedures outlined in Unit 3.
1. Stock must be held firmly on the table and against the fence for all crosscutting operations. The ends of long boards must be supported level with the table.
2. Before turning on the motor be certain that all clamps and locking devices are tight and the depth of cut is correct.
3. Keep the guard and antikickback device in position. Do not remove them without your instructor's permission.
4. Always return the saw to the rear of the table after completing a crosscut or miter cut. Never remove stock from the table until the saw has been returned.
5. MAINTAIN A 6 IN. MARGIN OF SAFETY. To do this you must keep your hands 6 in. from the path of the saw blade.
6. Shut off the motor and wait for the blade to stop before making any adjustments.
7. Be sure the blade has stopped before you leave

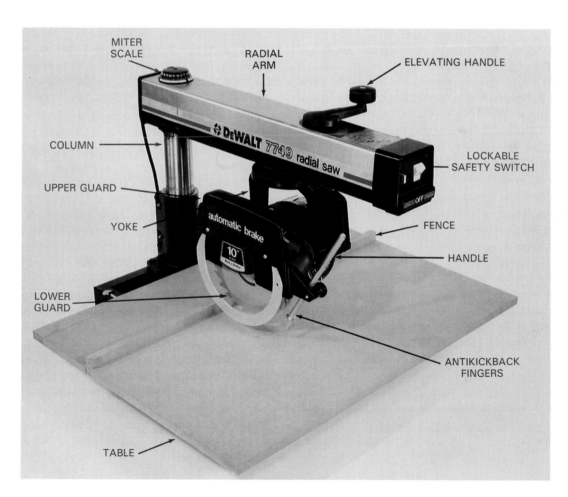

Fig. 14-59. Parts of a 10 in. (254 mm) radial arm saw. (DeWalt, Div. of Black and Decker)

the machine.

8. The table should be kept clean and free of scrap pieces and excessive amounts of sawdust.

9. Secure approval from your instructor before making ripping cuts or other special setups. When ripping stock it must be flat and have one straight edge to move along the fence.

10. When ripping, always feed stock into the blade so that the bottom teeth are turning toward you, Fig. 14-60. This will be the side opposite the antikickback fingers.

## CROSSCUTTING

Use a crosscut or combination blade. Set the radial arm so it is perpendicular to the table fence and lock the motor in a horizontal position. Adjust the elevating handle until the blade is about 1/16 in. below the surface of the table. Be certain that the yoke locating pin is tight. Move the saw over the table and check to see that the guard rides easily over the table fence.

With the saw against the column, place your work on the table and align the cut. Hold the stock firmly against the table fence with your hand at least 6 in. away from the path of the saw blade. Turn on the motor, grasp the saw handle and pull the saw firmly and slowly through the cut, Fig. 14-61. The saw may tend to "feed itself." You must maintain complete control over the rate of feed. This is especially true when cutting very hard wood or stock that is thick. If the rate of feed is not controlled properly, the saw will advance too rapidly and "climb" over the work resulting in an accident, ruined piece, or at the very least, a poor cut. When the cut is complete, return the saw to the rear of the table and shut off the motor.

Fig. 14-61. Crosscutting with lower guard in position. Antikickback fingers are raised about 1/4 in. above the work. (Delta International Machinery Corp.)

Duplicate parts can be cut to length by using stops clamped along the fence. Always make certain that the stock is against the fence before starting the cut. The saw can be operated either with the left or right hand, with the other hand holding the work. The long part of the work should always be on the side of the holding hand. When working with small pieces where the hand cannot be kept at least 6 inches away from the cutting line, the work should be clamped to the table or cut with hand tools.

## MITERS, BEVELS, AND COMPOUND MITERS

The radial arm saw is ideal for making miter and bevel cuts, is easy to handle on large pieces, and makes precision cuts easily.

To cut miters, swing the radial arm to the required angle, then follow the same procedure as for crosscutting, Fig. 14-62. The lower guard can be used for cuts of this kind.

Bevel cuts across the grain are made with the radial arm at right angles to the table fence. Elevate the arm so the blade will clear the table and then tilt the motor to the required angle. Lower the arm until the blade will cut about 1/16 in. below the table surface and proceed as in regular crosscutting, Fig. 14-63. The lower guard cannot be used for this operation when the bevel angle approaches 45 degrees.

COMPOUND MITERING combines the two previous operations. Tilt the motor to the required angle and then swing the radial arm into position. Be certain all clamps are securely locked. Make the cut as shown in Fig. 14-64.

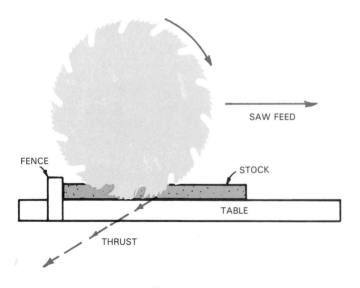

FENCE

SAW FEED

STOCK

TABLE

THRUST

Fig. 14-60. Blade rotation and feed.

Fig. 14-62. Cutting a miter. Lower guard has been removed to show operation.

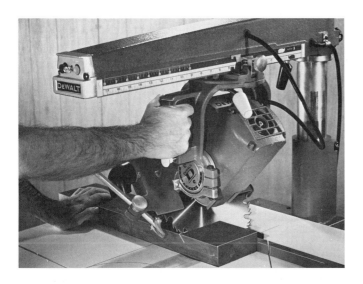

Fig. 14-63. Making a bevel cut across the grain.

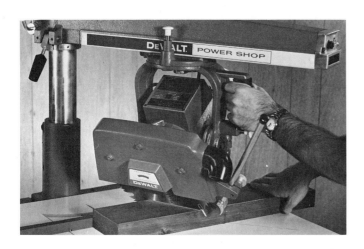

Fig. 14-64. Cutting a compound miter. Lower guard cannot be used.

*When crosscutting or making miter or bevel cuts, always return the saw unit to the rear of the table immediately after completion.*

## RIPPING CUTS

To set up for ripping cuts, release the yoke and turn the motor 90 deg. so the blade is parallel with the fence. Lock the yoke and move the saw along the radial arm to secure the correct measurement between the fence and the blade. Lock the saw unit in place and adjust its height so the blade will cut just under the surface of the table. Adjust the guard and set the antikickback fingers so they will ride on the top surface of the stock.

Study the diagram in Fig. 14-65, so you will be certain to feed the stock in the correct direction. If the stock is fed into the saw from the wrong direction, the saw will climb on top of the board possibly causing damage to the saw and injury to the operator. Turn on the motor and feed the stock, Fig. 14-66. Use push sticks. Do not place your hands closer than 6 in. to the operating blade.

Bevel ripping is shown in Fig. 14-67. To make the setup, raise the radial arm and tilt the motor unit to the required angle. Then lower it until the blade just touches the table and set it for the required width of cut. Be sure to adjust the guard and antikickback fingers for the thickness of your stock. Use push sticks and push boards to finish the cut or have a helper "tail" the stock from the other side.

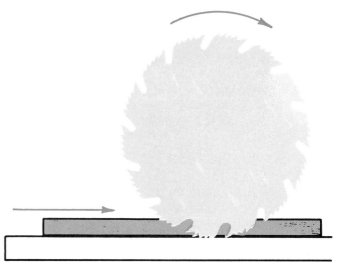

Fig. 14-65. Feed direction for ripping cuts. View is from column side.

Fig. 14-67. Ripping a bevel.

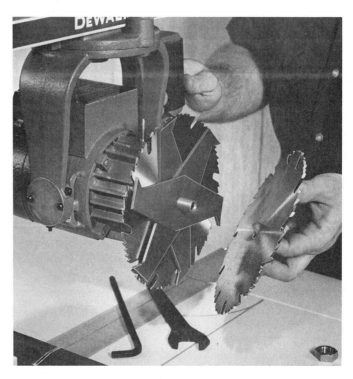

Fig. 14-68. Mounting a dado head.

Fig. 14-66. Top. Making a ripping cut. Bottom. View at rear of blade showing position of splitter and antikickback fingers.

## DADOS AND GROOVES

*across grain* *with the grain*

Mount a dado head on the saw arbor, following about the same procedure used for the table saw. On some machines an Allen wrench is used to hold the arbor when tightening the nut, Fig. 14-68. When a full width dado head is used, it may not be possible to use the outside collar because you must have the nut turned on the full depth of its threads. Replace the guard and check its clearance.

Set the radial arm and other adjustments as described for crosscutting. Lower the dado until it will cut the correct depth in your stock. Measure the distance for this setting and then make a trial cut in waste material that is the same thickness as your stock. Also check the width of the dado cut.

Place the stock on the table with the layout lines turned up and the edge against the fence. Pull the dado head up to the edge of the fence and align the stock. Now push it back, turn on the motor, and pull it slowly through the cut, Fig. 14-69. Always return the motor unit to the rear of the table immediately, and then remove the stock or set up additional cuts. Use stop blocks set along the fence to position duplicate parts.

Fig. 14-69. Cutting a dado. Lower guard can be used.

*Unless you have had a great deal of experience on the radial arm saw, have your instructor check each special setup before you perform the work.*

To cut grooves, Figs. 14-70 and 14-71, the machine is set up in the same manner as for ripping and the same procedures and precautions are followed. Fig. 14-71 shows a safe procedure being used to cut a groove in the edge of stock, with the motor unit turned in a vertical position. A rabbet cut can be made with the same setup by simply raising the saw unit.

Fig. 14-70. Back view of a groove being cut.

Fig. 14-71. Cutting an edge groove. Note the special guard.

## PORTABLE CIRCULAR SAW

The portable circular saw is used extensively by carpenters for framing and for other rough construction work. It may be used in shops for cutting stock to rough size. Fig. 14-72 shows the parts of a standard model.

The size is determined by the diameter of the largest blade it will carry. Sizes range from a 4 1/2 in. blade powered with a 1/6 hp motor to a 12 in. blade powered with a 1 1/2 hp motor. A practical size is 7 in. which will cut to a depth of slightly over 2 in. and can be used for rough framing work. The depth of cut is adjusted by raising or lowering the position of the motor on the base using the depth adjustment knob. On most saws it is possible to tilt the base so that bevel cuts can be made. The angle of tilt is set with the tilt adjustment knob. Some models have a ripping guide or fence.

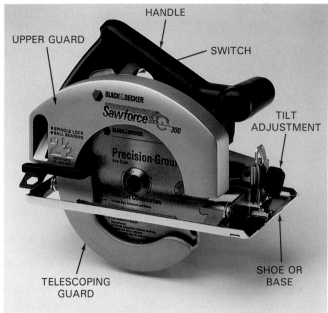

Fig. 14-72. Parts of a portable circular saw. During operation, telescoping guard is pushed back by stock. When cut is completed, a spring returns the guard.  (Black & Decker)

Portable saws are normally guided along the cutting line "freehand" and require extra clearance in the saw kerf. Blades are set at least 2 1/2 gauges on each side to provide this extra clearance.

Fig. 14-73 shows a cut being started with a portable saw. Note the direction of blade rotation and the movement of the saw. As the blade enters the cut, the telescoping guard is pushed back by the stock. A spring returns the guard to closed position when the cut is complete.

## PORTABLE CIRCULAR SAW SAFETY

These safety rules should be observed, in addition to the power equipment safety rules explained in Unit 3.

1. Stock must be supported in such a way that the kerf will not close and bind the blade either during the cut or at the end of the cut.
2. Support thin materials on benches. Small pieces should be clamped in a vise, or onto a bench top or sawhorse.
3. Be careful not to cut into the bench, sawhorse, or other supporting devices.
4. Adjust the depth of cut to the thickness of the stock, PLUS about 1/8 in.
5. Check the base and angle adjustment to be sure they are tight. Plug cord into a grounded outlet. Make certain it will not become fouled in the work.
6. Always place the saw base on the stock with the blade clear before turning on the switch.
7. During the cutting operation, stand to one side of the cutting line.
8. Large saws will have two handles. Keep both hands on them during the cutting operation. Small saws should also be guided with both hands whenever possible.
9. Do not lay the saw down until the blade stops moving. Some newer saw models have a brake that quickly stops the blade once the motor is turned off.
10. Always unplug the machine to change blades or make major adjustments.
11. Always use a sharp blade with plenty of set.

## USING THE PORTABLE CIRCULAR SAW

When using a portable saw, make layout lines that can be easily followed, or clamp straightedges to the surface of the work that will guide the saw. Some saws have a ripping fence. It should be used for ripping cuts.

Grasp the handle of the saw firmly in one hand with the forefinger ready to operate the trigger switch. The other hand should be placed on the stock, well away from the cutting line. Some saws will require both hands on the machine. Rest the base on the work and align the guide mark with the layout line. Turn on the switch, allow the motor to reach full speed and then feed it smoothly through the cut, Fig. 14-74. Release the switch as soon as the cut is finished. Remember to hold the saw until the blade stops.

The portable saw may be used to make cuts in assembled work. For example, flooring and roofing boards are often nailed into place, then the ends are trimmed. Fig. 14-75 shows plywood being accurately ripped on a panel saw. The sawing head is similar to a portable saw. It is mounted on a carrier which slides (or locks in place) on steel rails.

### Power Miter Box Saw

A power miter box saw is used for cutting miters on trim and molding, Fig. 14-76. It is similar to a portable circular saw mounted on a spring-loaded

Fig. 14-73. Blade rotation and feed. (Porter-Cable Corp.)

Fig. 14-74. Making a cut across the grain.    (Black & Decker)

Fig. 14-75. A custom-built panel saw that will crosscut or rip large panels. (Mark Clauss)

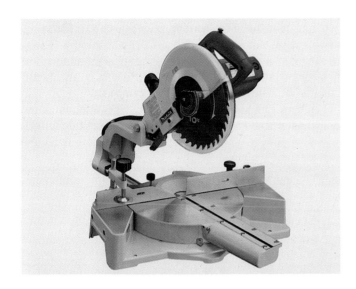

Fig. 14-76. This power miter box is ideal for cutting miters on trim and molding pieces. (Makita U.S.A., Inc.)

arm. This saw will make very accurate cuts by pulling downward on the handle after the angle has been set using the angle scale. A trigger control in the handle turns the motor on and off.

A fine-tooth crosscut blade is used on the power miter box for smooth cuts at a higher rpm than regular circular saws. Saw size is determined by the largest diameter blade that it will accommodate. The most common sizes are 9 inches and 10 inches.

## POWER COMPOUND MITER SAWS

Power compound miter saws have evolved from simple trim saws to sophisticated tools that can cut a wide variety of material—large boards to small trim, Fig. 14-77.

New machines have large blades (12''), two-way bevel tilt mechanism, sliding support arm, and a turntable that pivots to cut a 60 degree right or left miter. These machines can cut large crown moldings without reversing the stock. (Older saws tilt only to the left because the motor housing extends straight from the right side of the blade and would contact the workpiece if tilted.) Traditional miter saws limit the turntable's swing to 45 degrees right and left, but some models provide for a 60 degree swing to either side.

Fig. 14-77. This power compound miter saw is truly a modern tool that far exceeds the capabilities of the power miter box. (Makita U.S.A., Inc.)

## FRAME AND TRIM SAW

The frame and trim saw is supported on a pair of overhead shafts or guides, Fig. 14-78. The support rotates left and right slightly more than 45 degrees to make crosscuts and miter cuts. It is capable of all sawing operations except ripping. Typical capacity is 16 inches in width on crosscuts and 12 inches on miter cuts of 45 degrees. Maximum thickness of stock is 2 inches. An extension table allows one operator to cut long stock alone.

### INDUSTRIAL MACHINES

Circular saws, like those you have learned to use in the school shop, are also used in industry. Table saws and radial arm saws are among the basic power equipment found in smaller woodworking plants and cabinet shops. Patternmarking shops will also have about the same power woodworking machines as the school shops. Fig. 14-79 shows a table saw with a power feed that is used in manufacturing. In large production plants, the cutting principles of these basic machines are applied in the design of huge automatic machines that handle hundreds of board feet of lumber per hour.

## CUTOFF SAWS

Industrial cutoff saws operate in about the same way as the radial arm saw, except that they have a power feed and cannot be adjusted for angle cuts.

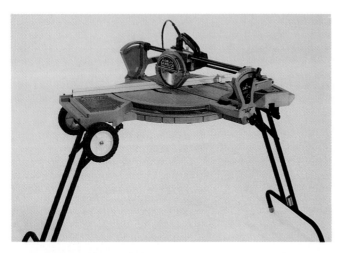

Fig. 14-78. Frame and trim saw is capable of all sawing operations, except ripping.     (Delta International Machinery Corp.)

Fig. 14-80 shows a model in which the feed is operated by hydraulic power. A touch of the foot pedal moves the blade through the cut at a controlled speed and then returns it to the back position. The length of the stroke is adjustable for any length up to 36 in. The cutoff saw requires extension tables on both sides (shown).

Rough crosscutting is sometimes done with a swinging cutoff saw. It differs from the previously described saw in that the sawing head is mounted on an overhead swing arm. It is pulled through the stock by hand.

Modern production machines require rugged, long lasting blades. Teeth with carbide tips are used because they stay sharp longer than those on conventional type blades. Carbide blades require precision sharpening equipment. The carbide tip is too hard to be ground with a conventional abrasive, so a special diamond wheel is used.

## STRAIGHT LINE RIP SAW

Straight line rip saws, Fig. 14-81, will rip boards very accurately. The motor and blade are located in the table. An endless chain on each side feeds the stock in a straight line. Overhead is an assembly of rollers that apply pressure to the stock and hold it firmly on the table and feed chains.

The straight line rip saw, Fig. 14-82, is also designed with the blade and motor unit located

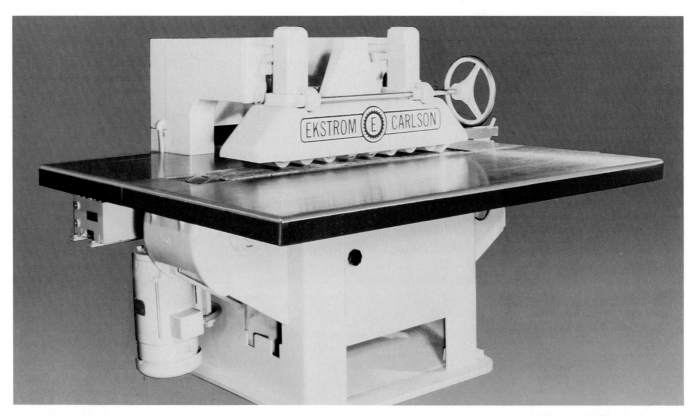

Fig. 14-79. High performance rip saw used in production operation.     (Ekstrom Carlson and Co.)

above the table. The endless feed belt located in the table makes a slight dip as it moves directly under the blade.

Cutoff and rip saws are used in combination with facers and planers to rough mill and prepare stock for finished machine operations, Fig. 14-83.

## GANG RIP SAW

The gang rip saw operates similarly to the straight line rip saw, except that a number of blades are

Fig. 14-80. Modern cutoff saw setup for production sawing. (Speed Cut, Inc.)

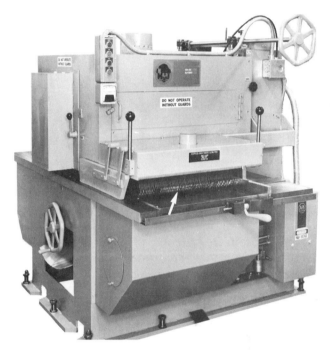

Fig. 14-81. When using a straight line rip saw, the fence is not required. Power feeder moves material through cut in straight line. (Campbellrhea Mfg., Inc.)

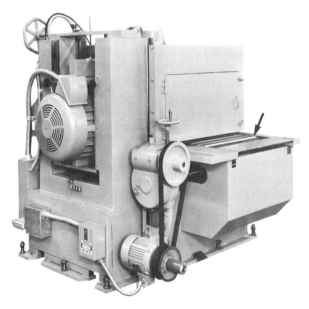

Fig. 14-82. Top. Straight line rip saw with arbor located above table. Note antikickback fingers (arrow). Bottom. Rear view shows variable speed drive for slat bed (arrow). More than one blade can be mounted on arbor. (Mereen-Johnson Machine Co.)

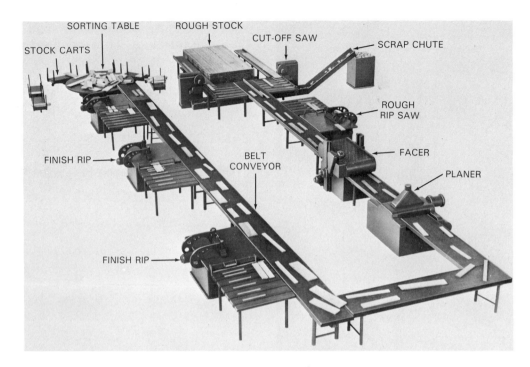

Fig. 14-83. Scale models used to plan a milling layout. (C.O. Porter Machinery Co.)

mounted on the saw arbor. To permit blades to operate at various positions across the table, rollers are used instead of a belt or chain to feed the stock. All of the rollers are powered and operate somewhat like those on a planer. This machine, like the straight line rip saw, will cut boards accurately. Fig. 14-84 shows a heavyduty model that can be equipped with a 150 hp arbor motor. As many as 10 cuts can be made at one time through hardwoods 3 in. (76 mm) thick.

## DOUBLE END SAWING MACHINES

These machines consist of feed chains that carry the work past sawing heads located on each side. The chain is often equipped with rubber pads that protect the surface of finished material. Rubber-tired rollers hold the stock securely on the feed chains. The sawing heads can be set at various angles for beveling and other special work. See Fig. 14-85.

Two double end machines are sometimes placed together with a special conveyor unit between, Fig. 14-86. This makes it possible to cut panels and doors to finished size in one operation. The work is fed into one machine and is cut to width. It then moves out on conveyor rolls and is picked up by the second machine, then cut to finished length.

## MULTIPLE CUTTING AND GROOVING EQUIPMENT

These machines usually have a long saw arbor that extends across either a conveyor chain or a slat bed, Fig. 14-87. Small rubber-tired or composition

wheels hold work firmly against the conveyor. Blades and dado heads can be set at various positions along the arbor to cut stock to size and form grooves and dados in cabinet and furniture parts.

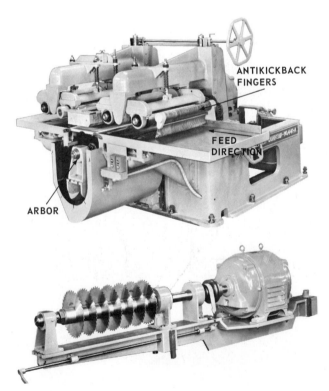

Fig. 14-84. Top. Gang rip saw. Arbor is located below the table. Bottom. Motor, arbor, and blade assembly. As many as 10 blades can be mounted at one time. (Mereen-Johnson Machine Co.)

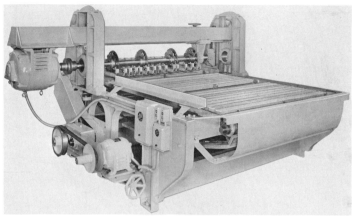

Fig. 14-87. Multiple cutting and grooving machine with slat bed. View shows setup for multiple drawer front ripping and grooving. Blade and dado combination cuts part to size and forms joint. (Mereen-Johnson Machine Co.)

Fig. 14-85. Basic double end sawing machine. Space between sawing heads is adjustable for various widths of material. (Speed Cut, Inc.)

Like the double end sawing machine, multiple cutting and grooving equipment can be combined for various operations. Fig. 14-88 shows two machines set up for cutting particle board panels.

A variation of the previously described machine is shown in Fig. 14-89. Here blades are mounted on swinging arms and are driven by belts from

VARIABLE SPEED DRIVE

SCORING SAW HEADS

Fig. 14-86. Two double end machines set up for a precision hardwood panel sizing operation. As the panel moves through the unit in the foreground (crossgrain cut), scoring cuts are made before the regular cut to prevent splintering of the edge. (Kohler General, Inc.)

Fig. 14-88. Cutting 5 x 10 ft. (1.5 x 3) particle board panels into smaller pieces. Two machines, each like the one shown in Fig. 14-87, are being used. They are set at a 90 degree angle to each other with a special conveyor unit moving the panels from one machine to the other.

pulleys mounted on the main drive shaft. The blades can be positioned anywhere across the slat bed and raised or dropped into the work by switches on the operator's console.

## PANEL CUT-UP SYSTEMS

Tremendous amounts of panel material (plywood, hardboard, vinyl-surfaced particle board, and plastic laminates) are used in woodworking plants. Special machines and systems have been developed to cut standard panels into required sizes with speed and accuracy.

Fig. 14-90 shows a system where the cutting units consist of a sawing head that travels under the table. At the end of each cut the blade is automatically lowered below the table surface and returned rapidly to the starting point. The hold down

Fig. 14-89. Infeed side of multiple cutting and grooving machine with slat bed. Arrow points to one of the arms that carry blades or dado heads. Arms are raised and lowered by pneumatic cylinders and controlled from operator console. (Kohler General, Inc.)

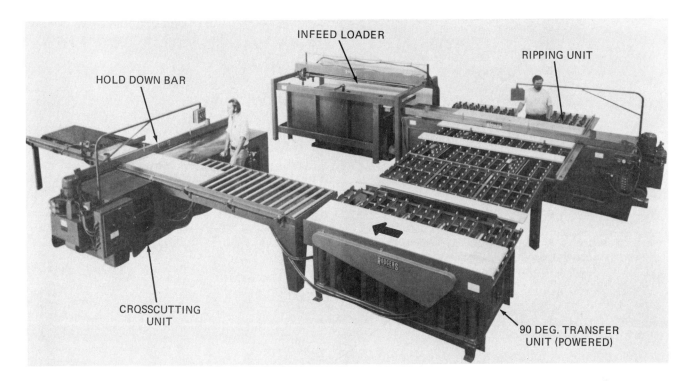

Fig. 14-90. Panel cut-up system. Material from the ripping unit moves by gravity to the 90 degree transfer unit which is powered. Cutting stroke can be varied from 10 to 110 fpm (3 to 33 mpm). (Rogers Machinery Mfg. Co., Inc.)

bar is also automatically released so that the operator can move the panel into position for the next cut.

Another modern system combines a traveling rip saw with multiple crosscut sawing units attached to an overhead beam or gantry, Fig. 14-91. High production rates are attained mainly because an entire stack of panels are cut in a single pass of the saw blade. These machines are generally designed to handle a stack up to 3 in. (76 mm) high.

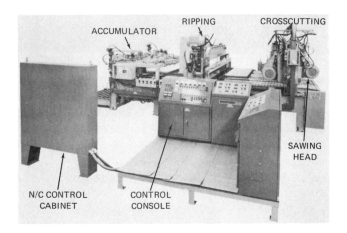

Fig. 14-91. Major parts of a panel cut-up system capable of processing thousands of panels per day. Materials include plywood and hardboard, as well as vinyl and high-pressure laminated particle board. (Mereen-Johnson Machine Co.)

In operation, panels are fed into an accumulator which lays up a perfectly aligned stack (also called a BOOK OF PANELS). The stack is then automatically moved into position for ripping cuts. After each ripping cut, the segment of stacked panels is clamped together and moved to a reciprocating table that feeds it through the crosscut saws. The crosscut sawing heads can be laterally adjusted between each set of cuts in order to produce various panel sizes.

Machine systems like the one previously described can be controlled manually or by a computer. To set the machine manually, the operator dials in the sawing positions on the control panel. Saws and guides are positioned automatically and digital readouts show their exact position. For N/C operation, perforated tape is inserted into the reader on the console and the starter switches are turned on. Fig. 14-92 shows the discharge end of a panel cut-up system used in a modern plant.

### TEST YOUR KNOWLEDGE, Chapter 14

Please do not write in the text. Place your answers on a separate sheet of paper.
1. A table saw with two arbors is called a _____ saw.
   a. Universal.
   b. Circular.
   c. Variety.
   d. None of the above.

Fig. 14-92. View shows discharge end of tape controlled panel cut-up system. Note the crosscut sawing heads located on both sides of beam. Motors (arrow) turn precision lead screws that move sawing heads to various positions along beam.
(Black Brothers)

2. What five items must be given to completely specify a circular saw blade?
3. The _____ will indicate blade size and coarseness of the cut.
4. The rip teeth on standard combination blades are known as:
   a. Hook teeth.
   b. Rakers.
   c. Arbor teeth.
   d. None of the above.
5. Stock must be surfaced and at least one edge must be jointed before it can be safely cut on the table saw. True or False?
6. Which direction should an arbor nut be turned in order to loosen it?
7. What is resawing?
8. When cutting duplicate pieces, why is it important to support stock with the miter gauge throughout the operation?
9. The dado head can be used to cut rabbet joints. True or False?
10. _____ is the operation that makes all teeth the same height.

11. In general, blades used on table saws are given _____ gauges of set on each side.
    a. Five.
    b. One-half.
    c. Two.
    d. None of the above.
12. What is gumming?
13. What is the largest size blade a 10 inch radial arm saw can carry?
14. What is compound mitering?
15. When ripping stock on a radial arm saw, the teeth on the blade rotate _____ (toward, away from) the operator.
16. The frame and trim saw is capable of all the sawing operations except:
    a. Beveling.
    b. Crosscutting.
    c. Ripping.
    d. None of the above.
17. List three types of industrial machines used in large woodworking shops.

## ACTIVITIES

1. Study manufacturers' catalogs and select a table saw that would be appropriate for a home workshop. Prepare complete specifications of the machine. Include the size of the blade, arbor, table, and motor. Also include adjustment features and accessories that would be desirable. Prepare a cost estimate.
2. Prepare double-size profile drawings of a number of rip teeth styles. Study manufacturers' bulletins for information.
3. Make arrangements to visit a home construction site to interview a carpenter. Secure information about the operations performed with a portable circular saw and the kinds and sizes of saws preferred. Summarize the interview in a written paper or an oral report.
4. Design an interlocking joint that could be used to join drawer fronts and sides. Prepare a set of drawings like the ones in Fig. 14-43. Show the cutting sequence you would follow.

This production setup uses a large radial arm circular saw. (Speed Cut, Inc.)

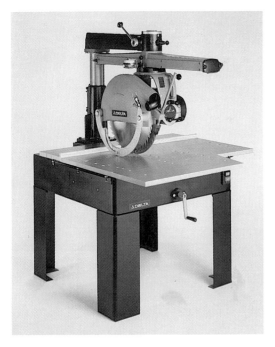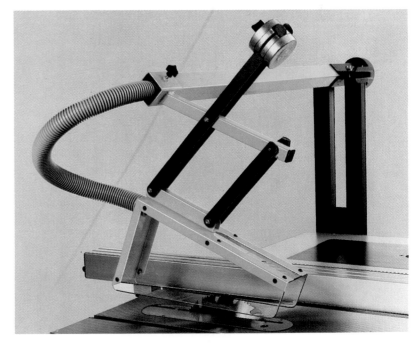

Left. Heavy duty 18'' radial arm saw. (Delta International Machinery Corp.) Right. This overarm blade cover can be used with most table saws. The built-in dust collection system helps control airborne dust that is created by the saw blade. (Excalibur Machine and Tool Company)

Steady hands, attention to detail, and quality machinery were necessary to produce this project. A jig saw was used to cut the design from 6/4'' hardwood. (AMI, Ltd.)

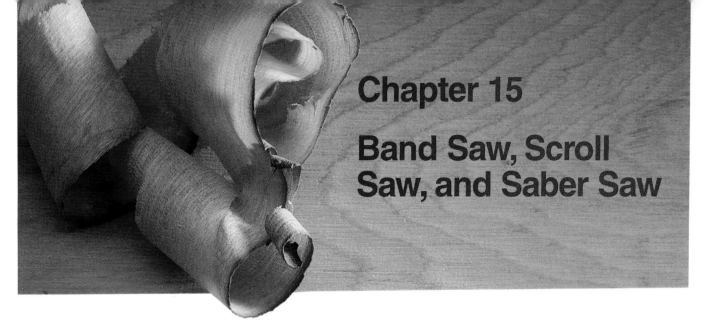

# Chapter 15

# Band Saw, Scroll Saw, and Saber Saw

The band saw, scroll saw, and saber saw are all designed especially for cutting curved outlines, but they also can be used for straight cuts not needing great accuracy. They are somewhat safer than circular saws because the cutting action is perpendicular to the surface of the stock. Therefore, there is no possibility of kickback. BAND SAWS cut large curves in thick stock while SCROLL SAWS cut intricate patterns and designs in thin material. The SABER SAW is especially helpful when cutting large sheets of plywood or hardboard, where it is easier to move the tool than the work.

Laser cutting tools provide a means of making straight or curved cuts as well as engraving. They offer repeatable precision and fine detail.

## BAND SAW

### SIZE AND PARTS

The size of a band saw is determined by the diameter of its wheels. Band saws like those shown in Figs. 15-1 and 15-2 are designed principally for cutting curved work, and are called NARROW BAND SAWS. They range in size from 10 to 42 in. and carry blades under 1 1/2 in. in width. The wheels are fitted with rubber tires that cushion the blade and prevent it from slipping. The top wheel adjusts up and down to permit some difference in blade length and to provide tension. It can also be tilted in or out so that the blade will run in the center of the wheel surface.

A blade guide assembly is located above and below the table. The assembly holds the blade in position and prevents it from being pushed off of the wheel during a sawing operation. The guide located above the table, Fig. 15-3, can be moved up and down to adjust for various thicknesses of stock. When properly adjusted, the guides do not touch the blade except when a piece of wood is being cut.

The cutting speed of a band saw is given in surface feet per minute (S.F.M.). It can be calculated if the wheel diameter (D) and rpm are known. Use the following formula:

$$S.F.M. = \frac{D \times 3.14 \times RPM}{12}$$

## BLADES

To specify a certain band saw blade you must list the width, length, gauge, tooth style, and tooth

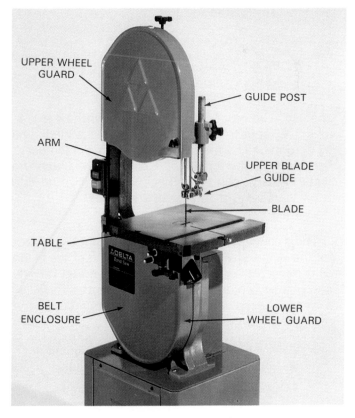

Fig. 15-1. Parts of a standard band saw.
(Delta International Machinery Corp.)

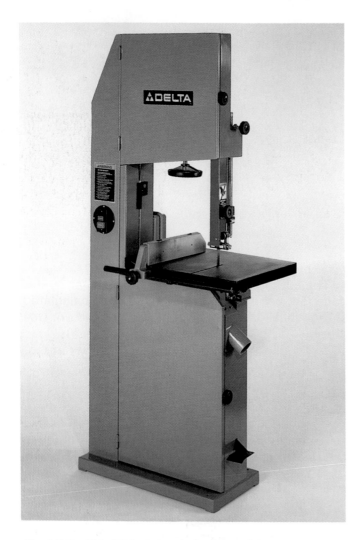

Fig. 15-2. This 20 inch band saw has a 2 hp motor to provide the power to cut through stock up to 19 in. wide and 11 in. thick. (Delta International Machinery Corp.)

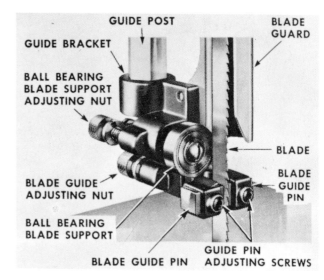

Fig. 15-3. Parts of upper guide. Lower guide is similar.

Tooth size and spacing will be determined by the kind of work required. Coarse teeth will provide a faster but unsmooth cut. For all-purpose work a 4, 5, or 6 point blade is generally used. Blades are specified by listing the numbers of points, or teeth per inch. Fig. 15-4 shows a close-up view of two general purpose blades.

Band saw blades are sold either in given lengths that are joined and ready for use, or in rolls of 100 ft. or longer. When purchased in rolls the correct length is cut and the ends are welded together with a machine, Fig. 15-5. Most band saw blades are thrown away when they become dull.

## Sharpening and Coiling

Band saw blades have many teeth and, therefore, considerable time is required to set and file them by hand. Small shops often prefer to use skip tooth blades with hardened teeth which stay sharp longer

spacing. The most commonly used widths are 1/4, 3/8, 1/2, and 3/4 inch. The length of the blade will be determined by the particular machine being used. To calculate the length of a blade, take twice the distance between the wheel centers (H) and add 3.14 times the diameter of the wheel (D), or:

$$L = 2H + 3.14 D$$

The thickness (gauge) of a blade must be correct for the wheel size. The continual flexing of the blade as it passes over the wheels causes metal fatigue and occurs rapidly when the blade is too thick for a given wheel diameter. Manufacturers recommend the following gauges:

| Wheel Diameter | Recommended Thickness |
|---|---|
| 10—20 inches | 25 gauge |
| 24—30 inches | 22 gauge |
| 36—40 inches | 21 gauge |
| 40 and over | 20 gauge |

Fig. 15-4. Top. Standard 1/2 in. blade. Bottom. Skip tooth blade. These teeth are hardened and will stay sharp longer.

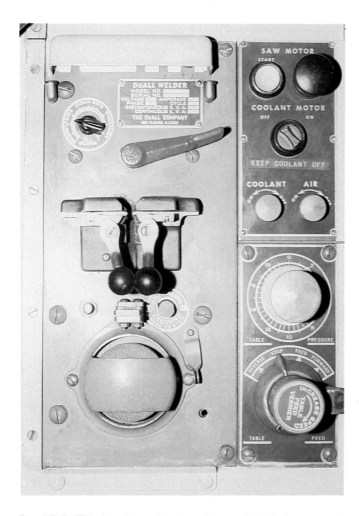

Fig. 15-5. This band saw blade welder welds blades up to 1 in. wide. It is also adjustable for various gauges.

used for hand filing can be mounted in an automatic filing machine, Fig. 15-7.

Storing, shipping, and handling blades is easier if they are coiled. Fig. 15-8 shows the sequence to follow.

A. With the teeth pointing away from you, grasp the blade in the palms of your hands and step on it with one foot. Your index fingers should point down along the back of the blade.

B. Using your index fingers, push the two lower sections away from you and permit the upper loop to swing toward you.

C. Continue the motion with the lower loops swinging toward each other and the upper loop swinging downward and underneath. Raise your foot so the blade can turn on edge.

D. Cross the loops and release the blade. It will fall together in three equal loops.

Long blades may be coiled into additional loops by enlarging one of the three loops and holding it as shown in Fig. 15-9. Repeat the above procedure and the blade will then be coiled in five loops.

## Mounting Blades

It is important to install band saw blades carefully and keep them in adjustment if the full life of the blade is to be secured. The steps listed should be followed.

1. Disconnect the electrical power and open the wheel guard doors. Pull the table alignment pin and remove the throat plate if necessary.

2. Loosen the upper and lower guide assemblies and push them back out of line with the wheels.

than regular blades. They cannot be filed and are discarded when they become dull.

Regular blades are filed and set in about the same way as a hand rip saw. The shape and angle are shown in Fig. 15-6. A special band saw file should be used. It has rounded edges that keep the bottom of the gullets round and minimizes checks and cracks in the blade. The same type of file that is

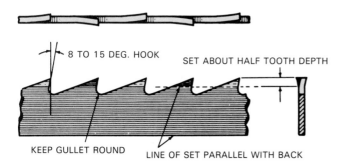

Fig. 15-6. Shape and angle of band saw teeth. (Simonds Saw and Steel Co.)

Fig. 15-7. Automatic filing and setting machine with attachments for band saw blades. (Foley-Belsaw Co.)

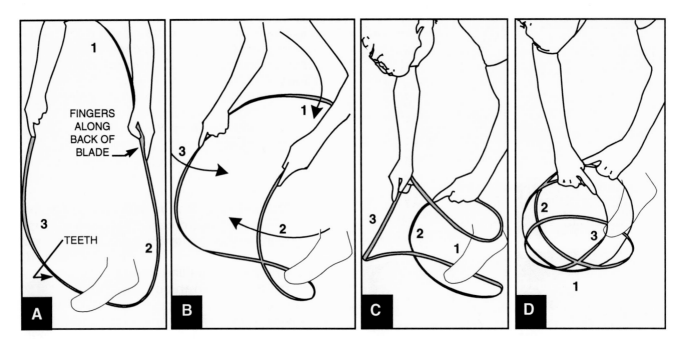

Fig. 15-8. Coiling a band saw blade. A—Starting position with teeth pointing away from you. B—Loops 2 and 3 pushed away and swinging toward the center. Loop 1 swings back and downward. C—Motion continued. Loop 1 swinging downward and underneath. D—Loop 2 and 3 now overlapped and on top of loop 1. Release blade.

3. Uncoil the blade and place it on the wheels with the teeth to the front and pointing down over the table. If the teeth are in the wrong direction turn the blade inside out.

4. Raise the top wheel to apply tension. Most machines have a scale to show the correct tension for various blade widths, Fig. 15-10.

5. Roll the machine by hand and adjust the top wheel with the tilting mechanism until the blade tracks smoothly near the center of the tires.

6. Move the saw guides forward until the front edges of the jaws are even or slightly back of the tooth gullets. The blade should move evenly between them with about 1/64 in. clearance on each side, Fig. 15-11. Lock the guide assemblies in position.

7. Move the blade support wheel forward on each guide assembly until it is 1/64 in. away from the back edge of the blade. Lock them in place.

8. Again roll the machine by hand and check all adjustments and clearances. Have your instructor check the adjustments. Replace the throat plate and pin and close the wheel guard doors.

9. Connect the power, turn on the machine, and make a trial cut.

**Band Saw Maintenance**

Keep the blade free of gum and pitch. It can be cleaned by wiping with a cloth saturated with a pitch and gum remover or mineral spirits. The band saw tires may gather an accumulation of sawdust and gum and should be cleaned occasionally with a stiff brush. As tires become grooved from blade wear they can be smoothed with coarse abrasive

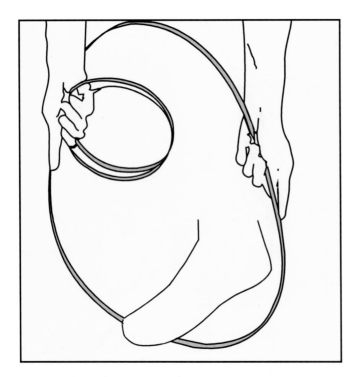

Fig. 15-9. Starting position for coiling five loops.

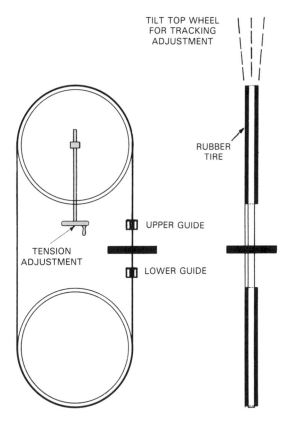

Fig. 15-10. Adjustments for mounting blade.

Lubrication requirements will vary with different machines. Check the operator's manual furnished by the manufacturer for recommendations. This manual will also provide information concerning wheel alignment, tire replacement and other maintenance aspects. The occasional application of a coat of paste wax to the table will prevent rust and help keep the surface smooth and clean.

## BAND SAW SAFETY

Follow these safety rules, in addition to the power equipment safety rules given in Chapter 3.
1. Wheel guard doors must be closed and the blade properly adjusted before turning on the machine.
2. Adjust the upper guide assembly so it is 1/4 in. above the work.
3. Allow the saw to reach full speed before feeding the work.
4. The stock must be held flat on the table.
5. Feed the saw only as fast as the teeth will easily remove the wood.
6. Maintain a 2 in. margin of safety. This means that the hands should always be at least two inches away from the blade when the saw is running, Fig. 15-12.

paper glued to a large block of wood. The lower wheel can be easily and safely dressed by removing the blade and running the wheel under operating power. The top wheel should be turned by hand. Driving the top wheel with a blade for this operation is extremely hazardous and should be undertaken only by a skilled operator.

Tire shape can be maintained longer if the blade tension is released when the saw is to stand idle for a considerable length of time.

Fig. 15-12. This operator is demonstrating safe practice on the band saw. His hands are at least 2 in. away from the blade, the upper guide assembly is within 1/4 in. of the surface of his workpiece, and he is wearing safety glasses.
(Delta International Machinery Corp.)

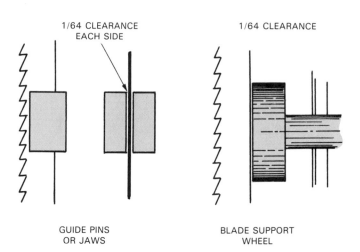

Fig. 15-11. Guide clearance.

7. Whenever possible plan saw cuts to avoid backing out of curves.
8. Make turns carefully and do not cut radii so small that the blade is twisted.
9. Stop the machine before backing out of a long curved cut.
10. Round stock should not be cut unless mounted securely in a jig or hand screw.
11. If you hear a clicking noise, turn off the machine at once. This indicates a crack in the blade. If the blade breaks, shut off the power and move away from the machine until both wheels stop.
12. Turn off the machine as soon as you have finished your work. If the machine has a brake, apply it smoothly. Do not leave the machine until it has stopped running.

Fig. 15-14. Roughing out parts before making finished cuts.

## ROUGHING CUTS

Since there is no tendency for kickback, the band saw can be used to cut rough lumber to length and width. Pieces that are warped should be handled carefully. It is usually best to turn the concave side down so the stock will rest firmly on the table without rocking.

When making cuts in rough lumber, lay out cutting lines with chalk. Adjust the upper guide to about 1/4 in. above the thickest part of the stock. If you are right handed, make a ripping cut by standing to the left of the cutting line. Feed the work with the right hand and guide it with the left hand. Move the work through the cut at a smooth, even speed. The rate of feed will vary with the kind and thickness of the wood and the blade size and speed, Fig. 15-13. For rough crosscutting, it is usually best to stand to the right of the sawing line, holding the stock in the right hand and feeding it with the left.

Fig. 15-14 shows roughing out cuts being made after stock has been surfaced and finished cutting lines drawn. Holes have been bored to free the blade for sharp turns. Stay well away from the cutting lines so that there will be sufficient stock for the finished cuts.

## STRAIGHT FINISHED CUTS

Some band saws are equipped with a fence and miter gauge. They are adjusted and used in the same general way as the table saw. Since their purpose is to guide the work accurately through the cut, the stock must be surfaced so it will be flat on the table and have a straight edge against the fence or gauge. The blade must be properly sharpened, otherwise it may crawl or lead away from the line of cut. The table can be tiled for making angle cuts.

## CUTTING CURVES

The basic purpose of the band saw is to cut curved work. The size of the curve (radius) that can be cut without straining or twisting the blade will be determined by the width of the blade and the amount of set in the teeth. A sharp blade with normal set will cut the following curves:

| Blade Width | Minimum Circle |
|---|---|
| 1/4 in. | 2 in. dia. |
| 3/8 in. | 3 in. dia. |
| 1/2 in. | 4 in. dia. |
| 3/4 in. | 6 in. dia. |

The curves will likely vary in size in a given piece of work. In Fig. 15-15 a finished cut is being made along a larger curve while a sharp point was passed by. It will be cut later. Note the relief cuts made before the main cut was started, to free the blade in the sharp curve.

The teeth of a band saw blade are chisel shaped

Fig. 15-13. Ripping rough stock to remove some of the cup.

Fig. 15-15. Making a finished cut along large curves. Details will be cut after this cut is completed.

and do not leave a smooth surface. For many jobs, the kerf should be located in the waste stock and far enough from the line to allow for smoothing. This allowance will vary with the coarseness of the blade but should seldom be less than 1/16 in., Fig. 15-16.

Feed the work straight into the blade and do not try to change the position of the cut by applying side pressure. Keep your eye on the line a little ahead of the blade so you can see how to adjust the position of the work to feed correctly.

Small curves can be cut with a wide blade by using one of the methods shown in Fig. 15-17.

*Applying side pressure, or cutting too small a radius will damage the saw blade. Burned marks on the cut surface of the work indicate that improper procedures were used.*

## CUTTING SEQUENCE

When working with complicated patterns, always study the sequence of cuts you will use. Often it

Fig. 15-16. Cutting on waste side of the line with a 1/16 in. allowance.

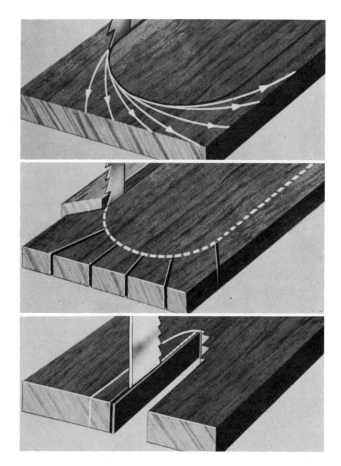

Fig. 15-17. Cutting sharp curves with a wide blade. Top. Tangent cuts. Center. Relief cuts. Bottom. Nibble cuts. (Jam Handy Organization)

is worthwhile to number the cuts on the work. Chalk marks along the finished line can indicate the direction of the cut and the order in which it will be made. Fig. 15-18 suggests a sequence of cuts to follow in cutting out the part shown. It will be necessary to back out of only two short straight cuts.

## MULTIPLE SAWING

To save production time, duplicate parts can be stacked together and cut in a single operation. This is called MULTIPLE or PAD SAWING. The layers can be held together by several methods, Fig. 15-19. If you use nails be certain that they are located well away from the cutting line.

## COMPOUND SAWING

This operation involves two sets of cuts, usually made at right angles to each other. In Fig. 15-20, the hull of a sail boat is formed by laying out the pattern on the top and sides and then making the two sets of cuts shown. After the first cut is made, the waste is spot glued back to support the stock

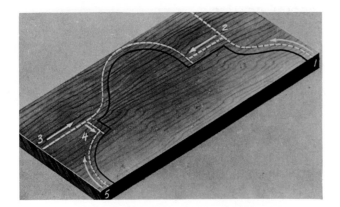

Fig. 15-18. Cutting sequence. (Jam Handy Organization)

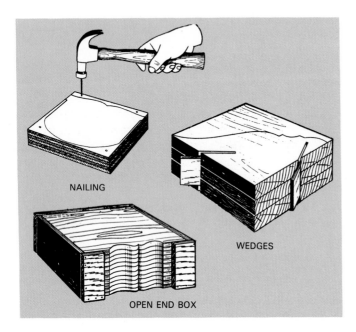

NAILING

WEDGES

OPEN END BOX

Fig. 15-19. How stock can be held for multiple sawing.

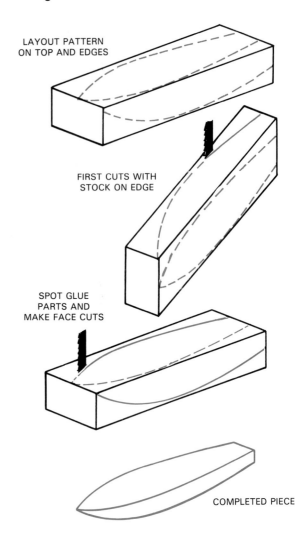

LAYOUT PATTERN ON TOP AND EDGES

FIRST CUTS WITH STOCK ON EDGE

SPOT GLUE PARTS AND MAKE FACE CUTS

COMPLETED PIECE

Fig. 15-20. Compound sawing.

during the final cut. Nails can be used to rejoin the work if carefully placed. Compound sawing can be applied to more complicated shapes such as cabriole legs or carving blanks.

## RESAWING

Stock can be resawed on the band saw to produce two or more thinner pieces as shown in Fig. 15-21. A simple guide should be used to control the thickness and help hold the stock on edge. Use a sharp blade, at least 1/2 in. wide. Band saw blades are thinner than circular saw blades and thus reduce the amount of waste in a resawing operation. On wide boards however, it is often helpful to first make circular saw cuts in from each edge and then finish the operation on the band saw.

Band saws can be equipped with a resawing fix-

Fig. 15-21. Resawing, using a simple guide clamped to the table.

Fig. 15-22. Top. Resawing attachment. Bottom. Resawing attachment in operation. (Northfield Foundry and Machine Co.)

ture or attachment, as shown in Fig. 15-22. This fixture or attachment consists of a special fence and pressure rolls. They are used to guide and hold the work. They will insure that accurate cuts will be produced.

## SPECIAL SETUPS

A wide range of special setups can be made on the band saw to produce duplicate parts in production work. One of these is pattern sawing where the work is mounted on a master pattern which moves along a stop or guide as the cut is made. Some setups are produced on an auxiliary table that has slots or grooves. Pins on the underside of a carrier move through these slots and control the direction and position of the cut. The work is held or clamped on the carrier.

## SCROLL SAW

### SIZES AND PARTS

The size of a scroll saw (sometimes called a jig saw) is determined by the distance from the over arm to the blade. The one shown in Fig. 15-23 is a 24 in. size. It is a standard model that provides different cutting speeds. Variable speeds are usually available that range from about 600 to 1800 C.S.M. (cutting strokes per minute). A pitman drive moves the lower chuck (not shown) up and down. The upper chuck is attached to a bar that moves inside the tension sleeve. The tension sleeve includes a spring that keeps the blade from buckling on the up stroke. It can be adjusted up or down for various blade lengths.

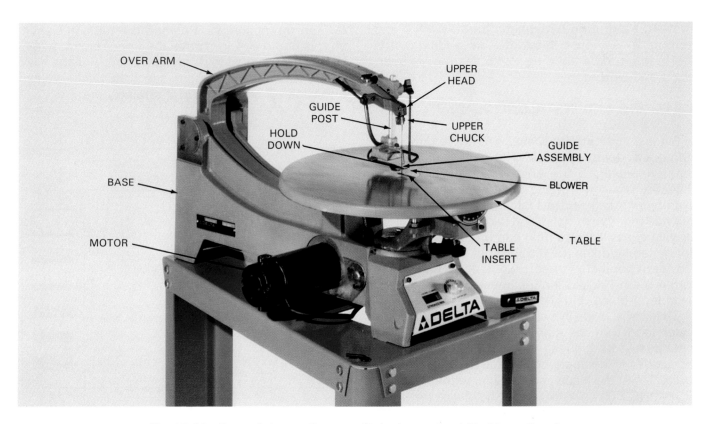

Fig. 15-23. Parts of the scroll saw. (Delta International Machinery Corp.)

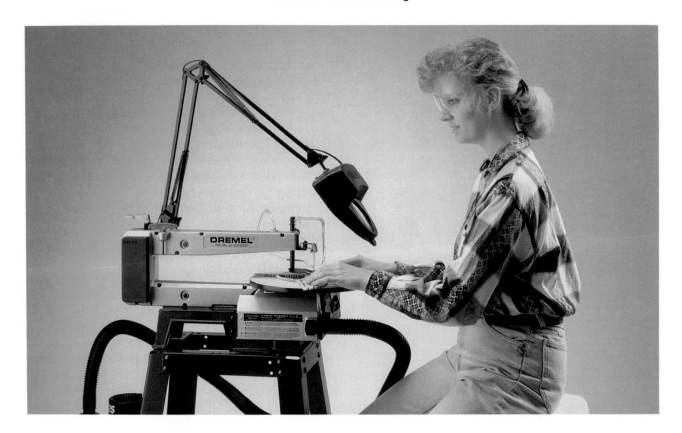

Fig. 15-24. This scroll is excellent for use with precision work. (Dremel)

Fig. 15-24 shows another type of scroll saw. This model is very useful for precision work. It has eight blade speeds through a two-stroke, four-speed belt system, along with a magnetic on/off switch and automatic sawdust blow-off. In addition, the worktable can be tilted up to 45 degrees, is over-sized and slotted.

## SELECTING AND INSTALLING BLADES

Blades vary in thickness, width, length, and number of teeth per inch. They are usually 5 in. long, however, 6 in. lengths are available. Fig. 15-25 gives some of the common sizes used for woodworking. Select the largest blade that will still provide the type of finish and width of cut required. It will be less likely to heat and break. A good size for general work is .020 thick and .110 wide with 15 teeth per inch. For soft wood use a blade with larger teeth (10 per inch suggested) and for hard woods, a blade with finer teeth.

To install a blade in a scroll saw, remove the table insert and turn the saw by hand until the lower chuck is at its highest point. Loosen the thumbscrew of the lower chuck and see that the jaws are clean. Insert the blade about 1/2 in. with the TEETH POINTING DOWNWARD. Hold the blade straight up and down and tighten the thumbscrew, Fig. 15-26. Replace the table insert.

Loosen the thumbscrew on the upper chuck. Pull the chuck down over the blade and tighten the thumbscrew. Do not use pliers or wrenches to tighten thumbscrews. Position the tension sleeve so it is about 3/4 in. above the upper chuck when the blade is moved to its highest point. Roll the saw over a few turns by hand to see if the blade is clear and runs up and down in a straight line.

| THICKNESS | WIDTH | NUMBER OF TEETH | |
|-----------|-------|-----------------|---|
| .008 | .035 | 20 | |
| .010 | .045 | 18 | |
| .020 | .085 | 15 | |
| .020 | .110 | 7 | |
| .020 | .110 | 15 | |
| .020 | .110 | 10 | |
| .028 | .187 | 10 | |

Fig. 15-25. Scroll saw blade sizes. They are listed in one-thousandths of an inch.

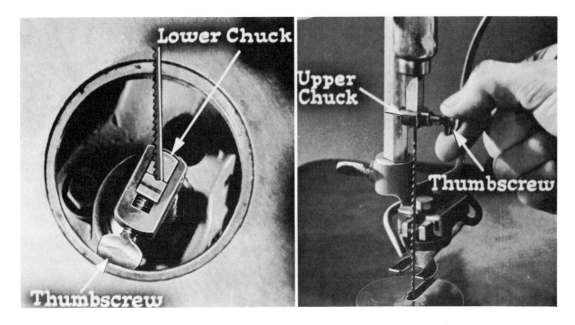

Fig. 15-26. Left. Blade mounted in lower chuck. Right. Tightening blade in upper chuck. (Jam Handy Organization)

Adjust the guide assembly so the blade runs freely on its sides, and the blade support roller just touches the back of the blade. Tighten the guide assembly, Fig. 15-27.

Saws of different makes will vary in exact requirements for adjustments and lubrication. Check the operator's manual for specific information.

## SCROLL SAW SAFETY

The following rules should be observed, along with the power equipment safety rules given in Chapter 3.

1. Be certain the blade is properly installed in a vertical position with the teeth pointing down.

2. Roll the machine over by hand to see if there is clearance for the blade and if the tension sleeve has been properly set.
3. Check the belt guard to see that it is closed and tight.
4. Keep the hold-down adjusted so the work will not be raised off the table.
5. When the saw is running, do not permit your fingers to get directly in line with the blade. Usually the work can be held on either side of the cutting line as shown in Fig. 15-28.

## CUTTING PROCEDURES

Stock to be cut on the scroll saw should be carefully prepared. Surfaces should be smooth and

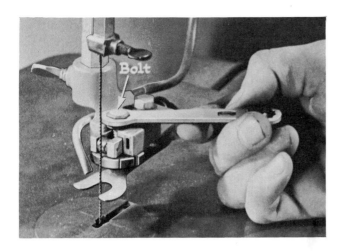

Fig. 15-27. Adjusting the guide assembly.
(Jam Handy Organization)

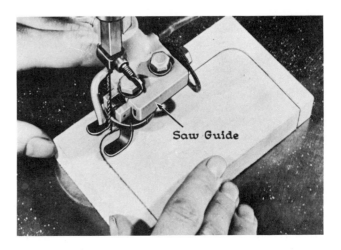

Fig. 15-28. Making a simple cut. (Jam Handy Organization)

cutting lines laid out with a sharp pencil. Curves are usually cut as the last step in the fabrication sequence. For example, in Fig. 15-29, the ends of a tray have been surfaced and squared to size and the miters for the corner joints have been cut and fitted.

Loosen the guide post and position the guide assembly so that the hold-down springs will rest on the top of the work. The stock can be placed at the side of the blade to make this setting. Start the saw and feed the work forward into the blade. You will get the smoothest cut possible if you feed the work slowly. Keep the blade cutting just on the outside or waste side of the line. Give the blade plenty of time to cut its way clear as you go around corners.

Before cutting complicated designs, you should work out the "route" you will follow, as was suggested for operating the band saw. This will often eliminate the need to back out of long cuts, or make sharper turns than the blade permits. Note the procedure in Fig. 15-30. The first cut was made all the way along the outline and then the details were cut. Drilling small holes in the waste stock at corners will often make the cutting easier.

### Internal Cutting

When the work includes internal curves and designs, drill or bore holes in the waste area and thread the blade through these holes. To thread the blade, first remove it from the upper chuck and raise the hold-down to its highest position. Roll the saw by hand so that the blade is at its lowest point and then thread the blade through the hole, Fig. 15-31. Replace the blade in the upper chuck, adjust the hold-down, and make the cut. When there are many internal cuts to make, it is faster to use a saber sawing setup. A shorter blade is clamped in only the lower chuck, Fig. 15-32. Since the blade will not be held taut by the upper chuck assembly, the blade must be heavy enough to resist the feed pressure.

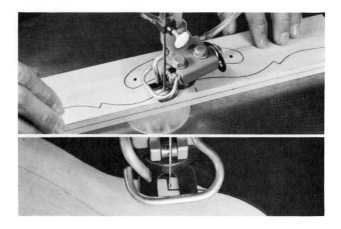

Fig. 15-30. Cutting procedure. Top. Cut along main outline and bypass details. Bottom. Cut details.

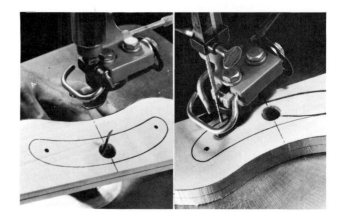

Fig. 15-31. Internal cutting. Left. Threading blade. Right. Making the cut.

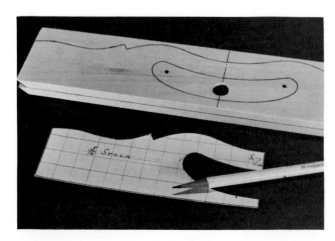

Fig. 15-29. Work prepared for cutting on jig saw. Note that the mitered corners have already been cut.

Fig. 15-32. Blade setup for saber sawing. Note that the chuck has been turned 90 deg. and the blade fastened in the V jaws. (Delta International Machinery Corp.)

*After changing blades or making any adjustments, always roll the jig saw several turns by hand to check movement before turning on the motor.*

## Marquetry and Angle Sawing

Marquetry is a method of forming designs. It is done by sawing two or more kinds of wood that are fastened together in a pad. These pieces are then interchanged, Fig. 15-33. A very fine blade must be used. Designs usually include internal cuts. A very small drill can be used for the threading hole or, because the blade is fine, it may be satisfactory to cut through the outside areas to reach the internal cuts. Intricate inlay pictures, consisting of many kinds of veneer, can be made by this method.

Marquetry and inlay work are sometimes sawed with the table at a slight angle so when the pieces are assembled, the saw kerf will be closed, Fig. 15-34. When cutting at an angle, the work must be kept on one side of the blade. The angle of tilt will vary with the width of the saw kerf.

Angle sawing can be applied to thick stock in such a way that the piece cut out will slip partially through the outside piece and fit tightly. It can be applied to such work as boat hulls, lamp bases, and other simple projects, Fig. 15-35.

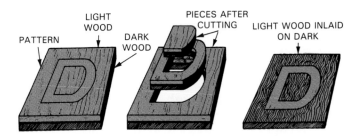

Fig. 15-33. Simple marquetry.

Fig. 15-34. The hold-down spring has been adjusted to compensate for table tilt.

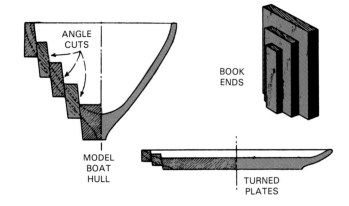

Fig. 15-35. Angle sawing ideas.

## SABER SAWS

### PARTS AND DESCRIPTION

The saber saw, also called a bayonet saw, is a portable electric jig saw used for a wide range of light work. It is used by carpenters, cabinetmakers, electricians, and home crafters. A standard model and its basic parts are shown in Fig. 15-36. The stroke of the blade is about 1/2 in. and it operates at a speed of about 4000 strokes per minute.

Various blades are available for wood cutting with a range of 6 to 12 teeth per inch. For general purpose work a blade with 10 teeth per inch is satisfactory. Always select a blade that will have at least two teeth in contact with the edge being cut. Saws will vary in the way the blade is mounted in the chuck, so you should study the manufacturer's manual. Also follow the lubrication schedule as specified in this manual.

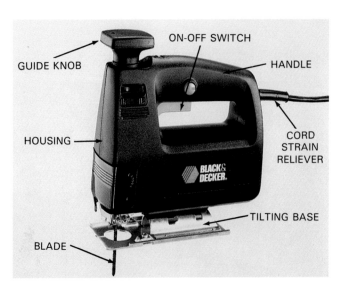

Fig. 15-36. Parts of a saber saw.    (Black & Decker)

## SABER SAW SAFETY

Observe the following safety guidelines when operating a saber saw. In addition to these guidelines, review the power equipment safety rules outlined in Chapter 3.

1. Make certain the saw is properly grounded through the electrical cord.
2. Select the correct blade for your work and be sure it is properly mounted.
3. Disconnect the saw to change blades or make adjustments.
4. Place the base of the saw firmly on the stock before starting the cut.
5. Turn on motor before blade contacts work.
6. Do not attempt to cut curves so sharp that the blade will be twisted. Follow procedures described for band saw operation.
7. Make certain the work is well supported and do not cut into sawhorses or other supports.

## USING THE SABER SAW

The saber saw can be used to make straight or bevel cuts as shown in Fig. 15-37. Curves are usually cut by guiding the saw along a layout line, Fig. 15-38. Circular cuts may be made more accurately with a special guide or attachment.

The blade cuts on the up stroke so splintering will take place on the top side of the work. This must be considered when making finished cuts, especially in fine hardwood plywood. Always hold the base firmly against the surface of the material being cut.

Cutting internal openings can be done two ways. A starting hole can be drilled in the waste stock, or the saw can be held on end so the blade will cut its own opening. This is called plunge cutting and must be undertaken with considerable care. Rest the toe of the base firmly on the work, turn on the motor, and then slowly lower the blade into the cut.

Fig. 15-38. When making a series of circular cuts with the saber saw, use a line to guide the cut. (Bosch Power Tool Corp.)

Another portable power tool is the reciprocating saw, Fig. 15-39. It is operated in about the same way as the saber saw. Fig. 15-40 shows a typical operation it will perform.

## LASER CUTTING TOOLS

Laser cutting of wood offers repeatable precision and fine detail. Lasers are different from conventional cutting tools in that they do not use a cutter, but apply a beam of light energy directly to the workpiece to vaporize the material.

Carbon dioxide ($CO_2$) lasers are used for wood cutting and engaving. Light energy is created by activating the $CO_2$ gas with an electrical current, which is concentrated into a beam and focused to a fine point (.003 in. to .006 in. diameter). The heat

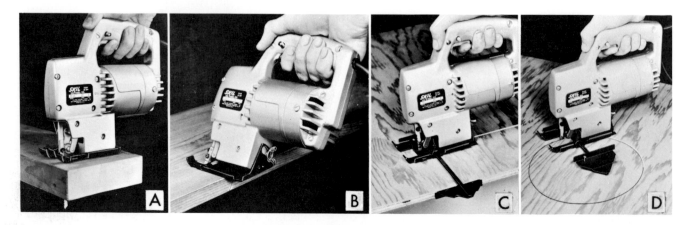

Fig. 15-37. Using a saber saw. A—Straight cutting. B—Angle cutting. C—Using a fence. D—Using a circle cutting guide.

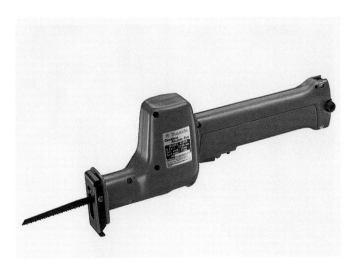

Fig. 15-39. Reciprocating saw. (Makita U.S.A., Inc.)

Fig. 15-40. Using the reciprocating saw to rough-in an opening. (DeWalt)

sirable for cut edges. The char, however, is what makes the laser an excellent engraving tool. The high cost of the laser is another disadvantage. Engravers cost up to $15,000 while more powerful lasers needed for wood cutting can cost over $60,000.

Cost effectiveness of laser machining depends on several factors—purchase price, quality control, the types and quantities of materials to be cut, settings and feed speeds, operator experience, and the nature of the woodworking activity. All of these factors affect the wear life and performance of a cutting tool and also determine whether it is a cost-effective choice.

## INDUSTRIAL MACHINES

Band saws somewhat larger, but otherwise similar to the ones you have operated in the school shop, are used to form curved parts and other work in commercial cabinet shops, patternmaking shops, and furniture factories, Fig. 15-41.

Fig. 15-41. Cutting tennis racket frames to finished thickness. The frame is mounted in a special carrier that moves across the table of a 42 in. band saw. (Wilson Sporting Goods Co.)

produced by the light beam does the cutting.

Laser cutting provides some advantages over conventional tooling due to the fact that they vaporize material rather than mechanically remove it. There is no tool wear, which might require sharpening or adjustments resulting from the reduced cutter size. Stress to the workpiece is reduced, allowing a woodworker to create fine detail on thick or thin materials. Pinpoint accuracy is possible with laser cutting, which lends itself to CNC positioning equipment. In addition, no sawdust is created.

Disadvantages of laser machining include the burned edge, called "char," which maybe unde-

Fig. 15-42 shows a large (27.5 in.) band saw with power feed. It is ideal for resawing work on large stock. Maximum width of the blade is 2.5 in. and throat depth is 26.7 in. A 10 hp motor is also standard on the saw.

Giant band saws are used to cut logs in lumber mills, Fig. 15-43. They are called BAND MILLS and include a carriage that moves the log through the cut. The carriage travels on steel tracks and is adjustable to various positions and rates of feed. These machines often use blades as wide as 16 in. and more than 60 ft. long.

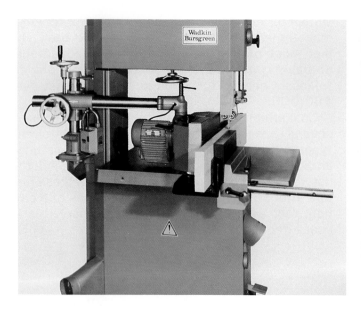

Fig. 15-42. Left. This large industrial band saw is equipped with power feed. It is an excellent tool for resawing work. Right. Close-up view of horizontal feed.

Fig. 15-43. Cutting logs in a lumber mill. Blade is 12 in. (305 mm) wide. All aspects of the sawing (turning log, movement of carriage, feed rates) are controlled by skilled operator seated at console. (Weyerhaeuser Co.)

## TEST YOUR KNOWLEDGE, Chapter 15

Please do not write in the text. Place your answers on a separate sheet of paper.

1. _____ saws are used to cut large curves, while _____ saws are used to cut intricate patterns and designs in thin material.
2. What is the formula for determining the cutting speed of a band saw?
3. Why are the wheels of band saws fitted with rubber tires?
4. To specify a band saw blade, what should NOT be listed?
   a. Tooth style.
   b. Gauge.
   c. Length.
   d. Cutting speed.
5. List five safety rules to observe when working with a band saw.
6. What is pad sawing?
7. _____ is done by sawing two or more kinds of wood that are fastened together in a pad.
8. The _____ _____ is a portable electric scroll saw that can be used for a wide range of light work.
9. The blade of the saber saw cuts on the down stroke. True or False?
10. What are four major advantages of cutting wood with lasers?

## ACTIVITIES

1. Calculate the cutting speed of the band saw in your shop. Also calculate the peripheral speed of the table saw blade. Compare the two speeds. Convert them into miles of kilometers per hour. Prepare a summary of calculations and include the formulas used.
2. Prepare a list of five manufacturers that produce narrow band saws and scroll saws. How do the saws of each manufacturer differ? Include the company's full name and address.
3. If you had a choice of either adding a band saw or a scroll saw to your home workshop, which would you select? Prepare a paper listing your reasons and considerations.

This simple shelf can be done on either the band saw or the scroll saw.    (Amerock Corp.)

Low-back chair. This solid rock maple chair shows the Shaker's sense of practicality—it was designed with a low two-slat back so that it could be tucked under the table after mealtime. Dimensions: 27'' back height, 17'' seat height, 18 3/4'' width, and 14'' depth.    (Shaker Workshops)

Top. This drilling assembly includes pneumatic drive and electric motor drive unit heads, mounted on framework built from Easi-rig System. (R.S. Brookman, Ltd.) Bottom. Typical work pieces of a modern double-end tenoner. (Wadkin PLC)

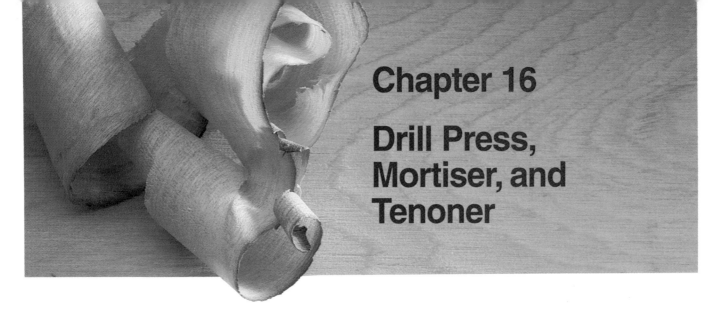

# Chapter 16

# Drill Press, Mortiser, and Tenoner

In wood fabrication, producing round holes and square and oblong mortises is important. The DRILL PRESS and MORTISER are power machines used to produce them. Large school shops will usually have both a drill press and mortiser, while smaller shops may have only a drill press and use an attachment for mortising operations. The TENONER is not a drilling or boring machine, but since industry uses it to cut tenons that fit into mortises, it is included in this section.

## DRILL PRESS

### SIZES, PARTS, AND ADJUSTMENTS

The drill press is a versatile power machine widely used in smaller woodworking shops, school shops, and home workshops. In addition to regular drilling and boring operations, it can be equipped with attachments for mortising, routing, shaping, and sanding. The drill press is available in either floor or bench models. Some have heads that adjust in or out from the support column and tilt at various angles. In production work, several drilling heads may be mounted on a single table.

Fig. 16-1 shows a bench model drill press. Its main parts consist of a base, column, table, and head. The table can be adjusted up and down on the column and can be tilted. The chuck is carried by a spindle that revolves inside a sleeve called a QUILL. The quill assembly can be moved up and down by a feed lever. It is spring loaded, so it will return to its uppermost position. The length of the stroke is adjustable.

Drill press sizes are given as twice the distance from the column to the center of the spindle. Sizes range from 12 in. to 20 in., with a 15 in. size often used in the school shop. Spindle speeds are usually varied by shifting a belt on step pulleys. However, variable speed drives are also available. For wood drilling and boring operations, speeds should range from 400 to about 1800 rpm.

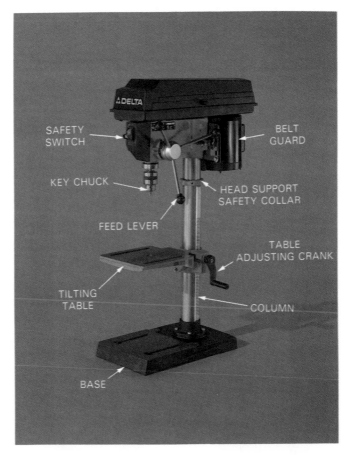

Fig. 16-1. Study the main parts of the standard bench model drill press. (Delta International Machinery Corp.)

### Wood Boring Bits

Fig. 16-2 shows some common boring bits. You will recognize several that look like regular auger bits used in the brace. Power bits seldom have a feed screw because the feed is controlled by the machine. Those with feed screws are mainly designed for use in portable drills. Most power bits have a brad point that centers the bit in the work, Fig. 16-3. The spur machine bit is the type most

273

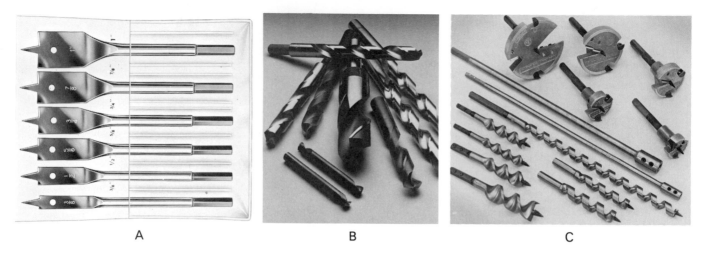

Fig. 16-2. Machine bits. A—Spade bits for a quick, rough hole. B—High speed twist drills. (Triumph Twist Drill Co.) C—From top to bottom: self-feeding, large-hole boring bits; 18 in. extenders; double twist bits (left); ship augers (right). (Black and Decker Ind./Const. Div.)

often used in the drill press. It is available in sizes from 1/4 in. to over 1 in., by thirty-seconds. Holes under 1/4 in. are drilled with a straight shank twist drill. It is ground to a somewhat sharper point than those used in metalworking. An included angle of about 80 deg. is recommended.

Power bits must be kept clean and sharp to do good work. They should be carefully handled and stored, and wiped off occasionally with a cloth saturated with light oil. Power bits are sharpened with a file in about the same manner as described for regular auger bits in Unit 6, with the exception that cutters are usually filed on the bottom side. When sharpening bits, always try to maintain the original angle and shape.

## DRILL PRESS SAFETY

Study the following safety rules for use with drill presses, in addition to reviewing the power equipment safety rules outlined in Chapter 3.

1. Check the speed setting to see that it is correct for your work. Holes over 1/2 in. should be bored at the lowest speed.
2. Use only an approved bit, Fig. 16-4. Bits with feed screws or those that have excessive length generally should not be used.
3. Mount the bit securely to the full depth of the chuck and in the center. Remove the key immediately.
4. Position the table and adjust the feed stroke so there is no possibility of the bit striking the table.
5. The work should be placed on a wood pad when the holes will go all the way through.
6. Work that will be held by hand should be center punched.
7. Small or irregularly shaped pieces must be clamped to the table or held in some special fixture.
8. Feed the bit smoothly into the work. When the hole is deep, withdraw it frequently to clear the shavings and cool the bit.
9. When using some special clamping setup, or a hole saw or fly cutter, have your instructor inspect it before turning on the power.
10. Always have your instructor check setups for routing and shaping.

FILING CUTTERS

MARGIN

FLUTE

SPUR

CUTTER

BRAD POINT

FILING SPURS

Fig. 16-3. Parts of a machine bit and sharpening operations.

Fig. 16-4. Forstner bit, brad point wood bit, and bit extension. These short bits are easy and safe to use. (Leichtung, Inc.)

Fig. 16-6. Boring a 3/4 in. hole.

## BASIC DRILL PRESS OPERATION

The speed setting will vary with the kind of wood and the size and type of bit. Bits over 1/2 in. in diameter should be used at low speeds (400 to 800 rpm) especially when boring hard wood. If large bits are driven at high speeds they will heat up and may be damaged.

Handle bits carefully. When inserting a bit in the chuck it is good practice to place a piece of wood on the table to protect the cutting edges and points if it should slip out of your hand or the chuck, Fig. 16-5. Adjust the height of the table to provide about 1/2 in. of clearance above the work.

When boring only a few holes, each one should be laid out and the center punched. The part can then be held and guided by hand. If the hole goes all the way through, support it on a flat piece of scrap stock as shown in Fig. 16-6. This will not only

protect the table but will also support the edges of the hole on the bottom side and prevent splintering.

Hold the stock firmly with one hand, turn on the motor, and bring the bit down close to the surface with the feed lever. Align the point of the bit with the punched hole and then feed the bit into the work with a smooth, even pressure. When the hole is through, raise the bit, clear away the cutting, and place the work in position for the next hole. Or, if your work is complete, stop the machine, remove the bit, and clear the table.

To bore a hole to a specified depth, use the depth stop. To make this setting, lower the bit along the edge of the work to the required depth, lock the quill in this position, and then set the stop. Unlock the quill and bore the hole. It is good practice to use the stop even though the hole goes through, as it will control the depth of the bit in the wood pad and insure against it striking the table.

Stock that is round or has irregular shapes must be clamped to the table or held in special supports, Figs. 16-7 and 16-8. In Fig. 16-7, the V-block is

Fig. 16-5. Mount the bit to the full depth of the chuck. Always remove the key after tightening the chuck.

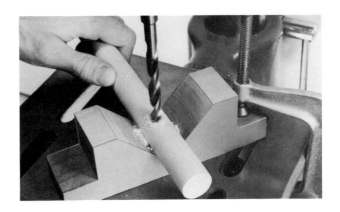

Fig. 16-7. Using a V-block to bore round stock.

275

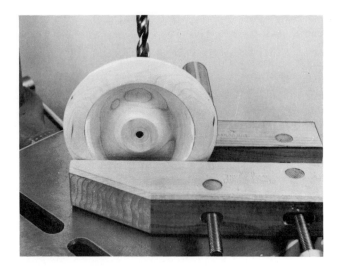

Fig. 16-8. Boring round stock clamped in a hand screw.

Fig. 16-10. Using a sliding T-bevel to set the table at an angle.

centered with the bit and then clamped in position to insure a hole through the center of the dowel. Metal vises are available that will rest on the table and hold irregularly shaped pieces.

When drilling holes in the end or edges of stock, it is often best to turn the table to a vertical position. The work can be supported on the lower table and held in position by the regular table, or it can be clamped to the regular table, Fig. 16-9. A straightedge can be clamped in a vertical position to serve as a fence. Holes through lamp stems or similar parts should be drilled in from each end. When drilling deep holes, raise the bit out of the work frequently to clear the cuttings and allow it to cool.

### Boring Holes at an Angle

To tilt the table, loosen the nut and pull the pin located underneath. Use a sliding T-bevel to position the table at the required angle, Fig. 16-10. The

miter gauge of the table saw can also be used. When the table is in the required position, tighten the nut.

The work should be clamped to the table or held against stops as shown in Fig. 16-11. Be careful! The bit will not easily feed into a slanted surface and may tend to tear the wood. For best results, clamp scrap stock over the position of the hole and bore through it, and then on into the work.

When you have completed your angle boring, level the table, replace the index pin, and tighten the nut.

### Cutting Large Holes

Large holes in thin stock can be cut easily and quickly with a HOLE SAW like the one shown in Fig. 16-12. Various size blade segments fit into grooves in the head and are held in place with a set screw. The center drill must be set deep enough to be thoroughly imbedded in the work before the saw

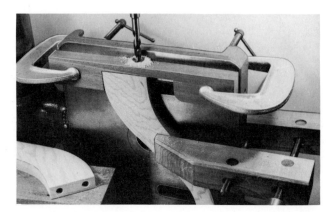

Fig. 16-9. Boring dowel holes in irregularly shaped parts. Table is turned to a vertical position.

Fig. 16-11. Boring a hole at an angle.

Fig. 16-12. Hole saw.

Fig. 16-14. Cutting a large hole with the fly cutter. Always clamp the work securely to the table.

comes in contact with the surface. Fig. 16-13 shows the hole saw in operation. Use the lowest speed (about 400 rpm).

A FLY CUTTER, Fig. 16-14, is sometimes used to cut a large hole. The cutter is mounted on a beam that is adjustable through the center hub. As with the hole saw, the center drill must be well imbedded in the stock before the cutter comes in contact with the surface. This tool is somewhat hazardous, so take extra precautions. Always clamp the work securely to the table and operate the machine at its lowest speed. Have your instructor check the setup before turning on the power.

**Boring Duplicate Parts**

When a number of equal size pieces require the same boring operation, you will save time and produce more accurate work by building a fixture or making a special setup. A simple arrangement consists of an auxiliary table with a stationary fence. By clamping it in the correct position, a series of holes can be bored along a straight line. Stops can be set along the fence to locate the exact position of the hole as shown in Fig. 16-15. Or instead of a stop, a previously bored hole can be used to space the next hole, Fig. 16-16.

Fig. 16-15. Boring duplicate parts. Top. Part held against the fence and a stop. Bottom. Spacer block used to locate second hole.

Fig. 16-13. Cutting 1/8 in. hardboard with a hole saw.

Fig. 16-16. Fixture for boring equally spaced holes. Taper the lower end of the dowel pin slightly so it can be easily slipped into the previously bored hole.

Pins and stops of various sizes and shapes can be attached to the auxiliary table to position work, Fig. 16-17. Small parts may require some kind of a clamping device to hold them during the boring operation, Fig. 16-18. Fig. 16-19 shows a fixture that was used to bore holes at an angle in lamp bases for a mass production project. After the first hole was bored, it was aligned with the index point to position the second hole. The second hole was then used to align the third.

Fig. 16-17. A simple fixture being used to locate holes at the corners of a square piece.

Fig. 16-18. Clamping device to hold small parts during a boring operation.

Fig. 16-19. Fixture for boring holes at an angle in a circular part.

## MORTISING ATTACHMENT

The mortising attachment for the drill press, Fig. 16-20, uses about the same kind of hollow chisel and bit as a regular mortising machine. The length of the bit is usually shorter. The bit fits inside the hollow chisel and cuts a round hole, while the square hollow chisel cuts out the corners as the assembly is forced through the wood. Hollow chisels and matching bits for drill press attachments are available in sizes from 1/4 in. to 3/4 in., in increments of 1/16 inch.

Fig. 16-21 shows a standard attachment when installed. To make the installation, use the following procedure:

1.  Remove the depth stop bracket from the quill and mount the chisel holder. Then attach the depth stop.

Fig. 16-20. Hollow chisel and hollow chisel bit. (Greenlee Bros. and Co.)

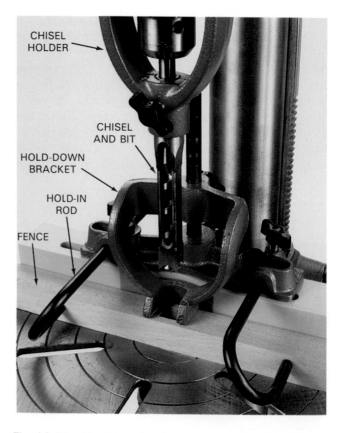

Fig. 16-21. Mortising attachment mounted on the drill press. (Grizzly Imports, Inc.)

2. Attach the fence and hold-down bracket to the table. It is best to include an auxiliary wood table larger than the drill press table.
3. Mount the hollow chisel into the holder as far as it will go.
4. Thread the matching bit into the chisel and tighten it in the chuck with the spurs of the bit extending 1/16 in. below the points of the chisel.
5. Have your instructor check the settings and clearances, and then make trial cuts.

## CUTTING A MORTISE

Adjust the fence to the correct position from the chisel and also align the sides of the chisel so they are parallel to the fence, Fig. 16-22. Set the depth stop to the required setting. Adjust the hold-down so it will just touch the top of the work without scarring or denting the surface. Stops can be clamped to the fence to control the position of the mortise. Check the settings by making a trial cut in extra stock of equal size.

Align the chisel at one end of the mortise and make the cut. Then move the work and make the cut at the other end as shown in Fig. 16-23. Stops

Fig. 16-22. Set the front face of the chisel parallel with the fence.

Fig. 16-23. Cutting a mortise with a hollow chisel mortiser. (Delta International Machinery Corp.)

can be used at either end of the table or fence to position these cuts. Now make cuts along the mortise according to the pattern shown in Fig. 16-24. Alternating strokes will equalize the side pressure on the bit; cutting four sides on the first pass and two on the second. This procedure is especially important when using chisels 1/2 in. and smaller, since unequal pressure will cause the chisel to bend and rub on the rotating bit.

When mortises meet at a corner, like the one shown in Fig. 16-23, it is best to cut the first mortise just deep enough to meet the line of the second mortise and then cut the second mortise to the full depth. This will prevent the internal corner from splitting off.

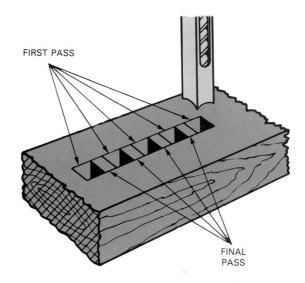

Fig. 16-24. Sequence of cuts for making a mortise. (Greenlee Bros. and Co.)

## POCKET CUTTER

Angled screws have been used in the assembly of tables, chests, and other objects of wood for a long time. However, the process of drilling the pilot holes for angled screws has been difficult. The use of a jig such as the one shown in Fig. 16-25 makes the job much easier and more accurate. The jig, clamp, and special drill provide a total system for this method of attachment.

Another device, called the POCKET CUTTER, was developed to eliminate angled screws altogether. Using a pocket cutter, both the pocket hole and the screw pilot hole are cut parallel to the face of the work. This enables the pieces to be joined with no chance of the screw tip breaking through the front face frame. The cut is made with a router bit and a square-drive pan-head screw is used to join the pieces.

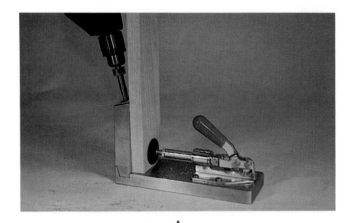

A

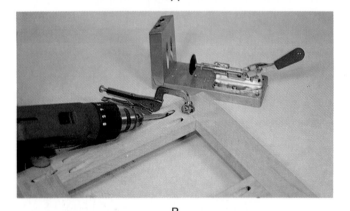

B

Fig. 16-25. A—Workpiece is clamped in the jig while angled holes are drilled in the proper orientation. B—Square-drive head screws are used to securely fasten the pieces together. (Kreg Tool Company)

## SANDING, ROUTING, AND SHAPING

Fig. 16-26 shows a drum and sanding arrangement for the drill press. An auxiliary table with an open throat is used to support the work. As a section of the sanding drum becomes worn it can be raised or lowered to a new position. A variety of drum sizes are available, for sharp or gentle curves, Fig. 16-27.

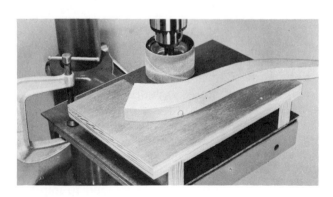

Fig. 16-26. Using an auxiliary table for a sanding operation.

Fig. 16-27. Sanding drums are ideal for sanding curved pieces on the drill press. A variety of sizes are available. (Leichtung, Inc.)

Drill presses that can reach speeds of at least 3000 rpm produce satisfactory routing jobs. The router bit must be mounted in a special adapter. Never attempt to mount and use a router bit in a regular key chuck. A fence or other type of guide should be used to control the work. Study and follow the directions for standard router operation. When the fence is behind the bit, the feed should be from left to right, Fig. 16-28.

Fig. 16-28. A routing operation on the drill press. Notice the feed goes from left to right. Routing and shaping setups on the drill press can be hazardous. Always have your instructor inspect and approve them before you turn on the power.

Light shaping operations can also be performed on the drill press. A fence and auxiliary table are needed, and a special adapter must be used to hold the shaper cutter. High speeds are essential for good work. Follow the procedures described in Chapter 18.

## PORTABLE ELECTRIC DRILL

The portable electric drill is manufactured in a wide range of types and sizes. The general size is determined by the chuck capacity. Sizes from 1/4 in. to 1 1/4 in. are available. However, 1/4, 3/8, and 1/2 in. are the most common. For general work in the school shop, 1/4 in. or 3/8 in. sizes are generally adequate, Fig. 16-29. The speed is fixed for each drill, with small sizes running at high speeds and large sizes at low speeds. Drills of 1/4 in. capacity usually operate at speeds of 1000—2000 rpm. Fig. 16-30 shows the parts and gearing of a standard model. Fig. 16-31 illustrates a power bit set for a portable drill.

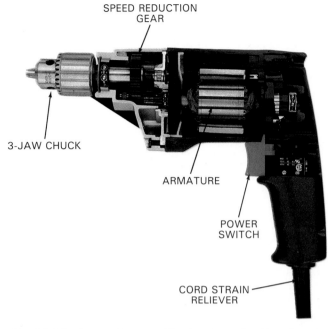

Fig. 16-30. Parts of a portable electric drill. (Skil Corp.)

Fig. 16-29. Typical 3/8 in. portable electric drill. (Black & Decker, Inc.)

Fig. 16-31. Power wood boring bit set for a portable drill. This set contains bits from 3/8 in. to 1 in. (Parker Mfg. Co.)

## PORTABLE ELECTRIC DRILL SAFETY

1. Select the correct drill or bit for your work and mount it securely to the full depth of the chuck, Fig. 16-32.
2. Make certain the stock to be drilled is held in a stationary position, so it cannot be moved during the operation.
3. Connect the drill to a properly grounded outlet.
4. Turn on the switch for a moment to see if the bit is properly centered and running true.
5. With the switch off, place the point of the bit in the punched layout hole.
6. Hold the drill firmly in one or both hands and at the correct drilling angle.

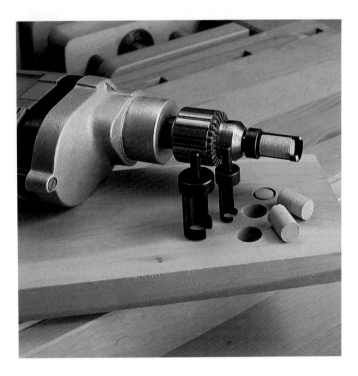

Fig. 16-32. This plug cutter is mounted in the chuck properly for safe operation. (Leichtung, Inc.)

Fig. 16-33. A combination square may be used to keep the drill in proper alignment during the drilling operation. (Black & Decker, Inc.)

7. Turn on the switch and feed the drill into the work. The pressure required will vary with the size of the drill and the kind of wood.
8. During the operation, keep the drill aligned with the direction of the hole, Fig. 16-33.
9. When drilling deep holes, especially with a twist drill, withdraw the drill several times to clear the cuttings.
10. Follow the same precautions and procedures as when drilling holes with a hand drill or the drill press.
11. Always remove the bit from the drill as soon as you have completed your work.

*Never operate a portable electric tool while standing on wet ground or any wet surface.*

### CORDLESS PORTABLE DRILL

Cordless portable drills are useful for many jobs and eliminate the hazard of electrical shock. They are used for general maintenance work and are sometimes used on production work where electrical cords would interfere with the operation.

Standard voltage has increased to 13.2 volts and the new tools can hold a charge for steady drilling for 30 minutes or more before recharging is required. Fig. 16-34 shows a state-of-the-art cordless drill.

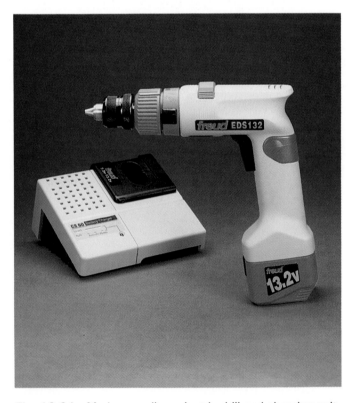

Fig. 16-34. Modern cordless electric drill and charging unit. (Freud, Inc.)

Fig. 16-35. Using a cordless drill to install cabinet hardware. (Black and Decker, Inc.)

Use of a cordless drill is shown in Fig. 16-35. Oftentimes, portable drills are powered with air motors, Fig. 16-36. They are lightweight and can be operated under heavy loads without danger of overheating.

Fig. 16-36. Two types of pistol air drills. (The ARO Corp., JET Equipment and Tools)

## INDUSTRIAL BORING MACHINES

Production boring machines have multiple spindles that produce a series of holes in a single stroke. On the gang borer, Fig. 16-37, the spindles receive power through vertical shafts with knuckle joints. The table remains stationary while the entire assembly of spindles and shafts are moved up and down by hydraulic power.

Fig. 16-38 shows a boring machine that can be adapted to a great variety of workpieces. Each boring head acts independently and is driven by an air motor. Heads can be placed in a vertical, horizontal, or angled position. Boring heads can also be located below the table. The model shown also has a trim saw unit.

FIXTURED TOOLS is a term generally given to equipment assembled from various self-contained units. An example is shown in Fig. 16-39. It consists of air clamps and self-feed drills mounted in

Fig. 16-37. Top. Gang boring machine. Drive shaft across the top is powered by an 8 hp motor. Bottom. Machine in operation. Knuckle joints permit flexibility in spindle arrangements. Strokes per minute can be varied from 0 to 36. (Greenlee Bros. and Co.)

283

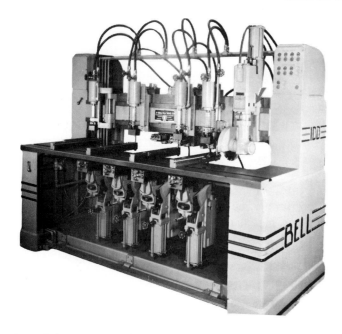

Fig. 16-38. Boring machine with individual air motors that can be adjusted to various positions or angles. Air cylinders feed the units into the work. It operates with 75 psi air pressure. (Nash—Bell—Challoner)

Fig. 16-40. This chair seat boring machine has 4 lower and up to 16 upper drilling heads, held in mounts which allow angling up to 30 deg. out of vertical. (R.S. Brookman, Ltd.)

a simple steel framework. Fixtured tools need few adjustments and are designed to perform a specific operation, Fig. 16-40.

## MORTISERS

The hollow chisel mortiser, Fig. 16-41, is widely used because it is compact, adaptable to light work, and useable in multiple head assemblies.

Fig. 16-39. Skilled operator adjusts air clamp on fixtured boring machine. Recommended operating pressure for the self-feed drilling units is 90 psi (621 kPa). (The ARO Corp.)

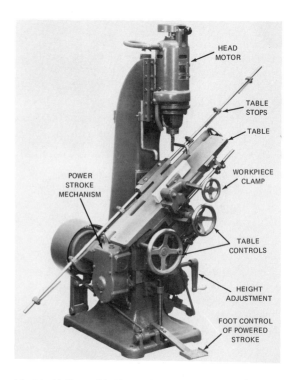

Fig. 16-41. Hollow chisel mortiser with table in tilted position. head motor (5 hp) is stroked up and down by a mechanism powered by a 1 hp motor. (Oliver Machinery Co.)

The mortiser table can be raised or lowered and tilted to various angles. It is moved horizontally by a rack and pinion attached to a handwheel. The motor head is lowered into the work by a separate motor. When fitted with regular bits, the mortiser can be used for boring.

The mortiser uses the same type of hollow chisels and bits described in the section on the drill press. Fig. 16-42 shows how a chisel and bit are mounted. The chisel bushing is set with a 1/32 in. spacer until the bit is mounted. After the bit setscrew is tightened, the spacer is removed, and the chisel bushing is moved up and set to provide clearance.

The regular mortiser is easier to use and more accurate than the drill press attachment. The table can be set up so that duplicate parts are clamped in place and the mortise cut by stroking the machine and turning the handwheel which moves the table to cutting positions between stops.

A multiple head mortiser is shown in Fig. 16-43. As many as 11 heads can be attached to the beam. Pneumatic power raises the table and work into the chisels. Each hollow chisel head is powered with a 1 1/2 hp motor.

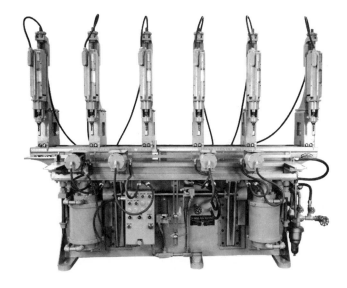

Fig. 16-43. Multiple head mortiser. Two 10 in. air cylinders raise the table up and down at rates from 0 to 30 strokes per minute. Length of stroke can be varied up to 8 in. (203 mm). Air cylinders clamp work in position. (Nash—Bell—Challoner)

## TENONERS

Tenoners are production woodworking machines used to cut plain tenons or tenons with shaped shoulders, like those found in panel doors or window sash. Besides these basic operations, they can be set up to cut various corner joints for cabinets, cases, and chests. With a dado attachment, grooves and dados can be cut in various locations in the surface of the work. Tenoners may be either single-end or double-end.

### SINGLE-END TENONERS

The standard design of a single-end tenoner consists of two tenoning heads, two coping heads, a cut-off saw, and a movable carriage, Fig. 16-44.

In operation, the stock is clamped or held to the carriage and moved forward through the tenoning heads which make the cheek and shoulder cuts. It then passes by the coping heads which are mounted on vertical arbors. These also form contours on the shoulders if it is necessary for them to fit over molded edges. Finally, the stock moves by the cut-off saw where the tenon is cut to length.

The cutting heads are powered by individual motors and can be adjusted to various vertical and horizontal positions. The coping heads may be tilted to secure angle cuts. Work can be moved through the machine at an angle by adjusting the carriage.

### DOUBLE-END TENONER

The double-end tenoner, as the name indicates, consists of two cutter assemblies. They are both mounted on a heavy base and one can be moved along the base to provide settings for various lengths or widths of work. Two feed chains carry

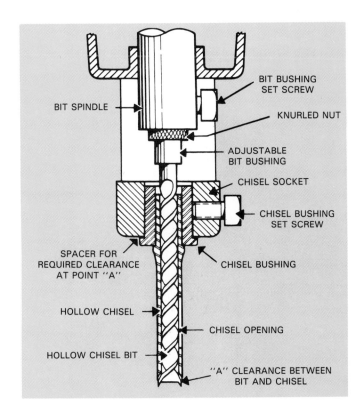

BIT SPINDLE

BIT BUSHING SET SCREW

KNURLED NUT

ADJUSTABLE BIT BUSHING

CHISEL SOCKET

CHISEL BUSHING SET SCREW

SPACER FOR REQUIRED CLEARANCE AT POINT "A"

CHISEL BUSHING

HOLLOW CHISEL

CHISEL OPENING

HOLLOW CHISEL BIT

"A" CLEARANCE BETWEEN BIT AND CHISEL

Fig. 16-42. A hollow chisel and bit, along with its parts and mounting. (Greenlee Bros. and Co.)

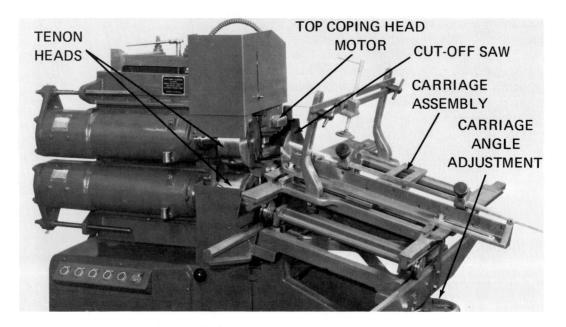

Fig. 16-44. Main parts of a single-end tenoner. Bottom coping head is located directly under top head.
(Oliver Machinery Co.)

the work through the machine at speeds from 15 to 60 fpm. A pressure beam, with a rubber padded chain, rides on top of the work and holds it down on the feed chain, Fig. 16-45.

In Fig. 16-46, the pressure beam has been swung away from the cutting heads to show their arrangement. In this particular machine, the work first moves by the cut-off saw and then scoring saws, before it reaches the tenoning and coping heads. The scoring saws rotate so they will cut into the

surface (climb sawing) and thus have no tendency to splinter the work.

The drawing and close-up view in Fig. 16-47, shows how the bottom check rail of a window sash is cut with the coping heads. The milled-to-pattern cutters are clamped into the coping head in about the same manner as the dado head in Fig. 16-48.

The versatility of cutter head design is coupled with the double-end tenoner to form the lock miter joint shown in Fig. 16-49. This joint is used to make

Fig. 16-45. Modern double-end tenoner. This machine is well suited for small or large manufacturing because it adjusts to a wide variety of work sizes. (Wadkin PLC)

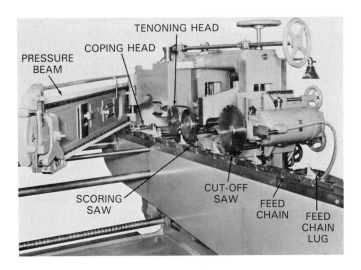

Fig. 16-46. Cutting units on one side of a standard double-end tenoner. Pressure beam is swung out to show assembly. (Greenlee Bros. and Co.)

all kinds of case goods: cedar chests, boxes, and other items that require light, strong corners. It requires precision machining with tolerances held to close limits. It is a good example of one of the many kinds of work the machine can perform.

Setting up and maintaining the double-end tenoner for work of this nature requires a skilled person who knows the characteristics of different woods and how joints are designed and proportioned. This person must also be an expert in the care and operation of woodworking machines. It is a highly satisfying experience to see fine, precision work moving off of a machine, and knowing that you were responsible for the setup. How would you like such a job?

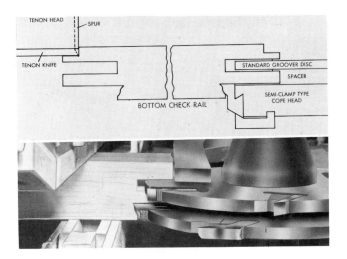

Fig. 16-47. Top. How the tenon head and coping head form the joint for a window sash rail. Bottom. Close-up view of coping head making the cut. (Wisconsin Knife Works, Inc.)

Fig. 16-48. Dado head used on a double-end tenoner. (Wisconsin Knife Works, Inc.)

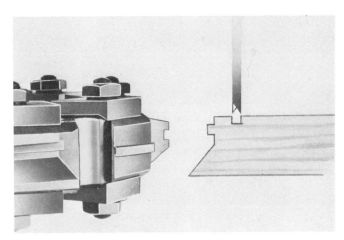

Fig. 16-49. Coping head equipped with special milled-to-pattern cutters from lock miter joints. (Wisconsin Knife Works, Inc.)

## TEST YOUR KNOWLEDGE, Chapter 16

Please do not write in the text. Place your answers on a separate sheet of paper.

1. The spindle of the drill press revolves inside a sleeve that is called a _____.

2. A 15 in. drill press will have a measurement of _____ in. from the center of the spindle to the column.
   a. 7 1/2.
   b. 15.
   c. 30.
   d. None of the above.
3. The spur machine bit generally has a _____ _____ instead of a feed screw.
4. List five safety precautions to follow when working with the drill press.
5. What two instruments can be used to cut large holes in thin stock?
6. What is mounted first in the chuck when installing a mortising chisel and bit?
7. When the fence is behind the bit in a standard routing operation, feed should be from _____ (left to right, right to left).

8. What is the proper procedure for starting a hole when using a portable drill?
9. What are fixtured tools?
10. As work is moved through the single-end tenoner, it is first cut by the tenoning heads and then by the coping heads. True or False?

## ACTIVITIES

1. Prepare a selected list of drill press attachments that would be practical for the home workshop. Include a complete description and estimated cost of each attachment.
2. Select or design a project, such as a cribbage board, that requires many holes. Prepare design sketches of a fixture that could be mounted on the drill press to drill or bore the holes with precision and speed.

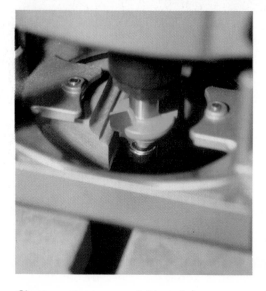

Shaper cutters are available to form most any shape on the edge of stock. (Top left and right. Freeborn Tool Company, Inc. Bottom left and right. CMT Tools)

These complex projects require the use of most of the machines found in a woodworking shop. (California Time/Westwood, Inc.)

Good design, careful selection of materials, and outstanding woodworking skill
are important to these projects. (Eldon Rebhorn)

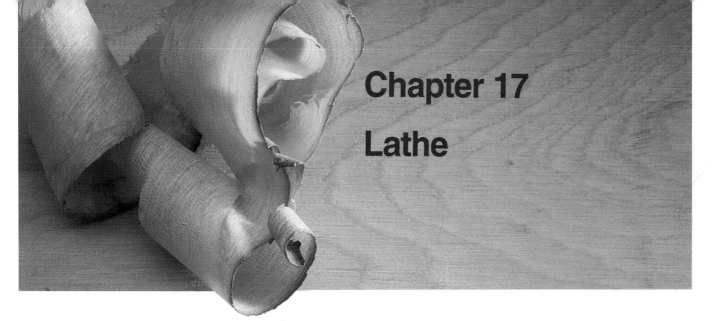

# Chapter 17

# Lathe

The operating principle of a hand-turning wood lathe is different from that of other power woodworking machines. The wood is mounted in the machine and rotated. The cutting edge of a hand held tool is then moved along the surface forming the part. Considerable skill is required to hold the tool in the correct position as well as control the feed and direction of the cut.

Production lathes operate on the same principle, except that a revolving cutterhead does the shaping, Fig. 17-1. Another type of production lathe has a shaped "back-knife" that is moved downward along the surface of the revolving wood blank. See page 307.

Hand-turning wood lathe sizes are determined by the swing and length of bed. The SWING is twice the distance from the center of the spindle to the bed. It indicates the largest diameter that can be turned. Variable spindle speeds are essential. Usually they range from about 600 to 3600 rpm.

## PARTS OF A LATHE

The basic parts of the lathe are shown in Fig. 17-2. It is advisable to study and learn the name of the lathe parts so you will be able to clearly understand the operating directions that follow.

The HEADSTOCK is rigidly fixed to the left end

Fig. 17-1. Close-up view of workpiece and cutterhead in a production lathe. Cutterhead revolves at a high speed and forms all of the contours in just a few moments. (Mattison Machine Works)

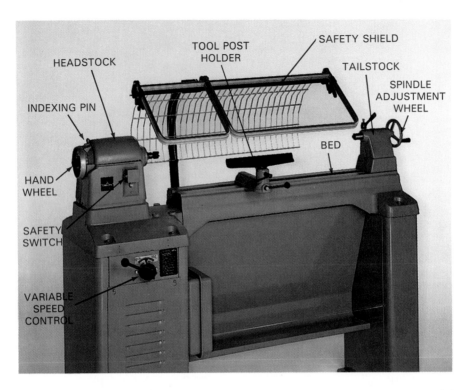

Fig. 17-2. Modern 12 inch woodworking lathe designed for industry, commercial shops, or schools. Speeds are possible from 340 to 3200 rpm with a special slow-start system. (Delta International Machinery Corp.)

of the lathe bed and carries a spindle that is threaded on both ends. The threads on the inside end are right-hand and those on the outside end are left-hand. They are used to attach the faceplates on which stock is mounted when turning projects such as disks and bowls. The spindle is hollow with the inside end tapered internally to carry the shank of the spur or live center.

The hollow spindle permits the use of a KNOCK-OUT BAR to remove the spur center or other taper shank tools.

The TAILSTOCK is movable and can be locked in any number of positions along the bed. It also has a spindle that is hollow and holds the CUP CENTER (also known as a DEAD CENTER). This spindle can be moved in and out of the tailstock by turning the handwheel. The cup center is removed by turning the handwheel counterclockwise until the spindle is completely retracted (withdrawn) into the tailstock.

The TOOL REST (also called a TOOL SUPPORT) clamps to the bed and can be adjusted up and down, at any position along the bed, as shown in Fig. 17-3. Tool rests are available in several different lengths. The top edge must be straight and smooth. This will insure that the lathe tools can be easily moved. To remove nicks and true this edge, use a mill file in about the same way as when sharpening a hand scraper.

## TURNING TOOLS

A set of turning tools (also called TURNING CHISELS) usually includes about six different shapes. Each shape or kind of tool is available in several sizes (widths), Fig. 17-4. The GOUGE, is a round-nose, hollow tool used for roughing out and making cove cuts. The SKEW is a double-ground, flat tool used to smooth cylinders and cut shoulders and beads. The PARTING TOOL is a double-ground tool used for cutting off work and making sizing

Fig. 17-3. The tool rest includes the base that clamps to the bed and the tool rest that clamps to the base. (Jam Handy)

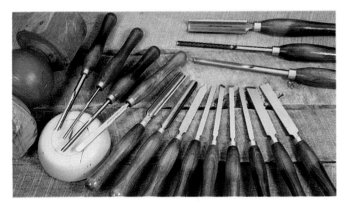

Fig. 17-4. Wood turning tools. Included are gouges, skew chisels, square chisel, diamond point chisel, square nose scraper, round nose scraper, parting tool, and diamond parting tool. (Woodcraft Supply Corporation)

cuts. The SPEAR POINT (also called a DIAMOND POINT), ROUND NOSE, and SQUARE NOSE are all single bevel tools used wherever their shape best fits the contour of the work.

### Sharpening Lathe Tools

In wood turning it is important to keep your turning tools sharp. When sharpening, follow about the same procedures used for sharpening plane blades and chisels. Gouges and round nose tools are difficult to sharpen; ask your instructor to help with these. Study the angles and bevels shown in Fig. 17-5. Try to maintain about the same shape when grinding your tools.

Most wood turners prefer to grind the skew with a flat bevel. To do this the grinding is done on the side of the abrasive wheel as shown in Fig. 17-6. If the wheel is true, each bevel can be ground to a perfect plane. Continue to grind until a fine wire edge appears and then hone on an oilstone. When honing the skew keep the ground bevel in contact with the surface of the stone.

The gouge should be ground on the side of the abrasive wheel with a rolling motion, Fig. 17-7. Be sure the bevel extends completely around to the sides. Remove the wire edge on the oilstone. Keep the bevel in contact with the stone, moving it back and forth and at the same time rolling it from side to side. Remove the wire edge from the inside surface with a slipstone, Fig. 17-7.

The parting tool and the square nose tool should be ground on the edge of the grinding wheel. This will form a slightly hollow-ground bevel that is desirable for these tools.

Using the side of the grinding wheel is considered good practice only when the cut is very light. It is more difficult to dress and reface the side than the edge. Heavy grinding and reshaping operations of any of the lathe tools should be done on the regular grinding edge.

### TURNING SPEEDS

Develop good judgment and exercise great care in selecting the proper turning speeds. The most important factor is the diameter of the work.

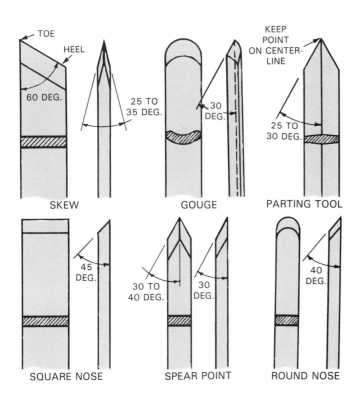

Fig. 17-5. Grinding angles for turning tools.

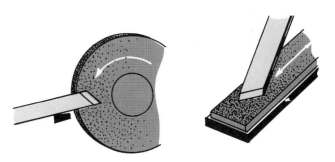

Fig. 17-6. Grinding and honing a skew.

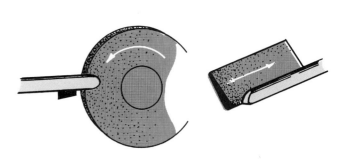

Fig. 17-7. Grinding and honing a gouge.

293

Consideration must also be given to the kind of wood being used and the type of cut being made. Check with your instructor if you have any doubt about the speed you have selected.

*To keep the tool from "burning" while it is being ground, dip it frequently in water. Lathe tools are made from steel that is heat treated and the temper may be damaged by excess heat.*

Always rough out work at a low speed (600-1000 rpm). After the work is round and true you can increase the speed. Stock that is 6 in. in diameter or larger should be turned at speeds under 1000 rpm. Diameters of 4 in. should not exceed speeds of 1500 rpm. Speeds over 2000 rpm should be limited to work 2 in. and under in diameter.

It is hazardous to exceed these recommendations, especially when turning thin walled bowls and disks. Because of CENTRIFUGAL FORCE (the force tending to make rotating bodies move away from the center of rotation), they may break and fly apart.

Slower speeds are quite satisfactory; the tools will stay sharp longer. This is especially true if the work is done by the scraping method, which rapidly wears away the tool edge. Sanding at high speeds causes the abrasive paper to heat and glaze, and results in excessive dust being thrown into the air.

High speed may be helpful, however, when applying a French polish finish. Heat generated by the friction aids in setting up and hardening the finishing material.

## DRAWINGS FOR TURNED OBJECTS

Turned objects often have many curves, beads, and coves that are hard to specify in a working drawing. Fig. 17-8 shows two methods commonly used. A half section has the advantage of showing both the inside and outside contour. Note the method of specifying diameters. In the second drawing a grid (a series of squares) has been drawn over the contour so that an accurate full-size template or pattern can be developed even though detailed dimensions are not included.

*Before starting work on the lathe, study the following rules carefully. Also review the general rules for power machine operation given in Chapter 3.*

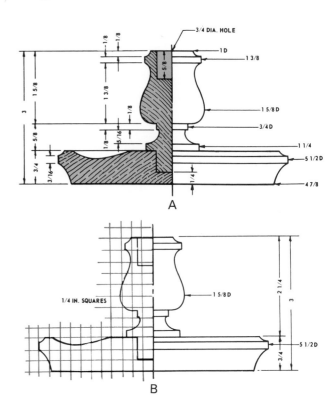

Fig. 17-8. Working drawings used for wood turning. A—Half section. B—Grid method.

## LATHE SAFETY

1. Before starting the machine, be sure that any spindle work has the cup center properly imbedded, tailstock and tool rest are securely clamped, and there is proper clearance for the rotating stock.
2. Before starting the machine for faceplate work, check to see that the faceplate is tight against the spindle shoulder and the tool support has proper clearance.
3. Wear goggles or a face shield to protect your eyes, especially when roughing out work.
4. Select turning speed carefully. Large diameters must be turned at the lowest speed. Always use the lowest speed to rough out work.
5. Wood with knots and splits should not be turned. Glued-up stock should cure at least 24 hours.
6. Keep the tool rest close to the work.
7. Remove the tool rest for sanding and polishing operations.
8. Use a scraping cut for all faceplate work.
9. Remove both the spur and cup centers when they are not in use.
10. When you stop the lathe to check your work, also check and lubricate the cup center.
11. Keep the lathe tools sharp, hold them firmly, and in the proper position.

12. Keep your sleeves rolled up and keep other loose clothing away from the moving parts of the lathe and work.

## SPINDLE TURNING

When the wood stock is mounted between the lathe centers, Fig. 17-9, the general operation is called SPINDLE TURNING. It is used to produce table and chair legs, lamp stems, ball bats, and other long round objects.

## MOUNTING STOCK

Select stock that is sound and free of splits and knots. The stock should be approximately square. Square the ends, allowing an extra inch of length so the piece can be trimmed after the turning is complete.

Locate the center of each end by drawing diagonal lines across the corners. If you are using hard wood, drill a hole about the size of the pin in the spur center on one end. Also use a handsaw or band saw to make saw kerfs about 1/8 in. deep, Fig. 17-10. The roughing out cuts will be easier to make if you plane off the corners of any stock that is over 3 in. square.

Hold the stock vertically with the dead center end resting on the lathe bed or other solid support. Drive the spur center into the hole and saw kerfs so that it is embedded about 1/4 in.

Insert the spur center, with the work attached, into the spindle of the headstock. Slide the tailstock into position so that the point of the cup center contacts the center of the work. Lock the tailstock to the lathe bed and turn the handwheel so that it forces the cup center into the wood.

With the lathe set on the lowest speed, turn on the power for just a moment and force the cup center deeper into the work. A beginner should turn the lathe by hand instead of using the power. This will form a "bearing" in the wood, the depth of which should be about 1/8 in.

Back out the cup center, lubricate with oil or wax, and move it back into position. Leave a slight clearance so that the lathe turns easily and then LOCK THE TAILSTOCK SPINDLE CLAMP. As you progress with the turning, check the cup center from time to time to be sure it has sufficient lubrication and is not overheating.

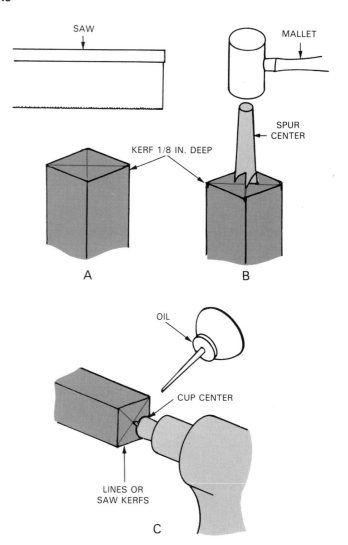

Fig. 17-10. Procedure for mounting stock between centers. A—Cut shallow saw kerfs across corners. B—Place a spur center in position. Hammer with a mallet to seat firmly. C—Place work between centers and position cup center with center of work.

## TURNING A CYLINDER

Adjust the tool rest so that it is about 1/8 in. above the centerline and clears the work by about 1/4 in. Rotate the lathe by hand to check this clearance. LOCK THE TOOL REST in this position.

Be sure the lathe is set at the lowest speed and then turn on the power. Select a large gouge and hold it firmly on the tool rest. First, make a series of individual cuts along the work, Fig. 17-11. These cuts will prevent long splinters from developing when a full pass is made.

You are now ready to make a cut the full length of the stock or as long as the tool rest will permit. Move the tool from left to right, holding it well up on the work so the ground bevel rides on the cut being made. Also roll the gouge so that the chips are thrown to the right. Study Fig. 17-12. Make

Fig. 17-9. Spur center and cup center.

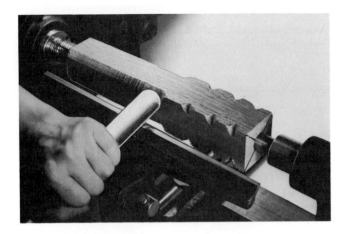

Fig. 17-11. First full roughing cut.

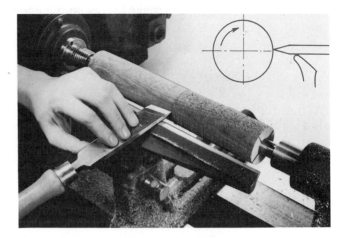

Fig. 17-13. Finishing cylinder with the skew in a scraping position.

Fig. 17-12. Final roughing cut.

Experienced wood turners use the skew to make shearing cuts because of the speed and quality of work that can be produced. For this type of cut, place a large skew slightly above the work and about 2 in. from the driven end. Slowly pull the tool back until the cutting edge touches the cylinder halfway between the heel and toe. Roll the tool just slightly until the edge starts to cut. Then move the tool along the work just as you did with the gouge, Fig. 17-14. Reverse the position of the tool and cut toward the headstock from where the first cut was started. When cutting properly, the GROUND BEVEL OF THE SKEW RIDES ON THE WORK. Therefore, it is important that the tool be carefully sharpened with a perfectly flat bevel.

## LAY OUT AND TURNING TO SIZE

With the lathe stopped, you can layout various lengths and positions on the work and check diameters with an outside caliper. If the stock is a

additional cuts until the stock is round. Stop the lathe and move the tool rest to a new position if the work is longer than the rest.

For a right-handed person, the right hand should grip the tool handle near the end. The left hand guides the tool along the rest and may be placed on top of the tool with the palm down or underneath with the palm up. Beginners usually like the "palm-down" position, especially for roughing out stock, as it provides a more positive grasp on the tool.

The cylinder can now be finished with a skew. Adjust the tool rest parallel with the work. The amount the speed can be increased depends on the diameter of the work. The skew can be used to make either a shearing or a scraping cut. Beginners may prefer to use the scraping cut, as shown in Fig. 17-13, since it is easier and requires less practice. When making a scraping cut the tool is held in a level position with the tool edge contacting the work even with or slightly above the horizontal centerline. The tool rest will need to be slightly below the centerline.

Fig. 17-14. Finishing a cylinder with the skew making a shearing cut.

light colored wood and you make heavy layout lines, you will be able to see them even when the lathe is running.

If the tool rest is placed close to the work, a rule can be placed on it and layouts can be marked while the work is rotating at a slow speed. Use considerable care when doing this.

The parting tool is used to cut positions and diameters into the work. It is a scraping type tool and is easy to use. A good cutting action is secured if it contacts the work above the horizontal center, Fig. 17-15. Work is often turned to size by holding the tool in one hand and the calipers in the other. Look ahead to Fig. 17-21. When parting tool cuts are deep, a CLEARANCE CUT MUST BE MADE about every 3/8 in. of depth to free the tool and prevent the point from overheating and burning. It is usually best to leave the sizing cut about 1/16 to 1/8 in. larger so that a finishing cut can be made after the contour is complete.

## TAPERS AND SHOULDERS

Lay out the length of a taper and then with the parting tool, turn to the required diameter at each end. Use the gouge to rough out to within about 1/8 in. of the finished size. Scraping tools can be used to finish the taper or a shearing cut can be made with the skew. Always cut from the larger part toward the smaller part.

A shoulder can be cut with the parting tool, and then a light cut (about 1/32 in.) can be made with the skew, Fig. 17-16. This will leave a smooth surface that will require very little sanding.

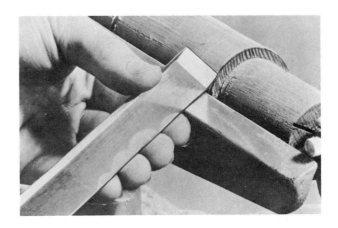

Fig. 17-16. Finishing a shoulder cut with the toe of the skew.

## BEADS AND V-GROOVES

Beads and V-grooves can be scraped or cut. The easiest way is to scrape them, using the spear point tool. It is usually best to separate beads with parting tool cuts, Fig. 17-17. Scraping is slower and the work will require considerable sanding but there is less danger of spoiling the work.

Cutting bead and V-grooves with the skew is the most difficult of the turning operations. However, when carefully done it will produce work that is so smooth that very little sanding is necessary. The beginner should expect to spend many hours of practice on sample pieces before producing finished work for a project.

First lay out the positions of each bead and make a vertical cut with the toe of the skew, Fig. 17-18. Now place the skew high on the work with the heel starting the cut as shown in Fig. 17-19. Rotate the tool from a horizontal to a vertical position, pulling it slightly toward you so that the heel will continue to cut. The entire cut is made with the heel of the skew. Keep the ground bevel riding on the work.

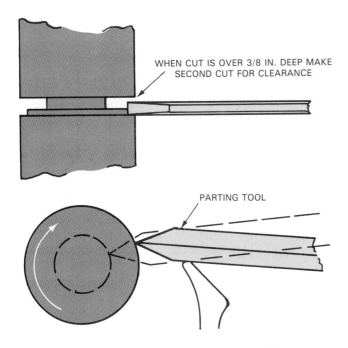

WHEN CUT IS OVER 3/8 IN. DEEP MAKE SECOND CUT FOR CLEARANCE

PARTING TOOL

Fig. 17-15. Using the parting tool to make sizing cuts.

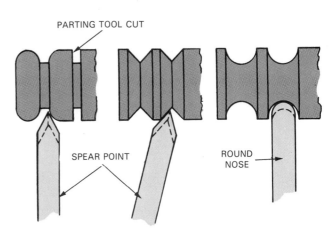

PARTING TOOL CUT

SPEAR POINT

ROUND NOSE

Fig. 17-17. Scraping beads, V-grooves, and coves.

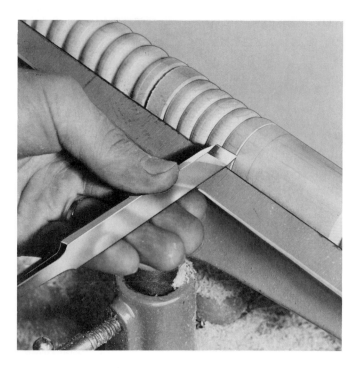

Fig. 17-18. First cut for forming a bead.
(Delta International Machinery Corp.)

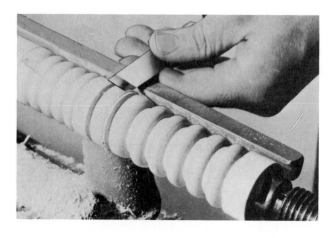

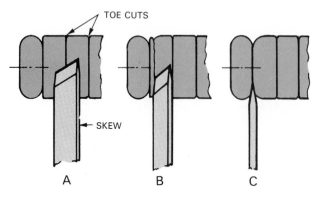

Fig. 17-19. Second cut for forming a bead. A—Place the skew flat against the surface and at a right angle to the work. B—Start the cut with the heel. Pull it slightly toward you so the heel can continue the cut. C—As cutting is complete, roll the tool into the groove.

Repeat the operation several times to secure the required depth. Now form the other half of the bead following the same procedure, but reverse the tool and movements.

V-grooves are formed in the same general way except that the skew is rocked straight into the work and not rotated. These cuts can also be made using the toe of the tool in about the same manner used in finishing a shoulder cut.

## COVES

Coves can be scraped with the round nose tool. Set the tool rest so the cutting edge will touch the work on a horizontal centerline or slightly above. Refer back to Fig. 17-17.

The gouge is used to cut a cove. First, lay out the position of the cove and then rough out the shape by feeding the tool straight into the work. Start the finishing cut by holding the gouge on edge and in a horizontal position, Fig. 17-20. Move the tool into the cut; at the same time roll it and lower the handle. KEEP THE GROUND SURFACE OF THE TOOL IN CONTACT WITH THE CONTOUR BEING CUT. Continue to the bottom of the cove and then cut the other half, coming in from the other side.

## TURNING DUPLICATE PARTS

When two or more pieces of the same size and shape are required, it is best to make a template. After the work is turned to a smooth cylinder, the template can be used to lay out the position of the diameters, Fig. 17-21. The parting tool and calipers are used to cut down to the various sizes and the contour is roughed out. Finished cuts are then made and the work carefully checked with the template as it nears completion.

Turning duplicate parts of a complicated design requires careful work. Remember that A GIVEN DEPTH OF CUT ACTUALLY REDUCES THE SIZE OF

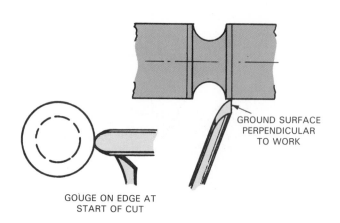

Fig. 17-20. Cutting a cove with the gouge.

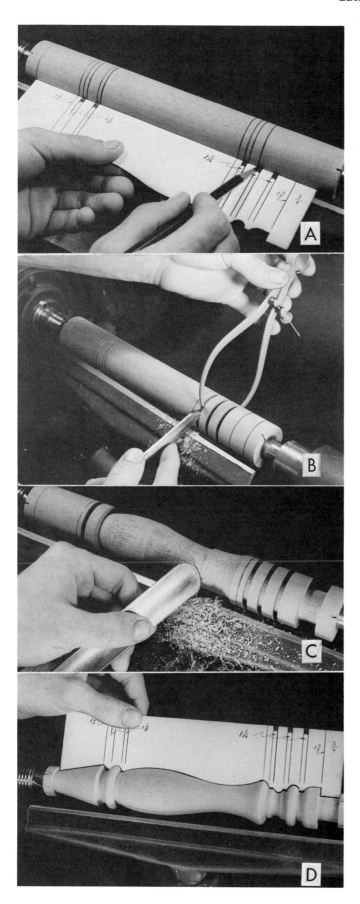

Fig. 17-21. Turning duplicate parts. A—Laying out the work. B—Sizing cuts with the parting tool and calipers. C—Roughing out the contour with the gouge. D—Checking with a template.

THE TURNING BY DOUBLE THAT AMOUNT. This means that to reduce the diameter 1/8 in., the depth of the cut must be only 1/16 in.

## Duplicating Attachments

Another method of making duplicate parts is to use a lathe duplicator attachment, Figs. 17-22 and 17-23. The duplicator shown in Fig. 17-22 is designed for shapes turned between centers. The pattern is mounted between centers at the back of the lathe. (The illustration shows the back of the lathe.) The follower beneath the handwheel guides the cutter to produce the desired shape.

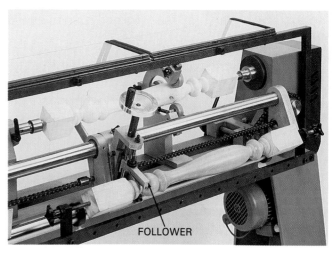

Fig. 17-22. This lathe duplicator uses a completed piece as the pattern. (AMI, Ltd.)

Fig. 17-23. The pattern for this bowl and spindle duplicator is a thin strip of metal. The cutter rides along this pattern, assuring uniform pieces. (AMI, Ltd.)

The duplicator shown in Fig. 17-23 is a bowl and spindle duplicator. The cutter is mounted on a hand-fed carriage; this permits the operator to make precise cuts as indicated by the pattern. The settings may be repeated time after time to produce identical parts.

## PARTIALLY TURNED SECTIONS

Sometimes a part of the turned piece includes a square section. For example, a turned table leg usually has a square section at the top where the rails join.

When such a piece is required, it must be squared to finished size and surfaced before turning. Be very careful to accurately center the piece in the lathe so that the square will meet turned rounds evenly on all sides.

Fig. 17-24 shows the procedure to follow. By making the layout and first cut with the skew, splinters are prevented from breaking off when the parting tool is used. The final cut on the square can be made with either the skew or spear point.

## PARTS WITH HOLES

On lamp stems and other parts that require a center hole, the center hole can be drilled after the turning is complete. If the stem is long it may be easier to drill the hole first, then plug the ends and drill out the plug after the turning is complete.

Deep holes are hard to drill or bore, especially in end grain. It may be best at times to rip the turning

blank apart, cut the grooves, glue the blank together again, and plug the holes, Fig. 17-25. This is an especially practical solution when gluing up two pieces of stock to secure required thickness.

The blanks for the salt and pepper set shown in Fig. 17-26, were first bored on the drill press. Then plugs were turned on the lathe to fit these holes. The hole in the midsection of the blank is smaller so that there are shoulders to keep the plugs from going all the way through. The plugs are inserted, and the blank turned. They are easily removed and can be used for turning additional pieces.

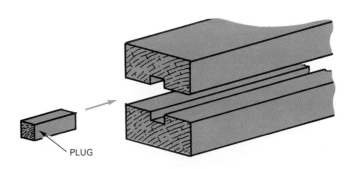

Fig. 17-25. Cut grooves, glue up, and plug ends of long pieces that require holes.

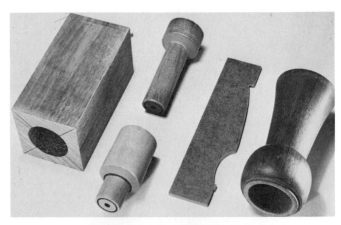

Fig. 17-26. Turning parts with large holes. Top. Blank, plugs, template, and finished turning. Bottom. Completed salt and pepper set.

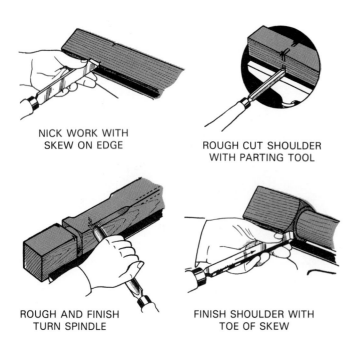

NICK WORK WITH
SKEW ON EDGE

ROUGH CUT SHOULDER
WITH PARTING TOOL

ROUGH AND FINISH
TURN SPINDLE

FINISH SHOULDER WITH
TOE OF SKEW

Fig. 17-24. Follow this procedure when turning work with a square section.

A long, thin turning will chatter and vibrate, unless it is supported with a steady rest. Such pieces may be turned in several sections and then assembled. Because of the tendency for slim pieces to vibrate, the SMALL DIAMETERS SHOULD BE TURNED LAST. It is also best to position the work in the lathe so that the SMALLEST DIAMETERS ARE NEAREST THE TAILSTOCK.

## SANDING LATHE WORK

Turnings can be sanded while they are rotating in the lathe. Work that has been scraped will require heavy sanding; you may need to start with a 100 (2/0) grade. Follow this with a 150 (4/0), then a final touch with a 180 (5/0) or 220 (6/0) grade. Work that has been produced with a shearing cut will require only light sanding.

A strip of abrasive paper held by the ends and at an angle with the work, Fig. 17-27, produces good results. Use narrow strips for small coves and fine details. A strip of paper held over a dowel or other wood forms may be helpful for sanding fine details.

Since you are actually sanding across the grain of the wood while the lathe is turning, you should use a very fine grade of paper to finish the work. When the contour will permit, you can secure the smoothest surface by stopping the lathe and hand sanding in the direction of the grain.

*Do not over-sand your work. This may washout details and spoil the appearance. Be sure to remove the tool rest when sanding.*

## FACEPLATE TURNING

### MOUNTING WORK ON FACEPLATES

When screw holes will not detract from the finished turning, the stock can be fastened directly to the faceplate. Usually, however, it is better to glue the work to a backing block.

Saw out the diameter of both the backing block and the stock for the finished turning. Check the surfaces to see that they are flat and will fit together smoothly. Spread glue on the surface of each piece, place a sheet of paper in the joint, and clamp together. Be sure they are carefully centered with each other. Allow the glue to harden overnight, then mount the work on a faceplate, Fig. 17-28.

After the turning is finished, use a large wood chisel to split the glue line. Keep the faceplate mounted on the lathe and work carefully all the way around the joint with the bevel turned toward the backing block.

### SCRAPING METHOD

All faceplate turning should be done using the scraping method; the tool rest should hold the

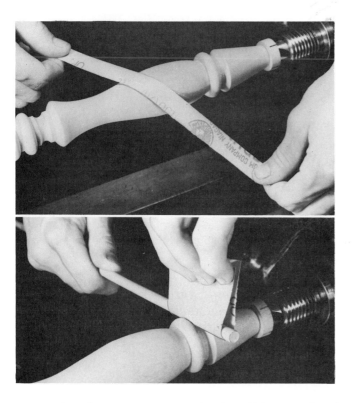

Fig. 17-27. Sanding spindle work. Top. Using a strip of sandpaper. Bottom. Sanding a cove with the paper formed over a dowel.

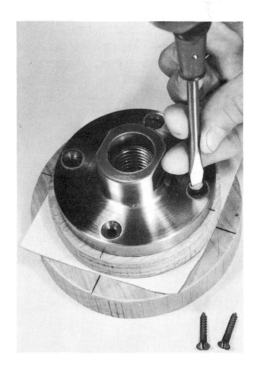

Fig. 17-28. Mounting work on a faceplate.

cutting edge of the tool on or slightly above a horizontal line through the center of the work. The spear point, round nose, or square nose are good tools to use. THE GOUGE SHOULD NOT BE USED ON FACEPLATE WORK.

Before turning on the power, screw the faceplate onto the lathe spindle until it is tight against the shoulder. Then set the lathe on the lowest speed and true the outside edge with a shoulder cut, using the spear point, Fig. 17-29A and B. Position the tool rest along the face of the disk and make a smoothing shoulder cut, once again using the spear point. Start at the outside edge and move the tool toward the center as shown in Fig. 17-29C. Diameters for the turning can be laid out with a rule and pencil while the lathe is running, Fig. 17-30. Be sure that the surface is smooth and that you use extra care while performing this operation.

Contours of the work can be formed by using various combinations of turning tools. Scraping cuts dull tools rather rapidly, so you will need to hone them often and regrind the bevel now and then.

## APPLYING FINISHES

Turned pieces that are a part of a larger assembly of cabinetwork are usually removed from the lathe and finished after final assembly. Small bowls, trays, and miniature turnings however, can be finished easily and quickly while the work is still spinning in the lathe. A shellac and linseed oil finish (French polish) is commonly used. REMOVE THE TOOL REST BEFORE PERFORMING ANY FINISHING OPERATIONS.

A ball of cotton folded inside a piece of cotton cloth makes a good pad. Saturate the pad with thin shellac and a little oil. Apply it to the work while it is turning at a slow speed. After the work is coated, increase the speed and pressure to smooth and harden the finish, Fig. 17-31. Building a very heavy (thick) finish will require considerable practice. Allow the first coat to cure and harden overnight, before applying a second coat. This method will make it easier for the beginner to secure a satisfactory finish.

Open-grained woods can be filled in the usual way. The work cannot be spun, however, until the filler has completely hardened; centrifugal force will throw it out of the wood pores. Other finishes can also be applied to turned parts and rubbed down while they are turning on the lathe.

## USING THE TAILSTOCK

When roughing out work that is mounted on a faceplate, it is often advisable to use the tailstock and cup center to provide additional support, Fig. 17-32. This can continue to be used as long as it

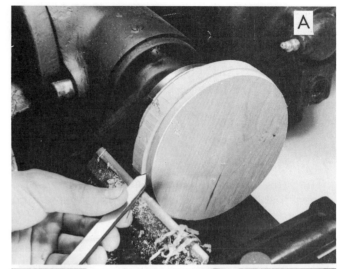

Fig. 17-29. Roughing out faceplate work. A—Making a shoulder cut with the spear point. B—Close-up view. Arrow shows direction of cut. C—Smoothing the face with a spear point.

does not interefere with the work. When you discontinue using the tailstock, move it well out of the way and remove the cup center. ALWAYS REMOVE THE CENTERS FROM THE LATHE WHEN THEY ARE NOT IN USE.

## DRILLING AND BORING HOLES

A drill chuck fitted with a tapered shank can be mounted in the tailstock and used for drilling and

Fig. 17-30. Laying out diameters with the lathe turning at a low speed.

Fig. 17-33. Drilling a hole in stock while on the lathe.

Fig. 17-31. Applying a French polish.

Fig. 17-32. Using the tailstock to rough out faceplate work.

boring, Fig. 17-33. The center should be marked and started with the spear point if you are using a large drill bit. With the lathe running at a slow speed you can advance the bit into the cut by turning the tailstock handwheel.

Before making this setup, check the position of the tailstock by inserting both centers and then bringing them together. The points of the spur center and cup center must align. If adjustment is necessary, secure help from your instructor.

## ASSEMBLING WORK IN THE LATHE

Fig. 17-34 shows a procedure that you can follow when making a candlestick or similar article. First turn the stem between centers. Then turn the base which is mounted on a faceplate. The hole for the stem can be turned with a round nose tool. Use considerable care in order to get a good fit. The parts can be assembled with glue, using the tailstock to both apply pressure and align the stem. After the glue has set up, further turning and finishing can be done.

## TURNED CHUCKS

After you have had success with standard faceplate turning, you may want to try the more advanced procedures that include the use of turned chucks to mount and carry the work. Fig. 17-35 shows a sequence of operations used to produce a small box with a fitted lid.

First, turn the inside of the lid, sand, and cut it off with the parting tool. After cutting off the lid, turn the inside of the main body (note the position of the tool support) and carefully form the rabbet so that you can press the lid tightly in place. Smooth the top of the lid and do further turning on the outside of the box if necessary. All of the outside surfaces can be sanded at this time.

Remove the lid and sand the rabbet so that there will be a little clearance. Also sand the inside of the box. Now cut off the main body of the box, again using the parting tool. Turn a rabbet (called a SPINDLE CHUCK) on the stock remaining on the faceplate. Reverse the box, press it on the chuck, and smooth and sand the bottom.

Securing the "press fit" between the chuck and the work is the most critical part of the procedure. Measure and turn carefully, providing excessive taper until the part starts to slip in place; then, reduce the taper gradually until you can press the part tightly against the shoulder. A beginner should

Fig. 17-34. Assembling work on the lathe. Left. Turning the stem. Center. Turning the base. Right. Parts glued and assembled.

plan the layout with enough extra stock so that if the first chuck is turned too small there will be sufficient stock to make another one. A strip of fine sandpaper can be used to ''shim-up'' a loose fit. When the work is fitted to an inside turning or chuck, the mounting is called a RECESSED CHUCK.

## USING METAL FASTENERS TO MOUNT WORK

The design of some turned objects will permit the use of screws or other metal fasteners in faceplate mounting. In Fig. 17-36 a hanger bolt has been carefully set in the base stock mounted on a faceplate. Drilled blanks are then fastened in place

with a washer and nut and the required contour is turned. The piece could be reversed for finishing the opposite side. The part being produced in Fig. 17-36 is the base for a small dresser lamp.

Fig. 17-37 shows wood screws being used to mount a blank which is being made into a glass coaster. The blank has been prebored on the drill press; the lathe is being used to enlarge the recess for the glass. The smaller outside hole will be enlarged to fit a stacking post. Always turn off center work at the lowest speed. Be sure the screws are flush or below the surface of the work.

In Fig. 17-38, a dowel screw (threaded on both ends) has been carefully set in the base stock. It

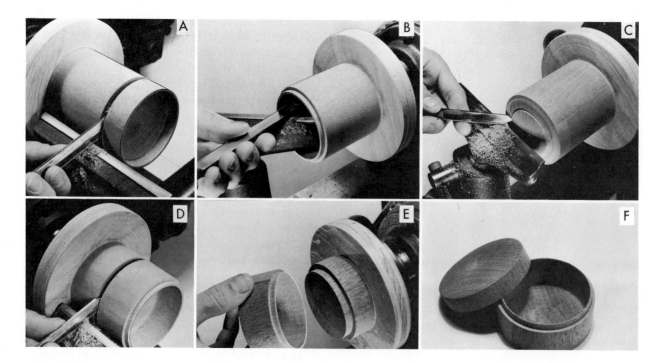

Fig. 17-35. Chucking and turning a small box. A—Cutting off the lid with the parting tool. B—Using a round nose to turn the inside. C—Top has been pressed in place and is being finished. D—Cutting off the main body of the box. E—Mounting box on a spindle chuck to finish the bottom. F—Completed box.

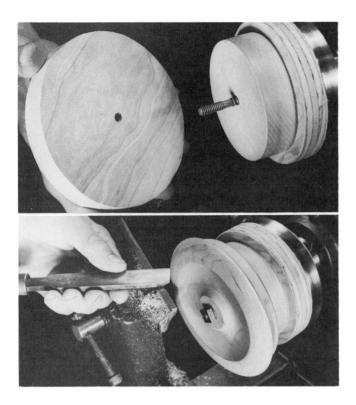

Fig. 17-38. A screw chuck for turning small knobs.

Fig. 17-36. Top. Mounting a drilled blank on a hanger bolt. Bottom. Turning the contour with a square nose tool.

is being used to mount small blanks that can be turned into drawer and door pulls. A disk of sandpaper glued to the surface of the chuck will help keep the blank from slipping.

## DRILL CHUCKS, DRIVE CHUCKS, MANDRELS, AND SPEED CHUCKS

A drill chuck mounted on a tapered shank can be placed in the headstock and used to turn small parts. In Fig. 17-39, a 3/8 in. dowel has been glued into a 1 in. dowel and then chucked for the turning as shown. The parts being produced (feet for a dresser lamp) were needed for a mass production project, so a specially formed tool was ground to shape from a section of an 8 in. mill file. The metal in file stock will hold an edge quite well, but it is very brittle. Tools made from it should be used only on small diameters.

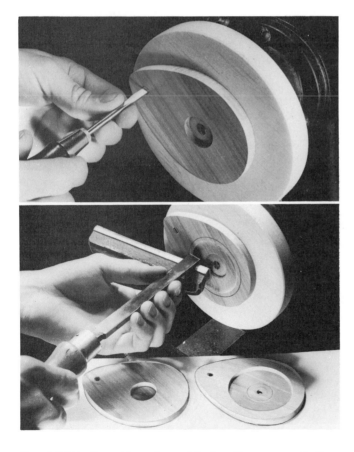

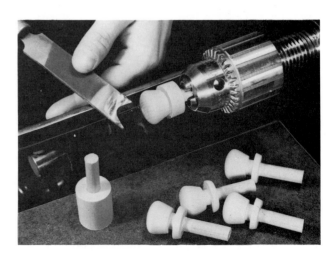

Fig. 17-37. Top. Mounting a blank with screws. Bottom. Turning the recess.

Fig. 17-39. Work mounted in a drill chuck.

A drive chuck provides a good way to mount small blanks for miniature turnings. In Fig. 17-40, top, a 13/16 in. hardwood square is being driven into a 1 in. hole about 1 1/4 in. deep. The chuck is made by mounting a piece of hardwood on the faceplate, turning it true, and then boring the hole with the round nose tool or a bit mounted in the tailstock. The faceplate is removed from the lathe and a smaller hole is drilled through the chuck, so the knock-out rod can be used to drive out the blank when the turning is finished.

Small tools are needed to make the miniature turnings shown in Fig. 17-40, bottom. These tools can be formed from discarded saw files. Grind and hone them in the same way you would the regular lathe tools.

Some small parts can be turned on a mandrel, Fig. 17-41. The square stock, driven into the drive chuck, has been turned to a slight taper so that a

Fig. 17-41. This mandrel is used for mounting and turning small parts from thread spools or dowel blanks.

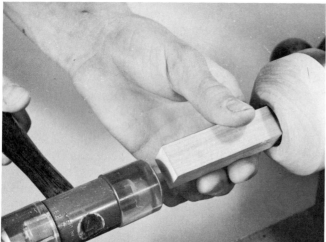

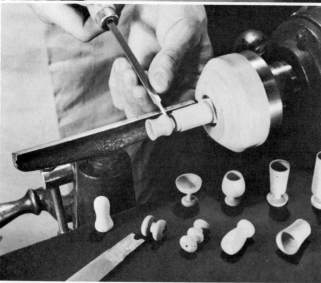

thread spool can be pressed on tightly. If the mandrel becomes compressed and the spools slip after working several pieces, the mandrel can be moistened with water and will swell back to its original size. Because wooden spools are becoming scarce, you may need to use dowels with holes bored through their center.

Speed chucks are the newest type of chuck, Fig. 17-42. They are designed to hold small turning on one end only. This chuck is ideal for objects that require external as well as internal material removal.

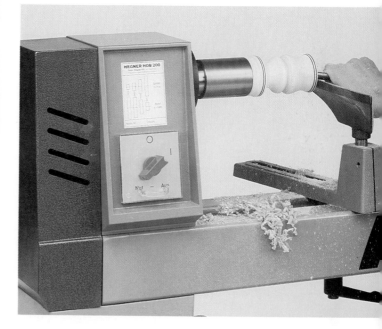

Fig. 17-40. Using a drive chuck. Top. Driving a 13/16 in. (20.5 mm) square into a 1 in. (25.4 mm) hole. Bottom. Turning miniature objects using a tool ground from a saw file.

Fig. 17-42. The speed chuck may be used to hold small turnings on one end for both internal and external machining. (AMI, Ltd.)

## INDUSTRIAL MACHINES

### AUTOMATIC LATHES

Large furniture and cabinet factories use automatic turning lathes to produce turned parts with speed and accuracy, Fig. 17-43.

With this machine, the wood blanks are placed in a hopper and are automatically centered between a headstock and a tailstock. (These are similar to those you have used, except that the tailstock also carries a spur center and is power driven.) The blank is then rotated at a speed of about 20 rpm. Behind this spindle is an arbor that carries cutterheads that can be made up in many shapes and sizes. This cutterhead assembly revolves at a high speed (2700—3600 rpm). In operation, the carriage with the slowly revolving blank of stock is moved backward, into the cutterheads, which form the desired shape in just a few seconds. Then the carriage is moved forward, the finished turning is released, and dropped out of the machine. Another blank is placed between the centers, and then the operation is repeated. Average production is about 2400 turnings in an eight hour day.

Fig. 17-44. Close-up of a cutterhead assembly. This assembly is used to produce lamp bases.    (Forest City Tool Co.)

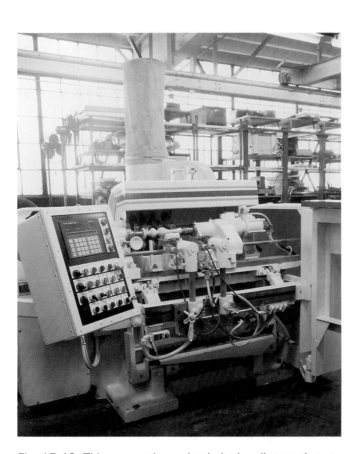

Fig. 17-43. This automatic turning lathe handles stock up to 4 in. (101.5 mm) square and 42 in. (1.06 m) long. The cutterhead turns at a speed of 2700 rpm. The feed chute and front cover are opened to show the basic mechanism. (Mattison Machine Works)

The cutterhead assembly is another machine used to turn parts quickly and accurately. It consists of many knives that overlap each other in such a way that smooth, even surfaces are formed. A cutterhead assembly used to turn a lamp base is shown in Fig. 17-44.

In Fig. 17-45, an octagonal shaped leg is being formed. To produce the eight sides, the carriage is moved in and out, changing the depth of cut. This action is controlled by a cam that is mounted on the spindle which turns with the workpiece.

The automatic back-knife lathe is specifically designed to turn small diameter work. Stock is mounted between centers and revolved at a high speed. A roughing-out cut is made with a gouge or V-knife held in a carriage. The carriage moves along a template resulting in a rough contour. As the carriage moves along the workpiece from right to left, a back-knife (ground to the required shape) moves downward along the back side of the workpiece. It produces the finished contour and surface with a smooth shearing cut.

### TURNING SANDER

In production woodworking, a special sander is used to smooth spindle turnings, Fig. 17-46. In operation, rotating spindles carry the workpieces

Fig. 17-45. Octagonal turning produced by cam action (arrow) varies depth of cut as workpiece rotates.

by sanding stations. The sanding station consists of brush backed strips of specially scored abrasive paper. The brush bristles hold the paper (which is very flexible) against the contour of the turning.

Machines can be equipped with several sanding stations (called racks). Each is loaded with a different grade of paper. The workpieces progess from course to fine sanding and are then released into the discharge chute. Production rates may run as high as 30 pieces per minute.

## CHUCKING AND BORING MACHINE

After furniture parts are turned and sanded, additional operations may still be required. For example, turned chair legs must be trimmed to length, holes must be bored for rungs, and a tenon must be formed on the top end to fit into the seat. Fig. 17-47 shows a machine designed to perform all of these operations automatically. Workpieces are loaded into a hopper and fed to spindles that carry each piece through the sequence of operations. They are then dropped into a discharge chute.

A specialized cutter (called a chuck) forms the tenon on the leg. This chuck is mounted on a revolv-

Fig. 17-46. A close-up of a turning sander capable of handling workpieces up to 2 in. (51 mm) in diameter and 32 in. (812 mm) in length. View shows workpiece on centering wyes, ready to be carried to sanding stations. Note the abrasive paper with stiff bristle brushes behind. Spindle speed is variable from 1300 to 2600 rpm. (Nash—Bell—Challoner)

Fig. 17-47. Chucking and boring machine setup for chair legs. Operations include boring rung holes, forming tenon on top end and trimming bottom end. Feeds and controls are operated by 80 psi (552 kPa) of compressed air. (Goodspeed Machine Co.)

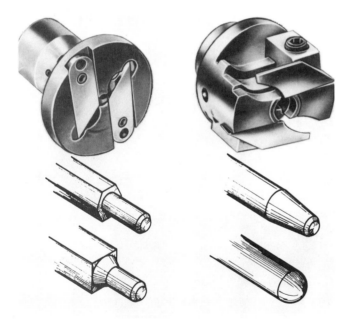

Fig. 17-48. Top. Two typical chuck designs. Bottom. Some shapes that can be formed by a chucking operation. (Nash—Bell—Challoner)

ing spindle and fed into the end of the leg, Fig. 17-48. These chucks are available in a variety of sizes and designs.

## TEST YOUR KNOWLEDGE, Chapter 17

Please do not write in the text. Place your answers on a separate sheet of paper.
1. The size of a lathe is determined by the

_____. It is _____ the distance from the lathe bed to the center of the spindle.
2. How is the cup center removed from the tailstock?
3. What is centrifugal force?
4. When the wood stock is mounted between the lathe centers, this is called:
   a. Faceplate turning.
   b. Spindle turning.
   c. Turning speed.
   d. None of the above.
5. Outline the procedure for mounting stock between centers.
6. When the skew is used to make a shearing cut, the _____ rides on the surface that is being cut.
7. Cutting beads and V-grooves with the skew is the easiest of the turning operations. True or False?
8. When turning duplicate parts, to reduce the diameter 1/2 in., the depth of cut should be:
   a. 1/4 in.
   b. 1 in.
   c. 1/2 in.
   d. None of the above.
9. In spindle turning, it is usually best to position the work so that the largest diameters are nearest to the _____ (headstock, tailstock) of the lathe.
10. Name the three tools most useful for faceplate turning.
11. Why is the tailstock sometimes used when roughing out faceplate work?
12. Drill chucks, drive chucks, mandrels, and speed chucks can all be used to turn _____ (small, large) pieces of wood.

## ACTIVITIES

1. Using suppliers' or manufacturers' catalogs, develop a complete set of specifications for a wood lathe.
2. Prepare a list of the basic equipment you would need to do wood turning in a home workshop. Secure a cost estimate.
3. Prepare a block chart calculating the surface feed per minute for various diameters and lathe speeds. List diameters of 1 to 12 in. across the top and speeds of 500 to 3000 rpm down the left side. Use the formula:

$$SFM = \frac{RPM \times \pi D}{12}$$

Convert some of the higher speeds into miles per hour. Also convert some of the speeds into meters and kilometers.

Top. Portable routers are available in a variety of sizes, shoapes, and types. (Black & Decker) Middle. Shaper cutters can be used to form a wide variety of edge shapes. (Freud, Inc.) Bottom. Typical moldings made by a high-production throughfeed molder.    (Wadkin PLC)

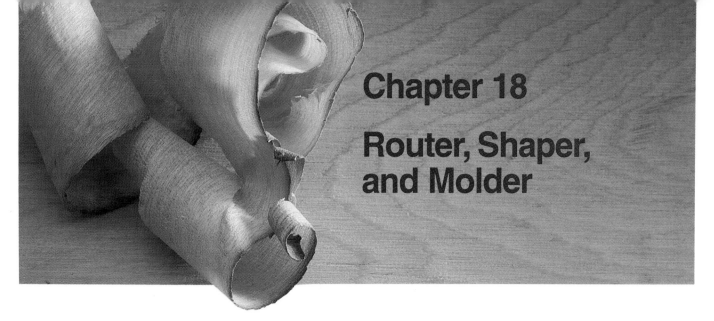

# Chapter 18

# Router, Shaper, and Molder

Routers, shapers, and molders are designed to cut irregular shapes and to form various contours on edges and surfaces. The shapes may be decorative in nature or they may form the joints for construction and assembly. Cutters travel at high speeds, producing smooth surfaces that require little, if any, sanding. The router and shaper are manufactured in sizes that are practical for the school shop. The molder, like the double-end tenoner, is a heavy production machine and is usually found only in large woodworking plants and factories.

## PORTABLE ROUTER

### PARTS AND DESCRIPTION

The portable router, Fig. 18-1, consists of a motor unit carried by an adjustable base. A collet type chuck is attached to the motor shaft and holds various cutting tools. The size of a router is given in horsepower rating. Sizes range from 1/4 hp to as large as 2 1/2 hp. The motors turn at speeds of 20,000 rpm or higher.

### PLUNGE ROUTERS

Plunge routers are ideal for mortising or cutting into the middle of a panel. Plunge routers were developed years ago, but early models were heavy, expensive machines intended for commercial applications. By adapting the plunge feature to the portable router, its versatility and popularity has increased because it can do all the jobs of a regular router plus cut clean mortises, make stopped cuts and template-guided cutouts.

There are many plunge routers available on the market in a wide variety of sizes and configurations. The most common plunge routers have the motor assembly housed in a carriage that rides on a pair of steel guide posts fixed to the base. Handles on the carriage enable the user to "plunge" the bit vertically into the work as well as move it in the horizontal direction. One or more springs move the carriage to its original position once the cut is completed. Most plunge routers have a locking device that holds the carriage at a fixed depth after plunging.

Depth of cuts are precisely set using a stop rod and scale/pointer mechanism on the router. A depth-stop turret facilitates quick and easy changes in cutting depth. Typical plunge depths are up to 3 inches on some machines. Some newer models contain a sophisticated electronic variable speed (EVS) package that allows the user to select the proper speed for the size of bit and application. Also, many plunge routers have a revolving depth stop that allows the user to set several predetermined plunge depths without having to reset the stop rod for each cut.

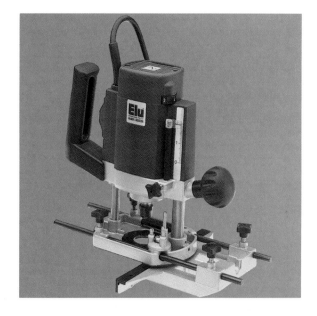

Fig. 18-1. A modern plunge cut router for general purpose work. (Black & Decker)

## ROUTER BITS

Router bits are available in a wide variety of shapes and sizes. They are made from two types of metals: carbon steel and carbide. CARBON STEEL BITS are easier to sharpen and less expensive, but they do not remain sharp as long as carbide cutters. CARBIDE CUTTERS perform well on hard, dense materials such as particle board and plastic laminates.

Router bits generally have three main parts: the shank, cutting edge, and pilot. Some bits do not have a pilot. Plain pilots and ball bearing pilots are available for some cutter designs. Router bits are produced in 1/4 in., 3/8 in., and 1/2 in. diameter shanks. The most popular size for portable routers is 1/4 in. diameter shank. One piece router bits are most common, but interchangeable pieces have the advantage of multiple setups with fewer cutters. Fig. 18-2 shows a router bit equipped with a ball bearing pilot. This pilot prevents burning on the edge of the board caused by a solid pilot.

Some of the most commonly used bits and cutters are shown in Fig. 18-3.

The STRAIGHT BIT has cutting edges on the end and sides. It is used for slotting, grooving, inlay work, and background routing. A VEINING BIT is similar to a straight bit except it has a rounded end.

The RABBETING BIT is used for joinery work and usually has a pilot tip that controls the depth of cuts.

ROUND-OVER BITS are made in a variety of radii and are used to shape rounded edges. They generally have a pilot the same diameter as the bottom of the cutter. BEADING BITS are similar in shape to round-over bits except the pilot is smaller in diameter and produces a step instead of a smooth transition.

ROMAN OGEE BITS produce an artistic curve that is popular for edges on tabletops and other furniture pieces. This cutter has a pilot to guide the cutter and to maintain the proper depth of cut.

CHAMFER BITS are designed to cut a standard angle chamfer (or bevel) on an edge. A 45 deg. angle is most common. Chamfer bits ALWAYS have a pilot.

ROUND BOTTOM or CORE-BOX BITS produce a rounded groove on the face of the board. This cutter does not have a pilot.

COVE BITS produce a concave edge. They also have a pilot.

V-BOTTOM BITS are used to cut a V-groove into the surface of a board. The standard angle is 45 deg. on either side of the groove.

DOVETAIL BITS are used to produce dovetail joints.

Other special purpose cutters include flush trim bits, tapered trim bits, louver slotting bits, and custom-shaped bits.

Fig. 18-4 shows the cuts made by some commonly used router bits.

Sharpening a router bit is fairly simple if you use a holding fixture, Fig. 18-5. This holds the bit in alignment while it is being ground on a smaller abrasive wheel mounted in the chuck of the router. The router must be firmly supported in an upside-down position. The bit can be held for freehand grinding, but this requires a great deal of skill. Router bits can be honed lightly with a small slipstone or oilstone. Always hone or grind the face of the cutter. Never try to sharpen the bevel side.

## PORTABLE ROUTER SAFETY

Observe these safety rules in addition to those given in Chapter 3.

1. The bit must be securely mounted in the chuck to a depth of at least 1/2 in. and the base must be tight.

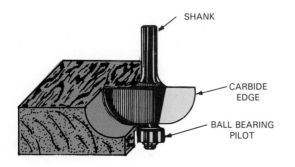

Fig. 18-2. This cove bit is equipped with a ball bearing pilot. (The Stanley Works)

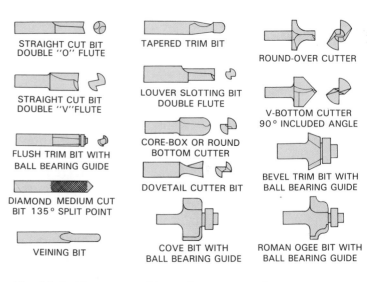

Fig. 18-3. These router bits and cutters are the most commonly used. The wide variety available makes the portable router a versatile tool.

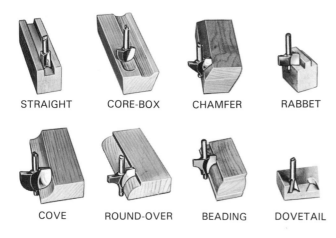

STRAIGHT    CORE-BOX    CHAMFER    RABBET

COVE    ROUND-OVER    BEADING    DOVETAIL

Fig. 18-4. The cuts produced by common router bits.
(The Stanley Works)

2. As with all portable tools, be certain that the motor is properly grounded.
3. Wear eye protection.
4. Be certain the work is securely clamped and that it will remain stationary during the routing operation.
5. Place the router base on the work or template, with the bit clear of the wood before turning on the power. Hold it firmly when turning on the motor to overcome starting torque.
6. Hold the router in both hands and feed it smoothly through the cut in the correct direction.
7. When the cut is completed, turn off the motor. Do not lift the machine from the work until the motor has stopped.
8. Always unplug the motor when mounting bits or making major adjustment.

## MOUNTING BITS AND ADJUSTING THE BASE

Select the correct bit for your work. Be sure the bit is sharp. The motor should be disconnected. The router base may be removed to insert the cutter on some models, but others (such as plunge routers) generally do not require removal of the base. Insert the bit at least 1/2 in. or to the full depth of the chuck, lock the motor shaft, and tighten the chuck using an approved type of wrench, Fig. 18-6.

Insert the motor unit into the base if removed, and lightly tighten the clamp. Measure and adjust for the correct depth of cut. Lock the base securely. Some routers have a special depth adjusting ring. When so equipped, the base is first set even with the bit and the adjusting ring is moved away from the base a distance equal to the depth. Resetting the base against the ring will then provide the required cut. Other routers have an adjusting thumbscrew mechanism with a locking device.

## USING THE ROUTER

Hold the router securely in both hands. When the power is turned on, the torque of the motor will cause the machine to twist out of your hands if not held securely.

The router motor revolves in a clockwise direction (when viewed from above) and, therefore, should be fed from left to right when making a cut along an edge facing you. When cutting around the outside of oblong or circular pieces, always move the machine in a counterclockwise direction so the cutter will rotate into the stock. This will produce a smooth cutting action.

The rate of feed will vary with the hardness of the wood and size of cut. Routers have an INDUCTION MOTOR which will slow down somewhat under load. Excessive loss of speed indicates too

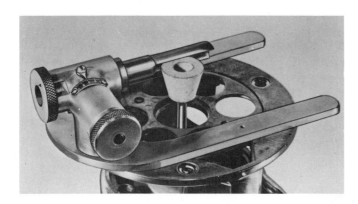

Fig. 18-5. Use a special holding fixture when sharpening router bits.

Fig. 18-6. When installing a router bit, the electric cord is unplugged.

heavy a cut. When the work is heavy, it is best to reduce the depth of the cut and maintain a good rate of feed. The depth of cut can then be increased and a second pass made over the work. Feeding router bits at a very slow rate causes them to heat and burn the wood as well as damage the cutter. This is most likely to happen when making cuts on end grain. Keep the router moving at all times.

For plain routing cuts the machine is sometimes guided along a layout line freehand. However, this is difficult to do; better work will usually be produced if some type of guide is used. Fig. 18-7 shows a standard guide attachment being used to cut a dado. The attachment includes a Vernier type adjustment that is helpful when making precision settings. In addition to dado cuts, it can be used for rabbets, grooves, and certain circular shapes, Fig. 18-8. In Fig. 18-9, a shop built guide is being used for a dado cut. The guide simply serves as a straightedge along which the router base can slide.

The router can be guided by a template. A guide tip is attached to the router base with the bit extending through its center. This tip guides the router along a template which is usually made of plywood or hardboard. The contour of the template must be larger for inside cuts and smaller for outside cuts, by an amount equal to the distance from the outside of the guide tip to the cutting edge of the bit. Fig. 18-10 shows a template ready for use.

## SHAPING EDGES

Most of the bits used for shaping an edge have a pilot tip that guides the router, Fig. 18-11. Edges must be perfectly formed since any imperfections will be followed by the tip. The design of the shaped edge must allow 1/8 in. of surface on which the tip can ride. Feed the bit smoothly in the correct

Fig. 18-8. Left. Series of router cuts needed to form a dado. Right. Cutting a groove. (The Stanley Works)

Fig. 18-9. Cutting a dado with a shop built guide.

Fig. 18-10. A template for routing.

Fig. 18-7. Using a guide to cut a dado.
(Porter-Cable Corp.)

Fig. 18-11. The pilot tip shown in the inset guides the router along the edges of the grooves in this sign.
(Leichtung, Inc.)

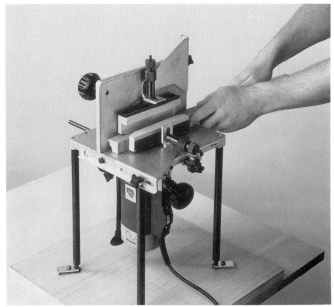

Fig. 18-12. Using a router table to produce small molding.
(Black & Decker)

direction and with just enough side pressure to hold the pilot tip against the edge. If too much pressure is used, the friction between the tip and the wood will cause it to burn. The tip should always be kept smooth and bright; an accumulation of pitch or gum will cause it to burn, even when light pressure is applied.

*Always set the router base firmly on the work with the bit clear of the cut before turning on the motor.*

Strips of small molding, Fig. 18-12, can be produced from rectangular stock using a router table and general-purpose router.

## CUTTING DOVETAIL JOINTS

Dovetail joints can be accurately cut using a special dovetailing attachment, dovetail bit, and a template guide tip. Use the following procedure when cutting a joint for a drawer side and front.

1. Clamp the dovetail attachment securely to the bench.
2. Fasten the template guide tip to the base of the router. Install the dovetail bit in the router (this must be done with the motor unit mounted on the base).
3. Adjust the depth of cut. A 9/16 in. dovetail bit is set to a depth of 19/32 in.
4. Clamp the stock in the attachment as shown in Fig. 18-13A. Piece A is the front of the drawer with the inside surface turned up. Piece B is the drawer side with the inside surface turned out. Each of the parts must be carefully aligned and located against the pins.
5. Place the template in position and tighten the clamp knobs, Fig. 18-13B.
6. Hold the router on the template with the bit clear of the work. Turn on the motor and carefully guide it in and out and around the ends of the fingers, Fig. 18-13C and D. When the cut is complete, turn off the motor and wait for it to stop before removing the router from the template. NEVER RAISE THE ROUTER OFF OF THE WORK WHILE THE MOTOR IS RUNNING.
7. Remove the parts and check the fit. If the fit is too loose, extend the bit slightly. If it is too tight, retract it. The depth of the fit can be adjusted by moving the template in or out.
8. Make trial cuts in extra pieces that are the same size as your work, until a satisfactory fit is obtained. Then cut the joints for your project. The joint for the right front drawer corner is made on the left end of the attachment and the left front corner is made on the right end.

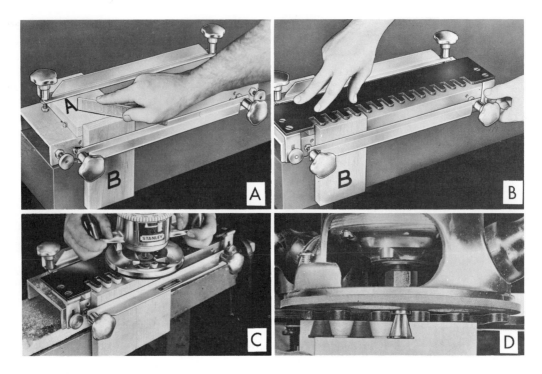

Fig. 18-13. Cutting a dovetail joint. A—Clamping stock in the fixture. B—Installing the template.
C—Making the cut. D—Close-up view. (The Stanley Works)

Fig. 18-14 shows another type of dovetail jig. This type provides for a wide variety of joints and variable spacing. Fig. 18-15 shows the cut when completed. Typical joints made with this jig are shown in the background.

When cutting dovetails in a rabbeted drawer front, Fig. 18-16, the drawer front and sides are cut separately. Mount the drawer front in the attachment, using a gauge block as shown, and then remove the gauge and cut the joint. Use a block the same thickness as the drawer front to set up the drawer side and leave it in place during the cutting.

## CUTTING GROOVES AND SPIRALS ON ROUND STOCK

The router may be used to cut grooves and spirals on lathe turnings, Fig. 18-17. An attachment is available which converts the standard router into a "router/lathe." It has an indexing head which allows straight grooves, evenly spaced, or spirals

Fig.18-14. Top. Half-blind dovetails used on a drawer front.
Bottom. Cutting the tails for a half-blind dovetail.
(Leigh Industries, Ltd.)

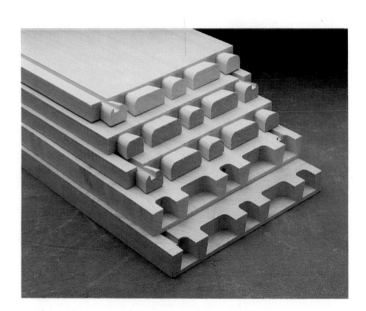

Fig. 18-15. Routing is complete using the setup shown
in Fig. 18-14.
(Leigh Industries, Ltd.)

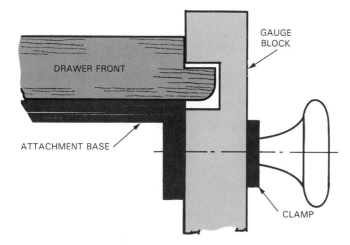

Fig. 18-16. Cutting dovetails in a rabbeted drawer front. Top. Using a gauge block to align the drawer front. Bottom. A completed joint.

cut along the length of a turned piece. Tapered pieces may also be grooved or spiraled using this attachment. A template is used to contour turn various shapes to specifications. Stock up to 3 in. square and 36 in. long may be machined in this attachment.

## BENCH SHAPER ATTACHMENTS

The portable router can be mounted under a router table to be used as a small bench shaper. Typical router bits may be used, or the collet chuck may be replaced with a small arbor or spindle that will carry regular shaper cutters. Some router tables can be tilted. This allows the router to make a greater variety of cuts using a given set of cutters. Circular pieces or irregular shapes are easily machined with attachments like the circle guide shown in Fig. 18-18.

## STENCIL AND PANTOGRAPH ATTACHMENTS

Stencils are available for the router to make two-dimensional letters, drawings, and other designs. These stencils or templates help even the inexperienced operator produce quality work with just a little practice. Pantograph attachments are available for both two- and three-dimensional work. Fig. 18-19 shows a two-dimensional pantograph setup in use. Again, a template or three-dimensional model is required for the pattern. These devices greatly extend the application of the router beyond its original use.

Fig. 18-17. A router with a jig was used to cut the grooves and spirals on these lathe turnings. (Leichtung, Inc.)

Fig. 18-18. Using a circular guide to control the depth of cut. (Millers Falls Co.)

## USING ROUTERS IN TRADES AND INDUSTRY

The building trades make extensive use of portable routers for such jobs as routing out stair stringers for risers and treads, Fig. 18-20. They are also a valuable tool for cutting the gain for hinges in doors and jambs, Fig. 18-21.

In millwork and furniture factories, heavy-duty routers are used for a wide range of work. Since the bit travels at such a high speed, it can be used to cut out various irregular shapes faster than a band saw and also produces a smoother edge. Templates and fixtures are used to guide the machine through the cut, Fig. 18-22. On large, heavy work, the router may be supported on swinging arms.

An overarm router/shaper, Fig. 18-23, can be set up for a variety of work in either industry or the school shop. The motor unit is mounted under the table for standard shaping operations. Production routers are often powered with air motors. They provide for continuous operation at high speeds and under heavy loads without overheating.

Pin routers are designed for routing and profiling flat sheets of plywood and composition material. The workpiece is placed on a carrier or fixture that has a groove or pattern on the bottom side, Fig. 18-24. The cut is made as the groove or pattern rides along a pin fixed in the machine table directly below the cutter.

A pin router is very useful for cutting curves and complex contours which must be repeated on several pieces. A fixture and pattern must be constructed to insure that each design will be identical. Tempered hardboard is generally used for the pattern. The pattern is attached to the underside of the fixture when a typical pin router is used. (The fixture is reversed for an inverted pin router because the cutter is mounted in the table instead of the overarm.) The fixture may be made using 3/4 in. plywood which is large enough to accommodate the

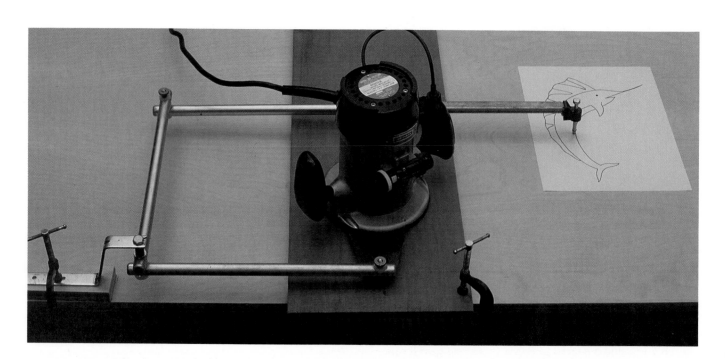

Fig. 18-19. This two-dimensional pantograph setup uses the router to make a decorative figure.

Fig. 18-20. Heavy-duty routers and stair templates are used to cut housed stringer. Stair treads and risers will be assembled in the grooves.

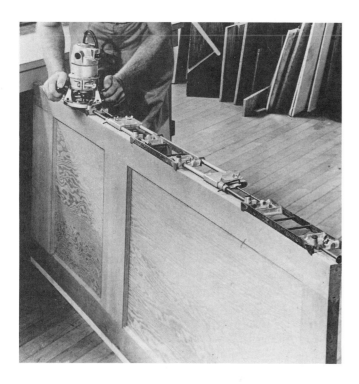

Fig. 18-21. Using a special template to cut the gain for passage door hinges. This template will also be used on the door jamb.

Fig. 18-22. This cabinet door template is equipped with a high-speed grooving indexer. (The Stanley Works)

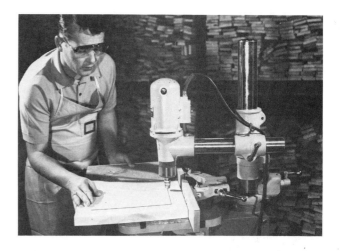

Fig. 18-23. Using an overarm router. Workpiece is guided by fence mounted on table. A foot pedal provides vertical table movement.

hold-down devices. The piece to be machined may be attached to the top side of the fixture with screws or fixture clamps. The work must be held securely on the fixture while machining. Study Fig. 18-24 to see the relationship of the pin, cutter, pattern, and workpiece to the fixture.

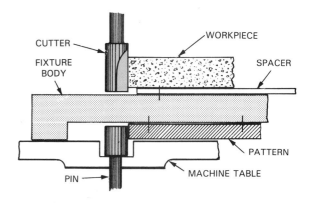

Fig. 18-24. Basic setup for cutting contours (profiling) on a pin router.

A pin router may also be used to make straight cuts. A fence is generally used when making straight cuts and no fixture is required.

Dados, rabbets, and other joints may be very accurately machined using the pin router. The cut is smooth and precise. A production pin router is shown in Fig. 18-25.

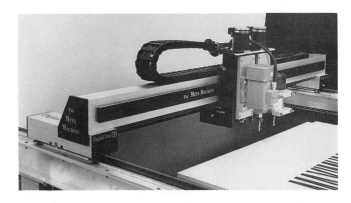

Fig. 18-26. This piece of equipment is a cost-effective computer-controlled automation center that can perform all the functions of a CNC machining center. It will drive one or two spindles that can cut out, drill, and groove panels in one continuous process.   (Digital Tool)

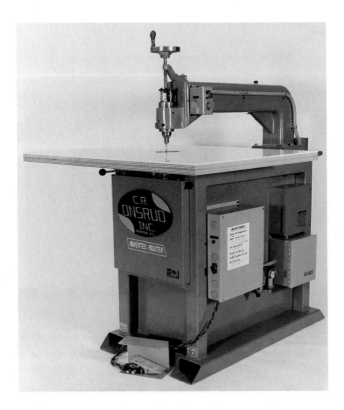

Fig. 18-25. Inverted pin router has the cutter mounted below the table with the pin in the arm above.   (C.R. Onsrud,Inc.)

## CNC ROUTERS

Computer-controlled woodworking equipment is widely used throughout larger manufacturing companies. However, most of this equipment is far too expensive for the small- to medium-size shop since prices range from $50,000 to $75,000.

Smaller, less expensive ($3000 to $10,000) CNC equipment is being developed for smaller operations, Fig. 18-26. Routing is the area that has received the most attention. Most of the CNC router centers are linked with a PC or minicomputer. CNC routers are very useful for carving, template routing, engraving, sign making, and other light machining tasks in wood, plastics, and nonferrous metals.

## SHAPER

### DESCRIPTION AND PARTS

The shaper can be used to perform many operations. Basically it is designed to cut molding and to form various decorative shapes on the edges of work. It can also be used to cut rabbet joints, tongue and groove joints, window sash joints, and many others. It consists of a vertical spindle that projects through a horizontal table. Work is moved over the table and the edge is fed into cutters mounted on the spindle. The depth of cut and position of the work is controlled by either the fence or by collars mounted on the spindle and pins set in the table. Various fixtures and special guides can also be used. Fig. 18-27 shows some of the important parts.

The spindle on small shapers is usually driven by a belt at speeds of 5,000 to 10,000 rpm. It can be moved up and down to provide various positions for the cutter. The motor has a reversing switch so the spindle can be revolved in either direction, thus extending the variety of setups that can be made.

Multipurpose machines can produce many standard molding shapes in a single pass, Fig. 18-28.

### SHAPER CUTTERS

There are two general types of shaper cutter: the assembled cutter and the solid wing cutter. The ASSEMBLED CUTTER (or an open-face cutter) is used on larger machines for production work. One type consists of flat knives with beveled edges that are ground to the required shape and then clamped between two collars. Extreme care must be used so the cutters project an equal amount and are securely locked in place.

SOLID CUTTERS, Fig. 18-29, are recommended for work in the school shop because they are safer

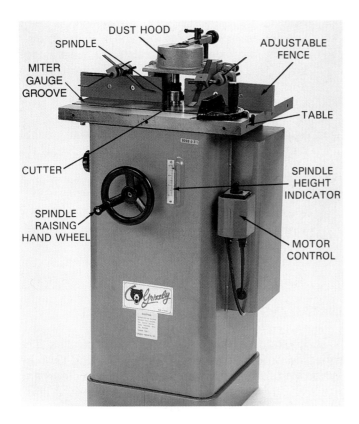

Fig. 18-27. Main parts of a standard 1 1/2 hp shaper. The fence and guard are shown in place.    (Grizzly Imports, Inc.)

Fig. 18-29. These solid wing shaper cutters produce the moldings shown. (Delta International Machinery Corp.)

to use. A wide range of patterns is available with the most common size designed to fit on a 1/2 in. spindle, Fig. 18-30.

Shaper cutters will stay sharp for a considerable length of time if they are kept clean and are carefully handled and used. The solid wing cutters are sharpened by honing the face while it is held flat on an oilstone, Fig. 18-31. If the edge is very dull it may be necessary to grind the face lightly. Use a fine grinding wheel and hold the front face of the cutter against the side of the wheel. Try to grind each wing the same amount. Do not attempt to grind or hone the beveled side of the edge.

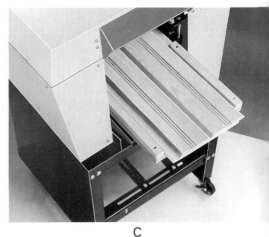

A                              B                              C

Fig. 18-28. This planer-molder is capable of producing a wide variety of standard molding shapes in a single pass. A—Crown molding. B—Tongue and groove. C—Individual design. (Foley-Belsaw Co.)

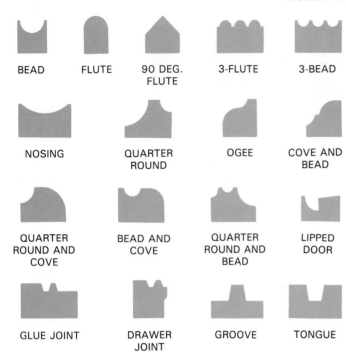

Fig. 18-30. Standard cutter shapes.

The shapes shown are: BEAD, FLUTE, 90 DEG. FLUTE, 3-FLUTE, 3-BEAD, NOSING, QUARTER ROUND, OGEE, COVE AND BEAD, QUARTER ROUND AND COVE, BEAD AND COVE, QUARTER ROUND AND BEAD, LIPPED DOOR, GLUE JOINT, DRAWER JOINT, GROOVE, TONGUE.

## SHAPER SAFETY RULES

The following rules should be observed in addition to the general safety rules given in Unit 3.

1. Be sure to get the instructor's permission before starting to set up and use the machine.
2. When possible, mount the cutter so that most of the cutting will be performed on the lower part of the edge. Any unused part of the cutter should be below the table.
3. An approved lock washer must be located directly under the spindle nut and the nut must be set tight.
4. Use the fence for all straight line shaping cuts. Be certain it is properly adjusted and securely locked in placed.
5. Use guards, feather boards, and hold-down devices whenever possible.

6. Maintain a 4 in. margin of safety when using the fence or miter gauge and a 6 in. margin when using depth collars. If the part is too small to allow this margin, design and build a special holder or push board.
7. Cut only new stock that is straight and true, and free of splits, checks, and knots.
8. Roll the spindle over by hand to check clearance of complicated settings. Snap the switch on and off quickly to check rotation of the cutter. Be certain the direction of feed is correct.
9. Have your instructor inspect the setup. Inform him or her of the direction and order of feed you plan to use.
10. Make a trial cut on an extra piece of stock that is the same thickness as your project work.

## INSTALLING SPINDLES AND CUTTERS

Some shapers have interchangeable spindles. The most common sizes are 5/16, 1/2, and 3/4 in. When installing a spindle, be certain it is clean and fits smoothly into the slots and keyways. A light film of oil should be applied to mating surfaces. Makes and models will vary in the way that the spindle is clamped and secured. The operator's manual should be studied for detailed directions. Also refer to the manual for other adjustments and oiling schedules. See Figs. 18-32 and 18-33.

To install a cutter, remove the table insert and raise the spindle to its highest point. Be certain the spindle, cutters, collars, and nut are clean and free of pitch and gum, Fig. 18-34. Mount the correct arrangement of collars and cutters on the spindle. Place the lock washer on the spindle and then turn on the nut and tighten it securely with an approved type wrench. ALWAYS PLACE THE LOCK WASHER

Fig. 18-31. Honing a shaper cutter.

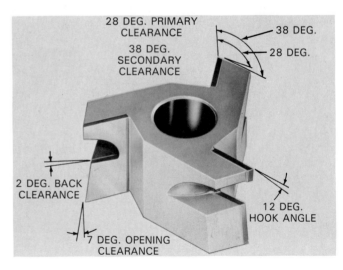

Fig. 18-32. Carbide-tipped lip door cutter. It will stay sharp much longer than a regular cutter.

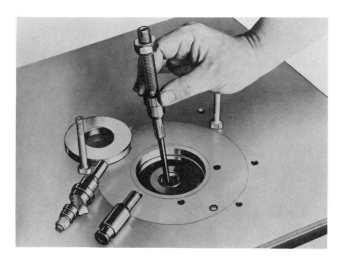

Fig. 18-33. Installing a spindle. Check operator's manual for detailed directions covering model being used. (Delta International Machinery Corp.)

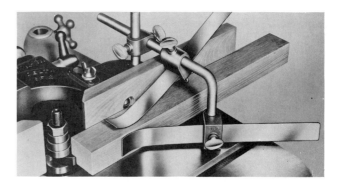

Fig. 18-35. Using the fence to guide straight cuts. (Delta International Machinery Corp.)

DIRECTLY UNDER THE NUT. Replace the table insert if it can be used. Check the clearance and adjust the cutter to the required height.

When installing spindles and cutters or making major adjustments on the shaper, the power should be disconnected.

## SHAPING WITH THE FENCE

All straight cuts should be guided along the fence as shown in Fig. 18-35. Mount the fence on the table and check the alignment of the two sides with a straightedge. When only a part of the edge is cut, the two sections are kept even and the part of the edge that is not cut continues in contact with the fence throughout the cut.

When the shaping cut removes all of the edge, the infeed section must be set back an amount equal to the depth of the cut. The work is first guided by the infeed fence. Then, after the edge is cut, it should align with and be guided by the outfeed section in the same way that the jointer tables operate, Fig. 18-36.

Adjust the fence to provide the correct depth of cut and lock it securely in position. Roll the cutter-head by hand to be certain it clears the fence. Adjust all guards and hold-downs to insure safety in the operation.

Work that is guided only by the fence should be at least 10 in. long to provide satisfactory control. To shape the end of parts that are less than 10 in. wide, use a miter gauge or guide block, Fig. 18-37.

WHEN ONLY PART OF THE EDGE IS SHAPED OUTFEED FENCE IS ALIGNED WITH INFEED FENCE

WHEN ALL OF EDGE IS SHAPED OUTFEED FENCE IS MOVED FORWARD TO SUPPORT THE WORK

Fig. 18-36. Fence adjustment. Note cutter rotation and direction of feed.

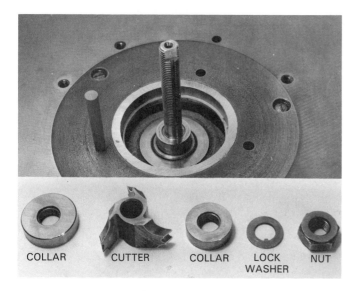

Fig. 18-34. This cutter setup is ready to be installed. Installation goes from left to right.

COLLAR   CUTTER   COLLAR   LOCK WASHER   NUT

323

Fig. 18-37. Using a miter gauge to shape the end of a panel frame.   (Freud, Inc.)

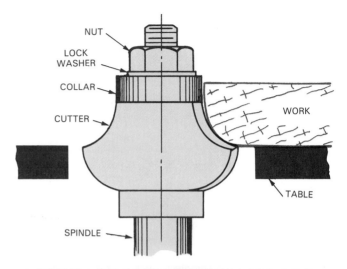

Fig. 18-39.   Top. The collar controls the depth of cut. Bottom. Set of standard collars.   (Freud, Inc.)

The shaper can be used to cut many types of joints. Fig. 18-38 shows a pair of cutters set up to form a stub tenon on a rail. Note that a supporting piece of stock is held against the back edge to prevent splintering the part at the end of the cut.

## SHAPING WITH DEPTH COLLARS

Parts with curves and irregular shapes are held against table pins or special forms, with the depth of cut controlled by a collar, Fig. 18-39. The collar must be clean and bright, and the contact surface should be at least 3/16 in. wide.

When possible, mount the cutter so that the lower part of the work will be shaped and the depth collar will be located on top. A table pin is used to position the work, especially at the start of the cut. Place it to the right of a cutter turning counterclockwise and left of one turning clockwise.

Fig. 18-40 shows a depth collar shaping operation. The cut should be started on the side grain and carried into the end grain. Start the cut by placing the work securely against the table pin. Swing it slowly into the cut and at the same time move it forward in the direction of the feed. After the cut is started, use of the table pin is not critical. However, it is often helpful in turning corners.

Hold the work firmly against the depth collar but avoid too much pressure as it may cause burning of the work and collar. Heavy cuts should be handled by making a first cut at about one-half the depth and then making a second pass around the work at a full setting.

*Always maintain a full 6 in. margin of safety and use the ring guard when shaping irregular pieces. Never hold the work along the edge that has just passed by the cutter as a sudden kickback could throw your hand into the cutter.*

Fig. 18-38. Cutting a stub tenon using the fence and miter gauge.

Fig. 18-40. Shaping a curved edge. Work is positioned against the starting pin. The collar controls depth of cut.

## PATTERN SHAPING

An irregularly shaped part can be cut to an exact outline and the edge can be shaped by using a pattern. The part should be cut to rough size on the band saw or jigsaw, mounted on the pattern, and held in place with clamps or pins. The pattern is designed to ride against the depth collar and guide the work through the cut, Fig. 18-41. Note the large collar mounted on top to help guard the cutter.

Use the same feeding procedure as for regular work with depth collars. Fig. 18-42 shows a pattern shaping setup where the pattern rides against a special table insert. One side is shaped, then the work is turned over in the holder to the other side.

## INDUSTRIAL MACHINES

DOUBLE SPINDLE SHAPERS can be used for a variety of work, Fig. 18-43, especially for shaping

Fig. 18-43. Double spindle shaper. Spindles are 1 1/4 in. (31.8 mm) in diameter and operate at speeds of 7200 rpm.

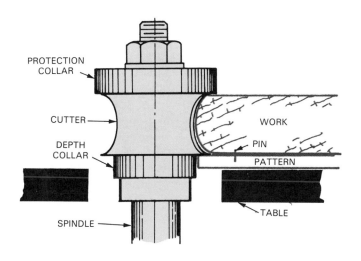

Fig. 18-41. Shaping with a pattern. 3/16 in. or 1/4 in. hardboard makes good pattern stock.

Fig. 18-42. Pattern shaping setup. The work is mounted in a holder and the depth of cut is controlled by a special table insert.

irregular curves. The spindles can be rotated in opposite directions making it easy to follow the grain of the wood by simply shifting the workpiece from one spindle to the other.

The CONTOUR PROFILER, Fig. 18-44, is a high production shaper. It consists of a table that moves back and forth and carries the workpiece along a high speed cutterhead. The cutterhead moves in and out as a roller guide follows the contour of a pattern or template attached to the table. See Fig. 18-45. Some machines have a cutterhead assembly on both sides which greatly increases the production rate for some parts.

In operation, the work (sometimes several layers) is stacked on the table, automatically clamped, then fed through the cut. At the end of the feed stroke the cutterhead retracts. The table returns rapidly to the starting position. An operator then unloads and

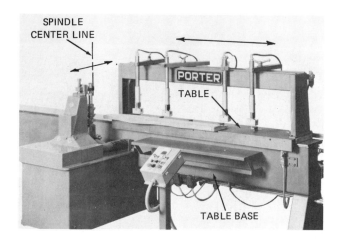

Fig. 18-44. Contour profiler. Arrows indicate table and spindle movement. Feed is from right to left at speeds adjustable from 0 to 60 fpm (18.3 mpm). (Porter Machinery Co.)

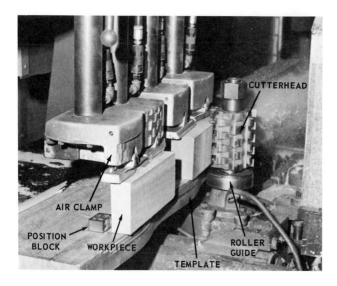

Fig. 18-45. Close-up view shows a contour profiler in operation. Feed is toward the rear of the view.

Fig. 18-47. Close-up view of spindle and air clamps. Cutterhead with straight knives produces a smooth surface and exact contour to edge of laminated particle board. Spindle rotation is 7200 rpm. (Danley Machine Corp.)

reloads the table for another cutting cycle.

Cutterhead rotation is in the feed direction (opposite to that shown in Fig. 18-36 for handfed shapers). This takes advantage of the "climb-cut" principle which prevents splintering along the cut. Such a cut is possible only when the workpiece is securely clamped and the feed rate automatically controlled.

A ROTARY PROFILER, shown in Fig. 18-46, is similar to the contour profiler. It has a revolving table that carries the workpieces. Templates or patterns are fastened to the table and the work held in place by air clamps. A roller, in contact with the template,

moves the cutterhead in and out as the table revolves. Compressed air is used to keep the roller in firm contact with the template. Table rotation is automatically controlled by a special cam that speeds up or slows down the movement for various sections of the workpiece. Sharp corners or curves usually require a slower speed. This type of machine is especially safe to use since the operator works on the side opposite the cutterhead location. Fig. 18-47 shows a close-up view of a cutter and roller

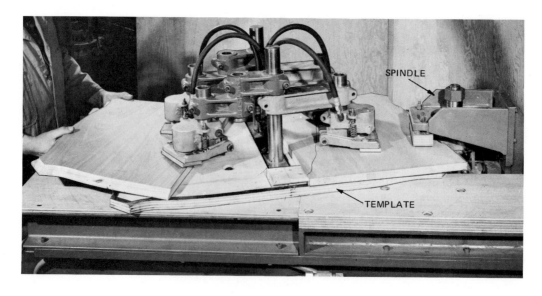

Fig. 18-46. Operator removes completed workpiece from rotary profiler. Clamps release automatically. Workpiece has been shaped to exact size and contoured on one side and both ends. Rotation is counterclockwise. (Danley Machine Corp.)

Fig. 18-48. Dual table shaper. The cutterhead is mounted on the center overarm which swings to first one and then the other revolving table. (Danley Machine Corp.)

guide. The roller guide is also called a FOLLOWER.

The DUAL TABLE SHAPER permits continuous production of smaller sized parts, Fig. 18-48. The operator unloads and loads one table while work on the other table is being shaped. The cutterhead and roller guide are mounted on an overarm which pivots between the two tables. As the cutting cycle is completed on one table, the operator presses a switch which causes the arm to swing to the second table and begin the cut.

A COMPUTER CONTROLLED ROUTER/SHAPER machine is fully automatic in its operation, Fig. 18-49. The machine has a fixed table with a moving gantry for continuous machining. Longitudinal (lengthwise) movement of the spindles is produced as the carriage rides on ways (slides) in the main base. Transverse (crosswise) movement results as the ram slides in and out on ways located in the carriage. Both of these motions are provided by lead screws. The lead screws are driven by hydraulic-servo mechanisms driven by the computer. Up and down indexing of the spindle can also be controlled by the computer.

Fig. 18-50 shows a close-up view of a shaping operation. The cutting cycle alternates between the two stations. Thus the operator can unload and load one station while the other is being machined.

## MOLDER

The molder produces moldings for furniture and interior trim. In a single pass through the machine, four cutterheads completely form such items as window sash stock, door casings, baseboard, base

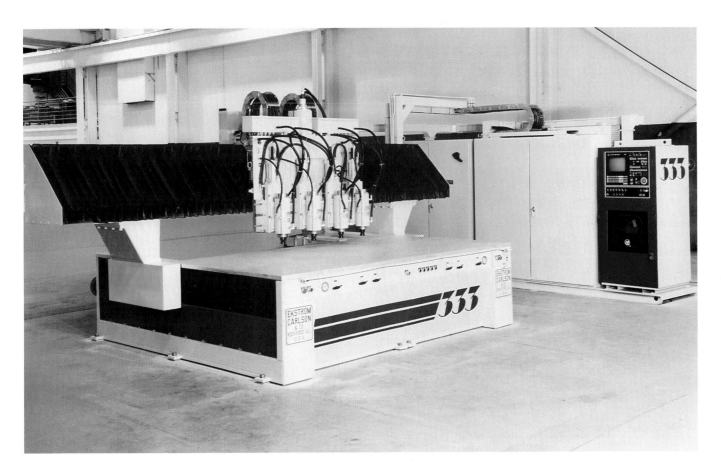

Fig. 18-49. Modern CNC three-axis contouring gantry router and production center. Travel is 150 in. on the X-axis, 60 in. on the Y-axis, and 8 in. on the Z-axis. Two shaping heads and four drills are standard in the machine. (Ekstrom, Carlson and Co.)

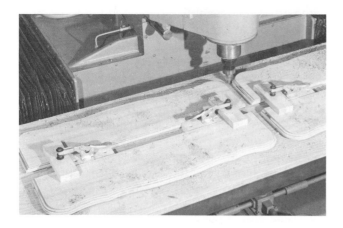

Fig. 18-50. Close-up view of workpieces on the table of a tape controlled router/shaper. Cutting cycle at each station requires 32 seconds, resulting in a production rate of 225 units an hour. (Ekstrom, Carlson and Co.)

Vinyl laminated particle board is widely used for low cost furniture and cabinetwork. V-fold construction of this material has resulted in high production rates. Basically, the fabrication process is simple. The laminated panel is notched with a 90 deg. groove down to the laminate but not through it. Glue is applied and the two pieces are folded together with the vinyl serving as a hinge. Most of the vinyl films applied to particle board have a simulated wood grain finish and are .007 in. (0.18 mm) thick.

Simple case construction, like a speaker cabinet, usually includes the forming of a finished edge. Fig. 18-52 shows a special cutterhead that can form the longitudinal grooves and surfaces required. After the cuts are made, the inside edges are coated with glue and folded together.

Fig. 18-53 shows a modern throughfeed molder with universal head and infeed straightening table. The operator's control panel is located at the infeed position. The machine is available with or without a sound enclosure as shown in the bottom photo.

## TEST YOUR KNOWLEDGE, Chapter 18

Please do not write in the text. Place your answers on a separate sheet of paper.

1. The bits of a portable router are held in a _____ type chuck.
2. Router sizes are given in:
   a. RPMs.
   b. Horsepower ratings.
   c. Router bit sizes.
   d. None of the above.

shoe, and tongue and groove flooring.

Modern woodworking plants use a tremendous variety of cutterheads. Many of them are carbide tipped or use throwaway inserts, Fig. 18-51. Noise reduction as well as smooth cutting and long life are all desirable characteristics of a good cutterhead.

Fig. 18-51. Cutterheads with carbide tipped throwaway inserts. These cutters are longer lasting and quieter than standard cutters. (Wisconsin Knife Works, Inc.)

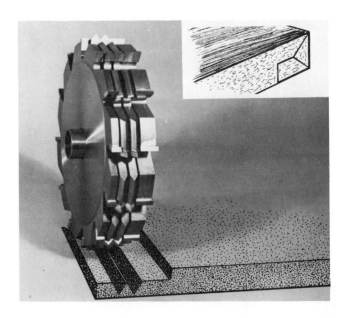

Fig. 18-52. Cutterhead produces segment that can be returned 180 deg. Inset shows how fold generates finished edge. (Herco, Inc.)

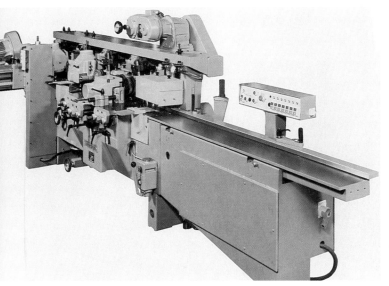

Fig. 18-53. Left. Throughfeed molder with universal head and infeed straightening table. This is a seven-head machine with three-position universal head. (Wadkin PLC) Right. This piece of equipment is a 10-spindle machine with nearly 40 spindle configurations available to meet a wide variety of requirements. (Michael Weinig, Inc.)

3. When cutting the outside edge of a circular piece, always feed the router in a _____ (clockwise, counterclockwise) direction.
4. Name the two types of metals from which router bits are made.
5. Why is a guide tip used when using a router with a template?
6. If a dovetail joint fits too tightly, should the depth of cut on the router bit be increased or decreased?
7. _____ _____ are designed for routing and profiling flat sheets of plywood and composition material.
8. The shaper can be used to:
    a. Cut rabbet joints.
    b. Cut moldings.
    c. Cut tongue and groove joints.
    d. All of the above.
9. Assembled cutters are recommended for work in the school shop because they are safer to use. True or False?
10. Solid wing cutters can be sharpened by honing the _____ (face, bevel).

11. When installing shaper cutters, what should be located directly under the nut?
    a. Collar.
    b. Cutter.
    c. Lock washer.
    d. None of the above.
12. _____ routers are ideal for mortising or cutting into the middle of a panel.
13. What has prevented small companies from using CNC equipment?

### ACTIVITIES

1. Prepare a visual aid by forming a milled-to-pattern knife out of wood. Demonstrate to the class how it is sharpened by sanding the bevel on a disk sander.
2. Visit a construction site or a local lumberyard and ask for small samples or waste cuttings of molding. Mount them on a panel with accurate and descriptive labels.

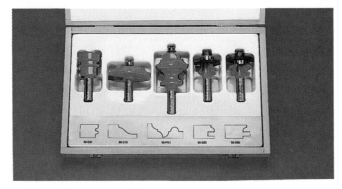

Left. Shaper collars. Right. Shaper cutters. (Freud, Inc.)

Sanding is an important operation in the production of any quality wood product. (Top. California Time/Westwood, Inc. Bottom. The Bartley Collection, Ltd.)

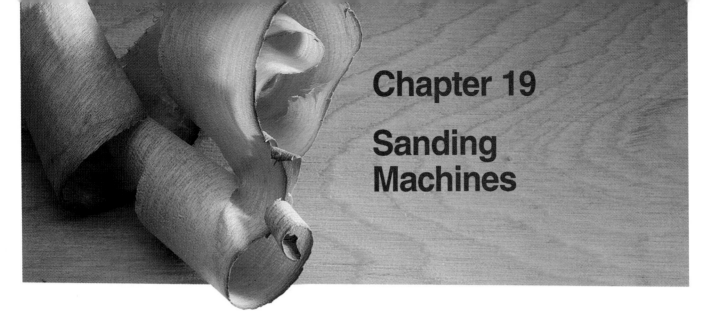

# Chapter 19
# Sanding Machines

There are many kinds and sizes of sanding machines, ranging from small portable tools to giant multi-belt machines weighing many tons.

Small stationary disk, belt, and drum sanders as well as various portable machines are practical for use in the school shop. Power sanders cut wood rapidly and create a great amount of dust. They should not be operated without proper and adequate connections to a central dust collection system or unit collectors.

## DISK SANDERS

Disk sanders, although not used extensively in production work, are a valuable tool in the pattern shop, small cabinet shop, and school shop. The stationary machine consists of a metal disk that carries the coated abrasive, and a table supporting the work. See Fig. 19-1. The table can be tilted at an angle and usually has a slot in which various guides can be used. The chief purpose of the stationary disk sander is to form and shape parts. The portable orbital sander, Fig. 19-2, is used mainly to prepare surfaces for finishing coats.

## SELECTING AND MOUNTING DISKS

Various grades of sanding disks are available, ranging from a No. 100 (smooth) to a No. 30 (coarse). For average work a No. 50 is satisfactory. Paperbacked sanding disks are used on stationary sanders, while portable sanders, with a flexible disk, require a cloth backing.

On sanders with a metal disk, the paper is held in place by a special nondrying adhesive. The old adhesive disk is peeled off and, if the surface of the metal disk is clean, the coating of adhesive can be reused. With the metal disk turning under power, run a stick of wood from the center to the outside edge to spread the adhesive evenly. Apply a coat of adhesive to the abrasive disk as shown in Fig. 19-3. Spread it thoroughly over the entire surface,

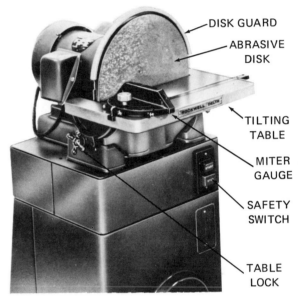

DISK GUARD
ABRASIVE DISK
TILTING TABLE
MITER GAUGE
SAFETY SWITCH
TABLE LOCK

Fig. 19-1. Disk diameter determines stationary disk sander size. (Delta International Machinery Corp.)

Fig. 19-2. Using a portable random orbit finishing disk sander to smooth a surface. (Porter-Cable Corporation)

Fig. 19-3. Applying adhesive to a sanding disk.

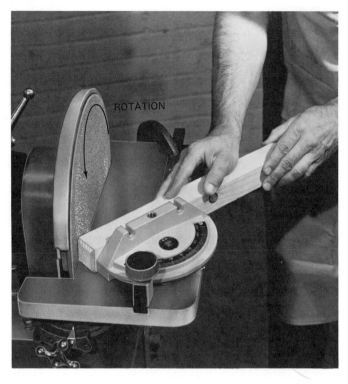

Fig. 19-5. Forming a chamfer with the workpiece held against the miter gauge.

then carefully mount the disk in position on the machine, and press it firmly in place. Be certain the edge of the abrasive disk is accurately aligned with the edge of the metal disk. On some machines it is best to remove the table for this operation.

## USING THE DISK SANDER

The disk sander is used mainly for edge sanding. Hold the work firmly on the table and move it lightly against the disk. USE ONLY THE HALF OF THE DISK THAT REVOLVES DOWNWARD PAST THE TABLE. Move the work along this surface. Do not hold it in one place or excessive heat will be generated, causing the abrasive to load with gum and pitch. This will shorten the life of the abrasive and also cause burn marks on your work.

Pieces of irregular shapes are usually guided freehand. For accurate work on straight edges, use a miter gauge placed in a table slot, as shown in Fig. 19-4. Other types of guides and auxiliary tables can be used for special work.

Fig. 19-5 shows a chamfer being sanded using a miter gauge. Fig. 19-6 shows a special fixture for sanding wooden disks.

If a large number of pieces are needed, it is better to have the auxiliary table slide in the machine table slot. Then various areas of the abrasive disk surface can be used.

A pattern sanding setup can be made by attaching a metal strip that extends above the edge of an auxiliary table, next to the surface of the disk. The pattern, which is slightly smaller than the finished part, rides along the metal strip and carries the work in about the same way as pattern shaping. Refer to Fig. 19-7.

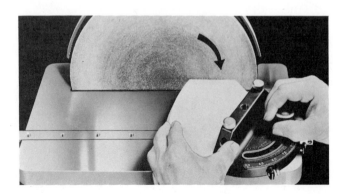

Fig. 19-4. Using the miter gauge in order to form an accurate, straight edge.

Fig. 19-6. Using a fixture to form disks of a specified size. The disk is held in place by a sharp pin in the dovetail slide.

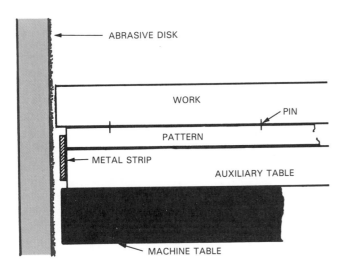

Fig. 19-7. Sanding duplicate parts. Items are limited to work with straight or convex edges.

To replace a belt, remove the end and side guard, retract the tension spring, and remove the belt. Select the new belt to be used. Note the travel direction arrow printed on the inside surface. Mount the belt so the travel arrow points in the correct direction, and adjust the tension. Roll the machine by hand to check the tracking of the belt. Replace the guards, turn on the machine, and readjust the tracking if necessary. Watch the tracking carefully for the first few minutes of operation.

Flat surfaces can be sanded by holding the work as shown in Fig. 19-9. Thin strips should be held against the belt with a wood pad, Fig. 19-10. When sanding long strips it is usually necessary to remove the end guard.

To sand small surfaces straight and true, use the table and miter gauge. A straightedge can be clamped to the table as shown in Fig. 19-11.

## BELT SANDERS

Fig. 19-8 shows a type of belt sander often used in the school shop. The belt runs over two drums, or PULLEYS, and rides on a platen. One drum is powered. The other can be adjusted so the belt will track in the center of the platen. The sander can be positioned vertically (as shown), horizontally, or at angles in between. Cloth belts are used. Grit sizes may range from No. 120 to No. 24 (coarse).

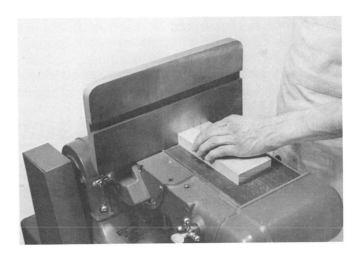

Fig. 19-9. Sanding a flat surface. Belt travel is toward the table which serves as a stop.

Fig. 19-8. Stationary belt sander. Sanding unit can also be turned to a horizontal position and other angles. Belt is 6 in. (152.5 mm) wide. (Powermatic)

Fig. 19-10. Sanding thin stock.

Fig. 19-11. Producing a square surface with the aid of the sander table and a straightedge.

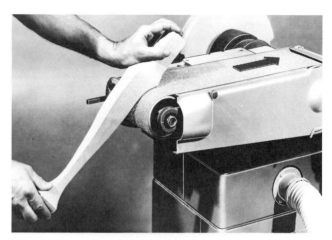

Fig. 19-13. Sanding a cabriole table leg on the idler drum. Belt rotation is in direction of arrow. Always replace the belt guard after this operation.

Curved edges are accurately sanded by using a shop-built fence, Fig. 19-12. Inside or concave curves may be sanded on the idler pulley or drum. The guard is removed and the work is held as shown in Fig. 19-13. Bevels may be sanded using the table tilted to the proper angle, Fig. 19-14. Irregular curves and small radii may be smoothed on a narrow belt sander, Fig. 19-15.

Dust control is an important factor when operating sanding machines. A UNIT (self-contained) COLLECTOR is shown in Fig. 19-16. Air is filtered through folds of special fabric.

## SANDING MACHINES SAFETY

Observe the following safety rules, in addition to those given in Chapter 3.

1. Be certain the belt or disk is correctly mounted. The belt must track in the center of the drums and platen. Do not operate the disk sander if the abrasive paper is loose.
2. Check the guards and table adjustments to see that they are in the correct position and securely locked in place.
3. Whenever possible, use the table, fence, and other guides to control the position of the work.
4. Small and irregularly shaped pieces should be held in a hand clamp, special jig, or fixture.

Fig. 19-12. Using a shop-built fence.

Fig. 19-14. Bevels and miters on an edge or end of a piece of stock can be sanded using the sanding table. (Delta International Machinery Corp.)

Fig. 19-15. The narrow belt on this disk and belt sander may be used to smooth curved surfaces. (Foley-Belsaw Co.)

5. When sanding the end grain of narrow pieces on the belt sander, always support the work against the table.
6. Sand only on the side of the disk sander that is moving down toward the table. Move the work along this surface so it will not burn.
7. Always use a pad or push block when sanding thin pieces on the belt sander.
8. Do not use power sanders to form and shape parts if the operations could be better performed on other machines.
9. Sand only clean, new wood. Do not sand work that has excess glue or finish on the surface. These materials will load and foul the abrasive.

Fig. 19-16. Combination disk and belt sander attached to a dust collector. (Delta International Machinery Corp.)

## PORTABLE BELT SANDERS

The portable belt sander is designed to sand flat surfaces. It consists of two pulleys that carry the belt over a shoe. The rear pulley is rubber covered and powered. Fig. 19-17 shows a standard model equipped with a dust collector.

The size of portable belt sanders is determined by the width of the belt. They usually range from 2 to 4 in. The length of belts vary with different makes and models. Belts are made of cloth and coated with various grades of aluminum oxide. For average work in the school shop a No. 60 or No. 50 grade is most often used.

To install or replace a belt on a portable sander, do the following.

1. Unplug the electrical cord, clean off the excess dust and lay the machine on its left side.
2. Retract the idler (forward) pulley. Different makes and models will vary in design so check the operator's manual for detailed directions.
3. Place the correct size of belt on the pulleys with the arrow (printed on the inside) pointing in the direction of travel.
4. Release the idler pulley so that correct tension is applied to the belt.
5. Support the sander on the heel of its base, turn on the switch, and turn the tracking adjustment so the belt travels in the center of the pulleys. Refer to Fig. 19-18. This adjustment may need to be corrected during the sanding operation. Never allow the belt to ride against the body of the sander.

Fig. 19-18.  The tracking adjustments knob is on the side near the front pulley.    (Makita U.S.A., Inc.)

## USING A PORTABLE BELT SANDER

Stock to be sanded should be firmly supported and held in position. The stock can be clamped in a vise or held by a stop mounted at the rear end of the work.

Be certain the switch is in the off position before plugging in the electric cord. Like all portable power tools, the sander should be properly grounded. Turn on the switch and check the travel of the belt to see that it is tracking properly.

Hold the sander off the work, then lower it carefully and evenly onto the surface. Move the sander forward and backward over the surface. At the end of each stroke, shift it sideways about one-half the width of the belt, Fig. 19-19.

Fig. 19-17. Main parts of a 3 in. (76 mm) portable belt sander. Notice the dust collector. It keeps work areas clean and catches dangerous wood and dust particles. (Robert Bosch Power Tool Corp.)

Fig. 19-19. Using belt sander. Note the direction of the sanding operation (arrow).

Continue over the entire surface, holding the sander perfectly level and sanding each area the same amount. Do not press down on the sander since its weight is sufficient to provide the proper pressure for the cutting action. If the sander is allowed to rock back on the rear pulley, the work will be damaged. When you complete the work, raise the machine from the surface and then stop the motor.

The portable belt sander can save sanding time, but a great deal of skill is required to operate it properly. See Fig. 19-20.

*Applying excessive pressure to the belt sander will cause the motor to heat and the belt to load and foul. Always lift the sander off of the work before starting or stopping the motor.*

Portable sanders are built with compact mechanisms that usually require special lubricants and extra attention to oiling schedules. Study and follow the recommendations given in the operator's manual. Always clean the sander and empty the dust bag before putting the sander away.

## PORTABLE FINISHING SANDERS

Finishing sanders are used for final sanding where only a small amount of material needs to be removed. They are also used for cutting down and rubbing finishing coats. There are two general types: orbital and oscillating. In the ORBITAL type, Fig. 19-21, the pad moves in a circular path about 3/16 or 1/4 in. wide, while the pad of the OSCILLATING sander moves back and forth in a straight line. The orbital type cuts faster and is used for general work. The oscillating type is best for fine

Fig. 19-21. An orbital sander used for finish sanding. (Black & Decker)

work, especially for rubbing down finishes.

Standard abrasive papers are attached to the sander pad with a clamp at the front and back edge. Many have pads that are sized so that one-third of a standard 9 x 11 in. sheet can be used. Grades and types of abrasive papers are selected with about the same considerations as for hand sanding. Be certain the paper is stretched tightly over the surface of the pad.

Start the sander while it is off the work, then move it back and forth with the grain in the same manner as the belt sander. It can be guided with either one or both hands; however, extra pressure beyond the weight of the sander should not be applied. Excessive pressure will slow down the motor, causing it to heat, and reduce the efficiency of the machine.

When you have finished working with the sander, clean it thoroughly before putting it away. Study the operator's manual for instructions on proper lubrication and adjustments.

Finishing sanders are often operated using compressed air, Fig. 19-22. The small oscillating air driven mechanism is lightweight and has no tendency to heat.

Fig. 19-20. Using a portable belt sander to polish a lacquer finish. Operation requires nylon fabric belt, special abrasive, and a skilled woodworker. (Black & Decker)

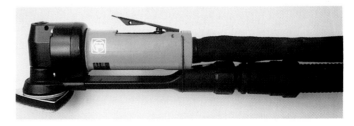

Fig. 19-22. This detail sander is operated with compressed air. An optional dust extraction unit is shown. (Fein Power Tools, Inc.)

## RANDOM-ORBIT SANDERS

A random-orbit sander's combination of rotation and random orbits allows you to remove large amounts of material while leaving the work surface fairly free of scratches and ready for final sanding, Fig. 19-23. Compared to standard orbital sanders, the random-orbit machines sand more aggressively and their paper stays clean longer. When you need to quickly sand narrow or curved surfaces, cabinet face frames or door frames, or sand off an old coat of paint, the random-orbit sander is a good choice.

The mechanism that provides the random-orbit motion is in the tool's drive system. A shaft rotates a counterweighted disk carrying an off-center thrust bearing.

The sanding disk may be attached to the backing disk one of two ways—pressure-sensitive adhesive (PSA) or hook-and-loops. Choose the type needed for your model of sander.

Random-orbit sanders are made in two basic designs—the right-angle and the in-line types, Fig. 19-24. The right-angle type is similar to right-angle grinders used in auto body work. Power is transmitted to the sanding disk through a set of bevel gears. In-line sanders have their motors mounted directly above the sanding disk with a gearless direct drive. In-line sanders are much quieter than the right-angle type.

Since sanders create a large amount of dust, dust collection may be needed. Some models incorporate a form of dust collection. (See Fig. 19-24 bottom.) One method uses a standard pattern of holes in the sanding disks that enables a vacuum created by the sander's fan or separate shop vacuum to pull sanding dust through the disk.

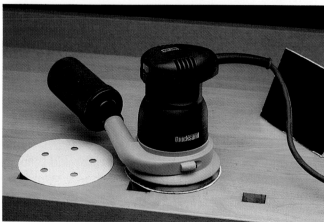

Fig. 19-24. Top. An example of a right-angle random orbit sander. (Porter-Cable) Bottom. An example of an in-line random orbit sander. (Woodcraft Supply Corporation)

## DETAIL SANDERS

A recent development in the area of sanding tools is the detail or corner sander, Fig. 19-25. Several manufacturers have developed these sanders for small spaces. The typical detail sander has a small triangular sanding pad that will reach into corners or other tight spaces. The sandpaper is easily attached and removed because hook-and-loops are used instead of pressure-sensitive adhesives.

### INDUSTRIAL MACHINES

The HAND STROKE BELT SANDER consists of a long belt that travels around two pulleys. A table, mounted on roller slides, is located under the belt. It can be moved in and out. The space between the belt and the table can be adjusted.

In operation, the workpiece is placed on the table and the space between it and the belt is adjusted to about one inch. Stops, set on the table, keep the workpiece in place. The moving belt is pressed against the surface of the stock with a block, Fig.

Fig. 19-23. A random orbit sander being used to perform finish sanding. (Porter-Cable)

Fig. 19-25. Left. This detail sander can reach small spaces that traditional sanders cannot. (Fein Power Tools, Inc.) Right. Using a detail sander with a two-sided sanding pad. (Fein Power Tools, Inc.)

Fig. 19-27. Heavy-duty belt sander with rubber faced drums. Notice that the abrasive belt is facing in, toward the drums. (Oliver Machinery Co.)

19-26. The block is moved along the entire length of the workpiece and then the table is repositioned (in or out) for the next stroke.

Some hand stroke belt sanders are designed so the abrasive side of the belt rides on the surface of the drums, Fig. 19-27. The belt return is located under the table. The result is less interference with the sanding operation.

Fig. 19-28 shows a close-up view of a sanding operation on this type of machine. Another close-up view, Fig. 19-29, shows the finish sanding of a shaped edge. For this kind of operation, a special flexible belt made of denim cloth must be used. Handblocks formed to match a certain shape are used to press the moving belt against the workpiece.

Fig. 19-28. Finish sanding with a hand stroke belt sander. Belt is No. 150 aluminum oxide abrasive on an E weight paper backing. (Norton Co.)

Fig. 19-26. Using a hand stroke belt sander to smooth a panel. Belt is 6 in. (152.5 mm) wide.

Fig. 19-29. Using a flexible belt and a contoured handblock to sand a shaped edge.

BRUSH BACKED SANDING WHEELS are used to smooth and polish irregular shapes, like the saw handle shown in Fig. 19-30. Strips of coated abrasives, located around the perimeter of a wheel, are backed with stiff bristled brushes. These bristles press the abrasive paper against the curved surfaces of the workpiece. Rolls of the abrasive are stored in the wheel. They can be quickly pulled out to replace worn strips.

RADIAL FLAP WHEELS (also called polishing wheels) are an assembly of coated abrasive strips attached to a center core. Each side of the core is fitted with a metal flange, Fig. 19-31. The wheels can be mounted on various machine shafts and arbors to sand flat or contoured surfaces. The strips of abrasive are usually J-weight cloth coated with garnet or aluminum oxide.

SLOTTED EDGE WHEELS can be used for a variety of special sanding operations, Fig. 19-32. Edges of a special blank of abrasive paper are tucked in a slot located on each side of the wheel. They are then clamped in place with a metal flange.

SPOOL SANDERS are often employed to smooth small, intricate edges and contours, Fig. 19-33. A special garnet cloth belt rides on the flat surfaces of idler pulleys. It flexes to match the contour of a drive pulley (called the spool).

SPINDLE SANDERS have a vertical drum that projects through a horizontal table. The drum revolves and also moves up and down (oscillates). The table can be tilted for working on angles. This type of sander is especially valuable in making wood patterns for metal casting, Fig. 19-34.

SANDING DRUMS are used to smooth curved

Fig. 19-30. Using a brush backed sanding wheel to smooth irregular curves.    (Merit Products, Inc.)

Fig. 19-32. Using a slotted edge wheel to sand flutes in a turned leg.

Fig. 19-31. Radial flap wheels. Sanding is done with the tips of the segments which bend slightly when workpiece is pressed against them. Recommended peripheral speed is about 3000 fmp (915 mpm). (3M Co.)

Fig. 19-33. In the spool sander a special abrasive belt runs between powered spool and overhead idler drum (not shown in view.)    (Norton Co.)

Fig. 19-34. This oscillating single spindle sander has a table with tilting capabilities. (Enlon Import Corp.)

Fig. 19-35. This two-spindle drum sander can be used to sand curved pieces. (Ekstrom, Carlson and Co.)

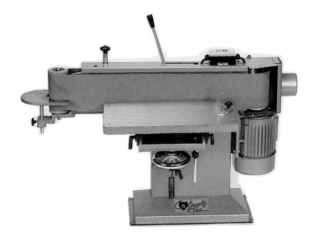

Fig. 19-36. A 6'' x 30'' edge sander. The sanding belt is mounted on two vertical drums; one a drive, the other an idler. The belt runs in a vertical plane while the workpiece is supported on a horizontal table during sanding. Edge belt sanders are used primarily to sand the edges of rectangular stock. (Grizzly Imports, Inc.)

pieces, Fig. 19-35. Abrasive cloth in the form of tubes is slipped over rubber drums which are then inflated. The pressure can be varied to provide the proper cushion for specific workpieces.

EDGE BELT SANDERS use a long belt carried in a horizontal position. The drums and platen of this type of machine oscillate up and down at a rate of about 130 cycles per minute. The side and end tables adjust vertically and can also be tilted. Straight edges and bevels are sanded on the side of the machine, Fig. 19-36. Curved edges can be worked against the idler pulley or drum.

The AUTOMATIC STROKE SANDER is similar to the hand stroke sander already described. In this machine, a stroking mechanism is used to carry the pressure block along the belt. Pressure and length of stroke is controlled by the operator, Fig. 19-37. The feed-through automatic stroke sander, shown in Fig. 19-38, has a conveyorized table that carries the work slowly through the machine as the belt is automatically stroked against the surface.

WIDE BELT SANDERS are high production machines used to sand plywood, particle board, and other kinds of panels or flat assemblies, Fig. 19-39.

Fig. 19-40 shows a wide belt sander being used to sand core stock for flush doors. Both the top and bottom surfaces are being smoothed in a single pass. In the diagram, Fig. 19-41, note the platen included in the top assembly of drums. The use of platens to press the abrasive belt against the surface of the work usually improves accuracy and

Fig. 19-37. Automatic stroke sander in operation.

Fig. 19-38. Feed-through automatic stroke sander. Workpieces are placed on the conveyorized table and carried slowly under the belt. (Mersman Bros.)

Fig. 19-40. The belts on this sanding unit are 20 ft. (6.1 m) long. Feed rates are adjustable up to 150 fpm (46 mpm). (Algoma Hardwoods, Inc.)

Fig. 19-39. A modern wide belt sander. (Sunhill Machinery)

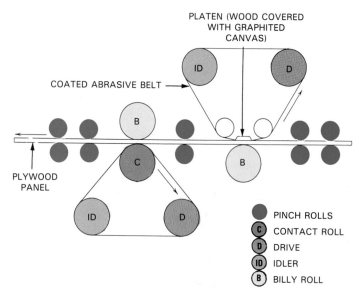

Fig. 19-41. Plywood panels proceed through the wide belt sander in this manner. (Norton Co.)

quality of finish.

Wide belt sanders are intended for high production. The plywood industry has replaced most of the older multi-drum units with this type of machine. Some have belts up to 72 in. wide, that travel at speeds up to 5000 fpm (1 524 mpm). Panels coming from the machine have a high quality finish. Thickness is controlled to within a few thousandths of an inch.

The shaper/sander shown in Fig. 19-42 replaces traditional two-step, raised panel production with one efficient, economical automatic machine operation. In a single pass, this machine shapes and sands one edge of a presized panel, and automatically returns the panel to the operator. The operator refeeds the panel until all four edges have been finished with the same profile.

Fig. 19-42. This machine shapes and sands one edge of a presized panel and automatically returns the panel to the operator for the next operation.
(Jenkins, Div. of Kohler General, Inc.)

## TEST YOUR KNOWLEDGE, Chapter 19

Please do not write in the text. Place your answers on a separate sheet of paper.
1. What is the main purpose of a stationary disk sander? What is the main purpose of a portable disk sander?
2. Explain the process for placing adhesive on a sander that has a metal disk.
3. When using the stationary disk sander, use only the half of the disk that revolves _____ past the table.
4. To track the belt on a sander, the _____ (idler pulley, powered drum) is adjusted.
5. What determines the size of a portable belt sander?
6. Explain briefly the proper stroking procedure when using the portable belt sander.

7. There are two types of finishing sanders. The _____ type moves back and forth in a straight line, while the _____ type moves in a circular path.
8. You should use the same grades of abrasive paper for a finishing sander as for hand sanding. True or False?
9. The hand stroke belt sander is adjusted so the belt runs about:
   a. 1 in. above the work.
   b. Even with the work.
   c. 1 1/2 in. above the work.
   d. None of the above.
10. Name and describe two industrial sanders. For what are they used?
11. What are the two advantages of a random-orbit sander?
12. What are the two basic types of random-orbit sanders?

## ACTIVITIES

1. Select a power sander that would be practical for a home workshop. List the factors you considered in making your choice. Prepare complete specifications for the machine and include cost figures.
2. Design a mounting or holder that would convert a portable belt sander into an edge sander. Try to include some of the features of the industrial machine described in this unit. Prepare working drawings of your design.
3. Design a small (2 in. or less in diameter) flap wheel that could be mounted in the chuck of the drill press. Develop a practical method for attaching the cloth or paper flaps to the hub. Prepare the necessary design sketches to clearly present your ideas.
4. Develop working drawings of a fixture that could be mounted on a stationary belt sander to finish long, thin, narrow strips. Use feather boards to apply pressure and some type of fence to guide the work. Include special guards to protect the worker.

These beautiful examples of woodworking art demonstrate outstanding work quality, good design, and careful attention to every detail. Excellence in work quality is a worthy goal. (Eldon Rebhorn)

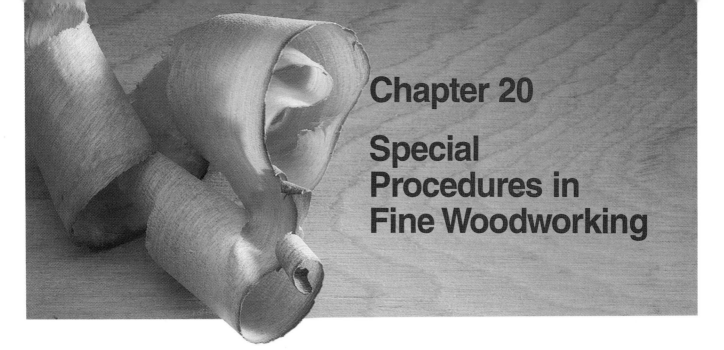

# Chapter 20

# Special Procedures in Fine Woodworking

The more experienced woodworker often selects projects using procedures and techniques that go well beyond those presented thus far. For example, the use of reeding and fluting to emphasize the shape or design of a table leg, or the application of marquetry to enhance a surface, frequently requires skills and techniques not covered in a typical woodworking course.

This unit will cover some of the special procedures used by advanced woodworkers to produce unique and creative pieces. Topics included are: reeding and fluting, carving, decorative joints, marquetry, decorative moldings, and tambours.

## REEDING AND FLUTING

Reeding and fluting are forms of surface decoration generally used on legs, posts, friezes, and panels. Reeding, or BEADING as it is sometimes called, consists of two or more reeds (convex shapes) which are cut close together and form parallel lines, Fig. 20-1. Reeds may be tapered, but the usual procedure is to make them parallel to each other. They may be either raised above the overall surface or cut flush with the surface.

Fluting is the reverse of reeding, Fig. 20-2. Here a series of concave shapes are formed in parallel lines. Fig. 20-3 shows a fine table and chair that use fluting for decoration.

Reeds and flutes may be made on flat or cylindrical surfaces using a router or simple hand tools. A router is faster and generally more accurate than hand tools.

## WORKING ON FLAT STOCK

One procedure for making reeds and flutes on flat stock is presented below.

1. Select a router with a reeding or fluting bit of the size required for the particular job. Plan to use either a straightedge or attachment to guide the router in a straight line.
2. Adjust the router bit to the proper depth and make a trial cut on a piece of scrap board. The usual depth of a reed or flute is between 1/8 and 1/4 in.

Fig. 20-1. Reeding a surface or edge may be accomplished with a reeding tool.   (Veritas Tools, Inc.)

Fig. 20-2. Fluted surface.

Fig. 20-3. Fluting has been used for decoration on this hand-crafted table and chair.
(Richard Scott Newman, Courtesy, Pritam and Eames)

3. Mark where the cuts are to be made on the workpiece. Use stop blocks to be sure that all cuts are exactly the same length.
4. Adjust the straightedge or guide to produce a cut in the proper location. Again, test on a piece of scrap.
5. Cut each reed or flute as planned, following procedures previously presented for the router.

## WORKING ON CYLINDRICAL STOCK

Cutting reeds and flutes on cylindrical pieces may be done on the lathe using an indexing head and router, or using custom-made fluting jigs and a router or shaper.

The procedure for reeding and fluting cylindrical pieces is the same whether done on the lathe or done using a fluting jig and router.

1. Divide the circumference of the workpiece by the number (usually six or eight) of flutes or reeds to be cut. For this, use the dividing head on the lathe, or make a plate with the desired number of stops for the custom jig. Fig. 20-4 shows one basic design for the jig which may be indexed to hold the workpiece at each desired position.
2. Build a cradle for the router. This should be securely attached to the lathe bed to produce straight and accurate cuts. See Fig. 20-5 for one type of cradle design.

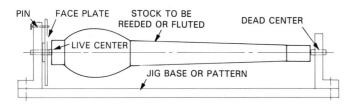

Fig. 20-4. An indexing jig for routing flutes or reeds on a turned part.

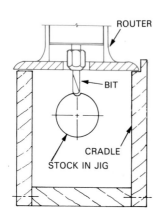

Fig. 20-5. Cradle design for routing flutes and reeds on the lathe.

3. Place a fluting or reeding bit in the router. Adjust the depth of cut with the router on the cradle, AFTER it has been secured to the lathe bed with clamps.
4. Make one cut of the proper length by sliding the router along the cradle. Release the pin on the indexing device (lathe or jig) and rotate the work piece to the next position for the second cut.
5. Lock the spindle in place by pushing the index pin into the appropriate face plate hole. Make the second cut. Repeat this procedure until all cuts are completed.

## USING THE SHAPER

Cutting reeds and flutes on a shaper will require a jig similar to the one described in Fig. 20-4, except that the base of the jig will be used as a pattern for the cut.

1. Cut the front edge of the base to the same contour as the workpiece. Be sure to calculate the proper distance from the spindle collar to the edge of the shaper cutter, so the depth of cut will be correct. Fig. 20-6 shows a typical setup. Adjust the height of the cutter to the midpoint of the workpiece.
2. Put the workpiece in the jig and lay out the number and length of flutes or reeds that need to be cut. Lock the indexing head in place for the first cut.
3. After the setup has been checked, the first cut may be made by moving the jig past the cutter, using the base as the pattern. Blocks may be clamped to the shaper table to insure the proper length of cut.
4. Rotate the work to the next indexing hole and secure the faceplate with the index pin. Make the next cut using the same procedure used for the first cut.

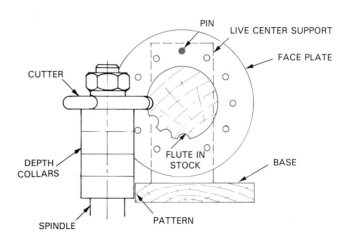

Fig. 20-6. Setup for cutting flutes and reeds on the shaper. Note the indexing plate with the desired number of stops.

5. Proceed with each cut until all reeds or flutes are completed.

Tapered cylindrical parts may also be fluted or reeded by following either of the procedures just outlined. The tailstock is set over as done when turning a taper on the lathe without a taper attachment.

## WOOD CARVING

Carving has long been an integral part of fine furniture making. It is an excellent technique for adding decoration, as well as function, to a project, as shown in Fig. 20-7.

Two basic types of carving that have the most application in general woodworking are CHIP CARVING and RELIEF CARVING. The basic techniques used in each type will be presented to encourage the serious woodworkers to incorporate carving into their work.

## CHIP CARVING

Chip carving is one of the oldest and simplest forms of decorative woodcarving. It is essentially the formation of complex geometric patterns from many small triangular incisions, Fig. 20-8.

To begin chip carving, you will need a straight-edged knife sharpened to a fine point. A skew-ground knife and a knife with an offset blade are also useful, but not necessary. Blades must be kept razor sharp since work appearance will depend on neat, crisp, clean lines. In addition, it is easier to control a sharp knife than a dull knife.

On paper, draw the pattern you wish to carve. Transfer the pattern to your workpiece using carbon paper, or by gluing the pattern directly to the wood using rubber cement. The pattern may also be drawn directly on the wood using a small straightedge. Do not make the lines any heavier than necessary, as they will be difficult to remove from

Fig. 20-7. Relief carving has been used on this American Georgian style highboy to enhance the design. (Drexel Heritage Furnishings, Inc.)

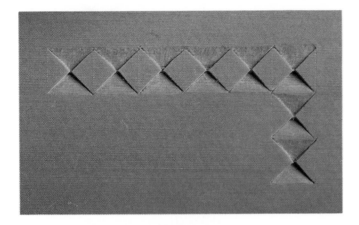

Fig. 20-8. Example of chip carving used to make a simple design.

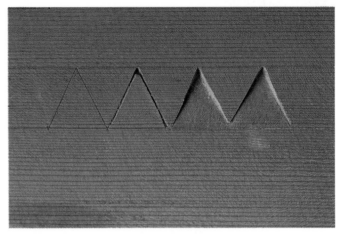

Fig. 20-10. Procedure for triangular chip carving. Left to right—draw the design; stab out shallow stop cuts; slice out the triangular chips; smooth sides and bottom.

the high points of the design.

Most traditional designs are made up from variations of two kinds of triangular chips. One kind of chip is made with three knife cuts while the other uses six cuts, Fig. 20-9. Many repetitions of the chips are used to produce the design.

The triangular chip (three cuts) is called the DREISCHNITT by German and Swiss carvers. It is used mainly for border designs. Begin this chip by stabbing out shallow stop cuts on two sides of each triangle, Fig. 20-10. Either the skew-ground knife or the straight-edged knife may be used. Firmly press the point of the knife into the APEX (the deepest part of the triangle) then vertically incise each wall. The cuts should slope up to the surface of the wood at the end of the line. Using the straight-edged knife, slice out the triangular chip of wood between the stop cuts. Designs are created by arranging these chips in various ways.

The six-cut chip is essentially three Dreischnitt cuts combined to form one large triangle, Fig. 20-11. Place the knife point in the center of the triangle and make a stop cut to each of its vertices. Slice out the three chips. The result will be a triangular carving with three sloping sides meeting at the center.

All chips should be relatively shallow; the deepest portion should be no deeper than 1/8 to 1/4 in. Keep both hands on the knife. This will allow better control and reduce the likelihood of getting cut.

Most any moderately soft, even-grained wood is good for carving. Examples include butternut, pine, bass, walnut, cherry, and red cedar. The grain of oak is generally too coarse to allow satisfactory chip carving.

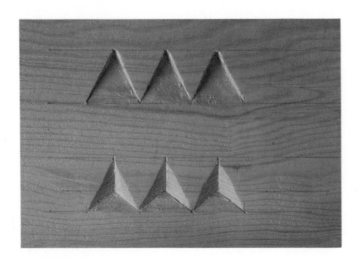

Fig. 20-9. The triangular chip (top) uses three cuts. The six-cut chip is essentially three triangles combined to form one large triangle (bottom).

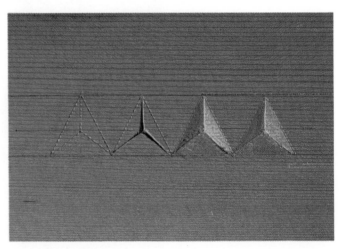

Fig. 20-11. Procedure for six-cut chip carving. Left to right—draw the design; stab out stop cuts to the center of the triangle; slice out three chips to produce a triangular carving; smooth sides and bottom.

## RELIEF CARVING

Relief carving is a method of creating a raised design. It appears to stand apart from the background, thus making it more prominent. Relief carving has been used for centuries to decorate furniture and architectural features of buildings, Fig. 20-12. Even though machine-made carvings are abundant, skilled woodworkers still take great pride in producing beautiful relief carvings.

Carving tools such as the V-tool, straight gouge, long bent grounder, spoon gouge, and flat or firmer gouge are generally used for relief carving, Fig. 20-13. The V-tool is used for outlining. Gouges are used for general shaping, and the long bent grounder for backgrounds. Tools should always be kept very sharp to cut cleanly and smoothly.

The first step in relief carving is to decide on an appropriate design. Once the design is selected, the proper scale must be determined. Because it is part of a larger whole, the size of a relief carving is very important. The design is then drawn on paper or on the wood itself, Fig. 20-14. If drawn on paper, transfer the pattern to the workpiece using carbon paper. Carefully think out each step of the carving, to produce the desired result.

After the design has been drawn to scale on the workpiece, carving can begin. First, cut around the design with the V-tool. This is called OUTLINING, Fig. 20-15. Outlining isolates the raised portion of

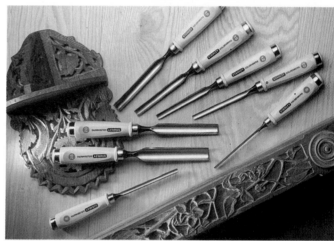

Fig. 20-13. Top. Carving tools commonly used for relief carving. Bottom. Gouges are used for general shaping. (Stanley Tools)

Fig. 20-12. These clock case panels, carved in relief, provide a decorative touch. (California Time/Westwood, Inc.)

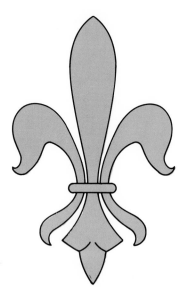

Fig. 20-14. A design for relief carving. It can be transferred to wood using carbon paper.

Fig. 20-15. Outlining a design with the V-tool.

down with a small flat firmer or gouge with a sweep similar to the curve of the design. This is called SETTING-IN the design, Fig. 20-16.

Once the outline is clearly defined, the background areas are taken down. This may be done with a router or by hand. When removing the background by hand, use a gouge or firmer and mallet, Fig. 20-17. Make a series of parallel cuts, generally across grain. After the background has

Fig. 20-16. Setting-in the design, using a gouge.

Fig. 20-17. Taking down the background with a bent firmer.

the design from the background. Make the cut 1/8 to 1/4 in. outside the design. Keep away from small details. If the grain splinters, try cutting from a different direction.

Once the design is outlined, use a gouge with medium sweep to make a series of cuts extending from the area outside the design toward the outline cut. The area made by these cuts will allow enough clearance to trim up the edges of the design. The walls of the design are made vertically. Cut straight

been roughed out, level and smooth using a regular or bent gouge.

Modeling can begin once the background has been leveled and smoothed. First make a rough outline of the design contours. Generally, this is done best with cuts that round off sharp angles from the top downward. Use a flat firmer for rounding outside curves. Use a gouge for inside curves. The lines that form valleys between elements of the design may be cut to depth with the V-tools and then rounded. Fig. 20-18 shows a portion of the design with the rough cuts completed.

Finish cuts are done using long, smooth cuts. Use both hands to steady the tool. Follow the curves of the design and direction of the grain, so that cuts will be smooth. Most fine carving shows slight tool marks and is not sanded. Light sanding, however, may be desirable in some instances. Fig. 20-19 shows the completed design.

## DECORATIVE JOINTS

Wood joints are a very important part of most woodworking projects. They hold the various parts together, provide strength and rigidity to the structure, and in some instances, contribute to the appearance of the finished product, Fig. 20-20.

## LAMINATED FINGER JOINT

While a common finger joint is both functional and interesting, it draws most attention to the corner

Fig. 20-19. The completed design still shows some tool marks.

Fig. 20-18. Modeling the design. A flat firmer is used on outside curves. A gouge is used on inside curves.

Fig. 20-20. This beautiful chest displays excellent work quality in its decorative joints.
(Richard Scott Newman, Courtesy, Pritam and Eames)

of the object rather than to the piece as a whole. A laminated finger joint, however, relates the joint to the total form, Fig. 20-21.

The following procedure is used for making the laminated finger joint.

1. Laminate a strip of veneer to the face of a wide board. This strip will form the stripe in the finished panel. The thickness of the board plus the veneer will determine the width of the fingers in the joint.

2. When the glue is dry, rip the board into strips equal to the thickness planned for each panel. Also rip a series of pieces to the same width from a similar board that does not have a veneered surface, Fig. 20-22.

3. Cut the pieces to proper length. The shorter boards will be equal in length to the inside dimensions of the box. They should be kept separate from the non-veneered board.

4. When all the pieces have been cut to length, a simple fixture can be used to maintain the staggered formation at the ends while gluing up each panel, Fig. 20-23.

5. When the glue has cured, the panels may be surfaced without affecting the joint.

6. Assemble the panels together to make the completed laminated finger joint.

## OUTLINED DOVETAIL JOINT

Because of their strength, dovetail joints have long been a favorite among skilled cabinetmakers. Generally, however, the joints are hidden from view in the completed piece, Fig. 20-24. But the OUT-LINED dovetail is designed to be very visible and decorative.

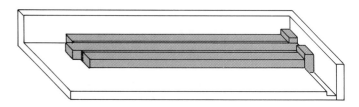

Fig. 20-23. Fixture for gluing up each panel in a laminated finger joint project.

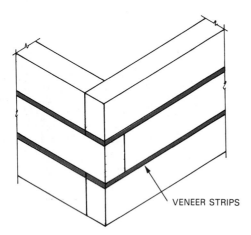

Fig. 20-21. Laminated finger joints are made by gluing veneers of contrasting colors between strips of lighter colored wood.

VENEER STRIPS

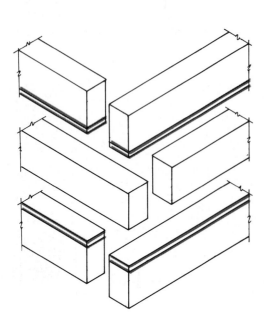

Fig. 20-22. Assembly of pieces found in a laminated finger joint.

Fig. 20-24. The dovetail joints in the cabinet are hidden from view, except when the drawers are open.
(James Krenov, Courtesy, Pritam and Eames)

The following procedure is one method of making outlined dovetail joints using a veneer of contrasting color.

1. Prepare the pieces as a typical dovetail joint would be prepared, but cut a shallow rabbet on the inside face of the mating pieces. Glue in strips of veneer on these pieces. Scrape or sand if needed. See Fig. 20-25 for rabbet and veneer location.
2. When the glue is dry, lay out and cut the dovetail in typical fashion. The veneer inlay will outline the base of the pins and tails.
3. Assemble the joint with glue and let it cure.
4. Use a saw which cuts a kerf just wide enough to receive a piece of veneer. This veneer is similar to that used for other parts of the joint. Cut along the glue line where the pins and tails come together. Refer again to Fig. 20-25.
5. Cut inlays from the veneer. Insert one in each of the saw kerfs with glue. When the glue is dry, trim and sand. This decorative joint requires more work than a plain dovetail, but is well worth the effort. Fig. 20-26 shows the completed joint.

## DOVETAIL PIN JOINT

The dovetail pin joint has several functions. It can be used with a miter joint, butt joint, or finger joint. The procedure explained will use the miter joint with dovetail pins. This joint is very decorative when used with contrasting color pins.

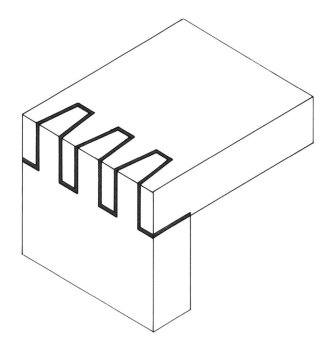

Fig. 20-26. Completed outlined dovetail joint.

1. Prepare the pieces as for a typical miter joint. Glue the assembly together.
2. Use the router with dovetail cutter to cut dovetail slots. The slots should be equally spaced along both faces of the mitered corner. The length of the cut should be consistent with the proportions of the surface, Fig. 20-27.
3. Make the pins by routing or sawing to proper size. Round the end of each pin on the disk sander.
4. Insert the pins in the dovetail slots with glue. When the glue is dry, scrape and sand the surface smooth.

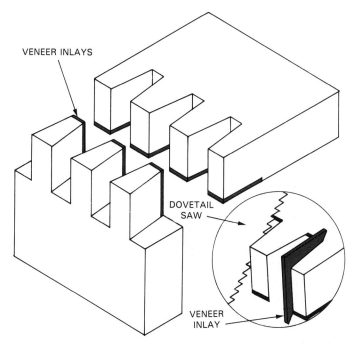

Fig. 20-25. Detail of outlined dovetail joint shows the location of veneer. Inset shows the method of cutting the kerf for veneer inlay between pins and tails.

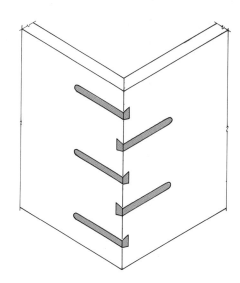

Fig. 20-27. Dovetail pin joint. Notice the consistent spacing of the pins.

## CURVED SLOT MORTISE-AND-TENON JOINT

Several types of mortise-and-tenon joints are used in cabinet and furniture construction. These joints are used to join rails and stiles, legs and rails of tables, and frame and panel construction. A well made mortise-and-tenon joint is one of the strongest wood joints.

Decorative curve slot mortise-and-tenon joints are made using a router and custom jig. This type of joint retains the strength of other mortise-and-tenon joints and is especially attractive.

To make the curved slot mortise-and-tenon joint, use the following procedure.

1. Cut the pieces to be joined to length as for a typical open mortise-and-tenon joint.
2. Cut the open mortise on the stile to the full depth, Fig. 20-28. Cut the rail on the back side (tenon cheek) typical fashion. Do not remove any material from the front face.
3. Cut a curve along the front side of the mortise with the router in a shop built jig. Build a jig that allows you to cut the desired curve on the rail and stile, Fig. 20-29.
4. Insert the rails and stiles into the jig and route the front curved shoulders to finished size.
5. The joint is assembled using glue. When the glue is dry, sand until smooth, Fig. 20-30.

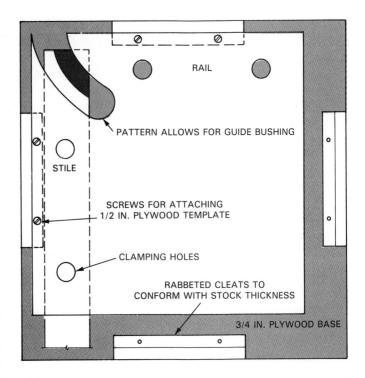

Fig. 20-29. This custom built jig cuts desired curves on the rail and stile.

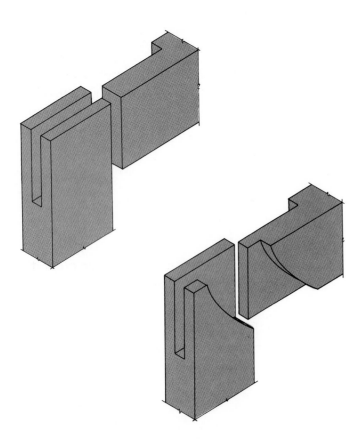

Fig. 20-28. Procedure for cutting the rail and stile for a curved slot mortise-and-tenon joint.

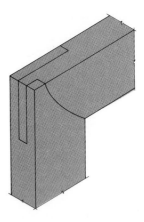

Fig. 20-30. Assembled curved slot mortise-and-tenon joint.

## DECORATIVE SPLINED MITER JOINT

The miter joint is considered a weak joint, but it does eliminate visible end grain. A splined miter joint is much stronger than a regular miter joint and is very decorative. Instead of hiding the spline, a wood of contrasting color can be used to emphasize the joint while adding strength, Fig. 20-31.

Use the following procedure to construct this joint.

1. Cut the pieces to length and miter the ends as in a typical miter joint.
2. Glue the corners together using a frame clamp or other suitable device. When the glue is dry,

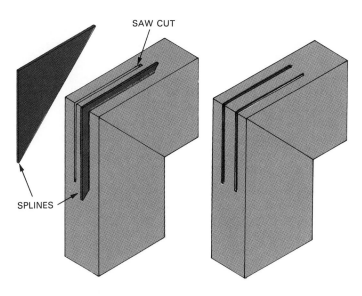

Fig. 20-31. A—Proper placement of splines in a decorative splined miter joint. B—Completed joint.

clean up the joint and sand until smooth.

3. Make a cradle to hold the mitered corner so that one, two, or three cuts may be made across the corner with a table saw, Fig. 20-32.
4. Set up the table saw and using the cradle, cut the desired number of kerfs across the corner of the mitered joint.
5. Cut splines from contrasting color wood to fit tightly in the saw kerf. Glue splines in place and trim after the glue dries.
6. Sand the completed joint.

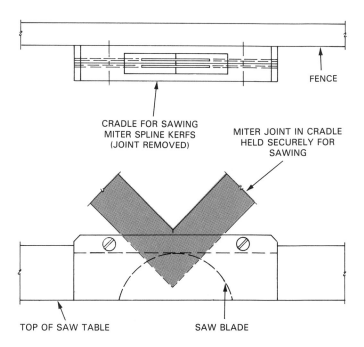

Fig. 20-32. Use a shop built cradle to cut decorative splined miter joints on the table saw.

## MARQUETRY

Marquetry is a surface covering process. It involves cutting pieces of thin wood veneers and assembling them into a design or picture. It should not be confused with INLAY, in which thin pieces of wood are glued into recesses cut into a surface. Marquetry seldom uses veneers over 1/16 in. thick. Colors and grain patterns of different veneers are used to complement the design, Fig. 20-33.

The basic operations in marquetry are selecting a design, cutting the veneer pieces to shape, gluing the pieces in place, and finishing the surface. One advantage of marquetry is that it requires very little equipment. Beautiful designs and pictures can be created with just a sharp knife. However, the jig saw with a 2/0 jeweler's blade speeds the work and often improves the quality. Most jig saws will require modification to use a jeweler's blade.

There are several methods of marquetry design: the single piece method, the pad method, the window method, and the double-bevel cut method.

Of these methods, the double-bevel cut offers the best speed and precision. After selecting a design, select veneers that possess the color and grain pattern that complement the picture. Remember that most veneer is 1/28 in. thick and must be cut very accurately to avoid gaps between pieces.

1. Trace the pattern on the background veneer using carbon paper. The background may be one or more pieces put together. Larger pieces will be cut out of the background first.
2. Before cutting out any piece of the background, tape the piece of veneer you wish to use for that element to the back in the proper position.
3. Use a sewing needle the same thickness as the blade to identify the starting point for sawing. Push the needle through both thicknesses of veneer on the cutting line. Pass the jeweler's blade through the hole with the teeth pointing downward. Attach the blade to the saw.
4. Tilt the table on the jig saw to about 13 deg. for a 2/0 blade. The tilting cut will compensate for the thickness of the blade and will eliminate any gap. If the angle is too great, the veneer will feather along the cut; if the angle is too little, the pieces will not fit tightly enough. You might have to experiment to determine the proper angle.
5. Cut out the part in either a clockwise or counterclockwise direction. Be consistent, however, because the cut pieces are not interchangeable and the table tilt will affect the results.
6. When the cut is done, the new piece of veneer will fit exactly in the place of the discarded background veneer. Fig. 20-34 shows how

355

Fig. 20-33. Left—Marquetry adds interest to this table. (Ed Zucca, Courtesy, Pritam and Eames) Right—This picture was created by carefully selecting the right veneers to ''paint'' the scene. (Eldon Rebhorn)

the double-bevel cut method works.

7. As each piece is cut out, tape it into place on the background. Continue this until the total design is completed.

8. After the parts have been cut and taped together, check that everything fits together as desired.

9. Particle board works well as a marquetry sub-base, but plywood is also acceptable. Gluing the marquetry design to the sub-base is similar to a typical veneering operation. A veneer press may be used or thick pieces of particle board may be clamped to the sub-base to form a press.

10. A good wood adhesive such as urea-formaldehyde should be used to attach the veneer picture. The tape is removed from the face of the design once the glue is dry.

11. Hand scrape the design and sand until smooth. Seal the surface with a sanding sealer that is compatible with the final finish.

## DECORATIVE MOLDINGS

Decorative moldings greatly affect the appearance of any piece of furniture or architectural element. The primary purpose is to visually relate one element to another and to add interest to the piece. Frequently, however, moldings also are used to hide joints and/or fasteners, cover end grain, and hold separate parts in proper relation to one another.

The simplest moldings are treatments used to smooth off edges. Fig. 20-35 shows several edge

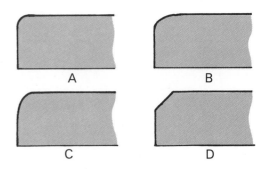

Fig. 20-35. Edge molding procedures affect the visual weight of an edge. A—Is neutral since the radius is equally distributed. B—Emphasizes top edge, making edge appear thinner. C—Calls attention to the side edge, making it appear thicker. D—Reduces the visual weight of the edge, making edge appear thinner.

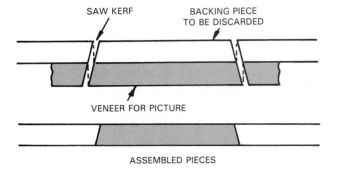

Fig. 20-34. The double-bevel cut method of marquetry.

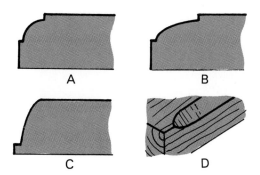

Fig. 20-36. These edge moldings are examples of the molding procedures shown in Fig. 20-35. A—Neutral edge. B—Thin edge. C—Thick edge. D—Thin edge.

moldings which affect the visual weight of an edge. Practical applications of these edge moldings are shown in Fig. 20-36.

Decorative moldings aid in the transition from one part of a piece to the next. For example, the armoire shown in Fig. 20-37 uses decorative molding to visually tie the two units together. Molding at the top, bottom, and across the doors gives a unity of feeling to the piece.

Decorative moldings are functional as well as decorative in the cabinetry shown in Fig. 20-38. The moldings on the door panels and dropped ceiling area over the sink are decorative. The moldings above eye level are mounted so the decorative elements face downward. The reverse is true for moldings at the base.

Molding design selected should relate to the nature of the piece and reflect the period of the design. Fig. 20-39 shows a few of the decorative moldings found on period French and English furniture. Variations of these and similar moldings can be developed using several standard architectural moldings fastened together or through creative use of the router or shaper.

### TAMBOURS

Tambours are flexible doors constructed from a series of thin wooden slats. The roll top desk shown in Fig. 20-40 uses tambours.

Tambours are constructed by gluing each strip to a fabric backing or threading strips together with wires. Each slat has a tongue at either end which slides in a groove cut into the carcass. Tambours may open vertically, as in a roll top desk, or horizontally, as in a cabinet or a buffet.

Tambours have several advantages over typical doors. They require less space to open since they do not swing out from the carcass. They provide more access to the inside than sliding doors which must overlap. And they can follow the curves of a furniture piece.

Fig. 20-37. Decorative moldings tie the two units together in this armoire. (Drexel Heritage Furnishings, Inc.)

### DESIGN AND CONSTRUCTION

The design and construction of tambours requires precise and thorough planning. The grooves must be smooth. The tongues must be shaped so they slide easily. The piece must be structurally sound. Tambour pieces generally have false tops, backs, and/or sides. They are used to conceal the back side of the tambour when open, and also to prevent the contents from obstructing movement of the doors. Fig. 20-41 shows a structural design detail of a false top in a tambour cabinet.

Tambour strips generally have a shoulder on the exposed side to conceal the tracking groove. This also allows the shape of each strip to be independent of the tongue shape. Tracking grooves vary in size from 3/16 in. to 5/16 in. widths. The grooves are slightly deeper than they are wide. A tongue which is wider than it is thick will slide more

Fig. 20-38. Molding is both decorative and functional in this modern kitchen. (Haas Cabinet Co.)

smoothly in the track. Be sure the strips are not too wide to travel around the sharpest bend. A scaled drawing can be used to check the tongue size.

The tracking groove is best routed using a template. Use the same template for both sides by turning it over. This will eliminate subtle differences in the curves if different templates are used. Particle board or hardboard may be used for a pattern.

ENGLISH

FRENCH

Fig. 20-39. Decorative moldings used in French and English period furniture and architecture.

Fig. 20-40. Contemporary tambour desk in padauk. (Robert March, Courtesy, Pritam and Eames)

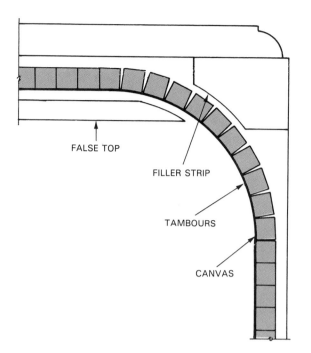

Fig. 20-41. Structural design detail of a false top in a tambour cabinet.

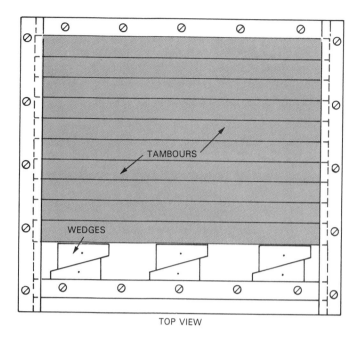

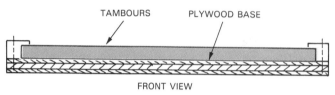

Fig. 20-42. Custom built jig for gluing fabric to the back of tambour slats.

The pattern can then be easily clamped into place for routing.

Tambour strips (slats) should be cut to shape but left longer than finished size until after they are glued to a fabric backing. The tambour may be cut to proper length with shoulders and tongues after the glue is dry. (It is best to keep the shape simple the first time. Rounded tambours are difficult to machine on the ends after they are glued to the fabric.)

Glue fabric to the tambours by cutting a piece of 3/4 in. particle board large enough to hold all of the strips with a frame around the assembly, Fig. 20-42. The frame pieces on the sides have a rabbet cut to hold the slats firmly to the particle board base. Slats are assembled with their back side up to receive the glue and fabric. Use wedges or some other device to force the slats closely together to prevent the glue from running through the cracks. This setup must be perfectly square or the tambour will not operate smoothly.

Fabric for a tambour backing can be unprimed canvas, leather, silk, or linen. Ten oz. canvas is readily available from most art supply stores, and works very well. The canvas should be wide enough to reach from tongue to tongue. The canvas will stretch about 3/8 in. on each side. Be sure to leave 2 or 3 inches of canvas over one end for a handle strip, if one is planned.

An aliphatic thermoplastic resin glue (yellow glue) is recommended for attaching the canvas. Brush the glue over the slats for even coverage. Use a flat object such as a veneer hammer or squeegee to even out the glue. Then attach the canvas. Work from the center toward the edges. Use light pressure and do not completely saturate the canvas with glue.

Once the glue is dry, the tambour can be cut to length on the table saw. Cut the shoulder of the tongues on the table saw and then route out the shoulder. Plan to route about 1/16 in. from the back side as well, to even out any variation that exists there, Fig. 20-43. Check for proper fit and hand sand until it moves easily. Attach the handle strip if you do not plan to use a finger recess on the first

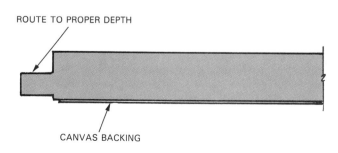

Fig. 20-43. Cutting the shoulder of the tongues on the tambour slats. Hand saw for best fit.

slat. Handle strips are generally attached with glue, and a strip of wood that is screwed to the back to secure the canvas. A finish is generally applied to the tambour before it is installed in the carcass. Finally, install a stop in the cabinet to prevent the tambour from going too far into the cavity or from putting pressure on the handle.

### TEST YOUR KNOWLEDGE, Chapter 20

Please do not write in the text. Place your answers on a separate sheet of paper.

1. Explain how reeding and fluting differ.
2. What tool is generally used to form reeds and flutes on a flat surface?
3. Name the two types of carving used the most in general woodworking.
4. _____ _____ is the formation of complex geometric patterns from many small triangular incisions.
5. Most chip carving designs are made from variations of two kinds of triangular chips. One uses _____ knife cuts, and the other uses _____ knife cuts.
   a. 3, 6.
   b. 2, 1.
   c. 2, 4.
   d. None of the above.
6. _____ _____ is a method of creating a raised design that seems to stand apart from the background.
7. What is meant by "setting-in" a design?
8. _____ is a surface covering process in which thin wood veneer pieces are cut and assembled in a design or picture.
9. Other than to decorate a piece, why is molding used on furniture?
10. What are tambours? Name several advantages associated with their use.

### ACTIVITIES

1. Design a decorative wood joint, then make a pictorial drawing of your design. Begin with a rather simple design. Specify the type of wood and contrasting veneer you would use.
2. Visit an antique furniture shop, flea market, museum, or other place where older furniture is displayed. Look for examples of hand carved work. If possible, photograph several pieces to show to your classmates. Learn as much about each piece as you can, and give your information in an oral report.
3. Start a collection of decorative moldings to be displayed on a panel. Determine the type of each molding in your collection. Describe how or where it was (is) used. Share the information with your classmates.

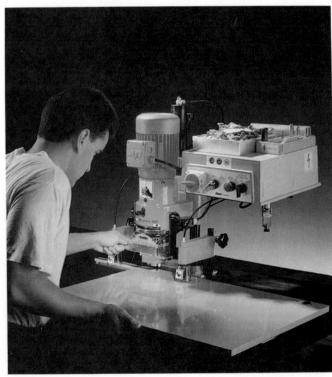

Left. Surface mounted and flush mounted RTA (Ready To Assemble) fittings for cabinets and furniture. Right. This "minipress" is basically a drill press with 5 spindles that is specifically designed to bore holes for press-in hardware. (Julius Blum, Inc.)

A beautiful example of the art of marquetry. (Ernie Ives)

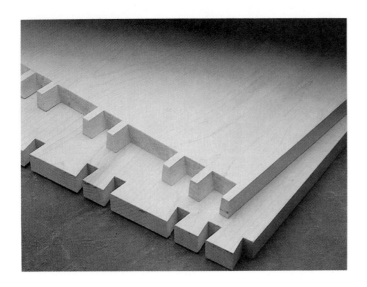
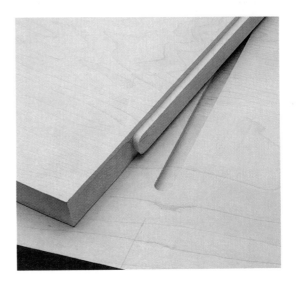

Left. Varying the spacing of dovetails adds interest to the project. Right. Sliding dovetails are particularly suitable for fitting shelves and partitions.   (Leigh Industries, Ltd.)

Left. This custom cabinet exhibits good form and design. (James Krenov, Courtesy, Pritam and Eames) Right. A functional patio cabinet made from plywood. (American Plywood Association)

The beautiful baby crib is an example of fine craftsmanship and good design.    (Mark Clauss)

# Chapter 21
# Furniture and Cabinetwork

FURNITURE is a term applied to movable articles such as chairs, tables, desks, and beds used to furnish rooms in homes and commercial or public buildings. CABINETWORK, although similar in nature, is a term usually applied to cases, cabinets, counters, and other interior woodwork that is fixed in place and is nonmovable after it is installed. Some pieces of furniture are called cabinets (TV, stereo, and storage), and this results in some confusion in the terminology.

Although methods of construction are often the same, cabinetwork in general does not require the high level of perfection in design, accuracy, and finish that is found in most furniture.

Today, nearly all furniture is produced in large factories. This is also largely true of cabinetwork. However, some is still made in smaller cabinet shops and by carpenters working on the construction site.

## TYPES OF CONSTRUCTION

FRAME construction consists of several similar pieces, that are usually fastened together at their ends. Examples include picture frames, bulletin boards, trays, mirror frames, and component parts of some furniture and cabinetwork, Fig. 21-1.

LEG AND RAIL is the type of construction used for tables, chairs, benches, and stools, Fig. 21-2. The basic parts (legs, rails, stretchers, braces) are nearly always made of solid stock and joined together with various joints. Mortise-and-tenon joints have been used for quality work through the years. But with so much improvement in adhesives, dowel joints are thought to be as strong, especially when reinforced with glue blocks or special metal fasteners.

BOX or CHEST AND CASE construction consists of sides, ends, top, and bottom, Fig. 21-3. Various joints are used in the corners while the bottom and top can be attached flush, or set in rabbets or grooves. If the structure is turned on its side it would be called CASE construction, with the

Fig. 21-1. Frame construction is used in this drafting table. (Dan Gratiot and Mark Hazel, Rhode Island School of Design)

Fig. 21-2. Leg and rail type construction is used in this fine vanity and stool. (David Welter)

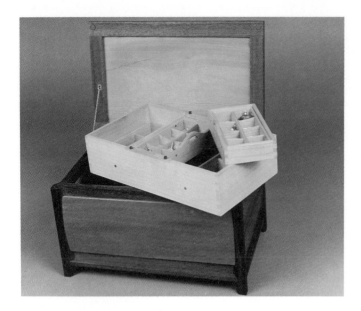

Fig. 21-3. The basic construction of this jewelry box consists of sides, ends, top, and bottom. (David Welter)

Fig. 21-4. This china cabinet is an example of carcass construction. Notice the framed glass panel doors covering the shelves. There are drawers behind the lower doors.    (David Welter)

bottom becoming the back and the sides becoming the top and bottom. Shelves could be installed and doors mounted on the front. This is the type of construction used for bookcases, cabinets, and built-ins. Because the surfaces are large and wide, plywood or other manufactured panels are used.

CARCASS construction is similar to case construction, but with more internal details. It usually includes drawers as well as doors. Instead of solid panels, framed panels are often used. It is the type of construction used in kneehole desks, dressers, and buffets, Fig. 21-4.

FRAME WITH COVER construction is used mainly in cabinetwork for such items as wardrobes, closets, and other built-in units. It consists of frames of various design that are then covered with thin plywood or hardboard to provide a finished surface.

## 32MM CABINET CONSTRUCTION

The 32mm system is a standard form of frameless case construction that provides a modular system of case assembly and hardware installation. In its purest form, the 32mm system utilizes European hinges, sliding panel saws, multispindle boring machines, dowel inserters, pneumatic clamps, edgebanders, and other items. Even so, the concept is rather simple—construction and fastening measurements are oriented around a 32mm grid. (The 32mm measurment being the minimum distance between the drill bits on certain boring machines.) This arrangement allows for interchangeability of components since all hardware holes are located on the grid. The European design generally refers to laminate box construction without face frames and produces a modern, seamless appearance.

The 32mm system utilizes several standard dimensions:
• Side panels have two vertical rows of holes on 32mm centers.
• The distance from the front or rear edge to hole center line is 37mm.
• System hole diameter is 5mm. Holes for assembly purposes may be 8mm, 15mm, and 35mm.
• Accurate hole location ensures a precise fit and proper operation of hardware.

The 32mm hinges are a major component of the system, Fig. 21-5. The levering arm folds into a hinge cup set into the back of the door. The hinges are almost invisible when the door is closed. Many are self-latching with 32mm locking hardware available. The hinges will open from 90 degrees to 270 degrees, depending on the manufacturer. Hinges can fit acute angles as well as wraparound

 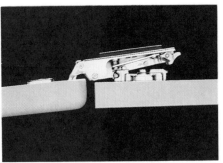 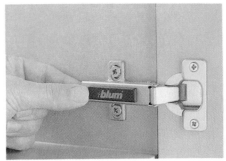

Fig. 21-5. Several types of hinges used in 32mm cabinet construction.　　(Julius Blum, Inc.)

doors. Some "clip-on" hinges provide for removal and reattachment in a matter of seconds without tools.

Small shops are using European 32mm hinges for their cabinets even though they don't have the large, expensive equipment required for the total system. Jigs and templates are available to facilitate the location of hinges (hinge-cut mortise and mounting plate). One of the most complete jigs available is shown in Fig. 21-6. This jig can be used to bore support holes, drawer slides, and other 32mm hardware as well as dowel holes for carcass panels and drawer parts. Fig. 21-7 through Fig. 21-12 provide a step-by-step procedure.

Fig. 21-7. Step 1. Cut the necessary panels and tape the exposed edges or apply solid wood edging. Step 2. Place the jig on a side panel and set the rails 37mm in from each edge using the gauge head.　　(Veritas Tools, Inc.)

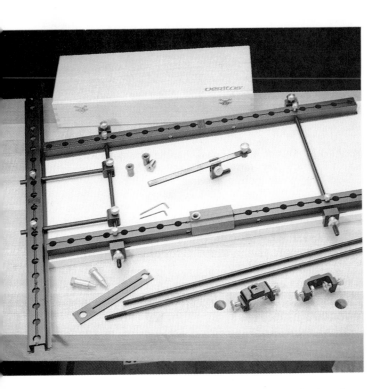

Fig. 21-6. This 32mm cabinetmaking system is suited to short runs and custom cabinets. The basic jig enables small shops to build cabinets based on the European system that requires very precise hole spacing and interchangeable panels. All holes are drilled in reference to the sides and ends of panels.　　(Veritas Tools, Inc.)

Fig. 21-8. Step 3. Using the gauge head, insert the center line of the end rail a distance equal to one-half of the material thickness. When doweled, top and bottom panels will be flush with side panels.　　(Veritas Tools, Inc.)

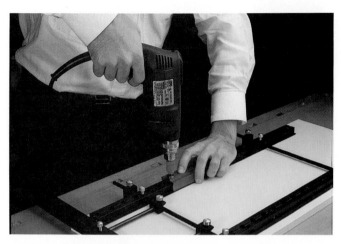

Fig. 21-9. Step 4. Drill as required for screw holes, shelf supports, or dowels. The jig is designed such that all holes are accessible at all times. (Veritas Tools, Inc.)

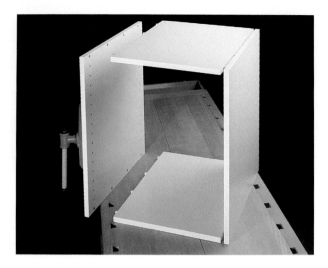

Fig. 21-12. Step 7. Assemble the case. The dowels make it easy to maintain squareness in assembly.
(Veritas Tools, Inc.)

Fig. 21-10. Step 5. Using the doweling jig bases and gauge head, clamp a rail on the top panel and drill the dowel holes. Repeat for the bottom panel. (Veritas Tools, Inc.)

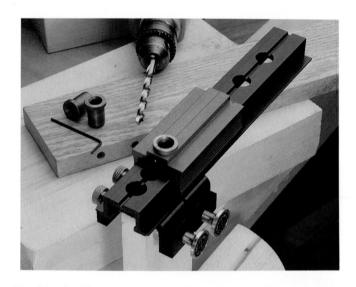

Fig. 21-13. This doweling jig will handle workpieces from 1/2 in. to 1 in. thick. The setting is accurate to a few thousandths of an inch. (Veritas Tools, Inc.)

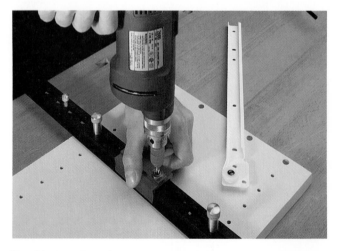

Fig. 21-11. Step 6. For heavy-load drawers, it is desirable to put at least one intermediate screw in the slide. Screws at the ends only allow too much flexing and distortion of the slide. (Veritas Tools, Inc.)

The doweling jig (Fig. 21-13), shelf-drilling jig (Fig. 21-14 left), and hinge-boring jig (Fig. 21-15 right) complete the system. The chief advantage of the 32mm cabinet system is the use of standardized cabinet components, one fastener size which increases efficiency, and fewer mistakes by less experienced employees. See Fig. 21-15.

Other more-sophisticated equipment is available for 32mm construction, Fig. 21-16. This machine is equipped with a 12-spindle boring head and "calibrator-fence" system that guarantees the centering of doors and side panels to the boring tool precisely and safely. The throat depth of 310mm allows boring to the middle line of base cabinets to mount drawer runners. Eight spindles are provided for the 32mm line boring.

Fig. 21-14. Shelf-drilling jig eliminates the time-consuming layout work usually associated with installing shelf supports. Right. A hinge-boring jig used for drilling 35mm holes for cup hinges. (Veritas Tools, Inc.)

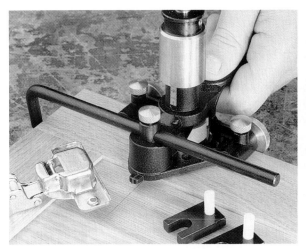

Fig. 21-15. Right. Drilling 35mm flap hinges. Left. Drilling standard 35mm hinges. (Veritas Tools, Inc,)

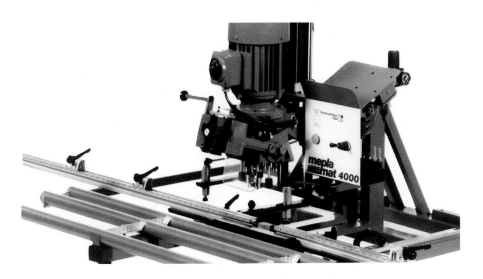

Fig. 21-16. 32mm equipment with a 12-spindle boring head and "calibrator-fence" system. (Mepla, Inc.)

## STANDARD SIZES

In the design and construction of furniture and cabinetwork, careful attention must be given to certain standard sizes. These sizes have been established from a study of human anatomy, and are intended to meet the needs of most people. These dimensions apply equally well to any style of furniture. Some sizes are critical for functional reasons, while others may vary. For example, the height of a dining table or home desk should be 29 to 29 1/2 in., while the width and depth of the desk top may vary considerably, depending on its purpose and use. Another important requirement for dining tables and desks is ample knee space. The distance from the seat of the chair to the underside of the top or rails must be at least 7 in. Leg room for kneehole desks should seldom be less than 24 in. wide.

Standard dimensions should be applied accurately to the design of chairs, Fig. 21-17. The height and depth of the seat are especially critical measurements. The angle of the seat and back are also important if maximum comfort is to be attained.

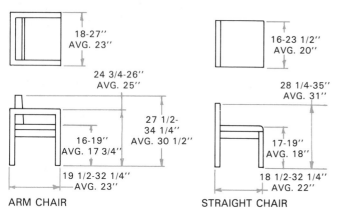

Fig. 21-17. Standard sizes used in chair construction.

## USING SOLID STOCK

Today, commercially produced furniture and cabinetwork includes a great amount of plywood, especially when working with wide surfaces. Using plywood saves production time because large panels are available with surfaces that are already sanded. The greatest advantage however, is that it provides a strong, stable material that is free from excessive swelling and shrinkage. Beautiful grain patterns are available in veneer covered plywood that may be used in place of the more expensive solid stock.

Solid wood, even though properly dried, is stable only in one direction—along the grain. Across the grain, expansion and contraction can be controlled

only by keeping the wood in the proper atmospheric environment. Interior wood products in service will dry out during the heating season and absorb moisture during the high humidities of summer months, causing a dimensional change across the grain of plus or minus 1/8 in. for each 12 in. of width. The hygroscopic nature of wood makes this a tremendous force that can result in joint failure and destruction of an assembly.

Waterproof finishes on the surface will slow down the expansion and contraction action somewhat but it cannot be prevented entirely. In the design and construction of your project, you should pay careful attention to this problem, especially when the width of solid stock parts is considerable.

Fig. 21-18 shows a night table built largely of solid stock. It is 20 in. wide, 15 in. deep, and 25 in. high. There is no problem of stability with the legs and rails that form the base. However, the top, shelf, bottom, and sides are all made of solid stock, and the direction of the grain must run as shown by the arrows. That way these members can all expand and contract together. A frame or plywood panel cannot be used for the bottom unless some flexible coupling is used to join it to the sides. The dimensions of the back will not change since it is bounded by edges running along the grain. Here a plywood panel must be used. The base will be stable in size and should be attached to the solid bottom of the main section with devices that will permit movement.

## FRAMED PANELS

For large areas in case and carcass construction, framed panels are often used, Fig. 21-19. Such construction is also used for doors (called panel doors) as it provides a stable assembly. The vertical members are called STILES and the horizontal members are called RAILS. The unit can be divided into several sections by using additional rails. The corner joints may be doweled but a stub tenon or

Fig. 21-18. Grain direction in solid wood construction. (Period Furniture, Inc.)

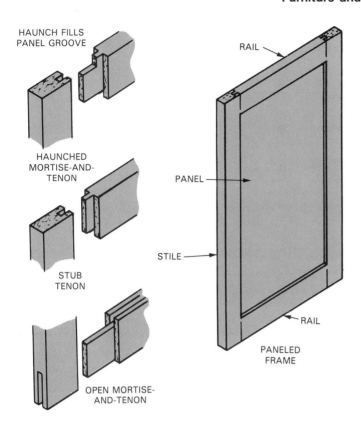

Fig.21-19. Joints used to construct a framed panel.

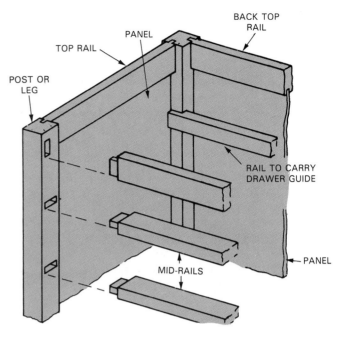

Fig. 21-21. Framed panels in carcass construction.

haunched mortise-and-tenon is used more often. A groove is cut around the inside of the frame to carry the raised panel, shown in Fig. 21-20. When framing glass doors, a rabbet and stop is used instead of the groove so that the glass can be replaced if broken.

Panel construction is a common form used in carcass assemblies and makes extensive use of the framed panel, Fig. 21-21. Corner posts or legs replace the stiles and can carry rails and/or panels on several faces. Rails are attached to the posts to frame openings for drawers or doors. It provides a strong, sturdy method of construction that is often used in quality furniture.

When the design requires flush panels, the corner posts are rabbeted to carry the panel and the rails are set behind the panel.

Fig. 21-22 shows extensive use of panel construction in kitchen cabinets.

## MAKING A MASTER LAYOUT

When working with complicated structures involving shelves, doors, and drawers it is good practice to make a full-size layout. This can be made on a piece of plywood or cardboard, Fig. 21-23.

Follow the dimensions of your working drawing carefully. Sectional views will usually be most helpful. Draw each member full size and show various clearances that may be required. This master layout will be especially valuable when cutting side or end panels to size and locating joints. It can also be referred to for exact sizes and locations of drawer parts and many other detailed dimensions that are not included in the working drawing.

## CONSTRUCTING WEB FRAMES

In case and carcass construction, internal framing components are often required. They are called WEB FRAMES, or usually just FRAMES. Plywood panels could be used but this would waste material

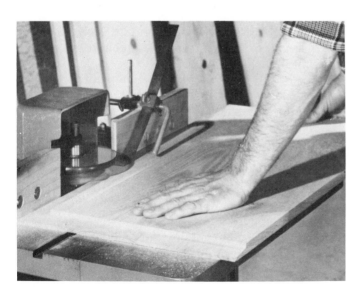

Fig. 21-20. Cutting the edge of a panel for standard panel construction. (Delta International Machinery Corp.)

Fig. 21-22. Panel construction has been used extensively in the construction of these kitchen cabinets. (Haas Cabinet Co.)

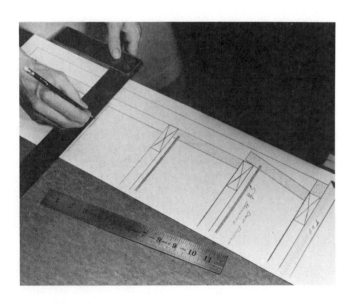

Fig. 21-23. Making a full-size layout on cardboard.

and might add excessive weight to the structure. Fig. 21-24 shows how a standard web frame fits into simple case construction. An alternate method is shown in Fig. 21-25.

Fig. 21-26 shows the joints being cut for a frame assembled with stub tenons. The required stock is cut to thickness and width, then cut to length, with each part about 1/8 in. longer and wider than required. In this particular assembly, the groove for the tenon is cut all the way across the front and back since it will be used to carry a center drawer guide. Normally, the groove could be cut in from each end just far enough for the tenon. The frames are then glued together, Fig. 21-27. Check carefully to see that they are square and lie in a perfect plane. After the glue has cured, the surfaces can be lightly sanded.

Frames should be trimmed to exact sizes, following the same procedure used for squaring a solid

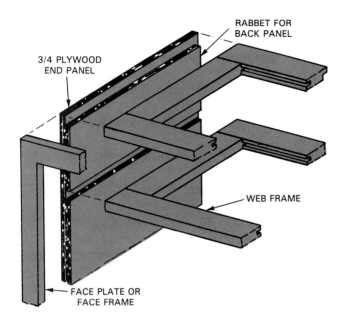

Fig. 21-24. Using web frames in case construction. Terminology used is as specified by the Architectural Woodwork Institute.

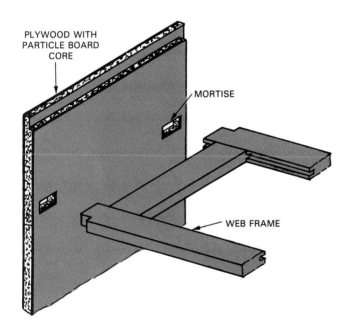

Fig. 21-25. Alternate method of joining web frame to side. This may be used when a full groove across the panel would weaken construction.

Fig. 21-26. Top. Cutting grooves in the front and back pieces. Push sticks are held in each hand to finish the cut. Bottom. Cutting the stub tenon using a dado head and fence pad.

Fig. 21-27. Gluing web frames.

panel. In some structures it may be necessary to separate the area by installing a hardboard or plywood panel in the frame. This is often done in chests of drawers and is referred to as DUSTPROOF CONSTRUCTION. The separation would also be important in banks of locked drawers since access to the drawer below could otherwise be gained by simply removing the drawer above.

Fig. 21-28. Top. Cutting dado joints in side or end panels. Bottom. Cutting a single shoulder tongue on the side of the frame, using a dado head.

## ASSEMBLING PANELS AND WEB FRAMES

If the side or end panels are of plywood, the frames can be set in dados and glued. The dados should be laid out and cut first, as shown in Fig. 21-28. It is best to make the depth of the groove, somewhat less than half the thickness of plywood. The edge of the frame is now cut to size to match the dado, using a setup as shown in Fig. 21-28, bottom. The dado could be cut to match the full thickness of the frame. However, it will be easier to secure an accurate fit by the method shown and the joint will be slightly stronger.

In Fig. 21-29, a trial assembly is being made of a drawer section for a kneehole desk. When constructing a unit like this, that has many parts, it is best to glue the frames into one side panel with the other side panel clamped in place dry. After the glued side of the assembly has set up, the other panel is removed and the glue applied.

When the drawer sections are complete, they are joined with the center section, Fig. 21-30, and the top, legs, and rear panels are attached. This general procedure and method of construction can be applied to cabinets, chests, and similar products. Side panels of solid stock could be used in these structures if the grain runs parallel to the frames.

## FINISHING PLYWOOD EDGES

When using plywood in the construction of furniture and cabinetwork, any exposed edges will need to be covered. This will include the edges of tops, case fronts, and may also include the edges of doors, shelves, and drawer fronts. In furniture factories, plywood is often made with a banding core of solid stock that matches the veneer. In this way, it is not necessary to cover the edges.

There are a number of ways to cover the edges of either veneer core or solid core plywood. One of the simplest ways is to apply a thin veneer. This can be purchased or produced in the shop. Any regular contact bond cement can be used. Porous woods should be double-coated.

Cut the veneer strips to size. It is usually best for the strip to be 1/16 to 1/32 in. wider than the edge of the plywood. A pair of sharp scissors or shears can be used to cut ends and miters. Apply the glue or cement, Fig. 21-31, allow it to dry, and then carefully place the strips in position. Press or roll them firmly. Water based glues, such as polyvinyl and urea resin, do not work well. This is because they tend to curl the veneer and the strips must then be clamped.

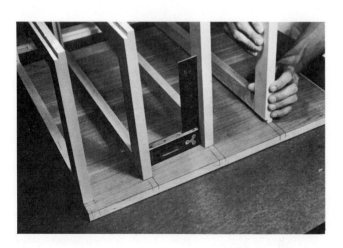

Fig. 21-29. Making a trial assembly of web frames and a side panel that will be used to make a kneehole desk.

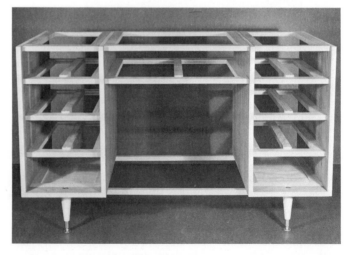

Fig. 21-30. Basic assembly of a kneehole desk. The bottom brace strips are removed after back panels and top are attached. (John Moeller)

Fig. 21-31. Veneering plywood edges. Top. Applying contact cement. Bottom. Placing veneer strips in position.

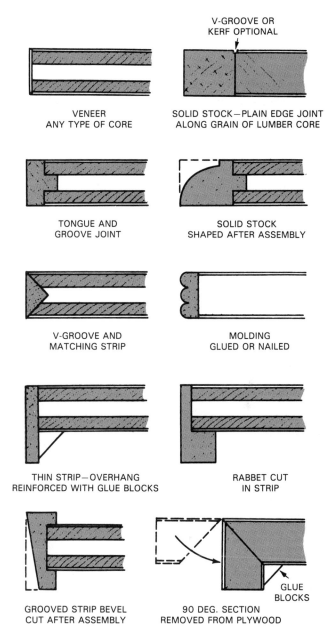

VENEER
ANY TYPE OF CORE

SOLID STOCK—PLAIN EDGE JOINT
ALONG GRAIN OF LUMBER CORE

V-GROOVE OR
KERF OPTIONAL

TONGUE AND
GROOVE JOINT

SOLID STOCK
SHAPED AFTER ASSEMBLY

V-GROOVE AND
MATCHING STRIP

MOLDING
GLUED OR NAILED

THIN STRIP—OVERHANG
REINFORCED WITH GLUE BLOCKS

RABBET CUT
IN STRIP

GROOVED STRIP BEVEL
CUT AFTER ASSEMBLY

90 DEG. SECTION
REMOVED FROM PLYWOOD

GLUE
BLOCKS

Fig. 21-32. Methods of trimming the edges of plywood.

Sometimes it is better to use solid wood strips for the banding and edge finish, Fig. 21-32. Larger strips can be glued in place and then shaped later. The V-strip provides an attractive appearance. It is especially valuable for veneer core doors where butt hinges will be used, since screws do not hold well in the edges. The solid strip may be applied so that it forms a wider width for an apron around a table top. Where solid edge banding meets at a corner, it should be mitered and carefully fitted. Use regular glue and clamps.

The banding strip could be cut from the plywood and a miter joint used. This makes it easy to secure a perfect match. With some woods, it is possible to make a 90 deg. V-cut just to the face veneer and then moisten and bend the edge into position.

## SHELVES

In some work, it may be necessary to fit and glue shelves into dados cut in the sides of a structure to provide additional strength. When possible however, it is better to make them adjustable, up and down, so that they can be used for various purposes.

Fig. 21-33 presents several methods of installing adjustable supports. Lay out the arrangement carefully so that the shelves will be perfectly level. It is usually best to do the cutting or drilling before the structure is assembled. This is essential when using a patented shelf standard, where slotted strips are set in grooves cut in the sides or back.

373

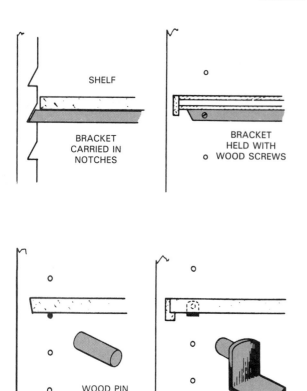

Fig. 21-33. Shelf supports.

Fig. 21-34. Top. Beautiful furniture top with a matched grain pattern. Bottom. Skilled craftsworker matches veneer and assembles it with a special taping machine.
(Drexel Heritage Furnishings, Inc.)

Standard shelving that is 3/4 in. thick should never be carried on supports that are spaced more than 42 in. apart. This applies especially to shelves that will carry books and other heavy loads.

## TOPS

The top is the most important surface of chests, tables, and cabinets. It should be smooth, attractive, and have a high resistance to abrasion and wear. Fig. 21-34 shows a skillfully matched grain pattern on a plywood table top with a banded edge of solid wood.

Tops can be made of plywood or solid stock, Fig. 21-35. Plywood offers the advantage of stability and warp resistance, but requires banding or other edge treatment. Solid tops should never be banded across the end grain. Special care must be given to the edge joints and grain match. In the school shop, table and desk tops of solid stock are usually glued and prepared after the base structure is complete, so they can be attached immediately, thus reducing the possiblity of warpage.

When design permits, tops should be attached as a separate component of a structure. This is usually possible in the construction of tables, desks, and some cabinets. Fig. 21-36 shows several methods that can be used. Solids should always be attached

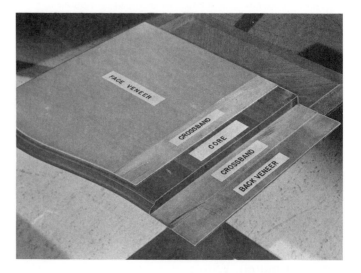

Fig. 21-35. Plywood fabricated especially for tops. The edge of the lumber core matches the face veneer.

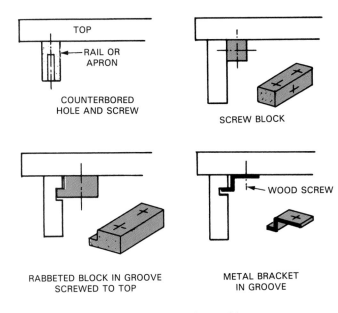

Fig. 21-36. Methods of attaching tops.

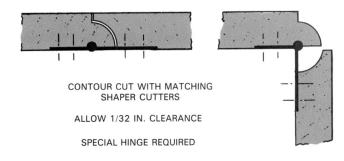

CONTOUR CUT WITH MATCHING
SHAPER CUTTERS

ALLOW 1/32 IN. CLEARANCE

SPECIAL HINGE REQUIRED

Fig. 21-38. Rule joint detail.

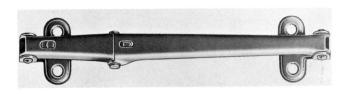

Fig. 21-39. Drop leaf support. (The Stanley Works)

in such a way that expansion and contraction across the grain can take place.

Tables are often designed with drop leaves so that space can be conserved when they are not in full use. The patented drop leaf table hinge, Fig. 21-37, improves the appearance when the leaf is down, since it eliminates the unsightly gap that would be formed by a conventional hinge. A rule joint, Fig. 21-38, is also used for this purpose. It is formed with special shaper cutters.

Tops may swing up to give access to the inside of the structure. Examples include stereo cabinets and toy chests.

Special hinges and self-balancing supports are available for use with drop leaves and for tops that swing up. They should be used during installation. See Fig. 21-39.

## LEGS

There are many ways to form and attach legs. In some structures, the corner posts are extended to serve as legs. In others, the legs are attached as individual units, Fig. 21-40, or secured to a separate frame or base, Fig. 21-41.

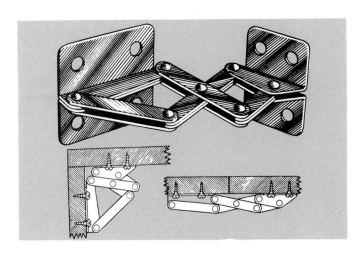

Fig. 21-37. Patented drop leaf table hinge.
(Selby Furniture Hardware)

Fig. 21-40. The legs of this table are attached to the top as individual units. (The Bartley Collection, Ltd.)

Fig. 21-41. The legs of this secretary are formed directly into the base of the unit. (Drexel Heritage Furnishings, Inc.)

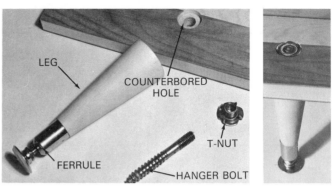

Fig. 21-42. Hanger bolt and T-nut provides a flush mounting.

Fig. 21-43. Splayed leg attached with a hanger bolt.

When the furniture is large or when it will carry considerable weight, it is best to attach the legs to a frame, using well designed mortise-and-tenon or dowel joints. If the legs are long, extra bracing may be required. This assembly is then attached to the main structure. One of the advantages of sub-assemblies like these is that they can be built and finished as separate units. This also makes handling, storing, and shipping easier.

Many leg attachment devices are available. Hanger bolts and T-nuts provide adequate strength and a trim appearance, Fig. 21-42. Splayed legs often present special problems. In Fig. 21-43, a hanger bolt is used to attach a leg to a rail that is set at an angle. The leg is also set at an angle on the face of the rail in order to form the required compound angle.

A unique method of attaching a shelf and leg, using a screw and screw eye in combination, is shown in Fig. 21-44. A commonly used bracket and hanger bolt, Fig. 21-45, also makes a strong joint.

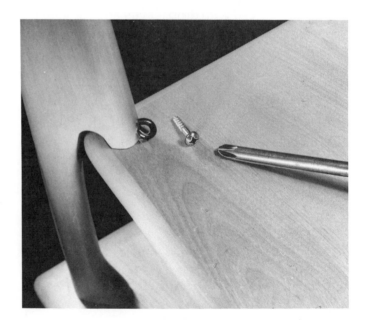

Fig. 21-44. Leg attached to a shelf with a screw eye and screw. View is from underside.

Fig. 21-45. Corner bracket and hanger bolt. Rails are fastened to top.

With the rails secured to the top, the leg can be quickly assembled or disassembled. Fig. 21-46 shows a leg of a traditional style table attached with screws and glue blocks.

## HARDWARE AND METAL TRIM

In addition to hinges, catches, and leg attachments, there is a wide range of other metal items used in furniture and cabinetwork. Much of it is exposed to view so it should be carefully selected. Give careful consideration to the size, style, material, and finish. Fig. 21-47 shows several unique styles and designs of quality knobs and pulls for drawers and doors.

Pulls and other metal trim should be fitted before the work is finished. In Fig. 21-48, a drawer knob which was prefitted, is being removed before the finishing operations.

Give careful attention to the location of pulls, knobs, and other surface hardware. Drawer pulls, for example, look best when they are placed slightly above the centerline. Be certain they are centered horizontally and are perfectly level. If you have a great deal to install, you can save time by making and using a drilling jig, Fig. 21-49.

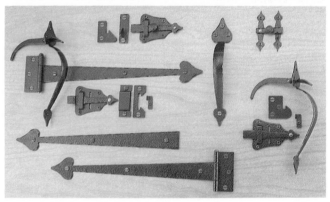

Fig. 21-46. Table leg attached with screws and glue blocks. (Drexel Heritage Furnishings, Inc.)

Fig. 21-47. An assortment of stylish knobs and pulls are available for cabinets, chests, and other pieces. (Amerock Corp.)

Fig. 21-48. Drawer pulls are removed before doing finishing operations. (Sherwin-Williams Co.)

Fig. 21-49. Using a jig to drill holes for drawer pulls.

## FURNITURE ASSEMBLIES

From your experience in woodworking, you will gain insight into and an understanding of furniture and cabinet construction that can be applied to commercially built units. Even though limitations in time, material, and equipment may prevent you from constructing sizeable or complicated pieces, take time to study the diagrams given in this unit to learn how various pieces are assembled.

Although plywood is used in most furniture today, especially to form large surfaces, some fine furniture is built entirely of solid stock. The exterior of the cabinet shown in Fig. 21-50 is solid stock. Study the construction details and note the provision made for expansion and contraction of the solid end panels and top.

Fig. 21-51 shows a modular unit (36 in. wide x 54 in. high x 19 3/4 in. deep) that is basic box construction. Note how different this construction is from the cabinet shown in Fig. 21-50.

## BUILT-IN CABINETWORK

The use of built-in cabinets and storage units is one of the most important developments in modern architecture and interior design. They provide more economical use of floor space than most furniture and, if carefully planned, result in greater efficiency and convenience, Fig. 21-52.

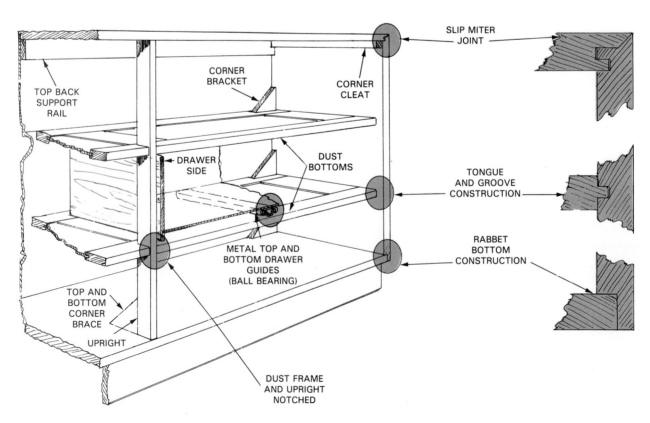

Fig. 21-50. Typical construction in which solid stock is used for the exterior of a cabinet. (The Lane Company, Inc.)

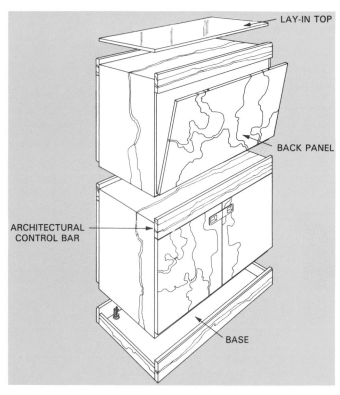

Fig. 21-51. Basic box construction has been used for this contemporary unit.

Modern built-in cabinetwork in the home includes kitchen cabinets, storage drawers and shelves, wardrobes, room dividers, and stereo/video cabinets. Kitchens are made very attractive and convenient with such built-in appliances and equipment as wall ovens, surface cooking units, refrigerators, dishwashers, and sinks, Fig. 21-53. Storage units are designed with attention to items that will be stored; space is carefully allocated and drawers, shelves, and other elements are proportioned to satisfy a specific purpose, Fig. 21-54.

Built-in units may be constructed "on the job" or produced in millwork plants and factories. Mass produced factory units are available in a wide range of sizes that can be adapted to various interior arrangements. Some are installed in basic framework that is built into walls and partitions of a building.

The architect's plan will show overall sizes and arrangements of built-in units, Fig. 21-55. Drawings are carefully scaled, eliminating the need for

Fig. 21-52. Built-in cabinetwork provides for efficient use of space. Without the cabinetwork, this room would have very little storage or shelf space. (Riviera Cabinets, Inc.)

Fig. 21-53. All of the appliances in this modern kitchen are built in for convenience and efficient use of space. (Haas Cabinet Co.)

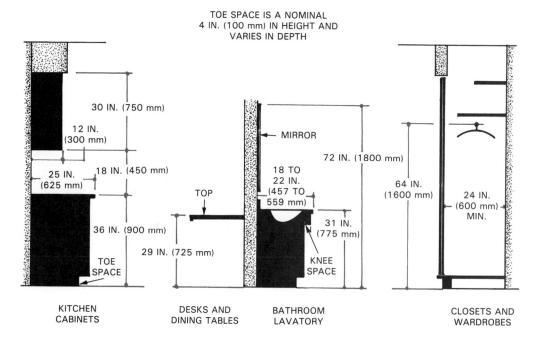

Fig. 21-54. Standard sizes for cabinetwork. Metric sizes are "rounded out" as generally proposed for building construction.

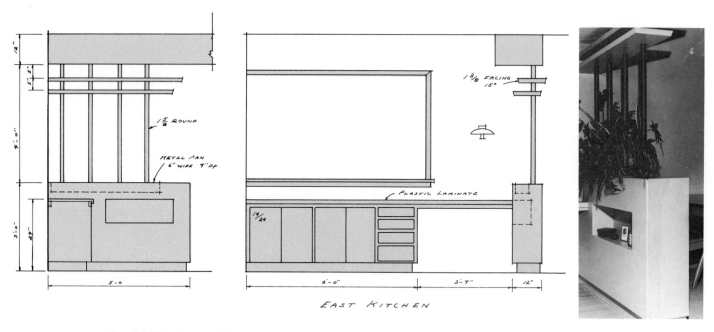

Fig. 21-55. Room divider and desk detail, plus photo of finished on-the-job built cabinetwork.

extensive dimensioning of views. They serve as a guide to the cabinetmaker or are followed in the selection of factory-built components. Joinery details and the structure of cabinets built on the job are designed by the cabinetmaker, who must work within the written specification requirements.

Factory-built cabinets are usually of high quality. Modern production machines can produce high quality work with unvarying accuracy and at moderate prices. Mass produced parts are assem-

bled with precision, using jigs and fixtures. Some factory-built cabinetwork is finished on the job; however in-plant finishes are usually of equal quality. In-plant finished cabinetwork can also be provided in various types and shades to match individual requirements, Fig. 21-56.

Manufacturers offer a wide range of standard units, especially in the area of kitchen cabinets, Fig. 21-57. Quite often they are also able to provide custom units to fill some specific requirement.

Fig. 21-56. An example of mass-produced cabinets with a factory applied finish. (Rivera Cabinets, Inc.)

## TEST YOUR KNOWLEDGE, Chapter 21

Please do not write in the text. Place your answers on a separate sheet of paper.

1. Explain the difference between furniture and cabinetwork.
2. _____ construction is similar to case construction, with more internal details.
3. When working with standard sizes, _____ dimensions are usually the most important and should receive the most consideration.
   a. Width.
   b. Height.
   c. Depth.
   d. None of the above.
4. List two advantages of using plywood in cabinetwork and furniture.
5. Is expansion and contraction of solid stock greatest along the grain or across the grain?
6. In a framed panel, the vertical members are called _____ and the horizontal members are called _____.
7. When should web frames be trimmed to exact size?
8. List four methods for attaching tops on cabinets or pieces of furniture.
9. A rule joint is formed with shaper cutters. True or False?

10. When should hinges, hardware, and other metal trim be fitted?
11. Why was 32mm used as the basis for the European system of frameless cabinet construction?
12. What is unique about the construction of all 32mm system hinges?
13. What device can a small shop use to make cabinets similar to those made using the 32mm system?
14. What is the chief advantage of the 32mm cabinet system?

## ACTIVITIES

1. Study the construction of the kitchen cabinets in your home. Then prepare a scaled sectional drawing of a typical base cabinet and include details of the joints used.
2. Prepare a check list of items to observe and examine when evaluating the quality of materials and construction in commercially built furniture.
3. Study an architectural standards manual, then prepare a drawing of a wardrobe unit. Include recommended sizes, heights, and space allotments for common clothing items (slacks, skirts, dresses, shirts, etc.).

Top. This cabinet uses a tambour door that spirals to the center. (Everett Bramhall, Rhode Island School of Design) Bottom. Kyoto and Geisha porcelain door knobs. (Baldwin Hardware Corp.)

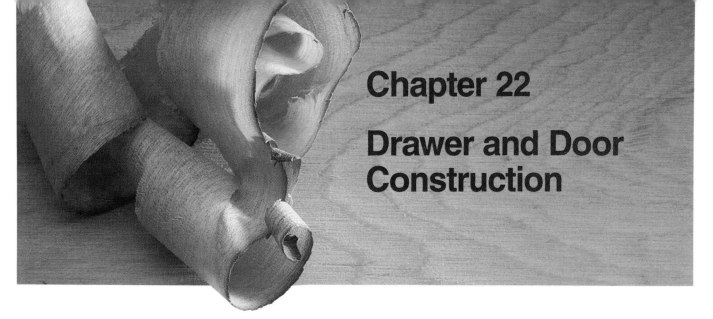

# Chapter 22

# Drawer and Door Construction

Drawers and doors are functionally and aesthetically important elements of most cabinets and enclosed furniture pieces. Several construction techniques are used and should be considered as a part of the total design. Drawers and/or doors frequently form the front of a piece of furniture or cabinet and, therefore, receive special emphasis.

## DRAWERS

There are two general types of drawers: LIP and FLUSH. They usually fit into framed openings of the structure. However, sometimes they are carried by special supports attached to the underside of a top or frame. Flush drawers, Fig. 22-1, are used in most furniture and must be carefully fitted. Lip drawers have a rabbet along the top and sides of the front which covers the clearance and permits greater freedom in the fit. They are used mainly in built-in cabinetwork.

Sizes and designs in drawer construction vary widely. Fig. 22-2 shows standard construction of several types of commonly used joints. The joint between the drawer front and the drawer side receives the greatest strain and should be carefully designed and fitted. In the highest quality work, each corner is dovetailed and the bottom grooved into the back, as well as the front and sides. Also the top edge of the drawer sides are rounded as shown in Fig. 22-3.

Drawers that are to be fitted very accurately may be constructed with the sides set about 1/16 to 1/8 in. deeper into the fronts so that a slight lug is formed. This lug is then trimmed to form a good fit.

## DRAWER CONSTRUCTION

Drawers are usually not constructed until after the case or cabinet in which they will fit has been assembled. The following procedure should be considered when building drawers for either furniture or cabinetwork.

Fig. 22-1. This contemporary cabinet uses flush type drawers. Rare mappa burls create the pleasing surface. (Thomasville Furniture Industries, Inc.)

1. Select the material for the fronts. Grain patterns should match or blend with each other. Solid stock or plywood may be used. Today, a variety of prefabricated drawer fronts are offered in many standard sizes. See Fig. 22-4.
2. Cut the drawer fronts to the size of the opening (if flush type), allowing a 1/16 in. clearance

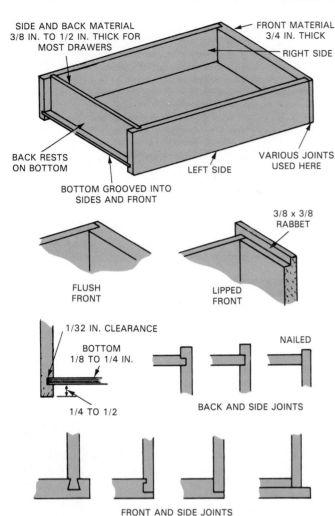

SIDE AND BACK MATERIAL
3/8 IN. TO 1/2 IN. THICK FOR
MOST DRAWERS

FRONT MATERIAL
3/4 IN. THICK

RIGHT SIDE

BACK RESTS
ON BOTTOM

LEFT SIDE

VARIOUS JOINTS
USED HERE

BOTTOM GROOVED INTO
SIDES AND FRONT

FLUSH
FRONT

3/8 x 3/8
RABBET

LIPPED
FRONT

1/32 IN. CLEARANCE

BOTTOM
1/8 TO 1/4 IN.

1/4 TO 1/2

NAILED

BACK AND SIDE JOINTS

FRONT AND SIDE JOINTS

Fig. 22-2. Standard drawer construction.

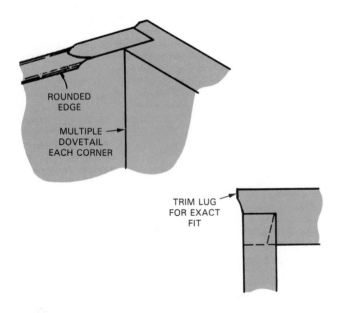

ROUNDED
EDGE

MULTIPLE
DOVETAIL
EACH CORNER

TRIM LUG
FOR EXACT
FIT

Fig. 22-3. Premium grade (highest) drawer details as established by the Architectural Woodwork Institute. Bottom is grooved into front, sides, and back. Sides and back must be of hardwood.

Fig. 22-4. Prefabricated drawer fronts are made in many designs. Top. Raised panel effect. Bottom. Ogee edge. (Frank Paxton Lumber Co.)

on each side and on the top. This clearance will vary depending on the depth of the drawer and the kind of material used. Deep drawers with solid fronts will require greater vertical clearance. For lip drawers, add the depth of the rabbets to the dimensions.

3. Select and prepare the stock for the sides and back. A less expensive medium hard wood can be used here. Plywood is usually unsatisfactory for these parts. Surface the stock to thickness, rip it to finished width, then cut it to the required length with allowance for the joints. The surfaces can be rough sanded either before or after cutting to length.

4. Select the material for the bottom. Hardboard or plywood should be used. The bottoms can be trimmed to final size after the joints for the other drawer members are cut.

5. Cut groove for bottom in front and sides.

6. Cut the joints in the drawer fronts that will hold the drawer sides. Fig. 22-5 shows a sequence

Fig. 22-5. Cutting lock joint in drawer front. Left. Cutting groove. Right. Trimming tongue to length.

for cutting a locked joint. For lip drawers, cut the rabbet first and then the required joint.

7. Cut the matching joint in the drawer sides. BE CERTAIN TO CUT A LEFT AND RIGHT SIDE FOR EACH DRAWER.
8. Cut the required joints for the drawer sides and backs, Fig. 22-6.
9. Trim the bottom to the correct size and make a trial assembly as shown in Fig. 22-7. Make

Fig. 22-6. Cutting dado in sides to hold drawer backs.

Fig. 22-7. Top. Trial assembly. Bottom. Parts ready to be glued.

any adjustments in the fit that may be required. The parts should fit smoothly. They should not be so tight that they will be difficult to assemble after the glue is applied.

10. Disassemble and sand all parts. The top edge of the sides are often rounded between points about 1 in. from each end.
11. Make the final assembly using one of several procedures. One method is to first glue the bottom into the front and then glue one of the front corners. This is shown in Fig. 22-8. Be sure the bottom is centered. The side grooves are usually not glued. Turn the drawer on its side and glue the back into the assembled side. Finally, glue on the remaining side as shown. Clamps or a few nails can be used to hold the joints together until the glue hardens.
12. Carefully check the drawer for squareness and then drive one or two nails through the bottom into the back. If the bottom was carefully squared, you should have little trouble with the operation. Wipe off the excess glue.

After the glue has cured, make a selective fit of each drawer to a particular opening. Install and adjust drawer guides. Place an identifying number and/or letter on the underside of the bottom so it will be easy to return the drawer to its proper opening after sanding and finishing operations. The inside surfaces of quality drawers should always be sealed and waxed.

## DRAWER GUIDES

Three common types of drawer guides are corner guides, center guides, and side guides, Fig. 22-9. The corner guide is often formed in the structure by the side panel and frame. However, it may be necessary to add a spacer strip.

The center drawer guide consists of a strip or runner fastened between the front and back rails. A guide, which is attached to the underside and back of the drawer, rides on this runner. The runner is attached to the frame or rails with screws. It can

Fig. 22-8. Gluing drawer. Left. Bottom in place and glue being applied to a front corner. Right. Placing the second side in position—final operation.

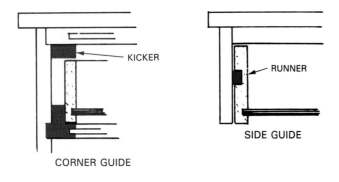

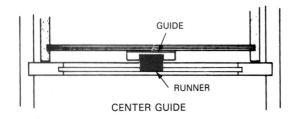

Fig. 22-9. Types of drawer guides.

be adjusted so that the clearance on each side is equal and the face of the drawer aligns with the front of the structure.

In drawer openings where there is no lower frame, a side guide may be the most practical guide to use. Grooves are cut in the drawer side before it is assembled and matching strips are fastened to the structure. This type of guide would be good to use for a drawer located directly under the top of a coffee table or an occasional table.

The drawer carrier arrangement may require a "kicker" or some other device to keep the drawer from tilting downward when it is pulled open, Fig. 22-10. Wooden drawer guides should be carefully fitted and the parts given a sealer coat of finish. If

the sealer on the moving parts is sanded lightly and then waxed, the drawer will work almost as smoothly as if it had been installed with one of the various patented nylon rollers or slides.

Fig. 22-11 shows a commercial back bearing for a center slide and how it is installed. For large drawers, or those that will carry considerable weight, a commercial, 3-roller drawer slide like the one shown in Fig. 22-12 might be used. It is available in several sizes and supports a weight up to 50 lbs.

## DOORS

There are two general classifications of doors: SWINGING and SLIDING, Fig. 22-13. Doors may be made of plywood, panel and frame, or a frame covered with thin plywood. Solid stock is seldom used, unless the door is very small. This is because it will very likely warp and, therefore, will require excessive clearances across the grain to prevent it from sticking during humid weather. Regardless of the material used, doors should be finished with the same sequence of finishing coats on both the inside and outside surface.

### SWINGING DOORS

Swinging doors may be hung flush with the opening, overlay the opening, or be inset part way like the lipped drawer front, Fig. 22-14.

The flush door fits into the opening and does not

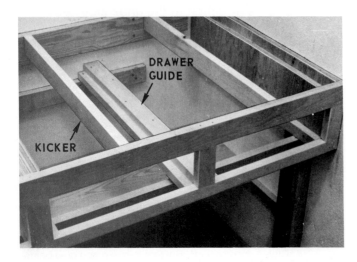

Fig. 22-10. Kickers prevent the drawer from tilting downward when pulled out.

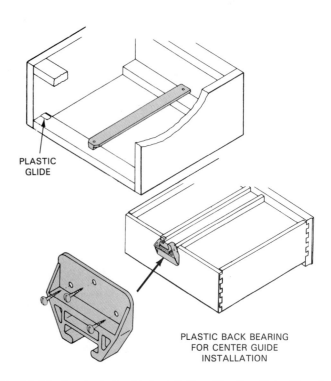

Fig. 22-11. A patented guide installation. (Ronthor Reiss Corp.)

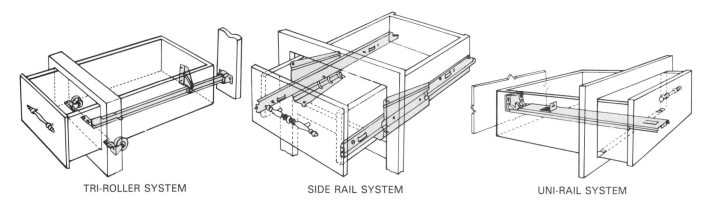

TRI-ROLLER SYSTEM          SIDE RAIL SYSTEM          UNI-RAIL SYSTEM

Fig. 22-12. Manufactured drawer slide assemblies are available in several designs. (Amerock Corp.)

project outward beyond the frame. The overlay door is mounted on the outside of the frame, completely or partially concealing it. The reverse bevel door is a variation of the overlay style. The lipped or inset door is rabbeted along all edges so that part of the door is inside the door frame. A lip extends over the frame on all sides, concealing the opening.

**Installing flush doors**

The flush door is usually installed with butt hinges. But, surface hinges, knife hinges, or various patented invisible hinges can be used, Fig. 22-15. Select a hinge that will be appropriate for the size of the door. The size of a hinge is determined by

Fig. 22-13. Swinging panel doors and sliding tambours are used in this modern bathroom cabinetry. (Haas Cabinet Co.)

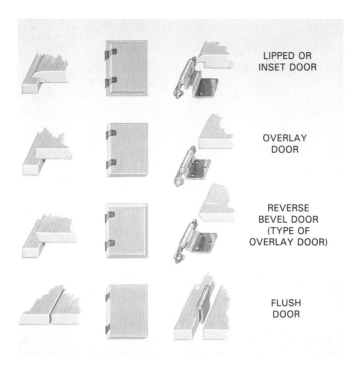

Fig. 22-14. Types of swinging doors used on cabinets. (Amerock Corp.)

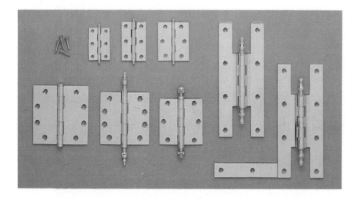

Fig. 22-15. Assortment of brass hinges for flush doors. (Baldwin Hardware Corp.)

its length and width when open. On large doors, three hinges should be used.

After the door is carefully fitted to the opening with about 1/32 in. clearance on each edge, it should be held in position with small wedges. Then mark the position of the hinges on the door and frame. Remove the door from the opening and lay out the position of the hinge leaf on the edge of the door and the frame. Also mark the depth and then cut the gain, as shown in Fig. 22-16. The total gain required for the hinge can be cut entirely in the door. However, for fine work it is best to gain equally into each member. On large doors it is practical to use the portable router for this operation.

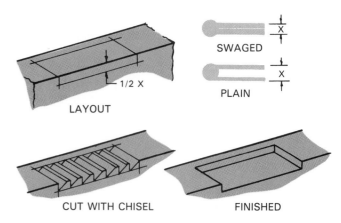

Fig. 22-16. Gain for a butt hinge.

Install the hinges on the door and then mount the door in the opening. Use only one screw in each hinge leaf. Make any necessary adjustments in the fit and then set the remaining screws. It may be necessary to plane a slight bevel on the edge of the door opposite the hinges.

Stops are set on the door frame so that the door will be held flush with the surface of the opening when closed. They may be placed all around the opening or just on the lock or catch side. On small doors, the catches used to hold them closed may also serve as stops, Fig. 22-17.

Flush doors on fine furniture and cabinetwork are sometimes installed with concealed hinges. The one shown in Fig. 22-18 is simply set in carefully aligned holes. After the hinge is inserted, a set screw is turned to create a wedge effect that fastens it securely in place. It can be mounted successfully in particle board, plywood, or solids.

Overlay doors provide an attractive installation in some contemporary styles of furniture. While butt

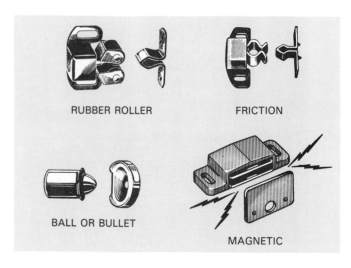

Fig. 22-17. Door catches.

Fig. 22-18. Fully concealed invisible hinge for flush doors. (Selby Furniture Hardware)

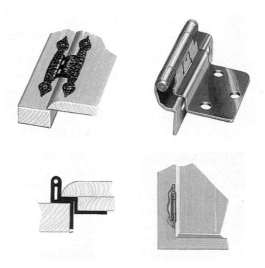

Fig. 22-20. Lipped (inset) hinges. (Amerock Corp.)

hinges can be used, those shown in Fig. 22-19 are especially designed for this type of door and are somewhat easier to install.

Lip doors are easier to cut and fit than flush doors because the clearance is covered. They are used for kitchen cabinets and other built-in cabinetwork. The door is cut to the size of the opening plus the width of the lip on each edge. Clearance of about 1/16 in. is provided on each edge with additional allowance for the hinge. Fig. 22-20 shows several types of hinges that are used on lip doors.

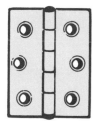

*Hinges and other hardware items should be installed, fitted, and then removed before finishing coats are applied.*

## SLIDING DOORS

Sliding doors are often used in furniture and cabinets where the swing of regular doors would be awkward or cause interference. They are adaptable to various styles and structural designs. See Fig. 22-21.

A sliding door arrangement can be constructed as shown in Fig. 22-22. Grooves are cut in the top and bottom of the case, before assembly. The doors are rabbeted so that the edge formed will match the groove with about 1/16 in. of clearance. Cut the top rabbet and groove deep enough that the door can be inserted or removed by simply raising it into the extra space. The doors will slide smoothly if the grooves are carefully cut, sanded, sealed, and waxed. Excessive finish should be avoided. Sliding glass doors are heavy and a special plastic or roller track should be used. Follow the manufacturer's recommendations for installation.

A wide range of sliding door track and rollers are available. Fig. 22-23 shows a self-lubricating plastic track that installs easily and provides smooth opera-

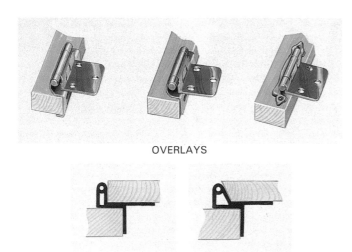

OVERLAYS

OVERLAY          REVERSE BEVEL

Fig. 22-19. Overlay and reverse bevel hinges. (Amerock Corp.)

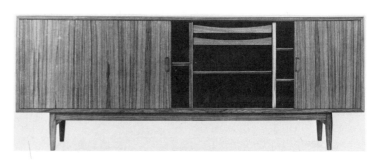

Fig. 22-21. Cabinet fitted with sliding doors. (George Tanier Inc.)

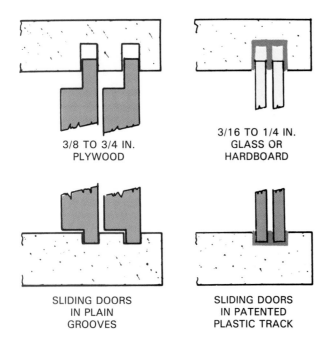

3/8 TO 3/4 IN.
PLYWOOD

3/16 TO 1/4 IN.
GLASS OR
HARDBOARD

SLIDING DOORS
IN PLAIN
GROOVES

SLIDING DOORS
IN PATENTED
PLASTIC TRACK

Fig. 22-22. Sliding door details.

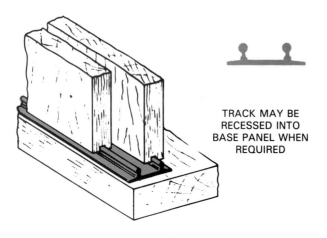

TRACK MAY BE
RECESSED INTO
BASE PANEL WHEN
REQUIRED

Fig. 22-23. Plastic door track installation.
(Ronthor Reiss Corp.)

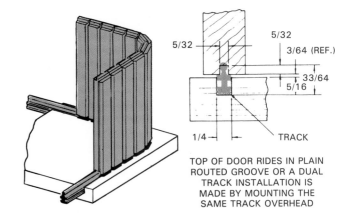

5/32

5/32

3/64 (REF.)

33/64

5/16

1/4

TRACK

Fig. 22-24. This tambour sliding door detail shows the use of plastic track.

TOP OF DOOR RIDES IN PLAIN
ROUTED GROOVE OR A DUAL
TRACK INSTALLATION IS
MADE BY MOUNTING THE
SAME TRACK OVERHEAD

Fig. 22-25. Sliding glass doors both protect and display objects in this wall cabinet.

tion for case and cabinet doors. Overhead track and rollers are used for large wardrobe doors and passage doors.

Fig. 22-24 shows the installation of a tambour door. Strips of wood with grooves in the ends are glued to a heavy cloth backing and ride on a plastic track. The track is set in a routed groove. It may be curved as shown. Installations of this type are a bit tricky; experiment with a small section of door and track before cutting and preparing the finished assembly.

Sliding glass doors are adaptable to wall units and add variety to an installation. Fig. 22-25 shows bypass (1/4 in. plate glass) sliding doors for a cabinet in a kitchen-dinette area.

## TEST YOUR KNOWLEDGE, Chapter 22

Please do not write in the text. Place your answers on a separate sheet of paper.
1. Explain the difference between lip and flush drawers.
2. What type of material is generally used for the bottom of most cabinet drawers?
3. Three common types of drawer guides include _____ guides, _____ guides, and _____ guides.
4. What is the purpose of a kicker?
5. List the four types of swinging doors that are often used in cabinetwork.
6. The _____ _____ door is a variation of the overlay door.
7. The size of a hinge is determined by its _____ and _____ when open.
8. Name three types of door catches.

## ACTIVITIES

1. Make a scale drawing of a well designed cabinet door in your home. Give a description of the materials and hardware used, and your reason for selecting that particular door for study.
2. Examine the types of cabinet hinges stocked at a local hardware store or lumber company. Give a written description of several of the hinges you examined. If available, collect literature on those particular hinges.
3. Examine cabinet and furniture drawers in your home. Sketch the construction used to attach the drawer front to the sides for each type you found. Which of these construction techniques is the best? Why?

Quality door and drawer construction is an integral part of these student wardrobes.    (Period Furniture, Inc.)

 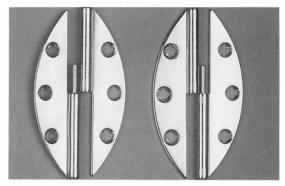

Left. Threaded inserts provide an effective means of assembly for furniture pieces. (Woodcraft Supply Corporation)
Right. Duplex hinge gain may be cut with a plate joiner.    (Lamello AG)

Two views of a dining/living room combination that takes advantage of the large, open space provided by both curved and straight laminated beams. (Potlatch Corp.)

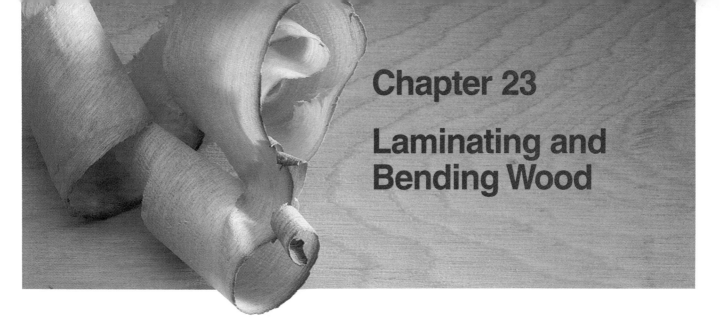

# Chapter 23

# Laminating and Bending Wood

Curved wood parts can be formed by cutting the stock to the required shape or by bending, Fig. 23-1. Cutting the curve with machines like the band saw is often wasteful of material and the part is seldom as strong as a bent piece. Wood can be bent either by PLASTICIZING (softening) it with steam or hot water, or by laminating and then clamping it in a form for drying and curing. While saw kerfs are sometimes cut on the concave side, parts produced by this method have very little strength.

WOOD LAMINATING is the process of forming parts (usually bent) by attaching two or more layers of wood together with the grain of each ply running in the same direction. Plywood is also composed of layers of wood, but with the grain direction running at right angles in each successive layer. Laminated wood is used for the curved parts of furniture, baseball bats, tennis rackets, golf clubs, boats, structural beams, and many other products.

Fig. 23-1. The graceful curves in the legs of the table, the chair, and the chair back were formed by bending the parts to shape. (David Ebner, Courtesy, Pritam and Eames)

## SELECTING AND CUTTING STOCK

Both hardwoods and softwoods can be laminated and bent; however, hardwoods have somewhat better bending characteristics. Hardwood species commonly used in industry for either solid or laminated bending include ash, birch, elm, hickory, maple, oak, sweet gum, and walnut. Laminated structural members are made from such softwood species as Douglas fir, southern yellow pine, white cedar, and redwood. More important than the kind of wood, is the quality and grain structure of a given specimen. Straight-grained stock that is free of knots, splits, checks, and other defects should be selected.

When a strip of wood is bent, the inside surface is made shorter (compressed) while the outside surface is stretched. The thicker the stock, the greater this difference will need to be. Wood fibers are difficult to stretch, but fairly easy to compress, therefore the greatest change usually occurs on the inside surface of the bend. Wood will bend across the grain or along the grain. Across-the-grain bends are seldom used in laminated parts; they apply mainly to curved or formed plywood.

In the school shop, veneers are often used to produce laminated parts. VENEER is defined as a thin wood sheet, 1/8 in. or less in thickness. Wood over 1/8 in. thick is simply referred to as STOCK, and is produced by resawing operations. Standard hardwood veneer thickness is 1/28 in. Other common thicknesses include 1/32, 1/20, and 1/16 in. In general, to save time and material, you should use layers of the thickest dimension that will still bend easily to the minimum radius of the part being produced. When the radius of bend is too sharp for the layer thickness, it may be necessary to moisten the surface and preform the wood before making the final assembly.

Laminating layers can be cut to rough size on the band saw or jigsaw. If 1/16 in., or thinner, veneers are used, the cutting can be done with a pair of heavy scissors or snips as shown in Fig. 23-2. Cross-grain cuts are easily made; cuts along the grain will tend to split the veneer. The splitting can be minimized by dampening the surface. After the plies are cut to size they should be arranged carefully, with the best surfaces on the outside.

## APPLYING GLUE

Urea resin glue fills the requirements for most laminating work done in the school shop. It has a sufficiently long assembly time, is strong, and stains the wood only slightly. Casein glue can also be used. It is less expensive, works best on oily woods, but has a staining characteristic that may be undesirable.

Glue can be applied by various methods. Fig. 23-3 shows urea resin being applied rapidly with a roller. As the layers are coated, they are stacked in the proper position. When the entire stack or laminate is coated, it is placed in a plastic (polyethylene film) bag or covered with wax paper. This is to prevent the excess glue or ''squeeze-out'' from touching the form.

Fig. 23-4 shows strips for a tennis racket being coated with adhesive and then formed in a special metal press.

Fig. 23-3. Top. Applying urea resin glue with a roller. Bottom. Placing the stack in a plastic bag.

## CLAMPING FORMS AND DEVICES

Fig. 23-5 shows the laminate placed in a form and pressure being applied with a shop-built press. A wide variety of forms and clamping devices can be designed and used. Some are fitted with machine bolts that are used to apply the pressure. The forms must be accurately shaped so pressure will be evenly distributed. Male-female types must be concentric when spaced for the given laminate. Alignment pins may be necessary to insure that the two parts come together correctly.

Surfaces of the form should be smooth and the curves should be free-flowing (faired). It may be helpful to use a rubber pad between the form and the laminate, or to line the surface with light sheet metal. Wood forms should be finished with a coat of sealer and paste wax, for easy cleaning and maintenance, Figs. 23-6 and 23-7.

## CURING

Allow the laminate to remain in the form until the glue has thoroughly set and is almost completely cured. At room temperature, this will require about

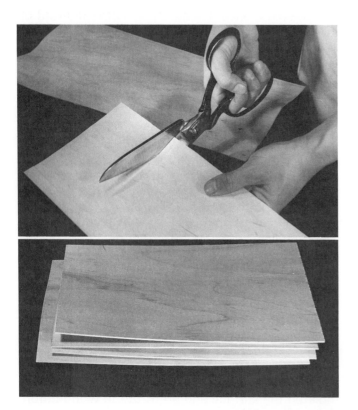

Fig. 23-2. Top. Cutting veneer to rough size. Veneer that is too dry (less than 6 percent moisture content) will splinter and break excessively. Bottom. Assemble the rough cut layers with the best surfaces to the outside.

Fig. 23-4. Left. Ash strips for a tennis racket emerge from a glue spreading machine. Right. Glue-coated strips in position around center form and ready for side clamps (arrow) to be closed. (Wilson Sporting Goods Co.)

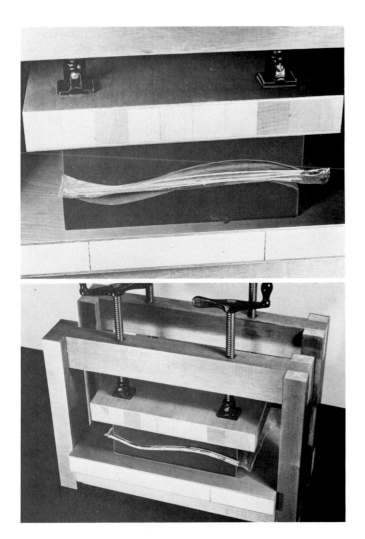

Fig. 23-5. Top. Laminate placed in the form. Bottom. Pressure applied in a shop-built press.

24 hours for urea resin glue. If higher temperatures are applied, this time can be greatly reduced. For example, urea resin will attain more than 90 percent of its total strength within one hour at a temperature of 140° F (60° C).

Since the glue will raise the moisture content of the wood, it is usually best to lay the part aside for several days before performing final shaping and finishing operations.

## CUTTING TO SIZE AND FINISHING

The edges of the laminate can be trimmed and shaped with various hand tools. The band saw, jigsaw, or sabre saw can be used if certain precautions are observed. Special jigs and fixtures may be required to properly support the work.

Surfaces can be smoothed with scrapers, files, and abrasive paper. Finishing coats can be applied in the same manner as other wood products.

 *When trimming the rough edges of a laminate, you should wear goggles or safety glasses to protect your eyes from flying particles of hardened glue and wood chips.*

## MOLDED PLYWOOD

Extensive use is made of molded plywood in furniture construction, especially for chairs and

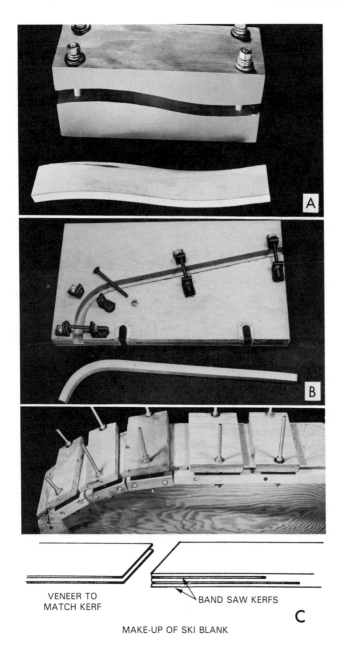

VENEER TO
MATCH KERF

BAND SAW KERFS

MAKE-UP OF SKI BLANK

C

Fig. 23-6. Clamping forms. A—Machine bolts are used to apply pressure and align the two parts of the form. Laminate consists of 7 layers of 1/16 in. veneer. B—Table leg. Six 1/8 in. laminations. C—Water ski. Two saw kerfs cut into the end of solid stock and then filled with veneer. Stagger the depth of the cuts and use a resorcinol glue.

Fig. 23-7. Open view of special high frequency press shown in Fig. 23-4. Bonding and curing of tennis racket has taken place in less than one minute.

Fig. 23-8. Chair seat and back made of molded plywood. (Herman Miller Inc.)

commercial seating. It is laid-up like regular plywood with the grain turned at right angles in alternate layers, and then pressed in special dies that form the required curved surfaces. The surfaces can be formed in a single-curved surface or a double-curved surface, like the seat and chair back in Fig. 23-8.

Single-curved molded plywood can be produced in the school shop with wooden forms and standard clamps. Fig. 23-9 shows a simple pressing arrangement to form a plywood seat for a TV stool from layers of 1/8 in. plywood. Also see Fig. 23-10.

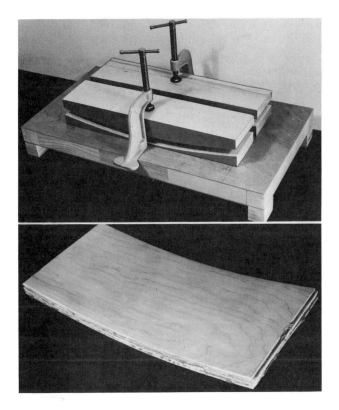

Fig. 23-9. Top. Plywood forming press. Bottom. Curved plywood blank made from five layers of 1/8 in. (3 mm) plywood. Individual layers of veneer could also be used.

## BENDING WITH KERFS

Thick stock can be bent easier if a series of saw kerfs is cut on the concave side. This reduces the size of the surface by removing some of the stock, rather than compressing it. However, a part produced in this manner is weak and should be used only in assemblies where it can be securely attached to other supporting members. For example, such a part might be used to form the trim apron of a tabletop, where the top itself, or other members, would provide the structural strength required. Another disadvantage results from the fact that the saw kerfs may telegraph (show through) on the outside surface. This can usually be avoided if the kerfs are not too deep and if the part is given a coarse sanding after the forming operation.

The depth, and spacing of the saw kerfs will vary with the kind of material and the radius of bend. You will need to experiment with a number of sample pieces to determine the best solution for your work. Fig. 23-11 shows a press used to form a part made from a piece of lumber core plywood. In this particular piece, a strip of veneer was glued to the inside surface. In some work the kerfed part could be attached directly to the structure with glue blocks set along the inside surface to hold it in place.

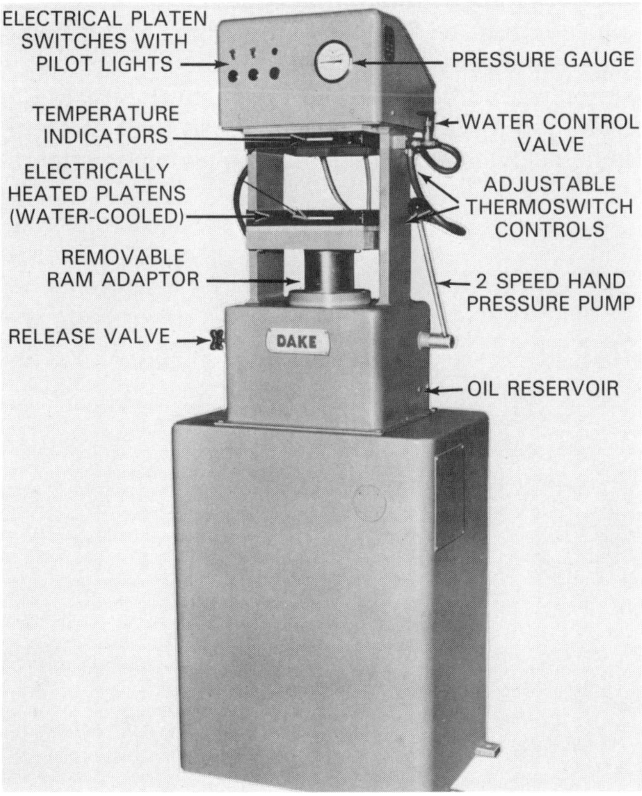

Fig. 23-10. Small hydraulic press for laboratories and school shops.

ELECTRICAL PLATEN SWITCHES WITH PILOT LIGHTS

PRESSURE GAUGE

TEMPERATURE INDICATORS

WATER CONTROL VALVE

ELECTRICALLY HEATED PLATENS (WATER-COOLED)

ADJUSTABLE THERMOSWITCH CONTROLS

REMOVABLE RAM ADAPTOR

2 SPEED HAND PRESSURE PUMP

RELEASE VALVE

DAKE

OIL RESERVOIR

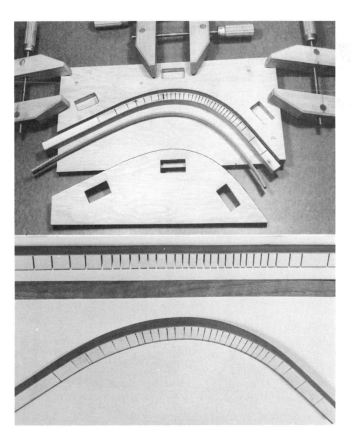

Fig. 23-11. Top. Forming press. Note sponge rubber pad. Bottom. Kerfed part, veneer strip, and finished piece.

## BENDING SOLID STOCK

Curved parts can be formed from solid stock by plasticizing the wood with moisture and heat, then bending and clamping the wood in the required shape until it cools and dries. This process is used extensively in industry, Fig. 23-12. It is not easily adaptable, however, to work in the school shop, except for small parts.

Stock for solid bending should be selected with about the same consideration as for laminated work. Air-dried stock with a moisture content of 12 to 20 percent will work best. Machine the stock to size, providing allowances for shrinkage and finishing. The ends should be seal-coated to prevent excessive absorption of moisture during the steaming process, and to minimize end checking during the drying and fixing process. For severe bends, cut the stock so that the annual rings are perpendicular to the plane of the bend.

The length of time required for steaming or boiling the wood varies with the kind of wood, initial moisture content (M.C.), thickness of the stock, and the degree of curvature required. In general, most wood will need to be steamed or boiled for about one hour for each inch of thickness. Plasticizing with steam, at or near atmospheric pressure, until the M.C. of the wood reaches 20 to 25 percent, will normally produce satisfactory results.

There are two broad classes of bends: those made with end pressure, and those made without end pressure (free bends). Free bending is feasible only for slight curvatures. Bending with end pressure causes the wood fibers to be properly compressed on the inside of the bend and reduces tensile failures on the outside surfaces. Also there is less tendency of "spring-back" after the work is removed from the clamps. End pressure is usually applied with a metal strap (galvanized iron or stainless steel) that is equipped with end fittings. This strap is applied to the convex side of the stock. As the bend is made, it absorbs the tensile stress, and the wood cells are subjected only to compression forces. See Fig. 23-13.

The work must be held in the clamps until it has cooled and dried, or SET. On heavy work this may take several days, even in specially heated drying rooms. In production work, bent parts are removed from the bending apparatus soon after they have cooled and are then placed in special retaining clamps to hold them in position until the set is complete. The amount of time or drying that is necessary to set a bend varies with kinds of wood and types of work.

## STRUCTURAL LAMINATES

The wood laminating process is applied to a wide range of structural members used in large buildings where it is necessary to have clear space, unobstructed by supports. Laminated construction allows the architect a wide latitude in creating forms adapted to and expressive of the function and purpose of the structure. In addition, laminated construction greatly extends the use of wood—the most abundant, beautiful, and economical building material available. Fig. 23-14 shows curved arches, formed by the laminating process and incorporated into a dignified, functional design.

In addition to flexibility in design, wood beam construction also provides a high fire resistance factor. Wood beams do not transmit heat like unprotected metal beams, which lose their strength and quickly collapse under extremely high tempera-

Fig. 23-12. Bending solid wood furniture parts in special metal clamps.

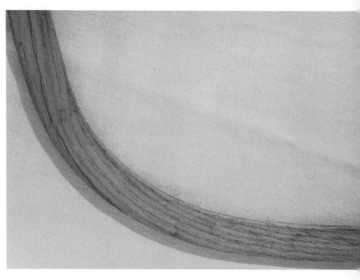

Fig. 23-13. Steam bent white oak strip. Note the smooth curve with little or no distortion; this is due to compression.

Fig. 23-14. The curved support beams of this modern structure are laminated beams. They provide great strength and freedom of design. (Potlatch Corp.)

Fig. 23-16. Scientific testing of a laminated arch design. (Forest Products Laboratory)

tures. Exposure of a wood beam to flame results in a very slow loss in its strength. It is weakened only in proportion to the slow reduction in cross section due to charring. This takes place slowly and thus provides precious time that may save life and material, Fig. 23-15.

Laminated beams and arches must be carefully designed so that they will provide the strength required. Fig. 23-16 shows a sample arch being submitted to an extensive series of tests. Data gathered from these tests will be compiled and used in future design problems. The parts and general design of a typical V arch are shown in Fig. 23-17.

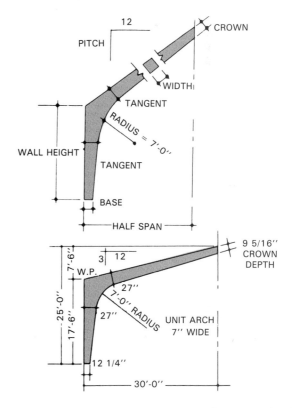

Fig. 23-15. This photo, taken after a fire, shows wood beam supporting twisted steel I beams. (Forest Products Laboratory)

Fig. 23-17. Parts of a laminated V arch. (Unit Structures, Inc.)

Most laminated structural members are made of softwoods. They are manufactured in industrial plants specializing in such production and then shipped, prefinished and ready for erection, to the building site.

Figs. 23-18 to 23-22 show in-plant views of the fabrication of beams and arches. Lumber is carefully selected and machined to size. To secure the required length, pieces must be end-jointed. Since end grain is hard to joint, a finger joint is used. In large laminates, a number of these joints may be required in each ply. They are always staggered at least 2 ft. from a similar joint in an adjacent layer.

Waterproof adhesives are applied and the layers are then clamped to forms. Because of the size of the units, it is seldom practical to utilize heat in the curing process. After the beam or arch has cured, the edges and faces are machined to size. Today, many of the beams and arches are finished in the factory to specifications that will match the interior of the completed building. Prefinished units are carefully wrapped and handled so they will arrive at the construction site free of damage.

Fig. 23-19. Gluing a laminated arch in a special clamping device. (Forest Products Laboratory)

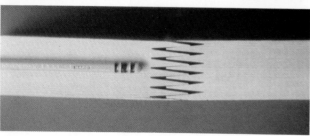

Fig. 23-18. Top. Assembling laminations for a straight beam 65 ft. long. Bottom. Finger joint used to join ends of laminations. Individual laminations should not exceed 2 in. in net thickness. (American Institute of Timber Construction)

Fig. 23-20. Final sanding and inspection of giant laminate arches. After coats of finish are applied, they will be wrapped in a waterproof covering for shipment to the construction site. (John Walker)

Fig. 23-21. Laminated beams provide a clear span of 48 ft. Purlins, spaced at 8 ft., will support 4 x 8 ft. prefabricated roof panels. Note the metal connections used to fasten the purlins to the beams. (Boise-Cascade Corp.)

Fig. 23-22. Construction worker attaches beam brackets to steel drum. The drum serves as a hub for assembling major beams. (Koppers Co., Inc.)

## TEST YOUR KNOWLEDGE, Chapter 23

Please do not write in the text. Place your answers on a separate sheet of paper.

1. When a piece of wood is bent, the outside surface is stretched and the inside surface is _____.
2. Veneer is generally defined as thin sheets of wood under _____ in. in thickness.
3. Why is polyvinyl glue not satisfactory for laminating work?
4. When making a curved male-female type form for laminations, not only the curve but the _____ of the lamination must be considered.
5. The spacing and depth of kerfs for bending solid stock will vary with the kind of wood and _____ of the bend.
6. Which type of stock is preferrable for steam bending?
7. The length of time required for steaming wood for bending will vary with the kind of wood, initial M.C., radius of curve, and _____.
8. Wood beam construction provides flexibility in design and a high _____ _____ factor.

## ACTIVITIES

1. Prepare a proposal for experimental work in laminating, using thin hardboard core stock and veneer or plastic laminates for the surface layers. Suggest articles or projects for which this type of laminate would be appropriate.
2. Develop a design for a heated laminating form that could be used in the school shop. Consider the use of a heating pad or the heating element of a discarded electric iron.
3. Secure descriptive folders from a company that manufactures laminated beams, arches, and trusses. Your local lumber dealer may be able to furnish addresses. Prepare a written report describing the various types, uses, design data, and finish. Also include information concerning appropriate roof decking materials, and methods of application.

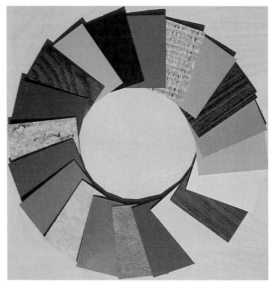

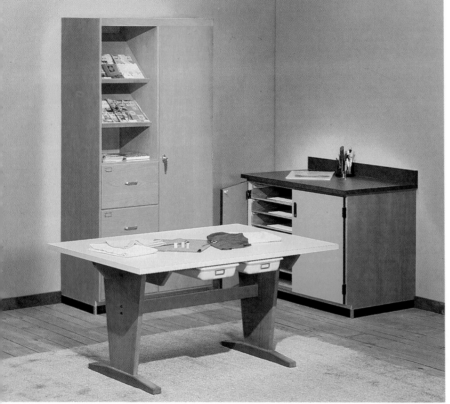

Top. Sample colors and textures available in plastic laminates. Center. The countertop, doors, and tabletop are just three of the many colors and textures available in plastic laminates. (Campbellrhea Mfg. Co.) Bottom. This decorative countertop is made from Formica ColorCore. Any thickness may be made by laminating several layers together. (Formica Corp.)

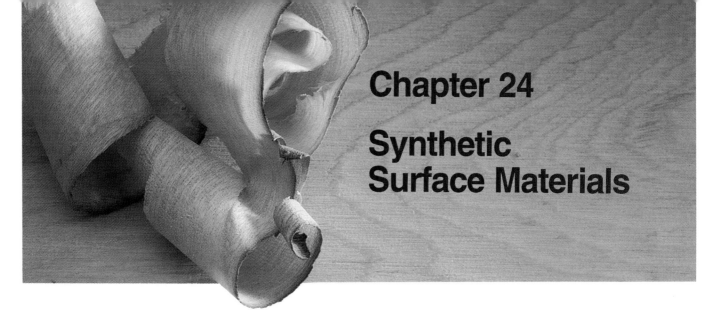

# Chapter 24

# Synthetic Surface Materials

High-pressure plastic laminates and solid surface materials provide a hard, smooth sheet of synthetic material that is highly resistant to wear and scratching. They are unharmed by boiling water, alcohol, oil, grease, and ordinary household chemicals. Because of these characteristics, plastic laminates and solid surface materials are widely used as a surface material for tops of furniture and cabinetwork, Fig. 24-1. They are also used for wainscotting and wall paneling in the home, and are especially practical in commercial and institutional buildings where surfaces may be subjected to a great amount of wear, Fig. 24-2.

Fig. 24-1. The countertops in this kitchen are decorative and resistant to wear and scratching. Oil, grease, boiling water, and most household chemicals will not harm the surface. (Riviera Cabinets, Inc.)

Fig. 24-2. Top. Heavy use of countertops and cabinet doors requires a material which is durable. Plastic laminate met this requirement for use in this test kitchen. Bottom. Countertops used as work surfaces in school laboratories should be smooth and resistant to chemicals. (Campbellrhea Mfg., Inc.)

Fig. 24-3. Postformed countertops may be purchased in ready-to-install form, with back splash and formed lip.

Fig. 24-4. Construction of a high-pressure plastic laminate.

## HIGH-PRESSURE PLASTIC LAMINATES

High-pressure plastic laminates are available in three types: GENERAL PURPOSE, VERTICAL, and POSTFORMED. There are subcategories and additional special purpose laminates within each of these categories. General purpose laminates (1/10 and 1/16 in. thick) are commonly used for exposed surfaces of countertops, door fronts, etc. Vertical laminates (1/32 in. thick) are used for door backs and other light-duty uses. Postforming laminates (1/16 in. thick) are used to make formed countertops, Fig. 24-3, and edgebond curved pieces. Unlike general purpose laminates, postformed laminates bend when heat is applied.

Some plastic laminates are also available in thicknesses of 1/10 to 1/32 in. 1/16 in. is most commonly used. They consist of seven layers of paper, similar to that used in common paper bags (Kraft paper), impregnated with phenol-formaldehyde resin, Fig. 24-4. On top of these is a pattern sheet, made in various colors, designs, and wood grains. A transparent sheet, impregnated with melamine resin, is placed over the pattern sheet. The entire build-up is bonded in huge presses at temperatures of over 350° F and pressure of 1,000 lbs. per sq. in. A polished stainless steel plate is used next to the top lamination which imparts a perfectly smooth surface to the laminate, Fig. 24-5.

Fig. 24-5. Processing paper to be used as the layers in a plastic laminate. (Formica Corp.)

Although the laminate is very hard, it does not possess great strength and is serviceable only when bonded to plywood, particle board, hardboard, or other backing. This base or core material must be smooth and dimensionally stable. Hardwood plywood (usually 3/4 in. thick) makes a satisfactory base; however, some plywoods, especially fir, have a coarse grain texture which may TELEGRAPH (show through). Particle board, which is less expensive than plywood, provides a smooth surface and adequate strength, and is therefore used extensively.

When the core or base is free to move and is not supported by other parts of the structure, the laminated surface may warp. This can be avoided by bonding a backing sheet of the laminate to the second face. It will minimize moisture penetration or loss, and provide a balanced unit with identical materials on either side of the core. For premium grade (highest) cabinetwork, Architectural Woodwork Institute standards specify that a backing sheet be used on any unsupported area exceeding 4 square feet. Backing sheets are like the regular laminate without the decorative finish and are usually thinner. A standard thickness for use opposite a .060 in. (1/16) face laminate is .020 in.

## LAYOUT AND CUTTING

Plan your work carefully so that the position of the pattern will be correct and there will be a minimum amount of waste. Plastic laminates are available in standard widths of 24, 30, 36, 48, and 60 in. Standard lengths include 5, 6, and 8 ft.

However, lengths of 10 and 12 ft. are also available. A soft lead pencil can be used to make layout lines. When working with dark colors, place a strip of masking tape in the layout area and then draw the line on the tape.

Plastic laminates can be cut to rough size with a handsaw, table saw, portable saw, or portable router, Fig. 24-6. Use fine-toothed blades and support the material close to the cut. Regular woodworking tools will grow dull rapidly so it is best to use carbide tipped tools whenever a large amount of laminate is to be cut. Laminates 1/32 in. thick, which are used on vertical surfaces, can be cut with tin snips. Always wear appropriate eye protection when cutting plastic laminates.

When using the table saw to cut plastic laminates, attach a wood strip to the fence to keep the laminate from slipping under the fence. Feed the material at a moderate rate into the blade with the decorative side facing up.

It is best to make the roughing cuts 1/8 in. to 1/4 in. oversize and then trim the edges after the laminate has been mounted. Handle large sheets carefully; they can be easily cracked or broken. Also be careful not to scratch the decorative side.

*Always wear adequate eye protection when cutting a plastic laminate with power equipment. The cuttings are hard and sharp, and fly from the machine at high speed.*

## APPLYING ADHESIVES

Although various types of adhesive can be used, contact cement is preferred because no sustained pressure is required. This is applied with a spreader, roller, or brush to both surfaces to be joined. In production work, contact cement is often sprayed.

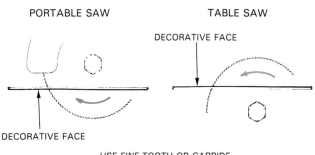

PORTABLE SAW                    TABLE SAW

DECORATIVE FACE

DECORATIVE FACE

USE FINE-TOOTH OR CARBIDE TIPPED BLADE

Fig. 24-6. Cutting plastic laminate with circular saws.

On large horizontal surfaces it is easiest to use a spreader. For soft plywoods, particle board, or other porous surfaces, the spreader is held with the serrated edge perpendicular to the surface. On hard nonporous surfaces and the plastic laminate, hold the edge at a 45 deg. angle, Fig. 24-7. A single coat should be sufficient.

An animal hair or fiber brush may be used to apply the adhesive to small surfaces or those in a vertical position. Apply one coat, let it dry thoroughly, then apply a second. All of the surface should be completely covered with a glossy film. Dull spots, after drying, indicate that the application was too thin. Another coat should be applied.

Stir the adhesive thoroughly before using and follow the manufacturer's recommendations. Brushes or other types of applicators may need to be cleaned in a special solvent.

*Some types of contact cement are extremely flammable. Nonflammable types may produce harmful vapors. Be sure to read the label on the container. Follow the manufacturer's directions and observe precautions.*

## DRYING AND BONDING

Let both surfaces dry for 15 minutes or longer. You can test the dryness by pressing a piece of paper lightly against the coated surface. If no adhesive sticks to the paper, it is ready to be bonded. This bond can be made any time within an hour (time varies with different manufacturers). If the assembly cannot be made within this time, the adhesive can be reactivated by applying a thin coat of adhesive to each surface.

Because they cannot be shifted once contact is made, bring the two surfaces together in the exact position required. When joining large surfaces, place a sheet of heavy wrapping paper (called a slip-sheet) over the base surface and then slide the laminate into position. Withdraw the paper slightly so one edge can be bonded and then remove the entire sheet and apply pressure. Some manufacturers recommend the use of dowel rods or a backing sheet instead of the paper separator.

Total bond is secured by the application of momentary pressure. Industry uses pinch rollers or rotary presses, Fig. 24-8. Hand rolling provides satisfactory results if the roller is small (3 in. or less in length), Fig. 24-9. Long rollers apply less pressure per square inch. Work from the center to the outside edges and be certain to roll every square inch of surface. In corners and areas that are hard to roll,

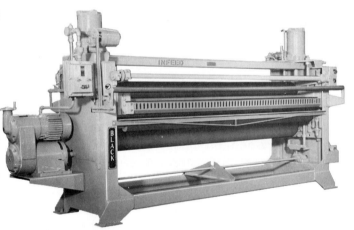

Fig. 24-8. A rotary press may be used to bond plastic to a base material. Pressure is applied by pneumatic cylinders. (Black Brothers)

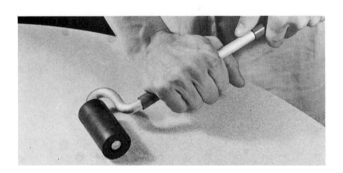

Fig. 24-9. Applying pressure to the laminate with a hand roller. Press down hard with both hands.

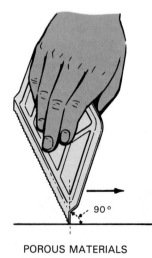

POROUS MATERIALS

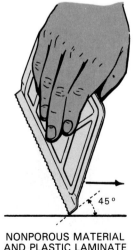

NONPOROUS MATERIAL AND PLASTIC LAMINATE

Fig. 24-7. Using a spreader to apply contact cement.

hold a block of soft wood on the surface and tap it with a rubber mallet.

## TRIMMING AND FINISHING

Trimming and smoothing edges is one of the most important steps in the application of a plastic laminate. A block plane or file can be used; however, an electric router equipped with a carbide tipped bit will produce precision work at a much faster rate. When using a router, some device must be used to control the depth of cut. An adjustable patented guide can be used, Fig. 24-10, or you can clamp or screw a wood guide block to the router base, as shown in Fig. 24-11. Make the adjustment carefully so the bit will cut even with the surface, with about 1/64 in. clearance.

The corners of a plastic laminate application should be beveled, Fig. 24-12. This will make them smooth to the touch and wear better.

The angle can be formed with a smooth mill file, as shown in Fig. 24-13. Stroke the file downward. Be careful not to damage the surface of the edge trim strip. Some routers can be equipped with an adjustable base or a special bit that will make this cut. Final smoothing and a slight rounding of the bevel should be done with a 400 wet-or-dry abrasive paper. Fig. 24-14 shows a finished countertop.

When working with plastic laminates, be especially careful that files, edge tools, or abrasive papers do not scratch or otherwise damage the finished surfaces.

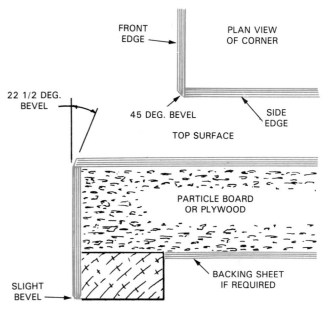

Fig. 24-12. Bevels for plastic laminate corners are important in the production of quality work.

Fig. 24-10. Trimming an edge with a router, using an adjustable guide. (DeWalt)

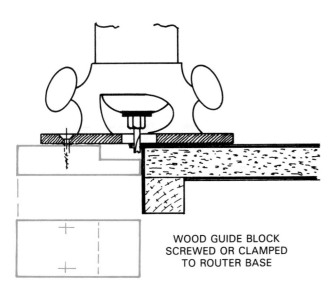

WOOD GUIDE BLOCK SCREWED OR CLAMPED TO ROUTER BASE

Fig. 24-11. Trimming an edge with a router, using a shop-made guide block.

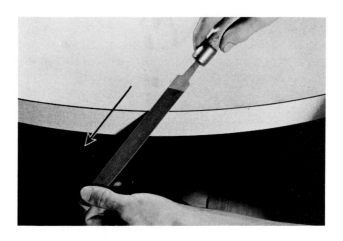

Fig. 24-13. Filing a corner bevel.

Fig. 24-14. Heat resistance makes plastic laminates an ideal surface material for counters and other areas subjected to high temperatures and hot objects. (Formica Corp.)

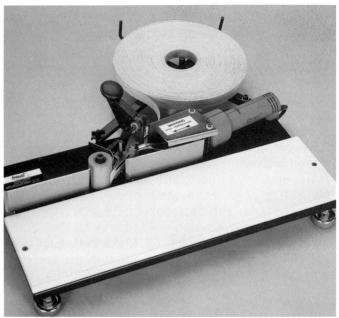

Fig. 24-15. This edgebanding machine enables wood and polyester edge finishes to be applied to veneered or plastic laminate boards with ease. The edgebanding is coated with a hot-melt adhesive on the backside and is softened as it passes the hot air of the heat gun. A pinch roller then presses the edgebanding against the veneered or laminated board. The adhesive creates a permanent bond in seconds. The system is ideal for the small shop or for large shops in situations wwhere time is critical. Edgebanding is availale in rolls of plastic or veneer from popular woods. (Freud, Inc.)

## EDGEBANDING

Most small and medium-size woodworking shops cannot afford an automatic edgebander. At least two alternatives are available—a tabletop edgebander that can trim and buff wood veneer and plastic laminate and a hand-held edgebander that applies preglued veneer tape.

High-quality tabletop edgebanders are available that can perform single-trim and single-buff operations on edgebanding less than 1/8 in. in thickness.

A less-expensive option is possible when preglued veneer tape is to be used, Fig. 24-15. It uses hot air to melt the glue and may be used on panels of almost any size. It can also apply tape to curved edges. Edgebanding tapes are available in several standard widths—13/16 in., 1 5/8 in., 2 in., and 3 in.. The 13/16 in. tape is most popular as it is used with 3/4 in.-thick material. Wood edgebanding tape is made from 1/40 in.-thick veneer that is backed with a resin-impregnated paper, which is a hot-melt glue.

## NEW SURFACING LAMINATE—NUVEL

A new surfacing material called Nuvel™ offers both cold- and hot-forming options, which are not possible with typical laminates, Fig. 24-16.

Nuvel is a compromise between high-pressure laminates and solid surface products, but has post-forming options not possible with either of those materials. It is available in sheet form with a thickness of .090 in. and sizes of 30 in. x 96 in., 30 in. x 120 in., 30 in. x 144 in., 48 in. x 96 in., and 60 in. x 144 in.. The new material has a uniform color throughout.

Nuvel is made from a polyester resin called Valox™, which was developed for automobile body components. Experimentation with the material has demonstrated cold-forming to a 4 in. radius and with heat a radius of 1/4 in. was achieved. Contact cement used with high-pressure laminates also works with Nuvel. Carbide tooling designed for solid surface materials also work on this material. Nuvel's solid color makes it a renewable surface that can be cleaned or repaired by sanding or buffing the damaged area.

Fig. 24-16. Nuvel™ is a solid color material that can be cold-formed to a 4 in. radius and to a 1/4 in. with heat. (Formica, Inc.)

## SOLID SURFACE MATERIALS

Solid surface materials like Avonite™, Corian™, Fountainhead™, Gibraltar™, and Surell™ are now being used by consumers and builders alike, Fig. 24-17. Solid surface materials consist of acrylic and/or polyester resins (depending on the brand) mixed with fillers and coloring agents. They usually are available in sheets measuring 1/2 in. thick by 31 in. wide by 145 in. length. The material may also be cast into sinks or moldings at the factory. Solid surface material costs several times more than typical high-pressure laminate.

Solid surface materials are frequently made to look like natural stone, but they are also available in a variety of solid and flecked colors. Countertops made with solid surface materials don't require a substrate like traditional plastic laminates. Solid surface countertops are generally attached to the cabinet frame using spots of silicone sealer to provide for expansion and contraction of the material.

Solid surface materials can be cut or shaped with common woodworking tools. Carbide router bits and saw blades are recommended. Inside corners should have a radius of at least 1/4 in. to avoid stress fractures. Seams should be placed no closer than 1 in. from the inside corners and 3 in. from sink cutouts. Seams should always be supported on the backside.

Pieces of solid surface material may be joined or "built-up" along the edge using manufacturer-supplied seam kits. The kits are available in colors that match the material. Seams that are done correctly disappear when sanding and buffing are completed. The seam kits have a catalyst and colored resin in a two-compartment plastic bag. The contents are mixed together by kneading the bag thoroughly with your hands. The cement is then ready to use. Cover both surfaces with an ample amount of the seam material after cleaning the surfaces with alcohol. Push the joint together with your hands until the cement squeezes out over the full length of the joint. Hold the pieces together with tape supported over the joint. As the seam material dries it will shrink, therefore, normal clamping procedures may not keep steady pressure on the joint. Spring clamps may be used for narrow strips because they will apply a steady pressure and cannot be clamped too tight. Too much pressure will squeeze the bonding resin out of the joint.

Allow the seam material to dry for 45 minutes to 1 hour and then remove the excess material with a flat-bottomed router bit. Two blocks under the router base, which straddles the joint, works well. Use 600-grit wet-or-dry sandpaper to finish the joint surface. Follow the manufacturer's directions to achieve a satisfactory finish.

Fig. 24-17. Solid surface materials, though more expensive than traditional high-pressure plastic laminates, produce nice renewable surfaces. Solid surface materials are 1/2 in. thick and do not require a substrate. (Wilsonart)

## TEST YOUR KNOWLEDGE, Chapter 24

Please do not write in the text. Place your answers on a separate sheet of paper.
1. The common thickness of standard plastic laminate is:
   a. 1/32 in.
   b. 1/16 in.
   c. 1/10 in.
   d. None of the above.
2. What are backing laminates used for?
3. How do postformed plastic laminates and standard laminates differ?
4. Why is a base required for plastic laminates?

5. What is meant by telegraph?
6. According to the Architectural Woodwork Institute, backing sheet is necessary in premium grade cabinetwork on any unsupported area exceeding:
   a. 4 square in.
   b. 4 square ft.
   c. 1/4 square ft.
   d. None of the above.
7. Because regular woodworking tools will grow dull rapidly, it is best to use _____ blades whenever cutting a large amount of laminate.
8. Contact cement is generally used to attach plastic laminate to particle board and plywood. True or False?
9. Name two methods for trimming the edge of a plastic laminate application.
10. Identify the three types of synthetic surface materials.

11. How are solid surface countertops generally attached to the cabinet frame?
12. What is used to join pieces of solid surface materials?

## ACTIVITIES

1. Collect samples of plastic laminates. Display each type along with an explanation where each might be used.
2. Design a project which utilizes a plastic laminate surface. Explain why this material was chosen for this particular application.
3. Visit a local cabinet shop. Report on procedures used to make custom countertops, the cost of materials and labor, and the type of jobs performed at the shop.

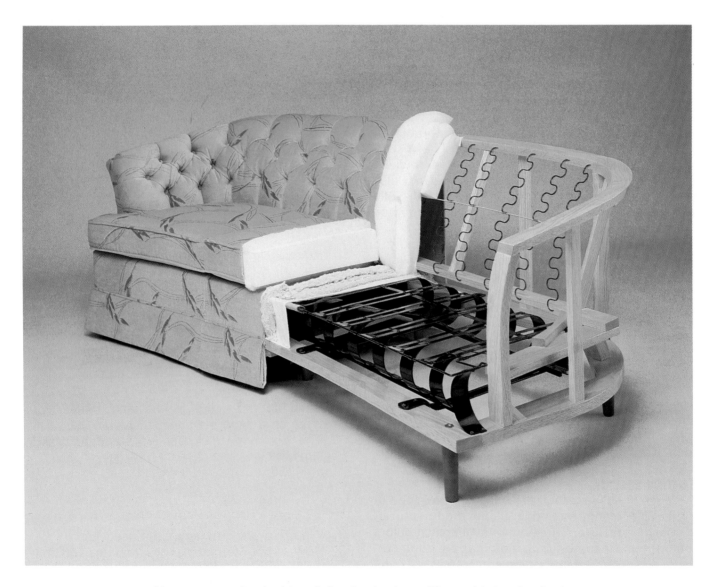

Many steps are involved in upholstering furniture. (Flexsteel Industries, Inc.)

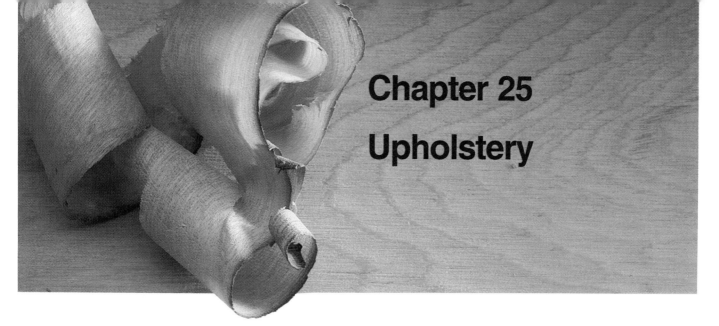

# Chapter 25

# Upholstery

New and improved materials have simplified upholstery methods and procedures, Fig. 25-1. Sinuous (sagless) springs, rubber webbing, and latex and plastic foam eliminate such time consuming operations as installing webbing, sewing and tying springs, and packing hair. There is still, however, much more to upholstery than can be presented in this short section. Study some of the upholstery books that are available before undertaking any major project.

## TOOLS AND MATERIALS

Some of the basic tools, in addition to those usually available in the school shop, are shown in Fig. 25-2. One of the basic tools you will need is an upholsterer's hammer, Fig. 25-3, in addition to

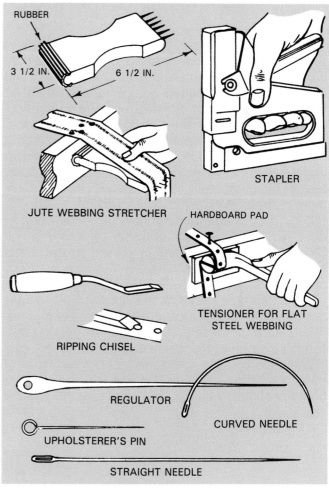

Fig. 25-2. Special tools for upholstery.

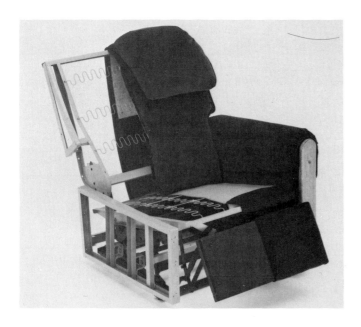

Fig. 25-1. This modern recliner utilizes a metal frame for spring attachment, which improves performance and speeds construction. (No-Sag Spring Div.)

a pair of heavy-duty shears. A flexible steel tape is often helpful when measuring irregular surfaces or curved contours.

JUTE WEBBING is a stout, closely woven strip, 3 to 4 in. wide. It is used to form the base for coil springs and stuffing materials. STEEL WEBBING is available in several types, with a 3/4 in. width being

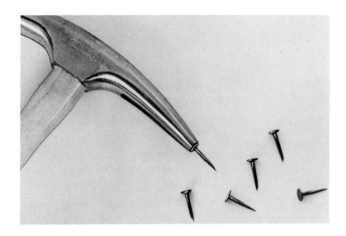

Fig. 25-3. Magnetic upholsterer's hammer. Tacks are picked up as shown and set in position with a short, accurate stroke. The hammer face is then used to finish the driving.

the most common. It is perforated for nails and may be corrugated with small loops through which coil springs can be attached. PLASTIC and RUBBER webbing are used in modern furniture to support cushions or to form the finished seating surface.

BURLAP is a coarse fabric made from jute or hemp fibers. A 40 in. width is commonly available in various weights (ounces per sq. yard). The 10 oz. weight is satisfactory for covering springs or webbing, or for forming rolled edges. DENIM is a strong, twilled cotton fabric which has excellent wearing qualities. It can be used for a seat surface that will be covered with cushions or sewed to the finish fabric for "pull strips." MUSLIN is also made of cotton and is used to cover stuffing materials. The unbleached type is satisfactory. CAMBRIC, a light cotton cloth, is made dust proof by sizing or glazing. It is used to enclose the underside of upholstered furniture to give it a finished appearance.

Coil springs are used for seats, backs, and cushions. They are available in various sizes and degrees of stiffness, Fig. 25-4. Sinuous springs are

available in continuous rolls or precut lengths. They do not require webbing or other bases, and are attached to the top side of the rails with special clips, Fig. 25-5.

Padding or stuffing materials cover the springs to form soft, smooth contours, Fig. 25-6. Rubberized hair and Spanish moss are often used. Latex foam (also called foam rubber) and plastic foam are used extensively in modern furniture. These newer materials are waterproof, durable, and come in a wide range of thicknesses and degrees of softness. A layer of cotton batting is often used between the stuffing material and the final cover. This is available in rolls 27 in. wide and in thicknesses of 3/4 in. and 1 in. Cotton batting is usually torn, instead of cut with shears, since this forms a tapered edge.

Regular upholsterer's tacks are blued and range in size from No. 1 (3/16 in.) to No. 16 (13/16 in.), Figs. 25-7. Webbing tacks have barbs to give them greater holding power. Fancy or decorative tacks are available in a wide range of designs, Fig. 25-8.

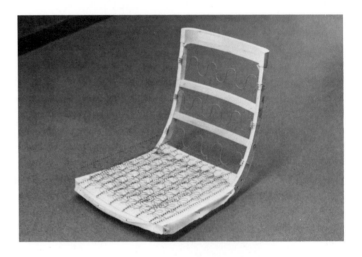

Fig. 25-5. Sinuous springs are used to provide support in this chair back. (No-Sag Spring Div.)

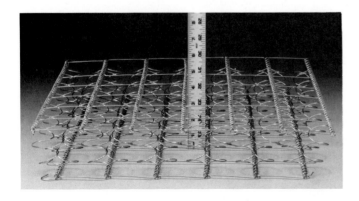

Fig. 25-4. One of the many types of a coil spring seat cushion. (No-Sag Spring Div.)

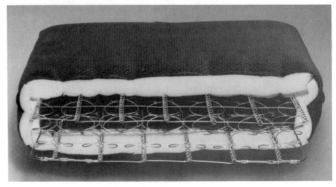

Fig. 25-6. Padding is used to cover the springs and add a cushion of comfort to this chair. (No-Sag Spring Div.)

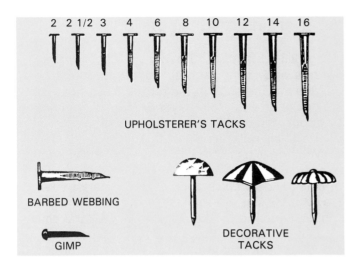

Fig. 25-7. Upholsterer's tacks. (Upholsters Supply Co.)

## FRAMES

Wood used to construct frames that will be upholstered should take and hold tacks well. Select a soft-textured hardwood that will provide sufficient strength and use sturdy joints that are reinforced with screws, dowels, and glue blocks. After the frame is assembled, round sharp edges and corners where they will contact the upholstery materials. See Fig. 25-9.

Seat frames, or other frames that will carry springs, are usually made of five-quarter stock. Exposed surfaces should be finished before the final cover is applied. Sometimes it is practical to pre-finish wood trim strips and attach them after the covering is complete.

## DETACHABLE SEATS AND BACK

Chairs like those in Fig. 25-10 are easy to upholster. The seats and backs are held in place with screws and can be easily attached or removed. The padding material is either supported on webbing attached to a frame or placed directly on a plywood base.

For an open base frame, first attach webbing to the top side and then cover it with a layer of burlap. It is best to include an edge roll when using loose-fill stuffing materials. The thickness of the padding is usually about 1 in. A layer of cotton batting can be applied over the stuffing materials and all of the padding is then held in place with a muslin cover. Nailing or tacking can be done on the underside, Fig. 25-11. Follow the procedure shown later in this unit, for attaching the finish fabric.

Fig. 25-8. Decorative tacks are used to cover the seam in the fabric and to create a design. (Kimball International)

Fig. 25-9. The sturdy wood used in the frame of this sofa will provide firm attachment for springs, padding, and fabric. Notice the reinforced joints on the frame. (No-Sag Spring Div.)

Fig. 25-10. Chairs with slip seats.

Fig. 25-11. Left. Tacking muslin cover in place. Right. Replacing slip seat. (Natural Rubber Bureau)

## TIGHT SPRING CONSTRUCTION

Fig. 25-12 shows cutaway views of typical coil springs and foam padding construction. Sinuous springs may be substituted for the webbing and coil springs or an extra thick layer of foam padding could be supported on webbing attached to the top edge of the chair rails, as shown in Fig. 25-12, left.

Webbing is used to provide a resilient foundation or base to hold springs or padding. Strips are spaced at least 1/2 in. apart and applied in various ways, Fig. 25-13. To determine the correct tension for rubber webbing, make a mark on the strip that is 10 percent shorter than the span, and then pull the webbing until this mark is aligned with the inside edge of the frame. When applying either jute webbing or rubber webbing, always try to secure equal tension in each strip.

Sinuous springs are easy to install and eliminate the webbing and twine tying required when using coil springs. Use a No. 9 gauge for chair seats, and a No. 11 gauge for backs and lighter work such as foot stools. The springs should run up and down on backs and from the front to the back on seats. See Figs. 25-14 and 25-15.

Measure the inside distance between the rails and

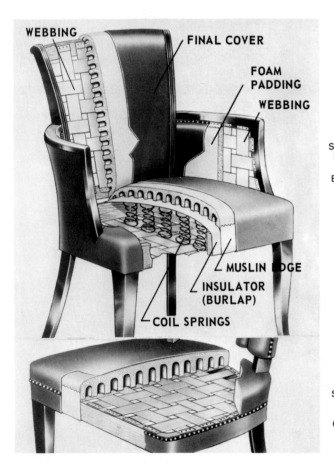

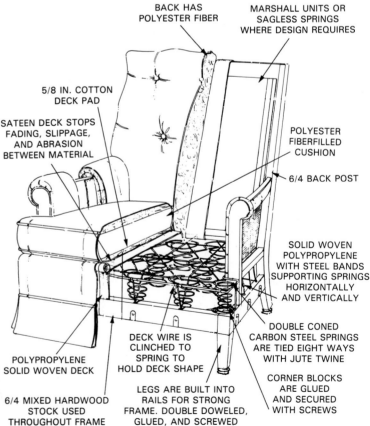

Fig. 25-12. Top left. Tight spring construction. Bottom left. Rubberized webbing and latex foam padding. (U.S. Rubber Co.) Right. Seat base uses double coned, carbon steel springs tied with jute twine. Cushions are filled with polyester. (Knob Creek)

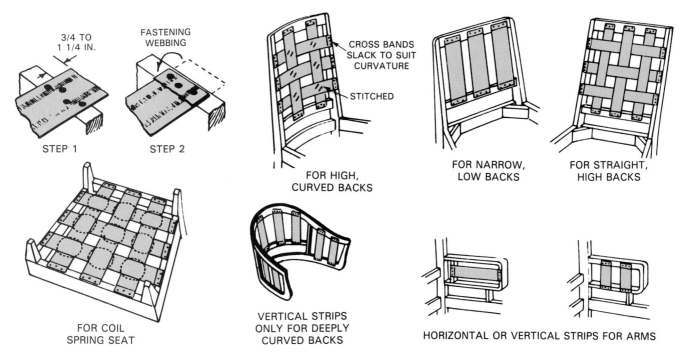

Fig. 25-13. How to apply and use webbing.

then cut the spring so it is about 1/2 in. longer. Hold the spring down flat on the work bench when measuring this length. When the spring is attached, it should have a crown of about 1 1/4 in. to 2 in. Each 1/2 in. increase or decrease in the spring length will change the crown height by about 1/4 in. Bend the ends of the spring, Fig. 25-14.

*Use care when holding sinuous springs straight for measuring, when cutting, and when installing. The tempered steel could snap back and cause an injury.*

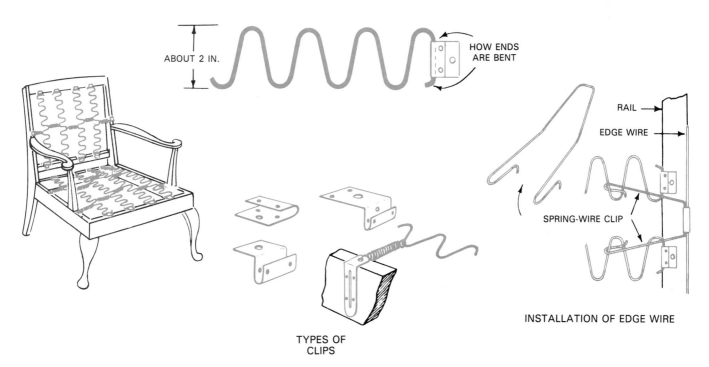

Fig. 25-14. Sinuous (sagless) springs.

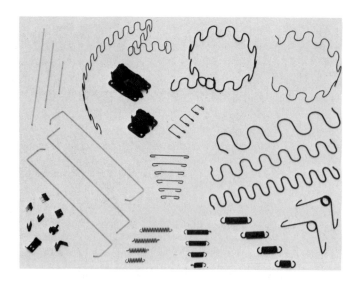

Fig. 25-15. Sinuous spring clips and helical springs. (No-Sag Spring Div.)

Fig. 25-17. Modular torsion bar type spring used to support seat cushions; it is adaptable to several furniture designs. (No-Sag Spring Div.)

The springs are fastened to the frame with clips and spaced about 4 in. on center. The clip is then fastened with one nail so it projects over the inside edge of the frame 1/8 in. The other nails are driven after the spring is in place. Alternate the position of every other sinuous spring, so the helical springs can be installed in a straight line, Fig. 25-16. The number of helical springs required is not critical. They should be attached with the opening turned inward so they will not snag or tear the padding. The helicals on the outside edge can be attached to the frame with nails or special clips.

Another approach to providing support for seat cushions, is to use a modular torsion bar type spring, like the one shown in Fig. 25-17. It is simple in design and adaptable to a wide range of furniture designs.

## PADDING

The spring or webbing base is covered with a layer of burlap to protect and hold the padding. When using latex or plastic foam it is usually best to include an "insulator" of cotton felt, canvas, or sisal to bridge the springs and further protect the stuffing.

Edge rolls, Fig. 25-18, are fastened to the edge of the frame to prevent loose stuffing materials from working thin. Commercially produced rolls are available in various sizes, or you can make your own by wrapping a roll of stuffing material in a strip of burlap or muslin.

Padding, also called stuffing, is available in loose or pad form. It is placed in position and usually stitched to the burlap spring cover. Pads are 1 to 1 1/2 in. thick and made of curled hair or rubberized fiber. Layers of cotton batting are placed over the stuffing material and held in position with a muslin cover.

Latex or plastic foam is easy to apply and since it is so resilient it is often used without a spring foundation. These materials are available in various types, shapes, and densities, Fig. 25-19. A pattern of the shape to be covered is prepared and 1/2 in. is added on each edge. The pattern is then laid out on the foam with a wax pencil or ball-point pen as shown in Fig. 25-20. Thicknesses of 2 in., or less, can be cut with scissors, Fig. 25-21. Thick slabs can be cut with a band saw.

The foam pad is held in position with muslin strips. The strips are cemented to the foam and then tacked to the frame. Brush the muslin and the latex foam with a liberal coat of rubber cement. Let this

Fig. 25-16. Installing sinuous springs. (No-Sag Spring Div.)

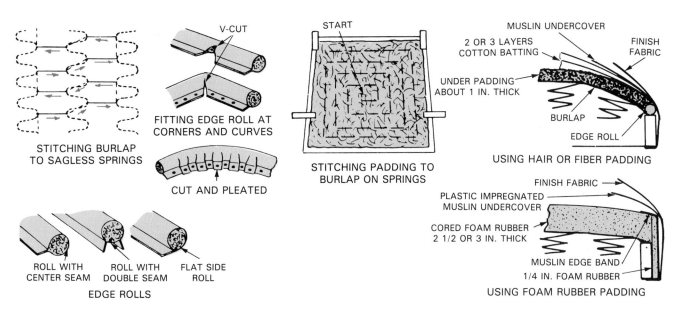

V-CUT

FITTING EDGE ROLL AT
CORNERS AND CURVES

STITCHING BURLAP
TO SAGLESS SPRINGS

CUT AND PLEATED

START

STITCHING PADDING TO
BURLAP ON SPRINGS

MUSLIN UNDERCOVER

2 OR 3 LAYERS
COTTON BATTING

FINISH
FABRIC

UNDER PADDING
ABOUT 1 IN. THICK

BURLAP

EDGE ROLL

USING HAIR OR FIBER PADDING

ROLL WITH
CENTER SEAM

ROLL WITH
DOUBLE SEAM

FLAT SIDE
ROLL

EDGE ROLLS

FINISH FABRIC

PLASTIC IMPREGNATED
MUSLIN UNDERCOVER

CORED FOAM RUBBER
2 1/2 OR 3 IN. THICK

MUSLIN EDGE BAND

1/4 IN. FOAM RUBBER

USING FOAM RUBBER PADDING

Fig. 25-18. Application of burlap, edge rolls, and padding.

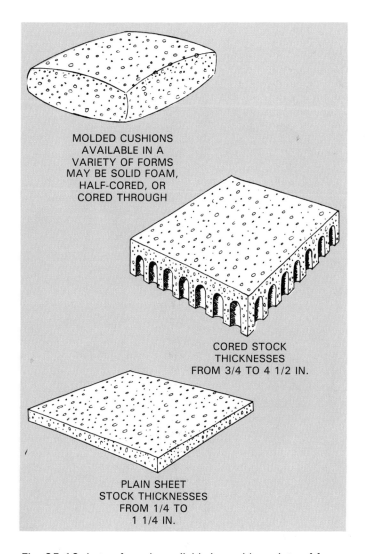

MOLDED CUSHIONS
AVAILABLE IN A
VARIETY OF FORMS
MAY BE SOLID FOAM,
HALF-CORED, OR
CORED THROUGH

CORED STOCK
THICKNESSES
FROM 3/4 TO 4 1/2 IN.

PLAIN SHEET
STOCK THICKNESSES
FROM 1/4 TO
1 1/4 IN.

Fig. 25-19. Latex foam is available in a wide variety of forms
and sizes. Grades of compression include soft, medium, firm,
and extra firm.

Fig. 25-20. Top. Laying out pattern on foam material. Add 1/4
to 1/2 in. (6 to 13 mm) to all edges. Bottom. Cutting with large
scissors. (Natural Rubber Bureau)

Fig. 25-21. To form a tapered edge, cut a bevel on the
underside of the foam material. (Natural Rubber Bureau)

417

coat become dry and then apply a second coat. When the second coat becomes tacky, press the strips firmly in place, Fig. 25-22. Allow this assembly to dry for about 1 hour before tacking it to the frame. Pieces of latex foam can be joined together with rubber cement in the same manner as used to apply the muslin.

When mounting latex or plastic foam directly to a plywood base, you should drill 3/8 in. holes, spaced about 3 in. apart, to permit free passage of air through the material. It is usually best to cover foam padding with a muslin cover, especially when the finish fabric is plastic, leather, or a loosely woven or stretchy material. See Fig. 25-23.

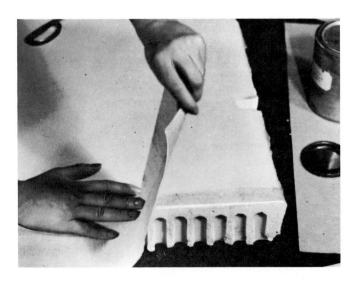

Fig. 25-22. Using rubber cement to attach a tacking strip. Use a strip about 1 in. (25.4 mm) wide to reinforce the edge of cutouts for arm and back supports.

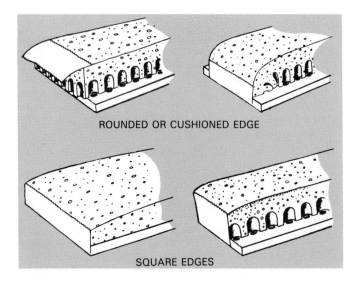

ROUNDED OR CUSHIONED EDGE

SQUARE EDGES

Fig. 25-23. How edges are formed. Strip is either tacked or stapled to frame or base.

Fig. 25-24. A—Tacking the muslin cover. B—Final covering in position and temporary tack in the center of each side. C—Sides tacked to within about 2 in. of corners. D—Corners folded under, trimmed, and tacked.

## FINAL COVERING

There are many kinds of fabrics and plastic materials suitable for the final covering. Select a color, texture, and pattern that will be appropriate for the design and the decor of the room in which it will be used. Most fabrics are available in 54 in. widths. You should develop patterns of the pieces needed and then arrange them carefully on the material to secure economical cuts. Be certain to align the pattern of the back with the seat and, when possible, run the warp threads up and down, and front to back, to provide for the greatest wear.

The covering is first placed in position and carefully aligned. Then the center of each side is tacked as shown in Fig. 25-24. Start from the center and tack toward the corners. Do not pull the cover too tight, as this will make a hard surface and place unnecessary strain on the fabric. On most work, the edge should be turned under as it is tacked. Pull the cover into position and then drive the tack or staple half way between the last fastener and the spot where you are pulling the cloth. Fasten the material to within about 2 in. of the corners and then fold the corners under and tack and/or sew, Fig. 25-25.

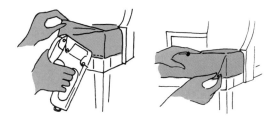

Fig. 25-25. How to form a corner. Left. Pull the material around the corner, lift up the excess, and staple. Then pull the remaining cloth straight down and trim to size. Right. Fold the remaining edge underneath and tack or staple it in place. It may be necessary to sew the vertical slit shut. Use thread that matches the fabric and will not show. (Natural Rubber Bureau)

Fig. 25-26. Covering the tacked edge with gimp. Apply droplets of glue to the gimp and use temporary tacking to hold it in place until dry.

To cover the staples or tacks, a decorative cloth or plastic banding, called GIMP, is used. It is about 1/2 in. wide and is attached with glue or small headed gimp tacks. When gluing gimp, use temporary tacking to hold it in place until the glue sets. See Fig. 25-26.

Fig. 25-27 shows some details and procedures used to cover large pieces of upholstered furniture.

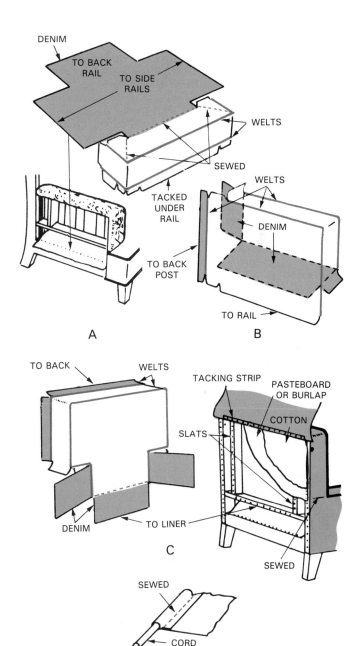

Fig. 25-27. Steps and details for attaching final covering. Denim strips, sewed to finish fabric, serve as pull and tacking strips, reducing amount of fabric required. Tinted portions are pull strip material. A—Sewing corners, attaching pull strips and welting to seat deck. B—Attaching pull strips and welting to arm sections. C—Attaching pull strips and welting to back sections. D—Sewing cordage inside welting.

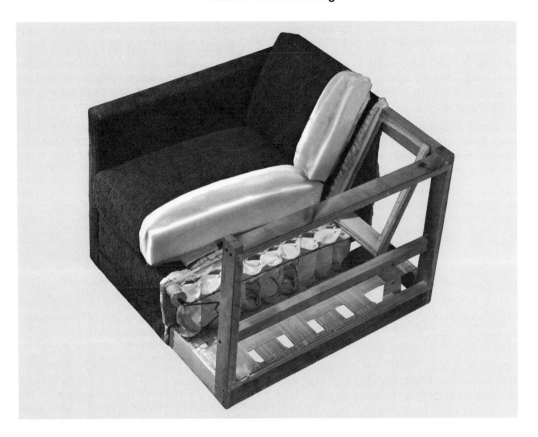

Fig. 25-28. Cutaway view of chair shows the details of overstuffed construction method.

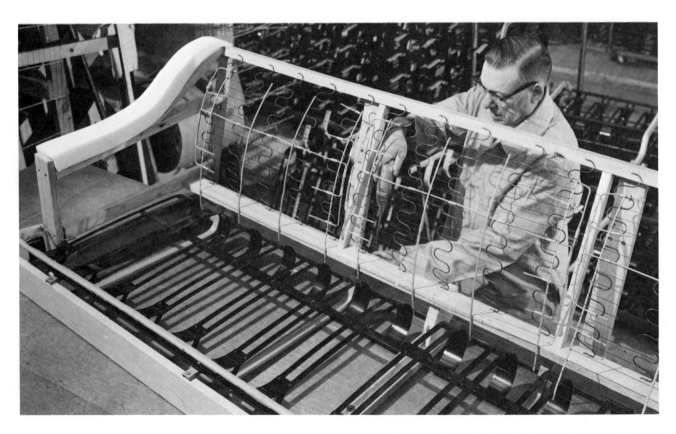

Fig. 25-29. Skilled upholsterer uses an air-powered screwdriver to install seat spring unit in sofa frame. Hardwood frame is constructed with double-doweled joints and reinforced with corner blocks. (Flexsteel Industries, Inc.)

It is unlikely that you will undertake an upholstery project of this size; it is included mainly for study, to gain some understanding of how such work is done. Fig. 25-28 shows how overstuffed chairs are constructed. Also see Fig. 25-29.

## TEST YOUR KNOWLEDGE, Chapter 25

Please do not write in the text. Place you answers on a separate sheet of paper.
1. What is the purpose of jute webbing?
2. Burlap is specified by weight in ounces per:
   a. Square foot.
   b. Square inch.
   c. Square yard.
   d. None of the above.
3. Explain the procedure used for determining the correct tension for rubber webbing.
4. Each 1/2 in. increase or decrease in the length of a sinuous spring will change the crown height about _____.
5. Helical springs should be attached with the opening turned outward so they will not snag or tear padding. True or False?
6. What are edge rolls?
7. Cotton batting is usually held in place with a _____ cover.
8. When mounting latex or plastic foam directly to a plywood base, what is the purpose of drilling 3/8 in. holes in the plywood?
9. A decorative cloth or plastic banding used to cover staples or tacks is called a _____.

## ACTIVITIES

1. Prepare a detailed, step-by-step procedure for replacing the cover and padding materials of a chair with a slip cover.
2. Secure small samples of various types of latex foam, polyurethane foam, and some of the newer synthetic padding materials. Mount them on a display board with descriptive labels listing their properties, application methods, and costs.
3. Visit a local upholstery shop. Prepare a report describing the types of tools and equipment used in the shop, the type of articles being upholstered, methods for determining costs, etc. If possible, photograph the processes involved in upholstering a single article.

Upholstery is an important part of the sofa, love seat, and chair in this contemporary wood furniture grouping. (Period Furniture, Inc.)

Additional plans for this building are shown in Figs. 26-1, 27-1, and 27-7.

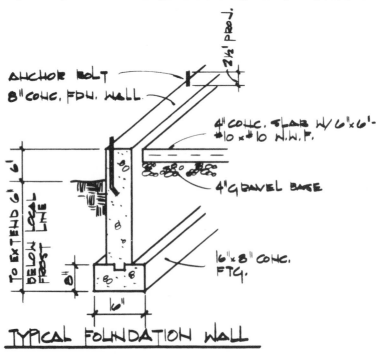

TYPICAL FOUNDATION WALL

Top. Pictorial of two-car garage with finished loft. Plans for this structure are shown in the following units. (National Plan Service, Inc.) Bottom. Typical foundation detail showing footing, foundation wall, and floor slab of the garage.

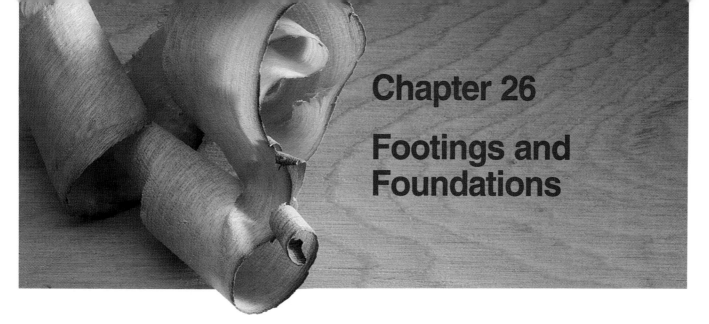

# Chapter 26

# Footings and Foundations

The construction of most structures requires carpenters to work closely with other tradespeople, the architect, and the owner. Carpenters may be required to stake out the location of the building and supervise the excavation. They build the forms for footings and concrete foundation walls. Those in the carpentry trade must have a working knowledge of standards and practices used in concrete work. This chapter illustrates the close relationship of footings and foundations to the remainder of the structure and to the carpentry trade.

## STAKING OUT BUILDING LOCATION

The PLOT PLAN gives structure location on the site, along with the distances from the structure to the property line. The specific dimensions of the foundation are shown on the FOUNDATION PLAN, Fig. 26-1. Locating the building on the site and laying out the foundation is done with a measuring tape, contractor's level and transit (if required). When angles other than 90 deg. must be measured, the surveyor's transit is used.

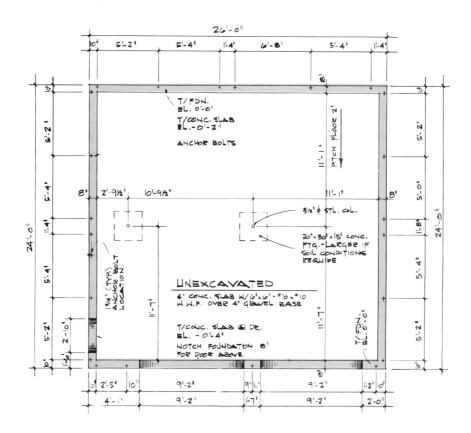

Fig. 26-1. The foundation plan provides information necessary for staking out the building lines and constructing the foundation. (National Plan Service, Inc.)

The first step in staking out the building is to locate each corner by laying off the distances indicated on the plot plan. A stake is driven into the ground at the location of each corner of the foundation to identify its position. Square corners may be laid out using the 9-12-15 unit method, Fig. 26-2. These proportions define a right triangle and establish a 90 deg. corner angle. The position of all corners should be checked for accuracy by diagonal measurement, Fig. 26-3.

BATTER BOARDS are used to retain the location of the foundation during excavation and construction. These are constructed of 2 x 4 stakes

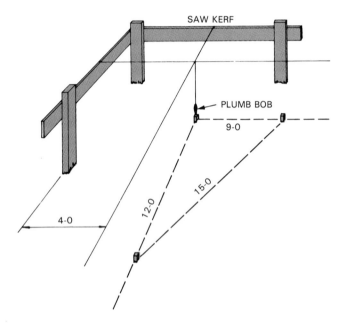

Fig. 26-2. Squaring a corner using the 9-12-15 unit method.

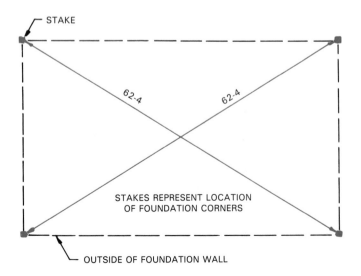

Fig. 26-3. Layout accuracy may be checked by measuring the diagonals. They must be equal.

sharpened on one end and driven into the ground about 4 feet outside the footing line. A 1 x 6 board is nailed horizontally to the stakes so all are level and in the same horizontal plane. (They will have the same elevation.) A strong cord or string is stretched across the boards at opposite ends of the building and located directly above the corner stakes. A plumb bob is used for accurate placement of each stake. This is done for each side of the building. A saw kerf is usually made at the exact point on the horizontal batter board where the string is located. This prevents movement of the string along the board. After cuts are made in all eight batter boards, the lines of the house will be located, Fig. 26-4.

## EXCAVATION

Building sites located on steep slopes or rugged terrain should be rough graded before the building is laid out. Top soil should be removed and piled where it will not interfere with construction. This can be used for the finished grade after the building is complete.

Where no grading is needed, the site can be laid out and batter boards erected, Fig. 26-5, bottom.

Stakes marking the outer edge of the rough excavation are set and the lines are removed from the batter boards during the work. For regular basement foundations, the excavation should extend beyond the building lines by at least 2 ft. to allow clearance for form work. Foundations for structures with a slab floor or crawl space will need little excavating beyond the trench for footings and walls.

The depth of the excavation can be calculated from a study of the vertical section views of the architectural plans.

It is important that foundations extend below the frost line. If footings are set too shallow, the moisture in the soil under the footing may freeze. This could force the foundation wall upward causing cracks and serious damage. Local building codes usually cover these requirements.

It is common practice to establish both the depth of the excavation and the height of the foundation by using the highest elevation on the perimeter of the excavation. This is known as the CONTROL POINT, Fig. 26-6.

Foundations should extend about 8 in. above the finished grade. Then the wood finish and framing members will be adequately protected from moisture. The finished grade should be sloped away from all sides of the structure so surface water will run away from the foundation.

The depth of the excavation may be affected by the elevation of the site. It may be higher or lower than the street or adjacent property. The level of sewer lines also affects the depth of the excava-

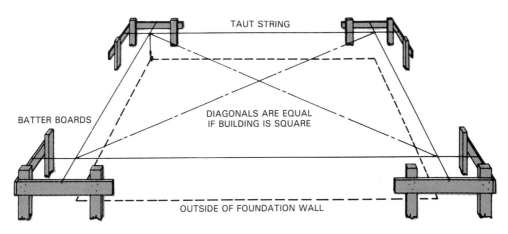

Fig. 26-4. Batter boards in place around the location of the proposed foundation.

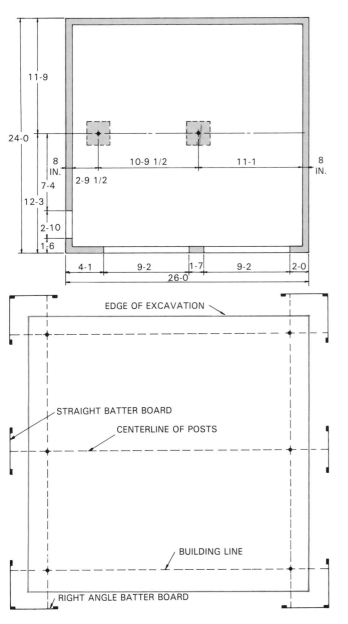

Fig. 26-5. Top. Plan showing overall dimensions. Bottom. Sketch of building lines set up around area to be excavated.

tion. Normally, solving these problems is the responsibility of the architect. Information on grade, foundation, and floor levels is usually included in the working drawings.

## FOUNDATION SYSTEMS

All structures settle to some degree during and after construction. In a properly designed and constructed foundation, the distribution of the load will work in such a way that any settling that occurs will be negligible, or at the least, uniform.

Foundations used in residential construction are usually of two types: basement or crawl space foundations and slab foundations, Fig. 26-7. These foundations are types of SPREAD foundation. A spread foundation uses walls, piers, pilasters, and/or columns to spread the load onto the footings, Fig. 26-8. The footings, in turn, transfer the load into the soil.

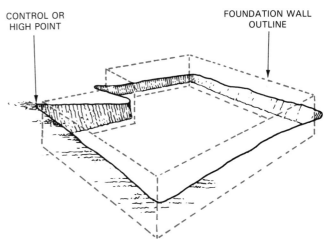

Fig. 26-6. Highest elevation outside the excavation is used to establish depth of excavation.

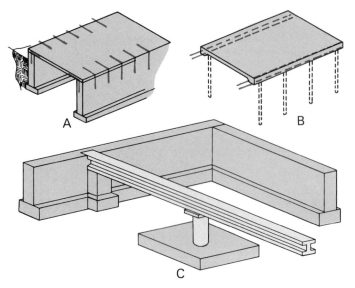

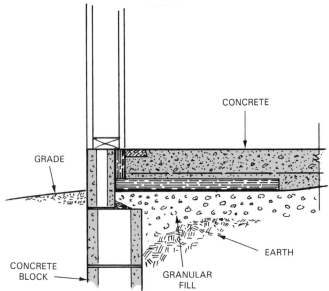

Fig. 26-7. Examples of foundation types. A—Slab on foundation is used in cold climates. B—Slab-on-ground is popular in warm climates. Piers (dotted lines) can be used as support in unstable soils. C—Crawl space foundation is similar to basement foundation.

Fig. 26-9. Concrete slab floor construction.

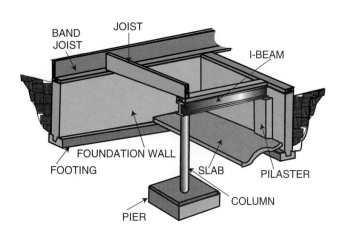

Fig. 26-8. Elements of a typical foundation. Footings and piers spread the load over a wide area.

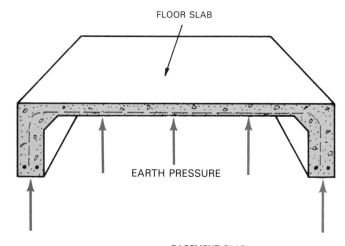

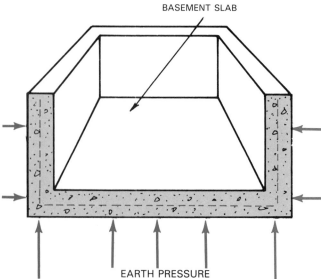

Fig. 26-10. Types of monolithic (single unit) foundations. Top. Matt foundation. Bottom. Raft foundation.

## SLABS

Slab foundations take several forms. The slab can be used with other elements such as walls, piers, and footings, as shown in Fig. 26-7B. This is called a STRUCTURALLY SUPPORTED slab. A second type is laid directly on top of the ground like those shown in Fig. 26-9. These are known as GROUND SUPPORTED slabs.

Some slabs, particularly those used in warmer climates, are constructed in one continuous pour. There are no joints or separately poured sections. These are called MONOLITHIC POURS. This type of construction is appropriate over soils with low-bearing capacity, Fig. 26-10.

## FOOTINGS

PLAIN footings carry light loads and usually do not need reinforcement. REINFORCED footings have steel rebar in them for added strength against cracking. They are used when the load must be spread over a large area, or when the load must bridge over weak spots, such as excavations for sewer lines.

A STEPPED footing changes grade levels at certain intervals to accommodate a sloping lot or varied floor levels inside the structure. See Fig. 26-11. Vertical sections should be at least 8 in. thick. Horizontal distance between steps should be at least 2 ft. If masonry units are to be used over the footing, distances should fit standard brick or block modules.

## FOOTING DESIGN

Footings must be wide enough to spread a load over sufficient area. In residential and smaller building construction, the usual practice is to make the footing twice as wide as the foundation wall, Fig. 26-12. Average thickness is about 10 in.

Footings under columns and posts carry heavy, concentrated loads and are usually from 2 to 3 ft. square. The thickness should be about 1 1/2 times the distance from the face of the column to the edge of the footing.

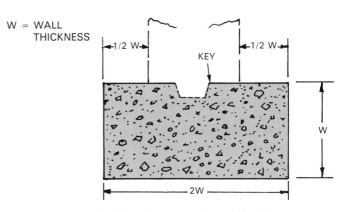

Fig. 26-12. Standard footing design for residential construction. Footing should be twice the width of the wall.

Reinforced footings are used in regions subject to earthquakes, and where footings must extend over soils containing poor load-bearing material.

Some structural designs may also require reinforcing. The common practice is to use two No. 5 (5/8 in.) bars for 12 x 24 in. footings. At least 3 in. of concrete should cover the reinforcing at all points.

In a single story dwelling where chimney footings are independent of other footings, they should have a minimum projection of 4 in. on each side. For a two-story house, chimney footings should have a minimum thickness of 12 in. and a minimum projection of 6 in. on each side. Exact dimensions will vary according to the weight of the chimney and the nature of the soil. Where chimneys are a part of outside walls or inside bearing walls, chimney footings should be constructed as part of the wall footing. Concrete for both chimney and wall footings should be placed at the same time.

Footings that must support cast-in-place concrete walls may be formed with a recess forming a keyed joint as illustrated in Fig. 26-13.

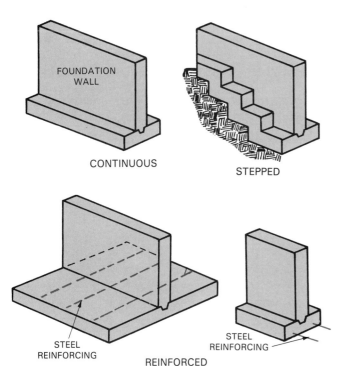

Fig. 26-11. Different types of footings are needed for varying slope and soil conditions. Vertical runs of stepped footing should not exceed 3/4 of horizontal run between steps.

Fig. 26-13. When a concrete foundation is to be poured, the footing should be keyed. Key is formed by placing a wooden strip in the form during or immediately after the pour. (Portland Cement Association)

## FOOTING FORMS

After the excavation is completed, the footings are laid out and forms are constructed. Lines are replaced on the batter boards and corner points are dropped with a plumb bob to the bottom of the excavation.

Drive stakes and establish points at the corners of the foundation walls. Set up a builder's level at a central point in the excavation. Drive a number of grade stakes (level with the top of the footing) along the footing line and at approximate points where column footings are required. Corner stakes can also be driven to the exact height of the top of the footing. Connect the corner stakes with lines tied to nails in the top of the stakes.

Working from these building lines, construct the outside form for the footing. The form boards will be located outside the building lines by a distance equal to the footing extension (usually 4 in. for an 8 in. foundation wall). See Fig. 26-14. The top edge of the form boards must be level with the grade stakes.

Transfer the measurement from the grade stakes to the form. Use a carpenter's level. After the outside form boards are in place, it will be relatively easy to set the inside sections.

Forms constructed of 1 in. boards should be supported with stakes placed 2 to 3 ft. apart. Stakes may be placed farther apart when 2 in. material is used. Spacers or spreaders used to locate the inside form will save measuring time, Fig. 26-15.

Bracing of footing forms is sometimes desirable. Usually it is not necessary unless 1 in. lumber is used for forming. If this is the case, attach the brace to the top of a form stake and to the bottom of a brace stake located about a foot away. Refer back to Fig. 26-15.

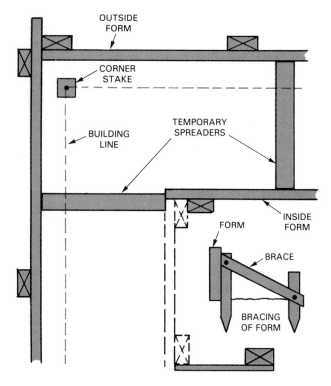

Fig. 26-15. Properly located footing form. Note that it extends beyond corner stake and building line. Precut spreaders were used to locate the inside form boards.

Stepped footings require additional form work. Vertical blocking must be nailed to the form to contain the concrete until it sets, Fig. 26-16.

Column (isolated) footings are pads of concrete which will support stringers resting on columns. They carry weight transmitted to the column from the center beam of a building. Fig. 26-17 shows a typical form for an isolated footing.

Forms for column footings are usually set after the wall footing forms are complete. These are

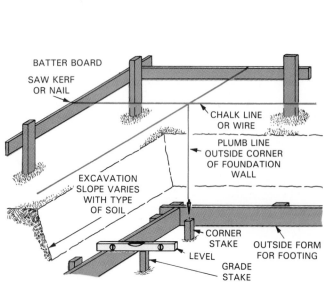

Fig. 26-14. Laying out forms for footings. The outside forms are built first. They must be level with grade stakes.

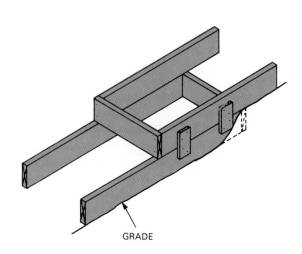

Fig. 26-16. Form for a stepped footing.

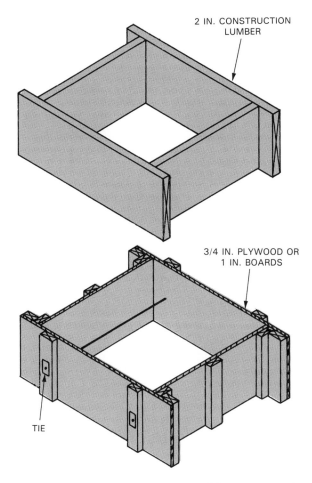

Fig. 26-17. Isolated footing forms made of 2 in. construction lumber and 3/4 in. plywood.

located by direct measurements from the building lines. Forms are leveled to grade level stakes previously set.

Form boards are temporarily nailed to stakes and to each other. Duplex (double-headed) nails may be used for easy removal. If regular nails are used, they should be driven only partway into the wood. Do not nail from the inside as this will make form removal difficult.

When the forms are completed, check again for accuracy and sturdiness. Remove the line, line stakes, and grade stakes. The concrete may now be placed.

## ERECTING WALL FORMS

Several types of wall forming systems are available. All of these systems require certain considerations, in order to achieve quality work.

The forms used must be tight, smooth, defect-free, and properly aligned. Joints between form boards or panels should be tight. This prevents the loss of the cement paste, which tends to weaken the concrete and cause honeycombing.

Wall forms must be strong and well braced to resist the side (lateral) pressure created by the plastic concrete. This pressure increases tremendously as the height of the wall is increased. Regular concrete weighs about 150 lb. per cu. ft. If it were immediately poured into a form 8 ft. high, it would create a pressure of about 1200 lb. per sq. ft. along the bottom side of the form.

In practice, this amount of pressure is reduced through compacting and hardening of the concrete. It tends to support itself. Thus, the lateral pressure will be related to the amount of concrete placed per hour, the outside temperature, and the amount of mechanical vibration.

Low wall forms, up to about 3 ft. in height, can be assembled from 1 in. sheathing boards or 3/4 in. plywood, supported by 2 x 4 studs spaced 2 ft. apart. The height can be increased somewhat if the studs are closer together, Fig. 26-18. For walls over 4 ft. high, the studs should be backed with wales to provide greater strength, Fig. 26-19.

## REESTABLISHING THE BUILDING LINE

Before setting up the outside foundation wall form you will need to mark the building line on top of the footing. Set up your lines on the batter boards once more. Then drop a plumb line from the intersections (corners) of the building lines to the footing. Mark the corners on the footing. Snap a chalk line from corner to corner on the footing. This line will be the outside face of the foundation wall. As you set up the foundation forms, align the face of the outside form with the chalk line.

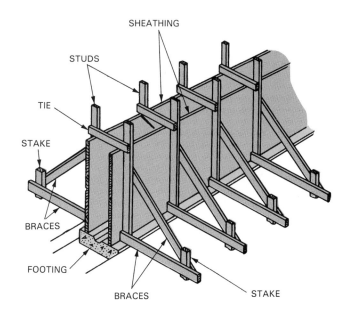

Fig. 26-18. Design for wall forms up to 3 ft. high. Use plywood sheathing and space studs 2 ft. apart.

429

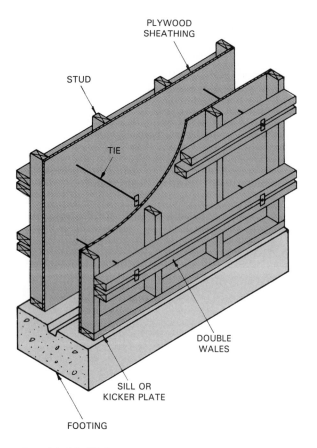

Fig. 26-19. Wales greatly strengthen a wall form.

## FORM HARDWARE

Wire ties and wooden spreaders have been largely replaced with various manufactured devices. Fig. 26-20 shows three types of ties. The rods go through small holes in the sheathing and studs. Holes through the wales can be larger for easy assembly or the wales can be doubled as shown.

The snap tie is designed so that a portion of it remains in the wall. Tapered ties are removed and should be coated with release. Bolts in the coil ties should also be coated with release.

The coil spreader is assembled with a cone of wood, plastic, or metal, and a lag screw. The cone provides smooth contact with the form and leaves a recess that is easy to fill.

Taper ties are threaded at both ends for easy removal. The threaded plate is removed from the small end and the rod is pulled free from the other.

Corners of concrete forms can be secured by corner locks. Two types are shown in Fig. 26-21.

After the concrete has set, the clamps can be quickly removed and the forms stripped. A special wrench is used to break off the outer sections of the snap tie rod. The rod breaks at a small indentation located about 1 in. beneath the concrete surface. The hole in the concrete is patched with grout or mortar.

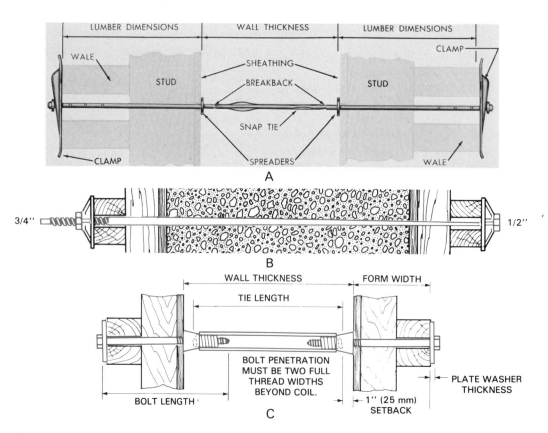

Fig. 26-20. Form ties combine the functions of ties and spreaders. A—Snap tie. (Universal Form Clamp Co.) B—Taper tie. C—Heavy duty coil tie. (The Burke Co.)

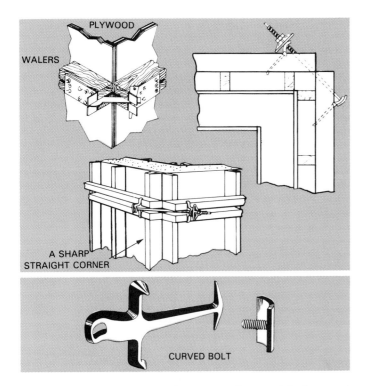

Fig. 26-21. Corners of wall forms must be carefully fastened so they will withstand pressure of poured concrete. This can be done by interlocking the wales or using patented locks. Top. A high speed corner lock. Clamps are attached with 6 to 8 penny duplex (double-headed) nails and lag screws. Bottom. A corner lock requiring no nails or screws. (The Burke Co.)

## PANEL FORMS

Currently, prefabricated panels are used for most wall forming. The panels, made from a special grade of plywood, are attached to wood or metal frames. Refer to Fig. 26-22.

Carpenters can build their own panels, using 3/4 in. plywood and 2 x 4 studs, to form 2 ft. or 4 ft. by 8 ft. units. For standard columns and other units, prefabricated forms will save time, Fig. 26-23.

Tubular fiber forms may also be purchased. These are usually found in heavy construction, Fig. 26-24.

Since panel forms, with rare exception, are designed to be used many times, they should be treated to prevent the concrete from sticking to the surfaces. Use special form release coatings.

Manufacturers have developed many forming systems to replace or supplement panel forms built by the carpenter. For residential work they usually consist of steel frames and exterior grade plywood panels. Sometimes the plywood is coated with a special plastic material to create a smooth finish on the concrete and prevent it from sticking to the surface. The panel units are light, for easy handling and transporting from one building site to another. Specially designed devices are used to assemble and space the components quickly and accurately. See Fig. 26-25.

Fig. 26-22. Modular form components are produced in several sizes (dimensions are in feet): 2 x 2, 2 x 4, 4 x 2, 4 x 4, 8 x 2, and 8 x 4. Plywood facing (3/4 in.) is attached to a steel frame. (Symons Corp.)

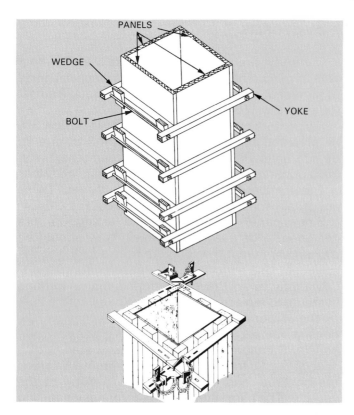

Fig. 26-23. Prefabricated column forms save construction time. Top. Yoke and wedge arrangement. Bottom. Scissor clamps. (The Burke Co.)

Fig. 26-25. Manufactured forms are easy to erect and strip. Top. Form designed for residential foundation. Wedge-bolt connectors are tightened or loosened with a light blow of the hammer. (Symons Corp.) Bottom. Close-up of system having patented corners and form ties. (Universal Form Clamp Co.)

Fig. 26-24. Column form made of fiber paper. The form is only used once because it is destroyed by the removal process. (Sonoco Products Co.)

## WALL OPENINGS

Several procedures are followed in forming openings in foundation walls for doors, windows, and other holes. In poured walls, forms or stops are built into the regular forms. Nailing strips may be attached to the form and cast into the concrete. Frames are then secured to these strips after the forms are removed. Fig. 26-26 shows several methods for framing openings.

Special framing must also be attached inside the form for pipes or for voids carrying beams. As with windows and doors, form work for these structures must be attached to the outside wall form before the inside form is erected.

Tubes of fiber, plastic, or metal can be used for small openings. They are held in place by wood blocks or plastic fasteners which are attached to the form. Larger forms made of wood can be attached with duplex nails driven through the form from the outside.

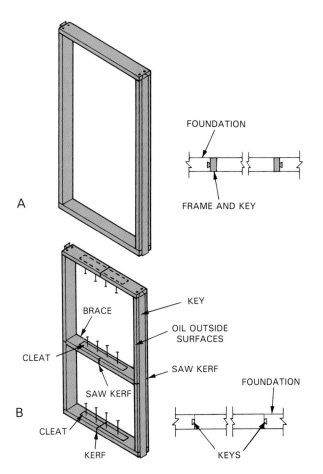

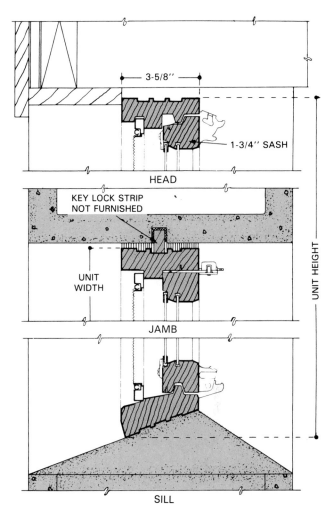

SCALE: 3'' EQUALS 1'-0''

Detail above shows typical basement installation in concrete block wall with poured sill. Note key lock strip at side jamb to secure unit in opening. Strip is nailed to back of jamb in slot provided before installation.

Fig. 26-26. Forms used to frame openings in foundation wall can be constructed by the carpenter. A—Permanent frame will be left in the wall. B—Removable frame is called a buck. Members are cut part way through for easy removal. Cleats and braces reinforce members at saw cuts. Bucks and frames are nailed to the form with duplex nails from the outside.

In concrete block construction, door and window frames are set in place. The masonry units are constructed around them. The outside surface of the frames has grooves into which the mortar flows, forming a key. Basement windows are usually located level with the top of the foundation wall. The sill carries the weight of the structure across the opening, Fig. 26-27.

## ANCHORS

Wood plates are fastened to the top of foundation walls with 1/2 in. anchor bolts or straps. They are spaced not more than 4 ft. apart, Fig. 26-28. In concrete walls, they are set in place as soon as the pour is completed and leveled off.

Anchor bolts are set in the cores of a concrete block wall. They should be about 18 in. long. A piece of metal lath is placed in the second horizontal joint below the top of the wall to hold the grout or mortar. Bolts are installed after the wall is completed. Anchor clips are installed in the same way.

Fig. 26-27. Installing windows in basement walls. Top. Detail of basement window unit that can be placed in a concrete or masonry foundation wall. Bottom. Unit installed.
(Andersen Corp.)

433

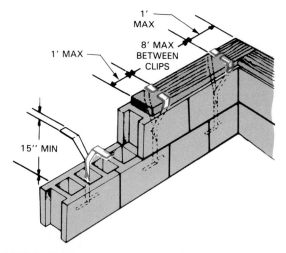

Fig. 26-28. Anchor bolts and straps are installed about the same way. Top. Anchor strap is embedded in the next-to-top block. Bottom. Embedding an anchor bolt in concrete or mortar.

## CONCRETE BLOCK FOUNDATIONS

In some localities, concrete blocks are used for foundation walls and other masonry construction. The standard block is made from Portland cement and aggregates such as sand, fine gravel, or crushed stone. It weighs about 40 or 50 lb.

Lightweight units are made from Portland cement and natural or manufactured aggregates. Among these are volcanic cinders, pumice, and foundry slag. A lightweight unit weighs between 25 and 35 lb. It usually has a much lower U factor. (This is a measurement of the heat flow or heat transmission through materials.)

### SIZES AND SHAPES

Blocks are classified as solid or hollow. A solid unit is one in which the core (hollow) area is 25 percent or less of the total cross-sectional area.

Blocks are usually available in 4, 6, 8, 10, and 12 in. widths and 4 and 8 in. heights. Sizes are actually 3/8 in. shorter than their nominal (name) dimensions to allow for the mortar joint. For example, the 8 x 8 x 16 block is actually 7 5/8 x 7 5/8

x 15 5/8. With a standard 3/8 in. mortar joint, the laid-in-the-wall height will be 8 in. and the length 16 in. Fig. 26-29 shows some of the sizes and shapes, with names that indicate use.

## LINTELS

Masonry that is carried across the top of openings is supported by a structural unit called a lintel. A lintel can be a precast concrete unit that includes metal reinforcing bars, or steel angle irons. Both are shown in Fig. 26-30.

Another method is to lay a course of lintel blocks across the opening (supported by a frame). Then add reinforcing bars and fill the blocks with concrete, Fig. 26-31.

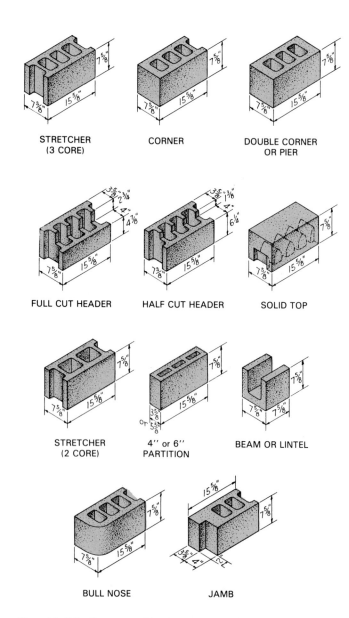

Fig. 26-29. Concrete blocks are manufactured for many different purposes. These are typical.
(Portland Cement Association)

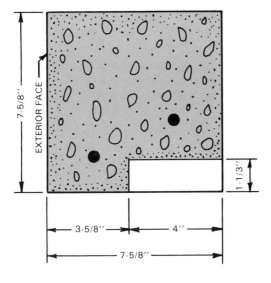

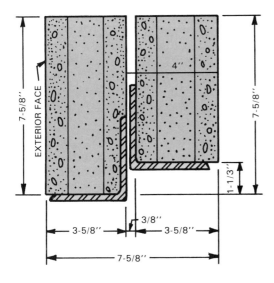

Fig. 26-30. Lintels for block walls. Top. Precast unit. Bottom. Standard block units supported by angle steel. Notches are for window or door frames.

## WATERPROOFING

In most localities, the outside of poured concrete or concrete masonry basement walls should be waterproofed below the finished grade and drain tile installed. See Fig. 26-32.

Masonry (block) walls may be waterproofed by an application of cement plaster followed by several coats of an asphaltic or other waterproofing material. A cove of plaster should be formed between the footing and wall. This precaution prevents water from collecting and seeping through the joint.

To waterproof poured walls, bituminous waterproofing is generally used without cement plaster. Polyethylene sheeting is often used as a waterproofing material. It should cover wall and footing in one piece.

Fig. 26-33 shows a drain tile along the side of the footing. The drain should lead away from the foundation to an outlet that always remains open.

Fig. 26-32. A cove of mortar is formed over the footing to prevent water from entering. (Portland Cement Association)

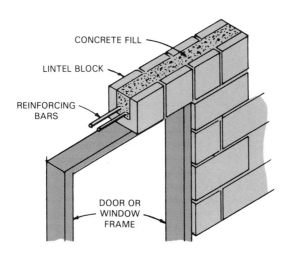

Fig. 26-31. Lintel blocks are laid over a supporting frame. Then the cavity is filled with reinforced concrete.

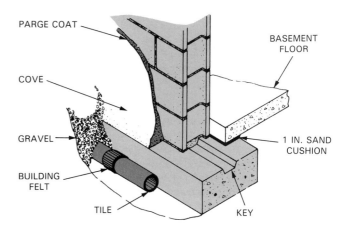

Fig. 26-33. A basement wall may be waterproofed by applying a parge coat and placing drain tiles along the footing.

In some areas, perimeter drains may be connected to a sump pump. Tiles or perforated pipe should be covered with a 6 to 8 in. layer of coarse gravel or crushed stone.

As an energy conservation measure, plastic foam board may be added to the outside face of the foundation wall. In such cases, no back plastering or waterproofing should extend any higher than 2 in. below the final grade.

## SLAB-ON-GROUND FOUNDATIONS

Many commercial and residential structures are built without basements. The main floor is formed by placing concrete directly on the ground. Footings and foundations are somewhat similar to those for basements. However, they need to extend down only to solid soil and below the frost line, Refer to Fig. 26-34.

In slab-on-ground construction, insulation and moisture control are essential. The earth under the floor is called the SUBGRADE and must be firm and completely free of sod, roots, and debris.

A coarse fill, at least 4 in. thick, is placed over the finished subgrade. The fill should be brought to grade and thoroughly compacted.

This granular fill may be slag, gravel, or crushed stone, preferably ranging from 1/2 in. to 1 in. in diameter. The material should be uniform without fines to insure maximum air space in the fill. Air spaces will add to insulating qualities and reduce capillary attraction of subsoil moisture (action by which moisture passes through fill).

In areas where the subsoil is not well drained, a line of drain tile may be required around the outside edge of the exterior wall footings.

While preparing the subgrade and fill, various mechanical installations should be made. Under-floor ducts, where used, are usually embedded in the granular fill. Water service supply lines, if placed under the floor slab, should be installed in trenches deep enough to avoid freezing. Connections to utilities should be brought above the finished floor level before pouring the concrete.

After the fill has been compacted and brought to grade, a vapor barrier should be placed over the sub-base. A vapor barrier is essential under every section of the floor. Its purpose is to stop the movement of water into the slab.

Among materials widely used as vapor barriers are 55 lb. roll roofing, 4-mil polyethylene film, and asphaltic-impregnated kraft papers. Strips should be lapped 6 in. to form a complete seal.

Perimeter insulation is important. It reduces heat loss from the floor slab to the outside. The insulation material must be rigid and stable while in contact with wet concrete. Fig. 26-35 shows a foundation design with perimeter insulation typical of residential frame construction.

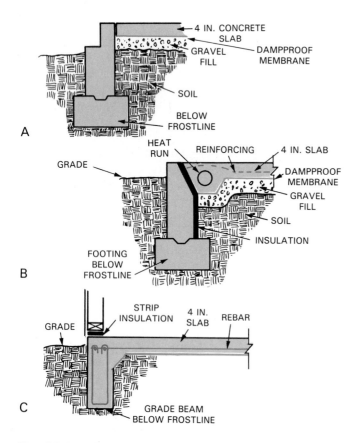

Fig. 26-34. Three types of slab-on-ground foundations. A—Unreinforced slab with loads supported by footing and wall. Used where soil is coarse and well drained. B—Slab is reinforced with welded wire fabric. Inside foundation wall is insulated because of perimeter heat duct in slab. C—Monolithic slab. This type is used over problem soils. Loads are carried over a large area of the slab.

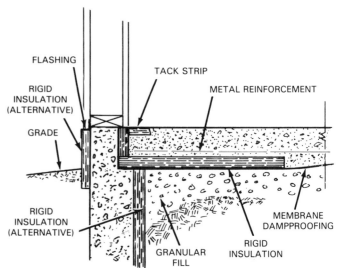

Fig. 26-35. Perimeter insulation is important when using slab-on-ground construction in cold climates.

Insulation thickness varies from 1 to 2 in., depending on outside design temperature. The insulation can be placed horizontally, vertically, or in both directions along the foundation wall.

When the insulation, vapor barrier, and all mechanical aspects are complete, reinforcing mesh, if used, is laid. Check local building codes for requirements. Usually a 6 x 6 x 10 ga. mesh is sufficient for residential work. This should be located from 2 to 2 1/2 in. below the surface of the concrete.

Many of the considerations mentioned for slab-on-ground floors also apply to basement floors. They are poured after the superstructure of the building is in place and after the waste-plumbing lines are laid.

## STEPS, SIDEWALKS, AND DRIVEWAYS

Some steps are poured against a wall while others are placed between two existing walls. Others are cast on sloping terrain. Fig. 26-36 shows several methods of forming steps.

Generally, sidewalks and driveways are placed after the finished grading is completed. The grade should be settled before proceeding.

Main walks should be at least 4 ft. wide with secondary walks 3 ft. or less. Thickness is usually 4 in. with the forms constructed from 2 x 4 or 2 x 6 lumber. Sand fill should be used under walks and drives to reduce moisture under the slab when placed on heavy soils.

Driveways should be 5 or 6 in. thick, with reinforcing mesh. A single driveway should be at least 10 ft. wide and a double driveway a minimum of 16 ft. Turning radii should be 18 ft. Control joints are necessary to prevent uncontrolled cracking, Fig. 26-37. In sidewalk and driveway construction, control joints are generally spaced at intervals equal to the width of the slab, but not more than 20 ft. apart.

## PAVING

Brick paving can be installed either as a rigid or flexible system, Fig. 26-38. Rigid paving is easily recognized by its mortar joints. A properly designed rigid paving system consists of a well-compacted subgrade, a properly prepared base, a reinforced concrete slab, a mortar setting bed, and brick paving with mortar joints between the pavers.

Flexible paving has a greater variety of design options than rigid paving. A flexible system consists of a well-compacted subgrade beneath a layer of crushed stone, a sand setting bed, and fine sand between the pavers. A rigid edge restraint must be used to prevent creep (horizontal movement).

Heavy traffic areas such as driveways should use 2 1/4 in. pavers. Patios and sidewalks may use 1 1/2 in. pavers on a flexible base. Paving should be

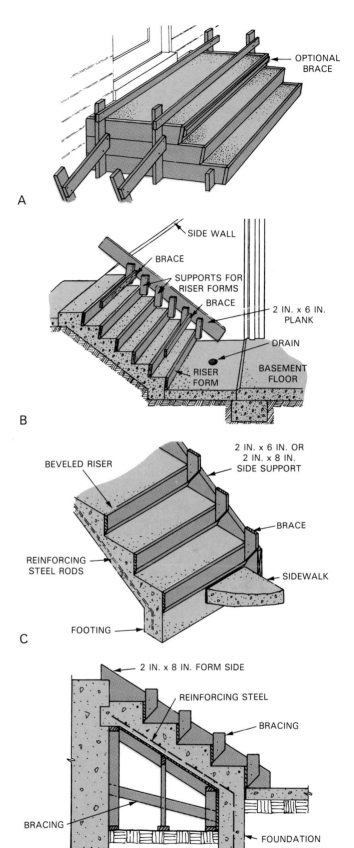

Fig. 26-36. Typical methods of building forms for steps. A—Constructing forms for steps. Nosing is formed by tilting form boards inward at the bottom. B—Form for steps located between two walls already in place. C—Form for steps cast on sloping terrain. D—Form for free-standing concrete steps.

Fig. 26-37. Jointing a slab helps control any cracking due to shrinkage caused by dryness or temperature change. (Portland Cement Association)

Fig. 26-38. Brick paving can be installed either as a rigid or flexible system.

sloped at least 1/8 in. to 1/4 in. per foot to provide drainage. An expansion joint should be provided every 20 ft. for rigid paving and every 30 ft. for flexible paving. Solid curbs that prevent drainage should have weep holes every 16 in. along the length. All concrete, mortar, and brick should conform to recognized standards.

## WOOD FOUNDATIONS

The All-Weather Wood Foundation system is so named because it can be installed in almost any weather. It provides comfortable living space in basement areas because the stud wall can be fully insulated. All wood parts are pressure treated with chemical solutions. This makes the fibers useless as food for insects or as a spot for fungus growth. Pressure-treated wood foundations have been approved by major code groups and accepted by the Federal Housing Administration (FHA), the Department of Housing and Urban Development (HUD), and the Farmers Home Administration (FmHA).

For a regular basement, the site is excavated to the regular depth. Plumbing lines are installed and provisions made for foundation drainage according to local requirements.

A sump (pit for water collection) will be required where ground water is a problem. Discharge from the sump may be connected to a storm sewer or other positive drainage. The subgrade is covered with 6 to 8 in. of porous gravel or crushed stone. This layer must be carefully leveled. Footing plates of 2 x 8 or 2 x 10 material are installed directly on the gravel base. Walls are erected on these plates. A typical wood foundation system is illustrated in Fig. 26-39.

Nails and other fasteners should be made of either silicon bronze, copper, or hot-dipped zinc coated steel. Special caulking compounds are used to seal all joints in the plywood sheathing.

Before pouring the basement floor, the porous gravel or crushed stone base is covered with a polyethylene film (6 mil. thick) and a screed board is attached to the foundation wall.

The first floor joists or trusses are installed on the double top plate of the foundation wall with special attention given to methods of attachment, so that inward forces will be transferred to the floor structure. See Fig. 26-40. Where joists run parallel to the wall, blocking should be installed between the outside joist and the first interior joist.

Before backfilling, attach a 6-mil polyethylene moisture barrier to sections of the wall below grade. Bond the top edge of the barrier to the wall at grade level with a special adhesive. Install a treated wood strip over this and caulk it. (Later it will serve as a guide for backfilling.)

Lap vertical joints of at least 6 in. in the polyethylene film. Seal joints with the same adhesive.

Do not backfill until basement floor and first floor are installed. Let the basement floor cure.

As with any foundation system, satisfactory performance demands full compliance with recommended standards covering design, fabrication, and installation. Standards for wood foundations are contained in a manual published by the National Forest Products Association, 1619 Massachusetts Avenue, N.W., Washington, D.C. 20036.

Carpenters installing wood foundations should make certain that each piece of treated lumber and plywood carries the mark, ''AWPB-FDN.'' This means the materials meet requirements of code organizations and federal regulatory agencies.

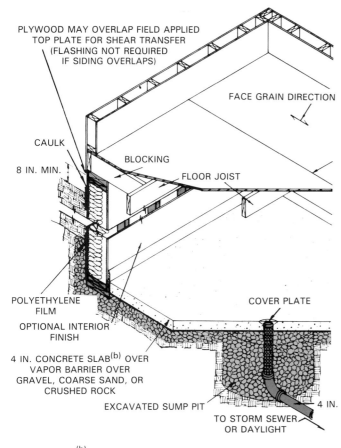

PLYWOOD MAY OVERLAP FIELD APPLIED
TOP PLATE FOR SHEAR TRANSFER
(FLASHING NOT REQUIRED
IF SIDING OVERLAPS)

FACE GRAIN DIRECTION

CAULK

BLOCKING

8 IN. MIN.

FLOOR JOIST

POLYETHYLENE
FILM

OPTIONAL INTERIOR
FINISH

COVER PLATE

4 IN. CONCRETE SLAB(b) OVER
VAPOR BARRIER OVER
GRAVEL, COARSE SAND, OR
CRUSHED ROCK

EXCAVATED SUMP PIT

4 IN.

TO STORM SEWER
OR DAYLIGHT

(b)A WOOD BASEMENT FLOOR SYSTEM IS
AVAILABLE, WRITE APA FOR DETAILS

Fig. 26-39. Typical wood foundation in cutaway. Note drainage sump which keeps the subsoil dry around the foundation. (American Plywood Association)

Fig. 26-40. Truss joists being installed over wood foundation. Use of 10d nails is recommended so inward pressure on wall is transferred to the floor system. (Osmose)

## TEST YOUR KNOWLEDGE, Chapter 26

Please do not write in the text. Place your answers on a separate sheet of paper.

1. A _____ indicates structure location on a site, along with distances from structure to property line.
   a. Foundation plan.
   b. Plot plan.
   c. Floor plan.
   d. None of the above.
2. What is the use of batter boards?
3. What is a control point?
4. Explain the situations in which each of the following footings would be used: plain, reinforced, and stepped.
5. What is the standard width of a footing for an 8 in. thick foundation wall?
   a. 4 in.
   b. 32 in.
   c. 16 in.
   d. None of the above.
6. What are the components of a standard concrete block?
7. Name three types of slab-on-ground foundations.
8. The typical thickness of a sidewalk is _____.
9. What is the purpose of pressure treating lumber with a chemical solution for use in a wood foundation?
10. What are the two basic systems of installing paving?
11. Which paving system provides greater design options?

## ACTIVITIES

1. Question a local building contractor about the difference between concrete block and cast concrete foundations. Cover such things as cost, time required, resistance to leakage, supporting strength, work quality, ease of modification, applications, etc.
2. Secure reference materials prepared by such organizations as the Portland Cement Association, National Concrete Masonry Association, and the Mason Contractors Association of America. Prepare a detailed report on the following aspects of control joints: function, location, and construction.
3. Visit your local building inspector to discuss the advantages and disadvantages of wood foundation walls. Secure requirements for the location of your home. Visit a building and loan association and discuss wood foundations with them to determine their willingness to finance structures utilizing wood foundations. Report your findings.

Top left. Engineered wood floor trusses used as floor frame. (Southern Forest Products Association) Bottom left. Pressure treated 2 x 6 southern yellow pine decking. (Southern Forest Products Association) Right. Using a power nailer to install a door trimmer. (Paslode Co., Div. of Signode)

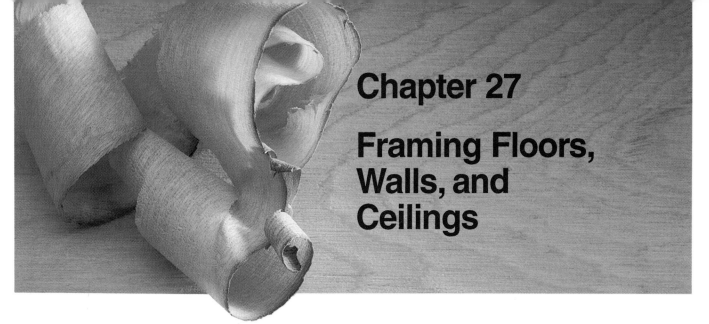

# Chapter 27

# Framing Floors, Walls, and Ceilings

After the foundation is completed, work can begin on the floor framing. Even though carpenters prefer to have the backfill completed before they begin the floor framing, this should not be done. Frequently, foundation walls are damaged by backfilling too soon, even when braced heavily inside. Delay backfilling until the floor platform is in place and the foundation has some weight on it.

## FLOOR FRAMING

Before beginning work on the floor framing, carpenters should study the floor plan(s) of the building, Fig. 27-1, and floor framing details if included in the drawings. Generally, the floor plan or foundation plan will indicate the direction, size, and spacing of the joists or floor trusses. Become very familiar with the basic dimensions of the building and any special features which it has.

## TYPES OF FRAMING

Methods of floor framing vary from one section of the country to another. Even builders in a given area may use different methods, based on personal preference and experience. In some parts of the country, buildings must be constructed to resist high winds and/or rain. Earthquakes and heavy snow loads are considerations in other areas. All buildings should resist fire. Framing methods are also determined by the basic design of a structure. Fig. 27-2 shows several basic house designs that affect floor framing methods.

The basic types of floor framing are PLATFORM

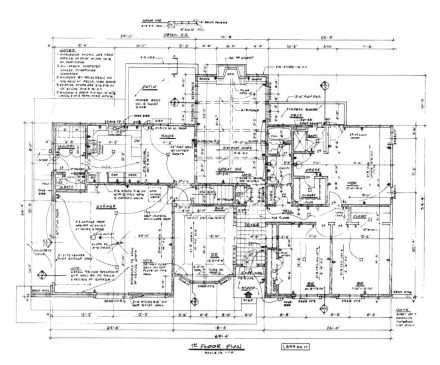

Fig. 27-1. Floor plans contain vital information related to framing floors and walls. These plans are studied before the framing is started. (The Garlinghouse Company)

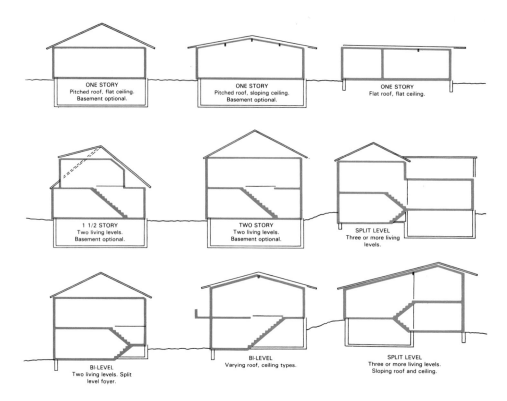

Fig. 27-2. How a house will be framed depends on the type, how spaces are tied together, and the kinds of materials used. These are basic types.

(also called western framing) and BALLOON framing. Of these two, platform framing is used more extensively. Plates, sills, joists, and studs are structural members used in both types of framing.

## Platform framing

Platform framing is used in most residential construction. The first floor is built directly on the foundation walls, just as though it were a platform. This platform becomes a work area for the carpenter. Wall sections can be assembled and raised safely and accurately. The wall sections are one story high. These sections and various partitions support a platform for the second story. Each floor is framed separately, Fig. 27-3.

Platform framing can be used on both one and two-story structures, and is easily and quickly constructed. Shrinkage is uniform throughout the structure. A firestop is automatically provided.

In platform framing, the sill is the starting point in constructing a floor. A SILL is the lowest member of the frame of a structure, resting on the foundation and supporting the floor joists.

Platform framing utilizes a method of sill construction known as BOX SILL construction, Fig. 27-4. The box sill consists of a 2 in. x 6 in. plate, and a header which is the same size as the floor joists. Fig. 27-5 shows a detail of the first and second floor of a structure using platform framing and box sill construction.

The only firestopping needed in platform framing is built into the floor frame between floors. It prevents the spread of fire in a horizontal direction, Fig. 27-6. Here it also serves as solid bridging, holding the joists in a plumb (vertical) position with even spacing.

Fig. 27-3. Example of platform framing on a house. The platform (arrow) supports the wall sections for the next floor. (American Plywood Association)

442

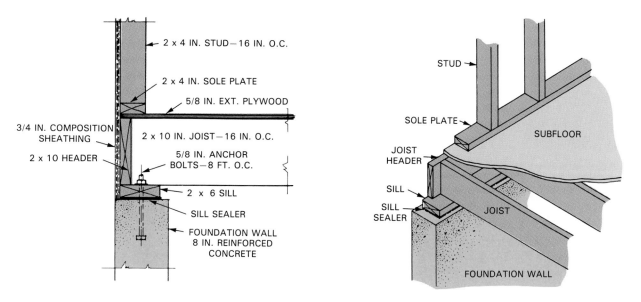

Fig. 27-4. Left. Detail of box sill construction showing first floor framing at the foundation wall. Right. Pictorial view. This type of construction is called platform or western framing.

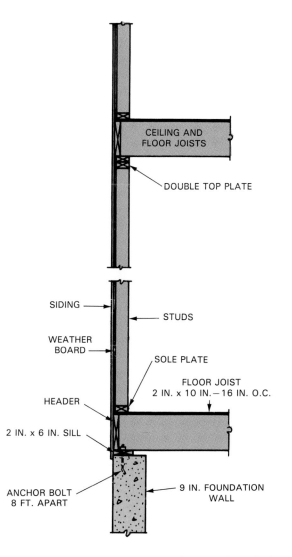

Fig. 27-5. Detail of first and second floors using platform framing and box sill construction.

The type of framing is usually shown or specified in the architectural plans. A longitudinal section through the entire building, Fig. 27-7, or more localized details will provide this information.

## Balloon framing

Balloon framing was once used extensively, but in recent years has diminished in importance. Its distinguishing feature is that the wall studs rest directly on the sill plate. In balloon framing two types of sill construction are used, the solid or standard sill and the T-sill, Fig. 27-8.

In solid sill construction, the studs are nailed directly to the sill and joists. No header is used.

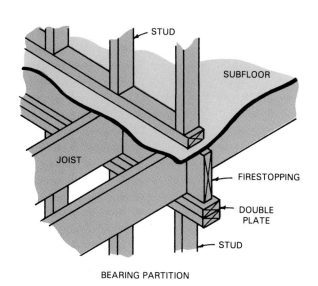

Fig. 27-6. Firestopping needed in platform framing to resist horizontal spread of fire.

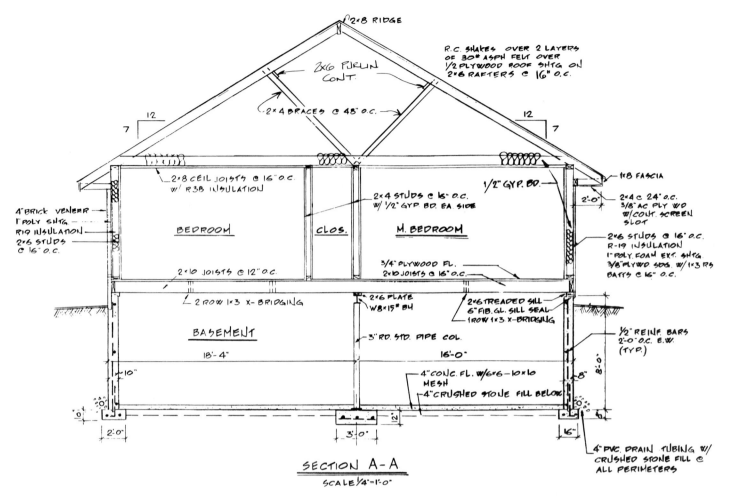

2x8 RIDGE

R.C. SHAKES OVER 2 LAYERS
OF 30# ASPH FELT OVER
1/2" PLYWOOD ROOF SHTG. ON
2x8 RAFTERS @ 16" O.C.

2x6 PURLIN
CONT.

2x4 BRACES @ 48" O.C.

12
7

12
7

2x8 CEIL. JOISTS @ 16" O.C.
W/ R3B INSULATION

2x4 STUDS @ 16" O.C.
W/ 1/2" GYP. BD. EA. SIDE

1/2" GYP. BD.

1x8 FASCIA

BEDROOM

CLOS.

M. BEDROOM

2'-0"

2x4 @ 24" O.C.
3/8" AC PLY WD
W/CONT. SCREEN
SLOT

4" BRICK VENEER
1" POLY SHTG
R19 INSULATION
2x6 STUDS
@ 16" O.C.

2x6 STUDS @ 16" O.C.
R-19 INSULATION
1" POLY. FOAM EXT. SHTG.
3/8" PLYWD SDG. W/ 1x3 R3
BATTS @ 16" O.C.

2x10 JOISTS @ 12" O.C.

3/4" PLYWOOD FL.
2x10 JOISTS @ 16" O.C.

2 ROW 1x3 X-BRIDGING

2x6 PLATE
W 8x15# BM

2x6 TREADED SILL
6" FIB. GL. SILL SEAL
1 ROW 1x3 X-BRIDGING

BASEMENT

18'-4"

3" RD. STD. PIPE COL.

16'-0"

1/2" REINF. BARS
2'-0" O.C. E.W.
(TYP.)

8'-0"

10"

4" CONC. FL. W/6x6-10x10
MESH
4" CRUSHED STONE FILL BELOW

8"

2'-0"

3'-0"

2"

16"

4" PVC DRAIN TUBING W/
CRUSHED STONE FILL @
ALL PERIMETERS

SECTION A-A
SCALE 1/4"=1'-0"

Fig. 27-7. This sectional view through the entire structure indicates that platform framing is to be used.
(The Garlinghouse Company)

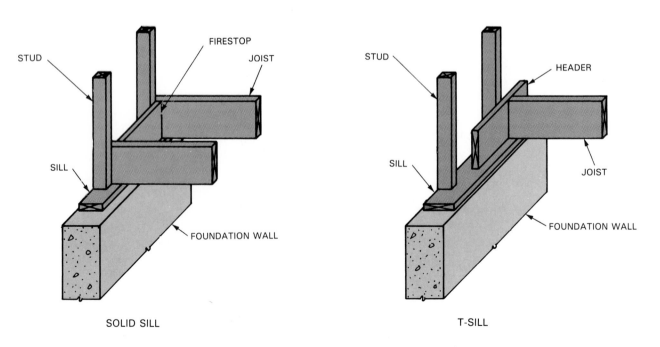

STUD

FIRESTOP

JOIST

STUD

HEADER

SILL

JOIST

SILL

FOUNDATION WALL

FOUNDATION WALL

SOLID SILL

T-SILL

Fig. 27-8. Two types of sill construction used in balloon framing.

Joists are supported by a ribbon and nailed to the studs on the second floor level, Fig. 27-9. A firestop must be provided between the studs using pieces cut to the proper length.

T-sill construction uses a header which also serves as a firestop. The studs rest on the sill plate and are nailed to the header as well as the sill plate. The sill plate in T-sill construction may be eight or ten in. wide to provide broader base support upon which the joists may rest. Solid sill construction is used more extensively in two-story homes.

Two advantages of balloon framing are small potential shrinkage and vertical stability. Balloon framing is suitable for two-story structures with brick veneer or stucco exterior wall finishes. The vertical shrinkage in a two-story house using platform framing is sometimes great enough to cause cracking. This, however, is usually not the case with balloon framing.

Disadvantages of balloon framing include a less than desirable surface to work on during construction and the need for firestop blocks.

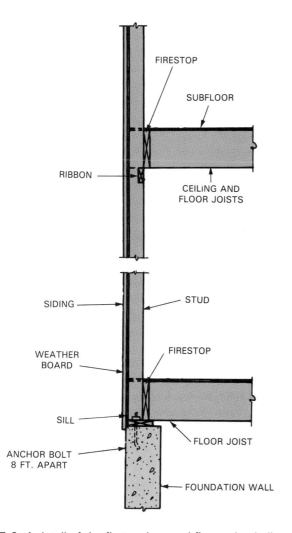

Fig. 27-9. A detail of the first and second floor using balloon framing and solid sill construction.

## GIRDERS AND BEAMS

Joists support the floor surface and rest on the top of the foundation wall. Usually the span (distance between the walls) is so great that support is needed between opposite foundation walls. Girders or beams provide the required support. Generally, a girder rests on the foundation wall on either end and gains support from one or more posts or columns along its length. Wood girders may be solid timber, built-up lumber, glue-laminated beams, or parallel strand lumber. Steel beams are commonly of two types: S beam and wide-flange beams.

To find the approximate size of a girder complete the following steps.
1. Determine the distance between the girder supports.
2. Find the girder load width. A girder must support the weight of the floors on each side of it to the midpoint between the girder and foundation wall.
3. Determine the "total floor load" per square ft. supported by joists and bearing partitions to girder. This will be the sum of loads per sq. ft. listed in the diagram, Fig. 27-10. This does not include roof loads. These are carried on the outside walls unless braces or partitions are placed under the rafters. Then a portion of the roof load is carried to the girder by joists and partitions.
4. Find the total load on the girder. This is the product of girder span times the girder load width times the total floor load.
5. Select the proper girder size according to the code in your area. The table in Fig. 27-11 is typical. It indicates safe loads on standard size girders, for spans from 6 ft. to 10 ft. Shortening the span is usually the most economical way to increase the load a girder will carry.

Built-up girders can be made using three or four pieces of 2 in. lumber, nailed together with 20d nails.

## STEEL BEAMS

In many localities, steel beams are used instead of wood girders, Fig. 27-12. Sizes depend on the load. It can be calculated in the same way as the wood girders.

Two types of steel beams are illustrated in Fig. 27-13. The W (wide-flange) beam is the type generally used in residential construction. While wood beams vary in depth, width, species, and grade, steel beams vary in depth, width of flange, and weight.

After the approximate load on a steel beam has been determined, the correct size can be selected. Fig. 27-14 lists a selected group of steel beams commonly used in residential structures. For

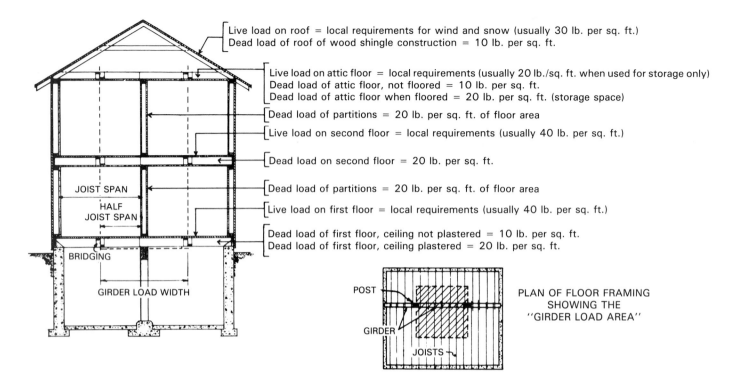

Live load on roof = local requirements for wind and snow (usually 30 lb. per sq. ft.)
Dead load of roof of wood shingle construction = 10 lb. per sq. ft.

Live load on attic floor = local requirements (usually 20 lb./sq. ft. when used for storage only)
Dead load of attic floor, not floored = 10 lb. per sq. ft.
Dead load of attic floor when floored = 20 lb. per sq. ft. (storage space)

Dead load of partitions = 20 lb. per sq. ft. of floor area

Live load on second floor = local requirements (usually 40 lb. per sq. ft.)

Dead load on second floor = 20 lb. per sq. ft.

Dead load of partitions = 20 lb. per sq. ft. of floor area

Live load on first floor = local requirements (usually 40 lb. per sq. ft.)

Dead load of first floor, ceiling not plastered = 10 lb. per sq. ft.
Dead load of first floor, ceiling plastered = 20 lb. per sq. ft.

JOIST SPAN

HALF JOIST SPAN

BRIDGING

GIRDER LOAD WIDTH

POST

GIRDER

JOISTS

PLAN OF FLOOR FRAMING SHOWING THE "GIRDER LOAD AREA"

Fig. 27-10. Diagram shows method of figuring loads for frame of a two-story home.

| GIRDERS | SAFE LOAD IN LB. FOR SPANS FROM 6 TO 10 FEET | | | | |
|---|---|---|---|---|---|
| SIZE | 6 FT. | 7 FT. | 8 FT. | 9 FT. | 10 FT. |
| 6 x 8 SOLID | 8,306 | 7,118 | 6,220 | 5,539 | 4,583 |
| 6 x 8 BUILT-UP | 7,359 | 6,306 | 5,511 | 4,908 | 4,062 |
| 6 x 10 SOLID | 11,357 | 10,804 | 9,980 | 8,887 | 7,997 |
| 6 x 10 BUILT-UP | 10,068 | 9,576 | 8,844 | 7,878 | 7,086 |
| 8 x 8 SOLID | 11,326 | 9,706 | 8,482 | 7,553 | 6,250 |
| 8 x 8 BUILT-UP | 9,812 | 8,408 | 7,348 | 6,544 | 5,416 |
| 8 x 10 SOLID | 15,487 | 14,782 | 13,608 | 12,116 | 10,902 |
| 8 x 10 BUILT-UP | 13,424 | 12,768 | 11,792 | 10,504 | 9,448 |

Fig. 27-11. Table indicates typical safe loads for standard size wood girders.

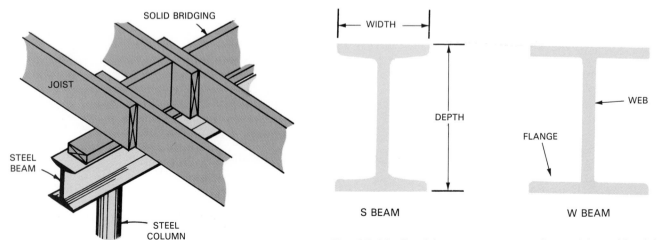

SOLID BRIDGING

JOIST

STEEL BEAM

STEEL COLUMN

Fig. 27-12. Floor joists supported by a steel beam and column.

WIDTH

DEPTH

WEB

FLANGE

S BEAM

W BEAM

Fig. 27-13. Steel beams are commonly used in residential construction. An S beam (formerly called an I beam) is a standard shape. A W beam is a wide-flange shape.

| DESIGNATION WT./FT. | NOMINAL SIZE DP. x WD. | SPAN IN FEET | | | | | | | | | |
|---|---|---|---|---|---|---|---|---|---|---|---|
| | | 8' | 10' | 12' | 14' | 16' | 18' | 20' | 22' | 24' | 26' |
| W8x10 | 8x4 | 15.6 | 12.5 | 10.4 | 8.9 | 7.8 | 6.9 | — | — | — | — |
| W8x13 | 8x4 | 19.9 | 15.9 | 13.3 | 11.4 | 9.9 | 8.8 | — | — | — | — |
| W8x15 | 8x4 | 23.6 | 18.9 | 15.8 | 13.5 | 11.8 | 10.5 | — | — | — | — |
| W8x18 | 8x5 1/4 | 30.4 | 24.3 | 20.3 | 17.4 | 15.2 | 13.5 | — | — | — | — |
| W8x21 | 8x5 1/4 | 36.4 | 29.1 | 24.3 | 20.8 | 18.2 | 16.2 | — | — | — | — |
| W8x24 | 8x6 1/2 | 41.8 | 33.4 | 27.8 | 23.9 | 20.9 | 18.6 | — | — | — | — |
| W8x28 | 8x6 1/2 | 48.6 | 38.9 | 32.4 | 27.8 | 24.3 | 21.6 | — | — | — | — |
| W10x22 | 10x5 3/4 | — | — | 30.9 | 26.5 | 23.2 | 20.6 | 18.6 | 16.9 | — | — |
| W10x26 | 10x5 3/4 | — | — | 37.2 | 31.9 | 27.9 | 24.8 | 22.3 | 20.3 | — | — |
| W10x30 | 10x5 3/4 | — | — | 43.2 | 37.0 | 32.4 | 28.8 | 25.9 | 23.6 | — | — |
| W12x26 | 12x6 1/2 | — | — | — | — | 33.4 | 29.7 | 26.7 | 24.3 | 22.3 | 20.5 |
| W12x30 | 12x6 1/2 | — | — | — | — | 38.6 | 34.3 | 30.9 | 28.1 | 25.8 | 23.8 |
| W12x35 | 12x6 1/2 | — | — | — | — | 45.6 | 40.6 | 36.5 | 33.2 | 30.4 | 28.1 |

Fig. 27-14. Allowable uniform loads for W beams. Loads are given in kips (1 kip = 1000 lb.). (Grosse Steel Co.)

example, if the total load on the beam (evenly distributed) is 15,000 lb. and the span between supports is 16 ft., than a W8-18 beam should be used. This specifies an 8 in. beam weighing 18 lb. per lineal foot. The width of the flange is 5 1/4 in.

## FRAMING OVER GIRDERS AND BEAMS

Common methods for framing joists over girders and beams are shown in Fig. 27-15. In Fig. 27-15A, the top of the girder is flush with the top of the sill plate. In Fig. 27-15B, the girder is used with ledger strips to increase headroom below the girder. Fig. 27-15C is similar to B, except joist hangers are used instead of ledger strips. The setup shown in Fig. 27-15D is used when the girder is raised to provide additional headroom. The joists are supported by the ledger strips. Finally, Fig. 27-15E shows the most typical setup. The top of the beam is flush with the top of the foundation wall.

## POSTS AND COLUMNS

For ordinary wood posts (not longer than 9 ft. or smaller than 6 x 6 in.), it is safe to assume that a post whose greatest dimension is equal to the width of the girder it supports will carry the girder load. For example, a 6 x 6 in. post would be suitable for a girder 6 in. wide. For a girder 8 in. wide, a 6 x 8 in. or 8 x 8 in. post should be used.

Wood posts should be supported on footings which extend above the floor level and which provide a secure anchor. A 1/2 in. diameter reinforcing rod or bolt may be used for this purpose. Be sure the rod extends about 3 in. into the bottom end of the post. See Fig. 27-16.

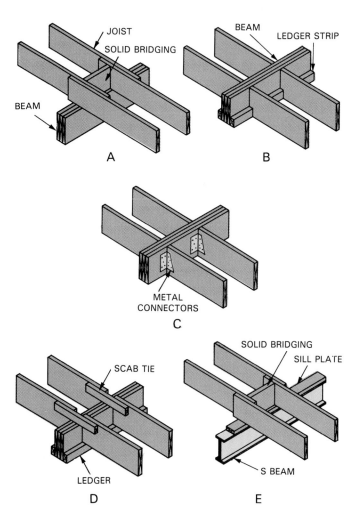

Fig. 27-15. Common methods for framing over beams and girders. A—Joists lapped over built-up beam. B—Beam with ledger strip supporting joists. C—Metal connectors used to secure joists to beam. D—Joists resting on ledger connected with scab tie. E—Joists supported by steel beam with sill plate.

447

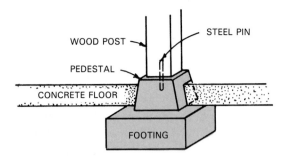

Fig. 27-16. Footings for wood columns should extend above the concrete floor for moisture protection.

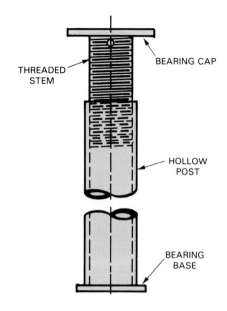

Fig. 27-18. Steel posts with threaded top section are easy to install and adjust.

Another method of securing the bottom of a wood post is to use a post anchor, Fig. 27-17. This device will hold a post securely and support it above the floor, protecting it from moisture. Post anchor strength is far less than that method previously described. Post anchor securing should be used in light-load situations.

A built-up wood post may be made by nailing together three 2 x 6 boards. Choose pieces that are free from defects. Nail them securely.

Steel posts are usually chosen to support girders and beams. The post should be capped with a steel plate to provide a good bearing surface and good anchorage to the beam (if needed). Some steel posts are adjustable, such as the one shown in Fig. 27-18. These are very popular because they are easy to install and adjust.

## INSTALLING SILLS

Two basic types of sill anchors are generally used. Both are shown in Fig. 27-19. With the strap type anchor, position the sill and attach the straps with nails. Some types must be bent over the top of the sill; others are nailed on the sides.

When anchor bolts are used, remove the washers and nuts. Lay the sill on top of the foundation wall against the anchor bolts. Remember, the edge of the sill may be set back from the outside of the foundation a distance equal to the thickness of the sheathing.

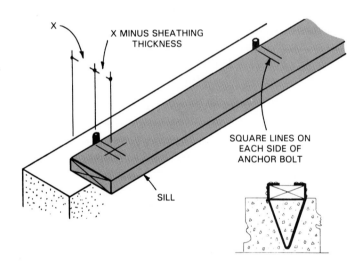

Fig. 27-19. Procedure for laying out anchor bolt holes in a sill plate. An anchor strap (inset) is nailed to the sill. (TECO)

Fig. 27-17. Adjustable steel post anchor. (Timber Engineering Co.)

Draw lines across the sill on each side of the bolts as shown. Measure the distance from the center of the bolt to the outside of the foundation and subtract the thickness of the sheathing. Use this distance to locate the bolt holes. Separate measurements for each bolt will most likely be needed since they may be different.

Most carpenters prefer to snap a chalk line along the top of the foundation wall where the outside of the sill plate should be located. This will insure a straight floor frame. Slight variations between the outside surface of the sheathing and foundation wall can be shimmed when the siding is installed.

After all the holes are located, bore the holes. Most carpenters prefer to bore the hole about 1/4 in. larger than the diameter of the bolts, allowing some adjustment for slight inaccuracies in the layout. As each section is laid out and holes bored, position the section over the bolts.

When all sill sections are fitted, remove them from the anchor bolts. Install the sill sealer and then replace them. Install washers and nuts. As nuts are tightened, see to it that the sills are properly aligned. Also, check the distance from the edge of the foundation wall. The sill must be level and straight. While low spots can be shimmed with wooden wedges, it is better to use grout or mortar.

## JOISTS

Joists provide support for the floor. They are usually made from a common soft wood such as southern yellow pine, fir, larch, hemlock, or spruce. Joists are also available in aluminum and steel.

The sizes of floor joists range from a nominal size of 2 in. x 6 in. to 2 in. x 12 in. The size required for a given situation will depend on the length of space, load to be supported, species and grade of wood, and distance the joists are spaced apart. Spacing of floor joists may be 12, 16, or 24 in. O.C. (on center). A spacing of 16 in. O.C. is most common. Span data for floor joists is presented in the reference section. The span data presented assumes a maximum deflection of 1/360th of the span with a normal live load. This is the amount which most codes require. The normal live load for first floor area is 40 lb. per sq. ft. The chart shows that the following choices would be within the limits for a span of 13 ft. using #1 dense yellow pine: 2 in. x 8 in. joists—12 in. O.C. and 16 in. O.C.; 2 in. x 10 in. joists—12 in. O.C., 16 in. O.C., and 24 in. O.C.; 2 in. x 12 in. joists—12 in. O.C., 16 in. O.C., and 24 in. O.C. The obvious choice would be 2 in. x 8 in. joists, 16 in. O.C. These joists would span 13 ft. 7 in. which exceeds the span by 7 in.

### LAYING OUT JOISTS

Study the plans carefully. Note the direction the joists are to run. Also, become familiar with the location of posts, columns, and supporting partitions. The plans may also show the centerlines of girders.

The position of the floor joists can be laid out directly on the sill, Fig. 27-20. On platform construction, the joist spacing is usually laid out on the joist header rather than the sill. The position of an intersecting framing member may be laid out by marking a single line and then placing an X to indicate the position of the part, Fig. 27-21. Instead of measuring each individual space around the perimeter of the building, it is more accurate and efficient to make a master layout on a strip of wood (called a rod). Use it to transfer the layout to headers

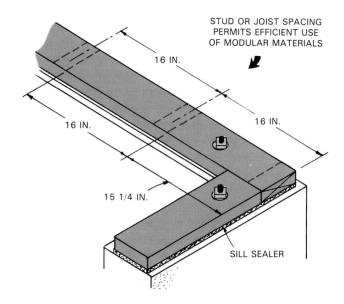

Fig. 27-20. After sill is attached to foundation, locations for studs or joists may be marked.

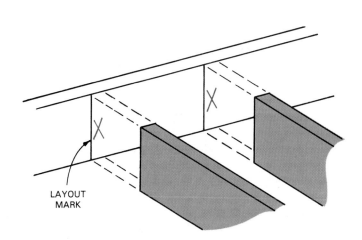

Fig. 27-21. Marking the actual location of framing members. The X indicates the side of the line where the member is positioned.

or sill. The same rod is then used to make the joist layout on girders and the opposite wall.

Joists are doubled where extra loads must be supported. When a partition runs parallel to the joists, a double joist is placed underneath. Partitions which carry plumbing or heating pipes are usually spaced far enough apart to permit easy access, Fig. 27-22.

Joists must also be doubled around openings in the floor frame for stairways, chimneys, and fireplaces. These joists are called TRIMMERS. They support the headers which carry the tail (short) joists, Fig. 27-23. The carpenter must become thoroughly familiar with the plans at each floor level so adequate support can be provided.

Select straight lumber for the header joist and lay out the standard spacing along its entire length. Add

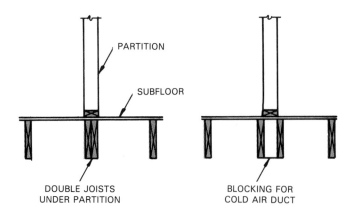

Fig. 27-22. Joists located under partitions are usually doubled. Spacing the joists apart (right) provides space for heating and plumbing runs. If the wall must hold a plumbing stack, the wall may be framed with 2 x 6 boards.

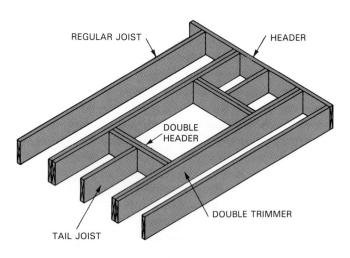

Fig. 27-23. Floor framing used around openings such as fireplaces and stairs.

the position for any doubled joists and trimmer joists that will be required along openings. Where regular joists will become tail joists, change the X mark to a T to prevent errors.

## INSTALLING JOISTS

After the header joists are laid out, toenail them to the sill. Position all full length joists with the crown (slight warpage called crook) turned up. Hold the end tightly against the header and along the layout line so the sides will be plumb. Attach the joists to the header using a nailing pattern consisting of three 16d nails.

Now fasten the joists along the opposite wall. If the joists butt at the girder (join end to end without overlapping), they should be joined with a scarf or metal fastener. If they lap, they can be nailed together using 10d nails. Also use 10d nails to toenail the joists to the girder.

To increase the accuracy of the floor frame, some carpenters first nail the joists to the headers. The headers are then carefully aligned with the sill or a chalk line on the foundation. Then the assembly is toenailed to the sill.

Nail doubled joists together using 12 or 16d nails spaced about 1 ft. along the top and bottom edge. First, drive several nails straight through to pull the two surfaces tightly together and clinch the protruding ends. Finish the nailing pattern by driving the nails at a slight angle. This will prevent them from going all the way through while increasing their holding power.

## FRAMING OPENINGS

Place boards or sheets of plywood across the joists to provide a temporary working deck to install header and tail joists. First set the trimmer joists in place. Sometimes a regular joist will be located where it can serve as the first trimmer. Fig. 27-24 is a plan view of the finished assembly.

The length of the headers can be determined from the layout on the main header joist. Cut headers and tail joists to length. Be sure to make cuts square, because considerable strength will be lost if the assembly is not tight. Lay out the position of the tail joists on the headers by transferring the marks made on the main header in the initial layout.

Small assemblies may be nailed together and then set in place. Usually, however, the headers are installed and then the tail joists are attached. One tail joist can be temporarily nailed to each trimmer for accurate location while it is being nailed into place.

Metal framing anchors are often used to assemble headers, trimmers, and tail joists, Fig. 27-25. They are made from 18 gauge zinc-coated sheet steel in a variety of sizes and shapes. The National Forest Products Association recommends the use of framing anchors or ledger strips to support tail joists that are over 12 ft. long.

## BRIDGING

Some recent studies have shown that bridging may be eliminated where joists are properly secured at the ends, and/or where subflooring is adequate and carefully nailed. However, many local building codes list requirements in this area; general standards suggest that bridging be installed at intervals of no more than 8 ft.

Regular bridging, sometimes called herringbone or cross bridging, is composed of pieces of lumber or metal braces set diagonally between the joists, Fig. 27-26. The purpose of bridging is to hold the joists in a vertical (on edge) position and to transfer the load from one joist to the next.

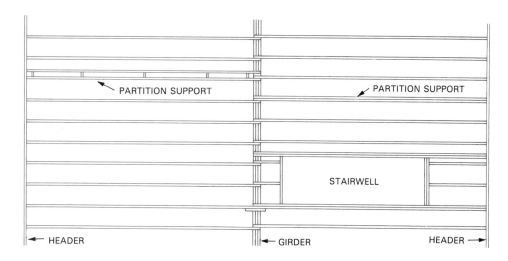

Fig. 27-24. Plan view of floor frame with rough opening for stairs and two types of partition support. A single header is used next to the girder since the distance between the header and girder is so short.

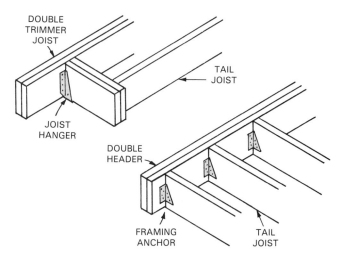

Fig. 27-25. Joist hangers and framing anchors are useful when assembling floor framing members.

To install bridging, first determine the position of the run, then snap a chalk line across the tops of the joists. Attach a piece to each side of every joist. Alternating the position of the two pieces, first on one side of the chalk line and then on the other side at the next joist, will make installation easy and correct. The lower ends of the bridging are not nailed until the subflooring is complete or until the under surfaces of the floor are to be enclosed.

Solid bridging, as the name implies, consists of solid blocks set between the joists. This is often used in odd-size spaces in a run of cross bridging. Solid bridging, also called blocking, improves an installation, Fig. 27-27. The chief purpose is to provide a nailer for the sheathing, but it also adds rigidity to the floor and keeps the joists vertical.

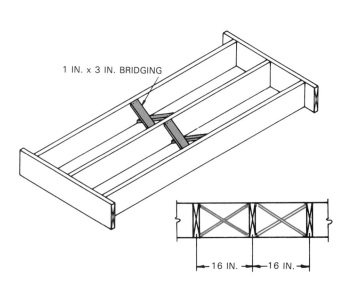

Fig. 27-26. 1 in. x 3 in. wood bridging. Bridging is a requirement of many codes.

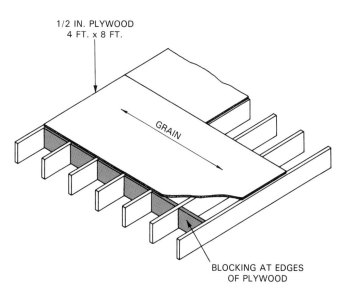

Fig. 27-27. Blocking is used to support the edges of 1/2 in. plywood used for subfloor.

Fig. 27-28. Metal bridging can be installed quickly.

Several types of prefabricated steel bridging are available that are easy to install. The type shown in Fig. 27-28 is manufactured from sheet steel. A V-shaped cross section makes it rigid. No nails are required on the bottom end and it is driven into place with a regular hammer. This design meets FHA Minimum Property Standards, and is approved by the Uniform Building Code.

After the bridging is installed, the floor frame should be checked carefully to see that nailing patterns have been completed in all members. After this is done, the frame is ready to receive the subflooring.

## SPECIAL FRAMING PROBLEMS

In modern residential construction, the design may include a section of floor that cantilevers (overhangs) a lower floor or basement level. When the floor joists run perpendicular to the walls, the framing is comparatively easy. It is only necessary to use longer joists. If, however, the floor joists run parallel to the wall, the construction must be framed with cantilevered joists as illustrated in Fig. 27-29.

Exact spacing and length of the members depends on the weight of the outside wall. Usually, cantilevered joists should extend inward at least twice

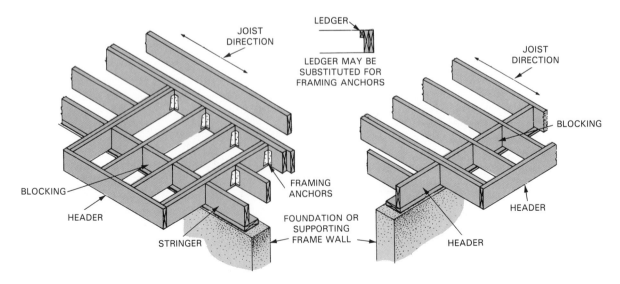

Fig. 27-29. Framing methods on overhangs depends on direction the joists run. Blocking holds the joists vertical, adds rigidity, and closes up the space.

as far as they stick out over the supporting wall.

Entrance halls, bathrooms, and other areas are often finished with tile or stone that is installed on a concrete base. To provide room for this base, the floor frame must be lowered. When the area is not large, this can be done by doubling joists of a smaller dimension or spacing the smaller joists closer together, Fig. 27-30. When the area is large, steel or wood girders and posts should be added.

## BATHROOMS

Bathrooms must support unusually heavy loads, heavy fixtures, and often the additional weight of a tile floor. The fixed dead load imposed by a tile floor will average around 30 lb. per sq. ft. The load from bathroom fixtures adds from 10 to 20 lb. per sq. ft., for a total of 40 to 50 lb. dead load. In addition, it is frequently necessary to cut joists to bring in water service and pipes. Special precautions must, therefore, be taken in framing bathroom floors to provide adequate support.

### Cutting floor joists

Before cutting joists to install plumbing, it is useful to know how stress affects floor joists. This knowledge will help you determine where to make holes and cut notches.

When the top of a joist is in compression and the bottom in tension, there is a point at which the stresses change from one to the other. At this point, there is neither tension nor compression.

In the usual rectangular joist, this point is assumed to be midway between the top and bottom. If there is neither compression nor tension at the center, then a hole no larger than one-fourth the width of the joist would have little effect on the strength. Weight produces the greatest bend if it is at the center of the span. Therefore, holes should

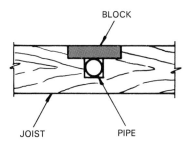

Fig. 27-31. When a large pipe such as a drain must pass through a joist, the joist should be blocked to prevent severe weakening of the member.

not be located at the center of the span if possible. When it is necessary to cut joists, the cuts should be made from the top. The loss should be compensated for by adding headers and trimmers or extra joists. Another method for solving the problem is illustrated in Fig. 27-31.

## FLOOR TRUSSES

Floor trusses are widely used in modern construction. They provide an easy-to-handle, light weight assembly and long, clear spans with minimum depth. The open webs provide room for plumbing, heating, and electrical systems. Sound transmission between levels is also reduced.

Modern engineered wood trusses are designed to meet loading requirements with a minimum of materials. Stress graded lumber is used in their construction and they are assembled under exacting conditions, Fig. 27-32.

## SUBFLOOR

Plywood, tongue-and-groove boards, and common boards are used for subfloors. The large size of plywood sheets (4 ft. x 8 ft.), and comparatively short time required to nail the sheets in place has drastically increased the use of plywood for subfloors. One-half in. thick plywood may be used when joists are spaced 16 in. O.C., but some builders prefer 5/8 in. stock. When plywood is used, it is important that the joist spacing be very accurate. All edges of the plywood must be supported.

The subfloor serves three purposes:
1. It adds rigidity to the structure.
2. It provides a base for finish flooring material.
3. It provides a surface upon which the carpenter can lay out and construct additional framing.

In some localities there is a trend to combine the subfloor and underlayment (usually 5/8 in. particle board) into a single thickness which is usually 1 1/8 in. thick for 16 in. O.C. joist spacing. The sheets have tongue-and-groove edges and require no blocking between the joists. This single layer

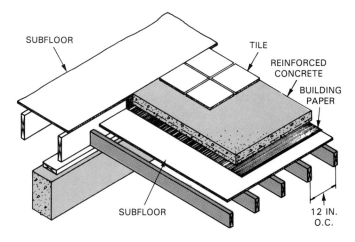

Fig. 27-30. Smaller joists are used when a concrete base is needed for tile or stone surfaces.

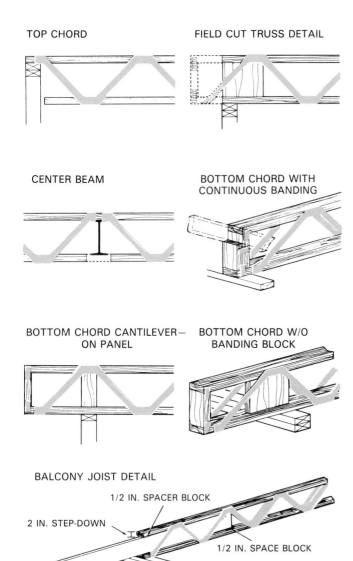

TOP CHORD

FIELD CUT TRUSS DETAIL

CENTER BEAM

BOTTOM CHORD WITH CONTINUOUS BANDING

BOTTOM CHORD CANTILEVER— ON PANEL

BOTTOM CHORD W/O BANDING BLOCK

BALCONY JOIST DETAIL

1/2 IN. SPACER BLOCK

2 IN. STEP-DOWN

1/2 IN. SPACE BLOCK

2 x 8 BALCONY JOIST

Fig. 27-32. Truss construction details. Chords are made of lumber; webbing is a patented galvanized steel design. Trusses provide wide nailing surface because chord is laid flat. (TrusWal Systems Corp.)

Fig. 27-33. Waferboard panels are engineered and approved for use in subflooring. The same application methods are used as for plywood. For non-textile resilient floor applications a 1/4 in. underlayment is recommended. (Louisiana-Pacific Corp.)

## GLUED FLOOR SYSTEM

In a glued floor system, the subfloor panels are glued and nailed to the joists. Structural tests have shown that stiffness is increased about 25 percent with 2 x 8 joists and 5/8 in. plywood. In addition, the system insures squeak-free construction, eliminates nail-popping, and reduces labor costs.

Before each panel is placed, a 1/4 in. bead of glue is applied to the joists, as shown in Fig. 27-34. Spread only enough glue to lay one or two panels. Two beads of glue are applied on joists where panel ends butt together. All nailing must be completed before glue sets.

When laying tongue-and-groove panels, apply glue along the groove, either continuously or periodically. Use a 1/8 in. bead so excessive squeeze-out will be eliminated. A 1/8 in. space must be provided at all end and edge joints. Material specifications and application procedures are published by the American Plywood Association.

## STEEL JOISTS

Several types of cold-formed steel joists are available for floor frames. They are used where long spans are required and in commercial construction. Their load bearing capacity is greater than wood joists of comparable size.

Steel joists are attached to steel headers with clips and screws. They may also be attached to regular wood headers and sills. Steel joists are sometimes set in pockets formed in poured concrete or masonry construction. Plywood subflooring is attached to the joist with a 3/8 in. bead of adhesive and self-drilling screws or flooring nails. Typical joist

provides adequate structural qualities and a satisfactory base for direct application of carpet, tile, and other floor finishes.

Special plywood subfloor-underlayment panels are also available for joist or beam spacing of 20, 24, or 48 in. Maximum support spacing is stamped on each panel.

Other sheet materials such as composite board, waferboard (also called waferwood), oriented strand board, and structural particle board are also approved for use as subflooring. These products have been rated by the American Plywood Association and meet all standards for subflooring. The specifications for application are the same as for plywood, Fig. 27-33.

Fig. 27-34. Applying adhesive for a glued floor system. A 1/4 in. wide band of glue applied to the top of the joist is sufficient. Two beads are applied where panels butt. (American Plywood Association)

spacing is 24 in. O.C. Fig. 27-35 shows a steel joist installation.

## WALL AND CEILING FRAMING

In modern light frame construction, walls and ceiling joists form one structural system. The walls support the joists or trusses, which form the ceiling and the next floor level. The walls are stiffened and held in place by the addition of the joists.

Outside walls serve as a nailing base for inside and outside wallcovering materials. Inside walls (called partitions) serve as a nailing base for inside wallcovering materials.

Fig. 27-35. These steel joists are attached to a steel header resting on the foundation. A plywood subfloor will be installed over the joists.

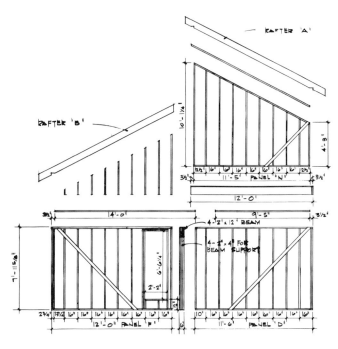

Fig. 27-36. Typical framing plans for the right side elevation of a garage with loft. (National Plan Service)

## FRAME WALL CONSTRUCTION

Frame wall construction involves the proper arrangement of the wall-framing members, Fig. 27-36, used in conventional construction. They include the sole plate, top plates, studs, headers (lintels), braces, and sheathing. Plates and studs are usually nominal 2 x 4 inch lumber. Headers or lintels are ordinarily constructed from larger stock. Bracing may be 1 x 4 or steel straps when the sheathing does not provide sufficient stiffness. Fig. 27-37 shows a frame wall with the framing members identified.

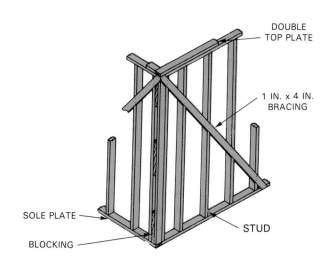

Fig. 27-37. A frame wall corner showing the various framing members and their relationship to each other.

Wall framing lumber must have good stiffness and nail-holding properties, be free from warp, and be easy to work. Species which meet these criteria include Douglas fir, southern yellow pine, hemlock, spruce, and larch. The most common lumber grade used is construction grade or its equivalent. Moisture content should be between 15 and 19 percent.

Frame wall construction usually begins with the sole plate. The spacing of the studs is marked off on the sole plate, Fig. 27-38. Conventional stud spacing of 16 in. or 24 in. has evolved from years of established practice. It is based more on accommodating the wallcovering materials than on the actual calculation of imposed loads.

Construction of the wall is ordinarily performed on the subfloor. Exterior frame walls are flush with the outside of the foundation wall or moved 1/2 in. inside to allow for the thickness of sheathing, weatherboard, or rigid foam insulation (3/4 in.), Fig. 27-39. The sole plate acts as an anchor for the wall and a nailer for interior and exterior wall sheathing. A wall panel may extend along an entire side of the building if sufficient help or equipment is available to raise the wall. Otherwise, the wall may be built in smaller sections.

Wall studs are cut to length (usually 7 ft. 9 in. when 1 1/2 in. material is used) and nailed to the sole and top plates. A second plate is added after the wall is in place. The distance from the top of the subfloor to the bottom of the ceiling joists is usually 8 ft. 1 1/2 in. This distance provides a finished wall height of 8 ft.

Openings for doors and windows are framed before the wall is moved to the vertical position. Headers are cut to length and nailed into position with cripple studs and trimmers firmly nailed to the sole and top plates, Fig. 27-40. CRIPPLES are studs

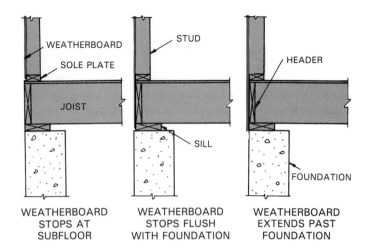

WEATHERBOARD STOPS AT SUBFLOOR

WEATHERBOARD STOPS FLUSH WITH FOUNDATION

WEATHERBOARD EXTENDS PAST FOUNDATION

Fig. 27-39. The weatherboard may terminate at the subfloor, the top of the foundation, or extend below the top of the foundation. The treatment used will most likely depend on the construction procedure.

which are not full length due to a wall opening. TRIMMERS are studs which support the header over an opening in the wall and stiffen the sides of the opening. Regular stud spacing is even and constant along the wall regardless of openings so that modular sheet material can be applied with little cutting.

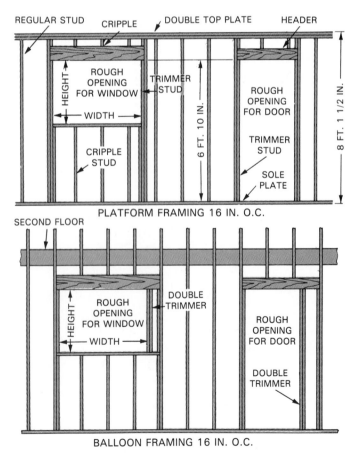

PLATFORM FRAMING 16 IN. O.C.

BALLOON FRAMING 16 IN. O.C.

Fig. 27-40. Wall sections of platform and balloon framing.

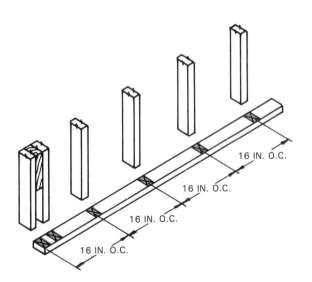

Fig. 27-38. A sole plate showing the location of studs.

## CORNERS

Typical methods of platform framing used to form exterior wall corners are shown in Fig. 27-41. The corner must have a nailing edge for the interior wall material and adequate support for the structure.

Interior frame walls are constructed the same way as exterior walls. They have sole plates and double top plates. Interior walls must be securely fastened to the exterior walls where they intersect. Again, a nailing edge must be provided for the plaster base or drywall. This can be done using a 2 x 6 secured to cross blocking or by doubling the exterior wall studs at the intersection of the partition. Fig. 27-42 shows both methods. The same arrangement is used at the intersection of all interior walls.

## ROUGH OPENINGS

Rough openings for windows and doors shown on the floor plan are dimensioned to the center of the opening. Specific dimensions are usually provided by the window and door schedule. The width is listed first and the height second. The rough open-

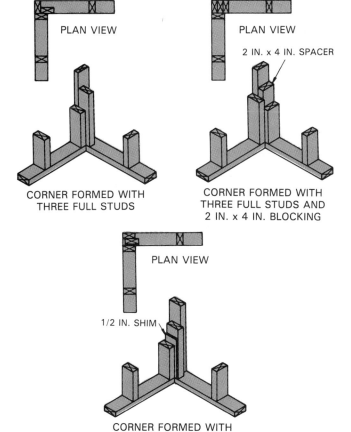

PLAN VIEW

CORNER FORMED WITH
THREE FULL STUDS

PLAN VIEW

2 IN. x 4 IN. SPACER

CORNER FORMED WITH
THREE FULL STUDS AND
2 IN. x 4 IN. BLOCKING

PLAN VIEW

1/2 IN. SHIM

CORNER FORMED WITH
THREE FULL STUDS
AND 1/2 IN. SHIM

Fig. 27-41. Corner posts are framed in a variety of ways. This illustration shows three methods.

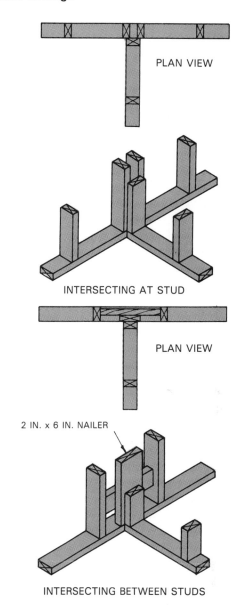

PLAN VIEW

INTERSECTING AT STUD

PLAN VIEW

2 IN. x 6 IN. NAILER

INTERSECTING BETWEEN STUDS

Fig. 27-42. The framing for the intersection of partitions and exterior walls is accomplished by using extra studs or blocking and a nailer.

ing height of most doors is 6 ft. 10 in. Tops of all windows will probably be the same distance above the floor and shown on the elevation drawings and/or details.

Each wall opening requires a header above the opening to support the weight above. Headers are formed by nailing two pieces of dimension lumber (2 x 6, 2 x 8, etc.) together with a 1/2 in. plywood spacer between to equal the stud width. The length of the header will be equal to the width of the rough opening plus the thickness of two trimmers, Fig. 27-43. Header sizes vary with the span and load requirements. Fig. 27-44 shows sizes for various spans. Check the code to be sure these specifications are permitted in your area. Special headers are required for openings wider than 8 ft. or in situations

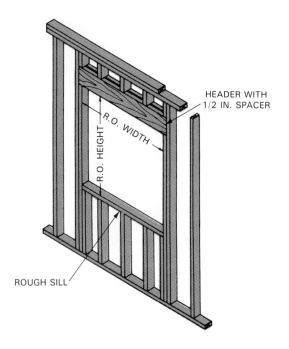

Fig. 27-43. The rough opening for a window is the area between the trimmers, and between the rough sill and header.

Fig. 27-45. "Glulams" or glue laminated beams are ideal for long spans and heavy loads.    (Boise-Cascade Corp.)

| MATERIAL ON EDGE | SUPPORTING ONE FLOOR, CEILING, ROOF (IN FT. & IN.) | SUPPORTING ONLY CEILING AND ROOF (IN FT. & IN.) |
|---|---|---|
| 2 × 4 | 3-0 | 3-6 |
| 2 × 6 | 5-0 | 6-0 |
| 2 × 8 | 7-0 | 8-0 |
| 2 × 10 | 8-0 | 10-0 |
| 2 × 12 | 9-0 | 12-0 |

Fig. 27-44. Recommended header spans. Check local code.

involving extremely heavy loads. Fig. 27-45 shows a wide opening supported by a glue laminated beam.

In modern platform construction, extra studs are included around rough openings as shown in the standard assembly, Fig. 27-46. The studs and trimmers support the header and provide a nailing surface for window and door casing. Some carpenters also double the rough sill to add a nailing base for window stools and aprons.

In balloon construction, found in older homes, studs extended from the sole plate to the roof plate. It was common practice to extend headers beyond the rough opening to the next regular stud.

## PLATE LAYOUT

Use only straight 2 x 4 stock for plates. Select two of equal length and lay them side by side along the location of the outside wall. Length should be determined by what can easily be lifted off the floor

and into a vertical position after it is assembled.

Lay out the plates along the main side walls first. Align the ends with the floor frame and then mark the regular stud spacing all the way along both plates, Fig. 27-47. Lay out the centerline for each door and window opening. Measure off one-half the width of the opening on each side of the centerline. Mark the plate for trimmer studs outside of these points. Include a full length stud on the outside of each trimmer stud. Identify the positions with a T for trimmers and X for full length studs. All the stud spaces between the trimmers will be marked with a C to designate a cripple stud.

Lay out the centerlines where intersecting partitions will butt the exterior wall. Add full length studs if required. When blocking between regular studs is used, the centerline will be needed as a guide for positioning the backing plate.

## LAY OUT OF ROUGH OPENING HEIGHTS

A master stud pattern, Fig. 27-48, is a time saver and frequently prevents errors. It is made from a straight 1 x 4 or 2 x 4 with the sole plate, double top plate, header(s), and rough sill heights marked off along its length. Lay out the headers. Lay out the height of the rough openings by measuring down from the bottom side of the header. Next, draw in the rough sill. The length of the various studs can now be taken directly from this master stud pattern.

## CONSTRUCTING WALL SECTIONS

Working from the master stud pattern, cut the various stud lengths. In modern construction, it is

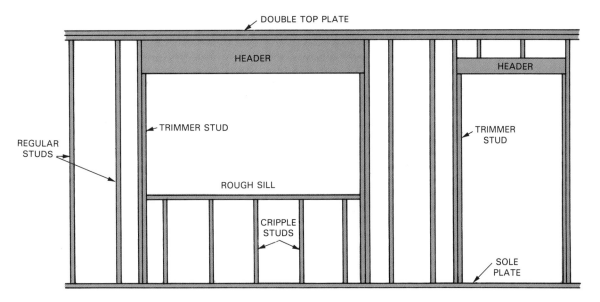

Fig. 27-46. Proper way to frame openings in walls. Trimmer studs carry the weight of the header. Header is wider than it needs to be. However, it is done this way to fill the space. It avoids labor or cutting and installing cripple studs and braces.

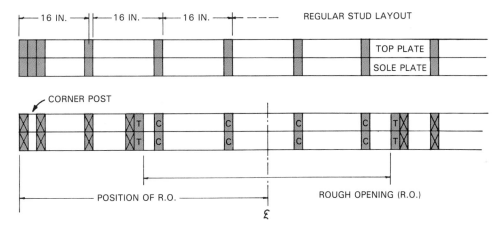

Fig. 27-47. Layout of sole and top plates. Top. Regular stud spacing has been marked. Bottom. Layout is converted for a window opening.

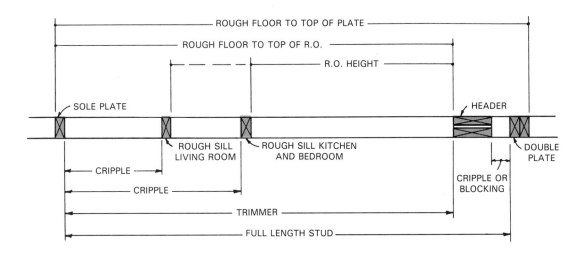

Fig. 27-48. Master stud pattern shows the various stud lengths.

seldom necessary to cut standard full length studs. These are usually precision end trimmed (P.E.T.) at the mill and delivered to the construction site ready to assemble.

Cut and assemble the headers. Their length, and also the length of the rough sill, can be taken directly from the plate layout.

The sequence to be followed in assembling wall sections, especially the rough opening, will vary among carpenters. Following is one of several procedures that could be used.

Move the top plate away from the sole plate about a stud length. Turn both plates on edge with the layout marks inward. Place a full-length stud, crown up, at each position marked on the plates. Nail the top plate and sole plate to the studs using two 16d nails through each end of each stud.

Set the trimmer studs in place on the sole plate and nail them to the full-length studs. Now place the header so it is tight against the end of the trimmer and nail through the full-length stud into the header using 16d nails. The upper cripples can be installed after the header is placed. Currently, carpenters sometimes omit cripple studs and run the header all the way to the top plate.

For window openings, transfer the position of the cripple studs from the sole plate to the rough sill, and then make the assembly using 16d nails. Some carpenters prefer to erect the wall section and then install the lower cripples and rough sill. When this procedure is followed, the lower ends of the cripple studs are toenailed to the sole plate.

Add studs or blocking at positions where partitions will intersect outside walls. Also install any wall bracing that may be required for special installations. Remember that the inside surface of the frame is turned down.

Wall sheathing is often applied to the frame before it is raised. The frame must be square before sheathing is applied. Diagonal bracing may be applied or the frame may be nailed to the floor to keep it square.

Materials used for exterior wall sheathing include plywood, composite board, fiberboard, and insulating panels. Many types of sheathing are available in standard sizes from 4 x 8 ft. to as large as 4 x 14 ft. Thickness varies with type of material selected and insulating value or strength desired. Corner bracing is required with fiberboard, gypsum sheathing, and rigid foam sheathing. Plain 3/4 in. board sheathing is seldom used in modern construction because of added labor cost.

Once the sheathing has been attached, the wall section may be raised into place, Fig. 27-49.

Fig. 27-49. Wall frames are assembled on the floor and then raised into position. (National Forest Products Association)

Smaller sections may be raised by hand. Larger sections may require wall jacks or other equipment. Immediately after the wall section is up, secure it with braces. Make final adjustments in the position of the sole plate, then nail it to the floor, Fig. 27-50. Plumb at corners and several points along the wall.

When one section of the wall is in place, build other sections and erect them. No special order needs to be followed.

## PARTITIONS

When the outside wall frame is completed, partitions are built and erected. At this stage it is important to enclose the structure and make the roof watertight. Only bearing partitions (those that support the ceiling and/or roof) are usually installed. Erection of nonbearing partitions can be done later.

Roof trusses, often used in modern construction, are supported entirely by the outside walls. When they are used, inside partition work is seldom started until the roof is complete.

The centerlines of the partitions are established from a study of the plans and then marked on the floor with a chalk line. Plates are laid out; studs and headers are cut; partitions are assembled and erected in the same way as outside walls. See Fig. 27-51. Erect long partitions first, then cross partitions. Finally build and install short partitions that form closets, wardrobes, and alcoves.

The corners and intersections are constructed as described for outside walls. The size and amount of blocking, however, can be reduced, especially in nonbearing partitions. The chief concern is to provide nailing surfaces at inside and outside corners for wallcovering material.

Fig. 27-51. Raising a main bearing partition. Note that a section of the double plate has been used to splice the top plate.

Nonbearing partitions do not require headers. Many openings can be framed with single pieces of 2 x 4 lumber, as shown in Fig. 27-52. Most carpenters, however, include trimmers around openings because they are more rigid. Furthermore, they provide additional framework for attaching casing and trim. Door openings in partitions (and outside walls) are framed with the sole plate included at the bottom of the opening. After the framework is erected, the sole plate is cut out. Rough door openings are generally made 2 1/2 in. wider than the finished door size.

Fig. 27-50. Using an air-powered nailer to secure sole plate to floor. (Senco Products, Inc.)

Fig. 27-52. Headers are not used on nonbearing partitions.

When framing walls and partitions, openings for heating ducts, Fig. 27-53, are easily cut and framed. Extra support for bathtubs and wall mounted stools should be added, Fig. 27-54. Support and nailers for recessed and wall-hung cabinets, tissue roll holders, drapery brackets, towel bars, shower rods, and similar devices should be added during the framing phase.

Special framing is frequently required for plumbing in walls. Large drain and vent pipes may require a wall built from 2 x 6 in. material to provide added wall thickness, Fig. 27-55. Other special framing

may require the study of construction details in order to proceed. The bay window shown in Fig. 27-56 is a good example of special framing.

The top plate is doubled to add support under ceiling joists and rafters. This also further ties the wall frame together. Joints in the upper plate should be at least 4 ft. from those in the lower top plate. Joints are lapped at the corners as shown in Fig. 27-57.

## CEILING FRAME

The assembly just below the roof that carries the ceiling surface is called the ceiling frame. On other levels, the ceiling cover is carried on the bottom side of the floor joists.

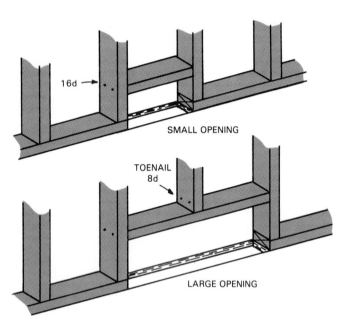

Fig. 27-53. Installing special framing for heat ducts.

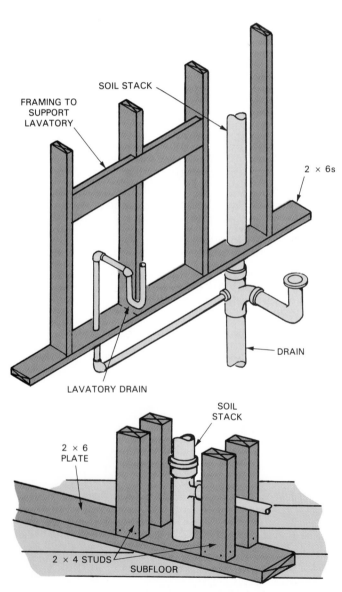

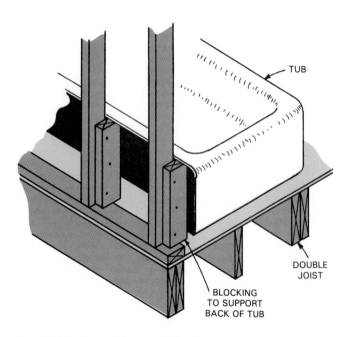

Fig. 27-54. Extra joists and blocking are needed to support tubs.

Fig. 27-55. A partition containing plumbing pipes may need to be constructed differently to provide room for plumbing. Top. Wall constructed of 2 x 6 studs and plate. Note special framing for supporting lavatory. Bottom. 2 x 4 studs on 2 x 6 plate eliminate need to notch or bore studs for lateral runs.

The main framing members are also called joists. Like floor joists, their size is determined by the length of span and the spacing used. To coordinate with walls and permit the use of a wide range of surface materials, a spacing of 16 or 24 in. O.C. is commonly used. Size and quality requirements must also be based on the type of ceiling finish (plaster or drywall) and what use will be made of the attic space, Fig. 27-58. The architectural plans will usually include specifications. These requirements should be checked with local building codes.

Ceiling joists usually run across the narrow dimensions of a structure. However, some may be placed to run in one direction and others at right angles, Fig. 27-59. By running joists in different directions, the length of the span can often be reduced.

In large living rooms, the midpoint of the joists may need to be supported by a beam. This beam can be located below the joists or installed flush with the joists. In the latter, the joists may be carried

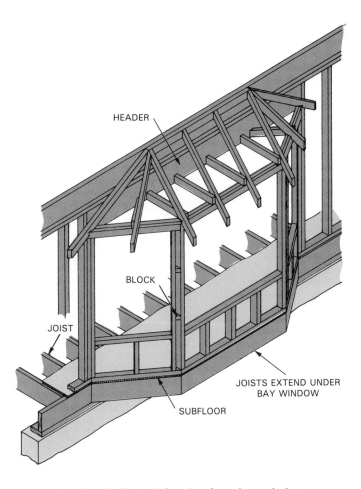

Fig. 27-56. Typical framing for a bay window.

| SIZE IN. | SPACING IN. | GROUP A FT. IN. | GROUP B FT. IN. | GROUP C FT. IN. | GROUP D FT. IN. |
|---|---|---|---|---|---|
| 2 × 4 | 12 | 9 - 5 | 9 - 0 | 8 - 7 | 4 - 1 |
| | 16 | 8 - 7 | 8 - 2 | 7 - 9 | 3 - 6 |
| 2 × 6 | 12 | 14 - 4 | 13 - 8 | 13 - 0 | 9 - 1 |
| | 16 | 13 - 0 | 12 - 5 | 11 - 10 | 7 - 9 |
| 2 × 8 | 12 | 19 - 6 | 18 - 8 | 17 - 9 | 14 - 3 |
| | 16 | 17 - 9 | 16 - 11 | 16 - 1 | 12 - 4 |
| 2 × 10 | 12 | 24 - 9 | 23 - 8 | 22 - 6 | 19 - 6 |
| | 16 | 22 - 6 | 21 - 6 | 20 - 5 | 16 - 10 |

Fig. 27-58. Spans for ceiling joists are figured for a normal dead load and a live load of 20 psf (pounds per sq. ft.). This permits the attic to be used for storage. Always check local codes. (National Building Code)

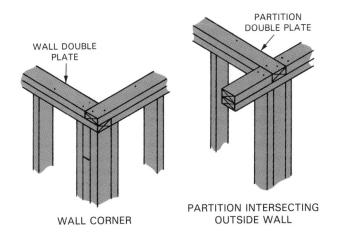

Fig. 27-57. Double plates are lap jointed for strength wherever they intersect.

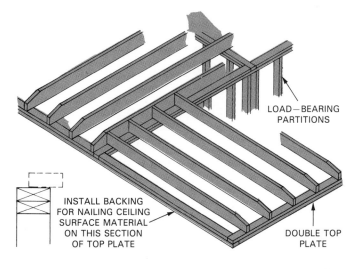

Fig. 27-59. Ceiling frame. Joists in foreground are turned at right angles to reduce the span.

Basic construction of ceiling framing is similar to floor framing. The main difference is that lighter joists are used and headers are not included around the outside.

When trusses are used to form the roof frame, a ceiling frame is not required. The bottom chords of the trusses carry the ceiling surface.

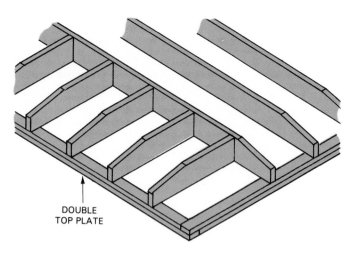

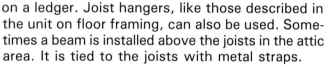

Fig. 27-60. Stub ceiling joists along the end wall. These are required for a low-pitched hip roof.

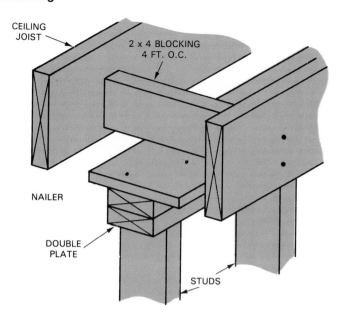

Fig. 27-61. Use special blocking to anchor partitions to the ceiling frame when they run parallel to the joists.

on a ledger. Joist hangers, like those described in the unit on floor framing, can also be used. Sometimes a beam is installed above the joists in the attic area. It is tied to the joists with metal straps.

When ceiling joists run parallel to the edge of the roof, the outside member will likely interfere with the roof slope. This often occurs in low-pitched hip roofs. The ceiling frame in this area should be constructed with stub joists running perpendicular to the regular joists, Fig. 27-60.

Lay out the position of the ceiling joists along the top plate, using a rod. When a double plate is used, the joists do not need to align with the studs in the wall. The layout, however, should put the joists alongside the roof rafters so that the joists can be nailed to them.

Ceiling joists are installed before the rafters. Toenail them to the plate using two 10d nails on each side.

Partitions or walls that run parallel to the joists must be fastened to the ceiling frame. A nailing strip or drywall clip (to carry the ceiling material) must be installed. Various sizes of materials can be installed in several ways. The main concern is that they provide adequate support. Fig. 27-61 shows a typical installation.

## STRONGBACKS

Long spans of ceiling joists may require a strongback. This is an L-shaped support, attached across the tops of joists to strengthen them and maintain the space between them. It also evens up the bottom edges of the joists so the ceiling will not be wavy after the drywall is applied. The strongback is built with two pieces of dimension lumber. One is usually a 2 x 4 and the other a 2 x 6 or 2 x 8. Fig. 27-62 shows a typical strongback, along with the procedure for construction.

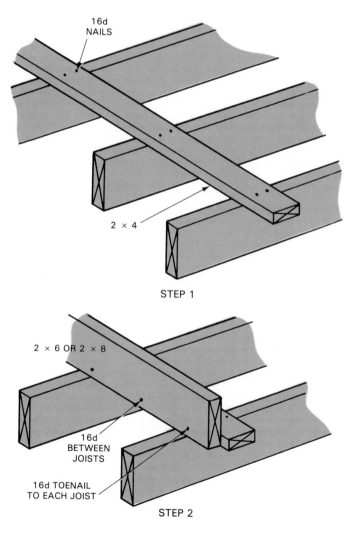

Fig. 27-62. Building a strongback. Step 1, nail the 2 x 4 to the joists. Step 2, turn the second 2 x 6 or 2 x 8 on edge and nail it to the 2 x 4 and to joists.

## METAL FRAMING

Metal framing has become very popular in residential construction. Many reasons have contributed to its popularity: increased lumber costs, decreasing quality of lumber, and builders looking for ways to improve overall quality and reduce cost. In addition, natural disasters such as hurricanes, fires, earthquakes, and floods have forced model building code officials to make changes to strengthen buildings. Metal framing performs well and has captured the interest of insurance companies, buildings, and home buyers. Finally, environmental concerns have helped to bring metal framing to the forefront because it is recyclable.

The steel component known as the structural "C", Fig. 27-63, is the predominant shape used for floor joists, wall studs, roof rafters, and ceiling joists. Standard dimensions are nearly identical to those of dimensional lumber. Flange widths are generally 1 1/2 in. and web depths range from 2 in. to 12 in. Gauges (metal thicknesses) from 12 to 22 are available. Standard metal framing members are available in lengths from 8 to 16 feet.

Metal framing is similar to wood framing in many respects. However, differences in installation tools and techniques exist. Metal members are fastened together with screws. These are typically 1/2 in. long, low-profile, zinc-coated, pan head screws. For protection, plastic grommets are required wherever electrical wiring is to pass through the framing. Metal framing is protected from corrosion by a zinc coating (galvanizing). Spacing of studs is usually 24 in. on center. Fig. 27-64 shows a typical residential application of steel framing.

Fig. 27-64. Interior of metal framed residence showing portion of kitchen soffit from which cabinets will be hung.

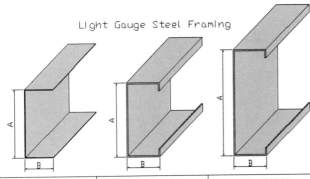

Light Gauge Steel Framing

| CHANNEL STUDS | | 'C' STUDS | | 'C' JOISTS | |
|---|---|---|---|---|---|
| A | B | A | B | A | B |
| 2 1/2" | 1" | 2 1/2" | 1 1/4" | 5 1/2" | 1 7/8" |
| 3 1/4" | 1 3/8" | 3" | 1 3/8" | 6" | 1 5/8" |
| 3 5/8" | | 3 5/8" | 1 1/2" | 7 1/4" | 1 3/4" |
| 4" | | 3 1/4" | 1 5/8" | 8" | 2" |
| 6" | | 4" | | 9 1/4" | 2 1/2" |
| | | 5 1/2" | | 10" | |
| | | 6" | | 12" | |
| | | 7 1/2" | | | |
| | | 8" | | | |

Fig. 27-63. Common sizes of the three predominantly used steel framing members.

## TEST YOUR KNOWLEDGE, Chapter 27

Please do not write in the text. Place your answers on a separate sheet of paper.

1. What two floor framing methods are used most often in current residential construction?
2. A _____ is the lowest member of the frame of a structure; it rests on the foundation and supports the floor joists.
3. Name three types of girders or beams used in residential construction.
4. How many pounds will a W8 x 10 beam support over a span of 12 feet?
   a. 10.4
   b. 13.3
   c. 40.6
   d. None of the above.
5. A _____ post would be used to support a 6 in. girder.
6. What is the purpose of a joist?
7. Joists that are doubled around openings in the floor frame for stairways, chimneys, and fireplaces are called _____.
8. Which of the following is NOT a purpose of bridging?
   a. To hold the joists in a vertical (on edge) position.
   b. To hold the joists in a horizontal position.
   c. To transfer the load from one joist to the next.
   d. None of the above.
9. Name two special framing problems and explain how they are solved.
10. A subfloor adds _____ to a structure, provides a base for _____ flooring material, and provides a surface the carpenter can use to lay out and construct additional _____.

11. What is a cantilevered floor section?
12. A _____ is an inside wall.
13. What is the purpose of a master stud pattern?
14. Name four types of exterior wall sheathing.
15. What is a strongback?
16. The steel component known as the structural _____ is the predominant shape used for floor joists, wall studs, roof rafters, and ceiling joists.

## ACTIVITIES

1. Obtain a set of house plans and identify the following:
   a. Size of floor joists required.
   b. Spacing of floor joists.
   c. Type of sill construction specified.
   d. Thickness and type of subfloor material to be used.
   e. Size of sill plate.
   f. Type and size of bridging.
   g. Species and grade of lumber specified for joists.
   h. Method of framing (balloon or platform).
   i. Type of construction details shown relating to sill and floor.

2. Secure a set of architectural plans for a one-story house. Study the details of construction, especially typical wall sections. Prepare a scale drawing of the framing required for the front walls. Be sure the rough openings are the correct size and in the proper location. Your drawing should look somewhat similar to one of the drawings in Fig. 27-40.

3. Secure literature about fiberboard, foamed plastic, and gypsum sheathing. Secure this material from local lumber dealers or write directly to manufacturers. Also study books and other reference materials.

4. Prepare a report for the class based on the information you obtain in Activity #3. Include grades, manufacturing processes, characteristics, and application requirements. Discuss current prices and purchasing information. Be prepared to discuss specifications given in the literature. Relate these "specs" to local code.

Roof design and roofing materials are important elements in the appearance and function of this structure.
(American Plywood Association)

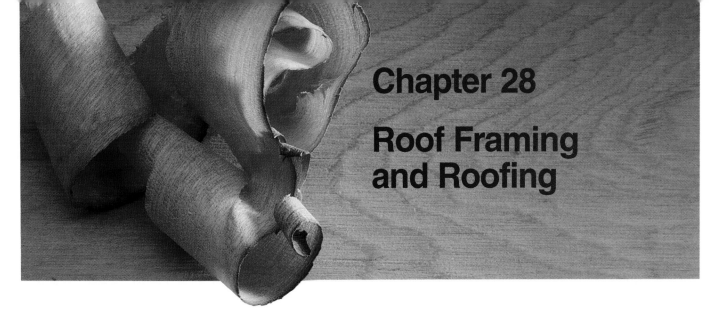

# Chapter 28

# Roof Framing and Roofing

Roof framing provides the support for sheathing and roofing materials. The frame must be strong enough to support the roof itself, wind, and/or snow loads. If the roof is skillfully designed and constructed, it will also contribute to the overall appearance of the structure.

## TYPES OF ROOFS

The overall appearance of a structure is greatly affected by the roof lines and materials used for roof construction. The designer has many standard designs from which to choose. He should be able to find one which will complement the basic design of the home being constructed. Fig. 28-1 shows several roof types commonly used in residential construction.

The GABLE roof is very popular. It is easy to build, sheds water well, provides good ventilation, is economical, and is attractive on a variety of house shapes and designs.

The HIP roof is slightly more difficult to build than a gable roof, but is still a popular choice. It does not provide for ventilation as well as some other designs. A hip roof also increases the chance for leakage due to hips and valleys. An advantage of the hip roof is the protective overhang formed over end walls and side walls.

A FLAT roof is generally the most economical roof to construct. It requires a ''built-up'' or membrane roof covering rather than conventional shingles or tile. A built-up roof consists of layers or roofing felt and tar topped with gravel. Actually, most so-called flat roofs are pitched at about 1/8 to 1/2 in. per foot

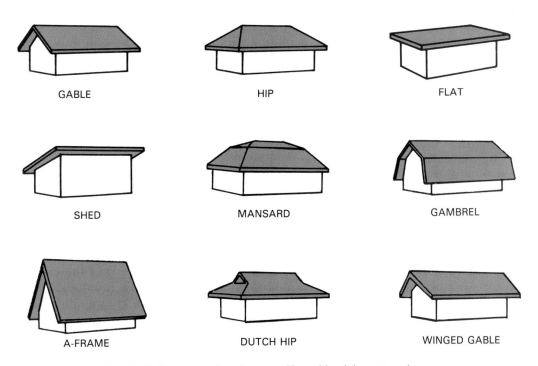

GABLE       HIP       FLAT

SHED       MANSARD       GAMBREL

A-FRAME       DUTCH HIP       WINGED GABLE

Fig. 28-1. Typical roof designs used in residential construction.

to aid in drainage. The flat roof is popular in warmer areas of the country where wide overhangs are desirable for shade and where there is little or no snow fall.

A SHED roof is similar to a flat roof, but has more pitch. It is frequently used for additions to existing structures or in combination with other roof styles. A built-up roof is generally required unless the roof has a pitch of over 3:12 (three feet of rise for each 12 feet of run).

The MANSARD roof is gaining in popularity after being used infrequently for several years. It is a French design that is more difficult to construct than the hip or gable. The main advantage is the additional space gained in the rooms on the upper level.

The GAMBREL roof is sometimes called a barn roof because it has been used extensively on barns. It provides the additional headroom needed for Dutch colonial and similar house styles. It permits more efficient use of the second floor level. Dormers are usually included.

The A-FRAME provides not only a roof but the walls of a structure. Originally it was used for cottages, but in recent years has been applied to homes, churches, and other structures.

The DUTCH HIP is a variation of the hip roof. The slope on either end is broken up by the addition of a small gable. This provides for ventilation and more interesting roof lines.

The WINGED GABLE is a variation of the gable roof. The ridge is longer than the eave line which produces the ''winged'' appearance. The purpose is to add interest to the simpler gable roof types.

## ROOF SUPPORT

The roof and all attachments must be supported by various parts of the structure. Typical rafter construction is usually supported by the outside walls and one or more interior bearing partitions. Roof trusses generally are supported by the outside walls.

## RAFTERS

The parts of a typical roof frame are shown in Fig. 28-2. Several roof types are combined in this illustration.

COMMON rafters run at a right angle from the wall plate to the ridge. A plain gable roof consists entirely of rafters of this kind.

HIP rafters also run from the plate to the ridge, but at a 45 deg. angle. They form the support where two slopes of a hip roof meet.

VALLEY rafters extend diagonally from the plate to the ridge in the hollow formed by the intersection of two roof sections.

There are three kinds of JACK RAFTERS. They are the following.
1. HIP JACK. This is the same as the lower part of a common rafter but intersects a hip rafter instead of the ridge.
2. VALLEY JACK. This is the same as the upper end of a common rafter but intersects a valley rafter instead of the plate.
3. CRIPPLE JACK. Also called a cripple rafter, it intersects neither the plate nor the ridge. Instead, it is terminated at each end by hip and

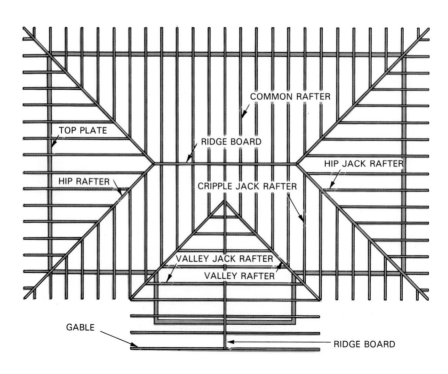

Fig. 28-2. Roof framing plan with structural members identified.

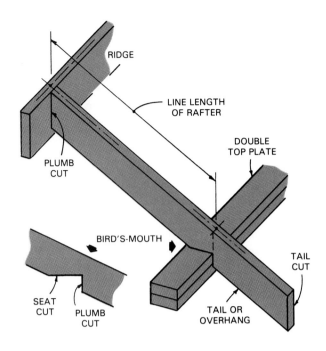

Fig. 28-3. Rafter parts. Various cuts and surfaces have special meaning.

valley rafters. The cripple jack rafter is also called a hip valley cripple jack or a valley cripple jack.

## PARTS OF A RAFTER

Rafters are formed by laying out and making various cuts. Fig. 28-3 shows the cuts for a common rafter and the sections formed. The RIDGE CUT allows the upper end to fit tightly against the ridge. The BIRD'S-MOUTH is formed by a seat cut and plumb (vertical) cut when the rafter extends beyond the plate. This extension is called the OVERHANG or TAIL. When there is no overhang, the bottom of the rafter is ended with a seat cut and a plumb cut.

Rafters are cut to the proper dimensions by locating the ridge cut, the seat cut, the plumb cuts, and the tail cut. The precise layout of these cuts is determined by either the slope or the pitch of the roof. Terms used when calculating the pitch or slope include rise, run, and span.

The RISE of a roof is the vertical distance measured from the top of the wall plate to the intersection of the centerline of the rafters. The RUN of a roof is one-half of the span. SPAN is the horizontal distance from the outside of one stud wall to the outside of the opposite stud wall, Fig. 28-4.

## SLOPE AND PITCH

These terms are often used incorrectly. They are not the same measurement. SLOPE gives the incline of a roof as a ratio of the vertical rise to the horizontal run. It is usually expressed as "X" distance in 12, where X is the rise. For example, a roof that rises 5 in. for each 12 in. of run, has a 5 in 12 slope. The slope of a roof is sometimes called the "cut of the roof."

Roof slope may be given on a drawing by showing a slope ratio diagram. This diagram, shown in the upper corner, Fig. 28-4, represents the ratio between the rise and run of the roof.

PITCH gives the incline of the roof as a ratio of the vertical rise to the span. The span is twice the length of the run. For example, a roof that rises 4 ft. in total and has a total span of 24 ft., has a pitch of 1/6 (4/24 = 1/6). Pitch is calculated using the formula:

$$\text{Pitch} = \frac{\text{Rise}}{\text{Span}}$$

Rafter sizes depend on the distance to be spanned, the spacing of the rafters, and the weight to be supported. Rafter span data is presented in

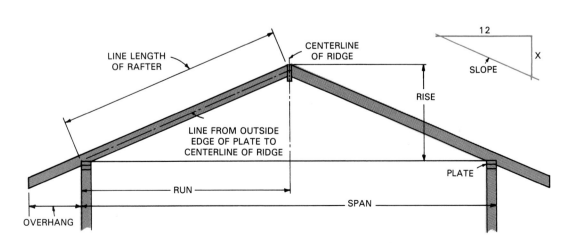

Fig. 28-4. These terms are basic to rafter layout.

| SIZE OF RAFTER (Inches) | SPACING OF RAFTER (Inches) | MAXIMUM ALLOWABLE SPAN (Feet and Inches Measured Along the Horizontal Projection) | | | |
|---|---|---|---|---|---|
| | | Group I | Group II | Group III | Group IV |
| 2 × 4 | 12 | 10-0 | 9-0 | 7-0 | 4-0 |
| | 16 | 9-0 | 7-6 | 6-0 | 3-6 |
| | 24 | 7-6 | 6-6 | 5-0 | 3-0 |
| | 32 | 6-6 | 5-6 | 4-6 | 2-6 |
| 2 × 6 | 12 | 17-6 | 15-0 | 12-6 | 9-0 |
| | 16 | 15-6 | 13-0 | 11-0 | 8-0 |
| | 24 | 12-6 | 11-0 | 9-0 | 6-6 |
| | 32 | 11-0 | 9-6 | 8-0 | 5-6 |
| 2 × 8 | 12 | 23-0 | 20-0 | 17-0 | 13-0 |
| | 16 | 20-0 | 18-0 | 15-0 | 11-6 |
| | 24 | 17-0 | 15-0 | 12-6 | 9-6 |
| | 32 | 14-6 | 13-0 | 11-0 | 8-6 |
| 2 × 10 | 12 | 28-6 | 26-6 | 22-0 | 17-6 |
| | 16 | 25-6 | 23-6 | 19-6 | 15-6 |
| | 24 | 21-0 | 19-6 | 16-0 | 12-6 |
| | 32 | 18-6 | 17-0 | 14-0 | 11-0 |

Fig. 28-5. Sample table showing maximum runs allowed for rafters sloped 4 to 12 or greater. Groups refer to species of wood. Secure this kind of information from local building codes.

Fig. 28-5. Normal rafters listed in the table are for slopes of 4 to 12 or greater. Rafters for low-sloped roofs may also serve as a base for the finished ceiling. In this instance, they are acting as rafters and ceiling joists, Fig. 28-6.

## LAYING OUT COMMON RAFTERS

When laying out rafters, a pattern rafter is first carefully laid out, checked, and cut. This rafter is used to mark other rafters of the same size and kind.

Usually the carpenter will stand on the crowned side that will be the top edge of the rafter to lay out the pattern. It is easier to hold and manipulate the framing square from that position. However, in order to be more easily understood, this position has been reversed. The rafter is shown in the position it will have WHEN INSTALLED.

To lay out a rafter by the step-off method refer to Fig. 28-7. Place the framing square on the stock and align the figures with the top edge of the rafter—unit run (12 in.) on the blade and unit rise on the tongue.

To insure accuracy, the correct marks on the square must be positioned exactly over the edge of the stock each time a line is marked. Be sure to use a sharp pencil to make the layout lines.

Start at the top of the rafter. Hold the square in position and draw the ridge line along the edge of the tongue. Continue to hold the square in the same position and mark the length of the odd unit (8 in. used in the example). Now shift the square along the edge of the stock until the tongue is even with the 8 in. mark. Draw a line along the tongue and mark the 12 in. point on the blade for a full unit.

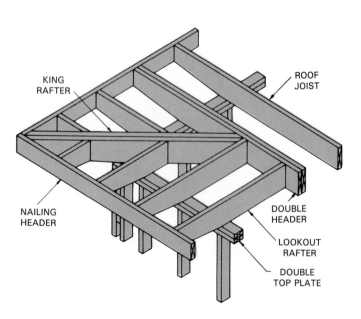

Fig. 28-6. Framing detail of the cornice for a flat or low-sloped roof.

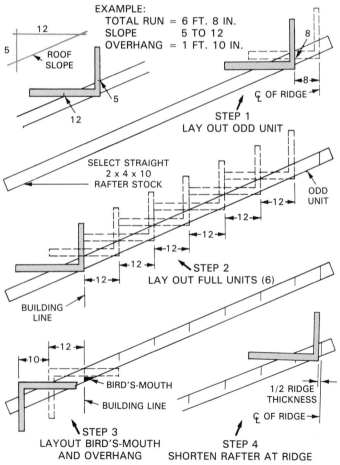

Fig. 28-7. Illustration of the step-off method for laying out a common rafter.

470

Move the square to the 12 in. point just marked and repeat the marking procedure. Continue until the correct number of full units are laid out. This number will be the same as the number of feet in the total run (six used in the example).

Form the bird's-mouth by drawing a horizontal line (seat cut) to meet the building line so the surface will be about equal to the width of the plate. The size of the bird's-mouth may vary depending upon the design of the overhang. Note that in Fig. 28-7, the square has been turned over to mark these cuts and also to lay out the overhang. This may or may not be necessary depending on the length of the rafter blank.

To lay out the overhang, start with the plumb cut of the bird's-mouth and mark full units first. Then add any odd unit that remains. The tail cut may be plumb, square, or a combination of plumb and level. Check the cornice details shown in the architectural plans for exact requirements.

The final step in the layout consists of shortening the rafter at the ridge. With the square in position, draw a new plumb line back from the ridge line half the thickness of the ridge, Fig. 28-7. Now make the ridge, bird's-mouth, and tail cuts you have laid out. Label the rafter as a pattern, indicating the roof section to which it belongs.

## FRAMING SQUARE RAFTER TABLE

You can calculate the length of a common rafter using the table on the framing square. See Fig. 28-8. Under the full-scale number that corresponds with the unit rise, find the number in the first line.

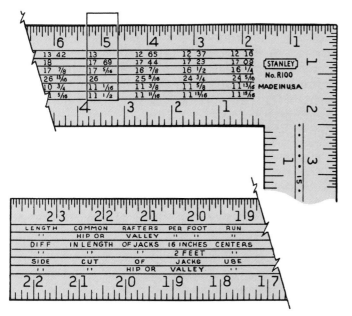

Fig. 28-8. The blade of the square carries tables for figuring length of rafters. For example, if unit rise is 5 in., you will find the rafter length for 12 in. of run is 13 in.

This is the line length of the rafter in inches for one foot of run. To find the length of the rafter from the building line to the center of the ridge, multiply the units of run by the figure from the table as follows:

Run = 6 ft. 8 in.      Slope 5 to 12
Run of 6 ft. 8 in. = 6 2/3 units
Table number      = 13
Rafter length      = 6 2/3 units x 13 in.
                          = 86 2/3 in.
                          = 7 ft. 2 2/3 in.

This example gives the line length of the rafter, running from the center of the ridge to the outside of the plate. The length of the overhang must be added, and half the ridge board thickness subtracted from the top end.

## FRAMING

### ERECTING A GABLE ROOF

It is generally considered good practice to lay out rafter spacing along the wall plate at the same time the lay out is made for the ceiling joists. Rafters are usually spaced the same as the joists, but when rafters are spaced 2 ft. O.C. and ceiling joists are spread 16 in. O.C., the layout is coordinated as shown in Fig. 28-9.

Long, straight pieces should be selected for the ridge. Rafter spacing is laid out on the ridge from the marking on the plate. Joints in the ridge should occur at the center of a rafter.

Begin roof frame assembly by placing the ridge between two rafters and nailing it in place temporarily. Move along the ridge about five rafter spaces and nail another pair in place. Plumb and brace the assembly. Install the remaining rafter pairs. Fig. 28-10 shows common rafters being installed.

### Gable end frame

Square a line across the end wall plate directly below the center of the gable. If a ventilator is to

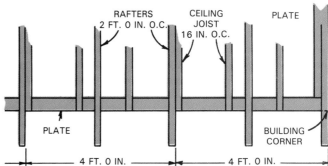

Fig. 28-9. Plan view of ceiling joist and rafter layout when joists are spaced 16 in. O.C. A joist is nailed to every other rafter to prevent walls from spreading.

Fig. 28-10. Installing common rafters. Be sure bird's-mouth is pushed tightly against the plate.
(Southern Forest Products Association)

be installed, measure one-half of the opening size on each side of the centerline, and mark for the first stud. Lay out the spacing for the remaining studs.

Hold up a stud at the first location and plumb it with a level. Mark the stud at the underside of the rafter. Repeat the operation at each stud location along one side of the gable. Cut pairs of studs for each length that is marked off. See Fig. 28-11.

Some roof designs include an extended rake (gable overhang). Fig. 28-12 shows the typical framing methods for extended rake.

When constructing the gable ends for a brick veneer structure, the frame must be moved outward to cover the finished wall. This projection can be formed by using lookouts and blocking attached to a ledger. Fig. 28-13 illustrates the framing method used when the top of the veneer is aligned on the sides and ends of the building.

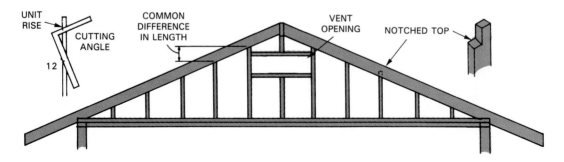

Fig. 28-11. Lay out studs for a gable end as shown.

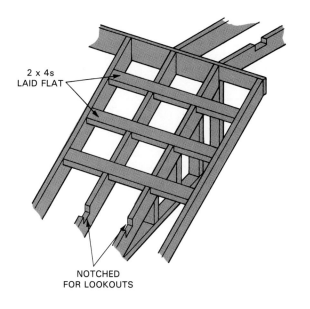

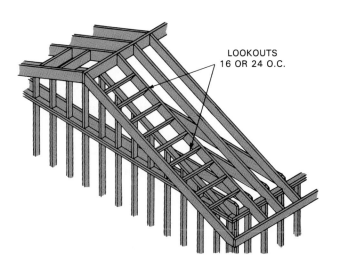

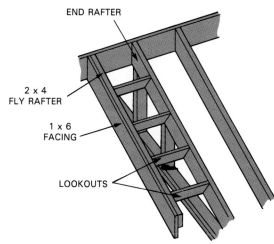

Fig. 28-12. Methods of framing gable overhang. Top, left and right. Lookouts laid flat over notched rafters. (Photo: American Plywood Association) Bottom, left. Plate atop framing studs supports lookouts. Be sure top of plate lines up with bottoms of rafters. Bottom, right. Small overhang with short lookouts supporting 2 x 4 fly rafter and face board.

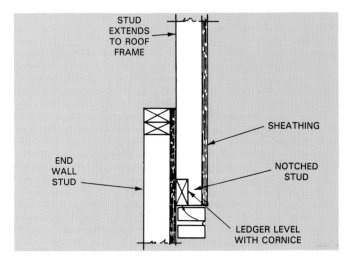

Fig. 28-13. Gable end framing for masonry veneered buildings.

## HIP AND VALLEY RAFTERS

The length of hip and valley rafters can be determined from rafter tables on the framing square. Secure the number from the second line. Using the same example as used for common rafters, the calculations would be as follows.

Run = 6 ft. 8 in.     Slope 5 to 12
Run = 6 ft. 8 in.  = 6 2/3 units
Table number     = 17.69
Hip or Valley length = 17.69 x 6 2/3
                    = 117.93
                    = 9 ft. 9 15/16 in.
                    = 9 ft. 10 in.

Hip and valley rafters must be shortened at the ridge by a horizontal distance equal to one-half of the 45 deg. thickness of the ridge, Fig. 28-14. The

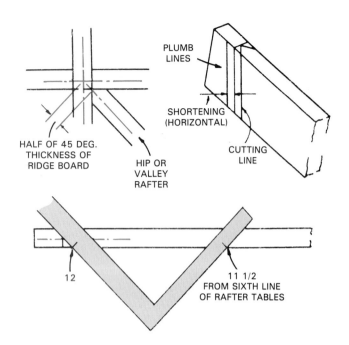

Fig. 28-14. Shortening a hip and valley rafter and laying out cheek cuts.

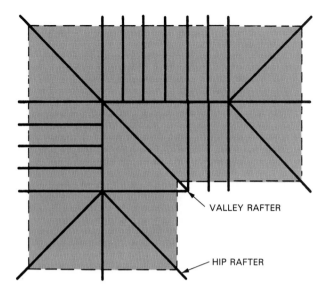

Fig. 28-15. Rafter plan showing hip and valley rafters in place.

cheek cuts are then laid out using the figures from the sixth line of the rafter table, Fig. 28-8 (example 11 1/2). All the figures on the table are based on or related to 12; therefore place 12 on the blade and 11 1/2 on the tongue along the edge of the rafter as shown, and draw the angle for each cut. Now draw plumb lines, using 17 on the blade and 5 on the tongue. The tail cuts at the end of the rafter are laid out using the same angle.

The top corners of a hip rafter will extend slightly above the plane of the roof. They could be planed off; however, it is easier to make the seat cut slightly deeper. The plumb cut of the bird's-mouth of valley rafters must be moved toward the tail by a distance equal to the 45 deg. thickness of the rafter. Hip and valley rafters are then added to the roof frame as shown in Fig. 28-15.

### Jack rafters

Hip jack rafters have the same tail or overhang as the common rafter. The length from the bird's-mouth to the hip rafter varies. The difference in length of adjacent rafters can be secured from the third or fourth line of the rafter table. For the example previously used, 26 in. is listed for rafters located 24 in. O.C.

For the first jack rafter down from the ridge, lay out the line length of the common rafter and subtract the common difference. Now shorten the length of one-half the 45 deg. thickness of the hip. Square this line across the top edge and draw the cheek cut using the number from the fifth line of the table. Move down the rafter the common dif-

ference and mark the cutting line for the next jack. Continue until they are all laid out and then use this rafter for a pattern. See Fig. 28-16.

Valley jacks will have a cheek cut at the lower end and a plumb cut at the ridge like a common rafter. Assemble the jacks in the roof frame as shown in Fig. 28-17.

Cripple jack layout and cutting is somewhat complicated and beyond the scope of this book. Study a carpentry textbook for information about their use and other special roof framing problems.

### ERECTING JACK RAFTERS

When all jack rafters are cut, assemble them into the roof frame, Fig. 28-18. Jack rafters should be erected in pairs to prevent the hip and valley rafters from being pushed out of line. It is good practice to first place a pair about halfway between the plate

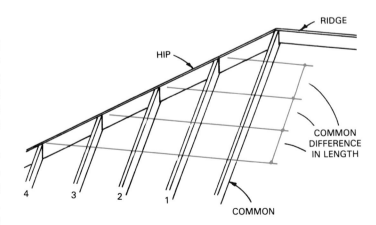

Fig. 28-16. When evenly spaced, hip jack rafters have a common and predictable difference in length from one to the next.

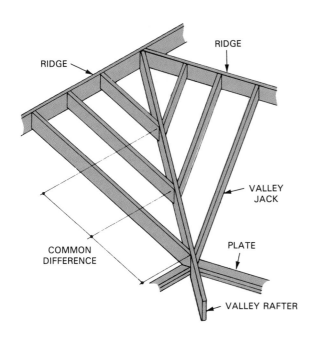

Fig. 28-17. Finding the common difference of valley jack rafters will be the same as for the hip jacks.

and ridge. Carefully sight along the hip or valley to determine that it is straight and true.

After rafters have been erected and securely nailed, check over the frame carefully. If some rafters are bowed sideways, they can be held straight with a strip of lumber located across the center of the span. Each rafter is sighted, and moved as needed.

## ROOF OPENINGS

Roof openings may be required for chimneys, skylights, and other structures. Use about the same procedures for large openings in the roof as was used in floor framing.

Small openings are constructed after the entire framework is completed. Large openings, such as for a chimney, may require special procedures during the roof framing phase. Fig. 28-19 shows the framing for a typical chimney. Use a plumb line to locate the opening on the rafters from openings already formed in the ceiling or floor frame. Rafters to be cut should be supported with a strip, which in turn is supported by two rafters on either side of the opening.

## ROOF TRUSS CONSTRUCTION

A truss is a framework that is designed to carry a load between two or more supports. The principle used in its design is based on the rigidity of the triangle. Triangular shapes are built into the frame in such a way that the stresses of the various parts are parallel to the members making up the structure.

Roof trusses are frames that carry the roof and ceiling surfaces. They rest on the exterior walls and span the entire width of the structure. Since no load bearing partitions are required, there is more freedom in planning and dividing interior space. They permit larger rooms without extra beams and supports. Surface materials can be applied to out-

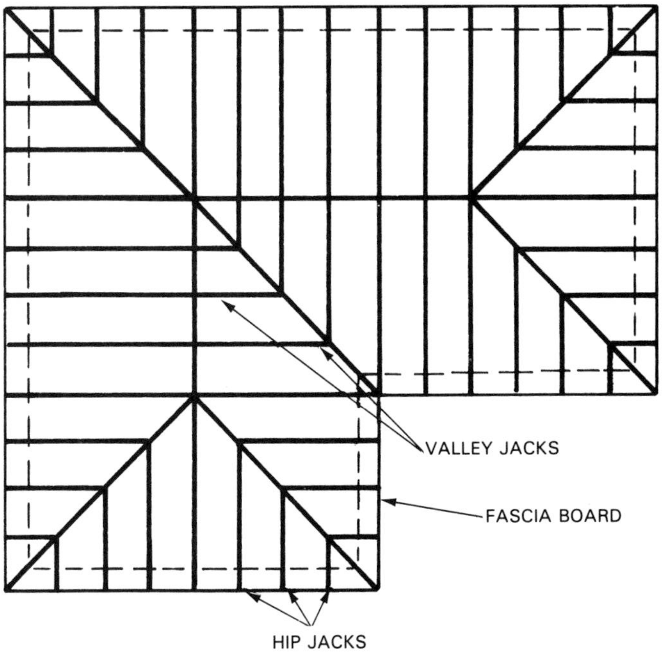

Fig. 28-18. Plan view of complete roof frame. All hip and valley jack rafters are assembled.

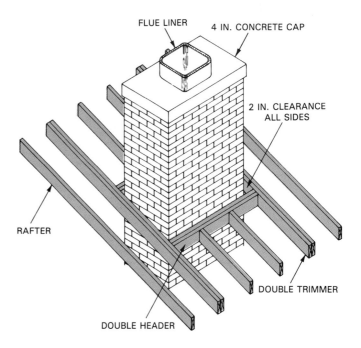

Fig. 28-19. Framing a roof opening for a chimney. Allow 2 in. clearance on each side and end. Note that the headers above and below the chimney are plumbed.

side walls, ceilings, and floors before partitions are constructed.

There are many types and shapes of roof trusses. Three commonly used in residential construction are the W or Fink truss, kingpost truss, and scissors truss, Fig. 28-20.

When built on the job, trusses should always be constructed according to designs developed from engineering data. There are several sources for such material. Usually included are detailed construction drawings and also specifications concerning materials and fasteners.

Roof trusses must be made of structurally sound lumber and assembled with carefully fitted joints. Although the carpenter is seldom required to determine the sizes of truss members or the type of joints, she or he should understand their design well enough to appreciate the necessity of first class work in construction.

Trusses are precut and assembled at ground level. Spacing of 24 in. O.C. is common. However, 16 in. O.C. and other spacing may be required in some designs.

When the truss is in position and loaded, there will be a slight sag. To compensate for this, the lower member, or BOTTOM CHORD, is raised slightly during fabrication of the unit. This adjustment is called CAMBER, and is measured at the midpoint of the span. A standard truss, 24 ft. long, will usually require about 1/2 in. of camber.

In truss construction, it is essential that joint slippage be held to a minimum. Regular nailing patterns are usually not satisfactory. Special connectors must be used. Various kinds are available. All of them hold the joint securely and are easy to apply, Fig. 28-21. Plywood gussets are applied with glue and nails to both sides of the joint.

When only a few trusses are needed, they can be laid out and constructed on any clear floor area. First make a full-size layout on the floor, snapping chalk lines for long line lengths and using straightedges to draw shorter lines. A portable truss assembly unit may also be used to build trusses. Refer to Fig. 28-22.

Trusses for residential structures can normally be erected without special equipment. Each truss is simply placed upside down on the walls near where it will be installed. Each truss is righted and nailed into place with adequate bracing until sheathing is attached.

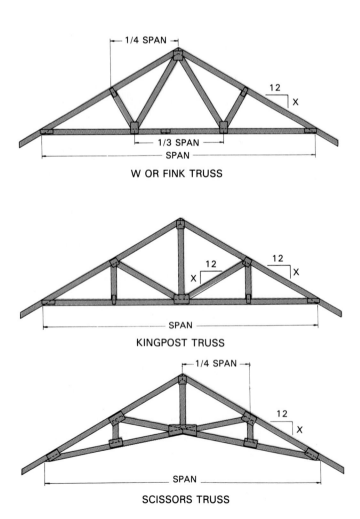

Fig. 28-20. Design data for a W or Fink truss, kingpost truss, and scissors truss.

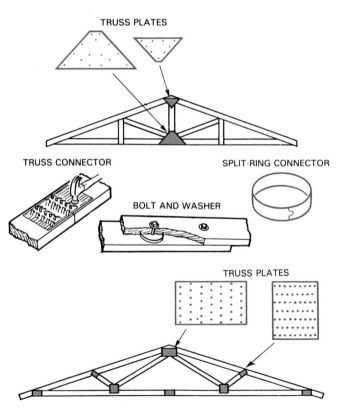

Fig. 28-21. Plates and connectors for roof trusses. Truss plates are made in many sizes, shapes, and types. Some are perforated for nails; some require no nails. Split-ring connectors fit into recesses bored in mating joints.

Fig. 28-22. Portable truss assembly unit adjusts to different sizes and designs.

Fig. 28-23. Sheathing boards can be spaced if wood shingles, corrugated metal, or tile are the covering materials. (Paslode Co., Div. of Signode)

## CODE REQUIREMENTS

Check local code for additional requirements. Special roof anchorage, for example, is frequently required in areas that experience high winds. Collar beams, which tie opposite rafters together, help to form a more rigid structure and may be required. Purlins are needed when the rafter span exceeds the maximum allowed. This member is attached to the underside of the rafters and is supported through bracing by a bearing partition below.

## ROOFING

### ROOF SHEATHING

Roof sheathing adds strength and rigidity to the roof frame and provides a nailing base for the roof covering material. Sheathing materials include plywood composites, oriented strand board, waferboard, particle board, shiplap, and common boards.

Sheathing must cover the entire roof area if asphalt shingles or other composition materials are used for the finished roof decking. For wood shingles, metal sheets, or tile, however, board sheathing may be spaced according to the course arrangement, Fig. 28-23.

When end-matched boards are used, the joints may be made between rafters. Joints in the next board must not occur in the same rafter space. Boards not long enough to be carried on at least two rafters should not be used.

Fit sheathing carefully at valleys and hips and nail it securely. This will insure a solid, smooth base for

the installation of flashing materials. Around chimney openings, the sheathing should have a 1/2 in. clearance from masonry. Framing members must have a 2 in. clearance. Always nail material securely around openings.

Structural panels are an ideal material for roof sheathing. They can be installed rapidly, hold nails well, resist swelling and shrinkage, and because the panels are large, add considerable rigidity to the roof frame. Plywood is laid with the face grain perpendicular to the rafters. End joints should be directly over the center of the rafter. Small pieces can be used but they should always cover at least two rafter spaces. For wood or asphalt shingles with a rafter spacing of 16 in., 5/16 in. solid sheathing is usually recommended. For a 24 in. span, a 3/8 in. thickness should be used. Slate, tile, and mineral fiber shingles require 1/2 in. thicknesses for 16 in. rafter spacing and 5/8 in. for 24 in. spacing.

A patented panel clip is available to strengthen roof sheathing panels between rafters, Fig. 28-24. The clips are slipped onto the panels midway between the rafter or truss spans. Two clips should be used where supports are 48 in. O.C.

### ROOFING MATERIALS

Roofing materials protect the structure and its contents from the sun, rain, snow, wind, and dust.

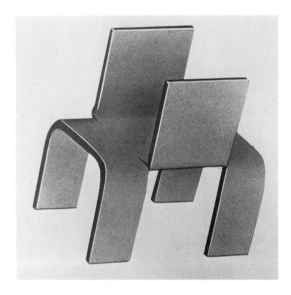

Fig. 28-24. Panel clips, sometimes called H clips, eliminate blocking on long truss or rafter spans. (Panel Clip Co.)

All items that will project through the roof should be built or installed before roofing begins. These structures include chimneys, vent pipes, and special facilities for electrical and communications service. Performing any of their work after the finished roof is applied may damage the roof covering.

## MATERIALS FOR PITCHED ROOFS

Several types of materials are commonly used for pitched (sloping) roofs. They include asphalt, wood, and metal shingles; slate and tile; and sheet products such as roll roofing, galvanized steel, aluminum, and copper.

A membrane system is used for flat roofs and low-sloped roofs. It consists of a continuous watertight surface, usually obtained through built-up roofs or seamed metal sheets.

Built-up roofs are fabricated on the job. Roofing felts are laminated (stuck together) with asphalt or coal tar pitch. Then this surface is coated with crushed stone or gravel.

Metal roofs of this type are assembled from flat sheets. Seams are soldered or sealed with special compounds to insure watertightness.

In addition to weather protection, a good roof should offer some measure of fire resistance and have a high durability factor. Due to the large amount of surface that is usually visible, especially in sloping roofs, the materials should contribute to the attractiveness of the building by adding color, texture, and pattern, Fig. 28-25.

When selecting roofing materials it is important to consider such factors as initial cost, maintenance costs, durability, and appearance. The pitch of the roof limits the selection. Low-sloped roofs require

Fig. 28-25. Roofing material has a significant impact on the finished appearance of a structure. (Manville Building Materials Corp.)

a more watertight system than steep roofs. Materials such as tile and slate require heavier roof frames. Any roofing material which weighs more than 4 lb./sq. ft. is considered a heavy roofing material.

Local building codes may prohibit the use of certain materials because they pose a fire hazard or because they will not resist high winds or other elements found in certain areas.

## Asphalt roofing products

Asphalt roofing products are widely used in modern construction. They include three broad groups: saturated felts, roll roofing, and shingles.

Saturated felts are used under shingles for sheathing paper and for laminations in constructing a built-up roof. They are made of dry felt soaked with asphalt or coal tar.

Saturated felt is made in different weights, the most common being 15 lb. The weight indicates the amount necessary to cover 100 sq. ft. of roof surface with a single layer.

Roll roofing and shingles are outer roof covering. They must be weather-resistant. Their base material is organic felt and/or fiberglass. This base is saturated and then coated with a special asphalt that resists weathering. A surface of ceramic coated mineral granules is then applied. The mineral granules shield the asphalt coating from the sun's rays, add color, and provide fire resistance.

Asphalt shingles are the most common type of roofing material used today. They are manufactured as strip shingles, interlocking shingles, and large individual shingles. For example, the three-tab square butt shingle is available in many qualities and colors, and in weights from 215 to 245 lb. per square. Dimensions of a standard three-tab strip shingle are shown in Fig. 28-26.

Many of the shingles are available with a strip of factory-applied, self-sealing adhesive. Heat from the sun will soften the adhesive and bond each shingle tab securely to the shingle below. This bond prevents tabs from being raised by heavy winds.

## Underlayment

An underlayment is a thin cover of asphalt-saturated felt or other material. It has a low vapor resistance. The purpose of underlayment is to protect the sheathing from moisture until the shingles are laid, to provide additional weather protection by preventing the entrance of wind-driven rain and snow, and to prevent direct contact between shingles and resinous areas in the sheathing.

Materials such as coated sheets of heavy felts, which might act as a vapor barrier, should not be used. They allow moisture and frost to gather between the covering and the roof deck. Although 15 lb. roofer's felt is commonly used for this purpose, requirements vary depending on the kind of shingles and the roof slope.

Do not put down underlayment on a damp roof. Moisture may be trapped, damaging the roof.

General application standards for underlayment suggest a 2 in. top lap at all horizontal joints and a 4 in. side lap at all end joints, Fig. 28-27. It should be lapped at least 6 in. on each side of the centerline of hips and valleys.

## DRIP EDGE

The roof edges along the eaves and rake should have a corrosion-resistant drip edge. Various shapes of galvanized steel, aluminum, or plastic are available, Fig. 28-28. They extend back about 3 in. from the roof edge and are bent downward over the edge. This causes the water to drip free of underlying cornice construction. At the eaves the underlayment should be laid over the drip edge. At the rake, place the underlayment under the drip edge.

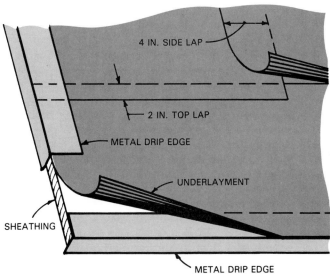

Fig. 28-27. Application of underlayment and metal drip edge. Underlayment goes under the drip edge on the rake; over it at the eaves.

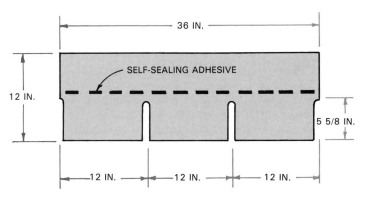

Fig. 28-26. Standard three-tab asphalt strip shingle. These dimensions are the most common.

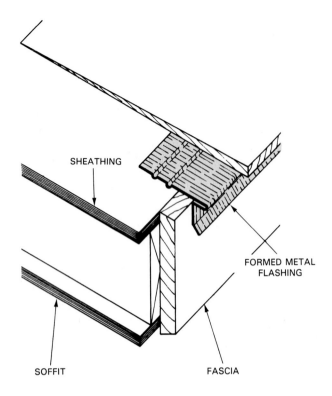

Fig. 28-28. Drip edge flashing prevents water from entering behind the shingles and protects the facia.

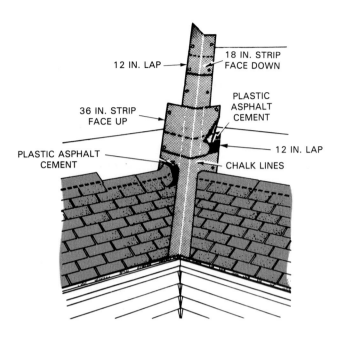

Fig. 28-29. Open valley flashing. Use two layers. Both layers should be 90 lb. roll roofing, mineral surfaced.

## OPEN VALLEY FLASHING

The installation of roofing materials is complicated by the intersection of other roofs, adjoining walls, and such projections as chimneys and vent stacks. Making these areas watertight requires a special construction, called FLASHING. Materials used for flashing include tin-coated metal, galvanized metal, copper, lead, aluminum, asphalt shingles, and roll roofing.

A VALLEY is the surface where two sloping roofs meet. Water drainage is heavy at this point and leakage would create a serious problem. Flashing is one method of leakproofing valleys. For asphalt shingles, the recommended flashing material is 90 lb. mineral-surfaced asphalt roll roofing, installed as illustrated in Fig. 28-29.

## WOVEN VALLEY FLASHING

Another method of flashing a valley when asphalt shingles are used is to weave the shingles across the valley. Strip shingles are the only type that can be used.

It is essential that a single unit be wide enough to straddle the valley with a minimum of 12 in. of material on either side. To provide this margin, it is necessary to cut some of the preceding shingle strips. Nails or other fasteners must stay at least 6 in. away from the valley centerline, Fig. 28-30.

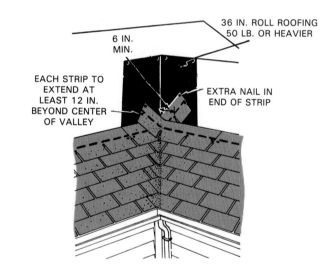

Fig. 28-30. Method of laying woven valley flashing. This is common during reroofing.

## FLASHING AT EAVES

In cold climates, it is highly recommended that flashing strips on eaves be installed over the underlayment and metal drip edge. This prevents leakage caused by water backed-up by ice dams on the roof.

The flashing strip can be smooth or mineral-surfaced roll roofing. It should also be wide enough to extend from roof's edge to about 12 in. inside the wall line.

## FLASHING AT A WALL

Metal flashing shingles should be used where the roof joins a vertical wall. They should be 10 in. long and 2 in. wider than the exposed face of the regular shingles. The 10 in. length is bent so that it will extend 5 in. over the roof and 5 in. up the wall as shown in Fig. 28-31.

As each course of shingles is laid, a metal flashing shingle is installed and nailed at the top edge as shown. Do not nail flashing to the wall as settling of the roof frame could damage the seal.

Wall siding is installed after the roof is completed and serves as cap flashing. Position the siding just above the roof surface to allow enough clearance to paint the lower edges.

## FLASHING AROUND A CHIMNEY

Flashing around the chimney must allow for some settling or shrinkage of the building frame. To provide for this movement, the flashing is divided into two parts:
1. The base flashing that is secured to the roof deck.
2. The counterflashing (also called cap flashing) that is secured to the chimney.

Before base flashing is applied, lay the shingles up to the front face of the chimney. Then lay out and cut, from 90 lb. mineral-surfaced roofing, the front section of flashing. A similar section can be cut for the back if there is no saddle, Fig. 28-32. Such a structure is not required when the chimney is small and located high on the roof near the ridge.

Cement the front base flashing into place. Then cut and apply the side pieces. The base flashing at the back of the chimney is applied last. All the sections are cemented together as they are applied.

Sheet metal is often used for base flashing. It should be applied by the step method previously

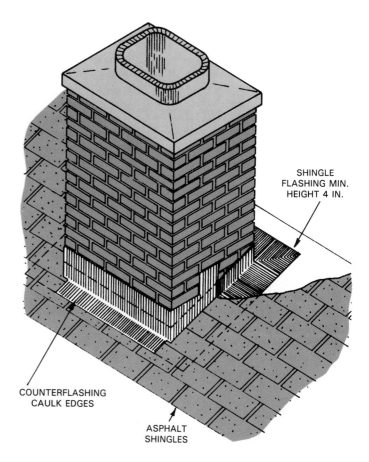

Fig. 28-32. Flashing around a chimney is composed of shingle flashing and counterflashing.

described in the section on wall flashing.

Metal sheets set into the mortar joints of the chimney during construction are known as COUNTERFLASHING. The metal strips are bent down over the base flashing. Then the metal is set into the mortar joints to a depth of 1 1/2 in. Counterflashing on the front of the chimney can be one continuous piece. On the sides it must be stepped up in sections to align with the roof slope, Fig. 28-32.

## CHIMNEY SADDLE

Large chimneys on sloping roofs generally require a saddle on the high side. The purpose of the saddle is to divert the flow of water and to prevent ice and snow from building up behind the chimney.

Fig. 28-33 illustrates one framing design for a chimney saddle. The frame is nailed into place and then sheathed. A small saddle could also be constructed from triangular pieces of 3/4 in. exterior plywood and nailed to the roof deck.

Saddles are usually covered with corrosion-resistant sheet metal. However, mineral-surfaced roll roofing could also be used. Valleys formed by the saddle and main roof should be carefully sealed in the manner used for regular roof valleys.

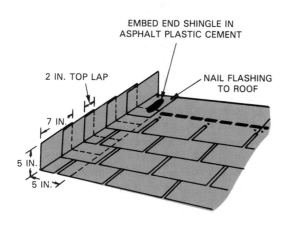

Fig. 28-31. Apply metal flashing shingles with each course. Follow these lap and bending directions.

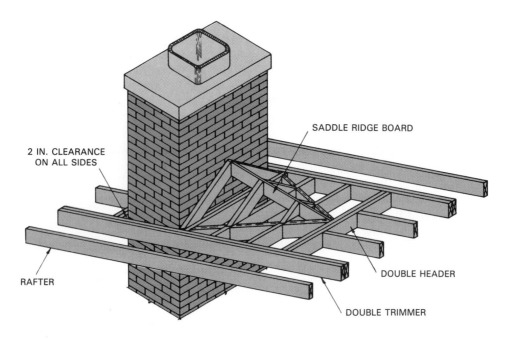

2 IN. CLEARANCE
ON ALL SIDES

SADDLE RIDGE BOARD

DOUBLE HEADER

DOUBLE TRIMMER

RAFTER

Fig. 28-33. The framing of this saddle illustrates the way water is shed away from the chimney.

## VENT STACK FLASHING

Pipes which project through the roof must also be flashed. Prefabricated flanges are available for this purpose. The roofing must be laid up to where the stack penetrates the roof. Cut and fill shingles around the stack. Then cement a flange in place. Lay the shingles over the top, Fig. 28-34. The flange must be large enough to extend at least 4 in. below, 8 in. above, and 6 in. on each side.

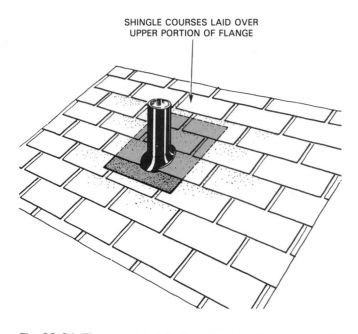

SHINGLE COURSES LAID OVER
UPPER PORTION OF FLANGE

Fig. 28-34. The proper installation of flashing for a vent stack.

## HIPS AND RIDGES

Special hip and ridge shingles are usually available from the manufacturer. The special shingles can be easily made, however. Cut pieces 9 in. by 12 in. from either square butt shingle strips or mineral-surfaced roll roofing that matches the color of the shingles.

Begin at the bottom of hips or at one end of the ridge. Lap the units to provide a 5 in. exposure. Secure with one nail on each side so that nails are not visible.

## OTHER ASPHALT ROOFING PRODUCTS

Individual asphalt shingles are available in several sizes and designs. One commonly used is 12 in. wide and 16 in. long. Hex shingles are equally as popular. These shingles are intended primarily for use over old roofing. The same procedure should be used for installation as for strip shingles.

Asphalt roll roofing is manufactured in several weights, surfaces, and colors. It may be used as a main roof covering or as a flashing material. Selvage edge roll roofing can be used on roofs with slopes as low as 1 in. per foot. It is 36 in. wide with a 17 in. wide, granular surfaced area and a 19 in. wide, smooth area. The overlap is cemented together to form a watertight membrane. Application is generally parallel to the eaves, Fig. 28-35.

Built-up roofing is designed for flat roofs or roofs with very little slope. Manufacturers of the materials for these roofs (saturated felt and asphalt) provide

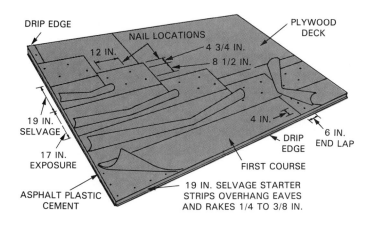

Fig. 28-35. Method for applying double-coverage, roll roofing parallel to the eaves. (Bird and Son, Inc.)

detailed specifications for installation. In general, however, a built-up roof is made by applying several layers (four or five) of saturated felt with asphalt mopped between each layer. Gravel or slag is cemented to the surface of the last layer of felt to protect it from the elements, Fig. 28-36.

## WOOD SHINGLES AND SHAKES

Wood shingles and shakes have been used for many years as a roofing material. Most wood shingles used now are fire-resistant because they are treated with fire-retardant chemicals. Common materials for wood shingles and shakes are western red cedar, redwood, and cypress. All are decay resistant and will last many years if installed and maintained properly.

Wood shingles and shakes are packaged in bundles (four bundles will cover 100 sq. ft.). Standard exposures of 5, 5 1/2, and 7 1/2 inches

are common. This will provide a minimum of 3 layers at all points on the roof. Fig. 28-37 shows wood shakes attached to a roof.

Wood shingles are taper-sawed and graded No. 1, No. 2, and No. 3, plus a utility grade. Butt ends vary in thickness from 1/2 to about 3/4 in. Lengths available include 16, 18, and 24 in.

Wood shakes have much greater surface texture than shingles. They are available hand-split and resawn, taper split, and straight split. Available lengths include 18, 24, and 32 in. Butt ends vary in thickness from 1/2 to 1 1/2 in. Cedar shakes are very durable.

Flashing is just as important with wood shingles and shakes as any other roofing material. Flashing materials used include tin plate, lead-clad steel, galvanized steel, lead, copper, and aluminum sheets. Recommended valley flashing for use with wood shingles and shakes is pictured in Fig. 28-38. Flashing around chimneys and where the roofs meets a wall is similar to that used for asphalt shingle roofs.

Shingled hips and ridges require good, tight construction to prevent leaks. Factory assembled ridge and hip units are available for quality construction. Fig. 28-39 shows a properly constructed hip using prefabricated units.

Fig. 28-37. Western red cedar shakes applied in the approved manner. 3 in. wide nailing strips may be used instead of solid sheathing, as shown here.
(Red Cedar Shingle and Handsplit Shake Bureau)

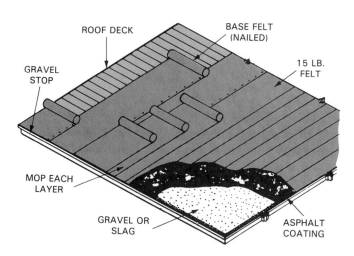

Fig. 28-36. The steps shown are generally followed in constructing a built-up roof. Proper materials are indicated layer by layer.

Fig. 28-38. Flashing should extend at least 7 in. on each side of the valley of a roof, with a 12:12 slope. Roofs with less slope use wider flashing.
(Red Cedar Shingle and Handsplit Shake Bureau)

Fig. 28-39. How wood cap shingles are installed at hips and ridges. Note how the angles are alternated.
(Red Cedar Shingle and Handsplit Shake Bureau)

Prefabricated 8 ft. panels with shingles or shakes already attached are available, Fig. 28-40. They are bonded to a backing of 5/16 in. exterior sheathing plywood. Either solid sheathing or nailing strips can be used under these prefabricated panels.

Fig. 28-40. Applying shingle panels to a roof. Panels are prefabricated in 8 ft. lengths. (Shakertown Corp.)

## TILE ROOFING

Tile roofing is made from clay, metal, and concrete. The most commonly used types in residential construction are manufactured from mixtures of shale and clay, molded into shapes, and hard-burned. These tiles are hard, fairly dense, and very durable. Most clay tiles used for roofing are unglazed. However, glazed roofing tiles are produced and used. Typical tile roof application details are shown in Fig. 28-41.

The roof frame must be securely supported and braced to support the weight of a clay tile roof. Fig. 28-42 shows a roof made with clay tiles.

## SHEET METAL ROOFING

Sheet metal roofing is manufactured from galvanized steel, aluminum, and terne metal sheets. Each is available in a variety of shapes and intended applications.

Only galvanized sheets heavily coated with zinc (2 oz. per sq. ft.) are recommended for permanent buildings. This material may be applied to roofs with a slope as low as 3:12. Supports may be 24 in. apart if 26 ga. sheets are used. Lead-headed nails are recommended for application.

Corrugated aluminum roofing should be laid on solid sheathing as it is soft and thin. Aluminum alloy nails are recommended, with a nonmetallic washer between the nail head and roofing. Aluminum roofing should not contact any other type of metal as this will produce a corrosive action.

Terne metal roofing is made from copper-bearing steel. (Terne metal is 80 percent lead and 20 percent tin.) A wide variety of sheet sizes and cross-sectional shapes are available. For longest wear, terne metal roofs must be painted.

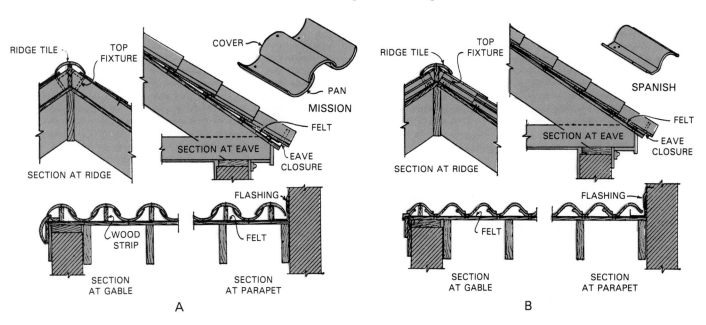

Fig. 28-41. Typical application methods for tile roofs. A—Two-piece pan and cover commonly known as mission tile. B—Spanish tile.

Fig. 28-42. This durable clay tile roof will withstand high winds, rain, and severe weather.

## Gutters

Gutters collect the water from the roof and direct it to an outlet. This prevents water from running directly off the eaves and splattering the house and running down the foundation wall. Gutters are usually pitched 1 to 1 1/2 in. in 20 ft. This slope permits even flow and prevents water from standing in the gutter.

Several styles of gutters and downspouts are available in copper, vinyl, aluminum, and galvanized sheet metal. Wood gutters are also made for residential construction. They are attractive on some home styles, but are diminishing in importance due to high original and maintenance costs.

The roof surface should extend over the inside edge of the gutter, with the front top edge at approximately the height of a line extending from the top of the roof sheathing. Wood gutters are generally almost level, to provide the proper appearance.

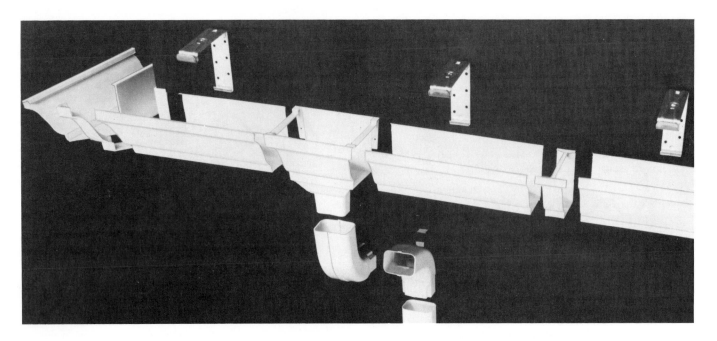

Fig. 28-43. Ogee style gutter made from vinyl plastic. (Bird and Son, Inc.)

Complete gutter systems are manufactured, making assembly and installation easy. Fig. 28-43 shows a vinyl plastic gutter system.

The size of gutter and downspouts relates to the amount of roof area to be drained. For roof areas up to 750 sq. ft., a 4 in. wide gutter is suitable; for roof areas up to 1400 sq. ft. a 5 in. gutter is sufficient; for roof areas larger than 1400 sq. ft., a 6 in. gutter is sufficient.

### TEST YOUR KNOWLEDGE, Chapter 28

Please do not write in the text. Place your answers on a separate sheet of paper.
1. A 3:12 roof pitch has a _____ of three feet and a _____ of twelve feet.
2. Name three types of jack rafters.
3. Define rise, run, and span.
4. _____ gives the incline of the roof as a ratio of the vertical rise to the span.
   a. Run.
   b. Slope.
   c. Pitch.
   d. None of the above.
5. Why should jack rafters be erected in pairs?
6. An area that experiences tornadoes _____ (would, would not) require roof anchors.
7. Give two reasons for the popularity of roof trusses.
8. _____ are used to strengthen roof sheathing panels between rafters.
9. What is an underlayment?
10. What two types of flashing are used around a chimney when roofing with asphalt or wood shingles?
11. What is the purpose of a chimney saddle?
12. From what is terne metal roofing made?

### ACTIVITIES

1. Working from a set of architectural plans for a residential structure, make a layout for a common rafter located in one of the roof sections. Use a good, straight piece of stock. If dimension lumber is not available, a piece of 1 in. material may be used. Make the layout by the step-off method and cover all operations including the shortening at the ridge. When completed, give a brief demonstration to the class, showing the procedure you followed.
2. Study the various types of roof trusses. Learn their names and the basic design patterns. List the advantages and disadvantages of each. Find out where they are most commonly used. Prepare a display board with line drawings of about eight of the most practical types and label each with an appropriate caption.
3. Study the kinds and qualities of asphalt shingles used in your area. Secure manufacturer's literature from a local builder's supply center. Prepare a report including information about kinds, grades, and costs. Also include information about materials for underlayment, valley flashing, hip and ridge finish, and fasteners.
4. Collect as many types of roofing materials as possible. Identify each one and describe its characteristics, cost, and application. Share your findings with the class.

This gable roof shows excellent design and construction. Notice the valley flashing and complete gutter system.

The roof structure of this residence is supported with glue laminated beams.    (American Plywood Association)

Top left. Large glass enclosures extend the living area and modify heat loss from the main structure. (Lord and Burnham) Center right. Main entry doors are metal-clad with foam fill. (Therma-Tru, Div. of LST Corp.) Bottom left. Several types of exterior materials are used on the facade of this house. (Carl Grooms)

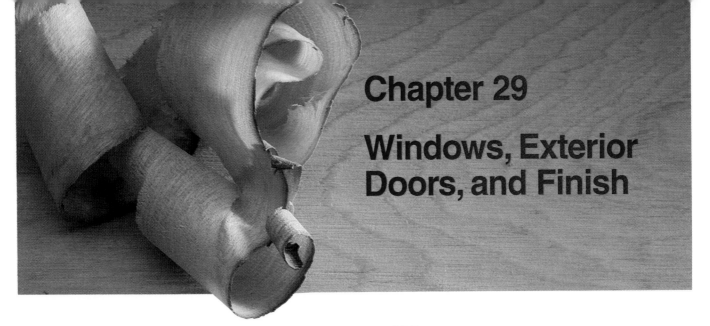

# Chapter 29

# Windows, Exterior Doors, and Finish

Once the structure has been framed, sheathed, and roofed, window, exterior doors, and exterior finish installation is next. Each of these elements is important to the function and appearance of the structure. Care should be taken in their installation.

## WINDOWS

Because windows are such an important part of most structures, much time is spent in selecting the type and location of the windows. Equally as important is the installation of the windows. Careful installation will insure proper operation of the windows and help to reduce air infiltration around each unit.

Today, most windows are built in large millwork plants to very exacting standards. They arrive at the building site as completed units ready for installation.

Windows used primarily for residential structures are made from wood, aluminum, and steel. Most, however, are made from wood. Wood transmits less heat (or cold) and, therefore, wood window frames are generally more energy efficient. One disadvantage however, is that wood will decay more readily than metal. It must be protected with paint or plastic covering.

Ponderosa pine is most commonly used in the fabrication of wood windows. It is carefully selected and kiln dried to a moisture control of 6 to 12 percent.

With steel or aluminum windows, it is possible to make smaller frame units than with wood. This is because metal is stronger than wood. Aluminum forms a protective oxide film which eliminates the need for paint or other protection. Metal windows generally require some type of protective coating.

## TYPES OF WINDOWS

In general, windows can be grouped under one or a combination of these three basic headings:

1. Sliding.
2. Swinging.
3. Fixed.

Each of these includes a variety of designs or methods of operation. Sliding windows include the double-hung and horizontal sliding. Swinging windows that are hinged on a vertical line are called casement windows while those hinged on a horizontal line can be either awning or hopper windows.

### Double-hung

A double-hung window consists of two sash that slide up and down in the window frame. These are held in any vertical position by a friction fit against the frame or by springs and various balancing devices. Double-hung windows are economical, simple to operate, and adaptable to many architectural designs. Fig. 29-1 shows an outside view of a double-hung window unit. Screen and storm sash are installed on the outside of the window.

Fig. 29-1. Typical double-hung window with screen in place. Nonfunctional shutters have been added for overall appearance. (Caradco Corp.)

489

## Horizontal sliding

Horizontal sliding windows have two or more sash. At least one of them moves horizontally within the window frame. The most common design consists of two sash, both of which are movable. See Fig. 29-2. When three sash are used, the center one is usually fixed.

## Casement

A casement window has a sash that is hinged on the side and swings outward on the other side. Installations usually consist of two or more units, separated by mullions, Fig. 29-3. Sash are operated by a cranking mechanism or a push bar mounted on the frame. Latches are used to close and hold the sash tightly against the weatherstripping.

The swing sash of a casement window permits full opening of the window. This provides good ventilation. Frequently, fixed units are combined with operating units in cases where a row of windows is desirable.

Because cranking mechanisms extend outward from the frame, it is easy to open and close windows located above kitchen cabinets or other built-in fixtures. Screen and storm sash are attached to the inside of standard casement windows.

## Awning

Awning windows, Fig. 29-4, have one or more sash that are hinged at the top and swing out at the bottom. They are often combined with fixed

Fig. 29-3. Casement windows are hinged on the side and are operated with a hand crank.

Fig. 29-2. Cutaway of a vinyl-clad horizontal sliding window. (Caradco)

Fig. 29-4. Awning windows are hinged on the top. (Andersen Corp.)

units to provide ventilation. Several operating sash can be stacked vertically so that they close on themselves or on rails that separate the units.

Most awning windows have a so-called projected action, where sliding friction hinges cause the top rail to move down as the bottom of the sash swings out. Crank and push bar mechanisms are similar to those on casement windows. Screens and storm sash are mounted on the inside. Awning windows are often installed side-by-side to form a "ribbon" effect. Such an installation provides privacy for bedroom areas and also permits greater flexibility in furniture arrangements along outside walls.

Consideration of outside clearance must be given to both casement and awning windows. When open, they may interfere with porches, patios, or walkways adjacent to outside walls.

### Hopper

The hopper window has a sash that is hinged along the bottom and swings inward, Fig. 29-5. It is operated by a locking handle located in the top rail of the sash. Hopper windows are easy to wash and maintain. However, they often interfere with drapes, curtains, and the use of inside space near the window.

### Multiple-use windows

The multiple-use window is a single outswinging sash that can be installed in a horizontal or vertical position. These windows are simple in design and do not require complicated hardware. One common unit includes two units installed vertically side-by-side to operate similar to a casement window. Screens and storms are attached on the inside.

### Jalousies

A jalousie window is composed of a series of horizontal glass slats held at each end by a movable metal frame. The metal frames are attached to each other by levers. The slats tilt together in about the same manner as a venetian blind. These windows provide excellent ventilation, but are poor insulators. They are used mainly in warm climates.

## FIXED AND SPECIAL-SHAPE WINDOWS

The fixed window unit can be used in combination with any of the movable or ventilating units. Its main purpose is to provide daylight, a view of the outdoors, or a design element. Typical fixed windows are large sheets of plate glass used to form window walls; special-shape windows such as triangles, trapezoids, or octagons; and circle-top windows, Fig. 29-6. The glass is set in a fixed sash mounted in a frame that will match the regular ventilating windows or are set in a special frame formed in the wall opening.

## WINDOW HEIGHTS

In residential construction, the standard height from the bottom side of the window head to the finished floor is 6 ft. 8 in. When this dimension is used, the heights of window (and door) openings will be the same. If inside and outside trim are to align, 1/2 to 3/4 in. must be added to this height for threshold and door clearances. Window manufacturers usually provide exact dimensions for their standard units. Fig. 29-7 shows a typical illustration from a manufacturer's literature.

## ENERGY EFFICIENT WINDOWS

The amount of glass area in a typical residential structure generally accounts for a large percentage

Fig. 29-6. Special-shape windows can be used with any movable window unit. (Andersen Corp.)

Fig. 29-5. Hopper window. (Andersen Corp.)

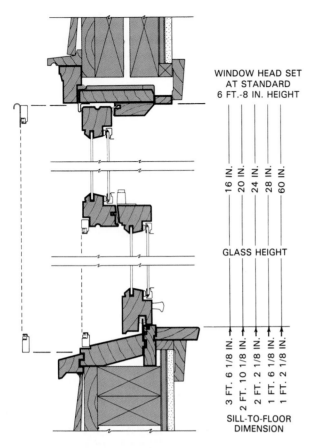

WINDOW HEAD SET
AT STANDARD
6 FT.-8 IN. HEIGHT

16 IN.
20 IN.
24 IN.
28 IN.
60 IN.

GLASS HEIGHT

3 FT. 6 1/8 IN.
2 FT. 10 1/8 IN.
2 FT. 2 1/8 IN.
1 FT. 6 1/8 IN.
1 FT. 2 1/8 IN.

SILL-TO-FLOOR
DIMENSION

Fig. 29-7. Manufacturer's product literature gives window head and sill heights. (Rolscreen Co.)

of the heat loss in winter and heat gain in summer. Glass is a poor insulator and readily transmits heat into or out of the building. The resistance to heat flow is measured in R-values. A low R-value means there is little resistance to passage of heat.

A single pane of typical window glass has an R-value of about 0.88. By adding another pane of glass with a 1/2 in. air space between them, the R-value can be increased to about 2.00. Traditionally, a storm sash has been attached to the outside of the window to reduce heat loss. Removal was then necessary to provide ventilation during the summer. New versions of the storm window have eliminated this bothersome task by storing the screen and storm sash in the frame. Other solutions are also available for various window types.

Double and triple glazing sharply increases resistance to heat flow. For a standard movable sash, two or three panes of 1/8 in. glass are fused together with a 1/4 to 1/2 in. air space between panes. Special seals are used to trap the air between panes. The air is dehydrated (moisture removed) and the space sealed at the factory. Fig. 29-8 shows several multiple glazing systems.

## WINDOW DETAILS

Because much of the actual construction of a window is hidden, sectional views are used to show

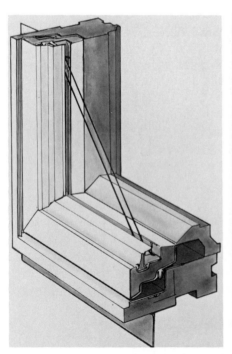
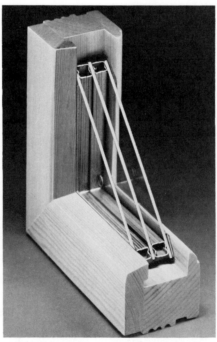

Fig. 29-8. These sealed glazing systems reduce heat flow through glass areas. They also help provide quieter interiors by transmitting less outside noise. Left. Sealed double glazed unit installed in a modern window sash. Note flange projecting from bottom of frame. It is used to mount frame in structural opening. (Andersen Corp.) Center. Sealed triple insulating glass is used in large, fixed glass windows and sliding glass doors. Two 5/16 in. air spaces are provided. Right. Double glazed unit with narrow slat blind set between glass panels. When closed, the blind increases R-value of window. (Rolscreen Co.)

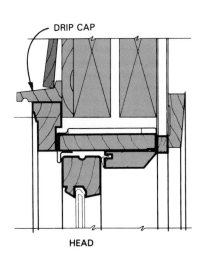
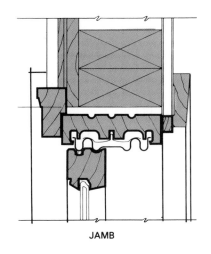
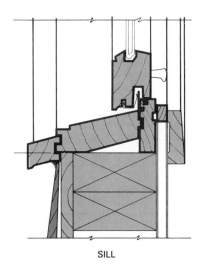

HEAD    JAMB    SILL

Fig. 29-9. Typical detail drawings shows a section through a window. Such details are included with the house plans. They help illustrate window installation.

the parts and how they fit together. It is standard practice to use sections through the top (head), side (jamb), and bottom (sill) of a window, Fig. 29-9. These drawings also include wall framing members and surface materials.

A sectional view of a typical mullion shows how window units fit together. A mullion is formed by the window jambs when two units are joined together as shown in Fig. 29-10.

A DRIP CAP, shown in the head section of Fig. 29-9, is designed to carry rain water out over the window casing. When the window is protected by a wide cornice, this element is seldom included.

## WINDOWS IN PLANS AND ELEVATIONS

It is common practice to locate the horizontal position of windows and exterior doors by including a dimension line to the center of the opening, Fig.

29-11. In masonry construction the dimension is given to the edge of the opening. This method is sometimes also used in frame construction.

Elevations will show the type of windows being used, Fig. 29-12, and may include glass size and heights. The position of the hinge line (point of dotted line) will indicate the type of swinging window. Sliding windows require a note to indicate they are not fixed units. Supporting mullions will be included in the plans and also in elevations.

## WINDOW SIZES

In addition to the type and position of the window, the carpenter should know the size of each unit or combination of units. Window sizes may include part or all of the following information: glass size, sash size, rough frame opening, masonry or unit opening. Fig. 29-13 shows the position of these measurements on window detail drawings

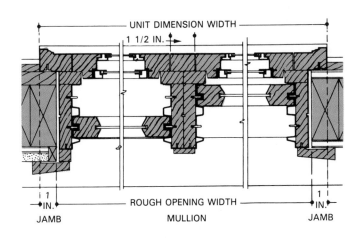

Fig. 29-10. Section drawing of a mullion. This is the area where two window jambs are joined. (Rock Island Millwork)

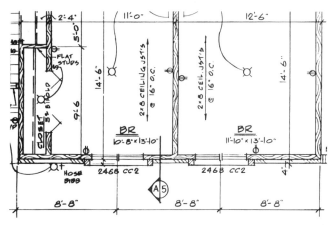

Fig. 29-11. The floor plan shows the location of windows.

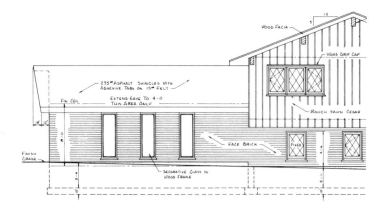

FRONT ELEVATION

Fig. 29-12. Elevations show dimensions to the top of windows, window style, and swing of windows.

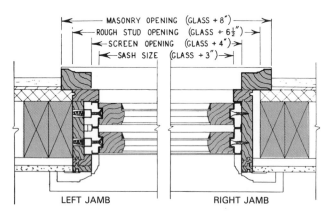

LEFT JAMB          RIGHT JAMB

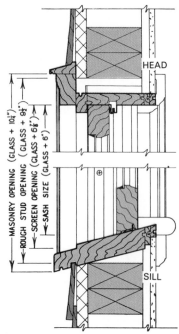

Fig. 29-13. Window sizes and location of measurements. The rough opening is larger than the overall size of the frame to permit alignments and leveling when unit is installed.

and how they are figured from the glass size. They may vary slightly from one manufacturer to another.

Detailed information about window size, rough opening, type, and manufacturer number is usually listed in a table called a WINDOW AND DOOR SCHEDULE. An identifying letter or number is located at each opening on the plan and a corresponding letter is then used in the schedule to specify the required unit and other necessary information.

## INSTALLING WINDOWS

Windows are easy to install if the rough openings are plumb, level, and the correct size. Follow the directions supplied by the manufacturer of that specific product.

If the window has not been primed at the factory, this may be done before installation. Weatherstripping and special channels should not be painted. Follow the manufacturer's recommendations. Although outside casings are usually attached, some windows, especially those with a metal frame, are set in the opening. The outside trim is then installed.

Most window units and multiple unit combinations are installed from the outside. Secure sufficient help to carry windows and handle them carefully, Fig. 29-14. Place the window in the opening and secure it temporarily.

Place wedge blocks under the sill and raise the frame to the correct height. Adjust the wedges so the frame is perfectly level.

Place wedge blocks not only at the ends but at several places in the center on large units to prevent sagging. Nail through the lower end of the side casing to secure the bottom of the frame.

Plumb the side jambs with the level and check the corners with a framing square. Usually the sash

Fig. 29-14. Windows must be handled carefully. Get help when installing larger units.

should be closed and locked in place. Drive nails temporarily into the top of the side casing. Now check over the entire window to see if it is square and level. Open the ventilating sash to see that they operate smoothly. A sag in the head or bow in the jambs should be straightened with a spacer strip.

Finally, nail the window permanently in place with aluminum or galvanized casing nails. Space the nails about 16 in. O.C. and be certain they are long enough to penetrate well into the building frame.

## EXTERIOR DOORS

Exterior doors, though similar to some of the interior types, have decided differences. They are usually thicker than interior doors and may have one or more glass panels to provide visibility.

Common exterior door types usually include flush, panel, glass sliding, and garage doors.

## TYPES OF DOORS

FLUSH DOORS are usually 1 3/4 in. thick and 6 ft. 8 in. high. Ordinarily, they are 3 ft. wide. Flush doors are one of the most popular exterior doors. They are made from birch, mahogany, oak, and several other woods. Moldings or other decorative mill work can be added to enhance its appearance, Fig. 29-15.

PANEL DOORS are available in a wide variety of styles. They are constructed from white pine, oak, fir, and various other woods. These doors are produced in the same sizes as flush doors. Refer to Fig. 29-16.

SLIDING GLASS DOORS have increased in popularity in recent years. They admit large amounts of light and extend living areas. Sliding glass doors are produced in both wood and metal units.

GARAGE DOORS are available in wood, metal, and plastics. Each material has its advantages and personal choice is usually the deciding factor in selection. Most residential garage doors are available in heights of 7 ft. and 6 ft. 6 in. Standard widths include 8, 9, 10, 16, and 18 ft. Two types of garage doors which account for most of the doors used are the overhead sectional and the one-piece overhead door.

Fig. 29-15. Exterior flush door with decorative molding and a leaded-glass light.     (Andersen Corp.)

Fig. 29-16. Wood panel door with insert and sidelights of leaded glass    (C.E. Morgan)

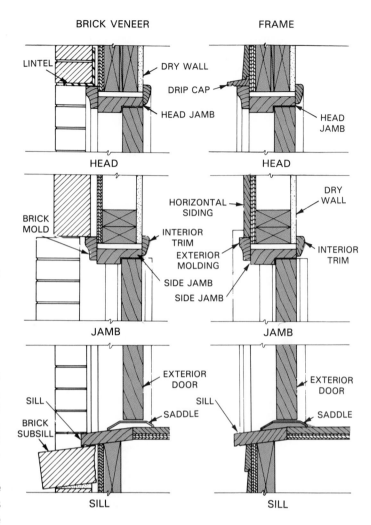

Fig. 29-17. Exterior door details for frame and brick veneer construction.

## EXTERIOR DOOR FRAMES

Exterior door frames are installed at the same time as windows. The procedure to follow is similar. Secondary and service entrances usually have frames and trim members to match the windows. Main entrances, however, often contain additional elements that add an important decorative architectural feature.

Exterior doors in residential construction are nearly always 6 ft. 8 in. high. However, 7 ft. sizes are also available. Main entrances usually are equipped with a single door that is 3 ft. wide. Narrower door sizes (2 ft. 8 in. and 2 ft. 6 in.) are used for rear and service doors. FHA Minimum Property Standards specify a minimum exterior door width of 2 ft. 6 in.

Outside door frames, like windows, have heads, jambs, and sills. The head and jambs are made of 5/4 in. stock since they must carry not only the main door but also screen and storm doors.

Door frames are manufactured at a millwork plant. They arrive at the building site either assembled and ready to install or disassembled. It is relatively easy to assemble door frames on the job when the joints are accurately machined and the parts are carefully packaged and marked.

While details of a door frame may vary, the general construction is the same for most. Fig. 29-17 shows a detail of the head, jamb, and sill of a door in brick veneer and typical frame with siding construction.

Door sills vary in design, but the top of the sill is always level with the finished floor. Sills may be made of wood, metal, stone, or concrete. Some of the finished floor, subfloor, and floor joist must be removed to make room for the sill. This is done when the door frame is installed.

### Installing door frames

Cut out the sill area, if necessary, so the top of the sill will be the correct distance above the rough floor. In some structures it may be necessary to install flashing over the bottom of the opening.

Place the frame in the opening, center it horizontally, and secure it with a temporary brace. Using blocking and wedges, level the sill and bring it to the correct height. Be sure the sill is well supported. For masonry walls and slab floors, the sill is usually placed on a bed of mortar.

With the sill level, drive a nail through the casing into the wall frame at the bottom of each side. Insert blocking or wedges between the studs and the top of the jambs. Adjust wedges until frame is plumb. Use a level and straightedge, Fig. 29-18.

Place additional wedges between the jambs and stud frame in the approximate location of the lock strike plate and hinges. Adjust the wedges until the side jambs are well supported and straight. Then, secure the wedges by driving a nail through the jamb, wedge, and into the stud.

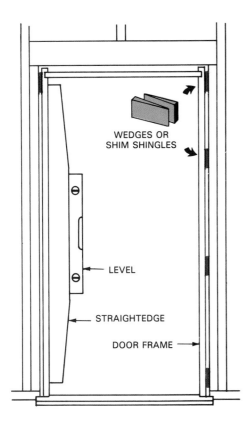

Fig. 29-18. Plumbing door jambs.

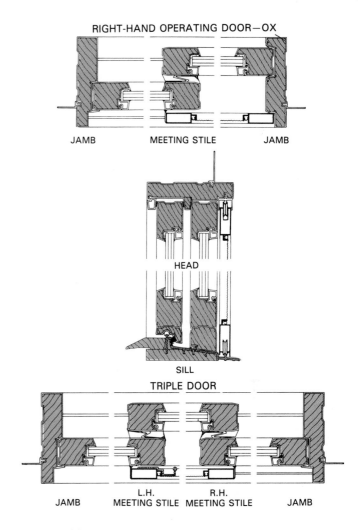

Fig. 29-19. Vinyl covered sliding glass door details.

Finally, nail the casing in place with nails spaced 16 in. O.C. Follow the same precautions suggested for window frame installation.

After the installation is complete, a piece of 1/4 or 3/8 in. plywood should be lightly tacked over the sill to protect it during further construction work. At this time, many builders prefer to hang a temporary combination door in order to secure the interior of the structure, thus providing a place to store tools and materials.

When a prehung door unit is installed, the door should be removed from its hinges and carefully stored to protect it.

## INSTALLING SLIDING GLASS DOORS

Sliding glass doors vary from one manufacturer to another. Therefore, be sure to study the construction details carefully. If detailed drawings or R.O. sizes are not included in the drawings, then the carpenter should secure the information from the manufacturer's literature. Fig. 29-19 shows the details of a typical sliding glass door unit.

The installation of sliding door frames is similar to the procedure described for regular outside doors. Before setting the frame in place, a bead of sealing compound should be laid across the opening to insure a weathertight joint. If heavy glass doors are to slide properly the sill must be level and straight.

Plumb side jambs and install wedges in the same way you would install regular door frames. After careful checking, complete the installation of the frame by driving weatherproof nails through the side and head casings into structural frame members.

At this point, many carpenters prefer just to check the fit between the metal sill cover and doors rather than installing them. These items are carefully stored away. The opening is enclosed temporarily with plywood or polyethylene film attached to a frame. Then, during the finishing stages of construction, after inside and outside wall surfaces are completed, the sill cover, threshold, doors, and hardware are installed.

## GARAGE DOOR FRAMES

Frames for garage doors include side jambs and a head similar to exterior passage doors. No rabbet is required. The frame is usually included in the millwork order along with windows and doors so the outside trim will match. The size of the frame opening is usually the same size as the door. However, the manufacturer's specifications and details should be checked before placing the order.

Fig. 29-20 shows a typical jamb section for wood frame or masonry construction. Note the thickness (2 in. nominal) of the heavy inside frame to which the track and hardware will be mounted. The width of this member should be at least 4 in. wide with no projecting bolt or lag screw heads.

The rough opening width for frame construction will normally be about 3 in. greater than the door size. The height of the rough opening should be the door height plus about 1 1/2 in. as measured from the finished floor.

## EXTERIOR FINISH

Exterior wall finish includes the construction and finish of cornice work and the materials used as an outside wall covering. Other elements of wall finish have been included in other sections.

## CORNICE DESIGNS

The cornice, or eave, is formed by the roof overhang. It connects the wall to the edge of the roof. Design requirements are determined, to a large extent, by the architectural style of the structure.

Three types of cornices are frequently used in residential buildings: the open cornice, boxed cornice, and close cornice. The OPEN CORNICE exposes the rafters and underside of the roof sheathing. The CLOSE CORNICE is used with some colonial style homes where little or no overhang is desired. The most popular type of cornice is the BOXED CORNICE. Fig. 29-21 shows several types of cornices in detail.

The RAKE is the part of the roof that overhangs a gable. The design and construction of the rake should match the cornice.

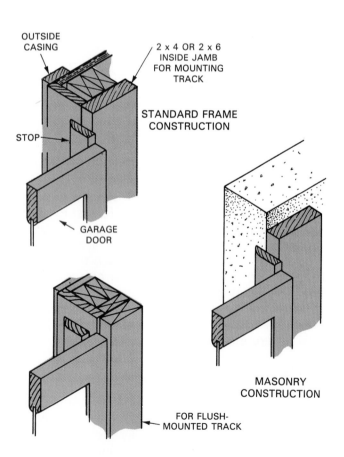

Fig. 29-20. Typical jamb construction for garage door frames for use with sectional door.

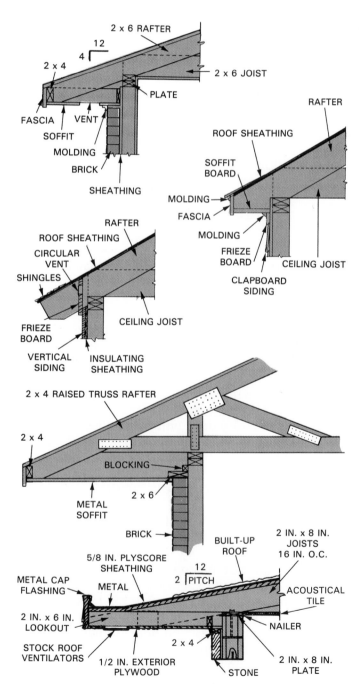

Fig. 29-21. Typical cornice details. These will be found in architectural plans.

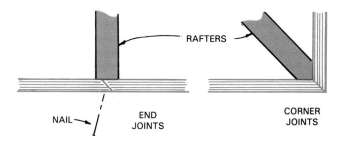

Fig. 29-22. Plan view of joints for fascia boards. Miter corners and make matching angled cuts on ends. Note how end joints are nailed.

## CORNICE AND RAKE CONSTRUCTION

In most construction, the fascia boards are installed on the rafter ends at the time the roof is sheathed. It is important that they be straight, true, and level with well-fitted joints. Corners of fascia boards should be mitered. End joints should meet at a 45 deg. angle, as illustrated in Fig. 29-22.

To frame a cornice with a horizontal soffit, first install a ledger strip along the wall if lookouts are to be used. With a carpenter's level, locate points on the wall level with the bottom edge of the rafter. Snap a chalk line between these points and nail on the ledger, Fig. 29-23.

Lookouts are usually made from 2 x 4 stock. Locate them at each rafter or every other rafter, depending on the kind of soffit material used. Cut the lookouts. Toenail one end to the ledger and nail the other end to the overhang of the rafter. When using thin material for the soffit, attach a nailing strip along the inside of the fascia to provide a nailing surface. Sometimes the back of the fascia is grooved to receive the soffit material.

After this frame is complete, apply the soffit. First cut the material to size and then secure it with rust resistant nails or screws.

The rake should be constructed to match the cornice using the same general procedure. Fig. 29-24 shows a completed cornice and rake.

## PREFABRICATED SOFFIT MATERIALS

Many builders prefer to use prefabricated soffit materials to save time. A variety of systems are available. It is important to plan for the use of a particular soffit system so that rafter length and cornice construction will be correct for the prefabricated soffit materials. Fig. 29-25 shows a popular prefabricated metal soffit system.

### TYPES OF FINISH

After the cornice and rake sections of the roof are covered, you can apply siding to the walls. When

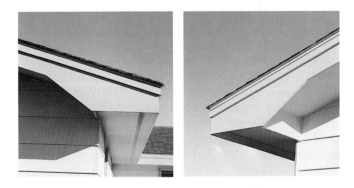

Fig. 29-24. Two views of a completed cornice and rake. Note continuous vent system in soffit. (Dickinson Homes, Inc.)

Fig. 29-23. Parts of a typical boxed cornice. Soffit materials are often prefabricated and usually hardboard, plywood, or metal.

Fig. 29-25. Prefabricated metal soffit system being installed on a wide boxed cornice. Each panel is 9 in. wide.

the structure includes a gable roof, the wall surface material is usually applied to the gable end before the lower section is covered. This permits scaffolding to be attached directly to the wall while siding the gable end.

All exterior trim members, if not factory primed, should be given a primer coat of paint as soon as possible after installation.

## HORIZONTAL SIDING

End views of a number of types of horizontal siding are shown in Fig. 29-26. Bevel siding is available in various widths. It is made by sawing plain-surfaced boards at a diagonal to produce two wedge-shaped pieces. The siding is about 3/16 in. thick at the thin edge and 1/2 to 3/4 in. thick on the other edge, depending on the width of the piece.

Wide bevel siding often has shiplapped or rabbeted joints. The siding lies flat against the studding, instead of touching it only near the joints as with ordinary bevel siding. This reduces the apparent thickness of the siding by 1/4 in. but permits the use of extra nails in wide siding and reduces the chance of warping. It is also economical, since the rabbeted joint requires less lumber than the lap joint used with plain bevel siding.

The rabbet, however, must be deep enough so that, when the siding is applied, the width of the boards can be adjusted upward or downward to meet window sill, head casing, and eave lines.

Rustic and drop sidings are usually 3/4 in. thick and 6 in. wide. They are made in a variety of patterns. Rustic siding has shiplap type joints, where drop siding usually has tongue-and-groove joints.

### Wood siding

One of the most common materials used for the exterior finish of homes is wood siding. Siding is usually applied over sheathing. However, in mild climates or on buildings such as a summer cottage, it is sometimes applied directly to the studs.

Cut and fit horizontal wood siding tightly against window and door casings, corner boards, and adjoining boards. Square butt joints are used between adjacent pieces of siding and should be staggered as widely as possible from one course to the next.

Wood siding can be given a coat of water-repellent preservative before it is installed, or the water repellent can be brushed on after the installation. In addition to this treatment, joints in siding may be bedded in a special caulking compound to make them watertight.

## VERTICAL SIDING

Vertical siding is commonly used to set off entrances or gable ends. It is also often used for the main wall areas. Vertical siding may be plain-surfaced matched boards, pattern-matched boards, or square-edged boards covered at the joint with a batten strip.

Matched vertical siding, made from solid lumber, should be no more than 8 in. wide. Backer blocks should be placed horizontally between studs to provide a good nailing base. The bottom of the boards are usually undercut to form a water drip.

Board and batten applications are designed around wide square-edged boards, spaced about 1/2 in. apart. Locate nails in center of batten so the shanks will pass between the boards and into the bearing.

Board and batten effects are made with large vertical sheets of plywood or composition materials. Simply attach vertical strips over the joints and at several positions between the joints. Fig. 29-27

Fig. 29-27. Textured plywood panels provide the basic siding material in this photo. Narrow strips of wood were added to cover the joints and add decoration.
(American Plywood Association)

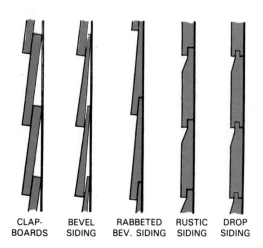

CLAP-BOARDS  BEVEL SIDING  RABBETED BEV. SIDING  RUSTIC SIDING  DROP SIDING

Fig. 29-26. Edge view of five types of horizontal siding.

shows an application of this type with solid wood strips being applied to the surface of exterior plywood sheets.

## WOOD SHINGLES

Wood shingles, Fig. 29-28, are sometimes used for wall covering as a large selection is available. Some are especially designed for sidewall application with a grooved surface and factory applied paint or stain. Shingles are very durable and can be applied in various ways to provide a variety of architectural effects.

Most shingles are made in random widths from 3 in. to 14 in. Standard lengths include 16, 18, and 24 in. depending on the exposure desired. The manufacturer's specifications should be followed.

Shingles on side walls are frequently laid in what is called DOUBLE-COURSING. This is done by using a lower grade shingle under the shingle exposed to the weather. The exposed shingle butt extends about 1/2 in. below the butt of the under course.

Solid sheathing is generally recommended for tight construction, but nailing strips can be used in mild climates. Roofing felt should always be used with nailing strips. Follow the manufacturer's instructions.

To obtain the best effect and to avoid unnecessary cutting of shingles, butt-lines should be even with the upper lines of window openings. Likewise, they should line up with the lower lines of such openings.

Shingles (and shakes) are available in panel form. The panels consist of individual shingles permanently bonded to a backing. Panels are available in various textures, either unstained or factory-finished, in a variety of colors. Special corner trim pieces are also available to match the panels.

## PLYWOOD SIDING

The use of plywood as an exterior wall covering permits a wide range of application methods and decorative treatments, Fig. 29-29. It may be used as the primary siding material or to complement other materials.

All plywood siding is made from exterior grade plywood. Douglas fir is the most commonly used species. However, cedar and redwood are also available. Panels come either sanded or with factory applied sealer or stain. Plywood siding is also available with special coatings and laminates which extend the useful life and serve as a finish.

Panels come in 48 in. widths and 8, 9, and 10 ft. lengths. A 3/8 in. thickness is normally used for direct-to-stud applications. A 5/16 in. thickness may be used over an approved sheathing. Thicker panels are required when the texture treatment consists of deep cuts.

Fig. 29-28. Wood shingles form a durable and attractive exterior wall covering. (Shakertown Corp.)

Fig. 29-29. Two examples of plywood siding styles with rough-sawn texture. (American Plywood Association)

Application of large sheets is generally made with the panels in a vertical position. This eliminates the need for horizontal joints. For unsheathed walls, the thickness of the plywood should not be less than 3/8 in. for 16 in. stud spacing, 1/2 in. for 20 in. stud spacing, and 5/8 in. for 24 in. stud spacing. Vertical joints must occur over studs and horizontal joints must be over solid blocking.

## HARDBOARD SIDING

Hardboard siding products now available are durable and applicable to various architectural designs. Installation methods are similar to those described for plywood sidings.

Hardboard sidings may expand more than plywood. Manufacturers, therefore, generally recommend leaving a 1/8 in. space where hardboard siding butts against adjacent pieces or trim members.

Siding panels are available in standard widths of 4 ft. and lengths of 8, 9, and 10 ft. Lap siding units are usually 12 in. wide by 16 ft. long. Narrower widths are also available. The most common thickness is 7/16 in. Like plywood, hardboard sidings are furnished in a wide range of textures and surface treatments, Fig. 29-30. Most panels have a factory-applied primer coat.

## ALUMINUM SIDING

Aluminum siding is a popular product, mainly because of its low maintenance cost. Aluminum siding produced today has a baked-on enamel finish and resembles painted wood siding. It can be used on new construction or over any existing exterior finish which is structurally sound.

A variety of horizontal and vertical panel styles in both smooth and textured designs are produced. An insulated panel is also produced. It has an impregnated fiberboard material laminated to the back surface.

Directions for the installation of a specific product are supplied by the manufacturer. These should be followed carefully. Fig. 29-31 shows a horizontal siding unit being fastened in place. Panels are fabricated with pre-punched nail and vent holes and special interlocking design. Standard strips are easily attached around windows and doors to provide a weathertight seal. Special corners and trim members are often formed on the job site.

Aluminum siding should be grounded as a precaution against faulty electrical wiring. Recommended procedures for this operation are available from the Aluminum Siding Association.

## VINYL SIDING

Vinyl siding is made from a rigid polyvinyl chloride compound that is tough and durable. This material, commonly called vinyl, is extruded into horizontal or vertical siding units.

Vinyl siding is usually installed with a backer board or insulation board behind each sheet. This backer adds rigidity and strength as well as insulation. Panels are designed with interlocking joints that are moisture-proof. Since the siding must be allowed to expand and contract slightly with temperature changes, the nail holes are slotted to permit movement.

## STUCCO

Stucco makes an attractive and satisfactory exterior wall finished. The finish coat may be tex-

Fig. 29-30. Home sided in shingle panels manufactured from hardboard. Panels are made in 8 ft. and 16 ft. lengths. (Masonite Corp.)

Fig. 29-31. Installing an aluminum siding panel. Lower edge interlocks with previously applied course. (Alcoa Building Products)

tured, colored, or painted with a suitable material. When stucco is used on houses more than one story high, the use of balloon framing for the outside walls is desirable to reduce shrinkage cracks.

In frame construction, the base for stucco consists of wood sheathing, sheathing paper, and metal lath, Fig. 29-32. The metal lath should be heavily galvanized and spaced at least 1/4 in. away from the sheathing so the base coat (called scratch coat) can be easily forced through, thoroughly embedding the lath. Metal or wood molding with a groove that "keys" the stucco is applied at edges and around openings. Galvanized furring nails, metal furring strips, and self-furring wire mesh are available.

## BRICK OR STONE VENEER

A brick or stone veneer is frequently used as the exterior wall finish material on a frame structure. The masonry units (brick, concrete, or stone) support only their own weight, not the weight of the structure as in a solid masonry wall.

The foundation must be designed to support the additional width (usually 4 in.) and weight of the masonry veneer. Fig. 29-33 illustrates the typical construction for a masonry veneer structure. Note that a base flashing of aluminum is positioned at the bottom of the sheathing; this extends up to 6 in. to protect the wall and floor materials from excessive moisture. A 1 in. air space is generally allowed between the sheathing and masonry

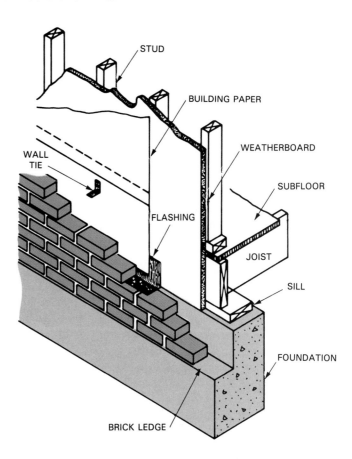

Fig. 29-33. Construction detail of a brick veneer wall section.

materials. Sheathing paper is not required if plywood or rigid foam insulation board is used.

Corrosion-resistant metal ties are used to attach the veneer to the wall frame. One tie is generally required for each 2 sq. ft. of area covered. Ties should be nailed to the studs every 16 in. vertically and 32 in. apart. Weep holes should be provided about every 4 ft. along the bottom course of masonry to permit the escape of excessive moisture.

Select a veneer material which is compatible with structure style and weather conditions. Clay bricks generally resist severe weathering because they absorb little moisture. Concrete masonry units are generally not recommended for exposure where severe freezing conditions exist. Most stone weathers well.

### TEST YOUR KNOWLEDGE, Chapter 29

Please do not write in the text. Place your answers on a separate sheet of paper.
1. Windows used for residential structures are made from what three materials?
2. Name the three basic types of windows.
3. Jalousie windows provide excellent ventilation. What is their biggest disadvantage?
4. The standard height from finished floor to the

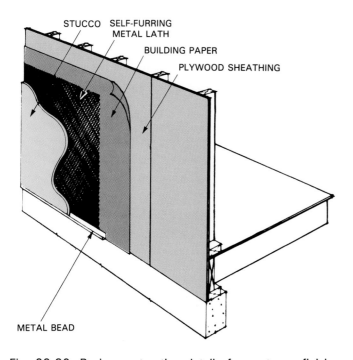

Fig. 29-32. Basic construction details for a stucco finish. Building paper, also called sheathing paper, is recommended for both interior and exterior plywood sheathing. (American Plywood Association)

bottom side of a window head is:
a. 8 ft. 6 in.
b. 6 ft. 8 in.
c. 6 ft.
d. None of the above.

5. A low R-value means there is little _____ to the passage of heat.

6. Adding another pane of glass to a window, with an air space in between the panes, would _____ (increase, decrease) the R-value.

7. Where would you look to find detailed information about window size, rough opening size, type of window, etc.?

8. Identify four common types of exterior doors.

9. FHA Minimum Property Standards specify a minimum exterior door width of:
a. 2 ft. 6 in.
b. 3 ft.
c. 2 ft. 3 in.
d. None of the above.

10. The rough opening width for a garage door in frame construction will normally be about _____ in. greater than the door size.

11. What is a rake?

12. Identify five types of exterior wall finish that are commonly used on residential structures.

13. In what type of exterior finish is double-coursing used?

14. Why are fixed windows generally used?

## ACTIVITIES

1. Build a scale model (1 in. = 1 ft.) of an exterior door, jambs, and rough framing. Identify the parts and standard dimensions.

2. Visit a local lumber company and examine the cut-away models of the windows they sell. Measure the various parts of one model and prepare a sketch of the construction. Identify the type of window and the manufacturer. Collect any specification data about the windows that you can and bring it to class for reference.

3. Start a collection of siding materials used in residential construction. Identify each by name and manufacturer. Determine the price per sheet, price per linear ft., etc. Record the R-value for each material. Share with the class your samples and information collected.

This modern residential structure has circle-top windows to increase light into the home and accent the overall design. (California Redwood Association)

Installing the fascia of a prefabricated soffit system.

The ceiling joists in this modern frame structure are engineered wood I-joists and the supporting beams are glue laminated beams. (American Plywood Association)

The interior finish of these two homes involved several materials. Each contributed to the functional as well as visual impact of the completed room. (Southern Forests Products Association, Wilsonart)

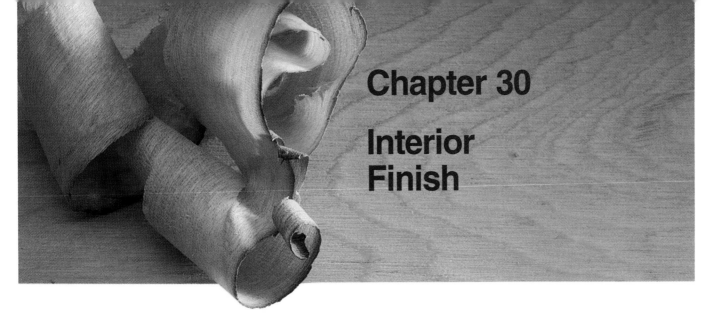

# Chapter 30

# Interior Finish

While carpenters complete the exterior finish of the house, other tradespeople are busy on the inside. Duct work is installed in the floor, ceiling, and walls for heating and air conditioning. The electrician strings rough wiring (or runs conduit) through the framework, then sets the boxes for convenience outlets, switches, and lighting fixtures. At this time, the housings for recessed fixtures are installed.

The plumber installs the drains, vent stacks, and pipes that will carry the water service. In the installation of the heating and plumbing ''rough-in,'' the tradesperson must often cut through the structural framework. The carpenter should check over this work and revise or reinforce framing members wherever necessary. Fig. 30-1 shows an interior view of a house with the rough-in almost completed. It is almost ready for insulation and wall finish.

Fig. 30-1. A residence during the rough-in phase. Several lighting fixtures and receptacles are in place and duct work is in process. Rough heating, plumbing, and electrical are installed before the insulation and interior wall finish is applied.

## INSULATION

Buildings that will be heated or air-conditioned should be insulated to maintain comfort and reduce fuel cost. In cold climates, the major concern is to retain heat in the building. In warm climates, insulation is needed to prevent heat from entering the building. Thermal insulation is located in the outside walls, ceilings, and sometimes the floors, Fig. 30-2.

### TYPES OF INSULATION

Insulation is made in many forms, grades, and thicknesses. The most common types inside are batt, blanket, loose fill, and rigid insulation. A reflective coating (usually metal foil) is available on all types except loose fill.

BLANKET INSULATION, Fig. 30-3, is usually packaged in rolls of convenient length and in widths appropriate for standard stud and joist spacing. Thicknesses of 3/4 in. to 6 in. are common. The most common material used for blanket and batt insulation is glass fibers. Other materials such as rock wool, slag, wood fiber, and cotton are also used. Blanket insulation is made with or without a vapor or reflective barrier on one side. Blanket insulation with a paper or reflective covering provides tabs along the sides for attachment. Unfaced blanket insulation is generally intended for use over an existing insulation layer which already has a vapor barrier.

BATT INSULATION is very similar to blanket insulation except it is packaged in short lengths (usually 24 or 48 in.) and is produced in greater thicknesses. Batts are available from 3 1/2 in. to 12 in. thick and in widths to match standard stud and joist spacing. The coverings used on blanket insulation are also available on batts, Fig. 30-4.

LOOSE FILL INSULATION is composed of various materials used in bulk form and supplied in bags or bales. It may be poured or blown in place. Loose fill insulation is commonly used to fill spaces in

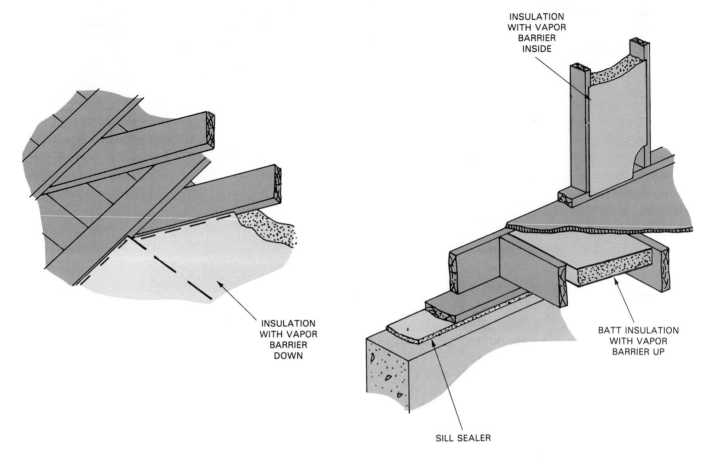

INSULATION
WITH VAPOR
BARRIER
INSIDE

INSULATION
WITH VAPOR
BARRIER
DOWN

BATT INSULATION
WITH VAPOR
BARRIER UP

SILL SEALER

Fig. 30-2. When insulation is properly installed, it will help increase the energy efficiency of heating and cooling units. Left. Attic insulation. Right. Foundation, floor, and wall insulation.

Fig. 30-3. Blanket insulation may be kraft paper faced, foil faced, or unfaced. This fiberglass blanket is 6 1/2 in. thick with an R-value of 19. (Owens-Corning Fiberglas Corp.)

Fig. 30-4. Batt with aluminum foil cover. Opposite side has a porous foil breather paper.

concrete blocks, fill spaces between studs, or to build up any desired thickness on a flat surface, such as an attic, Fig. 30-5.

Loose fill insulation is made from such materials as rock, glass, slag wool, wood fibers, shredded redwood bark, granulated cork, ground or macerated

Fig. 30-5. It is easy to level off poured insulation to a uniform depth with this setup. Strikeoff boards are installed permanently. (Vermiculite Institute)

(softened by wetting) wood pulp products, vermiculite, perlite, powdered gypsum, sawdust, and wood shavings. One of the chief advantages of this type is that when insulating an older structure, holes may be bored between each wall stud to blow the material into the walls. The holes are plugged with plastic plugs.

RIGID INSULATION, as ordinarily used in residential construction, is often made from expanded polystyrene (called styrofoam) or by reducing wood, cane, or other fiber to a pulp. The pulp is assembled into lightweight or low-density boards or panels that combine strength with heat and acoustical insulating properties. Thicknesses available for these products range from 1/2 in. to 1 in. for the fiber boards. Widths and lengths are designed for common applications. Rigid insulation is used for roof and wall sheathing, insulating foundation walls and slab floors, and as a base for plaster, Fig. 30-6. Only the polystyrene rigid foam should be used in areas where moisture exists.

REFLECTIVE COATED INSULATION is any insulation (blanket, batt, or rigid) which has a metal foil surface. For best results, the foil surface should be exposed to an air space, as found between a frame wall and brick veneer or the inside of a crawl space.

In addition to thermal insulation, it is essential that a vapor barrier be included to prevent the flow of moisture from the warm interior to the cold exterior of the building. This vapor barrier must be placed

Fig. 30-6. Perimeter of slab construction should be insulated with rigid insulation. (Owens-Corning Fiberglas Corp.)

on the warm side of the wall or insulation material. Plastic (polyethylene) films are widely used for this purpose. Copper and aluminum foil provides an effective vapor barrier and may also serve as a reflective insulator.

509

## PLACING INSULATION

Heated areas, especially in cold climates, should be surrounded with insulation. This should be placed in the walls, ceiling, and floors. Refer back to Fig. 30-2. It is best to have it as close to the heated space as possible. For example, if an attic is unused, the insulation should be placed in the attic floor rather than in the roof structure.

If attic space or certain portions of the attic must be heated, walls and ceilings should be insulated. If the insulation is placed between the rafters, be sure to allow space between the insulation and the sheathing for free air circulation. The floors of rooms above unheated garages or porches require insulation if maximum comfort is to be maintained.

When a basement is to be used as a living or recreation area, it will be necessary to insulate the walls, Fig. 30-7. This is highly recommended as an energy conservation measure, too. Not only does it save heat and provide comfort, it gives the basement better acoustical qualities as well.

Whether applied to basement walls or not, insulation should be installed over the band joists. (These are the floor framing members along the outside of the wall.) See Fig. 30-8. This section has little protection against heat loss.

Floors over unheated crawl spaces require the same degree of insulation as walls in the same

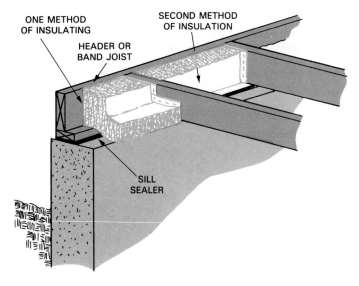

Fig. 30-8. Insulate behind headers atop basement walls. There is little protection from loss of heat through the header.

climate zone. If this space is enclosed by foundation walls and is ventilated, it will approach the outside temperature.

Many homes, as well as other structures, are built on concrete slab floors. Such floors should contain insulation and a vapor barrier to prevent heat loss along the perimeter. Little heat is lost into the ground under the center portion of the floor. Therefore, the vapor barrier should cover the total floor area, but only the perimeter needs to be insulated. The insulation can be placed horizontally under the floor (2 ft. wide) or vertically along the foundation walls, Fig. 30-9.

Fig. 30-7. Insulation with a moisture barrier backing is commonly applied to reduce heat loss in a basement. (Conwed Corp.)

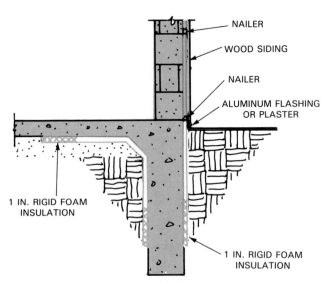

Fig. 30-9. Rigid foam insulation should be placed around the perimeter of a slab floor. This illustration shows the insulation in all possible locations: outside foundation, inside foundation, and under the slab.

Polystyrene panels must be protected against ultraviolet light, wear, and impact forces. An approved method is to cover the surface with special plaster made from cement, lime, glass fibers, and a water-resistant agent. This mixture is troweled onto the surface 1/8 in. to 1/4 in. thick. It should be extended down to at least 4 in. below finished grade. The buried portion of the polystyrene panel does not require protection.

Mineral fiber panels, exterior plywood, or other weatherproof panels can also be used to protect the insulation. These panels can usually be attached with an approved type of mastic adhesive and/or nailing strips. Their use is practical when only a small area of the insulation board projects above the finished grade.

Polystyrene insulation is available in panels that have a weatherproof coating of fiber-reinforced cement on one side. They are especially designed to insulate the outside surface of foundations. These panels must be cut with a circular saw equipped with a masonry blade.

In modern homes, considerable attention is given to sound control. Various insulation materials are placed around plumbing lines and installed in partitions and floors to reduce the transmission of unwanted noise.

## INTERIOR WALL AND CEILING FINISH

Several types of materials may be used to cover walls and ceilings. Some of the most common coverings include: gypsum wallboard; predecorated gypsum paneling; plywood and particle board paneling; hardboard and fiberboard; solid wood paneling; plaster; clay finishes; plastic laminates; ceiling tile; and suspended ceilings.

GYPSUM WALLBOARD, also known as DRYWALL, has a gypsum core with paper covering on either side. Common sizes include 4 x 7, 8, 9, 10, 12, and 14 ft. Thicknesses include 1/4, 5/16, 3/8, 1/2, and 5/8 in. for standard applications. Gypsum wallboard is used on walls and ceilings.

PREDECORATED GYPSUM PANELING is similar to regular gypsum wallboard, except a decorative finish is applied at the factory. These panels also have received special treatment so that no other finish work is required after installation. They are available in standard panel size.

PLYWOOD AND PARTICLE BOARD PANELING is available in standard panel sizes of 4 x 7, 8, 9, and 10 ft. It can be purchased with or without finish, Fig. 30-10. Plywood panels are available in hardwood or softwood veneers. Standard thicknesses include 1/4, 3/8, 7/16, 1/2, 5/8, and 3/4 in.

HARDBOARD AND FIBERBOARD are produced using wood fibers. Sizes are similar to plywood. The finished surface is designed to simulate wood,

Fig. 30-10. Top. Channel, roughsawn paneling may be purchased prefinished or ready for finish. (American Plywood Association) Bottom. Waferwood paneling is an attractive wall or ceiling covering. (Louisiana-Pacific Corp.)

leather, wallpaper, or other materials, Fig. 30-11. Hardboard and fiberboard can be used as a ceiling or wall finish.

SOLID WOOD PANELING uses boards or small pieces of solid wood. Generally, widths of boards range from 2 to 12 in.; thicknesses vary. Faces can be roughsawn, smooth, or molded in a variety of patterns. Wood shingles or shakes are sometimes used on interior walls.

PLASTER is a traditional wall and ceiling material. A plaster finish is supported on wood, metal, or gypsum lath. Gypsum lath has perforations for good adhesion, Fig. 30-12. Plaster can be textured, patterned, or trowled smooth for painting or wallpaper.

CLAY FINISHING products include brick, brick veneers, and ceramic tile. They are generally used for architectural and design emphasis or to protect

Fig. 30-11. Ceilings may be covered with a fiberboard product. In this room, it was prefinished to look like oak. (Armstrong World Industries, Inc.)

wall areas from heavy wear or damage. Kitchens and bathrooms are the most common locations for clay finishes, but they are popular in other areas of the home as well.

PLASTIC LAMINATES, usually bonded to particle board or hardboard, can be used as a wallcovering material. A common application is wainscoating. Refer to Fig. 30-13.

CEILING TILE is made in many sizes, types, and material contents. When selecting a product, consider its appearance, light reflection, fire resistance, sound absorption, maintenance, cost, and ease of installation. A standard size tile is 12 x 12 in. Follow manufacturer's instructions for proper installation, Fig. 30-14.

SUSPENDED CEILINGS can be used when a large amount of diffused illumination is desired, as in a kitchen or bath. They are also used when heating ducts and/or plumbing lines interfere with the application of a finished ceiling, as in a basement. Installation usually consists of a metal framework designed to support tile or ceiling panels. Fig. 30-15 shows the framework for a suspended ceiling.

## FINISH FLOORING

Finish flooring is the wear surface of a floor. Many materials and products are used for this purpose. Some of the more popular include wood flooring, resilient floor coverings, carpet, and ceramic tile.

WOOD FLOORING (especially hardwood) pro-

Fig. 30-12. Plaster is always applied over a supporting base. Old style wood lath has been replaced by several new products. The one used here is called perforated gypsum lath.

Fig. 30-13. These wall panels are manufactured from plastic laminate with a particle board base. (Formica Corp.)

Fig. 30-14. Staples can be used to attach tile to furring strips. (Duo-Fast Corp.)

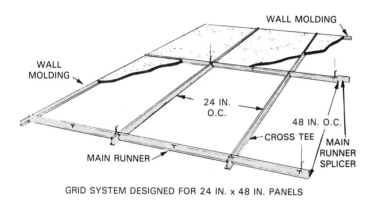

WALL MOLDING

WALL MOLDING

24 IN. O.C.

48 IN. O.C.

CROSS TEE

MAIN RUNNER SPLICER

MAIN RUNNER

GRID SYSTEM DESIGNED FOR 24 IN. x 48 IN. PANELS

Fig. 30-15. This sketch shows the typical framework used for suspended ceilings.

Fig. 30-16. Hardwood strip flooring produces a beautiful finish flooring that will withstand heavy use and maintain its beauty. (Memphis Hardwood Flooring Co.)

vides strength, durability, and attractive appearance. Three general types of wood flooring are used in residential structures: strip, plank, and block.

STRIP FLOORING, Fig. 30-16, consists of pieces cut into narrow strips with a tongue-and-groove on sides and ends. It is laid in a random pattern of end joints. Hardwood strip flooring is available in widths ranging from 1 1/2 to 3 1/4 in. Standard thicknesses include 3/8, 1/2, and 3/4 in.

PLANK FLOORING is frequently used in traditional homes to provide an informal atmosphere, Fig. 30-17. Plank floors are usually laid in random widths and plugged. Planks are usually 3/4 in. thick, and from 3 to 9 in. wide in multiples of 1 in.

BLOCK FLOORING looks like conventional parquetry, Fig. 30-18. The elaborate design is formed by gluing small blocks together. Unit blocks are produced in a 3/4 in. thickness. Squares are generally 6 3/4 x 6 3/4 in., 9 x 9 in., or 11 1/4 x 11 1/4 in.

RESILIENT FLOOR COVERING is a floor covering material rather than a flooring material (such as wood). These materials are termed resilient because

Fig. 30-17. The plank flooring in this home is attractive and functional. (Masonite Corp.)

Fig. 30-19. Left. Seamless vinyl floor covering. It is available in 6 and 12 ft. widths. (Gray and Rogers) Right. Vinyl tile floor covering. (Tarkett, Inc.)

Fig. 30-18. Wood block flooring forms a distinctive pattern and adds a feeling of warmth to the atmosphere. (Memphis Hardwood Flooring Co.)

Main stairs are often prefabricated in a factory, then assembled and installed on the site.

## TYPES OF STAIRS

Basically, there are three types of stair structure. They are straight run, platform, and winding. Within these structure types there are five common kinds

they return to their original shape. The group includes asphalt, cork, rubber, vinyl, and seamless floors. Most of the products are produced in tile and sheet form, Fig. 30-19.

CARPET is a very popular floor covering because of its beauty, versatility, and wear resistance. About 90 percent of the carpet produced today is made from four synthetic fibers: nylon, acrylic, polyester, and olefin (polypropylene). No single fiber is perfect for all types of carpeting. The advantages and disadvantages must be weighed against cost, application, and expected length of life.

CERAMIC TILE is a very durable flooring material. It is popular in high traffic areas and where moisture exists, such as foyers and bathrooms. However, it can be used anywhere in the home, Fig. 30-20.

### STAIRS

Stairs lead from one floor level to another through a stairwell opening. This should be framed during the rough construction. Rough stairs are built for use during construction, and then replaced with finished stairs after wall surfaces have been applied.

Fig. 30-20. Ceramic tile is available in a wide range of colors, textures, and shapes. This floor illustrates how unique designs can be formed. (Tile Council of America)

of stairs. Straight run stairs are of the straight run structure. L stairs, double L stairs, and U stairs are all types of platform stair structure. Spiral stairs and winder stairs are both types of winding stair structure. These stairs are illustrated in Fig. 30-21.

The STRAIGHT RUN STAIRS are used most often in home construction. They have no turns. These stairs are not as expensive to construct as other types of stairs.

The L STAIRS have one landing at some point along the flight of steps. If the landing is near the top or bottom of the stairs, the term LONG L is used. L stairs are used when the space required for a straight run stairs is not available.

DOUBLE L STAIRS require two 90 deg. turns along the flight. They may be used when space is not available for either the straight or L stairs.

U STAIRS may be constructed either as WIDE U or NARROW U stairs. Both have two flights of steps parallel to each other with a landing between. The difference between wide and narrow U stairs is the space between the two flights. Narrow U stairs have little or no space between the flights while wide U stairs have a well hole between.

WINDER STAIRS have pie-shaped steps which are substituted for a landing. This type is used when space is not sufficient for L stairs. If winder stairs are used, the width of the triangular steps should be sufficient at midpoint to provide a tread width equal to the regular steps. Winder stairs are not as safe as other types of stairs and should be avoided whenever possible.

SPIRAL or CIRCULAR STAIRS are used where little space is available. Most spiral stairs are made from steel and are welded together. However, it is possible to construct them from wood. Spiral stairs are, as a rule, not very safe since they usually have winder stairs.

## PARTS AND TERMS

Stairs are basically sets of risers and treads supported by STRINGERS. The height of the riser is called the UNIT RISE and the width of tread, nosing excluded, is called the UNIT RUN. The sum of all the risers is the TOTAL RISE and the sum of all the treads is the TOTAL RUN, Fig. 30-22.

Vertical space above the stair is known as HEADROOM. It is measured from a line along the front edge of the treads to the enclosed surface or header above. This distance is usually specified in local building codes. FHA requires a minimum headroom of 6 ft. 6 in. for main stairs and 6 ft. 4 in. for basement or service stairs.

## STAIR DESIGN

Most important in stair design is the mathematical relationship between the riser and tread, Fig. 30-23. There are three generally accepted rules for calculating the rise-run or riser-tread ratio. It is wise to observe them. They are as follows.

1. The sum of two risers and one tread should be 24 to 25 in.
2. The sum of one riser and one tread should equal 17 to 18 in.
3. The height of the riser times the width of the tread should equal between 70 and 75 in.

A riser 7 1/2 in. high would, according to Rule 1, require a tread of 10 in. A 6 1/2 in. riser would require a 12 in. tread.

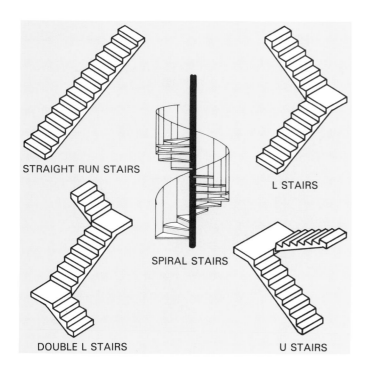

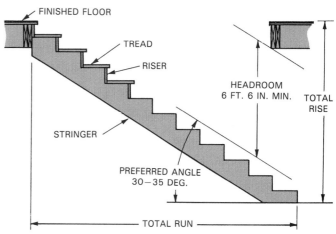

Fig. 30-21. The five general types of stairs commonly used in residential construction.

Fig. 30-22. Basic stair parts and terms. Total number of risers is always one greater than the total number of treads.

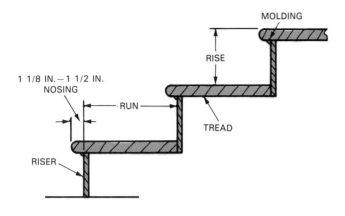

Fig. 30-23. Mathematical relationship between treads and risers.

In residential structures, treads (excluding nosing) are seldom less than 9 in. or more than 12 in. wide. In a given run of stairs it is extremely important that all of the treads and all risers be the same size. A person tends to measure (subconsciously) the first few risers and will probably trip on subsequent risers that are not the same.

When the rise-run combination is wrong, the stair will be tiring and cause extra strain on the leg muscles. Further, the toe may kick the riser if the tread is too narrow.

A unit rise of 7 to 7 5/8 in. high with an appropriate tread width will combine both comfort and safety. Main or principal stairs are usually planned to have a rise in this range. Service stairs are often steeper but risers should be no higher than 8 in. As stair rise is increased the run must be decreased.

## TREADS AND RISERS

A main stair tread is usually 1 1/16 or 1 1/8 in. thick. Either hardwood or softwood can be used, but hardwood is preferred.

Risers are generally cut from 3/4 in. stock. If the stairs are to be left uncovered, then the riser stock should match the tread material.

Where the top edge of the riser meets the tread, glue blocks are sometimes used. A rabbeted edge of the riser may fit into a groove in the tread. A rabbet and groove joint may also be used where the back edge of the tread meets the riser.

Stair treads must have a NOSING. This is the part of the tread that overhangs the riser. Nosings serve the same purpose as toe space along the floor line of kitchen cabinets. They provide toe room.

The width of the tread nosing usually varies from about 1 1/8 to 1 1/2 in. It seldom is greater than 1 3/4 in.

In general, as the tread width is increased, the nosing can be decreased. Cove molding may be used to hide the joint between the riser and tread.

## TYPES OF STRINGERS

Treads and risers are supported by stringers or carriages that are solidly fixed to the wall or framework of the building. For wide stairs, a third stringer is installed in the middle for added support.

The simplest type of stringer is formed by attaching cleats on which the tread can rest. Another method consists of cutting dados into which the tread will fit. Refer to Fig. 30-24. This type is often used for basement stairs where no riser enclosure is needed.

Standard cutout stringers (plain stringers) are commonly used for either main or service stairs. Prefabricated treads and risers are often used for this type of support. An adaptation of the cutout stringer, called SEMIHOUSED CONSTRUCTION, is illustrated in Fig. 30-25. The cutout stringer and backing stringer can be assembled and installed as a unit or installed separately.

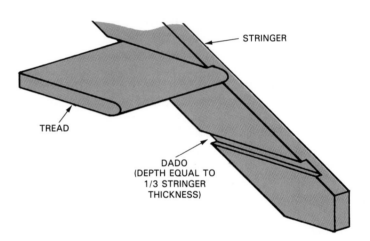

Fig. 30-24. Open riser stairs. Treads are set into dados cut in the stringer.

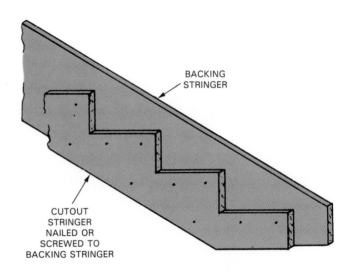

Fig. 30-25. Semihoused stringer construction.

A popular type of stair construction has a stringer with tapered grooves into which the treads and risers fit. It is commonly called HOUSED CONSTRUCTION. Wedges, with an application of glue, are driven into the grooves (dados) under the tread and behind the riser, Fig. 30-26. The treads and risers are joined with rabbeted edges and grooves or glue blocks. This type of construction produces a stair that is strong and will seldom squeak. Housed stringers can be purchased completely cut and ready for assembly or they can be cut on the job, using a router and template.

## INTERIOR DOORS

Interior doors may be classified in several ways depending on method of construction, use, location, function, and appearance. Some common types include flush, panel, bi-fold, sliding, pocket, double-action, and accordion doors.

FLUSH DOORS are smooth on both sides and are usually made of wood. Standard interior wood flush doors are 1 3/8 in. thick and 6 ft. 8 in. high. They are hollow core doors which have a wood frame around the perimeter and wood or composition material placed in the cavity to support the faces of the door. Interior flush doors are produced in a wide range of widths from 2 ft. to 3 ft. The standard increment width is 2 in. Both surfaces of the door are usually covered with 1/8 in. mahogany or birch plywood.

PANEL DOORS have heavy frames around the outside and generally have cross members which form small panels. The vertical members are called STILES and the horizontal pieces are RAILS. Panels which are thinner than the frame are placed in

Fig. 30-27. Standard interior panel door. In good residential planning, passage doors are located so they will swing open (90 deg.) against another wall, as shown. (C.E. Morgan)

grooves on the inside edges of the stiles and rails to enclose the space. The panels may be wood, glass, metal, or other material, Fig. 30-27. Panel doors are usually produced in white pine, but may be constructed of oak or other woods.

BI-FOLD DOORS are made of two parts which together form the door. They may be attached to the side jambs with conventional hinges or secured to the head jamb and floor using a pivot hinge, Fig. 30-28. Bi-fold doors may be flush, paneled, or

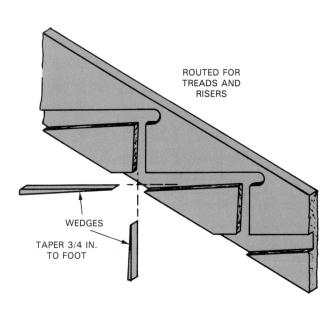

ROUTED FOR TREADS AND RISERS

WEDGES

TAPER 3/4 IN. TO FOOT

Fig. 30-26. Housed stringer.

Fig. 30-28. Bi-fold doors are often used to close off closet space. (C.E. Morgan)

louvered. They are popular as closet doors, and are seldom used for other applications. Bi-fold doors are installed in pairs with each door being the same width. Usual widths are 1 ft. to 2 ft.

Wood and metal bi-fold doors are made in the standard 6 ft. 8 in. height as well as 8 ft. The usual thickness is 1 1/8 in. for wood and 1 in. for metal.

SLIDING or BYPASS DOORS are popular where there are large openings, Fig. 30-29. They are frequently used as closet doors. Any number of doors may be used. The width is not critical, because the doors are hung from a track mounted on the head jamb. Door pulls are recessed to allow the doors to pass without interference. Glides are installed on the floor to prevent swinging.

Sliding doors may be flush, paneled, or louvered. They are usually constructed from wood, but other materials may be used. The major problem with wood sliding doors is warpage since they are not restrained by hinges.

POCKET DOORS are a type of sliding door. They are hung from tracks mounted on a head jamb and rest in a wall pocket when open, Fig. 30-30. Ordinarily, only one pocket door is used to close an opening, but two may be used for a large opening.

Pocket doors are frequently used between rooms such as the kitchen and dining room. The chief advantage is that they require no space along the wall when open. However, problems occur when outlets or cabinets are to be located on the wall space outside the pocket cavity. Pocket door frames of metal and wood are usually purchased assembled.

DOUBLE-ACTION DOORS are hinged so they can swing through an arc of 180 deg., Fig. 30-31. A special double-action, spring loaded hinge is mounted in the center of the side jamb. This door is generally used between rooms which experience a great deal of traffic and require the door closed most of the time. Double-action doors can be single

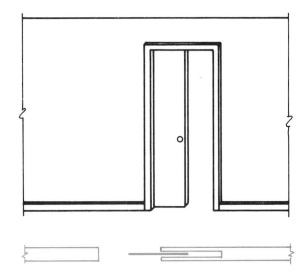

Fig. 30-30. Pocket door.

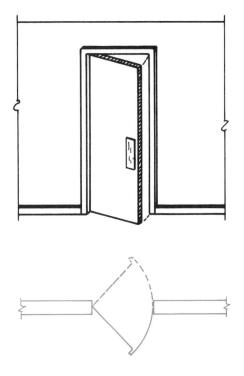

Fig. 30-31. Double-action door mounted in the center of the side jamb allows the door to swing in both directions.

Fig. 30-29. Bypass doors used for closet space. The doors open from either side. (C.E. Morgan)

or double doors. A flush, panel, or louvered door can be used.

ACCORDION DOORS are frequently used to close large openings where bi-fold or sliding doors would not be acceptable. They require little space and are produced in a large variety of materials and designs. They may be constructed from wood, plastics, or fabric. Individual hinged panels are sometimes used as well as a large folded piece of fabric or other material. The door is supported on a track mounted on the head jamb, Fig. 30-32.

Fig. 30-32. Accordion doors require less space to operate than swinging doors and provide unobstructed access to the interior space enclosed. (Rolscreen Co.)

## INTERIOR DOOR FRAMES

The door frame forms the lining of the door opening. It also covers the edges of the partition.

The frame consists of two side jambs and a head jamb, Fig. 30-33. Interior frames are simpler than exterior frames. The jambs are not rabbeted and no sill is included.

Standard jambs for regular 2 x 4 stud partitions are made from nominal 1 in. material. For walls of plaster, the jambs are 5 1/4 in. wide. For drywall, the jambs are 4 1/2 in. wide. The back side is usually kerfed to reduce the tendency toward cupping (warping). The edge of the jamb is beveled slightly so the casing will fit snugly against it with no visible crack.

Side jambs are dadoed to receive the head jamb. The side jambs for residential doorways are made 6 ft. 9 in. long (measured to the head jamb). This provides clearance at the bottom of the door for flooring materials.

Modern door frames are usually cut, sanded, and fitted in millwork plants. This allows quick assembly on the job. Door frames should receive the same care in storage and handling as other finished woodwork.

Installation of interior door frames is similar to exterior door frames. Refer to the section on exterior door frames for more information.

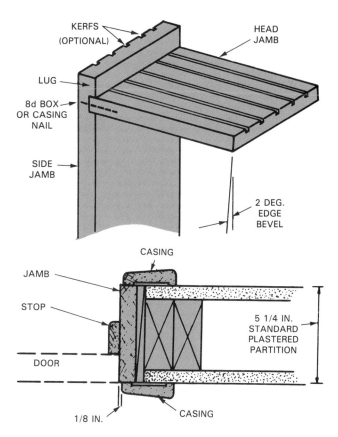

Fig. 30-33. Top. Section of interior door frame showing construction at junction of side and head jambs. Bottom. Section through side jamb of interior door.

## INTERIOR TRIM

Interior trim consists of decorative molding applied to window and door openings; intersections of walls, floors, and ceilings; and other structures such as mantels, cabinets, and stairs.

## MOLDINGS

Moldings are decorative wood or plastic strips designed for function as well as decoration. For example, window and door casings cover the space between the jamb and the wall covering. They also add strength to the installation.

Many types, sizes, and patterns of moldings are available for use in residential structures. Figs. 30-34 and 30-35 show several common moldings. Information on molding patterns, along with a numbering system and grading rules, is available from Western Wood Products Association, Portland, Oregon.

## WINDOW TRIM

Interior window trim consists of casing, stool, apron, and stops, Fig. 30-36. Millwork companies select and package the proper length trim members

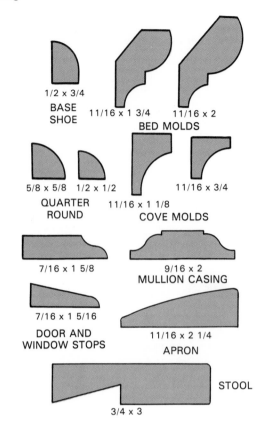

Fig. 30-35. Other typical molding patterns.

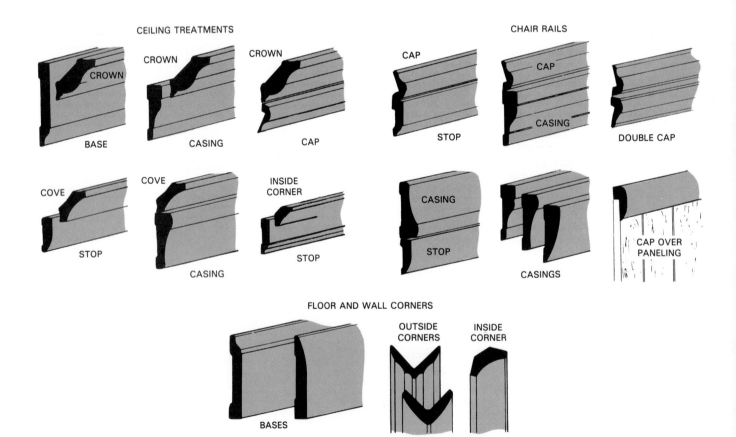

Fig. 30-34. Molding functions vary depending upon where they are used.    (Abitibi-Price Corp.)

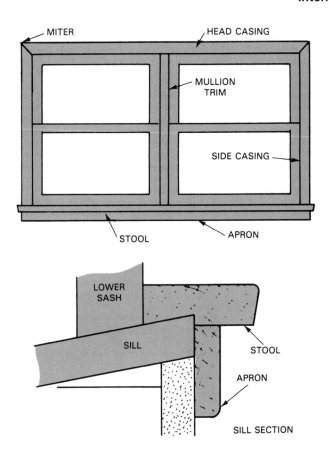

Fig. 30-36. Interior window trim.

Fig. 30-37. View of finished right-hand corner of window trim. Note nailing pattern especially for stool. Nail holes will be filled during finishing operations. Some carpenters nail the stool to the wall by toenailing it from underneath. This eliminates the nail hole.

to finish a given unit or combination of units.

The common procedure for trimming a window involves the following steps.

1.  Mark the stool for cutting by holding it level with the sill. Mark the inside edges of the side jambs and where it will fit against the wall.
2.  Cut the stool to size, checking for proper fit.
3.  After a light sanding, nail the stool in place.
4.  Install the side casings with the bottom against the stool. Be sure the miters are properly located and accurately cut.
5.  Measure and cut the apron to size. Its length is equal to the distance between the outside edges of the side casing, Fig. 30-37.

In some construction the stool and apron are sometimes eliminated. Instead, a piece of beveled sill liner is installed along with a standard piece of casing. This is commonly known as PICTURE FRAME trimming.

## BASEBOARD AND BASE SHOE

The BASEBOARD covers the joint between the wall surface and the finish flooring. It is among the last of the interior trim members to be installed since it must be fitted to the door casings and cabinetwork. BASE SHOE is used to seal the joint between

the baseboard and the finished floor, Fig. 30-38. It is usually fitted at the time the baseboard is installed but is not nailed in place until after surface finishes (lacquer, varnish, or paint) have been applied. Base shoe is often used to cover the edge of resilient tile or carpet.

Baseboards run continuously around the room between door openings, cabinets, and built-ins. The joints at internal corners should be coped. Those at outside corners are mitered. See Fig. 30-39.

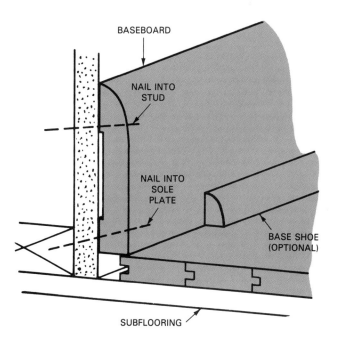

Fig. 30-38. Cutaway of baseboard and base shoe. They conceal the gap between flooring and finished wall.

521

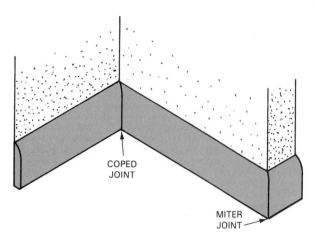

Fig. 30-39. Coped joints are suitable for inside corners; use mitered joint for outside corners.

Select and place the baseboard material around the sides of the room. Sort the pieces so there will be the least amount of cutting and waste. Where a straight run of baseboard must be joined, use a mitered-lap joint (also called a scarf joint). Be sure to locate the joint so it can be nailed over a stud.

## TEST YOUR KNOWLEDGE, Chapter 30

Please do not write in the text. Place your answers on a separate sheet of paper.

1. Heated or air-conditioned buildings should be _____ to maintain comfort and save energy.
2. Name and explain the four types of insulation used most often in residential construction.
3. What is reflective coat insulation?
4. With slab floors, the vapor barrier should cover the _____; insulation should cover the _____.
   a. Total floor area, perimeter.
   b. Perimeter, total floor area.
   c. Total floor area, total floor area.
   d. None of the above.
5. As what is gypsum wallboard commonly known?
6. How are hardboard and fiberboard produced?
7. _____ is a traditional wall and ceiling material.
   a. Solid wood paneling.
   b. Clay finishing.
   c. Plaster.
   d. None of the above.
8. When would you use a suspended ceiling?
9. Identify four types of finish flooring.
10. The four most popular synthetic fibers used in making carpets are _____, _____, _____, and _____.
11. What type of stairs have two parallel flights with a landing in between them?
12. List the three rules for calculating rise-run or riser-tread ratio.
13. What is nosing?
14. _____ doors are smooth on both sides and are usually made of wood.
15. _____ doors are a variation of the pocket door.
16. What is the purpose of adding trim around a door or window?

## ACTIVITIES

1. Visit your local building inspector and lumber company. Secure information and samples related to recommended amounts of insulation, proper installation, and R-values for various areas of the building structure. Prepare a comprehensive report on the subject and present your findings and samples to your class.
2. Collect samples of common wall and ceiling materials. Identify each one and explain its recommended use. Arrange the samples on a piece of plywood for display.
3. When applying moldings and trim, a coped joint is often used for inside corners. Secure information about this joint from reference books or visit with a carpenter. Prepare several sample joints.

Rigid polystyrene foam sheathing. Panels are 1 in. thick and 96 in. long. They have an R-value of 5.50.

The trim and molding used in this room set the mood for the space.     (NMC/Focal Point)

Post-and-beam construction opens up interior space by providing large spans that do not need support walls or posts.
(E.F. Bufton and Son)

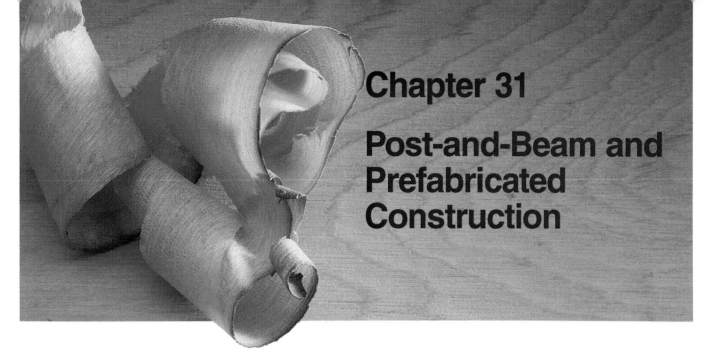

# Chapter 31

# Post-and-Beam and Prefabricated Construction

Post-and-beam construction uses large framing members—posts, beams, and planks, Fig. 31-1. They are spaced further apart than conventional framing members. Frames of this type are similar to mill construction which is used for barns and heavy timber buildings. It is used in residential construction because it permits greater flexibility than conventional framing methods, Fig. 31-2.

Post-and-beam construction is also known as PLANK-AND-BEAM construction. It is sometimes combined with conventional framing. For example, the walls may be built conventionally and the roof framed with beams and planks. In this case, the term plank-and-beam could be used to describe the roof structure. Similarly, it would be proper to refer to a floor structure as a plank-and-beam system.

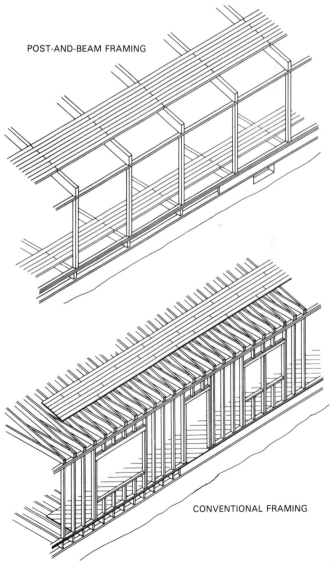

POST-AND-BEAM FRAMING

CONVENTIONAL FRAMING

Fig. 31-2. Comparison of typical post-and-beam framing and conventional framing. In post-and-beam construction, framing around large windows and doors is simplified since headers can be eliminated. (National Forest Products Association)

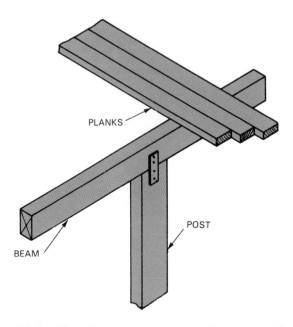

PLANKS

POST

BEAM

Fig. 31-1. The three components of post-and-beam construction.

## ADVANTAGES

Advantages of post-and-beam construction include the distinctive architectural effect created by the exposed beams in the ceiling and the added height, Fig. 31-3. The underside of the roof planks may serve as the ceiling surface thus providing a saving in material.

Post-and-beam framing may also provide some saving in labor. The pieces are larger, fewer in number, and can usually be assembled more rapidly than conventional framing.

One of the chief structural advantages is the simplicity of framing around door and window openings. Loads are carried by posts spaced at wide intervals in the walls. Large openings can be framed without the need for headers. Window walls, characteristic of contemporary architectural styling,

can be formed by merely inserting window frames between the posts. Another advantage is the wide overhangs that can be built by simply extending heavy roof beams.

Most limitations of post-and-beam construction can be resolved through careful planning. The plank floors, for example, are designed to carry moderate, uniform loads. Therefore, extra framing must be provided under bearing partitions and other places where heavy loads are likely to occur.

The framework, and especially the walls, must have good lateral stability. This can be provided with various types of bracing. It is more common, however, to enclose some of the wall area with large panels and use conventional stud construction. The installation of electrical wiring, plumbing, and heating is generally more difficult, since exterior wall panels are usually solid.

Fig. 31-3. An example of post-and-beam construction in a modern home. (California Redwood Association)

## FOUNDATIONS AND POSTS

Foundations for post-and-beam framing may consist of continuous walls or simple piers located under each post. Either type of foundation must rest on footings that meet the requirements of local building codes. Fig. 31-4 shows the front elevation of a post-and-beam building with footings indicated.

Posts must be strong enough to support the load and also large enough to provide full bearing surfaces for the ends of the beams. In general, posts should not be less than 4 x 4 in. nominal size. Where the ends of beams are joined over a post, the bearing surface should be increased with bearing blocks.

Distance between posts will be determined by the basic design of the structure and the size of materials used. This spacing must be carefully engineered. Usually posts are spaced evenly along the length of the building and within the allowable free span of the floor or roof planks. With the emphasis on modular dimensions, construction costs will be cheaper if post-and-beam positions occur at standard increments (multiples) of 16, 24, and 48 in.

In single-story construction, a plate is attached to the top of the posts in about the same way as conventional framing. The roof beams are then positioned directly over the posts as shown in Fig. 31-5.

## FLOOR BEAMS

Beams used for floor structures may be solid, laminated, steel reinforced, built-up, or box beams.

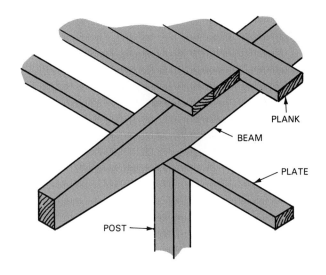

Fig. 31-5. Roof beams must rest directly over supporting posts.

See Fig. 31-6.

For one-story structures, where under-the-floor appearance is not critical, standard dimension lumber can be nailed together to form a large beam. Fig. 31-7 illustrates how 2 x 8s have been nailed together and then installed 4 ft. O.C. The decking being applied is 1 1/8 in. plywood with a special tongue-and-groove edge.

Design of sills for a plank-and-beam floor system can be similar to regular platform construction. When it is desirable to keep the silhouette of the structure low (floor level near grade level) the beams can be supported in pockets in the foundation wall.

In general, it is best to use solid timbers when

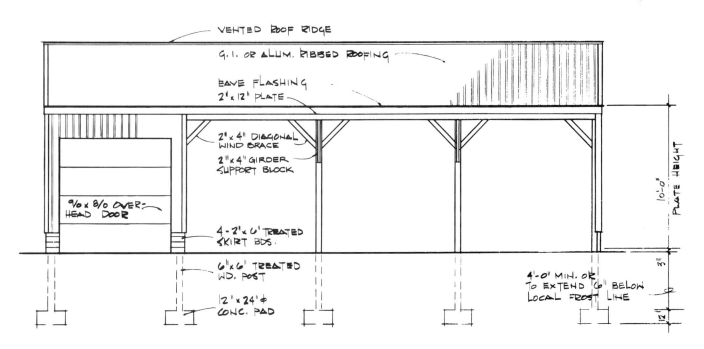

Fig. 31-4. Front elevation of a post-and-beam building which utilizes 6 x 6 in. treated posts and 24 x 24 x 12 in. footings. Footings are below the frost line. (National Plan Service, Inc.)

SOLID BEAM

HORIZONTAL
LAMINATED
BEAM

VERTICAL
LAMINATED
BEAM

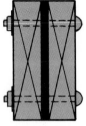
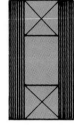

STEEL REINFORCED
BEAM

BOX BEAM

Fig. 31-6. A variety of beams used in post-and-beam construction.

## ROOF BEAMS

Two systems of beam placement are possible with post-and-beam roof construction:
1. Transverse beams that are similar to exposed rafters on wide spacing.
2. Longitudinal beams that run parallel to the supporting side walls and ridge beam. Fig. 31-8 shows both types.

LONGITUDINAL BEAMS, also called PURLIN BEAMS, are usually larger in cross section than transverse beams because they have greater spans and carry heavier loads. The longitudinal beam permits many variations in end-wall design. Extensive use of glass and extended roof overhangs are special features.

Both types of beam must be adequately supported either on posts or stud walls that incorporate a heavy top plate.

beam sizes are small and when a rustic architectural appearance is desired. Where high stress factors demand large sizes and a finished appearance is required, it is usually more economical to use laminated beams. They are manufactured in a wide range of sizes and finishes.

Solid timbers are available in several standard sizes beginning at 3 x 5 1/4 in. Lengths 6 ft. and longer in multiples of 2 ft. are also available.

Beam sizes must be based on the span (spacing between supports), deflection permitted, and the load they must carry. Design tables, available from lumber manufacturers, can be used to determine sizes for simple buildings.

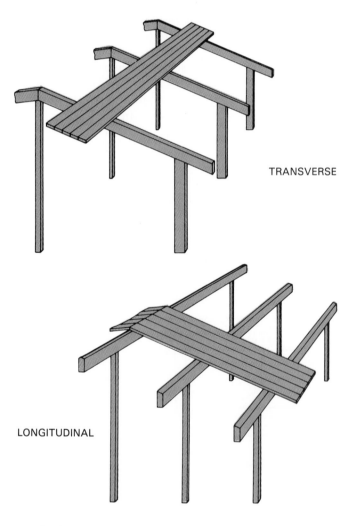

TRANSVERSE

LONGITUDINAL

Fig. 31-8. Top. Roof beams follow the roof slope and decking runs parallel to the roof ridge in transverse post-and-beam construction. Bottom. The roof beams are perpendicular to the roof slope in longitudinal post-and-beam construction. Planks are parallel to the roof slope.

Fig. 31-7. Laying 1 1/8 in. plywood with tongue-and-groove edge joints on beams spaced 4 ft. O.C. (American Plywood Association)

## FASTENERS

A post-and-beam frame consists of a limited number of joints. Therefore, the loads and forces exerted upon the structure are concentrated at these points. Regular nailing patterns used in conventional framing will usually not provide a satisfactory connection. Joints will need to be reinforced with special joints or metal connectors, Fig. 31-9. To increase the holding power of metal connectors, they should be attached with lag screws or bolts.

When connectors detract from the appearance of the structure, one or more alternatives may be considered. Concealed connectors, Fig. 31-10, or decorative fasteners can be used. Notches or gains can be cut in the structural members to provide the required anchorage or recess for the connector.

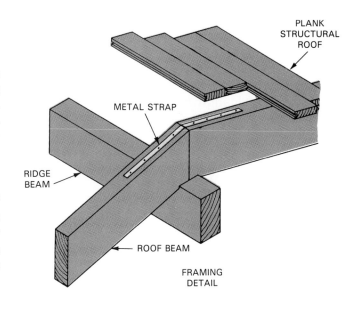

Fig. 31-10. The metal strap connector is hidden under the roof planks.

## PLANKS

Planks for floor and roof decking can be from 2 to 4 in. thick depending on the span. Edges may be tongue-and-groove or grooved for a spline joint that can be assembled into a tight, strong surface. Fig. 31-11 illustrates standard designs. When planks are end-matched, the joints need not meet over beams.

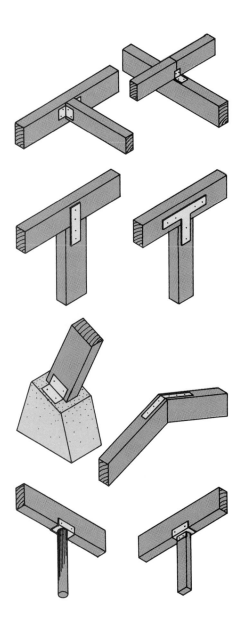

Fig. 31-9. Typical metal fasteners used to connect large beam segments.

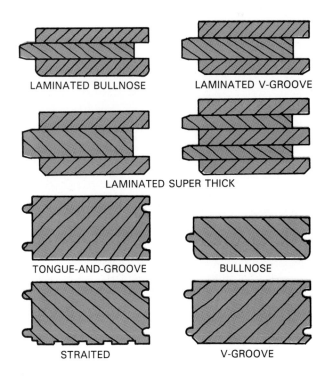

Fig. 31-11. Several plank designs produced commercially for use in post-and-beam construction.

Planks are stronger and stiffer if they continue over more than one span. This is also true of beams and other supports.

Roof planks should be selected carefully, especially when the faces will be exposed. Fig. 31-12 shows the application of planking with a V-joint along the edge.

In cold climates, plank roof structures located directly over heated areas require insulation and a vapor barrier. Thickness of the insulation will depend on the climate. The insulation should be a rigid type that will support the finished roof surface and workers. An approved vapor barrier should be installed between the planks and the insulation as shown in Fig. 31-13.

Several types of heavy structural composition board, 2 to 4 in. thick, are available for roof decks. The panel sizes are large, and the material is lightweight. Edges usually have some type of interlocking joint that provides a tight, smooth deck. When the underside (ceiling side) is prefinished, no further decoration is usually necessary. Always follow the manufacturer's recommendations when selecting and installing these materials.

## PREFABRICATED CONSTRUCTION

Prefabricated construction refers to cutting and assembling parts or sections in a factory. Prefabrication also refers to buildings that are partially or completely erected in the plant, Fig. 31-14.

Some of the advantages of prefabricated construction include uniform quality, more efficient use of materials, lower cost, stronger parts, and reduced

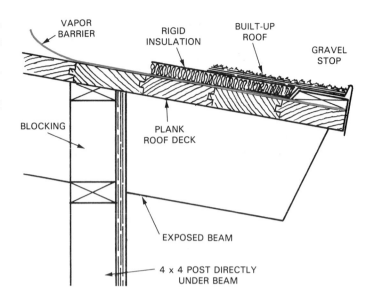

Fig. 31-13. Cross section shows application of vapor barrier and insulation to a plank decking. This type of covering is necessary when the deck is located directly over heated space.

installation time. Special handling equipment, precise measurements, and engineered construction account for the increased quality in prefabricated construction.

## FACTORY-BUILT COMPONENTS

Many components used in the construction of a modern dwelling are factory-built. Examples include windows, doors, soffit systems, stairs, cabinet units, and fireplace units.

Fig. 31-12. Laying 4 in. double tongue-and-groove planks on laminated beams.

Fig. 31-14. This factory-built home is a prime example of good quality and design which applies the principles of modular construction. (Scholz Homes, Inc.)

Framing components which are frequently factory-built are roof and floor trusses. These units must be carefully designed by structural engineers and built according to exact specification if they are to perform as desired. Special presses and jig tables are used to assemble the truss parts into a rigid structure, Fig. 31-15.

Wall and roof panels are factory-built in a wide variety of standard sizes and types. Panels provide structural strength in addition to forming inside and outside surfaces. Curved stressed-skin panels constructed of lumber ribs and plywood surfaces are shown in Fig. 31-16.

## PREFABRICATED BUILDINGS

There are four basic types of prefabricated dwellings: precut, panelized, sectionalized, and mobile home. Combinations of these are also used.

In a PRECUT HOME, the parts are cut to size,

numbered, packaged, and shipped to the building site for assembly and erection. Precut homes usually only include the materials needed to form the basic structure of the building and prefabricated items such as windows, doors, stairs, and cabinets. However, some manufacturers will supply a complete package.

Large panels for all flat sections of the structure are provided in PANELIZED HOMES. These sections are produced on production lines where the frame members are cut and fastened together, Fig. 31-17, with pneumatic nailers. Plumbing, wiring, and insulation may be installed as well as windows and doors, Fig. 31-18. Roof panels are made much the same as wall panels for post-and-beam construction or panelized wall structures designed to use them. Panels which form both the roof and ceiling can be painted before erection. Floor panels are also manufactured, but the first floor deck is generally

Fig. 31-15. This hydraulic press, with 40 ton capacity, is being used to install connectors in a flat girder truss 60 ft. long.

Fig. 31-16. Installing curved stressed-skin panels which copy some effects of vaulted ceilings.

Fig. 31-19. This kitchen module is being lifted into place. Other walls of the house will be located around it. Note the dishwasher, sink, and lighting fixtures have been installed.

Fig. 31-17. Wall panels under construction on a production line.

built by conventional methods.

Entire sections of SECTIONALIZED or MODULAR HOMES are built and finished in manufacturing plants. The complete kitchen shown in Fig. 31-19 is an example of a module. Other types of modules are even larger than the kitchen module. Widths up to 14 ft. wide and lengths up to 60 ft. are common in sectionalized units.

Most of the finish carpentry work can be completed in sectionalized construction at the factory. Walls, floors, and ceilings can be finished and built-in features installed. This is an advantage because close control can be exercised at the factory.

Fig. 31-18. A prefabricated wall panel is lifted into place. Notice that the electrical outlets, heating units, trim and wall finish have already been applied.

Fig. 31-20. A sectionalized module being lifted into place using a powerful crane. The module is essentially complete with electrical work, plumbing, heating, and interior finish installed at the factory. (American Plywood Association)

Fig. 31-22. Wooden floor frame is attached to steel chassis. Floor must be fully insulated. Note plumbing and electrical lines. (Redman Industries, Inc.)

Disadvantages of sectionalized prefabrication include: storage problems for these large units, transportation to the site, and need for large equipment to lift the units into place, Fig. 31-20.

MOBILE HOMES are totally complete housing units which are mounted on a chassis, Fig. 31-21. They do not require extensive site work or typical foundation. Common widths include 12 and 14 ft. Lengths up to 68 ft. are produced.

A welded steel chassis with a wood frame attached is typical floor construction, Fig. 31-22. Production methods used for standard prefabricated housing are used for walls and ceiling construction of mobile homes.

Fig. 31-21. Exploded view of a mobile home. All structural members above the steel chassis are wood. Plywood deck is securely screwed to floor frame which is assembled with glue. Outside walls consist of 2 x 3 studs with 1 x 2 horizontal rails glued in place. Inside surface is 3/16 in. prefinished plywood. Prepainted aluminum panels cover outside. (Redman Industries, Inc.)

## TEST YOUR KNOWLEDGE, Chapter 31

Please do not write in the text. Place your answers on a separate sheet of paper.

1. The three elements of post-and-beam construction are _____, _____, and _____.
2. Name three advantages of post-and-beam construction.
3. What two types of foundations are frequently used for post-and-beam construction?
4. Beams used for floor structures may be:
   a. Solid.
   b. Box.
   c. Built-up.
   d. All of the above.
5. Where high stress factors demand large sizes and a finished appearance is required, _____ beams are usually used.
6. Identify the two systems of beam placement in post-and-beam roof construction.
7. List two advantages of prefabricated construction.
8. Identify and briefly explain the four types of prefabricated dwellings.

## ACTIVITIES

1. Inquire at a local lumber company about sizes of timber and planks for post-and-beam construction. Report your findings to the class.
2. Build a typical section from the footing to the ridge of a post-and-beam structure. Use 1 in. = 1 ft. scale. Be sure to cut each piece to actual size. Label the parts and display your model.
3. Secure literature on prefabricated construction. Try to include examples of the four basic types: precut, panelized, sectionalized, and mobile home. Assemble the literature in a folder and make it available to the class.

Left. This construction represented a type of post-and-beam construction. (Boise-Cascade Corp.) Right. Heavy-duty joist hangers are used to attach members to a large supporting beam. (Boise-Cascase Corp.)

Sectionalized (modular) home being placed on its foundation. Each module is completely finished inside and out. (American Plywood Association)

Insulated sandwich panels are being used to form the roof of this large home.   (AFM Corporation)

Left. Patternmaker completing work on original wood pattern for an engine block. View shows a special tool being used to form a fillet around the base of a core print. Right. Patternmaker inspecting metal core box for an air-cooled engine head. Sample core is shown in foreground. Workers in background are checking full-sized pattern drawings. (Lear Siegler)

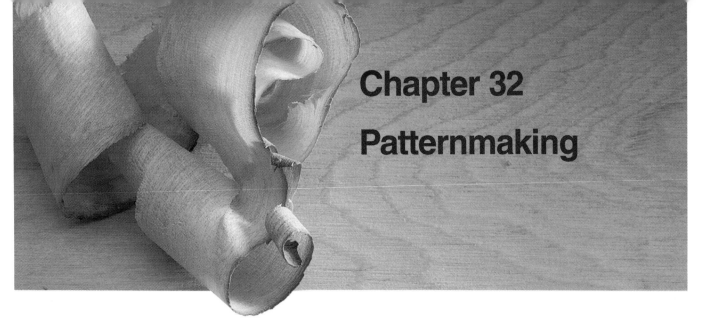

# Chapter 32
# Patternmaking

Patternmaking is the building and construction of models and forms (patterns) that are used in the foundry to make metal castings. Production work and automatic molding machines require metal patterns. However, wood is nearly always used to make the original or master patterns from which these metal patterns are produced, Fig. 32-1.

The knowledge and skills that you have gained in woodworking can be applied to this important area of work. Some of the first decorative patterns that you are likely to make (wall plaques, candlesticks, trays, etc.) will not require great attention to size. However, as you progress to advanced projects involving patterns of machine parts, you will need to work to exact dimensions. Patternmaking requires the highest level of accuracy.

Fig. 32-1. Patternmaker at work in plant that manufactures valves and controls for liquids and gases. The work of the patternmaker requires the highest level of accuracy of any of the woodworking trades. (Fisher Controls)

## THE MOLDING PROCESS

Patternmakers must be skillful, and have a broad knowledge of woodworking tools and materials. They must also understand foundry methods and procedures. Fig. 32-2 shows a sequence of basic steps that are followed in making a sand mold using a simple pattern.

The mold is made in a FLASK, which is either a wood or metal frame. It consists of two sections that are aligned with pins and sockets. The lower section contains the pins and is called the DRAG. The upper section is called the COPE. The separation between the two is called the PARTING. Complicated patterns may require additional sections (CHEEK FLASKS) between the cope and drag.

After placing the pattern on the molding board, it is dusted with a PARTING COMPOUND so that it will be easy to DRAW (remove) from the mold. Parting compound is also dusted over the drag before the cope is rammed so the two sections will not stick together.

The SPRUE PIN is used to make a hole in the cope. The metal is poured through this into the mold. The RISER PIN forms a hole for the metal to rise into when the mold is full. It permits air to escape from the mold and may absorb some of the shrinkage when the metal cools. The vent holes also allow air, steam, and gases to escape as the metal is poured.

The sprue and riser pins are removed from the cope and then the cope is carefully lifted from the drag. Sand along the edges of the pattern is swabbed (moistened) to make it firm. The pattern is rapped lightly to loosen it in the mold and then carefully drawn. Gates (channels) are made in the drag so the metal can flow from the sprue hole into the mold cavity and from the cavity to the riser. Cores, if required, are placed in the mold and loose sand particles are blown away. The cope is then returned to its position on the drag.

## SHRINKAGE, FINISH, AND DRAFT

When metal changes from a liquid to a solid state it contracts, or shrinks. The pattern, therefore, must be made oversize by an amount equal to this shrinkage. The amount of SHRINKAGE ALLOWANCE varies with the kind of metal or alloy, and the size of and shape of the casting. Application of these standard shrinkage allowances may vary, depending on the nature of the work being done.

The patternmaker uses a special shrink rule, Fig. 32-3. It is made slightly longer than a standard rule to compensate for the metal shrinkage. Shrink rules are available in a range of sizes to provide various allowances. In working with a shrink rule, select one that corresponds to the requirement of the casting for which the pattern is being made, then use it in the same way as a regular rule.

Castings for machine parts, especially those that will fit into assemblies, are machined to form smooth and accurate surfaces. Machining operations require extra metal in the casting. This FINISH ALLOWANCE must be added to the pattern. Finished surfaces of a part are designated on the working drawing by a V symbol on the edge view. The kind and quality of the machine operations is often specified with numbers and notes.

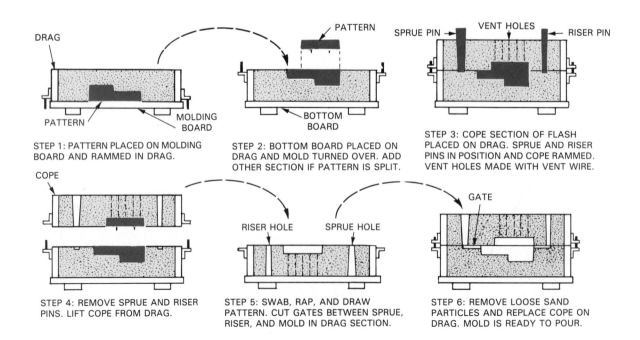

STEP 1: PATTERN PLACED ON MOLDING BOARD AND RAMMED IN DRAG.

STEP 2: BOTTOM BOARD PLACED ON DRAG AND MOLD TURNED OVER. ADD OTHER SECTION IF PATTERN IS SPLIT.

STEP 3: COPE SECTION OF FLASH PLACED ON DRAG. SPRUE AND RISER PINS IN POSITION AND COPE RAMMED. VENT HOLES MADE WITH VENT WIRE.

STEP 4: REMOVE SPRUE AND RISER PINS. LIFT COPE FROM DRAG.

STEP 5: SWAB, RAP, AND DRAW PATTERN. CUT GATES BETWEEN SPRUE, RISER, AND MOLD IN DRAG SECTION.

STEP 6: REMOVE LOOSE SAND PARTICLES AND REPLACE COPE ON DRAG. MOLD IS READY TO POUR.

Fig. 32-2. Steps for making a mold.

Fig. 32-3. A shrink rule (top) compared with a standard rule (bottom). This 9/32 size provides double shrinkage allowance, when building a master pattern from which an aluminum alloy pattern will be made for the production of a cast iron part.

The amount of finish allowance depends on the size and quality of the casting, the kind of metal, and the method of machining. General finish allowances may vary from 1/16 in. on small brass castings to 1/2 in. on large cast iron parts. Small aluminum castings produced in the school shop usually require about 1/8 in. finish allowance. Top surfaces of castings require greater finish allowances than bottom surfaces because slag and impurities will normally rise to the top of the mold.

DRAFT is the slant or taper formed on the vertical surfaces of the pattern so that it can be easily drawn from the mold, Fig. 32-4. Normal draft allowance is approximately one degree or 1/8 in. per ft., but additional amounts may be required when the surface is large or the wood grain runs in a horizontal direction. Additional draft must also be provided on the internal surfaces of recesses and pockets, especially if they are located in a position where the sand of the cope is lifted out when the mold is separated to remove the pattern.

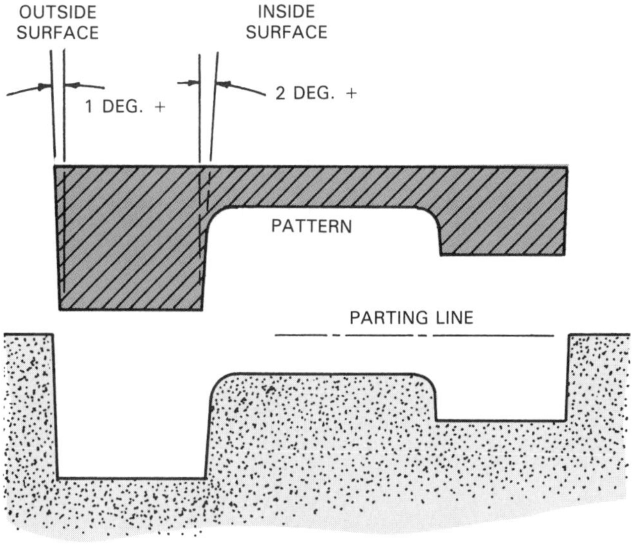

## MATERIALS AND TOOLS

Woods generally used for patternmaking are white pine, sugar pine, and mahogany. These are durable, stable, and have good working qualities. Patterns that will be subjected to hard usage or require extensive lathe work are often made of cherry wood. It is best to use plywood or laminated stock for large pieces that might warp if made of solid material.

Standard woodworking hand tools and machines are satisfactory for patternmaking. A spindle sander and disk sander are valuable for shaping parts and applying draft to inside and outside curves. Additional hand tools and supplies include shrink rules, fillet irons, brass dowels, rapping plates, metal letters and figures, and fillet material, Fig. 32-5.

## LAYOUTS

Some patterns can be produced by simply following the dimensions given on the working drawing. When the part is complicated and includes finish allowances and coring, it is best to make a full-size layout on cardboard or a wood layout board. This layout is then referred to for shapes and sizes during the construction of the pattern.

The patternmaker uses a soft pine layout board as shown in Fig. 32-6. Dimensions are laid out with a shrink rule and lines are cut into the surface with a knife and dividers. These lines are often traced with a sharp pencil to make them more readable. The edges of the board should be straight and true so squares can be used to lay out lines in the same

Fig. 32-4. Draft on the vertical surfaces of a pattern permits easy removal from the mold.

Fig. 32-5. Pattern letters and figures are used for identification purposes. Some have spurs or pins that are driven into the wood. Those with a plain back are cemented in place.

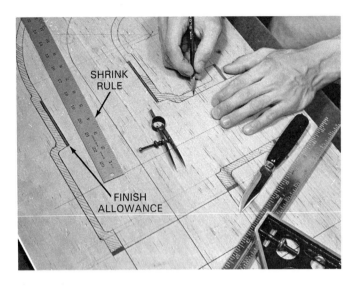

Fig. 32-6. Making a full-size drawing of the pattern on a layout board.

manner that a T-square is used on a drawing board. Sectional views are usually most valuable. Symmetrical parts may require only a half view. Details, such as spotfacing, milled slots, or drilled holes are not included in the layout.

A standard procedure to follow when making a pattern layout is shown in Fig. 32-7. It may include all or part of the following steps:

1. Determine the position of the pattern in the mold and select the parting line. Consider what coring will be required.

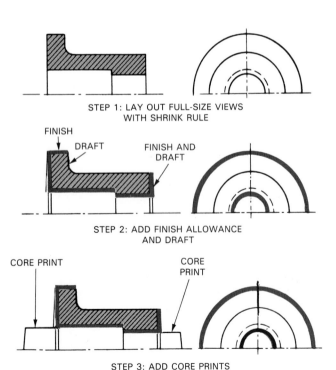

STEP 1: LAY OUT FULL-SIZE VIEWS WITH SHRINK RULE

FINISH
DRAFT
FINISH AND DRAFT

STEP 2: ADD FINISH ALLOWANCE AND DRAFT

CORE PRINT
CORE PRINT

STEP 3: ADD CORE PRINTS

Fig. 32-7. Procedure for making a pattern layout.

2. Lay out the exact shape and size of the part with a shrink rule.
3. Add finish allowances. Colored lines will help define these additions.
4. Add draft.
5. Lay out cored areas not already shown and add core prints.
6. Draw curves not included in the layout that may be needed for templates or checking the work.

## CONSTRUCTING THE PATTERN

Study the work carefully to determine the easiest and best procedure to follow. Most patterns are built by assembling separate pieces, rather than shaping them from solid stock. Segment and stave construction is used for large patterns that have circular or curved contours.

Start with the main parts and then add ribs, webs, bosses, and other details. Run the grain in the direction of the greatest length to minimize dimensional change in the pattern. When possible, form the draft on the parts by planing, sawing, or sanding before they are assembled. Check the parts by placing them directly on the layout board. Finish sand exposed surfaces before assembly, being careful to maintain true surfaces and accurate sizes.

Draw fine lines on the parts to show assembly points and glue them together. Check the work with squares and rules, Fig. 32-8. Some parts may need to be clamped or held with brads, but most parts can be set carefully in place and not handled until the glue has hardened, Fig. 32-9.

FILLETS and ROUNDS add to the strength and appearance of a casting, Fig. 32-10. Fillets also eliminate sharp corners in the mold that would otherwise "wash-off" when the metal was poured. Most rounded corners and edges are formed on parts before assembly, while fillets are added after assembly. Wax fillet stock is available. It is

Fig. 32-8. Assembling a pattern with glue.

Fig. 32-9. Final work on pattern in an industrial plant. A patternmaker must be highly skilled in the use of hand tools. (Fisher Controls)

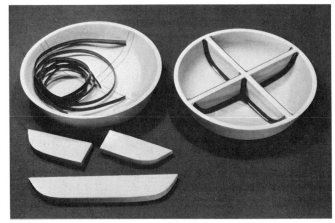

Fig. 32-11. Leather fillets applied to a one-piece pattern for a small-parts tray. Since the cope sand will extend down inside the pattern, the separating ribs must have considerable draft.

pressed into the corners and shaped with a hot fillet iron. Leather fillets are more durable than wax fillets and are available in various sizes. See Fig. 32-11. They are glued in place and smoothed with a cold fillet iron.

Many pattern shops use a fine grade of acetone base plastic wood for fillets. The material is formed into a roll of the required size, placed in the corner, and shaped with a regular fillet iron, Fig. 32-12. The fillet iron is dipped into lacquer thinner to keep the material from sticking to it and to help form a smooth fillet. Brushing a coat of lacquer thinner into the corner before applying the plastic wood may cause it to adhere better. After the fillet has hardened, it is sanded with fine abrasive paper.

When turning patterns on the lathe, fillets can be easily formed along with the required shape.

After the pattern is assembled, fillets are installed, and a final check is made of sizes, draft, and other allowances, the pattern should be lightly sanded and finished. Lacquers are used more extensively than shellac because lacquers are more durable and dry rapidly. A sealer coat should be applied and sanded, and then a final coat applied and rubbed smooth, so the pattern can be easily withdrawn from the mold.

Color coding of the various parts and surfaces is good practice. In the past, black was generally used to denote unfinished surfaces and the faces of core boxes. A new code recommends black for core prints and core areas while unfinished surfaces are given a clear coating. Red is always used to identify machined surfaces.

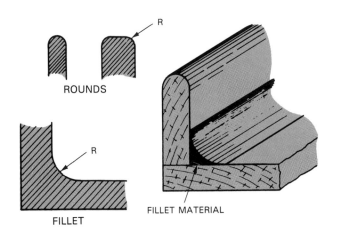

Fig. 32-10. Fillets and rounds are specified by the radius size.

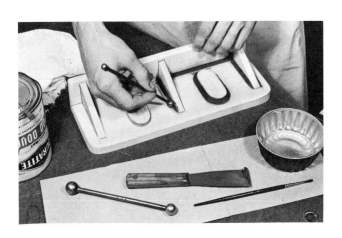

Fig. 32-12. Using a special plastic wood for fillet material. It is smoothed with a fillet iron dipped in lacquer thinner.

## SPLIT PATTERNS

Some patterns will need to be made in two parts, with one section located in the drag and the other in the cope. The dividing line or split is located at the parting line of the mold.

Cylindrical patterns that are turned on the lathe are usually designed in this way. Fig. 32-13 shows a sequence of steps to follow when constructing and turning a split pattern. The two sections are squared to size and wood or brass dowel pins are installed on the mating surfaces. The dowels must be tapered and carefully fitted so the parts will be held in proper alignment. Provide just enough clearance so easy separation can be made.

The two parts are then fastened together. Either corrugated fasteners or screws may be used. Glue may also be used in just the area of the waste stock. Center the piece carefully, so the parting line will be along the center of turning. After turning the main body to rough size, a recess is cut to receive the blocks that will form the flange. These blocks are first cut to size and then clamped together for

Fig. 32-14. Metal split pattern for production work. The flanges and core prints of the master wood pattern were turned as separate units and then attached to the main body. Metal core box is shown in background. (Fisher Controls)

boring of the center hole. Next they are glued in place and, after the glue has set, the turning is completed. Be sure the parting lines are properly aligned. See Fig. 32-14 for an example of a metal split pattern.

## CORES AND CORE PRINTS

Recesses, large holes, cavities, and interiors of castings are formed with cores, Fig. 32-15. Dry sand mixed with a special binder is formed in core boxes and then baked in an oven. Wire is often used to reinforce cores that are large and complicated. Cores made from a mixture of sand, water glass,

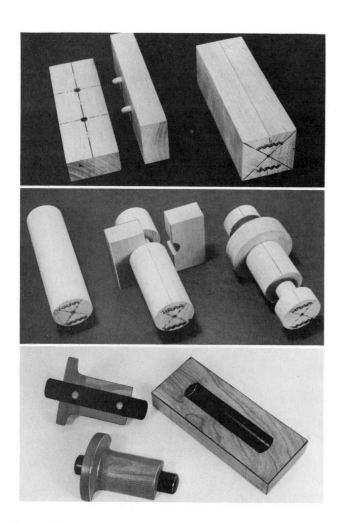

Fig. 32-13. Top. Preparation of stock for a split pattern. Center. Turning sequence. Bottom. Finished pattern and core box.

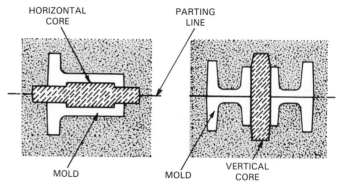

Fig. 32-15. Cores are used to form the interior of castings.

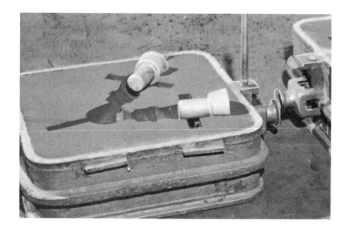

Fig. 32-16. Cores in position in the drag. Note that these particular cores are supported on only one end. (Fisher Controls)

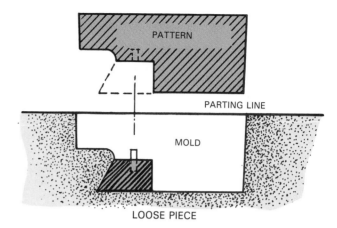

Fig. 32-18. A pattern with a loose piece. The main section of the pattern is drawn from the mold and then the loose piece is removed separately. Loose pieces can be held in place with pins, dowels, or dovetailed slots.

and carbon dioxide gas are satisfactory and require no baking. Simple cylindrical cores are available in various diameters and are used for production. The patternmaker designs the work to take advantage of stock sizes whenever possible.

CORE PRINTS are the projections added to patterns which make the impressions in the mold to seat and carry the core. The length and diameter of the core print depends on the size and weight of the core. The length of horizontal core prints for cores over 1 in. in diameter is usually equal to the diameter of the core. Core prints under 1 in. in diameter are maintained at a length of from 3/4 to 1 in. Horizontal cores are sometimes supported at only one end, Fig. 32-16, and it is then r ecessary to make the core print quite large to provide balance. Also see Figs. 32-17 and 32-18.

Vertical cores can be set in impressions made by core prints located in the drag. When these are anchored in both parts of the mold, the top, or cope end, of the core print and core are tapered 10-15 deg. This insures that the core can be easily aligned with the impression when the mold is closed. Vertical core prints, located in the cope, are often loose

so they can be removed while the drag section is being rammed.

## CORE BOXES

Fig. 32-19 shows a simple cylindrical core box and finished core. The box is rammed with the sand mixture and "dumped" to form a half core. After identical halves are baked they are bonded together with a flour paste to form the completed core. A complete core is formed in a single ramming by using a split core box, Fig. 32-20.

Plain cylindrical core boxes can be roughed out on the table saw as shown in Fig. 32-21. A diagonal fence guides the stock over the saw blade. The angle can be determined by raising the blade to the required depth, then setting the fence or guide strip at an angle that will provide twice this distance between the front and back edge of the blade. The cut is made by lowering the blade to about 1/8 in. above the table and making a pass over the machine. Additional passes are then made, raising the blade about 1/8 in. each time. This method forms an elliptical shape which must then be sanded

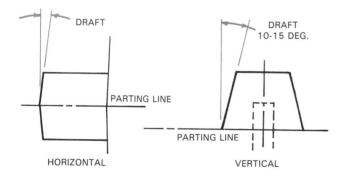

Fig. 32-17. Proportion and draft for cylindrical or rectangular core prints. Length of vertical core print is seldom over 1 in. (25.4 mm) even though cross section is large.

Fig. 32-19. Core box and dry sand core.

Fig. 32-20. Gear blank pattern and core box. The split core box is made by first setting the dowels and then clamping the pieces together to drill the hole.

Fig. 32-23. Patternmaker prepares a core box for the split pattern shown on the bench. Note the special type of vise that will clamp and support the workpiece in a variety of positions. (Fisher Controls)

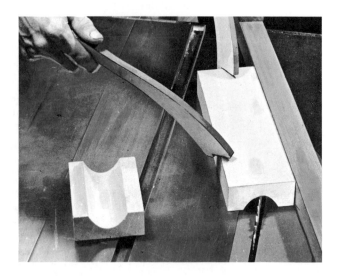

Fig. 32-21. Roughing out a core box on the table saw. Always set the guide strip so the thrust of the blade will be toward it. Be sure to have your instructor check the setup before turning on the machine.

finished outside dimensions. The required half-circles are then cut in each piece, after which the assembly is made. This same procedure can be applied to core boxes with internal shapes that are rectangular.

## MATCH PLATES

For production work in industry, patterns are mounted on metal plates, Fig. 32-24, which fit over the flask pins. They are called match plates because

to a half circle with a round form. An inside ground gauge of the correct size can also be used.

Cylindrical core boxes that include several diameters are made in layers, Figs. 32-22 and 32-23. The stock for each layer is first cut to

Fig. 32-22. This split core box forms a core with several different diameters. Note the brass dowel pins.

Fig. 32-24. A wood pattern mounted on a match plate. (Fisher Controls)

the two parts of a split pattern are mounted on each side in alignment, so the impressions in the cope and drag "match" after the pattern is drawn and the mold is closed.

In the school shop, the plate can be made of plywood. Fig. 32-25 shows a match plate for casting an anvil paperweight. To align the halves of the pattern, first drill two holes all the way through the pattern. Then use one of the halves to guide the bit for drilling the plate. Be sure to keep the bit perpendicular to the parting line. Insert dowel into the holes to align and hold the pattern. Gates,

runners, and impressions for sprue and riser pins are included on the plate.

For production work, multiple or gang patterns can be mounted on a single plate, Fig. 32-26. One-piece patterns can also be mounted on plates. This usually saves time in molding, especially if gates, runners, and sprue recesses are included.

Fig. 32-27 shows a multiple pattern match plate used for high volume production. The master pattern is made of wood and used to form the sand mold in the conventional way. The cope and drag are then separated by an appropriate amount, the edges are enclosed, and the mold poured. Gates and risers are included in the casting process. The master pattern must be built with double-shrink allowances; shrinkage for the metal pattern and shrinkage of the final casting.

Fig. 32-25. Match plate for casting an anvil paperweight as shown at bottom of photo.

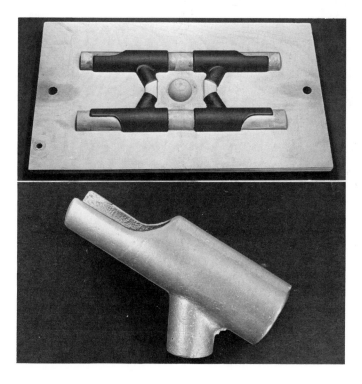

Fig. 32-26. Top. Multiple unit match plate for fishing rod holders. Bottom. Sample casting.

Fig. 32-27. Top. Master pattern of a flanged housing for a thrust bearing. Bottom. Metal match plate ready for the foundry. (Woodland Pattern Co.)

## TEST YOUR KNOWLEDGE, Chapter 32

Please do not write in the text. Place your answers on a separate sheet of paper.

1. A standard flask consists of two parts: the _____ and _____.
2. What is used to make the hole in the cope?
   a. Parting compound.
   b. Riser pin.
   c. Sprue pin.
   d. None of the above.
3. When molten metal cools and changes to a solid it _____ (expands, contracts) slightly.
4. Small aluminum castings usually require about how much finish allowance?
5. Does an internal or external surface include a greater amount of draft?
6. Name three types of wood most commonly used for patternmaking.
7. When should a layout board be used?
8. Most rounded corners and edges are formed on parts _____ assembly, while fillets are formed _____ assembly.
9. What is the difference between a core and a core print?
10. What are match plates?

## ACTIVITIES

1. Prepare a list of patternmaking and foundry terms. Include a definition of each.
2. Select a working drawing of a cast machine part from an advanced drafting book. Make a full-size drawing, following the procedure suggested for pattern layouts. Include finish allowances, draft, coring, and core prints. Prepare a written description of the procedure you would follow in the construction of the pattern and core boxes.

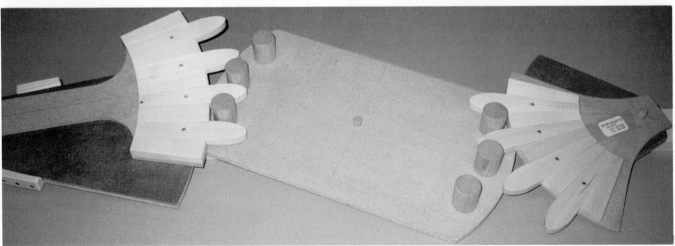

A full-size model of gears used to check for proper tooth shape. The gears will be used in a restored grist mill.    (Mark Clauss)

Finished casting of a valve body (center) surrounded by master and production patterns used in the foundry process.
(Fisher Controls)

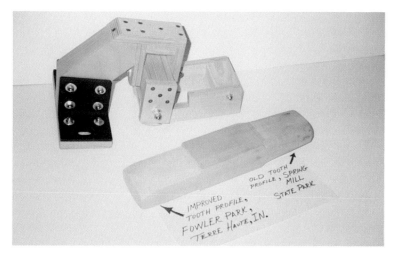

Grist mill gear tooth profiling fixture and trial gear blank.   (Mark Clauss)

Finish sanding a vanity with a portable orbital disk sander. (Campbellrhea Mfg., Inc.)

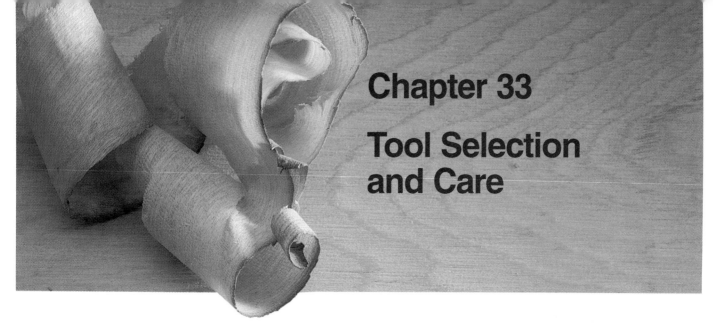

# Chapter 33

# Tool Selection and Care

The purpose of this chapter is to provide some assistance in the selection and care of common hand and power tools used in the home or school shop. A short section on setting up your own workshop is also included.

Tool selection is largely determined by the intended use of the tool or machine. For example, one who wishes to purchase a scroll saw for the primary purpose of cutting veneers for marquetry might very likely select a different machine than one who plans to cut complex shapes from 2 in. thick stock. Most quality scroll saws would perform either operation with ease, but each machine generally has features that give it a slight edge for certain operations. In addition, hand or power tool selection should include the best quality that can be afforded. Gadgets, accessories, or sales talk will not substitute for basic quality in work, design, and materials.

## HAND TOOLS

Hand tools can perform the same operations that portable power tools or stationary machines can perform. Most any woodworking project can be built using hand tools. Select quality hand tools and learn to use them well.

## HAMMERS

Selecting a quality hammer is just as important as choosing the proper hammer for a given task. The face of the head should be slightly convex and smooth. The convex shape permits nails to be driven flush with the surface without marring. Be sure to select the proper weight hammer. Hammer weight is based on the head weight. A 7 ounce hammer is common for light work. For general carpentry and woodworking use 13, 16, and 20 ounce hammers. The head should be drop-forged steel rather than brittle cast iron. Also, ''rim-tempering'' of the face reduces the chance of chipping. The handle should be comfortable, durable,

and securely attached to the head. Quality handles are available in steel, wood, and fiberglass. Examine the tool for quality and handle it to test for comfort and balance.

A quality hammer will last a lifetime when used properly and given reasonable care, Fig. 33-1. Do not use the hammer for jobs for which it was not intended. For example, never strike with the side

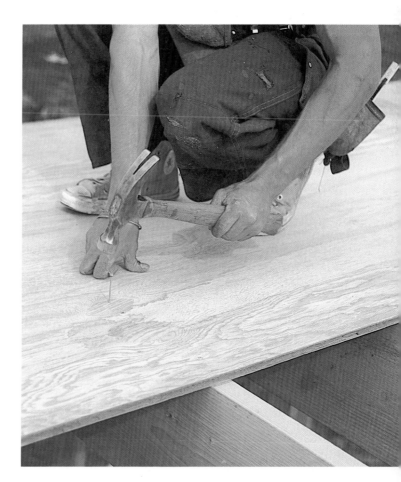

Fig. 33-1. The curved claw nail hammer is the most used tool on the construction site. (American Plywood Association)

of the head and do not hit anything harder than the face of the hammer. These practices may very likely damage the tool. Use a block under the head to provide added leverage on long nails. Do not try to pull very large nails that should be pulled with a wrecking bar. Do not store a hammer in a damp location. Excessive humidity causes a wood handle to swell, crushing the wood fibers and loosening the head. Excessive humidity may also cause the head to rust, unless coated with a light coat of oil. Extreme dryness shrinks wood handles, causing looseness.

## SAWS

Several types of saws are commonly used in a home and/or school shop: hand saws, backsaws, coping saws, and compass saws.

A quality hand saw should feel comfortable in your hand, Fig. 33-2. The teeth should be precision-ground to sharp points or to a sharp chisel edge in the case of a rip saw. The set should be uniform for making smooth, straight cuts. The number of teeth per inch will depend on the application. Choose a hand saw made from quality steel that is tough and durable, so it will hold an edge. The handle should be made from a hardwood, such as beech, and designed to fit the hand. The handle, frame, and any attachments must be secure.

Most of the considerations for choosing a hand saw apply to backsaws. However, the blade should not be taper ground because an absolutely rigid blade is needed.

Coping saw blades must be kept under high tension for accurate sawing. Blade attachment mechanisms should be simple, dependable, and provide for cutting in various positions.

The compass or keyhole saw has a tapered blade for cutting curves or starting from a bored hole. The same quality considerations used in selecting a hand saw apply to compass saws—quality steel, comfortable handle, and precision-ground teeth. In addition, the blade should be relatively stiff since it is narrower and may bend if too flexible.

As with any tool, never use a saw for any task for which it was not intended. Store it carefully to protect the cutting edge and prevent bending. Keep it out of high-moisture areas. Coat the blade with a light film of oil to prevent rust. This should be removed before use. Keep the blade clean and clear of pitch. Be sure nails and other metal fasteners are not in the cutting path, as this will damage the teeth. Keep the blade sharp and all connections secure. Hang up the saw when not in use, preferably in a cabinet. Never allow other tools to come in contact with the blade.

## CHISELS

A good chisel is nicely balanced, properly designed for the intended work, and holds an edge for a long time, Fig. 33-3.

Look for quality materials and construction. A new chisel should not require grinding before it can be used. Quality chisels are generally thicker at the shoulder than at the bevel end for added strength. A machine ground chisel is a mark of quality. The very highest quality chisels available are made from laminated steel (two distinct layers of steel). The flat side is a thin layer of very hard, high carbon steel designed to hold a keen edge for a long time.

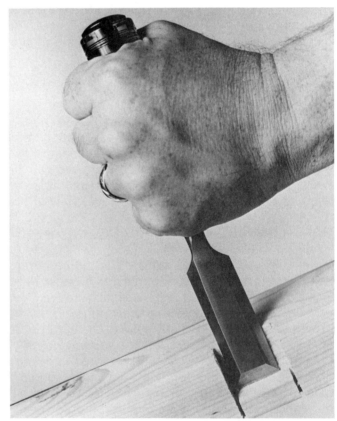

Fig. 33-3. Chisel handles should be able to withstand light hammer blows. (The Stanley Works)

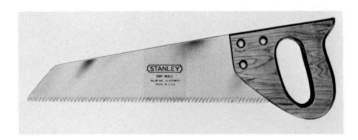

Fig. 33-2. This quality saw is used to cut drywall. (The Stanley Works)

Laminated to this hard layer is a much softer, but tougher, steel. This gives the chisel its strength. The cutting edge has a constant temper along its entire length where ordinary chisels drop from RC 58-62 at the tip to RC 25-30 at the tang or socket.

Keep chisels very sharp and store them boxed, in a rack on the wall, or in a tool roll. Putting them in a tool box will inevitably result in some damage to the cutting edge. Do not store metal tools in high-moisture areas, as this encourages rust. Keep chisels clean and free from mushroomed handles. Rough edges should be removed to prevent injury during use. Coat chisels with a thin film of oil if not in use for an extended period of time.

## MEASURING AND MARKING TOOLS

Selecting measuring and marking tools, Fig. 33-4, is a matter of taste, budget, and function. For most workshops the following would normally be desirable: folding wood rule, flexible steel tape, combination square, try square, framing square, T bevel, marking gauge (or mortise gauge), divider, and marking awl.

When purchasing measuring and marking tools, look for good construction and durable finish. Graduations should be scribed into the material rather than printed on the surface. Fasteners such

as thumbscrews and wing nuts should be easy to use and made from quality material, such as brass or steel. Tools with light weight stamped parts should be avoided. Handle each tool to see how it feels in your hands. If it feels clumsy or awkward, it is probably not the tool for you.

The accuracy of your work depends on the care of marking and measuring tools. Avoid dropping tools on the floor. Do not force movement when the parts are binding. Do not use pliers on thumbscrews or wing nuts. Protect the sharp points of scribes, dividers, and awls. Avoid piling other tools on them in a toolbox. Keep them in a dry place, preferably in a tool cabinet. Lubricate surfaces that require it. Keep all tools clean and in good repair.

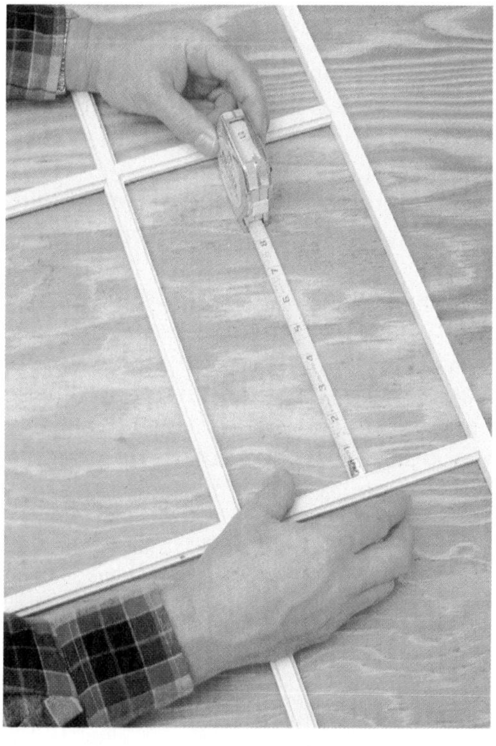

## HAND DRILLS AND BRACES

Hand drills and braces are used to drill and bore holes. The hand drill is a crank-operated tool. It provides adequate speed for drilling small holes (up to 1/4 or 5/16 in.) in soft materials using straight shank twist drills. The brace and bit is a hand operated tool that can bore large holes using a bit. See Fig. 33-5.

When choosing a hand drill, select one that has a quality chuck. Some of the better tools have a Jacobs chuck that can be tightened with a key. Others have a hand-tightened chuck. The key chuck will hold drills more securely than an un-keyed chuck. Highest quality hand drills have two pinion gears for smoother operation. Cast gear teeth usually indicate a lower quality tool. Wood handles

Fig. 33-4. Steel tape rules are available in lengths from 6 to 12 ft. They are useful for taking inside measurements. (The Stanley Works)

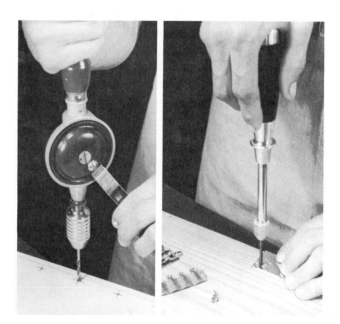

Fig. 33-5. Whether drilling holes with a hand drill or a push drill, use only the pressure you can apply with your hands.

and metal parts should have a durable finish. Some hand drills have a convenient hollow, detachable handle for storing extra drills.

A quality brace will be constructed from quality steel and have a ball bearing mounted head. Most are chrome plated for wear-resistance and include a ratchet. This is used for boring in tight places where a full turn of the handle is not possible. Wood handles should have a durable finish and be comfortable to hold. The standard brace has a SWEEP (diameter the handle turns) of 10 in. Sizes ranging from 8 to 14 in. are also available.

Store hand drills and braces to protect them from contact with other tools. Lubricate the moving parts occasionally. Wipe off sweaty hand prints to prevent rust and corrosion. Never try to use a bit in a three-jaw chuck or a straight shank drill in a two-jaw brace. Do not use pliers or wrenches on hand-tightened chucks. Use the proper drill or bit for the material you are working. Use only the force that you can apply with your hands.

## HAND PLANES

The variety of planes available can be confusing to the inexperienced woodworker, Fig. 33-6. However, it is not necessary to have every type of plane in your shop.

Once the decision on the type and size of plane is made, pay close attention to construction and quality. Make sure the parts are securely fastened together with quality fasteners, and that it is comfortable to handle. Check the machining of the sole. The sides should be square with it. The blade should

be properly machined and made from high quality steel. Laminated steel blades will hold a keen edge much longer than a conventional blade. The sole of the highest quality wooden planes are generally made from lignum vitae wood. This wood is very hard and contains natural oils, making the plane slide easily. The body is made from a quality hardwood such as beech, oak, or maple.

Be careful not to drop the plane. Such a jolt may crack the casting of a steel plane; it will surely dent or crush a corner of a wooden plane. Unplated metal surfaces should be coated with a light film of oil to prevent rust and stains from forming. Planes should be stored where the humidity is stable. Keep the blade sharp at all times and use the tool on clean, metal-free stock. Dented or slightly warped soles can be passed over the jointer to true the surfaces. Protect the blade by laying the plane on its side. Keep the sole clean.

## FILES AND RASPS

There are two basic kinds of files: single cut and double cut. Rasps differ from files in that teeth are formed individually and are not connected to one another. Files will cut smoother than rasps, but work much slower and clog more easily.

A typical wood shop should have a good selection of files and rasps, Fig. 33-7. For example, a smooth, single cut file may be used for sharpening or draw filing. Choose an appropriate file or rasp that is made from quality, hardened steel. A high-quality file will cost several times more than a file of lesser quality. Files and rasps should be sharp in order to cut well. Hold a new file up to the light to see if the light reflects off the cutting edge. If the light reflects then it is probably not sharp.

Keep files and rasps clean. Do not allow material to clog the teeth. A file card or brush is helpful in keeping a file clean. Never handle a file or rasp with moist hands. Moisture causes rust to form, ruining the cutting edges. Store files in a dry place and preferably in a slotted storage rack to protect the cutting edges. Attach a handle to each file for ease of use and increased safety. Never allow files to come in contact with one another or other hardened tools. Avoid dropping these tools as they may break

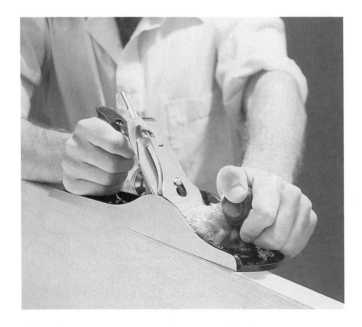

Fig. 33-6. Notice the quality construction of this plane. (The Stanley Works)

Fig. 33-7. The flat and the half-round are two types of standard wood files. (Nicholson File Co.)

or at the least, damage an edge. Do not file hardened metal with any file.

## VISES AND CLAMPS

Woodworker's vises are edge mounted on the bench, with their jaws flush with the bench top, Fig. 33-8. Some vises have a quick action device to eliminate handle-turning when the vise is wide open. Be sure to inspect this device carefully, because some types break easily. The jaws should close exactly parallel on all edges and provide even pressure between them. The handle should be made from metal or high quality hardwood. Smooth-operation is important. Be sure to examine the quality of this tool carefully. It will receive constant use and is an expensive item.

The beginning woodworker will need a variety of portable clamps. When selecting these clamps, do not skimp on quality. Check to see if the threaded shaft has been machined using a tough, durable steel. Threads should have a large bearing surface, especially on larger clamps. Handles should be designed to withstand all pressure you can apply with your bare hands. Castings should be smooth and free from defects. Fasteners should be tight and appropriate for the function.

Clamps and vises require very little attention. Lubricate the threads every few months or when they appear to need it. Keep the threads clean to reduce excessive wear and improve ease of operation. Never use a hammer, wrench, or other tool to tighten a vise or clamp. They are designed for hand use. Store your clamps in a rack. Keep them dry to reduce rust.

## PORTABLE POWER TOOLS

Portable power tools perform the same operations as stationary machines, but may be used anywhere in the shop or at remote locations. If stock is too large to handle or too big to move around in the shop, a portable power tool can be used. Portable power tools require less space and are less expensive than stationary machines. Most woodworkers have one or more of the following portable power tools in their shop.

### ELECTRIC DRILLS

The electric drill is frequently the first portable power tool that beginning woodworkers purchase, Fig. 33-9. It is versatile and saves much time and energy on many projects.

When choosing an electric drill, careful attention should be given to the design and workmanship of the chuck. A geared key chuck is necessary to withstand the torque. The three jaws must fit together very precisely and be able to hold a drill as small as 1/64 in. diameter. The horsepower of the tool should be compatible with the chuck size. Choose a drill that develops sufficient torque to perform desired operations. Speed usually varies

Fig. 33-8. This woodworking bench is equipped with two bench vises to handle most any job. (Leichtung, Inc.)

Fig. 33-9. A cordless electric drill is a versatile tool for a wide variety of tasks. (Makita U.S.A., Inc.)

with the size of the tool. A 1/4 in. drill runs at about 2000 rpm, while a 3/8 in. drill runs at about 1200 rpm. Higher speed is needed for sanding or polishing. The tool should be made from insulating material if the drill is not the grounding type.

Quality drills usually have a long cord with the chuck key attached to the cord. Inexpensive drills generally have a pigtail cord which requires an extension cord for use. Other types of drills available include air drills and cordless drills. They are not as popular as the electric drill.

With normal use, electric drills require little maintenance. Never allow sawdust to accumulate around the fan openings and be sure the openings are clear during operation. Do not overload the drill. This will make it run at low speed, burning the motor out in a short time. Lubricate the chuck periodically to insure smooth operation. Store the drill in a clean, dry place.

## CIRCULAR SAWS

Several factors should be considered when buying a portable circular saw for your shop. Select a saw that is large enough for the type of cutting you expect to do, Fig. 33-10. It is not advisable to purchase a saw for general purpose work which is less than 7 1/4 in. in diameter. The saw should have a dependable depth adjustment for making shallow cuts, an angle adjustment for cutting miters and bevels, and a ripping fence to guide the saw parallel to an edge. It should also have an automatic spring-activated blade guard. This guard retracts as the blade enters the stock and then covers the exposed blade when the cut is completed. Examine these features carefully to be sure they are functional and well-designed.

Examine the blade base to see if it is sturdy. A flimsy blade base will cause inaccurate cuts. Does the saw have a blade lock? This feature makes changing blades easier and safer. Choose a saw that develops enough torque to cut thick stock at a moderate rate. Some saws have a display light which indicates a dull blade or heavy cutting conditions. This can extend the life of the motor. Another feature for consideration is an external gear lubricator which eliminates the need to dismantle the saw to lubricate the gears. Double insulation for operation safety and a long electrical cord are also important features to consider.

Proper care of your portable circular saw will extend its useful life and maintain quality performance. Never remove the blade guard or ground prong. These devices are for your safety. Keep the tool clean and in top working order. Avoid working in damp or wet locations. When not in use, store the saw in a dry cabinet which can be locked to prevent unauthorized use. Protect the power cord to prevent damage during a cutting operation. Use the proper blade for each operation. An improper blade will produce a poor cut and may damage the saw.

## SABER SAWS

The saber saw is useful for making internal cuts, cutting curves, ripping, and crosscutting. It is a popular tool because of its versatility, Fig. 33-11.

A quality saber saw should provide smooth operation with minimum noise and vibration. The base should be adjustable, sturdy, and large enough for stable tool support. High quality saber saws fre-

Fig. 33-10. Portable circular saw.    (Makita U.S.A., Inc.)

Fig. 33-11. Many materials can be cut with these saber saw blades.

quently have a roller bearing blade support for added accuracy and long blade life. Double insulation provides added protection for the operator. Examine the blade attachment mechanism. Blades should attach securely and easily. Be sure the machine uses a standard blade which is readily available. Check to see if lubrication requires dismantling. This can be time-consuming. Select a saw that has bearings rather than bushings. Better saws use bearings for longer life.

Care of the saber saw includes lubricating the moving parts as often as needed. Protect the tool from moisture and excessive humidity. Keep the fan vents free from saw dust and dirt. When working outside, never lay the tool down on the ground. Lay the saw on its side when not in use. Protect the blade to prevent bending or breaking. Keep the cord clear of the blade at all times. Store the saw in a dry, secure place.

## ROUTERS

The portable router, Fig. 33-12, can be used to trim edges and laminates, cut coves, flutes, chamfers, decorative edges, rabbets, and dovetails.

Quality routers have permanently sealed precision ball bearings, micrometer depth adjustment, and smooth, non-marking bases. A flat top is desirable for fast, easy bit changes. The collet should be easy to reach. A shaft locking device eliminates the need for two wrenches. Easy and accurate depth adjustment is a must. Several techniques for adjusting the depth are available on modern routers:

spring loaded plunge-cut, micrometer adjustment, and threaded ring. Choose the type of router that best suits the work you will be doing. Be sure to buy a router that has a standard 1/4 in. split type collet. Some routers have collets which will accept 3/8 and 1/2 in. bits, but they are usually larger production tools. A double insulated case with a strain relief cord is desirable for added safety. Select a router which has a router guide for making straight cuts and arcs.

A quality router will need little maintenance beyond keeping it clean. Most require no lubrication since they have sealed bearings. Do not take cuts so heavy that the rpm's drop severely. This will burn out the motor. Remove the bit from the collet when you are finished. Always use a sharp router bit. Dull bits produce poor work and overload the motor. Keep the motor fan vent open and do not permit saw dust to accumulate there.

## SANDERS

Several types of portable sanders are useful in the home or school woodworking shop, Fig. 33-13. They include pad sanders, belt sanders, and disk sanders.

A quality pad sander should use a fourth, a third, or a half sheet of abrasive paper. The attachments which hold the paper should hold the paper securely and should be easy to use. The sander should have a quality rubber or felt pad to produce a smooth,

Fig. 33-12. Portable routers are available in a variety of sizes, shapes, and types. (Black & Decker)

Fig. 33-13. This portable sander is being used to smooth a surface for finish. (Bosch Power Tool Corp.)

even finish. The pad should be flush on all sides to allow sanding in corners. Select a pad sander which is comfortable to hold and easy to use. Double insulation or a grounded cord is necessary.

Belt or disk sanders are a larger investment than a pad sander. These tools may be purchased if the work being done requires this equipment. However, most home shops will not require these tools.

A pad sander should be cared for much the same as an electric drill or saber saw. Do not overload the motor by pressing too hard. Be sure that it is lubricated properly and kept clean. Store it in a dry, secure place.

## STATIONARY POWER TOOLS

Stationary power tools require a large investment. However, they reduce the labor required to produce a wood project and generally improve accuracy.

There are three basic factors for selecting specific brands of equipment: function, manufacturers' services, and appearance. This is the order of importance.

FUNCTION is related to the usefulness of the machine. For example, it is not wise to purchase a machine for operations that will seldom be performed. Multipurpose machines have not been commercially successful overall. MANUFACTURERS' SERVICES are often the primary difference between competing brands that have the same functional qualities. Services to consider include warranties offered, locations of service centers, availability of repair parts, and installation, operation, and maintenance support. APPEARANCE, although not as important as function or services, is important when designing a piece of equipment. There is no reason why a quality tool cannot be attractive.

The selection and care of several machines is discussed in the following paragraphs. These machines are among the most commonly used.

## TABLE SAW

When purchasing a table saw, Fig. 33-14, select at least a 10 in. saw, and a 1 hp motor. The arbor should tilt for angle cuts. The table should have a large extension on at least one side for cutting large panels or long pieces of wood. It should also have a well-designed rip fence and miter gauge.

Handles and operating levers must be large, slip-proof, shaped to fit the hand, and located logically on the machine. Surfaces that are grasped by hands should be painted, plated, or made of a corrosion-proof material.

The machine should not have any sharp-edged castings or fabricated parts, protruding set screws, or rough holes. The base or frame construction should be rigid enough to eliminate vibration. It

Fig. 33-14. A standard tilting arbor table saw. This type is found in many school and home shops.
(Enlon Import Corporation)

should also be shaped so as not to hamper the movements of the operator. An effective and easy-to-use guard and splitter should be provided with the table saw. The motor should have sealed bearings and a large shaft (arbor). A quality table saw should accept standard accessories used with table saws.

Proper care and maintenance of your table saw will extend its useful life. Keep all moving parts lubricated and free from sawdust build-up. Be sure the legs or base evenly supports the weight of the saw. This will reduce vibration and prevent unnecessary strain on the body of the saw. Never use the table as a work bench. The table is not designed to resist hammering, spilled glue, or paint. Keep the table top clean and free from rust, corrosion, and dirt. Be sure the proper voltage and overload protection are provided at all times. Keep the saw adjusted to reduce wear and improve performance.

## BAND SAW

A band saw is an indispensable tool. It cuts curves and irregularly shaped parts, as well as straight cuts and angles, Fig. 33-15.

A quality band saw should have a large, tilting table with a rip fence and miter gauge. Check the accuracy of these attachments. Wheels should be completely adjustable for tilt and blade tension. A good machine will have balanced wheels for vibration-free operation. Check each wheel to be sure it is perfectly round. Each wheel should have

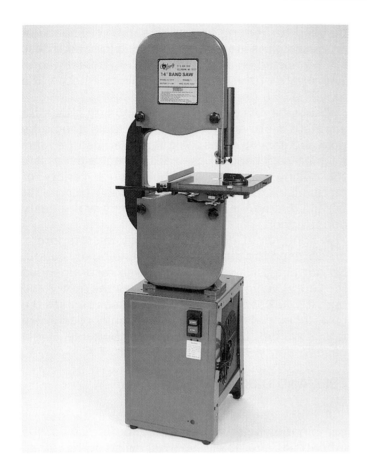

Fig. 33-15. A small 14 in. band saw, such as this one, is ideal for the home shop. (Grizzly Imports, Inc.)

a rubber tire that can be replaced when necessary. A blade tension and tracking adjustment is necessary on all band saws. Be sure these mechanisms work well and indicate the proper amount of tension required for a specific width blade. Examine the blade guides; they are extremely important for accurate cutting. All parts of the blade guides must be completely adjustable. The top blade guide should be supported on a sturdy arm that is easily raised and lowered for proper height. A dependable motor that develops sufficient power for cutting thick stock is necessary. Be sure the saw is not underpowered. Proper blade and belt guards should be provided with the saw for safe operation. Floor model saws should have a foot brake to stop the blade quickly if needed. A quality saw should provide for the easy removal and replacement of the blade.

Care of the band saw is similar to other machines. Keep it clean and lubricated. Do not allow pitch to build up on the tires or blade. Be sure the blade guides and blade tension are properly adjusted at all times. Release the tension if the saw is not to be used for a long period of time. This will help to keep the tires round and smooth. Never use a dull

blade. This places a heavy load on the motor and produces a poor cut.

## SCROLL SAW

The scroll saw (or jig saw) is used to make small radius cuts and straight cuts where great accuracy is not required. It is especially suited for making complete inside cutouts, Fig. 33-16.

Whatever type of scroll saw you choose, it should be a quality tool. The blade should be easy to attach and should maintain a relatively constant tension. Be sure the chuck will hold very fine blades as well as large blades. A variable speed saw is more useful than one with a constant speed. The table should be adjustable for angular cuts and preferably made from cast iron. All thumbscrews and adjustment nuts should be easy to reach and made from quality materials. Castings should be smooth and finished with no sharp edges.

Scroll saws require periodic lubrication and cleaning. Treat this machine as you would any other expensive tool. Follow proper procedures when using it. Keep it in good adjustment and protect it from rust and corrosion.

## JOINTER

The jointer is used to smooth or plane board edges and faces. It can also be used to cut rabbets, bevels, tapers, and other shapes, Fig. 33-17.

A quality jointer is expensive. It should be selected only after careful analysis. Be sure the tables are made from high quality cast iron which has been machined true in every dimension. The surface should be very smooth with no defects.

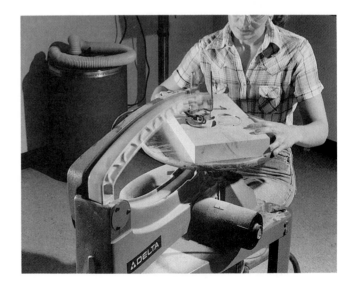

Fig. 33-16. This scroll saw is efficient and also attractive. (Delta International Machinery Corp.)

be used for routing and drum sanding. The major drill press parts are the base, table, and head. These are supported on a column for height adjustments. The length of the column determines whether the machine is a bench or floor model, Fig. 33-18.

Choose a drill press that has a quality chuck for accurate work and long life. The table should be rigid and easy to adjust. A crank to adjust the table height is very handy. Speed adjustment is necessary for drilling different size holes in a variety of materials. A quill lock is also a desirable feature for certain operations. Choose a machine with quality construction.

A lightweight drill press cannot tolerate lateral pressure on the quill as in drum sanding or routing. Do not use drills or bits larger than recommended for your machine. This will overload the motor and burn it out. Keep the machined surfaces such as the quill, table, and column clean and lightly oiled. Keep tables waxed. Do not hammer on the table. It is a casting and will break.

## BELT AND DISK SANDER

A home or school shop will most likely have a combination belt and disk sander before any of the other types available. This machine smooths, trims,

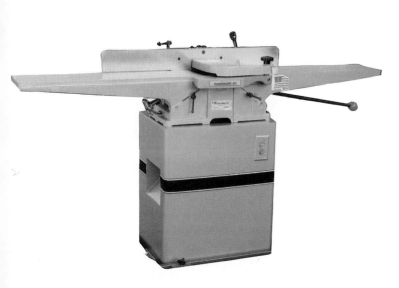

Fig. 33-17. The jointer is an ideal woodworking machine. (Powermatic)

Adjustment should be easy but snug. The cutter head must be perfectly parallel with the table surface. This can be checked with a dial indicator. The cutter head should be designed for three knives with adjustable gibs. The jointer should have a high quality fence. Most are also cast iron and machined smooth on the front side. The fence should tilt forward and backward to cut bevels and chamfers. Positive stops at 90 and 45 deg. which can be adjusted are very desirable on the fence tilting mechanism. The jointer should be equipped with a retractable guard which covers the cutterhead.

Proper use and care of the jointer includes never planing a board that may contain metal objects. This will damage the blades. Keep the blades sharp to produce smooth cuts. Feed stock at the proper rate so as not to overload the motor. Never hammer on the table. The casting may break or be damaged by the excessive force. Lubricate the ways as needed to provide smooth movement of the table. Never place heavy objects on the jointer table as this may cause it to droop. Keep the machined surfaces clean and free from rust or corrosion.

## DRILL PRESS

The drill press is designed for drilling and boring holes. Some machines, usually larger ones, can also

Fig. 33-18. A standard floor-type drill press. (Enlon Import Corporation)

and shapes, Fig. 33-19. The table (or tables) should be cast iron capable of tilting to 45 deg. The belt should be operable in the horizontal or vertical position. A dependable tracking mechanism is necessary for any belt sander. The motor should be dust-proof with sealed bearings. Choose as large a machine as you can afford and for which you have space.

Keep your sander clean and in proper adjustment. Allowing the sanding belt to run to the side will cut grooves in the side casting and damage the belt. Be sure the sanding disk is properly cemented to the disk plate. Loose paper will cut into the table and reduce sanding effectiveness and accuracy. Lubricate moving parts as needed. Regularly check to see that all parts are securely fastened.

## OTHER MACHINES AND TOOLS

Several other machines and tools available for the woodworking shop are of limited use, and, therefore, are not as popular as those discussed, Fig. 33-20. As with the purchase of any tool, research the subject well before making a final decision.

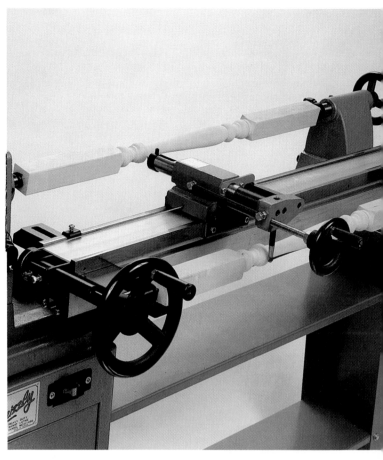

Fig. 33-20. General-purpose wood lathe with duplicator. (Grizzly Imports, Inc.)

Fig. 33-19. Combination belt, disk, and drum sander in use. The dust collector helps extend the useful life of the machine. (Delta International Machinery Corp.)

Compare models, sizes, types, etc. Make your decision based on facts. Collect literature from a variety of manufacturers. Talk to people who use the type of equipment in which you are interested. When possible, operate the machine before you buy. Above all, choose a quality machine and keep it in top condition.

## THE HOME WORKSHOP

Once you have decided on the tools and/or machines you will buy for home use, you may wish to plan an area in which to use them. You can apply the experience gained in the school shop to the planning and equipping of a home workshop. It is very likely that a friend or relative may want to help you. A corner of the basement or garage may provide the space.

You can make a start with a sturdy table or workbench and a tool panel, Fig. 33-21. Either or both of these items might make a good project for an advanced woodworking course. If the bench is large, it will be best to construct it in sections and make the assembly at home. Thick maple bench

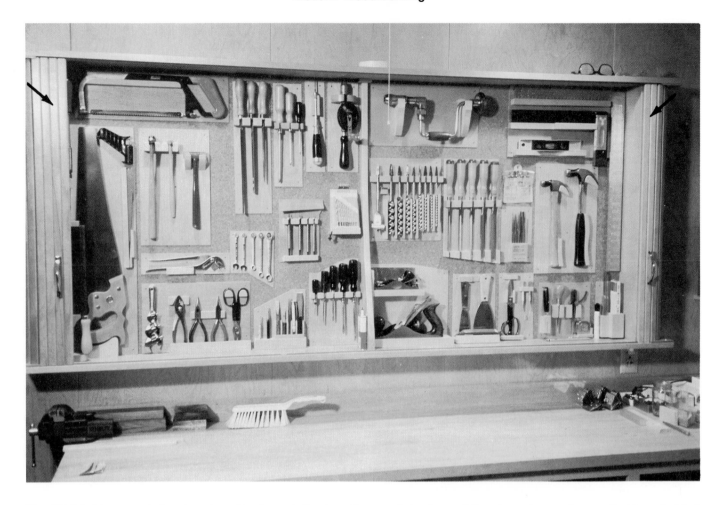

Fig. 33-21. Home workshop bench and tool panel. To close the panel, tambour sliding doors (arrows) are pulled from behind the panel to the front.

tops, like those in the school shop, are expensive and hard to make. A satisfactory top can be constructed from one or two layers of 3/4 in. plywood, covered with 1/4 in. tempered hardboard. After the tool panel and bench are completed and equipped, you can use them to build racks and cabinets for materials and supplies.

You may also want to design and build tool holders like those shown in Fig. 33-22. Custom-built holders are usually better to use than nails, screws, or metal clips. Attach the holder to a small subpanel and then mount the unit on the main panel with small screws. This way it will be easy to replace the holder or change its position when making a revision of the tool layout.

Even if you do not plan on a career in the woodworking industries, you may wish to continue woodworking as a hobby. Many people find that they quickly shed daily tensions as they become involved in some construction activity in their home workshop. Wood has always been a suitable material for a hobby because even those with limited skills can attain a fair degree of success with a relatively simple layout of tools and equipment.

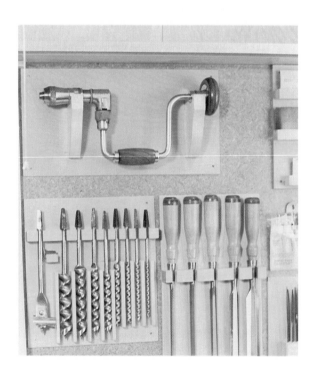

Fig. 33-22. Custom-made tool panel with individual tool holders. (Bill Wagner)

## TEST YOUR KNOWLEDGE, Chapter 33

Please do not write in the text. Place your answers on a separate sheet of paper.

1. Why is the face of a hammer head convex?
2. _____ _____ blades must be kept under high tension for accurate sawing.
3. Quality chisels are usually _____ at the shoulder than at the bevel end.
   a. Thinner.
   b. Thicker.
   c. Wider.
   d. None of the above.
4. Name three types of measuring and marking tools commonly found in a workshop.
5. Some of the better hand drills have a _____ chuck that can be tightened with a key.
6. Of what are high quality wooden plane soles made?
7. How do files and rasps differ?
8. When might you use a portable power tool?
9. What is the purpose of a spring-activated blade guard on a circular saw?
10. The saber saw is useful for:
    a. Making internal cuts.
    b. Cutting curves.
    c. Ripping and crosscutting.
    d. All of the above.
11. List three tasks that can be done with a portable router.
12. What are the three basic factors to consider when selecting stationary power tools?
13. A good _____ _____ will have balanced wheels for vibration-free operation.
14. What damage might result from stacking heavy objects on a jointer table?
15. The length of the _____ determines whether a drill press is a bench or floor model.

## ACTIVITIES

1. Select a common hand or power tool and collect literature from several manufacturers about that tool. Compare specifications, prices, and features. Choose the best tool for the price and explain why you chose it.
2. Prepare a maintenance schedule for five stationary machines in your shop. Indicate how each maintenance operation is done, how often it will be done, and the approximate time required to perform the operation.
3. Select one portable power tool to which you have access. Study the tool and prepare a list of its good design elements. Indicate areas that need improvement. Present your findings to your classmates for discussion.

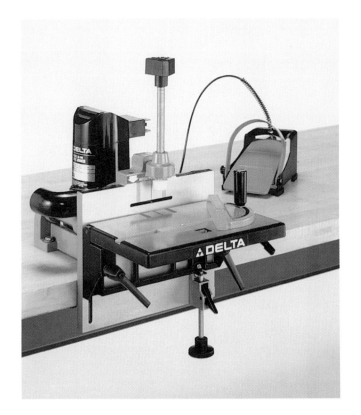

Left. Plate joiner attached to workbench. (Delta International Machinery Corp.) Right. Inserting a biscuit in a pocket cut, which was cut with the tabletop plate joiner. (Delta International Machinery Corp.)

Upper left. All of the parts for a mass-produced grandfather clock case. Each part has been machined to exact specifications to produce a quality product. Right. The completed project is 92 in. high by 28 1/2 in. wide by 16 in. deep. It has a hand-rubbed finish. Lower left. Close-up of decorative molding and fine work quality. (California Time/Westwood, Inc.)

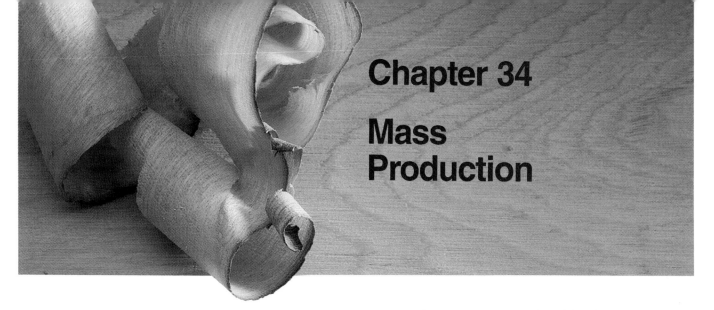

# Chapter 34

# Mass Production

Science and invention, coupled with industrial know-how, have made America a great nation. We have developed systems of mass production that provide us with a tremendous range of products that make life easier and more enjoyable. Items that were considered luxuries just a generation ago, are now available to everyone.

Although wood products are seldom produced at the high volume reached by such metal products as automobiles and refrigerators, the same general procedures, methods, and considerations must be applied to the manufacturing process.

All manufacturing plants, whether they are large or small, build a few custom products or mass produce items for wide distribution, include such departments and divisions as business and finance, product selection, design and engineering, production, inspection, storing, packaging, and shipping. In the mass production plant there are additional elements that receive special attention:

1. PRODUCT SIMPLIFICATION. Designing or redesigning the product so that it is easy to produce, yet still includes features that are attractive and functional.
2. STANDARDIZATION OF PARTS. Given parts will all be the same. They are interchangeable in an assembly. Worn or damaged parts can be easily replaced after the product is placed in service, Fig. 34-1.
3. SPECIAL MACHINES AND TOOLS. This includes jigs, fixtures, and special setups that can be applied to standard equipment so the equipment will perform a given operation with speed and accuracy, Fig. 34-2.
4. ORGANIZATION OF MACHINES, MATERIALS, AND WORKERS. Involves careful analysis of work, so that jobs can be broken down into simple operations and arranged in proper sequence. Controlled movement of materials and assemblies from one station to the next. Synchronization of all operations, so that the right things are at the right place at the right

Fig. 34-1. Standardized kitchen cabinets have interchangeable parts. Drawers are installed before units are given a final inspection, then they are individually boxed for shipment. (Bertch Wood Specialties)

Fig. 34-2. A specialized setup for cutting several fine grooves in a panel at once. Each piece cut in this manner will be exactly the same. (Campbellrhea Mfg., Inc.)

time. Assignment and coordination of workers and jobs.

Already you may have experienced in a small way the efficiency that can grow out of mass production. Possibly you have constructed a pair of matching end tables or similar project and found that you were able to produce them in less than double the time necessary to produce one.

Production time for each item can be further reduced as larger quantities are produced, especially if the work is carefully organized and attention is given to the development of special devices. For example, Fig. 34-3 compares several methods of cutting a dowel to a specified length. The hand sawing jig greatly improves the accuracy and quality of the work, which is very important for producing interchangeable parts. The sawing fixture mounted on the table saw provides the same accuracy, plus a higher production rate.

You may want to design and mass produce a small item working by yourself. If you carefully planned and organized the work, built a pilot model, and constructed a special jig or fixture for several of the key operations, you would gain considerable experience, even though you actually produced only a relatively small number of units.

It is likely, however, that your instructor may want to develop a mass production project involving a group of students or even the entire class. This will provide an experience more closely related to modern industry, that includes the careful control of material flow, production schedules, and the coordination of the efforts of many people.

## SELECTING AND DESIGNING

The selection and design of your individual projects will be determined largely by your personal interests and desires. When selecting an article to be mass produced and widely distributed, it will be especially important that you consider its function and appearance, and whether others will want to buy and own it, Fig. 34-4. Business and industry gives great consideration to this matter, and refers to it as MARKET RESEARCH. Manufacturers try to develop products that have a high level of consumer appeal. They give little attention to the personal whims off the designer or engineer.

After an article has been tentatively selected for mass production, study it carefully. Determine whether it can be adapted to mass production methods and efficiently built in the shop with standard tools and machines, Fig. 34-5. By designing and constructing special setups, this equipment can often be adapted to mass production requirements.

Parts that cannot be efficiently produced in the shop might be purchased from some outside source.

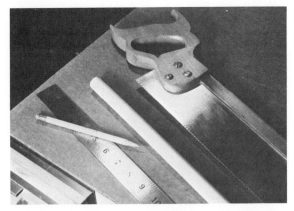

Using standard hand tools. Length is laid out with pencil and bench rule. Dowel stock is clamped in vise and cut made with backsaw. Accuracy and squareness of cut will vary depending on the skill of the operator. Production rate is about two pieces a minute.

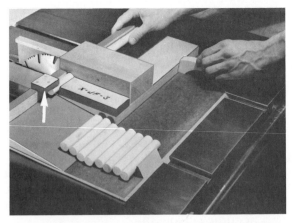

Using sawing jig mounted in bench vise. Dowel stock is fed through channel to stop, then clamped with eccentric (arrow). Backsaw rides in sawing slot and produces square cut. When cut is complete and saw raised, part rolls down sloping surface. Production rate is about five pieces a minute.

Using table saw fixture. Dowel stock is fed through holder to stop (arrow). Fixture, guided by strips riding in saw table slots, is moved forward through the cut as shown. When the cut is complete, the part drops slightly, clearing the stop. Fixture is returned to starting position and dowel stock is again fed through holder. This action pushes the completed part onto the ramp where it rolls back to stacking area. Production rate is about 15 pieces a minute.

Fig. 34-3. Comparison of three production methods.

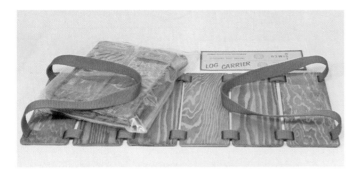

Fig. 34-4. This log carrier was designed and built in a classroom mass production setup.

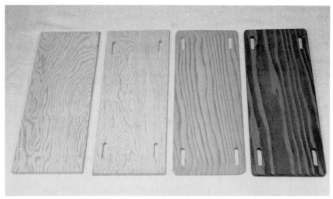

Fig. 34-6. These four panels represent successive operations in production of the finished part. From left to right: cut part to basic size, machine elongated hole for strap, round edges and sand the panel, and apply finish.

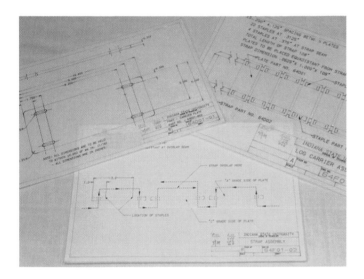

Fig. 34-5. Drawings of individual parts, production sequence plans, and assembly details are made and approved before production begins.

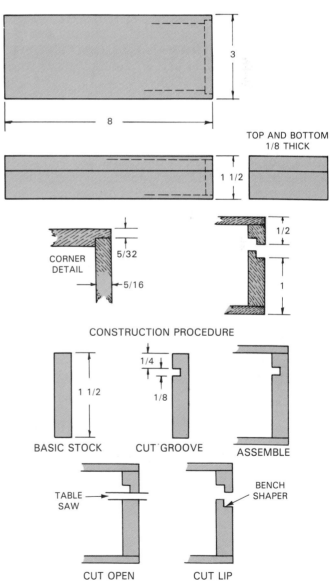

Fig. 34-7. Working drawing of card and pencil box to be mass produced.

Industry does this quite often. For example, some factories specialize in turned parts while others produce only formed plywood units. They then sell to companies that manufacture the finished items of furniture, cabinetwork, and other wood products.

Try to visualize the article in production. Determine if there can be easy movement of materials through the shop, with storage space for sub-assemblies and finished products, Fig. 34-6. Large pieces may create extra storage problems; it is usually best to select small articles which actually become advanced woodworking problems when planned and produced on a mass production basis.

After your sketches and ideas become stabilized, prepare a working drawing of the article. In addition to the usual details of construction, include the number that will likely be produced, along with suggestions on special procedures and setups that might be used to produce it in the most efficient way. See Fig. 34-7.

## PILOT MODELS AND PRODUCTION IDEAS

As soon as the working drawings are stabilized, build a sample unit or pilot model. This will provide a check on the design and may reveal certain improvements that can be made. As the various operations are performed they should be studied carefully to determine what special jigs or fixtures can be developed for the mass production setup, Fig. 34-8. Changes and improvements may be so extensive that several models may need to be built before a satisfactory solution is found. The original working drawing should, of course, be corrected and revised accordingly.

As you think of ways to mass produce the article, record your ideas in sketch form. These can be very simple drawings or diagrams. Instead of including dimensions, try to make the drawing to an approximate scale. Small details should be drawn full size. An example of such a sketch is shown in Fig. 34-9. The only "key," or exact dimension, is the size of the box. The sizes of the various parts of the jig are usually not critical and can be determined by the good judgment of the builder.

## OPERATIONAL ANALYSIS

During the construction of the pilot model, a great deal will be learned about the operations and procedures best suited for the production. Make a list of all the parts and subassemblies. Under each one list the detailed operations in the order they will be performed. Working from this analysis, prepare an operations flow chart, Fig. 34-10.

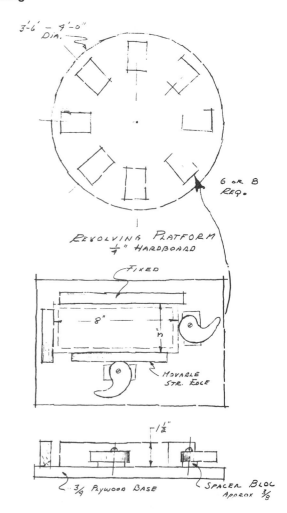

Fig. 34-9. Sketch of a gluing jig for card and pencil box. The only critical dimensions are those of the box. Sometimes colored lines are used to define the outline of the work from the jig or fixture.

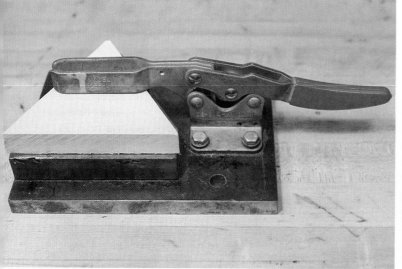

Fig. 34-8. Experimenting with various techniques for holding a part for machining. Left. Double-action clamp holds the part securely, but may interfere with the operation. Right. Special jig designed to hold the part while 15 holes are drilled in precise locations.

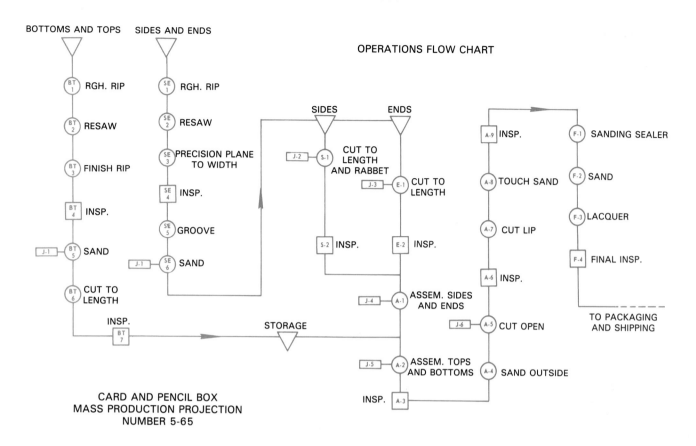

OPERATIONS FLOW CHART

CARD AND PENCIL BOX
MASS PRODUCTION PROJECTION
NUMBER 5-65

Fig. 34-10. Operations flow chart.

The symbols used in the sample chart are similar to those recommended by the A.S.M.E. (American Society of Mechanical Engineers). They show the sequence and order of operations, assembly points, and inspection points. Rectangles connecting to the operations indicate the construction of special jigs and fixtures. Numbering the operations makes it easier to assign workers and keep records. When the chart is complete it should be posted in the shop for easy reference by all students assigned to the project. See Fig. 34-11.

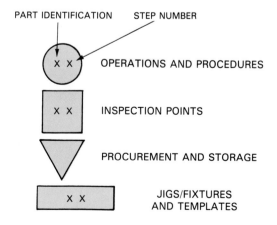

Fig. 34-11. Flow chart symbols.

The experience you have had in making PLANS OF PROCEDURE for your regular project work will be helpful as you prepare an operational analysis and a flow chart for mass production work.

## TOOLING-UP FOR PRODUCTION

Designing and constructing special tools, setups, jigs, and fixtures is one of the most important steps in developing a mass production project. It compares with the work of the tool designer in industry. The tool designer is a highly skilled mechanic and knows basic mathematics, drawing, and manufacturing methods. He or she must be able to analyze operations and then develop various tools, machines, and devices so these operations can be performed quickly, safely, and accurately. Fig. 34-12 shows a simple sanding jig used for rounding the corner of a production project (also shown).

The construction of the pilot model probably provided some ideas of what special tooling might be used. Now you will need to refine these ideas, develop the setups, and try them out. These devices are called jigs and fixtures. A JIG is a device that is attached to the work and guides the tool. A FIXTURE is usually mounted on or attached to the machine or tool, and holds and/or guides the work as the operation is performed. See Fig. 34-13.

567

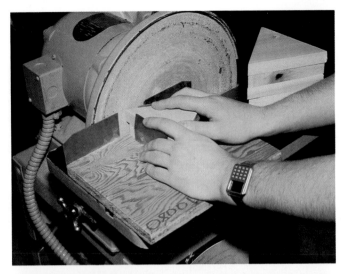

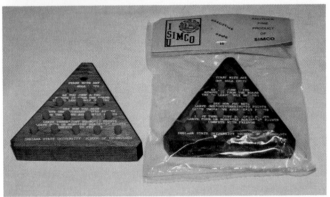

Fig. 34-12. Top. A simple sanding jig made in the shop for rounding the corners of a part. Bottom. The completed product ready for delivery.

There are three requirements a jig or fixture must meet. It must provide a way to make the part or perform the operation rapidly, it must be safe to operate, and it must also produce work that is accurate within the limits specified. The interchangeability of parts is an essential element in mass production and depends on this accuracy.

Note the jig construction in Fig. 34-14. You will always need to maintain a higher degree of accuracy in the jig and fixture building than will be required in the work that it performs. If the tolerance permitted in the fabrication of the part is 1/16 in., then you will usually need to construct the jig or fixture to within 1/32 in. of the size requirements. This is no doubt a higher level of accuracy than you have had to maintain in your regular project construction, where you worked with individual pieces and could easily adjust each part to secure the desired fit.

*When designing and building fixtures for power machines, be sure to include some type of guard arrangement. Guards should protect the operator, but not completely hide the cutting tool from view.*

The size of the production run (number of articles to be produced) will determine how extensive and complicated the jigs and fixtures should be. Production runs of 10 to 50 units will not justify the intricate tooling-up that would be required for runs of 100 to 1000. In industry the tooling-up process might include the purchase of additional equipment, specialized machinery, and require extra space and other facilities. All of this would be expensive; it would not become a profitable operation until many thousands of units had been produced and sold.

Fig. 34-13. Examine this setup. Determine whether it is a jig or fixture, based on the definitions given in the text. (Amerock Corp.)

Fig. 34-14. Building a jig.

In the school shop it is justifiable to develop far more extensive jigs and fixtures than the size of the run might indicate. They should be designed as small, separate units that can be quickly attached and set up for use on benches and machines, then easily removed and stored.

## EQUIPMENT LAYOUT AND PRODUCTION LINES

The selection and arrangement of equipment in industrial plants is so important that a special plant layout department is often included in the total organization. Members of this group are continually searching for new and better ways to refine and improve the flow of materials and the use of machines and equipment. They plan the arrangement of work stations and lay out production lines. PRODUCTION LINES are the areas where the product is assembled as it is carried along on continuously or intermittently moving conveyors. It requires a tremendous amount of careful planning to organize all of the tools, machines, supplies, materials, and workers in such a way that the product will be produced with speed and efficiency.

Woodworking plants generally do not make extensive use of moving production lines, except in the final assembly and finishing departments. See Fig. 34-15. Duplicate parts are usually stacked on stock trucks or carts and moved from one area or

Fig. 34-16. Cabinet drawer parts stacked on stock cart for easy movement to machine stations. Partially assembled frames are stacked on a pallet (arrow) that is usually moved by a fork-lift truck. (Bertch Wood Specialties)

work station to another, Fig. 34-16. A typical work station is shown in Fig. 34-17.

The average school shop is not designed for mass production work. It would be impractical to make extensive rearrangements for any particular product. It is worthwhile, however, to make a drawing

Fig. 34-15. Conveyor carries piano cabinets along the assembly line in a modern woodworking plant. (Kimball International)

Fig. 34-17. Workpieces moving out of a double-end tenoner. They have been trimmed to size. In addition, the edges have been rabbeted and the dado for the web frame has been cut. (Bertch Wood Specialties)

of the equipment layout as it exists, assign work stations, and draw coded lines indicating the flow of material. This assignment will be helpful, even though there may be overlapping of routes and other interference that would not be permitted in a regular industrial operation.

After the work stations have been established and the flow of materials and parts has been determined, try out each operation. It is especially important to check the time required at each station. If the time seems so long that a bottleneck (delay) may be created, one of the following adjustments should be made:

1. Refine the procedure or method.
2. Improve the operator's performance.
3. Break the operation down into two or more steps.
4. Duplicate the setup and add more operators (workers).
5. "Stock pile" or "bank" materials in overtime work sessions.

## HANDLING AND STORING MATERIALS

The transportation or flow of material and parts from one machine or work station to another requires special equipment. Woodworking industries use pallets, lift trucks, stock carts, roller conveyors, belt conveyors, and palletized conveyors. When machines are set up to produce a specific part, or certain subassemblies are being fabricated, many more units are produced than can be immediately used in the final assembly section. They are stockpiled and stored, Fig. 34-18.

In the school shop the movement of material, parts, and assemblies is limited to stock carts, tote trays, and stock boxes. A stock cart, Fig. 34-19, can be used to transport material from one station to another. It can also serve as a storage unit. At the beginning of the work period it can be quickly moved from the storage area to the work station and returned at the end of the session. Tote trays and boxes can be used in about the same way for small parts, Fig. 34-20.

Fig. 34-18. Parts and subassemblies in storage. (Kimball International)

Fig. 34-19. A stock cart that is adaptable to production work in the school shop.

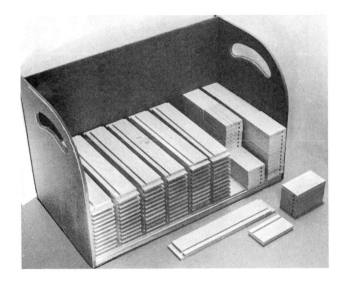

Fig. 34-20. A tote tray can be used for organizing, transporting, and storing small parts. If the parts are carefully stacked (as shown) it is easy to count and check them.

## INSPECTION POINTS

In the operations flow chart, you have probably noted the squares that are used to mark inspection points. They usually follow those operations where high accuracy and quality of work is especially important. You can readily see that it would be poor practice to just wait and see if the parts fitted properly at another station along the production line. By that time many defective pieces might have been produced, resulting in a great deal of wasted time,

materials, and money.

Inspection points will vary greatly as to the methods and procedures used. At some points, a visual check may be all that is needed. Parts are stacked together so that imperfect ones can be quickly spotted. Other points may require that each part, or every tenth part, or a certain percentage of parts be accurately checked with a rule, gauge, or some special measuring device or instrument. Industrial operations often require an entire department or group of experts to work in this area. It is known as QUALITY CONTROL.

The final inspection is very important in furniture and cabinetwork production. The unit must be square and true. Drawers, doors, and other working parts must fit smoothly and with the proper clearance. And the finish must also be carefully inspected. If a company wants to maintain a reputation for producing quality products, it is necessary to carefully inspect each unit before it is packaged and shipped.

## OPERATING THE PRODUCTION LINE

If the planning and preparation has been carefully done it will be enjoyable and exciting to actually get the article into production. A high level of perfection in timing and movement of work, however, should not be expected. Even in industrial plants, where personnel are highly trained and experts handle the work, it may require many weeks or months to perfect production lines and remove all the bugs (problems). Figs. 34-21 to 34-32 show a mass production project carried out in a school shop.

Workers can be assigned to the various work stations, using the coded numbers on the operations flow chart. Other systems can also be devised. Everyone should have an opportunity to practice their operations before the production run. Some workers may need special training and extra practice. When the run is of short duration, a given student may have several assignments, first at the beginning of the line and later at the end.

Fig. 34-21. Using a carrier board to plane stock to finished thickness.

Fig. 34-22. Precision planing stock to width on the shaper. Ring guard has been removed for this photo.

Fig. 34-23. Portable belt sander, held in a cradle to sand thin side strips.

Fig. 34-24. Fixture for cutting box ends to exact length. Regular saw guard is used for this operation.

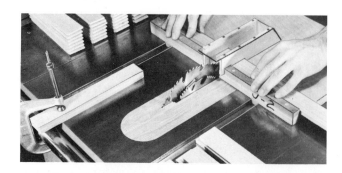

Fig. 34-25. Sides are cut to length and rabbeted in a single operation. A section of a dado head is mounted on each side of the saw blade. Note plastic-covered guard.

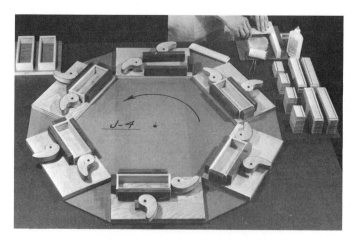

Fig. 34-26. Gluing setup for assembly of sides and ends. The polyvinyl glue makes an initial set in the time required for the subassembly to travel around the turntable.

Fig. 34-27. Rabbet joints are pressed against the applicator bar after glue has been spread on bar with roller.

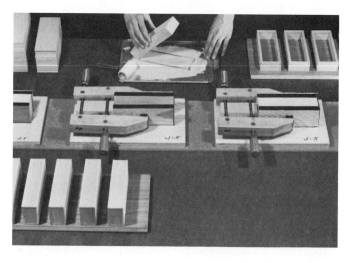

Fig. 34-28. Gluing tops and bottoms to the side and end assemblies. The clamping units are mounted on a carrier that is waxed on the underside and slides back and forth easily in front of the operator.

Fig. 34-29. Sanding outside surfaces on a stationary belt sander.

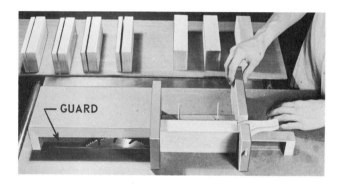

Fig. 34-30. Cutting the box open. Cut is made half way on one side and then the box is turned over to cut the othe side.

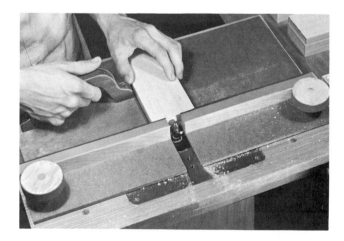

Fig. 34-31. Cutting a rabbet on the lower section to receive the lipped top. A small bench shaper is being used.

Parts that include time consuming operations and are likely to cause problems during the production run should be fabricated ahead of time. Also, all the basic stock should be selected and rough milled.

It will be quite a challenge to coordinate all the

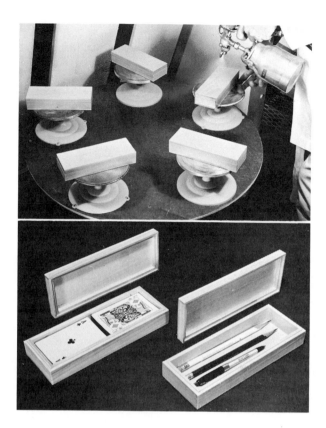

Fig. 34-32. Top. Spraying a final coat of lacquer on outside surfaces. Small turntables are mounted on the larger revolving table. Bottom. Finished boxes.

stations and keep the flow of work moving. Bottlenecks will very likely develop because of errors in planning, malfunctions in equipment, or inability of the workers. Sometimes the problems may be so severe that production will need to be closed down for the day. While supervisors or foremen make adjustments and repairs, the balance of the workers can return to their regular individual projects.

## RECORDS AND EVALUATION

At the end of the production run it will be especially valuable to review the total operation. Records should include such items as number of parts produced, total time required, percentage of waste or number of parts rejected, parts reclaimed or reworked, and total material and supplies used.

These records should be studied and evaluated along with a review of some of the problems and bottlenecks. Improved practices and organization will probably be evident. These should be discussed. Highlighted also, should be some of the operations or special jigs and fixtures that performed especially well. Those that did not meet expectations should also be pointed out, along with reasons for their failure. Fig. 34-33 shows several successful jigs and fixtures that were built in the school shop.

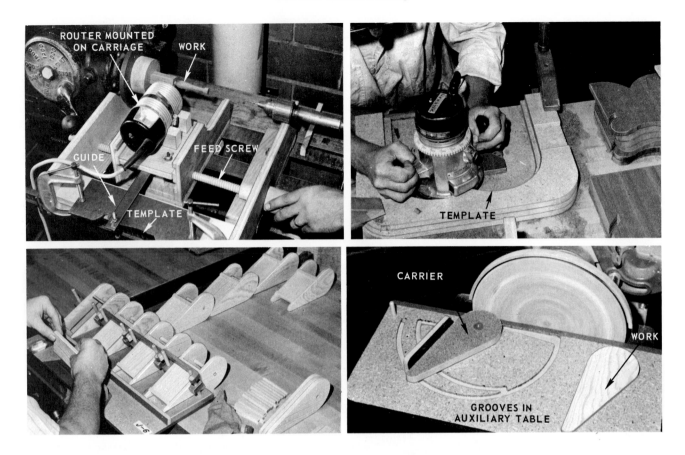

Fig. 34-33. Shop built jigs and fixtures used in mass production projects. Top left. Fixture mounted on lathe bed supports portable router. Spring (not visible) holds guide against template as carriage is fed along the cut from right to left. Top right. Blanking-out top contour of book holder end-piece. Router cut is guided as edge of base moves along template. Bottom left. Four place assembly and gluing jig. By the time the fourth compartment is filled, the first unit can be removed. Bottom right. Fixture on disk sander accurately smooths one side and both circular ends in a single operation. Carrier is guided by pins located on underside.
(Noel Mast, Dennis Marsh, Wilson Forbes)

## PRODUCTS

From the very start of a mass production project, a plan must exist for the use of the articles that will be produced. For short runs, the students involved in the work may want to divide the articles among themselves. On larger production runs it may be necessary to organize and establish a business committee. They can handle the distribution and sales, as well as control the money and pay for materials used.

Even though the emphasis in the school shop is directed toward the production aspects of a mass-produced article, some attention can be given to a study of such business and financial factors as capital outlay, raw material costs, labor costs, overhead and other expenses. Organization and control of all these, along with an efficient sales and distribution plan will be essential if the entire operation is to be profitable. In our modern industrial plants, the smooth running and efficient production line will help insure a profit only if it is a part of a sound and well-administered business structure.

## TEST YOUR KNOWLEDGE, Chapter 34

Please do not write in the text. Place your answers on a separate sheet of paper.
1. List four elements that receive special attention in mass production plants.
2. When consideration is given to the function, appearance, and consumer appeal of a product, this is known as _____ _____.
3. An experimental or sample unit of a product to be mass-produced is called a(n):
   a. Pilot model.
   b. Production idea.
   c. Operational analysis model.
   d. None of the above.
4. Rectangles used in an operations flow chart indicate the construction of special _____ and _____.
5. A square on the operations flow chart indicates procurement and storage. True or False?
6. What is the difference between a jig and a fixture?
7. What are some of the responsibilities of per-

sons working in the plant layout department?

8. List three reasons why bottlenecks are sometimes created on production lines.

9. Why is it important to detect defective products as soon as possible on the production line?

10. How valuable is it to review the total operation of a production run? Why?

## ACTIVITIES

1. Select or design a small article that can be mass produced in the school shop. Make an operational analysis and then prepare a flow chart.

2. Prepare sketches of a jig or fixture that could be used for some "key" operation in a mass production project. Include a written explanation of how it works and some of its features.

3. Design a gauge that could be used to check the thickness or width of mass produced parts to determine if they are within acceptable limits. Such a device is commonly called a "go and no-go" gauge. It has two gaps spaced so an acceptable part will slip by the first gap but not the second.

4. Study the history of the development of mass production. Learn of the contributions made by James Watt, Eli Whitney, and Henry Ford. Prepare a written or oral report for your class.

These solid wood chairs are excellent examples of mass-produced wood furniture pieces.    (Period Furniture, Inc.)

Top left. Logs debarked and ready for the mill. Right. Experimenting with cutter designs to attain a smooth surface and long lasting edge. (Kimball International) Bottom left. Construction of a light frame wood structure. Quality materials speed the work and produce a better finished product. (Southern Forest Products Association)

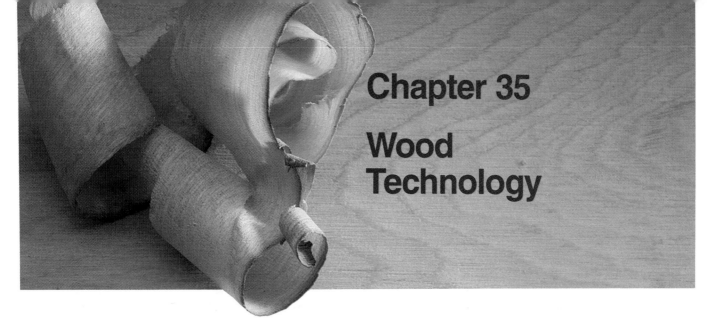

# Chapter 35

# Wood Technology

The successful woodworker must know and understand the properties and characteristics of wood. In this unit we will study wood technology and also learn something about forestry, lumbering, and wood products.

## PROPERTIES AND CHARACTERISTICS OF WOOD

### STRUCTURE AND GROWTH

Wood is not a solid material like steel or plastic. It is basically composed of many tubular fiber units, or cells, cemented together. Many properties of wood are related directly to its structure.

The long narrow tubes or cells (called fibers or tracheids) are no larger around than a human hair. Their length varies from about 1/25 in. in hardwoods to approximately 1/8 in. in softwoods. Tiny strands of cellulose make up the walls of the cells which are held together with a natural cement called lignin. This remarkable substance is unaffected by water, common chemical solvents, or heat. It is this cellular structure that makes it possible to drive nails and screws into the wood. It also accounts for the light weight, low heat transmission factors, and sound absorption qualities.

The growing, working parts of a tree are the tips of the roots, the leaves, and a layer of cells just inside the bark called the CAMBIUM. Water is absorbed by the roots and travels through the sapwood to the leaves, where it is combined with carbon dioxide from the air. Through the miracle of photosynthesis, sunlight changes these to food (carbohydrates). The food is then carried back to the various parts of the tree.

New cells are formed in the cambium layer, Fig. 35-1. The inside area of the layer (xylem) develops new wood cells while the outside area (phloem) develops cells that form the bark.

The growth in the cambium layer takes place in the spring and summer, forming separate layers

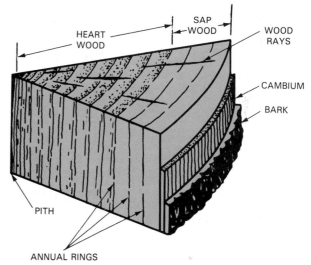

Fig. 35-1. Parts of a tree trunk.

each year. These layers are called annual rings, Fig. 35-2. In most woods the annual ring is composed of two layers, springwood and summerwood. In the spring, trees grow rapidly and the cells produced are large and thin walled. As the growth slows down during the summer months, the cells produced are smaller, thicker walled, and appear darker in color. See Fig. 35-3.

The change from springwood to summerwood may be either abrupt or gradual, depending on the kind of wood and growing condition. In such woods as maple, basswood, and poplar there is little difference in the cells formed. In oak, ash, and southern pine the difference is pronounced. These annual growth rings are largely responsible for the grain patterns that are seen in the surface of boards cut from a log. In tropical climates the growth of the tree is controlled more by wet or dry seasons than temperature changes. Generally the growth rings of woods grown in these areas are not as easily defined.

Fig. 35-2. Count the annual rings to learn the age of the tree. Drought, disease, or insects can interrupt the growth and cause an extra or false ring to be formed. (Forest Products Laboratory)

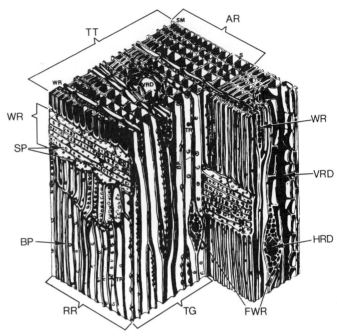

Fig. 35-4. Cell structure of a small block (1/32 in. square) of white pine softwood. (Forest Products Laboratory)

SAPWOOD contains living cells and may be several inches or more in thickness. Fast growing trees usually have a thicker layer. The HEARTWOOD of the tree is formed as the sapwood becomes inactive. It usually turns darker in color because of the presence of gums and resins. In some woods such as hemlock, spruce, and basswood there is little or no difference in the appearance. Sapwood is as strong and heavy as heartwood but not as durable when exposed to weather.

### Softwood cell structure

Fig. 35-4 is a drawing of a cell structure of a block of white pine. The drawing here shows a cube about 1/32 in. on a side.

The top of the block, TT, represents the transverse section. This is a plane parallel to the top surface of a stump or the end surface of a log. The rectangular units that make up this surface are sections through vertical cells, mostly tracheids. They are designated as TR. TRACHEIDS are elements that serve the dual function of transporting the sap and strengthening the wood. The walls of tracheids form the bulk of the wood substance in softwoods. Between the various cell units is the cementing layer, or MIDDLE LAMELLA. This thin, intercellular layer can be dissolved by certain chemicals, thus permitting the cells to be separated in making paper.

Springwood or earlywood cells, S, are formed

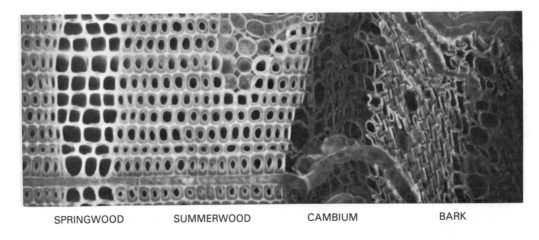

SPRINGWOOD          SUMMERWOOD          CAMBIUM          BARK

Fig. 35-3. Section through an annual ring, magnified about 220X. (Forest Products Laboratories)

during the early part of the year's growth. They are distinguishable by their greater size from the summerwood or latewood cells. These cells, SM, are formed during the later part of the growing period. Together, the earlywood and latewood cells make up the growth ring or annual ring, AR. One such ring is added each year on the outside of the wood previously formed, immediately under the bark.

Wood rays, WR, are strips of short horizontal cells that extend in a radial direction across the growth rings. The function of the wood rays is to store and to horizontally distribute the food material of the tree. They are mostly one cell wide. In softwoods that normally have resin ducts, however, fusiform wood rays, FWR, are present. They have a horizontal resin duct, HRD, at their center and are several cells wide. The large hole in the center of the top surface is a vertical resin duct, VRD.

The left side surface, RR, represents a vertical plane along the radius of the trunk. This surface is commonly called EDGE GRAIN in softwood lumber. It corresponds to the quarter-sawed surface in hardwoods.

The surface, TG, at right angles to the radial or edge grain surface, corresponds to the flat-grain or plain-sawed surface of lumber.

The symbol SP indicates a simple pit, an unthickened portion of the cell wall through which sap passes from ray cells to tracheids or vice versa. The bordered pits, BP, seen in section on surface TG, have their margins overhung by the surrounding cell walls. These structures allow the flow of sap from one tracheid to another.

## Hardwood cell structure

Fig. 35-5 is a drawing of a cell structure of yellow-poplar. It is an example of a block of hardwood. The drawing represents a block about 1/32 in. high.

The horizontal plane, TT, of the block corresponds to a minute portion of the top surface of a stump or end surface of a log. The vertical plane, RR, to the left corresponds to a surface cut parallel to the radius. The vertical plane, TG, to the right corresponds to a surface cut at right angles to the radius, or tangentially within the log. In hardwoods, these three major planes, along which wood may be cut, are known as end grain (TT), quarter-sawed (RR), and plain-sawed (TG) surfaces.

The hardwoods have specialized structures called VESSELS for conducting sap vertically, which on the end grain appear as holes or pores, P. Therefore, hardwoods are referred to as porous woods. This is in contrast to nonporous softwoods, in which the sap is transferred vertically only through cells called tracheids.

The vessels are made up of relatively large cells with open ends set one above the other. They continue as open passages or tubes for relatively long

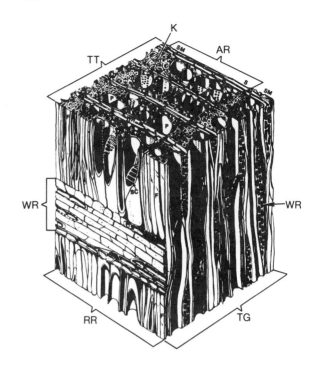

Fig. 35-5. Cell structure of a hardwood, yellow-poplar. The block of cells is about 1/32 in. square.
(Forest Products Laboratory)

distances.

The pores of hardwoods vary considerably in size. Some are visible without a magnifying glass in several species but not in others. In most hardwoods the ends of the individual cells of the vessels are entirely open, whereas in others, the opening has crossbars as indicated by SC on the radial surface.

Most of the smaller cells seen in the cross section of the drawing are wood fibers, F. They are the strength-giving elements of hardwoods. They are spindle-shaped cells, usually having small cavities and relatively thick walls. The thin places or pits, K, in the walls of the wood fibers and vessels allow the passage of sap from one cavity to another. The wood rays, WR, are strips of short horizontal cells that extend in a radial direction. They serve to store food and distribute it horizontally. In the drawing, most of the rays shown in the surface, TG, are pictured as being two cells wide. The width actually varies in different species of hardwoods, from 1 cell, as in the willows and cottonwoods, to over 50 cells in the oaks.

In woods of the temperate climate, the growth of one year is usually sharply defined from that of the previous or following year. As a rule, the springwood or earlywood is more porous than summerwood or latewood.

As with softwood, all the cells in hardwood are firmly cemented together by a thin layer, the middle lamella. This thin, intercellular layer can be dissolved by certain chemicals. This permits the fibers to be separated, as is done when making paper from wood.

## MOISTURE CONTENT AND SHRINKAGE

Before wood can be used commercially, a large part of the moisture (sap) must be removed. When a living tree is cut, more than half of its weight may be moisture. The heartwood of a "green" birch tree has a moisture content of about 75 percent. Most cabinet and furniture woods are dried to a moisture content of 7 to 10 percent.

The amount of moisture or moisture content (M.C.) in wood is expressed as a percent of the oven-dry weight. To determine the moisture content a sample is first weighed, then placed in an oven and dried at a temperature of about 212 to 220°F. The drying is continued until the sample no longer loses weight. It is weighed again. This oven-dry weight is subtracted from the initial weight. The difference is then divided by the oven-dry weight. See Fig. 35-6.

Moisture is contained in the cell cavities (free water) and in the cell walls (bound water). As the wood is dried, moisture first leaves the cell cavities. When the cells are empty but the cell walls are still full of moisture, the wood has reached a condition called the FIBER SATURATION POINT. This is about 30 percent for nearly all kinds of wood, Fig. 35-7.

The fiber saturation point is important because wood does not start to shrink until this point is reached. As the M.C. is reduced below 30 percent, moisture is removed from the cell walls and they become smaller in size. For a 1 percent moisture loss below the fiber saturation point, the wood will shrink about 1/30th in size. If dried to 15 percent M.C. the wood will have been reduced by about one-half the total shrinkage possible. A plain-sawed birch board that was 12 in. wide at 30 percent M.C.

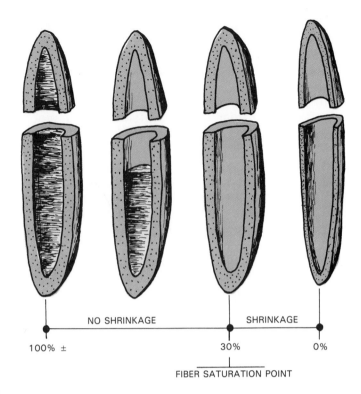

Fig. 35-7. How a wood cell dries. First the free water in the cell cavity is removed and then the cell wall dries.

will measure only about 11 in. wide at 0 percent. In general hardwoods shrink more than softwoods. Fig. 35-8 shows the shrinkage in a 2 x 10 joist.

Wood shrinks most along the direction of the annual rings (tangentially) and about one-half as much across these rings. There is practically no shrinkage in the length. How this shrinkage affects lumber cut from a log is shown in Fig. 35-9. As moisture is added to wood, it swells in the same proportion that the shrinkage has taken place.

## DRYING METHODS

Methods of drying or seasoning lumber vary with the use requirements. Today, because of the time saving and control factors, nearly all upper grades are kiln dried or dried by radio-frequency dielectric

12% - 18%

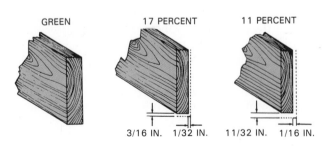

Fig. 35-8. Dimensional change in a 2 x 10 (50 x 250 mm). (Forest Products Laboratories)

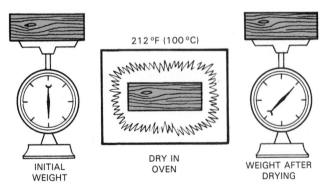

$$\text{PERCENT M.C.} = \frac{\text{INITIAL WT.} - \text{OVEN-DRY WT.}}{\text{OVEN-DRY WT.}} \times 100$$

Fig. 35-6. How to determine moisture content.

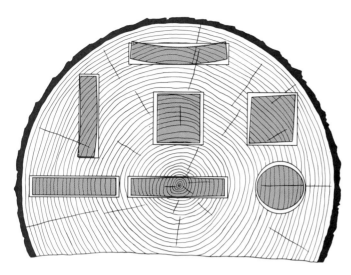

Fig. 35-9. The shrinkage and distortion of flat, square, and round pieces as affected by the direction of the annual rings. (Forest Products Laboratory)

heating. Sometimes lumber is first air dried before final drying.

## Air drying

In air drying, the lumber is simply exposed to the outside air. It is carefully stacked with STICKERS (wood strips) between each layer so air can circulate through the pile. Boards are spaced well apart in the layers so air can also move vertically. Fig. 35-10 shows lumber air drying in a sawmill yard.

The rate of air drying lumber can be partially controlled by varying the spacing between individual boards and the size of the pile. Because of the seasonal variations in climate and local weather condition, it is difficult to approximate the air drying time for any particular species or thickness. Lumber that might become dry in 30 to 60 days during an active drying period may require more than 6 months under unfavorable conditions. The moisture content of thoroughly air dried lumber, reduced during the spring, summer, or early fall will be about 12 to 18 percent.

## Oven drying

Lumber is kiln dried by placing it in an oven where the temperature and humidity are accurately controlled. The boards are stacked in about the same way as for air drying, Fig. 35-11. When the green lumber is first placed in the kiln, steam is used to keep the humidity high and the temperature is kept at a low level. Gradually, the temperature is raised and the humidity is reduced. Fans are used to keep the air in constant circulation over the surfaces of the wood. See Fig. 35-12.

A kiln schedule is a carefully compiled set of temperatures, humidities, and timings which are followed by the kiln operator. The schedule will vary depending on the size (cross section) and kind of wood, and its initial moisture content. One inch lumber can usually be kiln dried to a level of 6 to 10 percent in about three or four days.

Improper drying, either air or kiln, can result in such seasoning defects as splits, checks, warpage, loosened knots, honeycomb, and internal stresses, called case-hardening. Most of these are caused by drying the wood too rapidly. In case-hardening the surface layers dry, shrink, and become fixed or set

Fig. 35-10. Air drying lumber. Stacking method is called "flat piling." (American Forest Products Industries)

Fig. 35-11. Large kilns are used to season lumber at a sawmill. Note the "stickers" that separate the layers. (Kimball International)

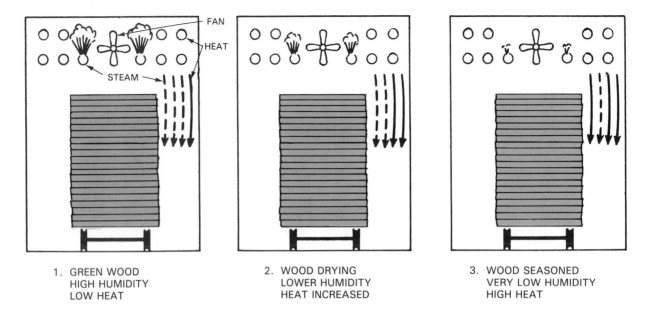

1. GREEN WOOD
HIGH HUMIDITY
LOW HEAT

2. WOOD DRYING
LOWER HUMIDITY
HEAT INCREASED

3. WOOD SEASONED
VERY LOW HUMIDITY
HIGH HEAT

Fig. 35-12. Kiln drying lumber. Temperatures range from a low of 110°F to a high of 212°F.

before the inside portion of the board. As the interior then dries below the fiber saturation point and starts to shrink, it pulls on the outside "shell," creating both compression and tension forces. When the board is cut these forces are released causing the kerf to close on (pinch) the saw blade or the stock to warp in various directions.

### Radio-frequency dielectric drying

Radio-frequency dielectric heating has helped to improve the finished quality of wood. It has improved the shear strength, impact resistance, checking resistance, and surface finish. Rapid drying is possible with this method that is not possible with kiln drying. For example, a drying time of 24 hours is possible for boards that have a beginning moisture content of 20% M.C. and an ending moisture content of 6% M.C.

Radio-frequency dielectric heating works by creating an electronic disturbance within the wood. This causes a uniform heat throughout each piece and eliminates the normal problems of case-hardening and checking.

A greater quantity of usuable lumber can be produced from wood dried by this method. With no distortion and uniform shrinkage, the dried size of each piece of lumber can be computed more accurately, therefore, reducing the need for large allowances required for kiln dried lumber.

Lumber dried by radio-frequency dielectric heating improves the color and other physical properties of wood. Staining is eliminated and end checking is reduced. Open-pored woods such as oak, ash, and walnut are ideal for this drying method. However, most softwood species do not respond well.

## MOISTURE METERS

The moisture content of wood can be determined by oven drying a sample as previously described, or by using an electric moisture meter. Although the oven drying method is the most accurate, meters are often used because readings can be secured rapidly and conveniently. They are usually calibrated to cover a range from 7 to 25 percent with an accuracy of plus or minus 1 percent of the moisture content.

Two types of meters are shown in Fig. 35-13. One determines the moisture content by measuring the electrical resistance between two pin-type electrodes that are driven into the wood. The other type measures the capacity of a condenser in a high-frequency circuit in which the wood serves as the dielectric (nonconducting) material of the condenser.

## EQUILIBRIUM MOISTURE CONTENT

A piece of wood will give off or take on moisture from the air around it until the moisture in the wood is balanced with that in the air. At this point the wood is said to be at EQUILIBRIUM MOISTURE CONTENT (E.M.C.). Since wood is exposed to daily and seasonal changes in the relative humidity of the air, it is continually making slight changes in its moisture content and therefore, changes in its dimensions. This is the reason doors and drawers often stick during humid weather but work freely the rest of the year.

Air can hold a certain amount of moisture at a certain temperature. RELATIVE HUMIDITY expresses

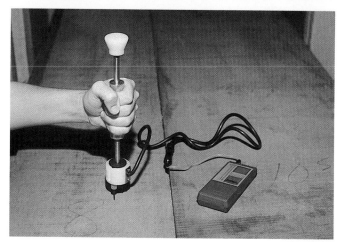

| MOISTURE CONTENT (E.M.C.) DESIRED (Percentage) | RELATIVE HUMIDITY REQUIRED (Percentage) |
|---|---|
| 5 | 24 |
| 6 | 31 |
| 7 | 37 |
| 8 | 43 |
| 9 | 49 |
| 10 | 55 |
| 11 | 60 |
| 12 | 65 |

Fig. 35-14. Relative humidities required to permit wood to remain in equilibrium at 72 °F.

Fig. 35-13. Top. Modern digital moisture meter. LED indicates correct moisture percentage. Middle. Probes inserted into end cut. Bottom. Hammer probe provides readings up to 1 in. below the surface. (Forestry Suppliers, Inc.)

what percentage of this maximum is actually being held by the air. Fig. 35-14 shows relative humidities needed for wood to remain in equilibrium at various moisture contents when the temperature is 72 °F.

Moisture changes in wood take place slowly under normal conditions. Paint and other finishes will slow this action still more, but will not prevent it entirely. Furniture and wood products should be made from wood with a moisture content equal to the average it will attain in service. Fig. 35-15 shows the average E.M.C. for interior woodwork throughout the United States. Figures for framing and exterior woodwork vary considerably but usually are several percentage points above those for interior work.

For fine furniture and fixture work the wood should be kiln dried to an M.C. somewhat below that which service conditions demand. It should then be stored in an atmosphere that will bring it to the required moisture content. The same atmospheric conditions should then be maintained throughout the manufacturing processes, until the finish is applied.

## WOOD IDENTIFICATION SAMPLES

The wood identification samples included in Unit 2 show both native and imported woods.

All of the samples shown are commercially available woods. Some are scarce and, therefore, quite expensive; others are moderate in price and used extensively in fine furniture and cabinetwork. Fig. 35-16 shows a map of North America and the general localities in which various hardwoods grow.

### FORESTRY

Forest lands constitute one of our greatest natural resources. Total area, including Alaska and Hawaii, is about 775 million acres. Nearly one-third of the continental United States is either in forests or well-suited by nature for their growth. Our forests provide the raw material for a wide range of wood-using industries. In addition to this, they help prevent excessive soil erosion, furnish ideal conditions

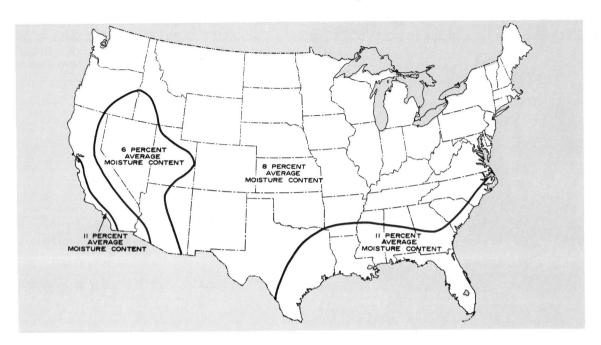

Fig. 35-15. Recommended E.M.C. averages for interior woodwork in various areas of the United States.

Fig. 35-16. Hardwoods of North America and where they grow. (Fine Hardwoods-American Walnut Association)

for wildlife, and provide areas for outdoor recreation. See Figs. 35-17 and 35-18.

Today, our supply of trees is no longer dependent entirely on nature. Sound forest management practiced by forest industries and others under the American Tree Farm System insures against the depletion of this important resource. Crops of trees are grown and harvested like other farm crops so our forests of today will also be our forests of tomorrow. Modern methods and equipment are used to plant tree seeds in nurseries, and then transplant them in the forests, Fig. 35-19.

Fig. 35-17. Cypress trees in South Florida grow to over four feet in diameter. They are especially resistant to decay from moisture.

Fig. 35-18. Fall foliage of hickory in Michigan. Hickory is used in furniture and tool handles.

Fig. 35-19. Millions of seedlings being grown at a tree farm nursery. (Mead Publishing Paper Division)

## LUMBERING

Trained foresters select and mark the trees that will be harvested. In addition to good timber, they also choose trees that are susceptible to insects and disease. Some trees are chosen because, when they are removed, a nearby tree will grow more rapidly. Trees selected for harvest are cut down with power saws or large hydraulic equipment, Fig. 35-20. Limbs are removed and the trunk is then cut into suitable lengths. This process is called BUCKING. See Fig. 35-21.

The logs are skidded to a central point with crawler tractors, where they are loaded on trucks or railroad cars for the trip to the sawmill, Fig. 35-22. In a few areas logs are still floated down streams to the mill.

Sawmills are located close to the forests and logs seldom need to be transported more than 100

Fig. 35-21. Removing the limbs and top with a chain saw. The log will then be cut into suitable lengths for transport to the mill. (Southern Forest Products Association)

Fig. 35-20. The hydraulic unit mounted on the front of this tractor is capable of cutting trees several inches in diameter, and then laying the tree down in the desired location for trimming. (Southern Forest Products Association)

Fig. 35-22. Huge logging truck moves out of timber area. This load will produce more than 12,000 board feet of lumber. The road is built and maintained by lumber company. (Weyerhauser Co.)

miles. Large mills are usually located on a river or lake so the logs can be stored in water until they are sawed. This prevents them from end-checking and insect damage. Also, it is easier to sort heavy logs by moving them around in the water. Some hardwood logs do not float very well. They are usually stacked in the mill yard where they are sprayed with water to keep them from drying out.

In large mills, logs are pulled up a jack ladder to the sawing deck where they are washed and the bark is sometimes removed, Fig. 35-23. Each log is then placed on the carriage of the headrig and moves through a giant band saw. This cuts the log into boards and timbers, Fig. 35-24. Small hardwood logs are often cut with a circular saw that may have a blade 4 feet or more in diameter.

From the headrig the boards move to smaller edger and trimmer saws that cut them to proper widths and lengths, Fig. 35-25. The rough boards are then sorted, graded, Fig. 35-26, and stacked either in the yard for air drying, or sent to huge

Fig. 35-24. Operator (called a sawyer) seated at control console of headrig. High speed bandsaw blade (arrow) produces slabs, timbers, and large rectangular pieces called "cants." (John Walker)

Fig. 35-23. Top. Logs are carried into the mill by the bull chain of a jack ladder. Bottom. Debarking a log before sawing. (Southern Forest Products Association)

Fig. 35-25. Rough boards are cut to various lengths with multiple trimmer saws.

Fig. 35-26. Grading boards as they come from the trimmer saws. (Southern Forest Products Association)

Fig. 35-27. Selected "peeler" logs, cut from the lower portion of the tree, are used for plywood. (American Plywood Association)

ovens for kiln drying. Large mills usually have a planing mill section where the dried lumber is surfaced and made into finished lumber. After leaving the planers the lumber is again graded, trimmed to remove defects, sorted by length and grade, and then prepared for shipment.

## PLYWOOD AND VENEER

Top quality softwood logs are selected for plywood fabrication, Fig. 35-27. Because of the limited supply, a large part of the total production of some of the fine hardwoods is cut into veneer. This is used to face high grade plywood panels. Veneer, both softwood and hardwood, is also used to manufacture boxes, crates, food containers, and other products that require thin pieces of wood. Such items as tongue depressors, mustard paddles, ice cream spoons, and Popsicle sticks are stamped from sheets of veneer.

Prior to cutting the veneer, the logs are cleaned and the bark removed. Hardwood logs are heated in hot water vats or steam chambers to make the cutting easier and help insure smooth unbroken sheets.

Nearly all veneer, especially softwood, is cut by the rotary method. The log is mounted in a huge lathe and revolves against a razor-sharp knife that peels off a thin continuous ribbon of wood. Fig. 35-28 shows a section drawing of the knife carriage of a veneer lathe. The angles and settings must be carefully controlled. Note that the thickness of the veneer is determined by the distance between the nose bar and the knife edge. As the veneer is cut, the wood fibers are compressed on one side

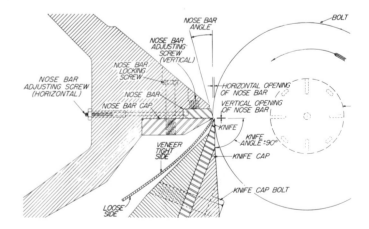

Fig. 35-28. Knife carriage of a veneer lathe. Angles and settings vary for different kinds and thicknesses of veneer. The nose bar is pressed tightly against the log. (Forest Products Laboratory)

and stretched on the other, forming what is called a tight side and a loose side, Fig. 35-29. The tight side should be used for the exposed face of plywood or veneer work.

Fig. 35-30 shows the steps in softwood plywood manufacturing. After the veneer is cut, giant knives, controlled by skilled operators, cut the veneer to proper width for full utilization. It then enters large ovens or dryers that operate at temperatures of about 350 °F. Travel time through a 100 foot dryer may vary from 6 to 20 minutes depending on the thickness of the veneer. When it emerges from the dryer, the moisture content (M.C.) will have been reduced to about 4 percent.

Next the sheets are patched, Fig. 35-31. Natural defects are cut out and replaced with solid wood, expertly glued into place. Some of the sheets then go through a glue spreader, Fig. 35-32, where an even coat of adhesive is applied to each side. These glue-covered pieces are stacked alternately with dry veneer to make up the plywood panel. There is always an odd number of veneers (3, 5, 7,) and the

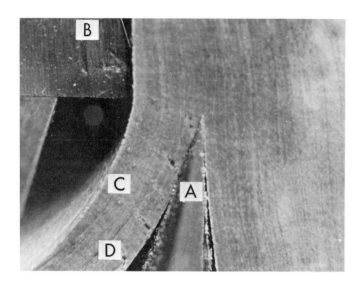

Fig. 35-29. Enlarged view of rotary veneer cutting. A—Knife. B—Nose bar. C—Tight side of veneer. D—Loose side and cracks in the veneer.

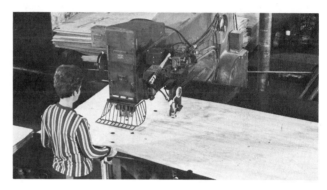

Fig. 35-31. Automatic machine (controlled by a pedal) stamps out knots and then glues patches into place.

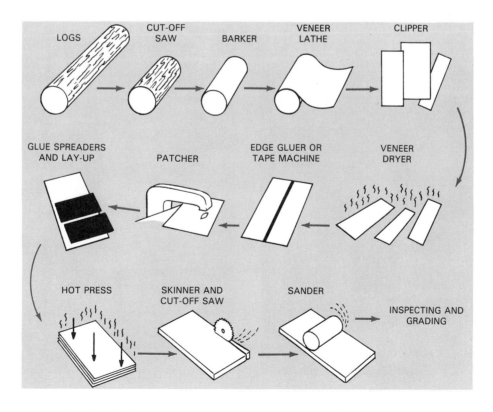

Fig. 35-30. Sequence in manufacturing plywood. (Weyerhauser Co.)

Fig. 35-32. Veneer sheets are fed through a glue spreader and placed in the "lay-up."

are heated to speed the setting of the glue. From the press, panels then move through double-end machines, Fig. 35-34. These trim the panels to exact size. Wide belt sanders are used to sand the panel faces. Finally comes inspection, the careful repair of blemishes, and final grading.

Hardwood plywood is manufactured in about the same way except that face veneers are more carefully matched, edge jointed, and glued. Quite often hardwood veneer is produced by slicing, Fig. 35-35. The flitch (log section) is moved downward against a knife edge, which cuts off sheets of the wood, Fig. 35-36. Because the veneer is forced abruptly away from the flitch by the knife, fine checks or breaks may occur on the knife side. This is similar to the loose side in rotary cutting and should be used for the glue side.

For fine furniture and cabinetwork, the grain and figure patterns of hardwood veneers are matched in various ways to produce panels of interesting design. Sometimes they are assembled to form symmetrical patterns called "book matched" and "diamond matched." The figure pattern in the veneer is determined by the kind of wood used, how the veneer is cut, and the portion of the tree in which it is located, Fig. 35-37.

direction of the grain is always placed at right angles to that of adjacent layers.

After the lay-up, panels go into powerful presses that exert pressure of more than 150 lbs. per square inch, Fig. 35-33. The platens (plates) of the press

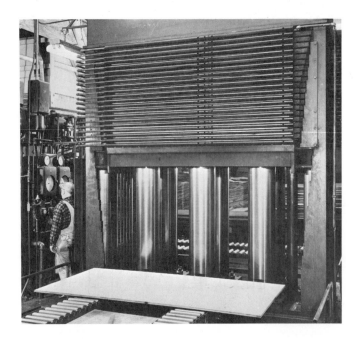

Fig. 35-33. Giant hydraulic press with heated platens and 20 openings (daylights). (American Plywood Association)

Fig. 35-34. Double-end machines trim the plywood panels to exact width and length.

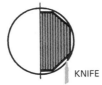

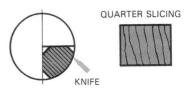

**Rotary**

The log is mounted centrally in the lathe and turned against a razor sharp blade, like unwinding a roll of paper. Since this cut follows the log's annular growth rings a bold variegated grain marking is produced. Rotary cut veneer is exceptionally wide.

**Plain Slicing (or flat slicing)**

The half log, or flitch, is mounted with the heart side flat against the guide plate of the slicer and the slicing is done parallel to a line through the center of the log. This produces a variegated figure.

**Quarter Slicing**

The quarter log or flitch is mounted on the guide plate so that the growth rings of the log strike the knife at approximately right angles, producing a series of stripes, straight in some woods, varied in others.

Fig. 35-35. Methods used to cut hardwood veneer. (Fine Hardwoods—American Walnut Association)

Fig. 35-36. Top. Slicing veneer. Flitch is clamped to machine table with hydraulic cylinders and moved up and down against a sharp knife. The machine operates at 80 strokes per minute. Veneer sheets are carried away on conveyor belts as shown. Bottom. Veneer plant worker stacks sheets of walnut veneer as they leave the end of the slicing machine. The veneer shown is 1/36 in. thick. (Bacon Veneer Co.)

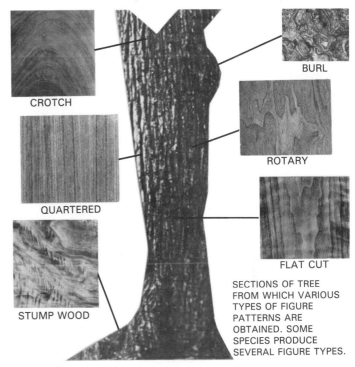

SECTIONS OF TREE FROM WHICH VARIOUS TYPES OF FIGURE PATTERNS ARE OBTAINED. SOME SPECIES PRODUCE SEVERAL FIGURE TYPES.

Fig. 35-37. Types of cuts and sections of tree from which various figure patterns are obtained. (Fine Hardwoods—American Walnut Association)

## MANUFACTURED BOARD

### Hardboard

Hardboard is a manufactured product made by bonding together wood fibers. The wood is reduced to individual fibers and then reunited with lignin, the natural cohesive substance found in all wood. Fig. 35-38 shows the process. Other composition board products are made with synthetic binders.

Various kinds of wood can be used to make hardboard. Residues (scrap and waste) from sawmills and plywood plants are used extensively. The wood

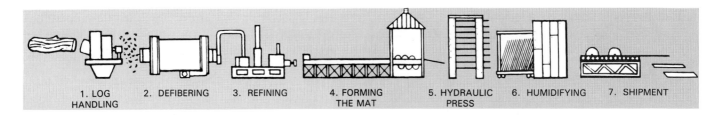

| 1. LOG HANDLING | 2. DEFIBERING | 3. REFINING | 4. FORMING THE MAT | 5. HYDRAULIC PRESS | 6. HUMIDIFYING | 7. SHIPMENT |

Fig. 35-38. Processes used in manufacturing hardboard.

is first chipped into thin pieces about 5/8 in. wide and 1 in. long. The chips are then reduced to individual fibers by either steam or special defibering machines. In the steam process the chips are placed in steam chests under tremendous pressure. When the pressure is suddenly released the chips explode into tiny fiber bundles, in about the same way some breakfast food cereals are formed, Fig. 35-39.

After certain refining processes are completed, the fibers are mixed in a tank of water and fed onto a moving screen to form a mat, Fig. 35-40. Another system is sometimes used, where the fibers are blown into a large metal cone and settle down (into a mat) like snowflakes. The thick blanket travels through rollers that compress the interlocking fibers. This compressed mat is cut into rough panel sizes and placed in multiple presses where heat and pressure produce the thin, hard, dry sheets. After the panels are conditioned through a humidification process, they are trimmed to size, Fig. 35-41.

The manufacturing process may include certain additives and heat treatments that result in a product with increased stiffness, hardness, and

Fig. 35-40. Checking the thickness of the "wet-lap." Rollers squeeze out water and compress fibers.

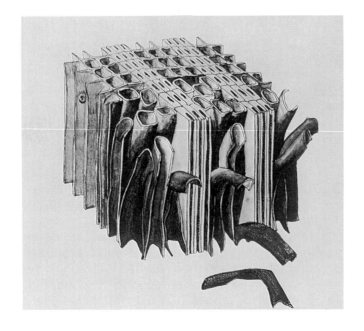

Fig. 35-39. This drawing illustrates how wood is reduced to individual fibers for hardboard production. (Forest Products Laboratory)

Fig. 35-41. Cutting and trimming the hardboard into standard size panels. (Masonite Corp.)

durability. This board is called tempered hardboard. Various surface textures and forms can be molded or cut into hardboard.

## Particle board

Particle board is made by combining wood flakes and chips with resin binders and hot-pressing them into panels, Fig. 35-42. This material, like hardboard, is a result of research and development in wood technology combined with modern adhesives and manufacturing equipment.

Special machines slice the wood flakes, Fig. 35-43, into the exact size required for the product being produced. The flakes are then mixed with a urea-formaldehyde resin adhesive. Boards that will be used in exterior applications are bonded with a phenolic resin.

This mixture is then formed into sheets, either by an extrusion process or a mat-forming process similar to that used for hardboard. The sheets are cut to rough size and bonded in huge hot presses. To complete the process, the edges are trimmed. The surface is sometimes filled and sanded or overlaid with various materials, Fig. 35-44.

## Waferboard

Waferboard panels are manufactured from poplar aspen that is roundwood cut into random width wafers, Fig. 35-45. The wafers are large and produce a slightly textured surface. They are approved for interior as well as exterior applications.

Fig. 35-42. Close-up view of a particle board panel surface. The flakes are still visible even though the surface is smooth.

Fig. 35-44. Sample of high-grade particle board surfaced with hardwood veneer. Note quality of machined edges. (Georgia Pacific Corporation)

Fig. 35-43. Dry wood flakes for particle board are sifted as they move along a conveyor. (National Particle Board Association)

Fig. 35-45. Waferboard panel products include sheathing, soffits, and several other applications. (Georgia Pacific Corporation)

## Oriented strand board

Oriented strand board is similar to waferboard in appearance, manufacture, and application. The primary difference between the products is that oriented strand board is made from longer strands of fibers. These are arranged in successive layers at right angles to one another, Fig. 35-46. The arrangement of the strands increases strength.

## OTHER FOREST PRODUCTS

In addition to lumber, poles, ties, veneer, plywood, and various composition boards, a total list of products from our forests includes many more items. For example, gums and resins harvested from living trees are used to make waxes, varnish, paint, driers, printing ink, rubber, insecticides, drugs, and chewing gum. More than 15 million cords of pulp wood are used annually for paper and cardboard, Fig. 35-47. Books, newspapers, magazines, food packages, shipping boxes, and countless other paper based products must be added to the list.

Through the magic of modern chemistry, wood cellulose is transformed into thousands of products such as lacquers, synthetic fibers for cloth, photographic film, plastics, linoleum, alcohol, and a component in the solid-fuels used in rockets.

## RESEARCH AND DEVELOPMENT

Although great progress has been made in the perfection of wood products and the full utilization of our forests, more new and spectacular developments will result from continuing programs of

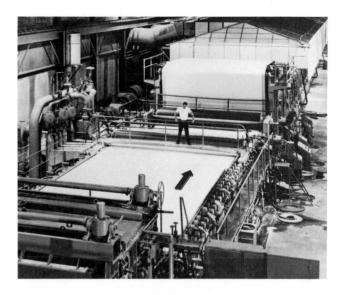

Fig. 35-47. ''Wet'' end of paperboard machine. Headbox, shown in foreground, controls the flow of wet pulp onto a moving mesh screen which extracts the water. The board is pressed and dried as it moves through heated rollers located under the enclosure in the background. (Potlatch Corp.)

research. Many commercial lumber companies conduct such programs. A major institution devoted to scientific experimentation and testing of wood is the Forest Products Laboratory in Madison, Wisconsin. It is a division of the Forest Service of the United States Department of Agriculture, Fig. 35-48.

Research conducted at the Forest Products Laboratory benefits producers, processors, distributors, and consumers of all kinds of wood products and by-products. Some research includes studies of wood structure and properties, grading, identification and classification, mill equipment, utilization of residues, seasoning and kiln schedules, adhesives, plywood and hardboard fabrication, paints, finishes, wood preservatives, joints and fasteners, sandwich panel construction, packaging, and tree growth. Research studies are also conducted on wood pulp, paper, and chemical products.

Current research is designed to reduce waste during the harvest operation and milling. For example, smaller logs are being used for lumber. Branches and wood residue are used in the production of particle board. Sawing techniques are now aided by computer to reduce waste and produce higher quality boards. Less waste is also possible with laser beam cutting which produces a very thin kerf, little noise, and no sawdust. This technique is still experimental commercially, but has been demonstrated in the laboratory.

Technical and scientific information about wood and wood products is available to industrial concerns, business people, farmers, teachers, and students.

Fig. 35-46. Oriented strand board. (Georgia Pacific Corporation)

Fig. 35-48. Forest Products Laboratory is a world center for wood research and development.

## TEST YOUR KNOWLEDGE, Chapter 35

Please do not write in the text. Place your answers on a separate sheet of paper.

1. The cellular structure of wood is held together with a natural cement called:
   a. Bark.
   b. Pith.
   c. Cambium.
   d. None of the above.
2. Where are new cells of wood and bark formed?
3. In some species of wood there is no difference in the appearance of sapwood and heartwood. True or False?
4. _____ are elements that serve the dual function of transporting sap and strengthening wood.
5. What is the initial M.C. of a wood sample that weighed 56 grams before oven drying and 50 grams after oven drying?
6. The fiber saturation point for nearly all kinds of wood is _____ percent M.C.
   a. 30.
   b. 35.
   c. 75.
   d. None of the above.
7. What are stickers?
8. What does E.M.C. stand for in woodworking?
9. Explain how radio-frequency dielectric heating works to dry wood.
10. Top quality softwood logs are selected for _____ fabrication.
11. The _____ (tight side, loose side) is used for the exposed face of plywood or veneer work.
12. How is hardboard manufactured?

## ACTIVITIES

1. Secure a sample of wood from your school shop stock room and determine the moisture content by the oven drying method. If you weigh the sample at school and dry it out at home, be sure to wrap it tightly in metal foil or plastic film so it will not gain or lose moisture between the weighing and drying operations.
2. Conduct a study of the E.M.C. of wood in your school or home workshop. Prepare a chart that will show daily, weekly, and monthly changes. A convenient way to secure M.C. readings is to prepare a wood sample (for pine about 3/8 x 3 x 10), dry it completely in an oven, and then reduce it in size until it weighs exactly 100 grams. As it gains moisture from the air you can make a direct reading of the M.C. For example, when it weighs 109 grams, the M.C. will be 9 percent.

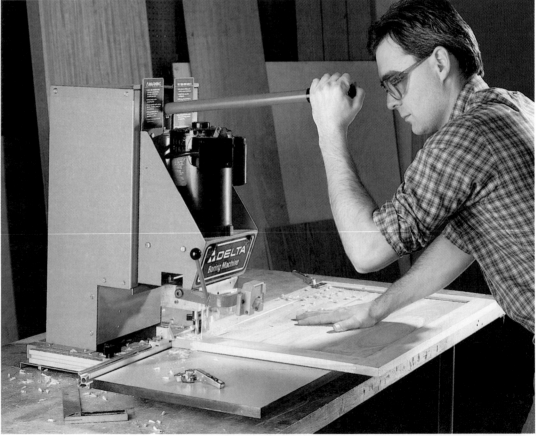

Top. Teamwork is a critical factor in your success on any job. (Marvin Windows) Bottom. A semiskilled worker prepares cabinet panels.   (Delta International Machinery Corp.)

# Chapter 36

# Career Opportunities

The wood and forest product industries offer a tremendous range of career opportunities. More than 2 million people are employed in the broad areas of forestry, lumbering, millwork, furniture manufacturing, wood construction, and the distribution of forest products. Wood, always a desired material for furniture and home interiors, continues to grow in importance and popularity. And, because wood is a natural resource from timberlands that are capable of renewing themselves, future growth in the industry will not be limited by a shortage of raw material.

## FORESTRY

If you enjoy the outdoors and like to work close to nature, you may wish to consider a career in this field. Basically, forestry covers the management of our forests so our supply of timber will be continuous. Many dedicated workers and specialists are needed for the operations of seeding, planting, fertilizing, and cultivating. Careful records are kept of tree growth so that procedures followed in these operations can be evaluated, Fig. 36-1. Other important programs in forestry cover fire control and the prevention of attacks by insects and disease.

Conservation in forest management is more than following practices that insure full use of our trees. It also includes growing more wood faster on existing areas. This is accomplished, to a large extent, through genetic research. Such research often includes artificial fertilization and grafting.

The forester and forester's assistants are trained to handle environmental problems. They know how to maintain the best growing conditions for trees, and at the same time protect against soil erosion which lowers the quality of the land and fouls rivers and lakes. Properly managed forest lands provide protection for wildlife and improved conditions for recreation. Write to the Forest Service, U.S. Dept. of Agriculture, Washington, DC 20250, for booklets on careers in forestry.

Fig. 36-1. Forester checks and records growth of Douglas fir trees seeded by helicopter. (John Walker)

## LUMBERING

The United States produces a third of the world's lumber, over half of its plywood and nearly half of its paper and paperboard. This requires a large lumbering industry.

Lumbering operations begin with the selection and cutting of trees, Fig. 36-2. Jobs include lumber jacks, fallers, limbers, and buckers. Highly skilled machine operators are needed to process the logs as they are moved into the sawmill. Lumber graders must have a great deal of experience and keep up to date on regulations and standards. The operation of modern dry kilns demands technicians who are experts in this area, Fig. 36-3.

Although large sawmills usually include a division

Fig. 36-2. Operating modern lumbering equipment requires skilled operators who enjoy the outdoors. (Southern Forest Products Association)

Fig. 36-3. Technician inspects pine lumber before it moves into dry kiln. (Georgia Pacific Corporation)

where plywood is made, many plants specialize in the manufacture only of plywood, Fig. 36-4. Sometimes a plant will simply produce the veneer which is then shipped to other mills or furniture plants for final processing.

There has been tremendous growth in the production of plywood as well as hardboard and particle board. This is partly because these materials permit greater utilization of timber resources and partly because sheet materials are generally easier to fabricate into finished products. This segment of the lumbering industry offers a wide range of job opportunities.

## PAPERMAKING

Papermaking is closely related to lumbering because about 95 percent of the raw material used is wood pulp. Although a large part of the pulp is produced from small logs, considerable use is made of wood residue (saw dust, chips, and waste). Papermaking is a highly complicated process and employs a wide range of processing equipment. The industry requires a great many skilled workers and technicians, Fig. 36-5.

Fig. 36-4. Skilled inspector makes final visual check of plywood panels. Conveyor line mechanism turns panel over so both sides can be viewed. (Weyerhauser Co.)

## MANUFACTURING

More than 5000 industrial woodworking companies are located throughout the United States and Canada. They manufacture furniture, doors and windows, cabinetwork, sports equipment, and many other products. Occupations in these industries include woodworkers, technicians, and professionals. Woodworkers are generally described as skilled or semiskilled.

Large woodworking plants employ many semiskilled workers. These jobs include moving and handling material and feeding machines, Fig. 36-6. Some of the operations along an assembly line are similar in nature and may require some on-the-job training, Fig. 36-7. As in other industries, the development of automatic and tape-controlled machines and equipment, is gradually reducing the demand for workers with this level of skill.

Important careers in the manufacturing of wood products include designing, industrial engineering, market research, and plant supervision, Fig. 36-8. People in these positions usually have college degrees and/or many years of experience. Technicians with know-how about new adhesives,

Fig. 36-5. Technician in glass enclosed booth monitors computer-controlled papermaking machine. (Georgia Pacific Corporation)

Fig. 36-6. Semiskilled worker feeds workpieces into double-end tenoner. (Campbellrhea Mfg., Inc.)

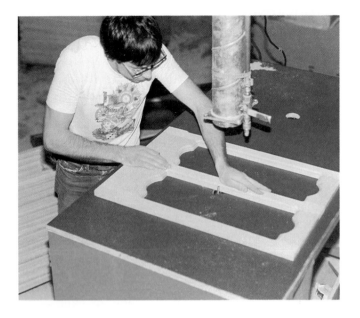

Fig. 36-7. Semiskilled assembly line worker routing a groove on the back side of a cabinet door frame. This task requires limited on-the-job training. (Bertch Wood Specialities)

Fig. 36-9. Skilled worker checks the setup on a shaper with power feed mechanism. (Bertch Wood Specialities)

finishes, abrasives, machines, and processes are in great demand. These technicians, along with highly skilled woodworkers are usually responsible for organizing production lines, directing the production schedule, evaluating processes, and checking the finished product. The skilled woodworker usually handles the work of building machine fixtures and of setting up and checking the machine operation, Fig. 36-9. It is exciting work adjusting and setting up production machines, and then watching them produce the workpieces with speed and accuracy.

More than 100 companies are engaged in the manufacture of woodworking machinery and equipment. Technicians and artisans in this field of work must be expert metalworkers. Further, they must have a thorough understanding of the wood and wood products that the machines will process. The latter is especially true of those who work in the area of sales and service. Machine manufacturers seldom produce the blades and cutterheads for their equipment. They depend on a number of companies which specialize in this field, Fig. 36-10.

Fig. 36-8. Plant executive discusses plans for a new product with the designer and production supervisor. (Kimball International)

Fig. 36-10. The workers in this company specialize in the manufacture and maintenance of blades and cutterheads. (North American Products Corp.)

Interesting career opportunities are available in upholstery and wood finishing. In most industries, these areas of work are performed as a part of the total manufacture of a product. Individuals who have skills and technical knowledge in these areas often establish their own businesses, offering custom upholstery or finishing and painting services in a local community.

Patternmaking demands the highest level of skill found in any of the woodworking trades. It requires about the same tools and machines you have used in the school shop, Fig. 36-11. Although some industries have a patternmaking department, most original wood patterns are produced by small companies that limit their work to this specialized field.

## CONSTRUCTION

Experts predict that the construction industry will continue to grow very rapidly in the years ahead. Construction will continue to require a higher proportion of skilled workers than any of the manufacturing industries. About one-third of all building construction artisans are carpenters, the single largest skilled occupation, Fig. 36-12.

Carpenters must be highly skilled in the use of hand and power tools. They must be able to read and interpret building plans, lay out foundations,

Fig. 36-12. Carpenter installing roof sheathing on a modern home. The work is physically demanding, but provides a sense of accomplishment when completed.
(Georgia Pacific Corporation)

Fig. 36-11. Patternmaker using a gouge to form a curved surface on a large circular pattern. (Fisher Controls)

construct wood frames, apply sheathing, install windows and doors, and perform inside and outsde finishing operations. Some carpenters specialize in either rough framing and structural work or finished interior trim and cabinetmaking.

Carpenters are usually the most important people on the residential building site. They must know the where, when, and how of nearly every kind of building material. Because of this broad knowledge, many have the opportunity to become general supervisors on major construction projects. Self-employment is common in carpentry. The experienced carpenter often moves into contracting work and becomes an employer of workers in the building trades.

To become a skilled carpenter you will need to complete high school. If available, you should enroll in technical school courses related to carpentry and building construction. You should then serve as an apprentice for a number of years, learning information and skills on the job, Fig. 36-13. A career as a carpenter is hard work, but it is interesting and profitable too. As a carpenter, you will experience a special feeling of satisfaction at the end of each day or week as you see buildings and structures develop, knowing it was partly due to your efforts.

## DISTRIBUTION

Many career opportunities are found in the distribution and sale of lumber and wood products.

There are over 30,000 retail building supply centers. There are some in every community. To secure employment in these centers you must have a good understanding of wood and wood products. Beyond that, you must be able to answer questions about their application and use. As you gain experience, you will likely be expected to read blueprints, prepare estimates, and figure building costs.

Managers and sales people in furniture stores should be able to identify various kinds of wood. They also need to know about wood joints, types of construction, and kinds and characteristics of modern wood finishes. These same requirements apply to the personnel in the growing number of kitchen cabinet planning and sales centers.

## WOOD SCIENCE AND TECHNOLOGY

Industrial companies and governmental agencies offer attractive career opportunities to wood scientists and technologists. People who qualify for these positions will devote most of their efforts to research and development activities. Typical projects include the continuing search for better and faster ways to grow trees; ways to reduce wood waste; and better methods of producing wood products. Specific activities might include the analysis of various species of wood to determine the best one to use for a given product. See Figs. 36-14 and 36-15.

Fig. 36-13. Apprenticeship programs provide on-the-job training. In this photograph, a carpenter is explaining fastening techniques to an apprentice.
(United Brotherhood of Carpenters and Joiners of America)

Fig. 36-14. Chemist looks at chromatographic analysis to study trace elements in given species of wood.

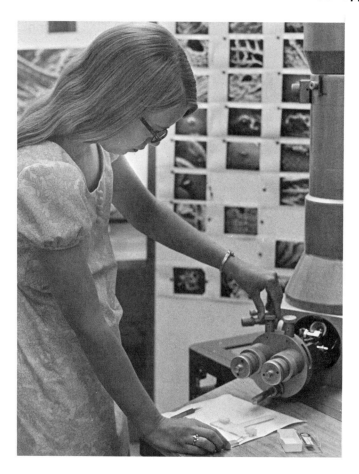

Fig. 36-15. Technician uses electron microscope to probe wood's fine structure. Microscope is capable of providing a magnification of 100,000X. (Forest Products Laboratories)

Fig. 36-16. Engineer connects strain gauge to hardboard web of wood beam. This is one of many devices used to evaluate design. (Forest Products Laboratories)

Trained technicians may be involved with the development of new and better adhesives and finishes for wood. Another interesting area covers the development and testing of new and more economical structural designs and building components. See Fig. 36-16.

College and university degrees are generally required for the wood scientist and for those who direct the work in forestry and forest product research. More than 40 schools located throughout the nation provide training in these fields of study. Technicians who assist in this kind of work can often get the basic training required in vocational/technical schools. If you enjoy working with young people, the teaching profession can offer you a rewarding career. Over 200 educational institutions offer teaching degrees in Industrial Technology and technical subjects, Fig. 36-17.

To prepare for any of the careers previously described you should, of course, complete your high school studies. Take as many woodworking courses as possible but do not neglect courses in other shop areas, especially drafting.

Students tend to minimize the importance of

Fig. 36-17. Shop instructor checks student's progress on wood turning lathe. (Rockwell International)

science, math, and English. This is unfortunate because top artisans and technicians in the field of woodworking need to adjust constantly to new scientific developments and advances in technology. They need to be competent in reading, writing, and speaking the English language.

Further preparation for the woodworking trades and occupations may be secured in vocational/technical schools and/or apprenticeship training programs. Visit or write to schools about their course offerings and secure information from industries and trade associations. Also visit with carpenters and the managers of any wood products industry that might be located in your community.

For information about careers in woodworking, write to: Director, Wood Industry Careers Program, National Forest Products Association, 1619 Massachusetts Ave., Washington, DC 20036.

## LEADERSHIP

The ability to lead and influence others is known as LEADERSHIP. A LEADER is someone who is in charge or command. Good leadership is necessary if an organization or business is to be successful.

There is no definition of a good leader. Studies tell us, however, that there are several qualities commonly found in all good leaders. They include the following:

VISION. This is the ability to know what needs to be done presently and in the future. Vision also includes the ability to set a schedule in order to achieve goals.

COMMUNICATION. A good leader is able to share information clearly and understandably. In addition, a strong leader is able to create an atmosphere of communication in the group he or she is heading.

PERSISTENCE. This is the ability to focus on overall goals and important points. Persistent leaders are not distracted from their goals very easily. They often work long, hard hours to reach their goals.

ORGANIZATIONAL ABILITY. Organizing and directing others is an important trait for good leadership. Organized leaders are capable of making changes based on past mistakes. They are also tactful but can command cooperation of the group when necessary.

RESPONSIBILITY. A responsible leader holds himself or herself responsible for his or her own actions. In addition, a responsible leader also gives credit to those who are deserving of it.

DELEGATES AUTHORITY. Good leaders are eager to give others, who are capable, tasks that will increase their leadership skills.

Many organizations offer the chance to gain leadership skills. Student organizations include the VOCATIONAL INDUSTRIAL CLUBS OF AMERICA

Fig. 36-18. Look for leadership opportunities in student organizations such as the Vocational Industrial Clubs of Amerca. (VICA)

(VICA) and TECHNOLOGY STUDENT ASSOCIATION (TSA). These organizations are helpful in developing leadership skills as they relate to the industrial/technical world, Fig. 36-18.

## TEST YOUR KNOWLEDGE, Chapter 36

Please do not write in the text. Place your answers on a separate sheet of paper.
1. What does conservation in forest management include?
2. Why has there been a large increase in the production of plywood, hardboard, and particle board?
3. In papermaking, about 95 percent of the raw material used is _____ _____.
4. A position as a semiskilled worker requires:
   a. Some on-the-job training.
   b. A college degree.
   c. Many years of experience.
   d. None of the above.
5. _____ requires the highest level of skill found in any of the woodworking trades.
6. Briefly explain how to go about becoming a carpenter.

## ACTIVITIES

1. Obtain job applications from several nearby businesses. Study the information they request. Prepare a bulletin board display of these applications. Ask the personnel director from one of

these companies to visit your class to discuss what it expected of their employees.

2. Compile an information packet on woodworking occupations. Use the Occupational Outlook Handbook as a source. Make this packet available to the class.

3. Write to the Wood Industry Careers Program (address is given in the unit) for information on various careers in woodworking. Make an outline of the type of schooling you would need in order to work in one of these areas. Include a timetable schedule to follow in order to meet these goals.

4. Conduct a student survey to learn if there is interest in starting a VICA or TSA group in your school. If there is sufficient interest, discuss with your instructor school policy and rules for starting such a group.

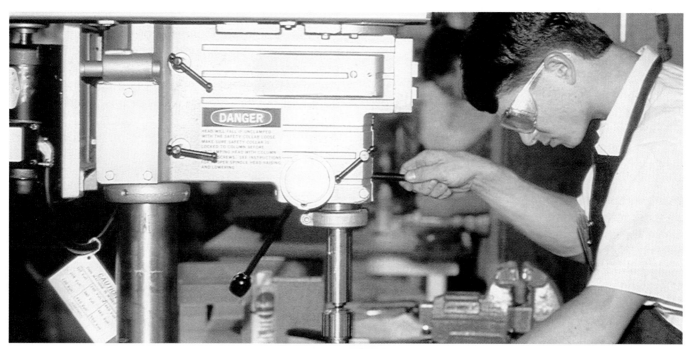

Students learn how to work and solve problems in woodworking classes.   (VICA)

# Glossary of Terms

**A**

**Acetone:** Very flammable solvent used for removing paint.

**Acrylic Resin Adhesive:** Water-resistant adhesive used to bond wood, metal, glass, and concrete (not recommended for plastics).

**Adhesive:** General term for a substance used to hold materials together by surface attachment. It includes cement, glue, paste, and mucilage.

**Air-Dried Lumber:** Lumber that has been piled in yards or sheds for a length of time. The minimum moisture content of thoroughly air-dried lumber is usually twelve to fifteen percent.

**Alkyd Resin:** Synthetic material which, when combined with a drying oil such as linseed oil or soybean oil, forms one of the most widely used vehicles for paints and enamels.

**Aluminum Oxide:** Abrasive made by fusing bauxite clay in an electric furnace; used in the manufacture of grinding wheels, sharpening stones, and abrasive papers.

**Anchor:** Any fastener used to attach parts, such as joists and trusses, to masonry or wood.

**Anchor Bolt:** Threaded rod used in construction to anchor the sill plate to the foundation.

**Annual Growth Ring:** Growth ring of a tree formed in a single year; composed of springwood and summerwood.

**Antiquing:** Process that ages the piece.

**Apron:** Trim used under the stool on interior windows.

**Arbor:** Short shaft or spindle on which another rotating part is mounted.

**Arch:** Curved structure that will support itself and the weight above its curved opening by mutual pressure.

**Areaway:** Recessed area below grade around the foundation that allows light and ventilation into basement window.

**Aromatic Red Cedar:** Similar characteristics to Western red cedar. Primarily used in construction of chests and closet linings because of its insect repellence.

**Arris:** Sharp edge formed when two planes or surfaces meet.

**Asphalt Shingles:** Composition roof shingles made from asphalt-impregnated felt covered with mineral granules.

**Atomization:** Breaking up of paint into finely divided tiny droplets; forming a fog or mist from a liquid, usually accomplished in spray painting.

**Awning Window:** Outward swinging window hinged at the top.

**B**

**Backfill:** Replacement of excavated earth into a trench around and against a basement foundation.

**Balloon Framing:** System of framing a building in which all vertical structural elements of the bearing walls and partitions consist of single pieces. These pieces extend from the top of the foundation sill plate to the roof plate and are fastened to all floor joists.

**Balusters:** Usually small vertical members in a railing used between a top rail and the stair treads or a bottom rail.

**Balustrade:** Series of balusters connected by a rail; generally used for porches and balconies.

**Banister:** Handrail with supporting posts used alongside a stairway.

**Bare-Faced Tenon:** Tenon shouldered on only one side.

**Baseboard:** Finish board covering the interior wall where the wall and floor meet.

**Base Shoe:** Molding used next to the floor in interior baseboards.

**Base Units:** In SI metric, the seven units which indicate the quantities of length, mass, time, electric current, temperature, amount of substance, and luminous intensity. Most other metric units are derived from them.

**Batt:** Roll or sheet of insulation installed between members of frame construction.

**Batten:** Strip of wood placed across a wood surface to cover joints or to strengthen the assembly.

**Batter Board:** One of a pair of horizontal boards

nailed to posts set at the corners of an excavation. Used to indicate the desired level and as a fastening for stretched strings to indicate outlines of foundation walls.

**Bay Window:** Window space projecting outward from the walls of a building.

**Beam:** Structural member transversely supporting a load.

**Beam Ceiling:** Ceiling in which the ceiling beams are exposed to view.

**Bearing Partition:** Partition that supports any vertical load in addition to its own weight.

**Bearing Wall:** Wall that supports any vertical load in addition to its own weight.

**Beech:** Whitish to reddish brown hardwood used especially in construction for interior and exterior cabinet parts.

**Birch:** Hard, heavy, light reddish brown hardwood. The most widely used hardwood veneer for flush doors, cabinetwork, and paneling. Mill products include interior trim, flooring, sash, and trim.

**Bleaching:** Lightening the color of wood by applying a chemical solution; removal of unwanted natural coloring from wood.

**Bleeding:** Movement of stain or dye from the wood into surface coats. For example, a mahogany oil stain under white enamel will bleed and develop pink spots.

**Blemish:** Any defect, scar, or mark that tends to detract from the appearance of a surface.

**Blind Nailing:** Nailing method in which the nail is not visible.

**Board Foot:** Method of lumber measurement using nominal dimensions of 1 in. thick, 12 in. wide, and 12 in. long.

**Boiled Linseed Oil:** Linseed oil that has been combined with blended drying agents to shorten the drying time.

**Bridging:** Small wood or metal members inserted in a diagonal position between the floor joists at midspan; acts both as tension and compression members for the purpose of bracing the joists and spreading the action of loads.

**Built-Up Finish:** Does not penetrate the wood but forms a film on the surface.

**Built-Up Roof:** Roof composed of three to five layers of asphalt felt laminated with coal tar, pitch, or asphalt. The top is finished with crushed slag or gravel. Generally used on flat or low-pitched roofs.

**Burl:** Swirl or twist in the grain of the wood, usually near a knot.

## C

**Caliper:** Tool for measuring the diameter of circular work.

**Cant:** Log with slabs cut off so that it is flat on two or four sides and ready to be cut into boards. Also called a **Flitch**.

**Capillary Action:** The resultant of adhesion, cohesion, and surface tension which causes liquids to rise in fine tubes or between closely spaced surfaces.

**Casement Window:** Hinged window, usually metal, that opens outward.

**Casing:** Moldings of various widths and thicknesses used to trim door and window openings at the jambs.

**Catalyst:** Substance which helps bring about a chemical action.

**Caul:** Metal or wood forms inserted between press platens to protect or shape a laminated assembly.

**Cements:** Waterborne contact cement and solvent-borne contact cement.

**Centrifugal Force:** Force tending to make rotating bodies move away from the center of rotation.

**Chalking:** Decomposition of paint into a loose powder on the film surface. Mild chalking, accompanied by satisfactory color retention in tinted paint, is desirable.

**Chamfer:** Beveled edge on a board formed by removing the sharp corner. Generally used on moldings, edges of drawer fronts, and cabinet doors.

**Checks:** Small splits running parallel to the wood grain, usually caused by improper seasoning.

**Chimney:** Vertical flue for passing smoke from a heating unit, fireplace, or incinerator.

**Chipped Grain:** Wood surface that has been roughened by the action of cutting tools. Considered a defect when surfaces are to be smoothly finished.

**Chord:** Horizontal member of a truss connecting the lower corners.

**Chuck:** Broad term meaning a device for holding a rotating tool or workpiece during an operation.

**Cleat:** Strip of wood fastened to another piece, usually to provide a holding or bracing effect.

**Collapse:** Seasoning defect resulting in the breakdown of wood cells, caused by too rapid or improper seasoning.

**Collar Beam:** Horizontal member which serves to tie together and stiffen pairs of common rafters.

**Concrete:** Mixture of cement, sand, and gravel with water.

**Concrete Form:** Temporary structure built to contain concrete during pouring and initial hardening.

**Cope:** Top half of a foundry flask. Also refers to the top half of the mold or pattern.

**Core:** The center of a plywood panel. Plywood cores may be of either sawed lumber or veneer.

**Corner Braces:** Diagonal braces placed at the corners of a frame structure to stiffen and strengthen the wall.

**Cornice:** Part of a roof that projects out from the wall.

**Counterboring:** Enlarging hole through part of its length by boring.

**Counterflashing:** Flashing used under the regular flashing.

**Countersinking:** Recess a hole conically for the head of a screw or bolt.

**Cove:** Molded trim of a concave shape used around cabinet construction and other built-ins.

**Crawl Space:** Shallow space below the floor of a house built above the ground, which is generally surrounded with the foundation wall.

**Cricket:** Device used at roof intersections to divert water.

**Cripple:** Structural member that is cut less than full length, such as a studding piece above a window or door.

**Cross Bracing:** Boards nailed diagonally across studs or other boards to make framework rigid.

**Cross-Linking PVAs:** Water-resistant adhesive that is widely used for radio frequency (RF) gluing.

**Crown molding:** Decorative molding used at the top of cabinets, at ceiling corners, and under a roof overhang.

## D

**Dado:** A groove cut across the grain of a board.

**Daylights:** In woodworking, it refers to the openings in a multiple press.

**Dead Load:** All the immovable weight in a structure and the weight of the structure itself.

**Decay:** Disintegration of wood substance due to the action of wood-destroying fungi.

**Degree Celsius:** Metric unit for measuring temperature within the range of the customary Fahrenheit scale. It is calibrated to zero for freezing and 100 for boiling point of water.

**Detail Sander:** Special portable sander designed to access corners or small spaces.

**Dimension Lumber:** Lumber two to five inches thick.

**Distressing:** Process of intentionally marring a wood surface to create the effect of longtime use and wear.

**Door Jamb:** Two vertical pieces held together by a head jamb forming the inside lining of a door opening.

**Double Glazing:** A pane of two pieces of glass, which is sealed with air space in between to provide insulation.

**Double Header:** Two or more timbers joined together for strength.

**Double Hung:** Refers to a window having top and bottom sashes each with the capability of movement up and down.

**Douglas Fir:** Yellow to pale reddish soft wood. The leading veneer wood primarily converted into plywood and widely used in building and construction. Also commonly used for sash, flooring, and doors.

**Drag:** Bottom half of a foundry flask or mold.

**Drier:** Catalyst added to a paint to speed up the curing or drying time.

**Drip Cap:** Molding placed above an exterior door or window, causing water to drip beyond the outside of the frame.

**Drying Time:** Time required for setting and curing a finish.

**Dry Wall:** Interior covering material, such as gypsum board or plywood, which is applied in large sheets or panels.

**Ducts:** In a house, usually round or rectangular metal pipes used for distributing warm air from the heating plant to rooms, cold air from a conditioning device, or as cold air returns. Ducts are also made of composition materials.

## E

**Earth Pigments:** Pigments mined from the earth such as ochre, umber, sienna, and Vandyke brown.

**Eccentric:** A circular part with the axis of rotation set off-center. Used to convert a circular motion to a back-and-forth motion.

**Edgebanding:** Application of thin strips such as wood veneer or preglued veneer tape to the edge of a workpiece.

**Emulsion:** Suspension of very small particles of oil in water, or water in oil, by the aid of an emulsifying agent.

**Emulsion Paints:** Various types of oils, resin, varnish, and lacquer mixed or emulsified so they can be thinned with water. They dry quickly and are practically odorless.

**Equilibrium Moisture Content (EMC):** Moisture content at which wood neither gains nor loses moisture when surrounded by air at a given relative humidity and temperature.

**Ethanol:** Denatured, ethyl or grain alcohol.

**Evaporation:** Change from liquid to gas, which occurs when solvents leave a wet paint film.

**Expansion Joint:** A bituminous fiber strip used to separate blocks or units of concrete to prevent cracking due to expansion as a result of temperature changes.

**Extender:** Filler substance added to paint or glue to increase coverage, provide body, or impart other desirable qualities.

## F

**Facade:** Front elevation or face of a structure.

**Face Size:** Exposed width of a molded piece of lumber after installation.

**Face Veneer:** Veneer selected for exposed surfaces in plywood.

**Fascia:** Vertical board nailed onto the ends of the rafters.

**Fence:** Adjustable metal bar or strip mounted on the table of a machine or tool to guide work.

**Fiberboard:** Building board made with fibrous material and used as an insulating board.

**Figure:** Pattern produced in a wood surface by annual growth rings, wood rays, and knots.

**Fill:** Sand, gravel, or loose earth used to bring a subgrade up to a desired level around a house.

**Filled Insulation:** Loose insulating material poured from bags or blown by machine into walls.

**Filler:** Liquid or paste material that contains finely powdered silica and a resin.

**Film Finish:** Finish that can be built up by repeated applications to achieve a hard, thick layer on the surface of the wood.

**Firestop:** Solid, tight closure of concealed space placed to prevent the spread of fire and smoke through such a space. In a frame wall, this will usually be a 2 x 4 cross blocking between studs.

**Fire Wall:** Wall designed to resist the spread of fire between sections of a house. Fire walls are commonly used between the main structure and an attached garage. Fire-resistant materials are designed specifically for this purpose.

**Fisheyes:** Small crater-like pockmarks in a finish.

**Fixed Windows:** Windows often used as a design element that cannot be opened or closed and provide daylight or a view of the outdoors.

**Flashing:** Sheet metal or other materials used around openings in roof or wall surfaces to prevent the penetration of water.

**Flatting Agent:** Ingredient used in lacquers and varnishes that reduces the gloss or gives a rubbed effect.

**Flexible Paving:** Paving technique used for light traffic areas such as patios and sidewalks.

**Flitch:** Portion of a log sawed on two or more sides intended for manufacture into lumber or sliced veneer. The term is also applied to the resulting sheets of veneer laid together in sequence of cutting.

**Floating Construction:** Method which permits wide panels in solid wood furniture to expand or contract without damage to the structure.

**Flue:** The space or passage in a chimney through which smoke, gas, or fumes exit.

**Flue Lining:** Round or square fireclay or terra-cotta pipe used for the inner lining of chimneys with the brick or masonry work around the outside.

**Fluting:** Parallel grooves or furrows cut out of the surface of wood, usually to secure a decorative effect.

**Fly Rafters:** End rafters of the gable overhang supported by roof sheathing and lookouts.

**Footing:** Masonry section, usually concrete, in a rectangular form wider than the bottom of the foundation wall or pier it supports.

**Forestry:** Science of developing, caring for, or cultivating forests, and management of growing timber.

**Foundation:** Supporting portion of a structure below the first-floor construction, or below grade, including the footings.

**Frieze:** In residential construction, a horizontal member connecting the top of the siding with the soffit of the cornice.

**Furring:** Narrow strips of wood attached to a base surface or frame upon which other materials are fastened.

## G

**Gable:** Portion of the roof above the eaves line of a double-sloped roof.

**Gain:** Recess or notch into which a door hinge fits flush with the surface.

**Gilding:** Addition of gold accents, especially on edges.

**Girder:** Large beam of wood or steel used to support concentrated loads at isolated points along its length.

**Glazing: 1:** Fitting window panes. **2:** Filling the pores of an abrasive stone with metal cuttings. **3:** Finishing process where transparent or translucent coatings are applied over a painted surface to produce blended effects.

**Gloss:** Finish that dries to a shiny or highly lustrous surface.

**Glue Blocks:** Small blocks of wood, usually triangular in shape, that are glued along the inside corner of a joint to add strength.

**Grain:** Direction, size, arrangement, appearance or quality of the fibers in wood.

**Graining:** Type of finishing technique that produces an opaque surface that resembles wood grain.

**Gram:** Metric measure equal to 1/1000 of a kilogram and to .035 oz.

**Gloss Topcoating:** Final coat that is shiny, smooth, and nearly transparent.

**Glue:** Various strong adhesive substances including: casein, liquid hide, hot animal glue, vegetable, blood albumin, and fish glue.

**Gusset:** Thin piece of metal or wood that forms a plate and is fastened to the surfaces of two or more structural members to secure or reinforce the joint.

## H

**Hanger:** Metal strap used to support piping or the ends of joists.

**Hardboard:** Manufactured material made by forming wood fibers into sheets using heat and pressure. The regrouped fibers are held together with the lignin in the wood.

**Hardwood:** Wood produced from broad-leaved trees or trees that lose their leaves. Examples include oak, maple, walnut, and birch.

**Header: 1:** Beam placed perpendicular to joists and to which joists are nailed into framing for chimneys, stairways, or other openings. **2:** Wood lintel.

**Hickory:** Hard and heavy brown to reddish brown hardwood. Used as face veneer for decorative interior plywood paneling and as solid lumber in special flooring applications. Pecan, a member of the hickory family, has similar properties and construction applications.

**Hip Rafter:** Diagonal rafter that extends from the plate to the ridge to form the hip.

**Hip Roof:** Roof that rises by inclined planes from all four sides of a building.

**Hollow Core Construction:** Sheet material such as plywood or hardboard (called skins) is bonded to a framed core assembly consisting of strips or various other forms of spaced support. Used in flush door construction.

**Housed Joint:** Joint formed by a recess that receives the entire end of the mating part. Similar to a mortise-and-tenon except that the tenon has no shoulders.

## I

**Inert Solvents:** Substances, such as mineral spirits and lacquer thinner, that reduce the viscosity of finishes and allow deeper penetration, faster drying, and more uniform application.

**Inlay:** Decoration where the design is set into the wood surface.

**Inspection:** Measuring and checking workpieces and assemblies at various stages of fabrication to determine if they meet specifications.

**Insulating Board:** Board suitable for insulating purposes; usually manufactured board made from vegetable fibers, such as fiberboard.

**Insulation:** Materials for obstructing the passage of sound, heat, or cold from one surface to another.

**Interchangeability:** Mass produced parts that have been made to specific dimensions and tolerances so that any one of them can fit and work in a final assembly.

**Interior Trim:** General term for all finish molding, casing, baseboard and cornice applied within the building.

## J

**Jack Rafter:** Rafter that spans the distance from the wall plate to a hip or from a valley to a ridge.

**Jalousie:** Type of window consisting of a number of long, thin, hinged panels.

**Jamb:** Side and head lining of a doorway, window, or other opening.

**Jig:** Device which holds the work and/or guides the tool while forming or assembling wood parts.

**Joist:** Horizontal structural member which supports the floor or ceiling system.

## K

**Kerf:** The split or space made by the blade of any hand or power saw.

**Kiln:** Heated chamber for drying lumber, veneer, and other wood products.

**Kiln-Dried Lumber:** Lumber that has been kiln-dried, generally to a moisture content of six to twelve percent.

**Kilogram:** SI metric base unit for mass (weight) which is equal to 2.2 lb.

**King Post:** Central upright piece in a roof truss.

**Knee Wall:** Low wall resulting from one-and-one-half-story construction.

**Knot:** Cross section of a branch or limb imbedded in the wood during the growth of the tree.

## L

**Lac:** Base for shellac, which is a natural resin secreted by insects that live on the sap of certain trees in oriental countries.

**Lacquer:** Finishing material made of nitrocellulose which dries by evaporation of the solvents.

**Lacquer Thinner:** Inert solvent that is used to thin lacquer.

**Laminate:** Form a product by bonding together two or more layers of material. Each layer is called a lamination or ply.

**Laminated Beam:** Beam made of superimposed layers of similar material. They are joined with glue and pressure.

**Lath:** Building material of wood, metal, gypsum, or insulating board that is fastened to the frame of a building to act as a plaster base.

**Lattice:** Framework of crossed wood or metal strips.

**Ledger:** Bearing strip attached to vertical framing (studs) on which horizontal members (joists) can be supported.

**Leveling:** In finishing, refers to the formation of a smooth film on either a horizontal or vertical surface, which is free of brush marks.

**Linear:** Pertaining to a line or consisting of lines. Linear measure refers to measurement along the length.

**Linseed Oil:** Vegetable oil pressed from the seeds of the flax plant. Used extensively in the manufacture of oil base paints and finishes.

**Lintel:** Horizontal supporting member spanning such openings as doors, windows, and fireplaces. May be made of stone, wood, or metal.

**Liter:** Metric measure of fluid volume, which is equal to one cubic decimeter ($dm^3$) or .26 gallon.

**Logger:** Worker who fells trees and prepares them for removal to saw mill.

**Log Grader:** One who grades logs for mill processing by notching or marking them for processing into veneer, pulp, or lumber.

**Lookout:** Short wooden framing member used to support an overhanging portion of a roof. It extends from the wall to the underside surfacing of the overhang.

**Lumbering:** Cutting, processing, and selling lumber.

## M

**Mandrel:** Shaft or spindle on which an object may be mounted for rotation.

**Maple:** Both hard and soft maple are generally light tan and used in construction where hardness is a major factor. Used for expensive cabinetwork, floor-ing, doors, and trim. Often used for interior railings, posts, and furniture.

**Marquetry:** Ornamental surface built up of various wood veneers to form a pattern or picture. Usually cut on the jig saw.

**Marbleizing:** Finishing technique that gives wood the appearance of marble.

**Masonry:** Stone, brick, concrete, hollow-tile, concrete-block, gypsum-block, and other similar building units or materials bonded together with mortar to form a wall, pier, buttress, or similar mass.

**Mastic:** Flexible adhesive for adhering building materials.

**Mesh:** Openings formed by crossing or weaving threads, strings, or wire.

**Metal Framing:** Use of metal studs, joists, and rafters to replace wood framing members.

**Meter:** Base unit for length in metric measure; one meter equals 1.09 yd.

**Millwork:** Refers to materials made in woodworking plants. Includes doors, windows, stairways, moldings, and wood trim.

**Mineral Spirits:** Petroleum solvent used as a substitute for turpentine.

**Miter:** Joining of two pieces at an evenly divided angle; cut made at an angle, usually 45 degrees.

**Moisture Barrier:** Material that retards the passage of vapor or moisture into walls and prevents condensation within the walls.

**Molding:** Strips of wood, usually shaped for decorative effect, that are applied to surfaces, corners, and edges of structures to provide a finished appearance.

**Mortar:** Mixture of cement, sand, and water used as a bonding agent for bricks and stone.

**Mortise:** Slot cut into a board, plank, or timber, usually edgewise, to receive the tenon of another board, plank, or timber to form a joint.

**Mosaic:** Surface decoration formed by small pieces of colored glass, stone, or tile, set in a ground of cement or mastic.

**Mottling:** Finishing technique that produces the visual effect of texturing even though the surface is smooth.

**Mullion:** Vertical separation between window units.

**Muntin:** Slender dividers between two or more panes of glass mounted in a single sash.

## N

**Naphtha:** Volatile, inflammable liquid used as a solvent or thinner for paint and varnish.

**Natural Resins:** Resins used in finishes that come

from trees or fossilized vegetable matter in the earth.

**Nominal Size:** Size of lumber before dressing rather than its actual size.

**Nonbearing Wall:** Wall supporting no load other than its own weight.

**Nosing:** Rounded edge of a stair tread.

**Nuvel™:** Solid color surface material made by the Formica Corporation.

## O

**On Center (O.C.):** Spacing of structural members from the center of one to the center of the next.

**Outlet:** Type of electrical box allowing current to be drawn from the electrical system for lighting or appliances.

**Overhang:** Projecting area of a roof or upper story beyond the lower part of the wall.

**Oxidize:** To unite with oxygen in a chemical reaction. Part of the drying process for some finishing materials.

## P

**Pallet:** Portable platform on which materials are stacked for storage or transportation.

**Panel:** In residential construction, a thin flat piece of wood, plywood, or similar material, framed by stiles and rails (as in a door) or fitted into grooves of thicker material with molded edges for decorative wall treatment.

**Particle Board:** Manufactured board made of wood chips held together with an adhesive.

**Partition:** Wall that subdivides space within a structure.

**Patina:** The mellowing and color changes that occur in wood over time.

**Pattern:** In metal casting, the woodpiece cut and shaped to give form to the mold in which the part will be cast.

**Patternmaker:** One who plans, lays out, and shapes wooden patterns of parts, which are to be cast in metal.

**Paving:** Process of covering a walkway or drive with masonry units.

**Penetrating Finish:** Natural oil finish such as linseed oil, tung oil, and wax or a synthetic finish such as alkyd and phenotic resin-oil coatings.

**Penetrating Stain:** Stain that contains dyes and resins that are almost completely absorbed into the wood.

**Peripheral Speed:** Speed of a point on the circumference of a revolving wheel or shaft. Usually given in feet per minute.

**Photosynthesis:** Process that takes place in the leaves of plants when they are exposed to light. Water and carbon dioxide are converted into carbohydrates.

**Pier:** Masonry pillar, usually located below a building, for support of the floor framing.

**Pigment:** Finely ground powders that are insoluble and provide color and body to a finishing material.

**Pigment Stain:** Stain containing insoluble powdered colors, which bond to the wood surface with resins.

**Pilaster:** Built-in projection in a straight masonry wall used for reinforcement.

**Pitch:** Slope of a roof usually expressed as a ratio.

**Pitch Pocket:** Opening extending parallel to the annual growth rings, containing, or having contained, liquid or solid resinous material.

**Plain-Sawed:** Lumber that is cut on a tangent to the annular growth rings.

**Plaster:** Mortar-like composition used for covering walls and ceilings; usually made of portland cement mixed with sand and water.

**Plate:** Horizontal framing member. **Sill Plate** is a horizontal member anchored to a masonry wall. **Sole Plate** is the bottom horizontal member of a frame wall. **Top Plate** is the top horizontal member of a frame wall supporting ceiling joists, rafters, or other members.

**Plate Joiners:** Portable power tool that is similar to a miniature power saw used to cut the kerf for a plate joint.

**Plate Joinery:** Method of making joints using plates, biscuits, or wafers.

**Plates:** Biscuits or wafers used in plate joints.

**Platform Framing:** Framing system in which floor joists of each story rest on the top plates of the story below, or on the foundation sill for the first story. The bearing walls and partitions rest on the subfloor of each story.

**Plumb:** Exactly vertical. Perpendicular to a level line.

**Plunge Router:** Used for mortising or cutting into the middle of a panel.

**Plywood:** Piece of wood made of three or more layers of veneer joined with glue, and usually laid with the grain of adjoining plies at right angles. Almost always an odd number of plies are used to provide balanced construction.

**Pneumatic:** Pertaining to, or operated by, air pressure.

**Pocket Cutter:** Device used to install angled screws or screws parallel to the surface of the workpiece.

**Polishing:** Process of buffing the surface with wax.

**Polymerization:** Chemical action in which the molecules of a substance interlock with each other in a special way. Part of the drying process of certain finishing materials.

**Ponderosa Pine:** Light reddish colored softwood used especially for sash, doors, and screens in the softer grades. Harder grades are used for joists, rafters, studdings, sills, sheathing, porch columns, posts, balusters, and stair rails.

**Post-and-Beam Construction:** Wall construction consisting of posts rather than studs.

**Prefabricated:** Built in sections or component parts in a plant and assembled at the site.

**Preframed Panels:** Fabricated panels consisting of precut lumber and plywood manufactured to standard dimensions ready for structural use.

**Preservative:** Substance that, for a reasonable length of time, will prevent wood decay of any wood properly coated or impregnated with it.

**Primer:** First step in preparing surfaces for opaque coatings.

**Pumice:** Porous volcanic lava that is crushed and graded and used for polishing finished surfaces.

**Purlins:** Horizontal roof members laid over trusses to support rafters.

## Q

**Quarter Round:** Molding with a cross section of one-fourth of a cylinder.

**Quarter-Sawed:** Lumber that is cut at a ninety degree angle to the annular growth rings.

**Quill:** Movable sleeve that carries the bearings and spindle of the drill press.

## R

**Rabbet:** Cut made in the edge of a board to form a joint with another piece.

**Radial:** Extending outward from a center or axis.

**Rafter:** One of a series of structural members of a roof designed to support roof loads. The rafters of a flat roof are sometimes called roof joists.

**Rapping Plate:** In patternmaking, a metal plate installed in the pattern to aid in rapping and drawing it from the mold.

**Ratchet:** Gear with triangular-shaped teeth that are engaged by a pawl, which imparts intermittent motion or locks against backward movement.

**Reactive Solvents:** Can dissolve stains or adhesives and strip finishes because they break apart the molecular bonds and cannot be used to thin paint.

**Red Cedar:** Reddish to dull brown softwood. Used for shingles in the United States because of its durability, working ease, and light weight. Also used for interior and exterior trim, sash, doors, and siding.

**Red Oak:** Rich light to medium brown, tough hardwood used for flooring, interior trim, stair treads, and railings. Popular as a face veneer plywood for paneling and cabinetwork.

**Reduce:** To lower the viscosity of a paint by the addition of solvent or thinner.

**Redwood:** Light to deep reddish brown softwood. Mill products include sash, doors, blinds, siding, and trim. Extensively used for garden furniture and exterior decking.

**Relative Humidity:** Ratio of water vapor actually present in the air as related to the greatest amount of vapor the air can carry at a given temperature.

**Resawing:** Ripping a board so the thickness is reduced or so that it is made into two thinner pieces.

**Respirator:** Shield for the nose and mouth that filters contaminated air.

**Retarder:** Solvent added to a paint to reduce the evaporation rate.

**Ridge:** Top edge of the roof where two slopes meet.

**Ridge Board:** Board placed on edge at the ridge of the roof into which the upper ends of the rafters are fastened.

**Rise:** Vertical height of a step or flight of stairs.

**Riser:** Each of the vertical boards closing the spaces between the stairway treads.

**Roof Sheathing:** Boards of sheet material fastened to the roof rafters on which the shingles or other roof covering is laid.

**Rotary Cut:** Method of cutting veneer in which the entire log is centered in a huge lathe and then turned against a broad knife.

**Rottenstone:** Decomposed siliceous limestone used for polishing finished surfaces.

**Rough Opening:** Framed opening in a structure into which doors, windows, and other finished trim are set.

**RPM:** Abbreviation for revolutions per minute.

**Run:** The net width of a step or the horizontal distance covered by a flight of stairs.

**Runs:** Irregularities in a surface finish. It is often caused by too heavy an application. Also called "sags" and "curtains."

## S

**Saber Sawing:** Cutting with a special blade mounted in only the lower chuck of the jig saw. Also applied to cutting with a portable saber saw.

**Saddle:** Two sloping surfaces meeting in a horizontal ridge, used between the back side of a chimney or other vertical surface and a sloping roof. Also called a cricket.

**Sandwich Construction:** Panels fabricated with high strength facing materials bonded to a low density core material or structure.

**Sash:** A single light frame containing one or more lights of glass.

**Satin Finish:** Final coat that has a distinct amount of surface texture which diffuses light reflection.

**Scaffold:** Temporary framework for supporting workers and materials during the erecting or repairing of a building.

**Sealer:** Thin, clear coat that fills wood pores and serves as a barrier coating.

**Semigloss:** Topcoating that is not as shiny or as clear as a clear gloss finish.

**Shake:** Defect in wood running parallel to the grain. Caused by the separation of the spring and summer growth rings.

**Sheathing:** Structural covering, usually wood boards or plywood, used over studs or rafters of a structure. Structural building board is normally used only as wall sheathing.

**Shed Roof:** Flat roof slanting in one direction.

**Sheen:** Degree of gloss in a cured finish.

**Shiplap:** Wood sheathing which is rabbeted so that the edges of the boards make a flush joint.

**Shoe Mold:** Small mold against the baseboard at the floor.

**Shoring:** Assembly of post and timbers used for bracing and support. Usually applied temporarily to units under construction.

**Siding:** Finish covering of the outside wall of a frame building. Made of horizontal weatherboards, vertical boards with battens, shingles, or other material.

**Silex:** Powdered quartz used as a base for paste filler.

Silicon Carbide: Produced by fusing silica (sand) and coke at high temperatures. Used as an abrasive.

**Sill:** Lowest member of the frame of a structure, resting on the foundation and supporting the floor joists or the uprights of the wall; member forming the lower side of an opening, such as a door sill.

**Skylight:** Opening in a roof covered by glass or plastic material to admit natural light.

**Sleeper:** Wood strips placed in or on a concrete base to which subflooring or finished flooring is attached.

**Sliced:** Method of cutting veneer where a section of a log is thrust down along a knife edge that sheers off the veneer in sheets.

**Soffit:** Underside of a cornice, beam, arch, or lowered section of a ceiling.

**Softwood:** Wood produced from coniferous trees. Pines are most commonly used but fir, spruce, redwood, and cedar are also included. The term has no reference to the actual hardness or softness of the wood.

**Solid Bridging:** Solid member placed between adjacent floor joists near the center of the span to prevent joists from twisting.

**Solid Color Surface Material:** Type of laminate made from polyester resin called valox.

**Solid Surface Material:** Type of material commonly used for cabinet tops. Available in sheets or may be cast into sinks or moldings.

**Solids:** Material remaining in a paint after the solvents have evaporated. Usually specified as a percentage of the initial weight.

**Solvent:** Any evaporating liquid that will dissolve a cured finish, stain, glaze, or paste-wood filler.

**Span:** Horizontal distance between supports for joists, beams, or trusses.

**Special Shape Windows:** Examples include triangles, trapezoids, and octagons.

**Splat:** Broad, flat, upright section in the middle of a chair back.

**Splayed:** Applies to the leg of a chair or table that makes an angle outward in two directions from the top or seat.

**Spline:** Thin strip of wood inserted in matching grooves cut on the joining faces of a joint. Also a flexible rod or rule used to draw curved lines.

**Spontaneous Combustion:** Self-ignition of combustible material through chemical action (as oxidation) of its constituents. A leading cause of woodshop fires.

**Spruce:** Pale yellowish softwood used for general building purposes such as planks, dimension stock, and joists. Millwork products include doors, sash, casing, and trim.

**Square:** Unit of measure usually applied to roofing material. Sidewall coverings are sometimes packaged and sold to cover 100 sq. ft.

**Stain:** Finish for wood containing dye or pigment.

**Stickers:** Strips of wood used to separate the layers in a lumber pile so air can circulate around each board.

**Stool:** Horizontal ledge or strip below an interior window which is a part of the frame.

**Story Pole:** Rod used for measuring and laying out door and window openings, siding, shingle courses, stairways, or cabinetry.

**Straightedge:** Straight strip of wood or metal used to lay out and check the accuracy of work.

**Stretcher:** Horizontal structural member used to reinforce the legs of chairs, tables, and desks.

**Structural "C":** Basic shape of metal framing members used for studs, joists, and rafters.

**Studs:** Vertical framing members of a wall.

**Subflooring:** Any material, usually 1/2 in. plywood, nailed directly to the floor joists. The finish floor is attached over the subflooring.

**Sugar Pine:** Similar in physical properties and uses in construction as white pine. See **White Pine.**

**T** —————————————————————

**Taper:** Gradual, uniform decrease in the size of a hole, cylinder, or rectangular part.

**Template:** A pattern, guide, or model used to lay out work or check its accuracy.

**Thermoplastic:** Resins that soften when subjected to high temperatures.

**Thermoset Adhesives:** Type of adhesive, including epoxy, polyurethane, reactive hot-melt, resorcinol/phenol-resorcinol, urea formaldehyde.

**Thermosetting:** Resins that can be cured with heat and, after setting, will not soften when heat is applied.

**Thinners:** Volatile liquids used to regulate the consistency (thickness) of finishing materials.

**32mm Construction:** Standard form of frameless case construction that provides a modular system of case assembly and hardware installation.

**Timbers:** Construction lumber with a cross section of five inches or more in both thickness and width.

**Toggle Clamp:** Type of "quick clamp" that is manufactured in a broad array of styles ranging from mechanical to pneumatic variations.

**Tongue:** Projecting bead cut on the edge of a board that fits into a groove on another piece.

**Topcoating:** Final protective film that resists moisture, dirt, chemicals, or other harmful substances.

**Tracking:** Refers to the alignment of a blade as it runs on the band saw wheel.

**Tread:** Horizontal board in a stairway on which the foot is placed.

**Trim:** General term that applies to the various wood strips and moldings used to finish door and window openings and corners where walls join the ceiling and floor.

**Trimmer:** The longer floor framing member around a rectangular opening into which a header is joined.

**Truss:** Structural members arranged and fastened in triangular units to form a ridge framework for support of loads over a long span.

**Tung Oil:** Drying oil used in water-resistant varnishes and high-gloss paints.

**Turpentine:** Volatile solvent used in wood finishes; made by distilling the gum obtained from the pine tree.

**U** —————————————————————

**Underlayment:** Material placed under finish coverings, such as flooring or shingles, to provide a smooth, even surface for applying the finish.

**V** —————————————————————

**Valley:** Internal angle formed by the junction of two sloping sides of a roof.

**Valley Rafter:** Diagonal rafter at the intersection of two intersecting sloping roofs.

**Varnish:** Composed of a gum or resin in a suitable carrying agent or vehicle such as linseed or tung oil. Solvent oils (usually turpentine) are added to make the varnish thin and fluid.

**Varnish Stain:** General-purpose interior varnish tinted with dye colors or pigments which stains and varnishes in one coat. Seldom used on quality furniture except as quick refinish.

**Vehicle:** Liquid part of a paint.

**Veneer:** Thin sheet of wood, either sliced, cut, or sawed. Veneer may be referred to as a ply when assembled in a panel.

**Vessels:** Wood cells of large diameter that are set one above another to form continuous tubes. The openings of the vessels on the surface of the wood are referred to as pores.

**Volatile Organic Compounds (VOCs):** Used in finishing materials such as clear finishes, sealers, fillers, stains, and paints.

**W** —————————————————————

**Wainscot:** Wood panels or other material applied to the lower part of an interior wall.

**Wane:** Presence of bark, or the lack of wood from any cause, on the edge or corner of a piece of lumber.

**Warp:** Variation from a true or plane surface. In lumber it may include bow, cup, crook, or wind.

**Washcoat:** Tin coat of sealer that is often applied before stain.

**Water Stain:** Colored dyes soluble in water.

**Water White:** Transparent like water. Used to describe a very clear lacquer or varnish.

**Weather-strip:** Strip of metal or fabric fastened along the edges of windows and doors to reduce drafts and heat loss.

**Web:** Thin section of a pattern connecting two heavier sections to provide added strength in the metal casting.

**White Oak:** See **Red Oak.**

**White Pine:** Softwood of light tan color used for door, sash, interior and exterior trim, siding, and panels. Lower grades are used for sheathing, subflooring, and roofing.

## Y

**Yellow Pine:** Softwood of medium texture, moderately hard and yellow to reddish brown in color. Used for joists, rafters, studding, and general construction where extra strength and stiffness are required.

# Reference Section

## WOOD SCREW TABLE

| LENGTH | GAUGE STEEL SCREW | BRASS SCREW | GAUGE NO. | DECIMAL | APPROX. FRACTION | APPROX. METRIC DRILL EQUIV. (mm) | DRILL SIZE A | B | C |
|---|---|---|---|---|---|---|---|---|---|
| 1/4 | 0 to 4 | 0 to 4 | 0 | .060 | 1/16 | 1.5 | 1/16 | | |
| 3/8 | 0 to 8 | 0 to 6 | 1 | .073 | 5/64 | 2.5 | 3/32 | | |
| 1/2 | 1 to 10 | 1 to 8 | 2 | .086 | 5/64 | 2.5 | 3/32 | 1/16 | 3/16 |
| 5/8 | 2 to 12 | 2 to 10 | 3 | .099 | 3/32 | 3.5 | 1/8 | 1/16 | 1/4 |
| 3/4 | 2 to 14 | 2 to 12 | 4 | .112 | 7/64 | 3.5 | 1/8 | 1/16 | 1/4 |
| 7/8 | 3 to 14 | 4 to 12 | 5 | .125 | 1/8 | 3.5 | 1/8 | 3/32 | 1/4 |
| 1 | 3 to 16 | 4 to 14 | 6 | .138 | 9/64 | 4.0 | 5/32 | 3/32 | 5/16 |
| 1 1/4 | 4 to 18 | 6 to 14 | 7 | .151 | 5/32 | 4.0 | 5/32 | 1/8 | 5/16 |
| 1 1/2 | 4 to 20 | 6 to 14 | 8 | .164 | 5/32 | 5.0 | 3/16 | 1/8 | 3/8 |
| 1 3/4 | 6 to 20 | 8 to 14 | 9 | .177 | 11/64 | 5.0 | 3/16 | 1/8 | 3/8 |
| 2 | 6 to 20 | 8 to 18 | 10 | .190 | 3/16 | 5.0 | 3/16 | 1/8 | 3/8 |
| 2 1/4 | 6 to 20 | 10 to 18 | 11 | .203 | 13/64 | 5.5 | 7/32 | 5/32 | 7/16 |
| 2 1/2 | 8 to 20 | 10 to 18 | 12 | .216 | 7/32 | 5.5 | 7/32 | 5/32 | 7/16 |
| 2 3/4 | 8 to 20 | 8 to 20 | 14 | .242 | 15/64 | 6.5 | 1/4 | 3/16 | 1/2 |
| 3 | 8 to 24 | 12 to 18 | 16 | .268 | 17/64 | | 9/32 | 7/32 | 9/16 |
| 3 1/2 | 10 to 24 | 12 to 18 | 18 | .294 | 19/64 | | 5/16 | 1/4 | 5/8 |
| 4 | 12 to 24 | 12 to 24 | 20 | .320 | 21/64 | | 11/32 | 9/32 | 11/16 |
| 4 1/2 | 14 to 24 | 14 to 24 | 24 | .372 | 3/8 | 9.5 | 3/8 | 5/16 | 3/4 |
| 5 | 14 to 24 | 14 to 24 | | | | | | | |

FLAT HEAD — LENGTH
ROUND HEAD — LENGTH
OVAL HEAD — LENGTH, GAUGE
C — A SHANK HOLE, B PILOT HOLE

## FIGURING PULLEY SIZES AND RPM

| TO FIND: | |
|---|---|
| RPM OF DRIVEN PULLEY | Multiply diameter of driving pulley by its rpm and divide by diameter of driven pulley. |
| DIAMETER OF DRIVEN PULLEY | Multiply diameter of driving pulley by its rpm and divide by rpm of driven pulley. |
| RPM OF DRIVING PULLEY | Multiply diameter of driven pulley by its rpm and divide by diameter of driving pulley. |
| DIAMETER OF DRIVING PULLEY | Multiply diameter of driven pulley by its rpm and divide by rpm of driving pulley. |

## MITER AND LOCK JOINTS

These patterns are made with special cutterheads.     (Wisconsin Knife Works)

## SHRINKAGE VALUE OF DOMESTIC WOODS

Shrinkage from green to oven dry moisture content. Percentage based on green dimension.

### HARDWOODS

|  | RADIAL PERCENTAGE | TANGENTIAL PERCENTAGE | VOLUMETRIC PERCENTAGE |
|---|---|---|---|
| ASH, WHITE | 4.9 | 7.8 | 13.3 |
| ASPEN | 3.3 | 7.9 | 11.8 |
| BASSWOOD | 6.6 | 9.3 | 15.8 |
| BIRCH | 7.3 | 9.5 | 16.8 |
| BUTTERNUT | 3.4 | 6.4 | 10.6 |
| CHERRY, BLACK | 3.7 | 7.1 | 11.5 |
| CHESTNUT | 3.4 | 6.7 | 11.6 |
| ELM, AMERICAN | 4.2 | 7.2 | 14.6 |
| HICKORY | 7.0 | 10.5 | 16.7 |
| HOLLY | 4.8 | 9.9 | 16.9 |
| MAPLE, SUGAR | 4.8 | 9.9 | 14.7 |
| OAK, RED | 4.0 | 8.6 | 13.7 |
| OAK, WHITE | 4.4 | 8.8 | 12.7 |
| POPLAR, YELLOW | 4.6 | 8.2 | 12.7 |
| SWEETGUM | 5.3 | 10.2 | 15.8 |
| SYCAMORE | 5.0 | 8.4 | 14.1 |
| WALNUT, BLACK | 5.5 | 7.8 | 12.8 |
| WILLOW, BLACK | 3.3 | 8.7 | 13.9 |

### SOFTWOODS

|  |  |  |  |
|---|---|---|---|
| CYPRESS | 3.8 | 6.2 | 10.5 |
| CEDAR, EASTERN, RED | 3.1 | 4.7 | 7.8 |
| CEDAR, WESTERN, RED | 2.4 | 5.0 | 6.8 |
| DOUGLAS-FIR | 4.8 | 7.5 | 11.8 |
| HEMLOCK | 4.2 | 7.8 | 12.4 |
| PINE, PONDEROSA | 3.9 | 6.2 | 9.7 |
| PINE, WHITE | 4.1 | 7.4 | 11.8 |
| REDWOOD | 2.6 | 4.4 | 6.8 |
| SPRUCE | 3.8 | 7.1 | 11.0 |

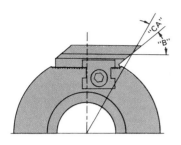 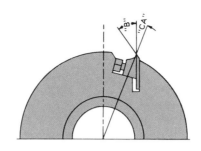 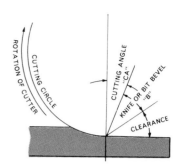

## CUTTING ANGLES

These sketches illustrate the cutting angle and knife and bit bevel relation on a typical milled-to-pattern head and a round head.

## CUTTING ANGLES

| | KILN DRIED 7% MOISTURE OR LESS | | WET OR GREEN MORE THAN 7% | |
|---|---|---|---|---|
| | CA | B | CA | B |
| Ash | 15° | 35° | 10° | 35° |
| Basswood | 10 | 30 | 20 | 30 |
| Beech | 10 | 35 | 15 | 35 |
| Birch | 10 | 35 | 15 | 35 |
| Cedar | 5 | 30 | 10 | 30 |
| Cherry | 10 | 35 | 15 | 35 |
| Chestnut | 5 | 35 | 10 | 35 |
| Cottonwood | 5 | 30 | 10 | 30 |
| Cypress | 5 | 30 | 10 | 30 |
| Elm, Hard | 0 | 40 | 5 | 40 |
| Fir | 10 | 35 | 15 | 35 |
| Gum | 20 | 35 | 25 | 35 |
| Hemlock | 15 | 35 | 20 | 35 |
| Hickory | 5 | 40 | 10 | 40 |
| Mahogany | 10 | 35 | 15 | 35 |
| Maple | 5 | 40 | 10 | 40 |
| Oak | 10 | 40 | 15 | 40 |
| Oak Qtd. | 10 | 40 | 15 | 40 |
| Pine, Yellow | 20 | 35 | 25 | 35 |
| Pine, White | 25 | 30 | 30 | 30 |
| Pine, Ponderosa | 25 | 30 | 30 | 30 |
| Poplar | 30 | 30 | 35 | 30 |
| Redwood | 5 | 30 | 15 | 30 |
| Spruce | 20 | 35 | 25 | 35 |
| Sycamore | 5 | 35 | 10 | 35 |
| Walnut | 5 | 35 | 10 | 35 |
| Elm, Soft | 5 | 40 | 10 | 40 |

## FINISH AND RATES OF FEED

**Knife Finish Ranges Generally Recommended according to wood species:**

| Kind of Wood | Knife Marks per Inch |
|---|---|
| Ash | 11 to 14 |
| Basswood | 8 to 12 |
| Beech | 12 to 14 |
| Birch (plain) | 12 to 14 |
| Birch (curly) | 13 to 16 |
| Cedar | 8 to 12 |
| Cherry | 12 to 14 |
| Cottonwood | 8 to 12 |
| Cypress | 8 to 12 |
| Elm (hard) | 10 to 13 |
| Elm (soft) | 8 to 12 |
| Fir | 8 to 12 |
| Gum | 9 to 13 |
| Hemlock | 8 to 12 |
| Hickory | 12 to 15 |
| Mahogany (plain) | 12 to 14 |
| Mahogany (figured) | 14 to 16 |
| Maple | 12 to 14 |
| Oak | 12 to 14 |
| Pine (yellow) | 9 to 13 |
| Pine (white) | 9 to 13 |
| Poplar | 9 to 13 |
| Redwood | 8 to 12 |
| Spruce | 8 to 12 |
| Sycamore | 11 to 14 |
| Walnut | 12 to 14 |

## RATES OF FEED

| R.P.M. | Knife Marks Per Inch | NUMBER OF KNIVES CUTTING | | | | |
|---|---|---|---|---|---|---|
| | | 1 | 2 | 4 | 6 | 8 |
| 3600 | 10 | 30 Ft. | 60 Ft. | 120 Ft. | 180 Ft. | 240 Ft. |
| | 12 | 25 | 50 | 100 | 150 | 200 |
| | 14 | 21 | 43 | 82 | 123 | 164 |
| | 16 | 18 | 37 | 73 | 112 | 146 |
| | 18 | 16.5 | 33.5 | 66.5 | 100 | 133.3 |
| | 20 | 15 | 30 | 60 | 90 | 120 |
| 4800 | 10 | 40 | 80 | 160 | 240 | 320 |
| | 12 | 33 | 66 | 133 | 200 | 266 |
| | 14 | 28 | 57 | 112 | 171 | 224 |
| | 16 | 25 | 50 | 100 | 150 | 200 |
| | 18 | 22.2 | 44 | 88 | 133 | 176 |
| | 20 | 20 | 40 | 80 | 120 | 160 |
| 6000 | 10 | 50 | 100 | 200 | 300 | 400 |
| | 12 | 41 | 83 | 166 | 250 | 332 |
| | 14 | 35 | 71 | 143 | 213 | 286 |
| | 16 | 31 | 62 | 125 | 185 | 250 |
| | 18 | 27 | 55 | 111 | 160 | 222 |
| | 20 | 25 | 50 | 100 | 150 | 200 |
| 7200 | 10 | 60 | 120 | 240 | 360 | 480 |
| | 12 | 50 | 100 | 200 | 300 | 400 |
| | 14 | 42 | 86 | 164 | 246 | 328 |
| | 16 | 36 | 74 | 146 | 224 | 292 |
| | 18 | 33 | 67 | 134 | 200 | 268 |
| | 20 | 30 | 60 | 120 | 180 | 240 |

$$*\frac{R.P.M. \times No. KNIVES}{FT. PER MIN. \times 12} = KNIFE\ MARKS\ PER\ INCH$$

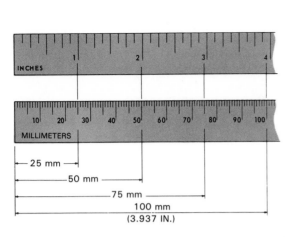

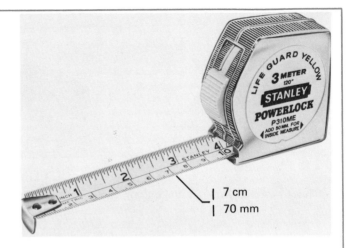

7 cm
70 mm

Length conversions can be made in two ways. Left. Align an inch-scale rule with a metric rule for equivalents. Right. Use a dual dimensioned rule. Numbers on the metric side are in centimeters (cm). Multiply these numbers by 10 to convert them to millimeters (mm).

## INCH TO MILLIMETERS CONVERSIONS

| EXACT | | ROUND OUT | |
|---|---|---|---|
| | | 0.5 mm | 1 mm |
| 1/32 IN. | 0.794 | 1 mm | 1 mm |
| 1/16 IN. | 1.588 | 1.5 mm | 2 mm |
| 1/8 IN. | 3.175 | 3 mm | 3 mm |
| 1/4 IN. | 6.350 | 6.5 mm | 6 mm |
| 3/8 IN. | 9.525 | 9.5 mm | 10 mm |
| 1/2 IN. | 12.700 | 12.5 mm | 13 mm |
| 5/8 IN. | 15.875 | 16 mm | 16 mm |
| 3/4 IN. | 19.050 | 19 mm | 19 mm |
| 7/8 IN. | 22.225 | 22 mm | 22 mm |
| 1 IN. | 25.400 | 25.5 mm | 25 mm |

## CONVERSION ACCURACY

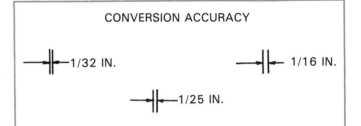

1/32 IN.          1/16 IN.

1/25 IN.

The size of a millimeter (1/25 in.) is about half way between 1/32 in. and 1/16 in. as shown above. For general woodworking, rounding a converted figure to the nearest millimeter is acceptable practice. When greater accuracy is required, round to the nearest 1/2 millimeter. See table at left. For sizes not listed, add combinations of figures (exact) and then round to accuracy desired.

## METRIC CONVERSIONS FOR LENGTH, AREA, AND VOLUME

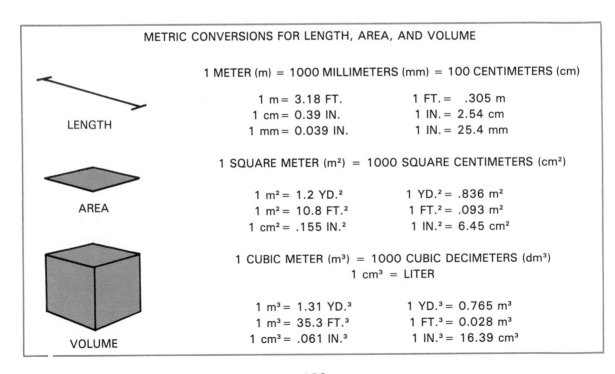

**LENGTH**

1 METER (m) = 1000 MILLIMETERS (mm) = 100 CENTIMETERS (cm)

| | |
|---|---|
| 1 m = 3.18 FT. | 1 FT. = .305 m |
| 1 cm = 0.39 IN. | 1 IN. = 2.54 cm |
| 1 mm = 0.039 IN. | 1 IN. = 25.4 mm |

**AREA**

1 SQUARE METER (m²) = 1000 SQUARE CENTIMETERS (cm²)

| | |
|---|---|
| 1 m² = 1.2 YD.² | 1 YD.² = .836 m² |
| 1 m² = 10.8 FT.² | 1 FT.² = .093 m² |
| 1 cm² = .155 IN.² | 1 IN.² = 6.45 cm² |

**VOLUME**

1 CUBIC METER (m³) = 1000 CUBIC DECIMETERS (dm³)
1 cm³ = LITER

| | |
|---|---|
| 1 m³ = 1.31 YD.³ | 1 YD.³ = 0.765 m³ |
| 1 m³ = 35.3 FT.³ | 1 FT.³ = 0.028 m³ |
| 1 cm³ = .061 IN.³ | 1 IN.³ = 16.39 cm³ |

# Reference Section

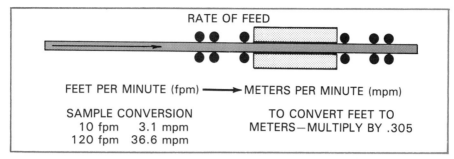

## RATE OF FEED

FEET PER MINUTE (fpm) → METERS PER MINUTE (mpm)

SAMPLE CONVERSION
10 fpm    3.1 mpm
120 fpm   36.6 mpm

TO CONVERT FEET TO
METERS—MULTIPLY BY .305

## STANDARD LUMBER SIZES AND METRIC CONVERSIONS

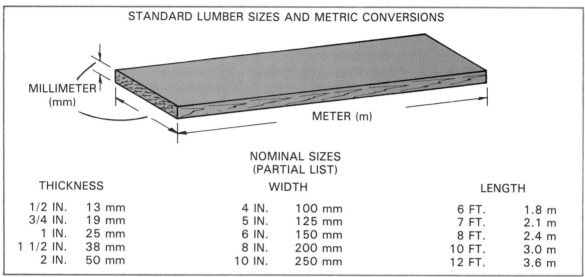

MILLIMETER (mm)

METER (m)

### NOMINAL SIZES
(PARTIAL LIST)

| THICKNESS | | WIDTH | | LENGTH | |
|---|---|---|---|---|---|
| 1/2 IN. | 13 mm | 4 IN. | 100 mm | 6 FT. | 1.8 m |
| 3/4 IN. | 19 mm | 5 IN. | 125 mm | 7 FT. | 2.1 m |
| 1 IN. | 25 mm | 6 IN. | 150 mm | 8 FT. | 2.4 m |
| 1 1/2 IN. | 38 mm | 8 IN. | 200 mm | 10 FT. | 3.0 m |
| 2 IN. | 50 mm | 10 IN. | 250 mm | 12 FT. | 3.6 m |

## METRICS IN CONSTRUCTION

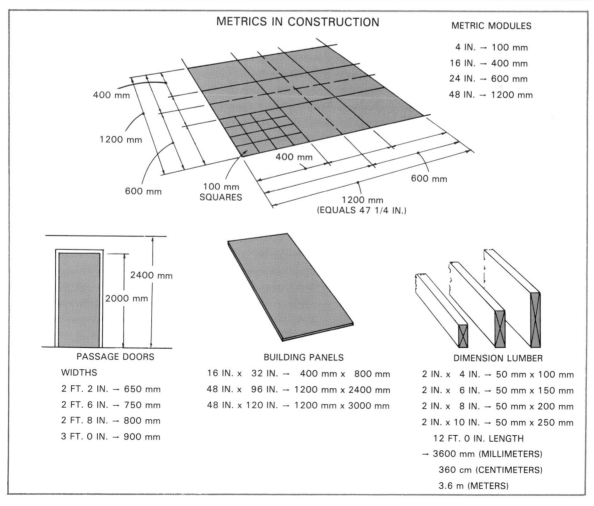

METRIC MODULES

4 IN. → 100 mm
16 IN. → 400 mm
24 IN. → 600 mm
48 IN. → 1200 mm

400 mm

1200 mm

600 mm

100 mm SQUARES

400 mm

600 mm

1200 mm
(EQUALS 47 1/4 IN.)

2400 mm

2000 mm

### PASSAGE DOORS
WIDTHS

2 FT. 2 IN. → 650 mm
2 FT. 6 IN. → 750 mm
2 FT. 8 IN. → 800 mm
3 FT. 0 IN. → 900 mm

### BUILDING PANELS

16 IN. x 32 IN. → 400 mm x 800 mm
48 IN. x 96 IN. → 1200 mm x 2400 mm
48 IN. x 120 IN. → 1200 mm x 3000 mm

### DIMENSION LUMBER

2 IN. x 4 IN. → 50 mm x 100 mm
2 IN. x 6 IN. → 50 mm x 150 mm
2 IN. x 8 IN. → 50 mm x 200 mm
2 IN. x 10 IN. → 50 mm x 250 mm

12 FT. 0 IN. LENGTH
→ 3600 mm (MILLIMETERS)
360 cm (CENTIMETERS)
3.6 m (METERS)

## INSTALLATION DATA OF COMMON ASPHALT ROOFING PRODUCTS (TILES)

| PRODUCT | Configuration | Per Square | | | Size | | Exposure | Underwriters Laboratories Listing |
|---|---|---|---|---|---|---|---|---|
| | | Approximate Shipping Weight | Shingles | Bundles | Width | Length | | |
| Self-sealing random-tab strip shingle 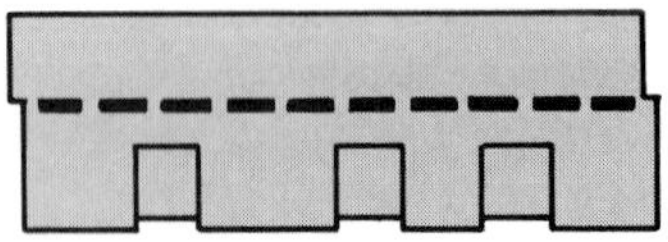 / Multi-thickness | Various edge, surface texture and application treatments | 285# to 390# | 66 to 90 | 4 or 5 | 11½" to 14" | 36" to 40" | 4" to 6" | A or C - Many wind resistant |
| Self-sealing random-tab strip shingle 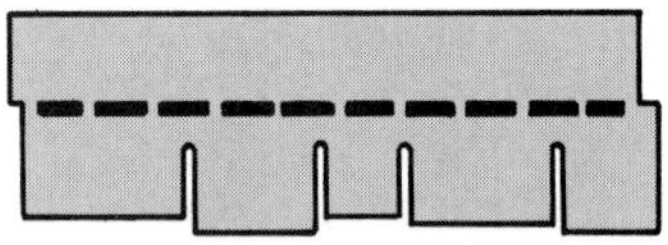 / Single-thickness | Various edge, surface texture and application treatments | 250# to 300# | 66 to 80 | 3 or 4 | 12" to 13¼" | 36" to 40" | 5" to 5⅝" | A or C - Many wind resistant |
| Self-sealing square-tab strip shingle 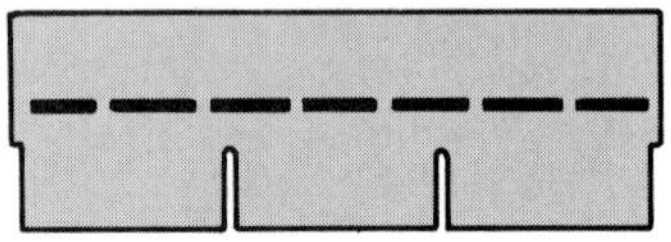 / Three-tab | Two-tab or Four-tab | 215# to 325# | 66 to 80 | 3 or 4 | 12" to 13¼" | 36" to 40" | 5" to 5⅝" | A or C - All wind resistant |
| | Three-tab | 215# to 300# | 66 to 80 | 3 or 4 | 12" to 13¼" | 36" to 40" | 5" to 5⅝" | |
| Self-sealing square-tab strip shingle 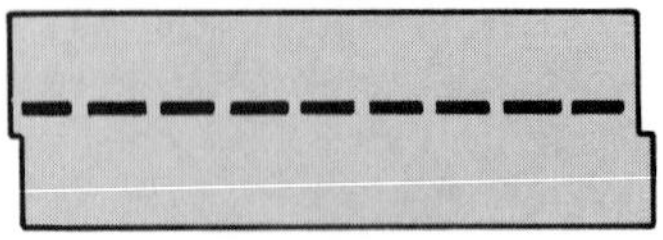 / No-cutout | Various edge and surface texture treatments | 215# to 290# | 66 to 81 | 3 or 4 | 12" to 13¼" | 36" to 40" | 5" to 5⅝" | A or C - All wind resistant |
| Individual interlocking shingle 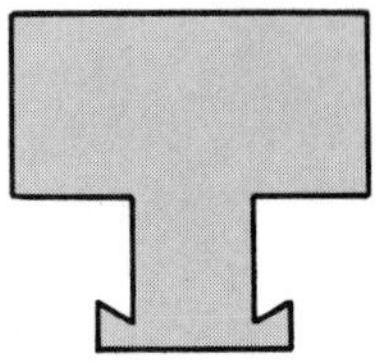 / Basic design | Several design variations | 180# to 250# | 72 to 120 | 3 or 4 | 18" to 22¼" | 20" to 22½" | — | C - Many wind resistant |

Installation data on common asphalt roofing products.

## INSTALLATION DATA FOR COMMON ASPHALT ROOFING PRODUCTS (ROLL)

| PRODUCT | Approximate Shipping Weight | | Squares Per Package | Length | Width | Side or End Lap | Top Lap | Exposure | Underwriters Laboratories Listing * |
|---|---|---|---|---|---|---|---|---|---|
| | Per Roll | Per Square | | | | | | | |
| Mineral surface roll | 75# to 90# | 75# to 90# | 1 | 36' to 38' | 36" | 6" | 2" to 4" | 32" to 34" | C |
| | Available in some areas in 9/10 or 3/4 square rolls. | | | | | | | | |
| Mineral surface roll (double coverage) | 55# to 70# | 110 # to 140 # | ½ | 36' | 36" | 6" | 19" | 17" | C |
| Smooth surface roll | 40# to 65# | 40# to 65# | 1 | 36' | 36" | 6" | 2" | 34" | None |
| Saturated felt (non-perforated) | 60# | 15# to 30# | 2 to 4 | 72' to 144' | 36" | 4" to 6" | 2" to 19" | 17" to 34" | None |

*UL rating at time of publication. Reference should be made to individual manufacturer's product at time of purchase.

## CONVERSION TABLE — ENGLISH TO METRIC

| WHEN YOU KNOW | MULTIPLY BY: * = Exact VERY ACCURATE | APPROXIMATE | TO FIND |
|---|---|---|---|
| **LENGTH** | | | |
| inches | *25.4 | | millimeters |
| inches | * 2.54 | | centimeters |
| feet | * 0.3048 | | meters |
| feet | *30.48 | | centimeters |
| yards | * 0.9144 | 0.9 | meters |
| miles | * 1.609344 | 1.6 | kilometers |
| **WEIGHT** | | | |
| grains | 15.43236 | 15.4 | grams |
| ounces | *28.349523125 | 28.0 | grams |
| ounces | * 0.028349523125 | .028 | kilograms |
| pounds | * 0.45359237 | 0.45 | kilograms |
| short ton | * 0.90718474 | 0.9 | tonnes |
| **VOLUME** | | | |
| teaspoons | | 5.0 | milliliters |
| tablespoons | | 15.0 | milliliters |
| fluid ounces | 29.57353 | 30.0 | milliliters |
| cups | | 0.24 | liters |
| pints | * 0.473176473 | 0.47 | liters |
| quarts | * 0.946352946 | 0.95 | liters |
| gallons | * 3.785411784 | 3.8 | liters |
| cubic inches | * 0.016387064 | 0.02 | cubic meters |
| cubic feet | * 0.028316846592 | 0.03 | cubic meters |
| cubic yards | * 0.764554857984 | 0.76 | cubic meters |
| **AREA** | | | |
| square inches | * 6.4516 | 6.5 | square centimeters |
| square feet | * 0.09290304 | 0.09 | square meters |
| square yards | * 0.83612736 | 0.8 | square meters |
| square miles | | 2.6 | square kilometers |
| acres | * 0.4046564224 | 0.4 | hectares |
| **TEMPERATURE** | | | |
| Fahrenheit | *5/9 (after subtracting 32) | | Celsius |

## CONVERSION TABLE — METRIC TO ENGLISH

| WHEN YOU KNOW | MULTIPLY BY: * = Exact VERY ACCURATE | APPROXIMATE | TO FIND |
|---|---|---|---|
| **LENGTH** | | | |
| millimeters | 0.0393701 | 0.04 | inches |
| centimeters | 0.3937008 | 0.4 | inches |
| meters | 3.280840 | 3.3 | feet |
| meters | 1.093613 | 1.1 | yards |
| kilometers | 0.621371 | 0.6 | miles |
| **WEIGHT** | | | |
| grains | 0.00228571 | 0.0023 | ounces |
| grams | 0.03527396 | 0.035 | ounces |
| kilograms | 2.204623 | 2.2 | pounds |
| tonnes | 1.1023113 | 1.1 | short tons |
| **VOLUME** | | | |
| milliliters | 0.06667 | 0.2 | teaspoons |
| milliliters | 0.03381402 | 0.067 | tablespoons |
| milliliters | | 0.03 | fluid ounces |
| liters | 61.02374 | 61.024 | cubic inches |
| liters | 2.113376 | 2.1 | pints |
| liters | 1.056688 | 1.06 | quarts |
| liters | 0.26417205 | 0.26 | gallons |
| cubic meters | 0.03531467 | 0.035 | cubic feet |
| cubic meters | 61023.74 | 61023.7 | cubic inches |
| cubic meters | 35.31467 | 35.0 | cubic feet |
| cubic meters | 1.3079506 | 1.3 | cubic yards |
| cubic meters | 264.17205 | 264.0 | gallons |
| **AREA** | | | |
| square centimeters | 0.1550003 | 0.16 | square inches |
| square centimeters | 0.00107639 | 0.001 | square feet |
| square meters | 10.76391 | 10.8 | square feet |
| square meters | 1.195990 | 1.2 | square yards |
| square kilometers | | 0.4 | square miles |
| hectares | 2.471054 | 2.5 | acres |
| **TEMPERATURE** | | | |
| Celsius | *9/5 (then add 32) | | Fahrenheit |

## MANUFACTURED 2 × 4 WOOD FLOOR TRUSSES

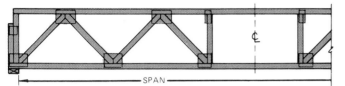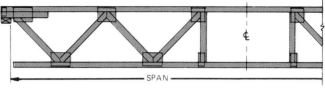

| Bottom Chord Bearing Type | | | |
|---|---|---|---|
| DEPTH | CLEAR SPANS | # DIAGONAL WEBS | CAMBER |
| 12″ | 7′-2″ | 4 | 0.063″ |
| | 9′-8″ | 6 | 0.063″ |
| | 12′-2″ | 8 | 0.063″ |
| | 14′-8″ | 10 | 0.134″ |
| | 17′-2″ | 12 | 0.237″ |
| | 19′-8″ | 14 | 0.365″ |
| | 21′-4″ | 16 | 0.507″ |
| 14″ | 9′-8″ | 6 | 0.063″ |
| | 12′-2″ | 8 | 0.063″ |
| | 14′-8″ | 10 | 0.095″ |
| | 17′-2″ | 12 | 0.178″ |
| | 19′-8″ | 14 | 0.288″ |
| | 22′-7″ | 16 | 0.449″ |
| | 24′-0″ | 18 | 0.569″ |
| 16″ | 12′-2″ | 8 | 0.065″ |
| | 14′-8″ | 10 | 0.070″ |
| | 17′-2″ | 12 | 0.132″ |
| | 19′-8″ | 14 | 0.228″ |
| | 22′-2″ | 16 | 0.346″ |
| | 25′-1″ | 18 | 0.505″ |
| | 26′-1″ | 20 | 0.596″ |
| 18″ | 14′-8″ | 10 | 0.065″ |
| | 17′-2″ | 12 | 0.120″ |
| | 19′-8″ | 14 | 0.176″ |
| | 22′-2″ | 16 | 0.268″ |
| | 24′-8″ | 18 | 0.367″ |
| | 27′-6″ | 20 | 0.600″ |
| | 27′-10″ | 22 | 0.630″ |
| 20″ | 14′-8″ | 10 | 0.063″ |
| | 17′-2″ | 12 | 0.081″ |
| | 19′-8″ | 14 | 0.140″ |
| | 22′-2″ | 16 | 0.226″ |
| | 24′-8″ | 18 | 0.327″ |
| | 27′-6″ | 20 | 0.451″ |
| | 29′-6″ | 22 | 0.630″ |
| 22″ | 17′-2″ | 10 | 0.066″ |
| | 19′-8″ | 12 | 0.114″ |
| | 22′-2″ | 14 | 0.184″ |
| | 24′-8″ | 16 | 0.266″ |
| | 27′-6″ | 18 | 0.367″ |
| | 30′-0″ | 20 | 0.520″ |
| | 31′-1″ | 22 | 0.630″ |
| 24″ | 17′-2″ | 12 | 0.063″ |
| | 19′-8″ | 14 | 0.095″ |
| | 22′-2″ | 16 | 0.153″ |
| | 24′-8″ | 18 | 0.235″ |
| | 27′-2″ | 20 | 0.325″ |
| | 30′-0″ | 22 | 0.431″ |
| | 32′-6″ | 24 | 0.630″ |

| Top Chord Bearing Type | | | |
|---|---|---|---|
| DEPTH | CLEAR SPANS | # DIAGONAL WEBS | CAMBER |
| 12″ | 6′-10″ | 4 | 0.063″ |
| | 9′-4″ | 6 | 0.063″ |
| | 11′-10″ | 8 | 0.063″ |
| | 14′-4″ | 10 | 0.122″ |
| | 16′-10″ | 12 | 0.233″ |
| | 19′-10″ | 14 | 0.376″ |
| | 21′-4″ | 16 | 0.507″ |
| 14″ | 9′-5″ | 6 | 0.063″ |
| | 11′-11″ | 8 | 0.063″ |
| | 14′-5″ | 10 | 0.088″ |
| | 16′-11″ | 12 | 0.167″ |
| | 19′-5″ | 14 | 0.273″ |
| | 21′-4″ | 16 | 0.429″ |
| | 24′-0″ | 18 | 0.569″ |
| 16″ | 12′-0″ | 8 | 0.063″ |
| | 14′-6″ | 10 | 0.067″ |
| | 17′-0″ | 12 | 0.126″ |
| | 19′-6″ | 14 | 0.219″ |
| | 22′-4″ | 16 | 0.337″ |
| | 24′-10″ | 18 | 0.489″ |
| | 26′-1″ | 20 | 0.596″ |
| 18″ | 14′-6″ | 10 | 0.063″ |
| | 17′-0″ | 12 | 0.098″ |
| | 19′-6″ | 14 | 0.170″ |
| | 22′-0″ | 16 | 0.260″ |
| | 24′-10″ | 18 | 0.378″ |
| | 27′-8″ | 20 | 0.617″ |
| | 27′-10″ | 22 | 0.630″ |
| 20″ | 14′-6″ | 10 | 0.063″ |
| | 17′-0″ | 12 | 0.079″ |
| | 19′-6″ | 14 | 0.136″ |
| | 22′-0″ | 16 | 0.221″ |
| | 24′-10″ | 18 | 0.337″ |
| | 27′-4″ | 20 | 0.442″ |
| | 29′-6″ | 22 | 0.630″ |
| 22″ | 17′-1″ | 12 | 0.065″ |
| | 19′-7″ | 14 | 0.112″ |
| | 22′-1″ | 16 | 0.181″ |
| | 24′-10″ | 18 | 0.275″ |
| | 27′-4″ | 20 | 0.381″ |
| | 30′-2″ | 22 | 0.534″ |
| | 31′-1″ | 24 | 0.630″ |
| 24″ | 17′-1″ | 12 | 0.063″ |
| | 19′-7″ | 14 | 0.093″ |
| | 22′-1″ | 16 | 0.150″ |
| | 24′-7″ | 18 | 0.231″ |
| | 27′-5″ | 20 | 0.335″ |
| | 30′-2″ | 22 | 0.443″ |
| | 32′-6″ | 24 | 0.630″ |

Wood floor trusses are typically manufactured from #3 Southern Yellow Pine. Pieces are joined together with 18 and 20 gauge galvanized steel plates applied to both faces of the truss at each joint. Where no sheathing is applied directly to top chords, they should be braced at intervals not to exceed 3′-0″. Where no rigid ceiling is applied directly to bottom chords, they should be braced at intervals not to exceed 10′-0″.

Manufactured wood floor trusses are generally spaced 24″ o.c. and are designed to support various loads. Typical trusses shown here were designed to support 55 psf (live load - 40 psf, dead load - 10 psf, ceiling dead load - 5 psf). A slight bow (camber) is built into each joist so that it will produce a level floor when loaded. Allowable deflection is 1/360 of the span.

Some of the longer trusses require one or more double diagonal webs at both ends. Wood floor trusses are a manufactured product which must be engineered and produced with a high degree of accuracy to attain the desired performance. See your local manufacturer or lumber company for trusses available in your area.

# Floor Joist Span Data

| 30 psi Live Load, 10 psi Dead Load, Def. <360 | | | | | | | | | |
|---|---|---|---|---|---|---|---|---|---|
| Species or Group | Grade | 2 x 8 | | | 2 x 10 | | | 2 x 12 | | |
| | | 12" oc | 16" oc | 24" oc | 12" oc | 16" oc | 24" oc | 12" oc | 16" oc | 24" oc |
| Douglas Fir and Larch | Sel. Struc. | 16'-6" | 15'-0" | 13'-1" | 21'-0" | 19'-1" | 16'-8" | 25'-7" | 23'-3" | 20'-3" |
| | No. 1 & Btr. | 16'-2" | 14'-8" | 12'-10" | 20'-8" | 18'-9" | 16'-1" | 25'-1" | 22'-10" | 18'-8" |
| | No. 1 | 15'-10" | 14'-5" | 12'-4" | 20'-3" | 18'-5" | 15'-0" | 24'-8" | 21'-4" | 17'-5" |
| | No. 2 | 15'-7" | 14'-1" | 11'-6" | 19'-10" | 17'-2" | 14'-1" | 23'-0" | 19'-11" | 16'-3" |
| | No. 3 | 12'-4" | 10'-8" | 8'-8" | 15'-0" | 13'-0" | 10'-7" | 17'-5" | 15'-1" | 12'-4" |

| 40 psi Live Load, 10 psi Dead Load, Def. <360 | | | | | | | | | |
|---|---|---|---|---|---|---|---|---|---|
| Species or Group | Grade | 2 x 8 | | | 2 x 10 | | | 2 x 12 | | |
| | | 12" oc | 16" oc | 24" oc | 12" oc | 16" oc | 24" oc | 12" oc | 16" oc | 24" oc |
| Douglas Fir and Larch | Sel. Struc. | 15'-0" | 13'-7" | 11'-11" | 19'-1" | 17'-4" | 15'-2" | 23'-3" | 21'-1" | 18'-5" |
| | No. 1 & Btr. | 14'-8" | 13'-4" | 11'-8" | 18'-9" | 17'-0" | 14'-5" | 22'-10" | 20'-5" | 16'-8" |
| | No. 1 | 14'-5" | 13'-1" | 11'-0" | 18'-5" | 16'-5" | 13'-5" | 22'-0" | 19'-1" | 15'-7" |
| | No. 2 | 14'-2" | 12'-7" | 10'-3" | 17'-9" | 15'-5" | 12'-7" | 20'-7" | 17'-10" | 14'-7" |
| | No. 3 | 11'-0" | 9'-6" | 7'-9" | 13'-5" | 11'-8" | 9'-6" | 15'-7" | 13'-6" | 11'-0" |

| 30 psi Live Load, 10 psi Dead Load, Def. <360 | | | | | | | | | |
|---|---|---|---|---|---|---|---|---|---|
| Species or Group | Grade | 2 x 8 | | | 2 x 10 | | | 2 x 12 | | |
| | | 12" oc | 16" oc | 24" oc | 12" oc | 16" oc | 24" oc | 12" oc | 16" oc | 24" oc |
| Southern Pine | Sel. Struc. | 16'-2" | 14'-8" | 12'-10" | 20'-8" | 18'-9" | 16'-5" | 25'-1" | 22'-10" | 19'-11" |
| | No. 1 | 15'-10" | 14'-5" | 12'-7" | 20'-3" | 18'-5" | 16'-1" | 24'-8" | 22'-5" | 19'-6" |
| | No. 2 | 15'-7" | 14'-2" | 12'-4" | 19'-10" | 18'-0" | 14'-8" | 24'-2" | 21'-1" | 17'-2" |
| | No. 3 | 13'-3" | 11'-6" | 9'-5" | 15'-8" | 13'-7" | 11'-1" | 18'-8" | 16'-2" | 13'-2" |

| 40 psi Live Load, 10 psi Dead Load, Def. <360 | | | | | | | | | |
|---|---|---|---|---|---|---|---|---|---|
| Species or Group | Grade | 2 x 8 | | | 2 x 10 | | | 2 x 12 | | |
| | | 12" oc | 16" oc | 24" oc | 12" oc | 16" oc | 24" oc | 12" oc | 16" oc | 24" oc |
| Southern Pine | Sel. Struc. | 14'-8" | 13'-4" | 11'-8" | 18'-9" | 17'-0" | 14'-11" | 22'-10" | 20'-9" | 18'-1" |
| | No. 1 | 14'-5" | 13'-1" | 11'-5" | 18'-5" | 16'-9" | 14'-7" | 22'-5" | 20'-4" | 17'-5" |
| | No. 2 | 14'-2" | 12'-10" | 11'-0" | 18'-0" | 16'-1" | 13'-2" | 21'-9" | 18'-10" | 15'-4" |
| | No. 3 | 11'-11" | 10'-3" | 8'-5" | 14'-0" | 12'-2" | 9'-11" | 16'-8" | 14'-5" | 11'-10" |

| 40 psi Live Load, 10 psi Dead Load, Def. <240 | | | | | | | | | |
|---|---|---|---|---|---|---|---|---|---|
| Species or Group | Grade | 2 x 6 | | | 2 x 8 | | | 2 x 10 | | |
| | | 12" oc | 16" oc | 24" oc | 12" oc | 16" oc | 24" oc | 12" oc | 16" oc | 24" oc |
| Redwood | Cl. All Heart | | 7'-3" | 6'-0" | | 10'-9" | 8'-9" | | 13'-6" | 11'-0" |
| | Const. Heart | | 7'-3" | 6'-0" | | 10'-9" | 8'-9" | | 13'-6" | 11'-0" |
| | Const. Common | | 7'-3" | 6'-0" | | 10'-9" | 8'-9" | | 13'-6" | 11'-0" |

*Span data are in feet and inches for floor joists of Douglas Fir/Larch, Southern Yellow Pine, and California Redwood. Spans are calculated on the basis of dry sizes with a moisture content equal to or less than 19 percent. Floor joists spans are for a single span with calculations performed based on the modulus of elasticity (E) and maximum fiber bending stress (Fb) allowed.*

## Ceiling Joist Span Data

### 20 psi Live Load, 10 psi Dead Load, Def. <240

Drywall ceiling, No future room development, Limited attic storage available

| Species or Group | Grade | 2 x 4 | | | 2 x 6 | | | 2 x 8 | | | 2 x 10 | | |
|---|---|---|---|---|---|---|---|---|---|---|---|---|---|
| | | 12"oc | 16"oc | 24"oc | 12"oc | 16"oc | 24"oc | 12"oc | 16"oc | 24"oc | 12"oc | 16"oc | 24"oc |
| Douglas Fir and Larch | Sel. Struc. | 10-5 | 9-6 | 8-3 | 16-4 | 14-11 | 13-0 | 21-7 | 19-7 | 17-1 | 27-6 | 25-0 | 20-11 |
| | No. 1 & Btr. | 10-3 | 9-4 | 8-1 | 16-1 | 14-7 | 12-0 | 21-2 | 18-8 | 15-3 | 26-4 | 22-9 | 18-7 |
| | No. 1 | 10-0 | 9-1 | 7-8 | 15-9 | 13-9 | 11-2 | 20-1 | 17-5 | 14-2 | 24-6 | 21-3 | 17-4 |
| | No. 2 | 9-10 | 8-9 | 7-2 | 14-10 | 12-10 | 10-6 | 18-9 | 16-3 | 13-3 | 22-11 | 19-10 | 16-3 |
| | No. 3 | 7-8 | 6-8 | 5-5 | 11-2 | 9-8 | 7-11 | 14-2 | 12-4 | 10-0 | 17-4 | 15-0 | 12-3 |

### 20 psi Live Load, 10 psi Dead Load, Def. <240

Drywall ceiling, No future room development, Limited attic storage available

| Species or Group | Grade | 2 x 4 | | | 2 x 6 | | | 2 x 8 | | | 2 x 10 | | |
|---|---|---|---|---|---|---|---|---|---|---|---|---|---|
| | | 12"oc | 16"oc | 24"oc | 12"oc | 16"oc | 24"oc | 12"oc | 16"oc | 24"oc | 12"oc | 16"oc | 24"oc |
| Southern Pine | Sel. Struc. | 10-3 | 9-4 | 8-1 | 16-1 | 14-7 | 12-9 | 21-2 | 19-3 | 16-10 | 26-0 | 24-7 | 21-6 |
| | No. 1 | 10-0 | 9-1 | 8-0 | 15-9 | 14-4 | 12-6 | 20-10 | 18-11 | 15-11 | 26-0 | 23-2 | 18-11 |
| | No. 2 | 9-10 | 8-11 | 7-8 | 15-6 | 13-6 | 11-0 | 20-1 | 17-5 | 14-2 | 24-0 | 20-9 | 17-0 |
| | No. 3 | 8-2 | 7-1 | 5-9 | 12-1 | 10-5 | 8-6 | 15-4 | 13-3 | 10-10 | 18-1 | 15-8 | 12-10 |

## Roof Rafter Span Data

### 20 psi Live Load, 10 psi Dead Load, Def. <240

Roof slope 3:12 or less, Light roof covering, No ceiling finish

| Species or Group | Grade | 2 x 6 | | | 2 x 8 | | | 2 x 10 | | | 2 x 12 | | |
|---|---|---|---|---|---|---|---|---|---|---|---|---|---|
| | | 12"oc | 16"oc | 24"oc | 12"oc | 16"oc | 24"oc | 12"oc | 16"oc | 24"oc | 12"oc | 16"oc | 24"oc |
| Douglas Fir and Larch | Sel. Struc. | 16-4 | 14-11 | 13-0 | 21-7 | 19-7 | 17-2 | 27-6 | 25-0 | 21-10 | 33-6 | 30-5 | 26-7 |
| | No. 1 & Btr. | 16-1 | 14-7 | 12-9 | 21-2 | 19-3 | 16-10 | 27-1 | 24-7 | 20-9 | 32-11 | 29-6 | 24-1 |
| | No. 1 | 15-9 | 14-4 | 12-6 | 20-10 | 18-11 | 15-10 | 26-6 | 23-9 | 19-5 | 31-10 | 27-6 | 22-6 |
| | No. 2 | 15-6 | 14-1 | 11-9 | 20-5 | 18-2 | 14-10 | 25-11 | 22-3 | 18-2 | 29-4 | 25-9 | 21-0 |
| | No. 3 | 12-6 | 10-10 | 8-10 | 15-10 | 13-9 | 11-3 | 19-5 | 16-9 | 13-8 | 22-6 | 19-6 | 15-11 |

### 20 psi Live Load, 15 psi Dead Load, Def. <240

Roof slope greater than 3:12, Light roof covering, Drywall ceiling, No snow load

| Species or Group | Grade | 2 x 6 | | | 2 x 8 | | | 2 x 10 | | | 2 x 12 | | |
|---|---|---|---|---|---|---|---|---|---|---|---|---|---|
| | | 12"oc | 16"oc | 24"oc | 12"oc | 16"oc | 24"oc | 12"oc | 16"oc | 24"oc | 12"oc | 16"oc | 24"oc |
| Douglas Fir and Larch | Sel. Struc. | 16-4 | 14-11 | 13-0 | 21-7 | 19-7 | 17-2 | 27-6 | 25-0 | 21-7 | 33-6 | 30-5 | 25-1 |
| | No. 1 & Btr. | 16-1 | 14-7 | 12-5 | 21-2 | 19-3 | 15-9 | 27-1 | 23-7 | 19-3 | 31-7 | 27-4 | 22-4 |
| | No. 1 | 15-9 | 14-3 | 11-7 | 20-9 | 18-0 | 14-8 | 25-5 | 22-0 | 17-11 | 29-5 | 25-6 | 20-10 |
| | No. 2 | 15-4 | 13-3 | 10-10 | 19-5 | 16-10 | 13-9 | 23-9 | 20-7 | 16-9 | 27-6 | 23-10 | 19-6 |
| | No. 3 | 11-7 | 10-1 | 8-2 | 14-8 | 12-9 | 10-5 | 17-11 | 15-7 | 12-8 | 20-10 | 18-0 | 14-9 |

### 20 psi Live Load, 10 psi Dead Load, Def. <240

Drywall ceiling, Light roofing, Snow load

| Species or Group | Grade | 2 x 6 | | | 2 x 8 | | | 2 x 10 | | | 2 x 12 | | |
|---|---|---|---|---|---|---|---|---|---|---|---|---|---|
| | | 12"oc | 16"oc | 24"oc | 12"oc | 16"oc | 24"oc | 12"oc | 16"oc | 24"oc | 12"oc | 16"oc | 24"oc |
| Southern Pine | Sel. Struc. | 16-1 | 14-7 | 12-9 | 21-2 | 19-3 | 16-10 | 26-0 | 24-7 | 21-6 | 26-0 | 26-0 | 26-0 |
| | No. 1 | 15-9 | 14-4 | 12-6 | 20-10 | 18-11 | 16-6 | 26-0 | 24-1 | 20-3 | 26-0 | 26-0 | 24-1 |
| | No. 2 | 15-6 | 14-1 | 11-9 | 20-5 | 18-6 | 15-3 | 25-8 | 22-3 | 18-2 | 26-0 | 26-0 | 21-4 |
| | No. 3 | 12-11 | 11-2 | 9-1 | 16-5 | 14-3 | 11-7 | 19-5 | 16-10 | 13-9 | 23-1 | 20-0 | 16-4 |

### 30 psi Live Load, 15 psi Dead Load, Def. <240

Drywall ceiling, Medium roofing, Snow load

| Species or Group | Grade | 2 x 6 | | | 2 x 8 | | | 2 x 10 | | | 2 x 12 | | |
|---|---|---|---|---|---|---|---|---|---|---|---|---|---|
| | | 12"oc | 16"oc | 24"oc | 12"oc | 16"oc | 24"oc | 12"oc | 16"oc | 24"oc | 12"oc | 16"oc | 24"oc |
| Southern Pine | Sel. Struc. | 14-1 | 12-9 | 11-2 | 18-6 | 16-10 | 14-8 | 23-8 | 21-6 | 18-9 | 26-0 | 26-0 | 22-10 |
| | No. 1 | 13-9 | 12-6 | 10-11 | 18-2 | 16-6 | 13-11 | 23-2 | 20-3 | 16-6 | 26-0 | 24-1 | 19-8 |
| | No. 2 | 13-6 | 11-9 | 9-7 | 17-7 | 15-3 | 12-5 | 21-0 | 18-2 | 14-10 | 24-7 | 21-4 | 17-5 |
| | No. 3 | 10-6 | 9-1 | 7-5 | 13-5 | 11-7 | 9-6 | 15-10 | 13-9 | 11-3 | 18-10 | 16-4 | 13-4 |

These spans are based on the 1993 AFPA (formerly NFPA) Span Tables for Joists and Rafters. These grades are the most commonly available.

*Ceiling joist and rafter span data are in feet and inches for Douglas Fir/Larch and Southern Yellow Pine. Spans are based on dry lumber size with a moisture content equal to or less than 19 percent. Calculations were based on the modulus of elasticity (E) and maximum fiber bending stress ($F_b$) allowed for ceiling joists. Rafter spans were based on the fiber bending stress ($F_b$) and allowable modulus of elasticity (E). Rafter spans are horizontal distances.*

## NAILS

### COMMON APPLICATIONS

| Joining | Size & Type | Placement |
|---|---|---|
| **Wall Framing** | | |
| Top plate | 8d common<br>16d common | |
| Header | 8d common<br>16d common | |
| Header to joist | 16d common | |
| Studs | 8d common<br>16d common | |
| **Wall Sheathing** | | |
| Boards | 8d common | 6" o.c. |
| Plywood<br>5/16", 3/8", 1/2" | 6d common | 6" o.c. |
| Plywood (5/8", 3/4") | 8d common | 6" o.c. |
| Fiberboard | 1¾" galv. roofing nail<br>8d galv. common nail | 6" o.c.<br>6" o.c. |
| Foamboard | Cap nail, length<br>sufficient for<br>penetration of ½"<br>into framing | 12" o.c. |
| Gypsum | 1¾" galv. roofing nail<br>8d galv. common nail | 6" o.c.<br>6" o.c. |
| **Subflooring** | 8d common | 10"-12" o.c. |
| **Underlayment** | (1¼" x 14 ga. annular<br>underlayment nail) | 6" o.c. edges<br>12" o.c. face |
| **Roof Framing** | | |
| Rafters, beveled or<br>notched | 12d common | |
| Rafter to joist | 16d common | |
| Joist to rafter and<br>stud | 10d common | |
| Ridge beam | 8d & 16d common | |
| **Roof Sheathing** | | |
| Boards | 8d common | |
| Plywood<br>(5/16", 3/8", 1/2") | 6d common | 12" o.c. and<br>6" o.c. edges |
| Plywood (5/8", 3/4") | 8d common | 12" o.c. and<br>6" o.c. edges |

*Aluminum nails are recommended for maximum protection from staining.

| Joining | Size & Type | Placement |
|---|---|---|
| **Roofing, Asphalt** | | |
| New construction<br>shingles and felt | 7/8" through 1½"<br>galv. roofing | 4 per shingle |
| Re-roofing application<br>shingles and felt | 1¾" or 2"<br>galv. roofing | 4 per shingle |
| Roof deck/<br>Insulation | Thickness of insulation<br>plus 1" insulation<br>roof deck nail | |
| **Roofing,<br>Wood Shingles** | | |
| New construction | 3d-4d galv. shingle | 2-3 per shingle |
| Re-roofing application | 5d-6d galv. shingle | 2-3 per shingle |
| **Soffit** | 6d-8d galv.<br>common | 12" o.c. max. |
| **Siding*** | | |
| Bevel and lap | Aluminum nails are<br>recommended for<br>optimum performance | Consult siding<br>manufacturer's<br>application<br>instructions |
| Drop and shiplap | | |
| Plywood | | |
| Hardboard | Galvanized hardboard<br>siding nail<br>Galvanized box nail | Consult siding<br>manufacturer's<br>application<br>instructions |
| **Doors, Windows,<br>Mouldings, Furring** | | |
| Wood strip to masonry | Nail length is determined<br>by thickness of siding and<br>sheathing. Nails should<br>penetrate at least 1½"<br>into solid wood framing. | |
| Wood strip to stud<br>or joist | | |
| **Paneling** | | |
| Wood | 4d-8d casing-finishing | 24" o.c. |
| Hardboard | 2" x 16 ga. annular | 8" o.c. |
| Plywood | 3d casing-finishing | 8" o.c. |
| Gypsum | 1¼" annular drywall | 6" o.c. |
| **Lathing** | 4d common blued | 4" o.c. |
| **Exterior Projects:** | | |
| Decks, patios, etc. | 8d-16d hot dipped<br>galvanized common | |

NOTE: Usage may vary somewhat due to regional differences and preferences.

## DRYWALL SCREWS

| Description | No. | Length | Applications |
|---|---|---|---|
| **Bugle Phillips** 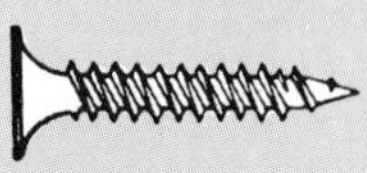 | 1E<br>2E<br>3E<br>4E<br>5R<br>6R<br>7R<br>8R | 6x1<br>6x1⅛<br>6x1¼<br>6x1⅝<br>6x2<br>6x2¼<br>8x2½<br>8x3 | For attaching drywall to<br>metal studs from 25 ga.<br>through 20 ga. |
| **Coarse Thread** 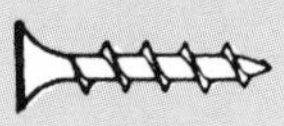 | 1C<br>2C<br>3C<br>4C<br>5C<br>6C | 6x1<br>6x1⅛<br>6x1¼<br>6x1⅝<br>6x2<br>6x2¼ | For attaching drywall<br>to 25 ga. metal studs, and<br>attaching drywall to<br>wood studs |
| **Pan Framing**  | 19 | 6x7/16 | For attaching stud to track<br>up to 20 ga. |

| Description | No. | Length | Applications |
|---|---|---|---|
| **HWH Framing**  | 21<br>22<br>35 | 6x7/16<br>8x9/16<br>10x¾ | For attaching stud to track<br>up to 20 ga. where hex<br>head is desired |
| **K-Lath** 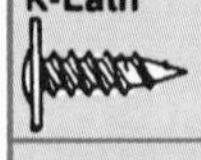 | 28 | 8x9/16 | For attaching wire lath,<br>K-lath to 20 ga. studs |
| **Laminating** 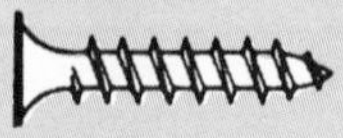 | 8 | 10x1½ | Type G laminating<br>screw for attaching<br>gypsum to gypsum,<br>a temporary fastener |
| **Trim Head**  | 9<br>10 | 6x1⅝<br>6x2¼ | Trim head screw for<br>attaching wood trim and<br>base to 25 ga. studs |

Nail chart shows common applications, size, type, and placement. (Georgia-Pacific)   Drywall screw chart gives description, number, length, and applications.   (Compass International)

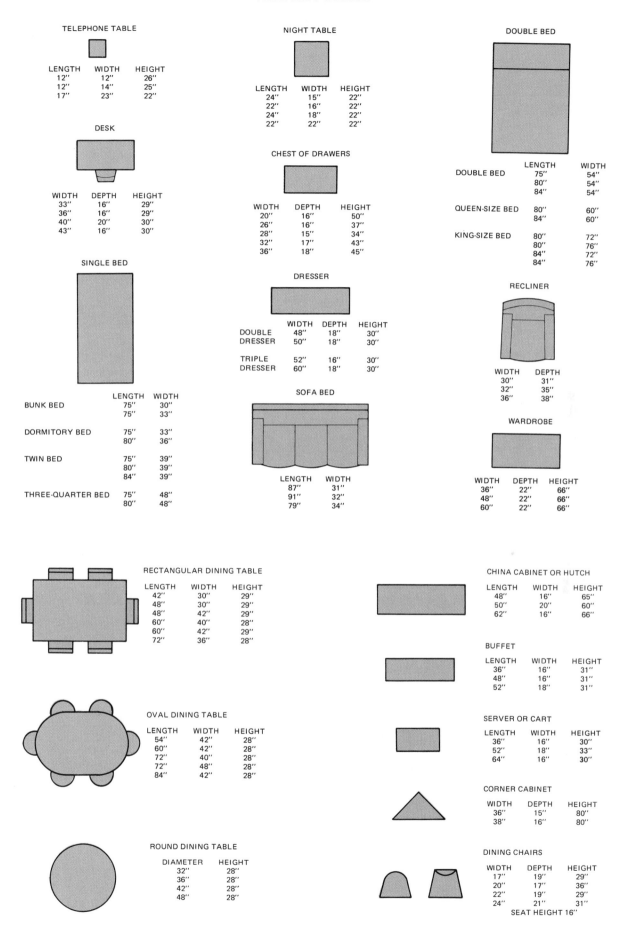

Fig. 21-5. Standard sizes of common bedroom, living room, and dining room furniture.

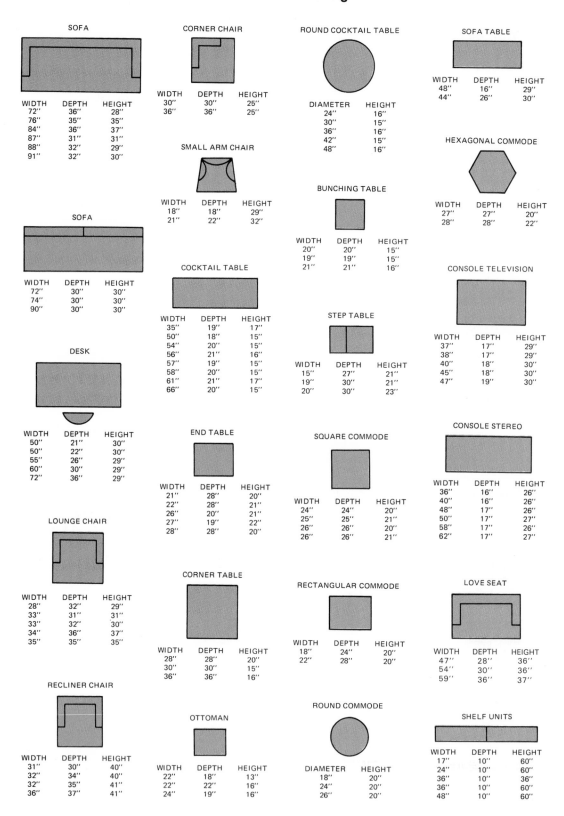

**SOFA**

| WIDTH | DEPTH | HEIGHT |
|-------|-------|--------|
| 72″ | 36″ | 28″ |
| 76″ | 35″ | 35″ |
| 84″ | 36″ | 37″ |
| 87″ | 31″ | 31″ |
| 88″ | 32″ | 29″ |
| 91″ | 32″ | 30″ |

**SOFA**

| WIDTH | DEPTH | HEIGHT |
|-------|-------|--------|
| 72″ | 30″ | 30″ |
| 74″ | 30″ | 30″ |
| 90″ | 30″ | 30″ |

**DESK**

| WIDTH | DEPTH | HEIGHT |
|-------|-------|--------|
| 50″ | 21″ | 30″ |
| 50″ | 22″ | 30″ |
| 55″ | 26″ | 29″ |
| 60″ | 30″ | 29″ |
| 72″ | 36″ | 29″ |

**LOUNGE CHAIR**

| WIDTH | DEPTH | HEIGHT |
|-------|-------|--------|
| 28″ | 32″ | 29″ |
| 33″ | 31″ | 31″ |
| 33″ | 32″ | 30″ |
| 34″ | 36″ | 37″ |
| 35″ | 35″ | 35″ |

**RECLINER CHAIR**

| WIDTH | DEPTH | HEIGHT |
|-------|-------|--------|
| 31″ | 30″ | 40″ |
| 32″ | 34″ | 40″ |
| 32″ | 35″ | 41″ |
| 36″ | 37″ | 41″ |

**CORNER CHAIR**

| WIDTH | DEPTH | HEIGHT |
|-------|-------|--------|
| 30″ | 30″ | 25″ |
| 36″ | 36″ | 25″ |

**SMALL ARM CHAIR**

| WIDTH | DEPTH | HEIGHT |
|-------|-------|--------|
| 18″ | 18″ | 29″ |
| 21″ | 22″ | 32″ |

**COCKTAIL TABLE**

| WIDTH | DEPTH | HEIGHT |
|-------|-------|--------|
| 35″ | 19″ | 17″ |
| 50″ | 18″ | 15″ |
| 54″ | 20″ | 15″ |
| 56″ | 21″ | 16″ |
| 57″ | 19″ | 15″ |
| 58″ | 20″ | 15″ |
| 61″ | 21″ | 17″ |
| 66″ | 20″ | 15″ |

**END TABLE**

| WIDTH | DEPTH | HEIGHT |
|-------|-------|--------|
| 21″ | 28″ | 20″ |
| 22″ | 28″ | 21″ |
| 26″ | 20″ | 21″ |
| 27″ | 19″ | 22″ |
| 28″ | 28″ | 20″ |

**CORNER TABLE**

| WIDTH | DEPTH | HEIGHT |
|-------|-------|--------|
| 28″ | 28″ | 20″ |
| 30″ | 30″ | 15″ |
| 36″ | 36″ | 16″ |

**OTTOMAN**

| WIDTH | DEPTH | HEIGHT |
|-------|-------|--------|
| 22″ | 18″ | 13″ |
| 22″ | 22″ | 16″ |
| 24″ | 19″ | 16″ |

**ROUND COCKTAIL TABLE**

| DIAMETER | HEIGHT |
|----------|--------|
| 24″ | 16″ |
| 30″ | 15″ |
| 36″ | 16″ |
| 42″ | 15″ |
| 48″ | 16″ |

**BUNCHING TABLE**

| WIDTH | DEPTH | HEIGHT |
|-------|-------|--------|
| 20″ | 20″ | 15″ |
| 19″ | 19″ | 15″ |
| 21″ | 21″ | 16″ |

**STEP TABLE**

| WIDTH | DEPTH | HEIGHT |
|-------|-------|--------|
| 15″ | 27″ | 21″ |
| 19″ | 30″ | 21″ |
| 20″ | 30″ | 23″ |

**SQUARE COMMODE**

| WIDTH | DEPTH | HEIGHT |
|-------|-------|--------|
| 24″ | 24″ | 20″ |
| 25″ | 25″ | 21″ |
| 26″ | 26″ | 20″ |
| 26″ | 26″ | 21″ |

**RECTANGULAR COMMODE**

| WIDTH | DEPTH | HEIGHT |
|-------|-------|--------|
| 18″ | 24″ | 20″ |
| 22″ | 28″ | 20″ |

**ROUND COMMODE**

| DIAMETER | HEIGHT |
|----------|--------|
| 18″ | 20″ |
| 24″ | 20″ |
| 26″ | 20″ |

**SOFA TABLE**

| WIDTH | DEPTH | HEIGHT |
|-------|-------|--------|
| 48″ | 16″ | 29″ |
| 44″ | 26″ | 30″ |

**HEXAGONAL COMMODE**

| WIDTH | DEPTH | HEIGHT |
|-------|-------|--------|
| 27″ | 27″ | 20″ |
| 28″ | 28″ | 22″ |

**CONSOLE TELEVISION**

| WIDTH | DEPTH | HEIGHT |
|-------|-------|--------|
| 37″ | 17″ | 29″ |
| 38″ | 17″ | 29″ |
| 40″ | 18″ | 30″ |
| 45″ | 18″ | 30″ |
| 47″ | 19″ | 30″ |

**CONSOLE STEREO**

| WIDTH | DEPTH | HEIGHT |
|-------|-------|--------|
| 36″ | 16″ | 26″ |
| 40″ | 16″ | 26″ |
| 48″ | 17″ | 26″ |
| 50″ | 17″ | 27″ |
| 58″ | 17″ | 26″ |
| 62″ | 17″ | 27″ |

**LOVE SEAT**

| WIDTH | DEPTH | HEIGHT |
|-------|-------|--------|
| 47″ | 28″ | 36″ |
| 54″ | 30″ | 36″ |
| 59″ | 36″ | 37″ |

**SHELF UNITS**

| WIDTH | DEPTH | HEIGHT |
|-------|-------|--------|
| 17″ | 10″ | 60″ |
| 24″ | 10″ | 60″ |
| 36″ | 10″ | 36″ |
| 36″ | 10″ | 60″ |
| 48″ | 10″ | 60″ |

Fig. 21-5 continued.

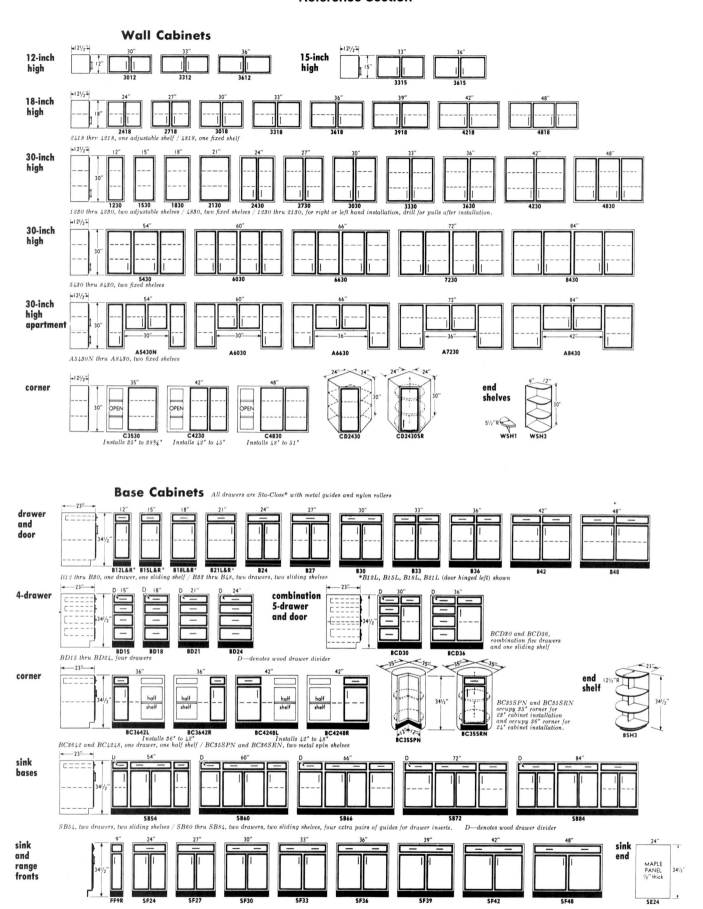

Fig. 21-47. Dimensions of standard base and wall units built by one manufacturer.
(I-XL Furniture Co.)

# Index